Handbook of Homework Assignments in Psychotherapy
Research, Practice, and Prevention
Research, Practice, and Prevention

Handbook of Homework Assignments in Psychotherapy

Research, Practice, and Prevention

Edited by

Nikolaos Kazantzis

Massey University
Auckland, New Zealand

Luciano L'Abate

Georgia State University
Atlanta, Georgia

 Springer

Nikolaos Kazantzis, Ph.D.
P. O. Box 3578
Shortland Street 1140
Auckland,
New Zealand

Luciano L'Abate
Professor Emeritus of Psychology
Georgia State University
Atlanta, Georgia
USA

Library of Congress Control Number: 2005936390

ISBN-10: 0-387-29680-8 (Hardbound)   e-ISBN 0-387-29681-6 (eBook)
ISBN-13: 978-0387-29680-7

Printed on acid-free paper.

10 9 8 7 6 5 4 3 2 1

springer.com

ACKNOWLEDGMENTS

We extend a warm acknowledgment to our contributors. It goes without saying that this *Handbook* would not exist without their contributions. We are fortunate to present their insights and teachings on homework in psychotherapy. The field's understanding regarding the role of homework in research, practice, and prevention will benefit from their work. In many instances, the chapters in this *Handbook* represent the first time that homework has been discussed within particular formulations or applications of psychotherapy. Special acknowledgements are extended to those colleagues who took on the difficult task of reading and commenting on the entire contents of this *Handbook*, we thank Larry Beutler, Louis Castonguay, Mark Harwood, Mike Lambert, and their graduate students for their fine concluding chapters.

We have had the opportunity to talk and work with many individuals who have contributed to the growing understanding of how homework can enable clients to achieve their therapeutic goals. Special thanks are extended to Judith Beck, Louis Castonguay, Frank Dattilio, Frank Deane, Keith Dobson, Anne Garland, Jennifer Hudson, Ian Evans, Lydia Fehm, Arthur Freeman, Guillem Fexias, Beverly Haarhoff, Pam Jezard-Clarke, Malcolm Johnson, Philip Kendall, Georgios Lampropoulos, Robert Leahy, Jay Lebow, Janet Leathem, Paul Merrick, Kathleen Mooney, Rona Moss-Morris, Frederick Newman, Robert Neimeyer, Christine Padesky, Kevin Ronan, Jan Scott, Gregoris Simos, George Stricker, and Michael Tompkins. We also thank our students, their enthusiasm, intelligence, and interest is always appreciated and valued. We look forward to our continuing collaboration on this important feature of psychotherapy.

We thank Margo Munro for producing the index. We thank Linda Kemp and Kathryn Lee for administrative support during the production of this book. We are also grateful for the editorial and production staff at Springer, in particular, Sharon Panulla (Executive Editor for Psychology) who skillfully guided the project through the merger between Kluwer and Springer-Verlag.

Last but not least, we thank our partners, families, and friends for their support and encouragement while we have been working on this project.

ABOUT THE EDITORS

Nikolaos Kazantzis, Ph.D., is a Senior Lecturer (Associate Professor equivalent) at the School of Psychology, at Massey University in New Zealand. He has published widely on the topic of homework assignments in psychotherapy, including serving as a Guest Editor for special issues in *Journal of Clinical Psychology* (2002), *Cognitive and Behavioral Practice* (2006), and *Journal of Psychotherapy Integration* (2006). He recently co-edited the book *"Using Homework Assignments in Cognitive Behavior Therapy"* (Routledge) with Dr. Luciano L'Abate. He has co-authored more than 50 articles and book chapters and has participated in national and international conferences related to his research interests. He is also a recipient of the Royal Society of New Zealand *Science and Technology Award for Beginning Scientists*, Australian Association for Cognitive Behavior Therapy (AACBT) *Tracy Goodall Early Career Award*, and Massey University's Research Medal—Early Career. Dr. Kazantzis is a licensed (registered) clinical psychologist and maintains a part-time practice in Auckland, New Zealand.

Luciano L'Abate, Ph.D., is Professor Emeritus of Psychology, Georgia State University, Georgia, Atlanta, USA where he was Director of the Family Psychology Training Program and the Family Study Center. He completed his Ph.D. at Duke University, with post-doctoral specialization at Michael Reese Hospital in Chicago. He worked in the Psychiatry Departments of Washington (St. Louis) and Emory (Atlanta) Universities Schools of Medicine before moving to Georgia State University, where he spent his entire academic career. He was in part-time private and consulting and clinical practice for 42 years. He published (author, co-author, edited, and co-edited) 37 books, with 3 books submitted for publication, as well as over 250 papers in scientific and professional journals.

CONTRIBUTORS

Timothy R. Apodaca, Ph.D., is a faculty member at Brown University Center for Alcohol and Addiction Studies

Fiona Barwick, is a graduate student at the Department of Psychology, at the Pennsylvania State University.

Donald H. Baucom, Ph.D., is Professor and Director of the Clinical Program at the Department of Psychology, University of North Carolina at Chapel Hill.

Judith S. Beck, Ph.D., is the Director of the Beck Institute for Cognitive Therapy and Research in suburban Philadelphia and Clinical Associate Professor of Psychology in Psychiatry at the University of Pennsylvania.

Larry E. Beutler, Ph.D., is Director of Training and Faculty Chair at Pacific Graduate School of Psychology and Consulting Professor, Department of Psychiatry and Behavioral Sciences at Stanford University.

Louis Castonguay, Ph.D., is Associate Professor of Psychology at the Department of Psychology, at the Pennsylvania State University.

Alex L. Chapman, Ph.D., is a Research Associate with Dr. Marsha Linehan at the University of Washington Department of Psychology, Behavior Research and Therapy Clinics.

Muriel Christianson is a doctoral candidate at the School of Psychology, Massey University, Wellington, New Zealand.

David A. Clark, Ph.D., is Professor Department of Psychology, University of New Brunswick and a Founding Fellow of the Academy of Cognitive Therapy.

Helen M. De Vries, Ph.D., is Associate Professor, at the Psychology Department, Wheaton College.

Hazel Dunn is Principal Cognitive Behavior Therapist at Psychological Services, Lancashire Care NHS Trust.

Jennifer A. Ellison is a doctoral candidate at the Department of Psychology York University.

Norman B. Epstein, Ph.D., is Professor and Director of the Marriage and Family Therapy Program at the University of Maryland, College Park.

Melanie J. V. Fennell, Ph.D., is Director of the Cognitive Behavior Therapy Training Programme at the Oxford University Department of Psychiatry, and Oxford Cognitive Therapy Centre, Warneford Hospital, England.

Nancy Gambescia, Ph.D., teaches and supervises psychotherapists in the assessment and treatment of sexual dysfunctions and couples therapy. She also maintains an active private practice specializing in relationship and sex therapy in Rosemont, Pennsylvania.

Leslie S. Greenberg, Ph.D., is Professor of Psychology and Director of the Psychotherapy Research Centre at York University.

S. Cory Harmon is a doctoral candidate at the Department of Psychology, Brigham Young University.

Mark T. Harwood, Ph.D., is Assistant Professor of Psychology at the Department of Psychology, Humboldt State University.

Steven C. Hayes, Ph.D., is Foundation Professor in clinical psychology, at the Department of Psychology, University of Nevada.

Jonathan D. Huppert, Ph.D., is an Assistant Professor of Clinical Psychology in Psychiatry at the University of Pennsylvania.

Malcolm Johnson is Associate Professor and Director of the Health Psychology Programme at the Department of Psychological Medicine, School of Medicine, University of Auckland, New Zealand.

Michael J. Lambert, Ph.D., is Professor of Psychology at the Department of Psychology, Brigham Young University.

Janet M. Leathem, Ph.D., is Professor of Neuropsychology and Coordinator of Clinical Psychology Training at the School of Psychology, Massey University, Wellington, New Zealand.

Jay Lebow,Ph.D., is a licensed clinical psychologist and research consultant at The Family Institute, and Adjunct Associate Professor at Northwestern University.

Deborah Roth Ledley, Ph.D., is Associate Director, Adult Anxiety Clinic of Temple at the Department of Psychology, Temple University.

Noam Lindenboim is a doctoral candidate at the Department of Psychology, University of Washington.

Marsha M. Linehan, Ph.D., is Professor, Department of Psychology and Director, Behavioral Research & Therapy Clinics at the University of Washington.

Peter M. Monti, Ph.D., is Professor of Medical Sciences and Director of the Center for Alcohol and Addiction Studies at Brown University.

Anthony P. Morrison, Ph.D., is Professor of Clinical Psychology at School of Psychological Sciences, University of Manchester, and Programme Coordinator at Psychology Services, Bolton Salford & Trafford Mental Health NHS Trust, England.

Laura Mufson, Ph.D., is Director, Department of Clinical Psychology, New York State Psychiatric Institute and Associate Professor of Clinical Psychology in Psychiatry Columbia University College of Physicians and Surgeons.

Dana D. Nelson is a doctoral candidate at the Department of Psychology, at the Pennsylvania State University.

Robert A. Neimeyer, Ph.D., holds a Dunavant University Professorship in the Department of Psychology, University of Memphis.

Gonzalo A. Pérez is a doctoral candidate at the Center for Family Studies at the Department of Psychiatry and Behavioral Sciences, University of Miami School of Medicine.

Heather M. Pierson is a doctoral candidate at the Department of Psychology, University of Nevada.

Kathleen Newcomb Rekart is a graduate student at Northwestern University.

Lawrence P. Riso, Ph.D., is Assistant Professor at the Department of Psychology, Georgia State University.

Michael S. Robbins, Ph.D., is a Research Assistant Professor at the Center for Family Studies at the Department of Psychiatry and Behavioral Sciences, University of Miami School of Medicine.

Tanya R. Schlam is a doctoral candidate at the School of Applied and Professional Psychology Rutgers University.

Karstin Slade is a doctoral candidate at the Department of Psychology, Brigham Young University.

George Stricker, Ph.D., is Professor of Psychology at Argosy University, Arlington VA after having retired from being Distinguished Research Professor of Psychology in the Derner Institute, Adelphi University, New York.

Joselyne M. Sulzner is a doctoral candidate at the Department of Psychology, Humboldt State University.

José Szapocznik, Ph.D., is Director, Center for Family Studies, Professor of Psychiatry & Behavioral Sciences, Psychology, Architecture, and Educational & Psychological Studies, and Chair, National Hispanic Science Network on Drug Abuse, Center for Family Studies at the Department of Psychiatry and Behavioral Sciences, University of Miami School of Medicine.

Michael E. Thase, M.D. is professor of psychiatry at the Western Psychiatric Institute and Clinic, University of Pittsburgh School of Medicine.

Michael A. Tompkins, Ph.D., is Director of Training at the San Francisco Bay Area Center for Cognitive Therapy is a licensed clinical psychologist and Assistant Clinical Professor at the University of California, Berkeley.

Michael P. Twohig is a doctoral candidate at the Department of Psychology, University of Nevada.

Gerald R. Weeks, Ph.D., is Professor and Chair of the Department of Counseling at the University of Las Vegas.

G. Terence Wilson, Ph.D., is Professor in the School of Applied and Professional Psychology, and Director of the Rutgers Eating Disorders Clinic at Wilson Rutgers University.

David Winter, Ph.D., is Professor of Clinical Psychology and Course Director of the Doctorate in Clinical Psychology at the University of Hertfordshire, and Head of Clinical Psychology Services and Coordinator of Research for the Barnet, Enfield and Haringey Mental Health Trust.

Marjorie C. Witty, Ph.D., is an Executive Faculty Member at Argosy University/Chicago's Illinois School of Professional Psychology.

Jami F. Young, Ph.D., is Assistant Professor of Clinical Psychology in Psychiatry Columbia University College of Physicians and Surgeons.

PREFACE

The aim of this *Handbook of Homework Assignments in Psychotherapy: Research, Practice, and Prevention* is to provide comprehensive resource on the role of homework assignments in psychotherapy and prevention. However, the process of generalizing in-session therapeutic work through between-session activity has a long history in psychotherapy. This *Handbook* is designed to elucidate and extend that history by presenting theoretical and clinically focused descriptions of the role of homework assignments in a range of psychotherapies, clinical populations, and presenting problems. Designed for both the beginning and the experienced psychotherapy practitioner, this *Handbook* assumes a basic knowledge of psychopathology and practice of psychotherapy and prevention. The *Handbook* aims to contribute to the professional resources for all psychotherapy practitioners and researchers, in private and public practice, graduate students in clinical and counseling psychology, couple and family therapists, as well as residents in psychiatry. This book does not aim to review the theories of psychotherapy in detail, specific treatments of psychopathology, clinical assessment, or basic psychotherapy and prevention processes that are currently available in numerous psychotherapy textbooks. This *Handbook* is a clinical resource designed to provide a focused coverage of how to integrate homework assignments into psychotherapy practice, and in the prevention of mental illness.

OUTLINE FOR THE HANDBOOK

This *Handbook* comprises four distinct parts. Part I of the book consists of nine chapters that describe the process of using homework assignments in a range of psychotherapy approaches (i.e., Chapters 1–9). As we were proposing a *Handbook* on homework assignments covering a range of different psychotherapy approaches, we made an effort to provide a broad guiding structure to facilitate consistency within this section. Thus, we invited primarily clinical chapters including the following; (a) brief overview of the therapeutic approach, (b) description of the role of homework assignments in the approach (main part of the chapter), (c) at least one relevant case study to illustrate how homework contributes to psychotherapy and prevention.

In Chapter 1, Deborah Roth Ledley and Jonathan Huppert extend their research contributions by describing the role of homework assignments in behavior therapy. In Chapter 2, Marjorie Witty presents a discussion on the role of client-instigated homework assignments in client-centered psychotherapy. In Chapter 3, Judith Beck and Michael Tompkins contribute to the cognitive therapy practice literature by presenting a description of homework assignments that emphasizes the role of the conceptualization and collaborative relationship. In Chapter 4, Jennifer Ellison and Leslie Greenberg present a description of the role of homework assignments in emotion-focused experiential therapy. In Chapter 5, Jami Young and Laura Mufson describe how homework assignments are integrated in interpersonal therapy. In Chapter 6, George Stricker dispels many misconceptions by explaining how homework assignments are integrated into psychodynamic therapy. In Chapter 7, Michael Twohig, Heather Pierson, and Steven Hayes describe how homework assignments are integrated by those practicing acceptance and commitment therapy. In Chapter 8, Michael Robbins, José Szapocznik, and Gonzalo Pérez outline how homework assignments are integrated into brief strategic family therapy. The final contribution to this section, Chapter 9, presents Robert Neimeyer and David Winter's account of how homework assignments can contribute to personal construct therapy.

Part II of the book consists of three chapters that describe the process of using homework assignments for different populations (i.e., Chapters 10–12). We again outlined fairly broad criteria for contributors' discussion of how homework is integrated into the process of psychotherapy, what difficulties are encountered with particular populations, and what homework assignments are helpful. We also encouraged chapter authors to briefly outline, as much as the literature permitted, the empirical support for the use or particular types of homework assignments being discussed. Thus, we invited primarily clinical chapters including the following; (a) an overview of common barriers to the successful use of homework, (b) empirically supported homework for the population, (c) types of homework assignments based on theoretical and empirical support, (d) at least one case study of psychotherapy and prevention including case formulation.

In Chapter 10, Helen DeVries outlines her approach to using homework assignments for older adults. In Chapter 11, Norman Epstein and Donald Baucom describe how they integrate homework assignments into couples therapy. In Chapter 12, Kathleen Newcomb Rekart and Jay Lebow discuss the use of homework assignments for families receiving psychotherapy.

Part III of the book consists of 10 chapters that describe the process of using homework assignments for a range of complex clinical problems (i.e., Chapters 13–22). Once again, we decided to outline fairly broad criteria for contributors' discussion of how homework is integrated into the process of psychotherapy, what difficulties are encountered with particular populations, and what homework assignments are often helpful. We asked contributors to follow the same guiding structure as that incorporated in Part II.

In Chapter 13, Noam Lindenboim, Alex Chapman, and Marsha Linehan describe how homework assignments are integrated into psychotherapy for borderline personality disorder. In Chapter 14, Lawrence Riso and Michael Thase outline how homework assignments are useful in psychotherapy for chronic depression. In Chapter 15, Malcolm Johnson presents his approach to the effective use of homework assignments for clients with chronic pain. In Chapter 16, Tanya Schlam and Terence Wilson discuss the use of homework assignments in psychotherapy for eating disorders. In Chapter 17, Melanie Fennell presents her approach to the use of homework assignments in therapy for low self-esteem. In Chapter 18, David Clark extends his contributions to the clinical practice literature in discussing the role of homework in therapy for obsessions and compulsions. In Chapter 19, Hazel Dunn and Anthony Morrison extend their research contributions by discussing the role of homework in therapy for psychosis. In Chapter 20, Nancy Gambescia and Gerald Weeks detail their approach to the use of homework in psychotherapy for sexual dysfunction. In Chapter 21, Timothy Apodaca and Peter Monti outline the use of homework in psychotherapy for substance abuse. Finally, in Chapter 22, Janet Leathem and Muriel Christianson present an account of how homework assignments can assist in psychotherapy to aid rehabilitation following traumatic brain injury.

The final part of the book consists of three concluding chapters designed to synthesize and propose directions the four preceding sections. In Chapter 23, Michael Lambert, Cory Harmon, and Karstin Slade present directions for research on homework in psychotherapy and behavior change. In Chapter 24, Dana Nelson and Louis Castonguay present directions for the integration of homework in psychotherapy practice. In Chapter 25, T. Mark Harwood, Joselyne Sulzner, and Larry Beutler present directions for homework in psychotherapy prevention.

CONTENTS

INTRODUCTION AND HISTORICAL OVERVIEW

Nikolaos Kazantzis and Luciano L'Abate

There has been substantive research into the effects of homework assignments on psychotherapy outcomes. Studies have examined the correlational effects of homework compliance, and contrasted comparable therapies with and without homework. In contrast, research into the processes and mechanisms by which homework produces its effects remains far less developed. Nevertheless, research into homework assignments is an essential and evolving enterprise to understanding how and when psychotherapy works.

Before discussing the findings from contemporary research on homework research, we present a brief historical overview in order to place the current research, and practice applications in this book in context of the evolving field of psychotherapy. This overview leads to a consideration of the theoretical underpinnings and empirical evidence supporting homework's role in psychotherapy.

HISTORICAL OVERVIEW

The use of between-session time for treatment purposes has its origins in psychoanalytic psychotherapy. Freud (1924) suggested that patients should face their fears in everyday situations once they had worked through their conflicts in psychoanalysis (cf. Dattilio, 2002). It is also noteworthy that early psychoanalytic and directive formulations of psychotherapy included the use of homework assignments as an additional component to in-session therapeutic work (e.g., Dunlop, 1936; Herzberg, 1941; Thorne, 1948). However, it is George A. Kelly's (1955) fixed role therapy that has been credited with the systematic integration of homework into psychotherapy. The systematic use of homework was next represented in behavior therapy formulations (Kanfer & Phillips, 1966; Shelton & Ackerman, 1974). In particular, the use of therapeutic assignments between sessions was popularized by therapists working with sexual dysfunction (i.e., Kanfer, 1970; Kanfer & Phillips, 1966) where homework was conceptualized as the beginning point of therapy structure (Heiman, Lo Piccolo, & Lo Piccolo, 1981). The advent of cognitive therapy as espoused by Aaron T. Beck and Albert Ellis further emphasized homework as a core and crucial feature of psychotherapy process (e.g., Beck, Rush, Shaw, & Emery, 1979; Ellis, 1962).

Within behavioral and cognitive-behavioral therapy approaches, homework is accorded the main responsibility for ensuring that patients practice, generalize, and maintain adaptive therapeutic skills. The emphasis on homework's role has been maintained in contemporary formulations of these approaches (Alford & Beck, 1994; Beck et al., 1990; Freeman & Davis, 1990; Hollon & Beck, 1994; March, 1997; Thase, 1996; Whisman & Jacobson, 1990) as well as in guides to clinical practice (Beck, 1995; Persons, Davidson, & Tompkins, 2000; Kazantzis, Deane, Ronan, & L'Abate, 2005).

However, the use of homework in psychotherapy is not limited to behavioral and cognitive-behavioral therapies. For instance, some insight-oriented practitioners explicitly encouraged the use of homework assignments (Carich, 1990; Halligan, 1995; Tanner & Connan, 2003), and the benefits of between-session assignments are emphasized in experiential therapy (Greenberg, Watson, & Goldman, 1988). It is also noteworthy that couples and family therapists consider homework integral to their work (Carr, 1997; Hansen & MacMillan, 1990; L'Abate, L'Abate, & Maino, 2005; Nelson, 1994; O'Connell & Gomez, 1995). Homework is used in rehabilitation counseling (Gandy, 1995), solution-focused therapy (Beyebach, Morejon, Palenzuela, & Rodriguez-Arias, 1996), and in self-help interventions (Jordan & L'Abate, 1995).

A range of psychotherapies integrate assignments to help patients extend the therapy to their daily lives, and it has been suggested that "homework" can be considered a common factor in psychotherapy (Garfield, 1997; Kazantzis & Ronan, in press). There is some empirical data to support this claim. A recent randomized survey of 827 practicing psychologists supported the assertion that homework assignments are commonly used to augment a broad range of psychotherapies in everyday clinical work (Kazantzis, Lampropoulos, & Deane, 2005). The survey found that 24% of the sample identified as psychodynamic, and 31% of that group reported using homework to augment therapy. This finding replicated earlier surveys (Fehm & Kazantzis, 2004; Kazantzis, Busch, Ronan, & Merrick, in press). Many psychodynamic practitioners ask their patients to remember dreams for in-session discussion and analysis, as well as by using a variety of activities between sessions to assist patients in attaining treatment goals (cf. Stricker, in press). However, homework has repeatedly been identified as an aspect of psychotherapy process used to distinguish between psychodynamic and cognitive-behavioral therapies in the empirical literature.

A comprehensive survey of the psychotherapy process literature found that homework was mentioned in the description of cognitive-behavioral treatments, but were not mentioned in the methods of psychodynamic psychotherapies (Blagys & Hilsenroth, 2002). This result mirrored earlier studies of therapist behaviors in delivering cognitive-behavioral and psychodynamic-interpersonal therapy sessions that showed homework clearly differentiated these treatments (Goldfried, Castonguay, Hayes, Drozd, & Shapiro, 1997; Goldfried, Raue, & Castonguay, 1998). Thus, there appears to be some discrepancy between the way in which homework assignments are integrated into studies of psychotherapy process and outcome, and the way in which homework assignments are integrated into psychotherapists' clinical practice.

At least some of the apparent discrepancy between what is described in psychotherapy research publications, and what is described as part of practice, may be due to the way in which homework is operationally defined. In the next section, we provide a brief discussion on what constitutes a psychotherapy "*homework*" assignment, and discuss further the notion that between-session (homework) assignments, in various forms, represent a widespread feature of psychotherapy process.

WHAT CONSTITUTES A PSYCHOTHERAPY HOMEWORK" ASSIGNMENT?

The term "homework" is known to produce negative reactions among patients (Dunn, Morrison, & Bentall, 2002; Kazantzis, MacEwan, & Dattilio, 2005), and is disliked by therapists (Fehm & Kazantzis, 2004). Often associated with "lessons" or schoolwork prescribed for completion at home, many patients report unpleasant memories and experience anxiety and other negative emotions when remembering homework during formative years of education. When used in therapy, the term generally carries with it the notion that an activity has been "assigned" by the therapist and the patient's role is to "comply" with it. The term also conveys the idea that the between-session therapeutic activity is a piece of work to be graded in some fashion, and that it can be "failed." These negative associations may account for the avoidance of the term "homework" by some researchers in the empirical and practice literature. Terms used to refer to homework include "self-help assignments" (Masters & Johnson, 1970), "between-session assignments," "home practice activities" (see also terms reviewed in Kazantzis, 2000).

The common rationale for engaging patients in activities between sessions has been to foster *learning* in one form or another. However, the specific nature of assignments, the way in which they are integrated into psychotherapy, varies considerably across psychotherapy approaches. Some psychotherapy formulations incorporate specific homework assignments with the aim of targeting emotions, behaviors, cognitions, as well as interpersonal relationships. Specific activity assignments can involve information gathering, application of insights, or generalization skills introduced in therapy session to be applied in the everyday situations in which patients' difficulties actually occur. In other psychotherapies, however, homework assignments are not specific "tasks," and may focus on their experiential qualities. In fact, some psychotherapy approaches, such as the client-centered approaches, exclusively encourage client-initiated homework assignments, and do not incorporate homework that is content or process-directed by the therapist. Whatever their nature, homework assignments are meaningful and intentional activities incorporated into psychotherapy to facilitate patient adjustment and benefit. All forms of therapy are charged with the task of ultimately transcending the boundaries of the consulting room if therapy is to have an impact on patients' lives. Making appropriate suggestions about how patients might facilitate their own learning between sessions can help achieve this goal.

THEORETICAL CONSIDERATIONS

As with other aspects of psychotherapy process, there has been little theoretical work to explain the mechanism by which homework can contribute to the benefit that patients experience in therapy (Orlinsky, 2006). Empirical work has progressed without a clear conceptual framework for understanding what leads patients to engage with between-session homework assignments, and *how* insights and learning from these activities make meaningful contributions to reduction in distress, unhelpful cognitions, behaviors, and overwhelming emotions. Some attempts have been made to devise such a framework (e.g., Detweiler & Whisman, 1999; Malouff & Schutte, 2004), but these have not comprehensively considered the theoretical basis to engaging in homework assignments (Kazantzis, Dattilio, & MacEwan, 2005). To date, the empirical work has been limited to fairly basic associations between ratings of homework compliance and symptom reduction. The purpose of this section is to consider the theoretical elements that would help determine patient *engagement* in homework assignments.

Classical and operant conditioning processes are involved in patient engagement with homework assignments (Kazantzis & L'Abate, 2005). Homework is linked with both antecedents and consequences that serve to create the conditions under which the homework task is increased or decreased. Extensions of classical conditioning have highlighted the importance of the predictive link between the conditioned stimulus and the unconditioned response, and the ability for a stimulus to serve as a "safety signal" by predicting when an aversive event will not occur (Rescorla, 1988). Behavioral theorists note that all "stimuli" in everyday life are comprised of elements that have a particular significance to an individual based on their previous experiences, and that these experiences may interfere with conditioning to novel elements in the environment (Bouton, 1988). In other words, there are usually particular situations or aspects of a situation in the patient's natural environment that indicate the application of a particular intervention would be beneficial.

In basic terms, operant conditioning theory states that contingencies that are positive will increase a behavior, those that are negative will decrease a behavior, and those that are neither positive nor negative will extinguish a behavior. Any behavior conceptualized as a maintaining factor to the presenting problems usually has a wide variety of functions for the patient. In operant terms, the patient has developed expectations that this behavior provides some benefits or rewards. Consequently, a key feature of integrating homework into therapy is to hypothesize, and then test, what the possible unique functions are that maintain behaviors such as subtle avoidance in panic, withdrawal in depression, or reassurance seeking in generalized anxiety. Thus, it is helpful for therapists to consider reinforcement and punishment contingencies (i.e., costs and benefits) as motivational variables that encourage a patient to dedicate time and energy on homework assignments that clearly produce adaptive outcomes.

Of particular relevance to homework in psychotherapy are core elements of generalization, where there is transfer of trained skills (or behaviors) to a new setting, or leads to the development of skills that were not specifically trained. If generalization were not possible, a patient would need to learn a new skill for every newly problematic situation. Furthermore, a particular homework activity may be shaped through a process of successive approximations towards a complex task (or chaining of successive operants), and the repeated intrinsic rewards of the intervention are considered to control its maintenance.

One important implication from these principles is that behaviors need to be practiced *on a regular basis* for the maintenance of therapeutic gains (L'Abate, 1997). A second important implication is that although therapists' praise, encouragement, and other extrinsic rewards may help patients engage in homework activities, such external reinforcement may not be reliable for sustained long-term change. Patients are likely to benefit more from activities that have clear intrinsic rewards in terms of their reduced experience of distress and increased experience of positive affect. Moreover, practical obstacles and the frequency of shaping contingencies serve to determine the extent to which a homework activity is generalized and maintained in the patient's everyday life. (See Alford and Lantka, 2000 for empirical support for this behavior theory.)

In addition to this behavioral theory, a number of foundations to engagement in homework assignments may be drawn from cognitive theories. Social learning theory would suggest that a patient's intention, or motivation, to engage in a homework assignment is mediated by their beliefs regarding its costs and benefits. In this context, the cost is the perceived difficulty and/or distress that might be caused by the activity, and the benefit being the perceived gain, understanding, and/or skill acquisition in of skill that would be expected. Patients' beliefs about the homework are highly idiosyncratic and make sense in the context of other cognitions that contribute to the etiology and maintenance of their presenting problems (e.g., Bruch, Heimberg, & Hope, 1991).

Hullian learning theory would suggest that homework assignments give structure, direction, and clarity to the often unstructured and unclear psychotherapeutic process (Hunt, Matarazzo, Weiss, & Gentry, 1979). To that extent, then, these three qualities tend to lower whatever anxiety level, conceived as "drive," may have been present from the outset of the process. Too much anxiety may interfere with learning, while too little anxiety would not provide sufficient motivation to learn. Hence, a certain level of anxiety is necessary to provide motivation for change. Anxiety reduction, therefore, increases the frequency and strength of positive behaviors (i.e., "habits" in Hullian parlance). The multiplicative function of "drive × habit" would tend to produce positive results (Rescorla & Holland, 1982).

Motivation to engage in homework activities can also be explained in social cognition theory terms (Curtis, 1984; Horvath, 1993; Miller, 1985). Patients' perceived confidence in their ability to engage in a task, also known as self-efficacy, is likely to serve as a determinant of their decision to engage (Bandura, 1989). Theory suggests that perceived confidence is based on prior experience of engaging in a task, observation of other people's experiences, receiving encouragement and feedback from others, and experiencing emotional triggers that cue the activity (Kazantzis & L'Abate, 2005). Theory also suggests that self-regulatory processes are likely to be operating, whereby patients reflect and form beliefs based on the utility of the homework task, and their degree of engagement and learning from having completed it. In other words, a number of cognitive factors mediate the process of learning through homework completion. These mediators are activated when patients make sense of learning from homework completion, as well as in determining whether a homework assignment will be carried out.

A further formulation of psychotherapy (L'Abate, 1997) sees its process as being based on novel stimuli not present in the patient's experiential and behavioral repertoire. Having someone listening to one's hurts and painful past experiences and traumas, being regulated and reassured by regular and repetitive pre-set appointments, feeling limited in a positive way by the 50 minute hour, receiving directions and hope in prescriptions present in homework assignments give patients new impetus to change. Thus, adding homework assignments to the concrete, structural aspects of therapy (regular and repetitive pre-set appointments and of time

duration of therapy sessions), and rehearsal and repetition of newly acquired positive behaviors, would tend to produce positive results, above and beyond so-called
"specific and non-specific factors," therapist's characteristics, and the therapeutic
alliance.

In this section, we have considered the theoretical foundations that underpin patient engagement with homework assignments. We acknowledge that this discussion
reflects our own cognitive-behavioral biases, but have attempted to present foundation that underpin any activities that patients engage in between sessions. We have
intentionally not discussed the implications of this theory for the actual integration
of between-session homework assignments into therapy sessions. Even more than
understanding the theoretical determinants of patients' regular practice of assignments, a therapists' integration of between-session assignments into sessions will be
influenced and guided by their theoretical approach and the population.

WHAT ARE THE ISSUES IN USING HOMEWORK
IN DIFFERENT PSYCHOTHERAPIES?

We suggest that there are several key issues to be considered for the integration of
homework assignments into a range of psychotherapy approaches. The first issue concerns the nature, or choice, of the specific homework activity. Homework assignments
can be based on clinical experience, the subjective judgment of the therapist, or they
can be based or directly or indirectly derived or driven from theory. When they are derived directly from a theory or model, as in Aaron T. Beck's system of psychotherapy
(Beck et al., 1979), there can be some degree of predetermined scheduling of assignments based on the theoretical model explaining the etiology and maintenance of the
patient's concerns. Additionally, published therapy resources also provide flexible
lists of homework assignments for various problems and populations (Bevilacqua &
Dattilio, 2001; L'Abate, 2005a). In this *Handbook*, the reader will find chapters where
homework assignments are administered according to a pre-conceived system or an
integrative method that links together most if not all assignments, according to a guiding, pre-ordained approach, be that approach behavioral, humanistic, psychoanalytic,
or systemic.

A second issue for the integration of homework assignments for a range of psychotherapies concerns the empirical "validation" or support for different assignments.
Taxonomies for the assignment of particular homework assignments for particular
problems have been proposed (i.e., Brown-Standridge, 1989; De Shazer, 1988; Hay &
Kinnier, 1998), but there is limited empirical support for specific assignments (see
review in Kazantzis, Deane, Ronan, & Lampropoulos, 2005). However, the notion
of considering empirically supported homework assignments is debatable. Even
if the assignment is theoretically identical, such as two patients scheduling activities as part of behavioral activation for depression, the real-life implementation
will differ between patients. That is, one patient may benefit from engaging in
the same activity three times daily for 30 minutes, whereas the other patient may
benefit from engaging in slight variations of the activity once per day for varying amounts of time. These differences are important for ensuring that the assignment can be practically carried out by the patient, given their idiosyncratic array
if weekly commitments, particular strengths and biases. Nonetheless, the field has

yet to evaluate many of the homework assignments championed as beneficial [1]. The line between individual tailoring of the same assignment, and a "different" homework assignment needs to be drawn. In this *Handbook,* the reader will find assignments ranging from those that do not involve any written or overt activity component, to those that are explicitly defined in terms of explicit or overt behavior.

A third issue for the integration of homework assignments for a range of psychotherapies concerns the method of integrating homework into therapy. A number of guides to the use of homework assignments in psychotherapy practice have appeared in the literature. As might be expected, cognitive theory and therapy (Beck, 1976; Beck et al., 1979) and traditional behavior therapy included a reasonable degree of guidance in the integration of homework into therapy sessions. Shelton and Ackerman (1974) devised a clinician's guide with a list of 150 homework assignments that could be used for behavioral problems. Shelton and Ackerman also provided guidance on how to integrate homework into the therapeutic process, later extended by Shelton and Levy (1981b) in a "model for practice." These early recommendations featured the following elements:

(a) homework is an interpersonal process that requires a strong therapeutic relationship
(b) homework should be relevant to the client's problems and goals for treatment
(c) homework should be within the client's ability
(d) homework should be practiced in-session
(e) homework compliance should be discussed, with successes praised, and problems considered
(f) private and public statements of commitments to homework are required
(g) homework should be assigned with a clear description of task variables—where, when, how often, and how long
(h) a written copy of the homework should be provided

However, a variety of recommendations have been published in the psychotherapy practice literature. Neimeyer (1999) outlined the following for the use of homework in narrative therapy: (a) develop a collaborative attitude; (b) respect the patient's "resistance"; (c) respect the patient's privacy; (d) integrate homework into the session; and (e) recognize the value of "being" as well as "doing." Broder (2000) outlined six strategies for the optimal use of homework in rational-emotive behavior therapy (Ellis, 1962) as follows:

(a) Communicate the importance of homework as early in treatment as possible with emphasis on its benefits to your client.
(b) If your sessions are limited, space them out in such a way as to make treatment as effective as possible by giving ample time to complete homework assignments and exercises. If you do that, make it clear that if your client runs into difficulty additional sessions can be scheduled. Make sure your client understands that sessions are precious commodities.

---

[1] Arguing that language can be distorted willfully or otherwise, and that talk cannot be controlled and it is subject to confusion and conflict, L'Abate (1999, 2004a, 2005b), for instance, has insisted in producing written homework assignments systematically related to clinical and non-clinical topics (L'Abate, 1996).

(c) Give lots of feedback and positive reinforcement when it becomes apparent that homework was completed.
(d) Help your client see how therapy supplements what is being done in between sessions as well as the reverse.
(e) Use both positive and negative contingencies to shape the completion of homework assignments.
(f) Begin sessions by following up on homework assignments. By not following up, homework may be perceived by clients as not being very important. In addition, following up gives you a built-in opportunity to reinforce whatever progress has been made in between sessions.

As illustrated by these examples, the recommendations offered for the use of homework assignments are strongly influenced by the theoretical orientation of the practitioners. There is limited discussion of between-session assignments in psychotherapies other than cognitive and cognitive-behavioral therapies. Thus, the broad aim of this *Handbook* is to provide a comprehensive resource on the use of homework assignments within the broad spectrum of psychotherapy approaches. The reader will see that some approaches incorporate homework assignments systematically, others use homework more reactively to address on patient needs.

THE PRACTITIONERS OF HOMEWORK
IN PSYCHOTHERAPY

Before proposing this project, we wanted to be sure that psychotherapy practitioners actually integrate the homework assignments into their practice so that such a resource would be useful for clinical work. We started by conducting local surveys of practicing psychologists and found that the majority reported integrating homework on a frequent basis (Deane, Glaser, Oades, & Kazantzis, 2005; Kazantzis & Deane, 1999). We also replicated this finding in a survey of German psychologists (Fehm & Kazantzis, 2004), and in a randomized sample of 830 North American psychologists (Kazantzis, Lampropoulos,& Deane, 2005). In addition, the use of homework is not limited to psychologists practicing psychotherapy; the prominent use of homework has also been found among case managers, counselors, nurses, psychotherapists, and social workers (Kazantzis, Busch, Ronan, & Merrick, in press; Kelly, Deane, Kazantzis, Crowe, & Oades, 2006). Thus, the use of homework in psychotherapy does not seem to be limited to a particular professional group providing psychotherapy.

CONTINUING RESEARCH ON
PSYCHOTHERAPY OUTCOMES

A wide variety of treatment outcome studies have included homework assignments within their treatment protocols, but a comparatively small proportion, 5% according to Shelton and Levy (1981b), actually measure the extent to which patients engage in homework. Nevertheless, studies have sought to examine the relationship between patient engagement in homework and therapy. The research has essentially progressed along two avenues. First, studies have sought to contrast therapies involving homework assignments, with comparable therapies consisting entirely of in-session work. These studies have intended to examine whether homework contributes a *causal* effect on therapy outcomes. If these studies are examined in terms of their being "statistically significant," then it appears as though the findings are inconclusive as only some report positive results at $p < 0.05$ (see Barlow, O'Brien, & Last, 1984; Edelman & Chambless, 1993; Fals-Stewart & Lucente, 1993; Kornblith, Rehm, O'Hara, & Lamparski, 1983; Lax, Basoglu, & Marks, 1992; Nelson & Borkovec, 1989; Startup & Edmonds, 1994). However, these studies have generally involved small samples and have been insufficiently sensitive to detect effects (Kazantzis, 2000). Quantitative reviews that bypass the limitations of low statistical power have concluded that the data support the hypothesis that homework produces positive effects on outcome (Beutler et al., 2004; Kazantzis, Deane, & Ronan, 2000).

The second avenue of research has involved the association between homework compliance and therapy outcome. This is a slightly different research question, namely, whether there is a *correlational* relationship between patient engagement in homework assignments and therapy outcome, given that the patient is involved in a therapy that incorporates homework assignments (e.g., Addis & Jacobson, 2000; Coon & Thompson, 2003; Edelman & Chambless, 1995; Leung & Heimberg, 1996). Because this correlational research question does not require the allocation of patients to different therapy conditions, this second group of studies has generally had greater power to detect a positive correlation between homework compliance and therapy outcome. Despite this positive link between patient engagement and outcome, there have been some key limitations in both avenues of research.

One limitation concerns the measurement of patient engagement in homework. Researchers have generally defined engagement as "compliance" or *quantity* of homework completion. Apart from the measures of compliance often involving retrospective single-item ratings at the end of therapy, these measures have not taken into account any of the theoretically relevant factors that are hypothesized to determine engagement and learning from homework (see review in Kazantzis, Deane, & Ronan, 2004). Some researchers have sought to assess the *quality* of homework completion, or degree of skill acquisition, and have generally found that this is a better predictor of outcome (e.g., Niemeyer & Feixas, 1990; Schmidt & Wollaway-Bickel, 2000). Thus, the measurement of homework completion has been limited in existing research and would benefit from integrating theoretically meaningful determinants of engagement for a more detailed examination of the mechanism by which homework produces its effects.

A second limitation of the existing data has been the focus on patient factors, and little consideration of therapist and the interaction with the patient. This seems particularly important given the growing body of evidence demonstrating that therapist competence is not a stable attribute, and does vary in the context of psychotherapy outcome studies (Dobson & Kazantzis, 2003; Kazantzis, 2003). It seems even more important when one considers the data showing therapist competence in reviewing homework assignments is linked with homework compliance (Bryant, Simons, & Thase, 1999) and competence in structuring therapy, including homework assignments, is linked with outcome (Shaw et al., 1999). Thus, future research would benefit from a more comprehensive examination of therapist competence of homework completion as a factor that influences the relationship between patient engagement in homework and therapy outcome.

A third limitation is that the large majority of empirical studies on the role of homework assignments have been conducted within behavioral and cognitive-behavioral therapies for anxiety and mood disorders. There is a need for more research on the mechanism by which homework contributes to the outcomes of a range of psychotherapies. Gathering data to ascertain whether the theorized foundations to patient engagement in homework would enable the field to move forward and provide practitioners with evidence-based recommendations for the integration of homework into psychotherapy. We hope that the theoretical, empirical, and clinical practice discussions outlined in this *Handbook* will encourage researchers to focus their attention on unraveling *how* homework produces its effects on outcome.

CONCLUSION

The purpose of this introductory chapter was to give an historical overview of how homework assignments fit within the context of the process and outcome of psychotherapy. Whatever their nature, homework assignments are meaningful and intentional activities incorporated into psychotherapy to facilitate patient adjustment and benefit. This book aims to provide readers with focused teaching on how to effectively use homework assignments in a range of therapy approaches and clinical populations heretofore absent in the psychotherapeutic literature. As the reader will note, the field is left with many unanswered questions about the role of homework assignments in psychotherapy. We hope that this *Handbook* will provide a step forward in the development of further theoretical and empirical work. Our patients are likely to benefit from the fields advancement towards defining the mechanism by which homework contributes to effective psychotherapy practice and prevention.

REFERENCES

Addis, M. E., & Jacobson, N. S. (2000). A closer look at the treatment rationale and homework compliance in cognitive behavioral therapy for depression. *Cognitive Therapy and Research, 24,* 313–326.

Alford, B. A., & Beck, A. T. (1994). Cognitive therapy of delusional beliefs. *Behaviour Research and Therapy, 32,* 369–380.

Alford, B. A., & Lantka, A. L. (2000). Processes of clinical change and resistance: A theoretical synthesis. *Behavior Modification, 24,* 566–579.

Bandura, A. (1989). Human agency in social cognitive theory. *American Psychologist, 44,* 1175–1184.

Barlow, D. H., O'Brien, G. T., & Last, C. G. (1984). Couples treatment of agoraphobia. *Behavior Therapy, 15,* 41–58.

Bevilacqua, L. J., & Dattilio, F. M. (2001). *Brief family homework planner.* New York: Wiley.

Beyebach, M., Morejon, A. R., Palenzuela, D. L., & Rodriguez-Arias, J. L. (1996). Research on the process of solution-focused therapy. In S. D. Miller, M. A. Hubble, & B. L. Duncan (Eds.), *Handbook of solution-focused brief therapy* (pp. 299–334). San Francisco: Jossey-Bass.

Beck, A.T. (1976). *Cognitive therapy and the emotional disorders.* New York: International Universities Press.

Beck, A. T., Rush, J. A., Shaw, B. F., & Emery, G. (1979). *Cognitive therapy of depression*. New York: Guilford.

Beck, A. T., Freeman, A., Pretzer, J., Davis, D. D., Fleming, B., Ottaviani, R., Beck, J. et al. (1990). *Cognitive therapy of personality disorders*. New York: Guilford.

Beck, J. (1995). *Cognitive therapy: Basics and beyond:* New York: Guilford.

Beutler, L. E., Malik, M., Alimohamed, S., Harwood, T. M., Talebi, H., Noble, S. et al. (2004). Therapist variables. In M. J. Lambert (Ed.), *Bergin and Garfield's Handbook of psychotherapy and behavior change* (5th ed., pp. 227–306). New York: John Wiley & Sons.

Blagys, M. D., & Hilsenroth, M. J. (2002). Distinctive features of cognitive-behavioral therapy: A review of the comparative psychotherapy process literature. *Clinical Psychology Review, 22,* 671–706.

Bouton, M. E. (1988). Context and ambiguity in the extinction of emotional learning: Implications for exposure therapy. *Behaviour Research & Therapy, 26,* 137–149.

Broder, M. S. (2000). Making optimal use of homework to enhance your therapeutic effectiveness. *Journal of Rational-Emotive and Cognitive Behavior Therapy, 18,* 3–18.

Brown-Stanridge, M. D. (1989). A paradigm for constructing of family therapy tasks. *Family Process, 28,* 471–489.

Bruch, M. A., Heimberg. R. G., & Hope, D. A. (1991). States of mind model and cognitive change in treated social phobics. *Cognitive Therapy and Research, 15,* 429–441.

Bryant, M. J., Simons, A. D., & Thase, M. E. (1999). Therapist skill and patient variables in homework compliance: Controlling a uncontrolled variable in cognitive therapy outcome research. *Cognitive Therapy and Research, 23,* 381–399.

Carr, A. (1997). Positive practice in family therapy. *Journal of Marital and Family Therapy, 23,* 271–293.

Carich, M. S. (1990). Utilizing task assignments within Adlerian therapy. *Individual Psychology, 46,* 217–224.

Coon, D. W., & Thompson, L. W. (2003). The relationship between homework compliance and treatment outcomes among older adult outpatients with mild-to-moderate depression. *American Journal of Psychiatry, 11,* 53–61.

Curtis, J. M. (1984). Motivational techniques for individual and group psychotherapy. *Psychological Reports, 54,* 271–277.

Dattilio, F. M. (2002). Homework assignments in couple and family therapy. *Journal of Clinical Psychology, 58,* 535–549.

Deane, F. P., Glaser, N. M., Oades, L. G., & Kazantzis, N. (2005). Psychologists' use of homework assignments with clients who have schizophrenia. *Clinical Psychologist, 9,* 24–30.

De Shazer, S. (1998). *Clues: Investigating solutions in brief therapy.* New York: Norton.

Detweiler, J. B., & Whisman, M. A. (1999). The role of homework assignments in cognitive therapy for depression Potential methods for enhancing adherence. *Clinical Psychology: Science and Practice, 6,* 267–282.

Dobson, K., & Kazantzis, N. (2003). The therapist in cognitive-behavioral therapy: Introduction to a special section. *Psychotherapy Research, 13,* 131–134.

Dunlop, K. L. (1936). *Elements of psychology.* St. Louis, MO: C V Mosby.

Dunn, H., Morrison, A. P., & Bentall, R. P. (2002). Patients' experiences of homework tasks in cognitive behavioral therapy for psychosis: A qualitative analysis. *Clinical Psychology and Psychotherapy, 9,* 361–369.

Edelman, R. E., & Chambless, D. L. (1993). Compliance during sessions and homework in exposure-based treatment of agoraphobia. *Behaviour Research and Therapy, 31,* 767–773.

Edelman, R. E., & Chambless, D. L. (1995). Adherence during sessions and homework in cognitive-behavioral group treatment of social phobia. *Behaviour Research and Therapy, 33,* 573–577.

Ellis, A. (1962). *Reason and emotion in psychotherapy.* Secaucus, NJ: Lyle Stuart.

Fals-Stewart, W., & Lucente, S. (1993). An MCMI-cluster typology of obsessive-compulsives: A measure of personality characteristics and its relationship to treatment participation, compliance and outcome in behavior therapy. *Journal of Psychiatric Research, 27,* 139–154.

Fehm, L., & Kazantzis, N. (2004). Attitudes and use of homework assignments in therapy: A survey of German psychotherapists. *Clinical Psychology & Psychotherapy, 11,* 332–343.

Freeman, A., & Davis, D. D. (1990). Cognitive therapy of depression. In A. S. Bellack., M. Hersen., & A. E. Kazdin (Eds.), *International handbook of behavior modification and therapy* (2nd ed., pp. 333–352). New York: Plenum.

Freud, S. (1924). Inhibitions, symptoms and anxiety. Reprinted in R. M. Hutchins (Ed.) *Great books of the western world* (pp. 718–734). Chicago: Encyclopedia Britannica.

Gandy, G. L. (1995). *Mental health rehabilitation: Disputing irrational beliefs.* Springfield, IL: Charles C. Thomas.

Garfield, S. L. (1997). Brief psychotherapy: The role of common and specific factors. *Clinical Psychology and Psychotherapy, 4,* 217–225.

Goldfried, M. R., Castonguay, L. G., Hayes, A. M., Drozd, J. F., & Shapiro, D. A. (1997). A comparative analysis of the therapeutic focus in cognitive-behavioral and psychodynamic-interpersonal session. *Journal of Consulting and Clinical Psychology, 65,* 740–748.

Goldfried, M. R., Raue, P. J., & Castonguay, L. G. (1998). The therapist focus in significant sessions of master therapists: A comparison of cognitive-behavioral and psychodynamic-interpersonal interventions. *Journal of Consulting and Clinical Psychology, 66,* 803–810.

Greenberg, L. S., Watson, J. C., & Goldman, R. (Eds.). (1988). *Process-experiential therapy of depression: Handbook of experiential psychotherapy* (pp. 227–248). New York: The Guilford Press.

Halligan, F. R. (1995). The challenge: Short-term dynamic psychotherapy for college counseling centers. *Psychotherapy, 32,* 113–121.

Hansen, D. J., & MacMillan, V. M. (1990). Behavioral assessment of child-abusive and neglectful families: Recent developments and current issues. *Behavior Modification, 14,* 255–278.

Hay, C. E., & Kinnier, R. T. (1998). Homework in counseling. *Journal of Mental Health Counseling, 20,* 122.

Heiman, J. R., Lo Piccolo, L., & Lo Piccolo, J. (1981). The treatment of sexual dysfunction. In A. S. Gurman & D. P. Kniskern (Eds.), *Handbook of family therapy* (pp. 592–627). New York: Brunner/Mazel.

Herzberg, A. (1941). Short-term treatment of neurosis by graduate tasks. *British Journal of Medical Psychology, 29,* 36–51.

Hollon, S. D., & Beck, A. T. (1994). Cognitive and cognitive-behavioral therapies. In A. E. Bergin & S. L. Garfield (Eds.), *Handbook of psychotherapy and behavior change* (4th ed., pp. 428–466). New York: John Wiley & Sons.

Horvath, A. T. (1993). Enhancing motivation for treatment of addictive behaviour: Guidelines for the psychotherapist. *Psychotherapy, 30,* 473–480.

Hunt, W. A., Matarazzo, J. D., Weiss, S. M., & Gentry, W. D. (1979). Associative learning, habit, and health behavior. *Journal of Behavioral Medicine, 2,* 111–124.

Jordan, K. & L'Abate, L. (1995). Programmed writing and therapy with symbiotically enmeshed patients. *American Journal of Psychotherapy, 49,* 225–236.

Kanfer, F. H. (1970). Self-monitoring, methodological limitations, and clinical applications. *Journal of Consulting and Clinical Psychology, 35,* 148–152.

Kanfer, F., & Phillips, J. (1966). A survey of current behavior and a proposal for classification. *Archives of General Psychiatry, 15,* 114–128.

Kazantzis, N. (2000). Power to detect homework effects in psychotherapy outcome research. *Journal of Consulting and Clinical Psychology, 68,* 166–170.

Kazantzis, N. (2003). Therapist competence in cognitive and behaviour therapies: Review of the contemporary empirical evidence. *Behaviour Change, 20,* 1–12.

Kazantzis, N., Busch, R., Ronan, K. R., & Merrick, P. L. (in press). Using homework assignments in psychotherapy: Differences by theoretical orientation and professional training? *Behavioural and Cognitive Psychotherapy.*

Kazantzis, N., Dattilio, F. M., & MacEwan, J. (2005). In pursuit of homework adherence in behavior and cognitive behavior therapy: Comment on Malouff and Schutte (2004). *The Behavior Therapist, 28,* 179–183.

Kazantzis, N., & Deane, F. P. (1999). Psychologists' use of homework assignments in clinical practice. *Professional Psychology: Research and Practice, 30,* 581–585.

Kazantzis, N., Deane, F. P., & Ronan, K. R. (2000). Homework assignments in cognitive and behavioral therapy: A meta-analysis. *Clinical Psychology: Science and Practice, 7,* 189–202.

Kazantzis, N., Deane, F. P., & Ronan, K. R. (2004). Assessing compliance with homework assignments: Review and recommendations for clinical practice. *Journal of Clinical Psychology, 60,* 627–641.

Kazantzis, N., Deane, F. P., Ronan, K. R., & L'Abate, L. (Eds.). (2005). *Using homework assignments in cognitive behavioral therapy.* New York: Routledge.

Kazantzis, N., Deane, F. P., Ronan, K. R., & Lampropoulos, G. L (2005). Empirical foundations. In N. Kazantzis, F. P. Deane., K. R. Ronan., & L. L'Abate (Eds.), *Using homework assignments in cognitive behavior therapy* (pp. 35–60). New York: Routledge.

Kazantzis, N., Lampropoulos, G. L., & Deane, F. P. (2005). A national survey of practicing psychologists' use and attitudes towards homework in psychotherapy. *Journal of Consulting and Clinical Psychology, 73,* 742–748.

Kazantzis, N., & L'Abate, L. (2005). Theoretical foundations. In N. Kazantzis, F. P. Deane., K. R. Ronan., & L. L'Abate (Eds.), *Using homework assignments in cognitive behavior therapy* (pp. 9–33). New York: Routledge.

Kazantzis, N., MacEwan, J., & Dattilio, F. M. (2005). A guiding model for practice. In N. Kazantzis, F. P. Deane, K. R. Ronan., & L. L'Abate (Eds.), *Using homework assignments in cognitive behavior therapy* (pp. 359–407). New York: Routledge.

Kazantzis, N., & Ronan, K. R. (Eds.). The use of between-session (homework) activities in different psychotherapy approaches [Special Issue]. *Journal of Psychotherapy Integration* (in press).

Kelly, G. A. (1955). *The psychology of personal constructs.* New York: W. W. Norton.

Kelly, P. J., Deane, F. P., Kazantzis, N., Crowe, T. P., & Oades, L. G. (2006). Use of homework by mental health case managers in the rehabilitation of persistent and recurring psychiatric disability. *Journal of Mental Health, 15,* 95–101.

Kornblith, S. J., Rehm, L. P., O'Hara, M. W., & Lamparski, D. M. (1983). The contribution of self-reinforcement training and behavioral assignments to the efficacy of self-control therapy for depression. *Cognitive Therapy and Research, 7,* 499–528.

L'Abate, L. (1997). The paradox of change: Better them than us! In R. S. Sauber (Ed.), *Managed mental health care: Major diagnostic and treatment approaches* (pp. 40–66). Bristol, PA: Brunner/Mazel.

L'Abate, L. (1999). Taking the bull by the horns: Beyond talk in psychological interventions. *The Family Journal: Therapy and Counseling for Couples and Families, 7,* 206–220.

L'Abate, L. (2004a). *A guide to self-help workbooks for clinicians and researchers.* Binghamton, NY: Haworth.

L'Abate, L. (2004b). The role of workbooks in the delivery of mental health services in prevention, psychotherapy and rehabilitation In L. L'Abate (Ed), *Using workbooks in mental health: Resources in prevention, psychotherapy, and rehabilitation for clinicians and researchers* (pp. 3–64). Binghamton, NY: Haworth.

L'Abate, L. (2005a). *Personality in intimate relationships: Socialization and psycho- pathology.* New York: Springer/Verlag.

L'Abate, L. (2005b). *What I really believe about psychotherapy.* Paper presented at a symposium on psychotherapy. Annual Meeting of the American Psychological Association, Washington, DC., August 19.

L'Abate, L. (1996). Workbooks for better living. www.mentalhealthhelp.com.

L'Abate, L, L'Abate, B. L., & Maino, E. (2005). A review of 25 years of part-time professional practice: Workbooks and length of psychotherapy. *American Journal of Family Therapy, 33,* 19–31.

Lax, T., Basoglu, M., & Marks, I. M. (1992). Expectancy and compliance as predictors of outcome in obsessive-compulsive disorder. *Behavioural Psychotherapy, 20,* 257–266.

Leung, A. W., & Heimberg, R. G. (1996). Homework compliance, perceptions of control, and outcome of cognitive-behavioral treatment of social phobia. *Behaviour Research and Therapy, 34,* 423–432.

Malouff, J. M., & Schutte, N. S. (2004). Strategies for increasing client completion of treatment assignments. *Behavior Therapist, 27,* 118–121.

March, P. (1997). In two minds about cognitive-behavioral therapy: Talking to patients about why they do not do their homework. *British Journal of Psychotherapy, 13,* 461–472.

Masters, W. H., & Johnson, V. E. (1970). *Human sexual inadequacy.* Boston, MA: Little & Brown.

Miller, W. R. (1985). Motivation for treatment: A review with special emphasis on alcoholism. *Psychological Bulletin, 48,* 84–107.

Neimeyer, R. A. (1999). Narrative strategies in grief therapy. *Journal of Constructivist Psychology, 12,* 65–85.

Neimeyer, R. A., & Feixas, G. (1990). The role of homework and skill acquisition in the outcome of group cognitive therapy for depression. *Behavior Therapy, 21,* 281–292.

Nelson, T. S. (1994). Do-overs. *Journal of Family Psychotherapy, 5,* 71–74.

Nelson, R. A., & Borkovec, T. D. (1989). Relationship of client participation to psychotherapy. *Journal of Behavior Therapy and Experimental Psychiatry, 20,* 155–162.

O'Connell, W. E., & Gomez, E. A. (1995). Marital and family therapy as an empowering of cooperation-as-equals. *Individual Psychology: Journal of Adlerian Theory, Research & Practice, 51,* 37–45.

Orlinsky, D. E. (2006). Comments on the state of psychotherapy research (as I see it). *Newsletter of the North American Society for Psychotherapy Research, January Issue.*

Persons, J. B., Davidson, J., & Tompkins, M. A. (2001). *Essential components of cognitive-behavior therapy for depression.* Washington, DC: American Psychological Association.

Rescorla, R. A., (1988). Pavlovian conditioning: It's not what you think it is. *American Psychologist, 43,* 151–160

Rescorla, R. A., & Holland, P. C. (1982). Behavioral studies of associative learning in animals. *Annual Review of Psychology, 33,* 265–308.

Schmidt, N. B., & Woolaway-Bickel, K. (2000). The effects of treatment compliance on outcome in cognitive-behavioral therapy for panic disorder: Quality versus quantity. *Journal of Consulting and Clinical Psychology, 68,* 13–18.

Shaw, B. F., Elkin, I., Yamaguchi, J., Olmsted, M., Vallis, T. M., Dobson, K. S., Lowery, A., Sotsky, S. M., Watkins, J. T., Imber, S. D. (1999). Therapist competence ratings in relation to clinical outcome in cognitive therapy of depression. *Journal of Consulting and Clinical Psychology, 67,* 837–846.

Shelton, J. L., & Ackerman, J. M. (1974). *Homework in counseling and psychotherapy: Examples of systematic assignments for therapeutic use by mental health professionals.* Springfield, IL: Charles C. Thomas.

Shelton, J. L., & Levy, R. L. (1981a). A survey of the reported use of assigned homework activities in contemporary behavior therapy literature. *The Behavior Therapist, 4,* 13–14.

Shelton, J. L., & Levy, R. L. (1981b). *Behavioral assignments and treatment compliance: A handbook of clinical strategies.* Champaign, IL: Research Press.

Startup, M., & Edmonds, J. (1994). Compliance with homework assignments in cognitive-behavioral psychotherapy for depression: Relation to outcome and methods of enhancement. *Cognitive Therapy and Research, 18,* 567–579.

Stricker, G.. Using homework in psychodynamic psychotherapy. *Journal of Psychotherapy Integration* (in press).

Tanner, C., & Connan, F. (2003). Cognitive analytic therapy. In J. Treasure, U. Schmidt, & E. van Furth (Eds.),*Handbook of Eating Disorders* (2nd ed., pp. 279–289). New York: Wiley.

Thase, M. (1996). Cognitive behavior therapy manual for treatment of depressed inpatients. In V. B. Van Hasselt & M. Hersen (Eds.), *Sourcebook of psychological treatment manuals for adult disorders* (pp. 201–231). New York: Plenum.

Thorne, F. C. (1948). Directive psychotherapy: Suggestion, persuasion, and advice. *Journal of Consulting and Clinical Psychology, 4,* 70–82.

Whisman, M. A., & Jacobson, N. S. (1990). Brief behavioral marital therapy. In R. A. Wells & V. J. Giannetti (Eds.), *Handbook of brief psychotherapies* (pp. 325–349). New York: Plenum.

Part I

PSYCHOTHERAPY APPROACHES

CHAPTER 1

BEHAVIOR THERAPY

Deborah Roth Ledley and Jonathan D. Huppert

Behavior therapy is an empirically based treatment approach that has demonstrated efficacy across numerous psychological disorders including mood disorders, anxiety disorders, eating disorders, and substance use disorders (Hersen & Bellack, 1999). Behavior therapy has also proven effective with numerous "problems with living" including weight management, smoking cessation, and childhood behavior problems. In behavior therapy, the therapist and patient work together to understand the factors that maintain problematic behaviors, and strategies are then initiated to help patients discontinue problematic behaviors and/or initiate new more, adaptive behaviors. Many treatment techniques fall under the umbrella of behavior therapy, from self-monitoring, to behavioral activation, to exposure, but all are meant to accomplish these same goals.

Behavior therapy is unique from other therapies in a number of ways. First, behavior therapy is time-limited. Some reasonably simple problems, like a specific phobia of spiders, can be treated in just a few hours (e.g., Öst, Ferebee, & Furmark, 1997). Even the most complex problems can often be treated in less than 20 sessions. Behavior therapy works efficiently because it is problem-focused and present-focused. Rather than spending a lot of time questioning where the problem came from, the focus is placed on the factors that currently maintain the problem and on changing these maintaining factors to ameliorate the problem. Another reason that behavior therapy can proceed relatively quickly is that much of the work of therapy actually occurs outside of sessions. Patients are typically assigned homework, and are generally encouraged to embrace opportunities to work on their difficulties in between sessions even beyond set homework assignments.

The concept of homework illuminates another important quality of behavior therapy—the patient and therapist are viewed as partners who each play an important role in treatment. Early on in treatment, the task of patients is to teach their therapists about the problems that they are experiencing; it is the therapist's task to teach patients about the behavioral model of understanding and treating their problems. Once the therapist and the patient are "on the same page" so to speak, they are ready to embark on the process of therapy together. While it is typical for the therapist to set session agendas and to assign homework early in treatment, patients are encouraged to take an increasingly active role as treatment progresses. This ensures that patients can serve as their own therapists once treatment is over, thereby facilitating continuing improvement as well as preventing relapse.

In this chapter, we will: 1) discuss the purposes of homework in behavior therapy; 2) describe different kinds of homework assignments; 3) show how to design and assign homework; 4) discuss how to ensure homework compliance and how to deal with noncompliance; and 5) describe how to adapt homework assignments when working with children and teenagers.

WHY HOMEWORK SHOULD BE ASSIGNED IN BEHAVIOR THERAPY

EMPIRICAL SUPPORT FOR THE USE OF HOMEWORK IN BEHAVIOR THERAPY

There are a number of reasons for why homework should be assigned in behavior therapy. Perhaps the most compelling reason is that homework compliance has been found to be associated with good treatment outcome across many disorders (see meta-analysis by Kazantzis, Deane, & Ronan, 2000). Homework compliance has also been associated with long-term maintenance of gains once treatment is over (Park et al., 2001).

CLINICAL RATIONALE FOR THE USE OF HOMEWORK IN BEHAVIOR THERAPY

A good way to communicate to patients the importance of homework is to share the research findings described above. It can also be helpful to share some hypotheses on the relationship between homework compliance and outcome. A simple explanation for the relationship is the old adage, "The more effort you put in, the more you get out." If patients only work on their difficulties during an hour-long, weekly therapy session, it is likely that they will get *something* out of treatment, but not nearly as much (and not nearly as efficiently) as if they put in time on their own in between sessions.

From a behavioral perspective, problematic behaviors are maintained because of learned associations between stimuli and responses. Behaviorally based treatment involves learning new, more adaptive responses; repeated practice strengthens this new stimuli-response association, while weakening the old, maladaptive responses. There are a number of reasons why these new associations are not learned as well if practice only occurs during sessions. The most obvious is that in-session time is limited. In order for these new associations to form, patients must practice them more frequently than would be afforded by a weekly therapy session. Patients might relate to the idea that behavior change is very much like learning a new language. Simply taking a language class would not lead to fluency. Rather, between classes, students should listen to language tapes, read newspapers or watch TV in the language, and practice conversing with a fellow student or someone fluent in the language. Students would probably benefit most from visiting a country where the language is spoken. This "extra" work outside the classroom is perhaps even more important than what is learned in the classroom.

Another advantage of homework is that it allows patients to try out new behaviors in different contexts, likely resulting in different learning experiences than what is gained from in-session work. Interestingly, animal models suggest that providing opportunities for learning in a variety of contexts promotes retention of new learning (e.g., Bouton, 1994). Take for example a patient with bulimia nervosa who had a long list of foods that she considered to be forbidden. This patient feared that if she ate these foods, she would lose control, overeat, and gain an immense amount of weight. She also feared that if she ate "bad" foods, even in moderation, other people would judge her negatively. At the time she came for treatment, she felt proud of her self-control and believed that her friends also placed value on this. During early therapy sessions, the therapist and patient worked through a hierarchy of forbidden foods, and homework assignments involved eating these same foods at home during the week. These exposures helped the patient learn that eating these foods in moderation would not lead to uncontrolled weight gain. Doing the exposures at home helped her to see that she would not lose control and overeat if the therapist were not present. Later homework assignments involved eating these same foods in the presence of friends in order to work on the belief that doing so would lead them to think less highly of her. In fact, when doing these homework assignments, the patient actually received positive feedback from her friends who were relieved to see her eat something besides salads and felt more at ease eating with her under these conditions. These very important learning experiences could not have occurred during sessions because the patient believed that the presence of the therapist would stop her from overeating and because she was not nearly as concerned by what the therapist thought of her as by what her friends thought of her. The combination of in-session and homework exposures helped her to set up a new association with her forbidden foods. Rather than associate them with fear and loss of control, she came to see that she could get some pleasure out of eating them in moderation—both from the food itself and from the improvement in her social relations that came about by being less restrictive around eating.

As was just mentioned, another important contextual difference between in-session work and homework is the presence/absence of the therapist. Sometimes patients believe that they were only able to engage in a new behavior because the therapist was present, offering reassurance and providing safety. For example, a patient with panic disorder who greatly feared riding the subway successfully did so with his therapist for the first time in 20 years. He had avoided doing so because he feared that he would have a panic attack while in the subway tunnel and that if he could not get out of the subway, he might go crazy. After the in-session exposure, the therapist asked the patient whether he was surprised that he did not have a panic attack (or go crazy). The patient responded, "Because you were there and I was distracted, I didn't get anxious enough to have a panic attack." The therapist then suggested that they get back on the subway, but that the therapist ride at one end of the car and the patient ride at the other so that the patient would not be distracted from his panic symptoms. During this exposure, the patient experienced some panic symptoms but they did not develop into full-blown panic, because he kept reminding himself that the therapist was there to help him if he needed it. It was essential in this situation for the patient to do this exposure on his own again for homework. Such an exposure would teach him two things: that the probability of him having a panic attack was lower than he expected and that if he were to have a panic attack, he could manage on his own, even if he could not get off the subway. Such experiences have a more powerful effect on feelings of self-efficacy than those that occur in the presence of a therapist.

Finally, homework is beneficial because it teaches patients to be their own therapists—a very important goal in behavior therapy which likely accounts for its good long-term efficacy. Over the course of therapy, patients have the opportunity to design homework assignments and carry them out while still receiving formal coaching from an expert. This means that patients will know not only how to maintain their treatment gains, but also how to deal with new problems once treatment is over. In other words, behavior therapy seems to have a preventative effect for the recurrence of problems once therapy formally ends.

TYPES OF HOMEWORK ASSIGNMENTS

There are several different kinds of homework assignments that can be given in behavior therapy. Most behavior therapy programs include psychoeducation, information gathering and treatment planning, and instruction on the core techniques of behavior therapy that are aimed at ameliorating the patient's problems. Homework can be integrated into all of these treatment components.

EARLY HOMEWORK: PSYCHOEDUCATION AND SELF-MONITORING

When psychoeducational material is covered in the first few sessions of treatment, patients can be given handouts to read for homework that cover this same material. Because patients can sometimes be overwhelmed in the first few sessions of treatment, it can be very beneficial to review psychoeducational materials at home. Homework handouts can be used to educate patients about the nature of their problems and the behavioral approach to treatment. When the patient is calmer and working at his own pace, it is likely that he will absorb more of this important information. In order to ensure that patients actively read handouts, they should be integrated into the subsequent session by inviting questions and asking patients to explain how the material covered in the handouts applies to their own situation.

Another excellent homework assignment for early on in treatment is self-monitoring of behaviors. In addition to psychoeducation, the first few sessions of behavior therapy are typically dedicated to gathering information about the patient's difficulties. Because many patients have a difficult time reporting their own behavior, self-monitoring serves as a means of accurately gathering information that will help the patient and therapist to understand the nature of the problem and how to treat it. Patients can be asked to monitor many different behavioral indices. Patients with depression are often asked to record their activities for a week, rating how much mastery they feel and how much pleasure they experience from each activity. Patients with bulimia nervosa can be asked to monitor episodes of binge eating, keeping track of the thoughts, feelings, and behaviors associated with binges. Similarly, patients with panic disorder can be asked to keep track of panic attacks for a week, also noting the thoughts, feelings, and behaviors associated with attacks. The information gathered from self-monitoring can then be reviewed and discussed during sessions so that the therapist and patient can come to an understanding of the factors maintaining the problematic behaviors. For example, when reviewing self-monitoring that was done for homework with a patient with bulimia, the therapist noted that the patient always binged at night and that she always noted feeling lonely before bingeing. When asked by the therapist how she feels *after* bingeing, the patient reported feeling disgusted in herself and convinced that no one would ever want to be friends with her or date her. This knowledge suggested that the patient binged in response to loneliness, but that by continuing to engage in binge eating the patient felt that it was even more likely that she would be alone forever. The insight gained from this self-monitoring homework informed the goals of treatment. The therapist and patient decided that the patient must find other behaviors to engage in when she was feeling lonely in the evenings besides bingeing. Establishing some social contacts was seen as a reasonable goal and one that would also resolve the feelings of loneliness that brought on binge eating behavior in the first place.

Assigning Specific Behavior Therapy Techniques

Once the patient and therapist come to an understanding of the maintaining factors for the problematic behaviors, specific behavior therapy techniques are taught to help patients break these patterns and establish new, healthier behaviors. These therapy techniques are assigned for homework along with continuing self-monitoring for the duration of treatment. As was already noted, many techniques lie under the umbrella of behavior therapy and, as such, homework assignments will look very different depending on the difficulties that each patient is having. A depressed patient might be asked to engage in a certain number of activities each day that provide a sense of mastery and/or pleasure. A patient with social phobia might be asked to attend a party and initiate conversations with two new people. A patient with marital difficulties might have a conversation with his spouse using assertive communication skills that he had learned and practiced in therapy. And, a patient with a high level of stress in his life might be asked to practice relaxation techniques like progressive muscle relaxation or positive imagery. Regardless of the specific technique, the key is that patients practice the skills in between sessions that they have learned during sessions to move them more effectively and efficiently through the therapeutic process.

DESIGNING AND ASSIGNING HOMEWORK

Before discussing the logistics of designing homework in behavior therapy, it is important to emphasize that homework should be a part of therapy right from the first session. Assigning homework at this stage sets the tone for therapy. It communicates to patients that therapy is a collaborative process. Behavior therapy is not a mysterious process—it is based on simple tenants that therapists teach to patients and that patients can then apply on their own. This ability to work on problems outside of the formal confines of the therapy sessions ensures that behavior therapy produces meaningful changes in a limited time frame. Another advantage of assigning homework right from the start of treatment is that patients leave the first session with something to work on that has a clear purpose—namely, to help them change the behaviors that they find troubling. They see that therapy has goals and that specific tools exist to propel them toward these goals—this sense of structure can be comforting and can "hook" patients into the therapy process.

Early homework assignments are simple to design—they tend to be consistent from patient to patient and do not involve a great deal of creativity on the part of the therapist. As noted above, these assignments typically include reading handouts and completing self-monitoring. Once a treatment plan is in place, however, homework will vary quite a bit from patient to patient depending on their idiosyncratic concerns. A general rule of thumb is that homework should mirror, or follow naturally from, what occurred in a treatment session. Approximately 10 minutes should be left at the end of a session to design homework and work out a plan for implementing it.

For the patient with panic disorder described above, homework for the week following this session in which he rode the subway with the therapist should also involve riding the subway. If it is too difficult for him to ride the subway alone right away, he could replicate the in-session exposure, going on the subway with a friend or family member who would gradually sit further and further away from him. If he felt quite confident after the in-session exposure, he could simply ride the subway alone or even try another mode of transportation that makes him anxious such as taking a taxicab. Having continuity between in-session work and homework solidifies learning.

Another key to effective homework design is that the assignment is clearly defined. Rather than sending the patient off to "take the subway a few times," it is best to specify how many times and under what conditions. For patients who have trouble following through with homework, this planning might even involve scheduling the homework at specific times, on specific days. Our patient and his therapist might decide that he will ride the subway to and from work at least twice in the upcoming week. They might further agree that he will ride the subway to work with his friend who lives and works in the same areas as him, but that he will ride the subway home from work alone. Structuring homework in this way makes it more likely that a patient will follow through than if assignments are left more open-ended.

The purpose of homework is not just for patients to *do* something, but to do something that will move along the therapy process. With this in mind, when homework is assigned, specific goals should be set and predictions advanced. Goals should be behavioral in nature—for our panic disorder patient, the goal should be to ride the subway to and from work on at least two days. This is very different from setting a goal of "not feeling anxious." Riding the subway might indeed make a patient feel anxious, but the goal of behavioral treatments is behavior change. While riding the subway repeatedly *will* make the patient feel less anxious, if he were to judge the success of his homework on this feeling, it is likely that many homework experiences would be considered a failure.

It is also helpful to have patients advance specific predictions about the assigned homework. While the goal of behavioral treatment is behavior change, behavioral change typically results in shifts in beliefs and feelings as well. Making specific predictions and then evaluating them once the homework is over makes patients more cognizant of these shifts and reinforces behavior change. Our panic patient predicted that there was an 80% chance that he would have a panic attack on the subway in the morning with his friend present and a 100% chance that he would have a panic attack at the end of the day when riding alone. After riding the subway to and from work on two days, he was amazed to see that he did not have a panic attack at all. This experience not only shifted his beliefs (that subways lead to panic attacks), but also reinforced his new behavior—riding the subway to work. Learning experiences are most powerful when patients have generated hypotheses before doing homework and evaluated their veracity afterward.

As we will discuss in more detail in the following section, an essential part of homework is reviewing it in the following session. If homework is assigned, but then never reviewed, patients will not view homework as an integral part of therapy. Approximately 10 minutes should be spent at the beginning of a session reviewing the homework, discussing whether or not the patient's goals were accomplished, and evaluating predictions. An excellent question to ask at the end of this review is: "What did you learn from the homework?" These learning experiences can be maintained on a running list that patients can refer to when they are having difficulties engaging in other behaviors. For our panic patient, he might write: "I don't *always* have panic attacks on subways; being alone on the subway isn't scarier than being with a friend; people look nice on the subway—if I did have a panic attack, I bet people would help me." These learning experiences could help him when confronting other feared situations, like going to see a movie or attending a sporting event.

Just as in-session work informs homework, homework can inform in-session work. While therapists will usually have a tentative agenda set prior to each session, they should be sufficiently flexible to adjust it based on what has happened with homework in the previous week. If our panic patient was supposed to ride the subway for homework, but was unable to, it would not be useful to move along to exposures to taxicabs in the following session. Rather, it might be best to re-do the exposure from the previous session, and add in an additional component to ensure homework compliance the following week. For example, the session might begin with the patient and therapist riding the subway together, then riding together but on opposite ends of the subway car, then in separate cars, and then on separate trains with a plan to meet a few stations down the line. This gradual exposure to riding alone might facilitate homework compliance the following week.

As has already been alluded to, the design of homework assignments should be a collaborative effort. While therapists will take a more active role early in treatment, they should gradually shift responsibility to the patient. When it is time to assign homework, the therapist can ask, "What do you think would be a useful homework assignment for you to do this week?" The therapist must balance involvement on the part of the patient with design of a useful assignment. In other words, if the patient designs a homework assignment that the therapist does not consider optimal, he or she should not criticize, but rather should use Socratic questioning to help the patient arrive at a better plan.

HOMEWORK COMPLIANCE

When determining homework assignments, the way that homework is assigned and the way in which it is integrated into the subsequent treatment session can facilitate compliance (see Bryant, Simons, & Thase, 1999). Patients will be most likely to comply if homework is reflective of the principles worked on during the session and relevant with their long-term goals. This will allow the patient to see the connection between the principles they have learned in session and the realization of their long-term goals in their "real lives." As we have already mentioned, patients will also be more likely to comply with assigned homework if it is reviewed carefully at the beginning of the next session. This demonstrates that homework is important, and reinforces the principles and lessons learned in the previous session. In our clinical experience, using and/or reviewing homework in the early sessions of treatment significantly facilitate later homework compliance.

BARRIERS TO COMPLETION OF HOMEWORK ASSIGNMENTS

Homework noncompliance can take many forms, and can end up being a major treatment issue. Overall, the behavior therapy approach to noncompliance is to try to determine how to better set up the contingencies in the therapy session such that patients will be reinforced for their compliance both by the therapist and, even more importantly, by the outcome of the homework. Noncompliance usually occurs because there was not a clear relationship between the assignments and the benefits of the therapy. We will address four common types of noncompliance that occur in behavior therapy: 1) misunderstanding the homework assignment; 2) outright refusal to do homework; 3) finding repeated excuses for why homework was not completed; 4) partial compliance. We will briefly discuss how to address each of these types of non-compliance.

Misunderstandings About Homework

When a patient does not complete his or her homework, there are many potential interpretations of such behavior. As behavior therapists, we assume that patients have various obstacles that are interfering with completing the homework, not that they are being resistant or passive aggressive. By determining whether the patient understood what was assigned to them and taking some responsibility for not having been clearer if the assignment was misunderstood, the therapist can avoid an accusatory stance and reinforce the collaborative stance of the therapeutic relationship. After determining what the patient did not understand, the therapist can then explain the assignment while clarifying the misunderstandings and even role-playing it with the patient in order to ensure the patient understands the assignment and the rationale for it. In addition, it can help to decrease misunderstanding if the patient repeats what the assignment is and describes how it is connected to the goals of the session and the treatment.

For example, a posttraumatic stress disorder (PTSD) patient came in after his first imaginal exposure homework assignment and stated that he did not feel anxious when repeatedly listening to the tape of the self-description of the trauma. The therapist asked about what the patient was doing while listening to the tape and for how long he listened to it. The patient reported that he had listened to the tape while driving to and from work. The therapist apologized for not having described the method of doing imaginal exposure for homework more carefully. Then, the therapist explained that the patient should do the imaginal exposure in a quiet place where he would not have any distractions for an extended period of time. The therapist asked the patient why that might be, and the rationale for imaginal exposure was reviewed. After this review, the patient completed the homework as planned and at the next session, the patient reported having felt engaged in the imaginal exposure and had habituated to the less intense parts of the tape.

Refusal to do Homework

There are a number of reasons why patients refuse to complete homework assignments in behavior therapy. Three of the most common reasons are misunderstanding the assignment, being assigned too much or too difficult homework, and overvalued ideation. Misunderstanding was addressed above. If a patient reports that she cannot do the homework, trying to convince the patient to comply by insisting or persisting until they give in is unlikely to lead to compliance once she gets home. Therefore, after making sure that the rationale is understood (if necessary), the therapist should try to strike a compromise with the patient that still helps her apply the principle that the other homework assignment was trying to achieve, even if at a lesser level. For example, a patient with obsessive-compulsive disorder (OCD) with contamination concerns conducted an exposure of putting items from the office trashcan on her body and clothing. However, she refused to take a contaminated paper home and touch her bed or other personal objects. She said she understood that it would help her if she did it, but that she was too overwhelmed to do it on her own at home, even if she had been able to contaminate herself in the office. Ultimately, she agreed to put the paper in the car the first day, then to bring it to one area of the house that was already thought to be contaminated on the third day. Bringing the paper to the rest of the house did not happen for homework during that week. However, after a scheduled home visit by the therapist (planned to generalize treatment from the office), the patient was able to continue to contaminate personal items as homework.

There are times when patients hold on to their beliefs so strongly about the consequences of confronting their thoughts or feared objects that they appear close to delusional. Such beliefs have been labeled as overvalued ideation in OCD (see Kozak & Foa, 1994), and likely apply to a range of psychopathology including eating disorders (Williamson, 1996), body dysmorphic disorder (Phillips, Kim, & Hudson, 1995), and other anxiety disorders besides OCD. Overvalued ideation can be a predictor of poor outcome in OCD, and is likely to be a predictor of poor outcome in other disorders as well. If a patient refuses to engage in an exposure for homework because he or she believes it will truly have significant negative consequences (e.g., he or she will really get fat from eating a single square of chocolate), these exposures can be emphasized during sessions where the therapist can model the exposure, and challenge the patient's motivation for change. For patients with overvalued ideation, the noncompliance is a reflection of a greater therapy issue that needs to be addressed carefully in session. For example, a patient concerned about getting AIDS from touching the sink in a public bathroom reluctantly engaged in the exposure with the therapist's guidance. However, the patient refused to do the exposure for homework. Further discussion led the patient to state that he believed that the sinks that the therapist selected must have been safe; the therapist would never put the patient (or himself) in harm's way. However, he believed that most bathrooms are contaminated and would lead to AIDS. At the next session, the therapist asked the patient to randomly pick five bathrooms around the area and then the therapist accompanied the patient to the first bathroom, modeling the exposure and having the patient engage in it after.

The next two exposures were done in the therapist's presence without modeling, and the last two were done with the therapist waiting outside the bathroom. During the following week, the patient was more willing to do the previously assigned exposures for homework.

Repeated Excuses for Noncompliance

If a patient repeatedly gives excuses for not completing the homework, the therapist should carefully consider this so as to give the patient the benefit of the doubt while still helping the patient understand that it is a problem. The therapist should discuss the patient's choices and motivation for change. A patient with social phobia came in stating that he had not conducted any of the homework exercises assigned to him regarding asking strangers questions such as directions or the time. The therapist asked what prevented him from asking any questions. The patient reported that he was too tired because he worked late every night. The therapist acknowledged that when one works extremely hard, it is hard to find time to do exposures. Then the therapist said, "So, it must be hard working so much that you don't have any time for yourself. Did you do anything outside of work this week?" The patient replied that he had gone running, watched a football game, and read a sports magazine. The therapist then asked how the patient could have incorporated the homework into his busy workday or his pleasure activities. After the patient generated some ideas, the therapist reinforced the patient for his creative thinking and suggested that the more the patient could problem-solve about doing his homework independently, the more likely it would be that his social anxiety would improve. The patient understood after this session, and completed most of his homework over the next few sessions and improved significantly.

Partial Completion of Homework

Partial completion of homework is very common. Some patients will only complete the monitoring and easier parts of homework (e.g., reading handouts); others may engage in some parts of the homework, but continue to engage in avoidance or other behaviors that may limit their success. Partial compliance can be due to a combination of the factors discussed above (misunderstanding, lack of motivation, anxiety, etc.). It is important to reinforce the part of the homework that was completed and then to carefully conduct an analysis of the factors that prevented completion of the rest of the assignment. For example, one patient completed all of his exposures but continuously refused to complete any monitoring. English was his second language, and even in his native language, completing the forms was difficult. However, the patient also became anxious when not doing things perfectly, and he did not think that he could complete the monitoring forms perfectly. The therapist asked the patient to complete the forms imperfectly, which lead to significant anxiety and continued noncompliance. The therapist therefore determined not to emphasize the completion of monitoring forms and only focused on the completion of exposure exercises for homework. The patient improved significantly. Another patient reported completing all of the exposures on her hierarchy, but was not habituating. The therapist carefully analyzed the way that the patient was engaging in exposures at home and determined that the patient was repeatedly telling herself that she was "ok" immediately after engaging in exposures. Engaging in this kind of safety behavior led to continued high levels of anxiety between sessions. After reviewing the rationale for eliminating avoidance behaviors including rehearsing positive reassurances and checking her anxiety, the patient was asked to do an exposure in session and refrain from all safety behaviors. The patient noted that this exposure felt different than when she had tried it previously, and habituation occurred between homework exercises once she did it the same way she did it in the office.

HOMEWORK ASSIGNMENTS WITH CHILDREN AND TEENAGERS

DESIGNING HOMEWORK FOR CHILDREN AND TEENAGERS

When treating younger patients, it is important that the process of assigning homework maintains a collaborative spirit, as children and adolescents are often sensitive to additional demands being placed upon them by adults in authority. Furthermore, children often view the notion of "homework" as aversive, or even a punishment. In order to prevent this from happening, the collaborative process should be emphasized early on in behavior therapy, encouraging young patients to be part of a team with the task of working toward goals that are viewed as desirable and rewarding (e.g., being able to play with friends without worrying). For children (ages 6–11), we try to make the session and homework engaging by phrasing it in the context of a game or challenge as much as possible. For example, a 9-year-old girl who had OCD concerns about "evening things" by touching things with her left hand if she touched them with her right was taught a game of "hot and cold" where the therapist would think of an object in the office and the girl had to touch different objects (with only one hand) until she guessed which one was selected. The therapist taught the game to the child's mother, and homework was to play the game each day.

In addition to making homework "fun," other strategies can increase homework compliance with young patients. Patients can be given the choice of homework assignments that are all equally "acceptable" to the therapist, ensuring that they feel they have some control over the therapy process. For example, a child with separation anxiety can be asked to choose from going to soccer, swimming, or piano one day after school the following week. As therapy progresses and children understand the approach to treatment, they can take an active role in designing their own homework assignments, just like adult patients. Therapists can take a less active role, serving as a "coach," who provides support and offers suggestions.

Teenagers typically do not need homework to be "fun" per se, but might respond to slightly different approaches than adults. When homework needs to be recorded (e.g., self-monitoring, activity monitoring), teenagers often like to do homework on the computer or sometimes in a nice journal with colored markers or pens. Because teenagers have their schoolwork to balance with therapy homework, they can also benefit from some help with time management. Because neither schoolwork nor therapy homework will be terribly fun for teenagers, they should be encouraged to break up tasks with rewarding activities. For example, patients can be encouraged to hold off on "instant messengering" their friends until they finish a difficult homework assignment or plan to do a difficult homework assignment in the half-hour prior to their favorite TV program.

Both children and teenagers can also benefit from one of the most commonly used procedures in behavior therapy—the reward chart. The use of monitoring charts at home, whether for completion of homework, for applying principles from the therapy, or for prosocial or otherwise positive behaviors, can be quite effective for both enhancing compliance and reducing opposition, even in externalizing disorders. However, the reward system to be used at home should be tailored and managed with full collaboration of the patient for best results. While stickers work for some children, points that add up to money or specific rewards (e.g., dinner in their favorite restaurant) are better for others, particularly teenagers. In addition to selecting effective reinforcers and coming up with a sufficient number to avoid habituation to the rewarding effects, consistent application by parents is one of the most important aspects of behavioral charts done at home. Rewards should be awarded as soon as possible after the completion of the goal, and should be applied on a daily basis. Oftentimes, parents will complain that such a system is not working, and it is because they have stopped applying it consistently. Finally, we find that positive reinforcement for most goals (rewarding positive behaviors) substantially increases patient motivation and participation in treatment more than negative reinforcement through removal of privileges or other positive aspects of a daily routine (punishing negative behaviors). However, there are times that removal of positive reinforcers is the only way to have the patient learn how their behaviors impact on others. The latter is especially the case when families have built whole systems of reward for the patient that require little effort for the patient to change (e.g., the whole family serving the child in order for him/her to avoid being contaminated).

The Role of Parents in Homework

When working with children, a common issue that arises is the role that parents should play in homework. Generally, younger children need more help with homework than older children and teenagers. Regardless of age, parents (and sometimes siblings) can serve as "allies" in the "battle for change." Just as the therapist does in session, parents can remind patients to do homework and can offer encouragement and support as it is completed.

One area in which parental involvement is essential with children (and partner involvement in adults) is reassurance seeking. Given that reassurance is a common method of avoiding feared outcomes for many individuals with anxiety and other disorders, it is essential to have strategies to apply at home to help modify this behavior. Once the patient and parent are clear about the role that reassurance plays in maintaining the disorder, we ask the patient and parents to come up with responses to use when patients ask for reassurance. These responses should not be critical nor angry, but helpful. Such responses as, "Your anxiety must be pretty strong right now," "Is that question an OCD question?," or "We agreed in the doctor's office that I shouldn't answer questions about how you look, right?" can be helpful.

When Parental Involvement Is Detrimental

Parents can play an enormously important role in facilitating homework compliance, but, at times, parental involvement is more detrimental than helpful. One common problem occurs when parents push their children past their point of competence and confidence. This pressure is often based in parents' desire for their children to get better very quickly. For example, parents of children with eating disorders often want them to be able to eat "normal" amount of a wide range of foods very soon after beginning treatment. This is incongruent with an approach to treatment that involves integrating feared foods gradually and learning that feared consequences from doing so will not occur. When children succeed at integrating a few feared foods, but are then criticized at home for not being able to eat anything, this denies children a very important success experience. Therapists must teach parents how to deal with their frustration in a more effective way (e.g., talking to their spouse in private) and how to support their children as they make difficult behavioral changes. If parents cannot hold back their criticism and frustration, it is often best for children to complete homework independently or with the help of another trusted adult (e.g., an older sibling or relative).

CASE EXAMPLES

USING HOMEWORK TO PREVENT RELAPSE

Leah was a 21-year-old woman who came for treatment of bulimia nervosa. Throughout high school, she had been worried about shape, weight, and eating, but it was not until college that she began to binge and purge. When she first came to college, she joined a sorority where thinness was highly valued. Like many other girls in her sorority, Leah went on a very restrictive diet, limiting her intake to fruit, vegetables, and whole grains. She also began to run five miles per day. After a few months on this highly restrictive diet, Leah began to binge eat periodically, typically in the company of her sorority sisters. She would become so upset after bingeing that she began to induce vomiting and also increased her exercise on days following binges to 8 miles of running, instead of 5. By the time Leah presented for treatment during the summer between her sophomore and junior years, she had been binging and purging at least once a day (and sometimes up to three times a day) for many months. She came for treatment after starting to get heart palpitations and worrying that this erratic eating behavior had become detrimental to her health.

Leah was compliant with treatment. She gradually normalized her food intake, learned to fight off urges to binge and to tolerate the feeling of fullness, and reduced her exercise to a three mile run, three days per week. For the most part, she was compliant with homework assignments, gradually integrating previously "forbidden foods" into her diet and practicing strategies for warding off her urges to binge or engage in compensatory behaviors. After a four-month course of treatment, Leah was eating a healthy range of foods, and had greatly reduced her binging and purging behaviors. In fact, the only trigger that remained for purging was eating at restaurants. If Leah cooked her own food, she felt comfortable because she knew what was in it, but despite repeated efforts, Leah refused to do exposures to eating restaurant food. When forced to eat at restaurants (e.g., when her parents came to visit her at school), she would come home and purge. For quite some time during treatment, Leah insisted that she could, for the most part, avoid eating out. She repeatedly told her therapist that it just was not important to her to work on this.

Near the end of treatment, Leah came to her therapy session with excellent news— she had been accepted to a semester abroad program in France. However, she would have to live in a dormitory with no cooking facilities and Leah was considering not going to France because she was so afraid of what she would eat there. She and her therapist agreed that if she did go to France with her continuing concern about eating out, she was at great risk for relapse after all of the hard work she had done during treatment. Therefore, they agreed that they would spend a few weeks intensely working on this concern. For the first few days, Leah's homework was to eat breakfast outside the home. This meal was the least anxiety-inducing for her because she could go to the local coffee shop and get coffee and a bagel, not much different from her breakfast at home. Once her anxiety to this habituated, her next homework assignment was to eat lunch out of the home. On the first day, Leah ordered a salad in the school cafeteria and it came with dressing, which she assumed was loaded with fat. She threw the salad out and left without eating. She called her therapist and they agreed that she should go back the next day and order the same salad and try to eat at least half of it. Leah did this, but came home and purged. Again, she called her therapist and without being prompted, Leah suggested she go back the next day to have the same lunch, but use the strategies she had learned during therapy to resist purging. She asked a trusted friend to join her for lunch, and after eating the salad, Leah and her friend went for a long walk until her urges to purge had dissipated. The following day, she returned to the cafeteria, had the same lunch, and again practiced resisting her urges. For another week after this successful exposure, Leah continued to eat lunch out, selecting different venues each day and trying to eat a variety of foods. Once she felt that she had a handle on lunch, she moved on to dinner. Again, she had some challenges at first, but persevered, and gradually could eat dinner out and not purge afterward. At this point, Leah's treatment was coming to a close, but she and her therapist worked out a plan to keep her on this good path until she left for France. While it was too expensive for her to eat out every day, she and her therapist agreed that she should eat a couple of lunches and dinners out each week to help her maintain her gains before she left for her semester abroad.

In this case, it would have been expensive and time-consuming for Leah and her therapist to work out this remaining problem together. Furthermore, if Leah's therapist had joined her for all of the exposures, she might have believed that she could only manage them because of the therapist's supportive presence. By assigning the exposures for homework, and by permitting contact with the therapist following difficult exposures, Leah was able to confront her fears many times a day, in different settings. She was also able to see that she had the skills to manage her anxiety about eating on her own. These last few weeks of homework-based exposure at the end of Leah's course of treatment were invaluable in terms of preventing a relapse of her eating disorder once she arrived in France.

The Relationship Between Homework Compliance and Progress in Treatment

David was a 37-year-old married man with panic disorder and agoraphobia. David was very concerned in situations that involved movement. Being on escalators, elevators, moving walkways, and so forth caused him to experience significant physical symptoms that often escalated into full-blown panic attacks. David found these feelings very uncomfortable and was also concerned that he might fall and hurt himself in these situations. This led David to avoid many situations. Another trigger for his panic was driving any faster than 25 miles per hour, restricting him to driving only on side streets in his neighborhood. This avoidance limited his work opportunities, prevented him from driving his children to activities, and put a strain on his marriage.

When David first came to treatment, he was resistant to working on his driving, but agreed to work on other "motion-related concerns." Five sessions were dedicated to riding escalators, elevators, moving walkways, and fast trains, and crossing busy streets, with the same tasks assigned for homework that were accomplished in the session. David experienced a great deal of anxiety in all of these situations, but did experience within-session habituation. However, when confronting the same situation the following week, David's anxiety was somewhat reduced, but still very significant. When reviewing his hierarchy during the sixth session of treatment, David reported that his anxiety about the situations he had confronted had only decreased a little bit.

There was a very simple explanation for David's lack of significant progress in treatment—he had done only minimal homework in between sessions. Each week, he had been asked to repeat the in-session exposure for homework, but in six weeks time had only managed to ride one escalator and go in a few elevators. David found it difficult to make time for exposures, and was also restricted because of his fear of driving. Therefore, he did not have the opportunity to learn that these situations were not dangerous, nor that his anxiety would go away with repeated exposure. He also believed that the exposures he had done were made easier by the presence of the therapist. In fact, his anxiety was so severe that he could not begin exposures without significant encouragement and prodding by the therapist. It remained unclear whether he could even initiate difficult exposures on his own at this point in therapy.

David's therapist shared her concerns with him, and questioned whether this was the right time for him to come to therapy. He explained that he very much wanted to get over his panic disorder, but that time was a real issue. He and his therapist then considered how he could seamlessly integrate exposures into his daily life. It turned out that this would be more easily accomplished with driving, rather than with the other situations he feared. They decided that for homework, he would drive his children to school using a different route each day and then go for a 15-minute drive on his way back home on a busy street with a speed limit over 25 miles per hour. He also agreed to begin taking more of the responsibility for driving when he and his wife went out. His therapist helped him prepare some coaching tips for his wife, so that she could be supportive during exposures and not push him to do things he was not yet ready to do.

David was able to start doing progressively more difficult driving exposures for homework. As he became more accustomed to the feeling of driving quickly, he became less afraid of other "motion-related" situations. As treatment progressed, he was able to take his children on a merry-go-round and on a train ride at the local zoo. In other words, exposure to one feared situation generalized to other situations that David feared. When David began to put effort into his treatment in between sessions, his progress greatly accelerated and by the end of treatment, he was able to drive anywhere on his own and manage a whole host of other situations that he previously feared and avoided.

CONCLUSION

Homework is an essential component of behavior therapy. Homework affords patients the opportunity to be their own therapists and to solidify the learning that took place during sessions. This opportunity to practice being one's own therapist likely plays an important role in maintaining treatment gains and preventing relapse once treatment is over. Given the relationship of homework to outcome, it is essential that therapists are careful about the way that they assign and review homework and take care of issues of noncompliance as soon as they arise.

REFERENCES

Bouton, M. E. (1994). Context, ambiguity, and classical conditioning. *Current Directions in Psychological Science, 3, 49–53.*

Bryant, M. J., Simons, A. D., & Thase, M. E. (1999). Therapist skill and patient variables in homework compliance: Controlling an uncontrolled variable in cognitive therapy outcome research. *Cognitive Therapy & Research, 23,* 381–399.

Hersen, M., and Bellack, A. S. (1999). *Handbook of comparative interventions for adult disorders, Second edition.* New York: Wiley.

Kazantzis, N., Deane, F. P., and Ronan, K. R. (2000). Homework assignments in cognitive and behavioral therapy: A meta-analysis. *Clinical Psychology: Science and Practice, 7,* 189–202.

Kozak, M. J., and Foa, E. B. (1994). Obsessions, overvalued ideas, and delusions in obsessive-compulsive disorder. *Behaviour Research and Therapy, 32,* 342–353.

Öst, L., Ferebee, I., and Furmark, T. (1997). One-session group therapy of spider phobia: Direct versus indirect treatments. *Behaviour Research and Therapy, 35,* 721—732.

Park, J-M., Mataix-Cols, D., Marks, I. M., Ngamthipwatthana, T., Marks, M., Araya, R., and Al-Kubaisy, T. (2001). Two-year follow-up after a randomized controlled trial of self- and clinician-accompanied exposure for phobia/panic disorders. *British Journal of Psychiatry, 178,* 543–548.

Phillips, K. A., Kim, J. M., and Hudson, J. I. (1995). Body image disturbance in body dysmorphic disorder and eating disorders: Obsessions or delusions? *Psychiatric Clinics of North America, 18,* 317–334.

Williamson, D. A. (1996). Body image disturbances in eating disorders: A form of cognitive bias? *Eating Disorders: The Journal of Treatment and Prevention, 4,* 47–58.

Chapter 2

CLIENT-CENTERED THERAPY

Marjorie C. Witty

Client-centered therapy, also called the person-centered approach, describes Carl R. Rogers' way of working with persons experiencing all types of personal disturbances or problems in living (Rogers, 1959; 1961; 1969; 1970; 1972; 1980a; 1986a). As early as 1939, Rogers developed his theory of psychotherapy with troubled children, and went on to expand his theoretical approach to include work with couples, families, and groups. His most comprehensive theoretical statement was published as a chapter in Sigmund Koch's *Psychology: A Study of a Science (Vol. III)* in 1959, and includes his theory of motivation and personality development, as well as theory of group interaction and interpersonal relationships (Koch, 1959, 184–256). Over his long career, Rogers extrapolated client-centered values to the education, marriage, group encounter, personal power, and conflict resolution (Rogers, 1969, 1970, 1972). Today, the person-centered approach is practiced in the United Kingdom, Germany, France, Greece, Portugal, Demark, Poland, Hungary, The Netherlands, Italy, Japan, Brazil, Mexico, Australia, and South Africa, as well as here in the United States and Canada. A world association, which can be contacted online, was founded in Lisbon in 1997 that reflects the growth and vitality of the approach entitled the World Association for Person-Centered and Experiential Psychotherapy and Counseling (WAPCEPC). Another international organization comprised of a diverse membership—lay persons, educators, business consultants, therapists, artists, psychologists—the Association for the Development of the Person-Centered Approach (ADPCA), is also accessible on the internet.

ROGERS' THEORY OF THERAPY

Based on his experience as a psychotherapist, Rogers postulated that persons possess resources of self-knowledge and self-healing, and that personality change and development are possible if a definable climate of facilitative conditions is present (Rogers, 1957; Rogers, 1980a, p. 115). The implication of Rogers' position is some persons and environments foster growth and development in human beings, and some undermine and inhibit growth. The person's inherent self-directive processes promote greater self-differentiation, more efficient self-regulation, self-understanding, and acceptance (Ryan & Deci, 2000). Rogers utilized the construct of the "actualizing tendency" to describe the organism's motivation to realize and enhance inherent potentials (Goldstein, 1940; Rogers, 1959; Bozarth & Brodley, 1991).

The therapeutic relationship has been identified repeatedly as a significant part of successful outcome in psychotherapy (Patterson, 1984; Smith & Glass, 1977; Smith, Glass, & Miller, 1980; Lambert, Shapiro, & Bergin, 1986; Lambert, 1992; Wampold, 2001). Regardless of therapeutic orientation, therapists who provide Rogers' core conditions at a high level are likely to attain better outcomes than therapists who do not.

THE ACTUALIZING TENDENCY

Rogers' theory of motivation emerged from his observations of clients' growth and development within the therapeutic relationship. The actualizing tendency was a theoretical construct proposed by the great holistic neurologist Kurt Goldstein (Goldstein, 1939; 1940, 1963). Rogers felt that this construct best described the unfolding of human potential he witnessed in his interviews with clients. This construct postulates that all living organisms are continually actualizing their potentials, even under unfavorable circumstances. By way of example, Rogers often illustrated the concept with reference to organisms in the natural world. He wrote about a potato in the root cellar of his boyhood home:

> The actualizing tendency can, of course, be thwarted or warped, but it cannot be destroyed without destroying the organism. I remember that in my boyhood, the bin in which we stored our winter's supply of potatoes was in the basement, several feet below a small window. The conditions were unfavorable, but the potatoes would begin to sprout pale white sprouts, so unlike the healthy green shoots they sent up when planted in the soil in the spring. But these sad, spindly sprouts would grow 2 or 3 feet in length as they reached toward the distant light of the window. The sprouts were in their bizarre, futile growth, a sort of desperate expression of the directional tendency I have been describing. They would never become plants, never mature, never fulfill their real potential. But under the most adverse circumstances, they were striving to become. Life would not give up, even if it could not flourish . . . . This potent constructive tendency is an underlying basis of the person-centered approach (Rogers, 1980, 118–119).

The actualizing tendency functions as an axiom in Rogers' theory. To the extent that the therapist holds the hypothesis that the client possesses the capacity for self-determination he or she is more likely to perceive the client's ideas, feelings, and actions as aspects of growth instead of pathology. It should be stated that the actualizing tendency does not mean that Rogers believed that people are "good," simply that organisms realize their potentials limited only by internal and external environmental constraints (Rogers, 1951, 1959, 1961; Brodley, 1998). Rogers recommended that novice therapists attempt to hold the hypothesis that clients have the inner resources to meet life's difficulties, recognizing that to discard that hypothesis would open the way for the therapist's exerting influence over the supposedly less competent client. This hypothesis, he acknowledged, was most difficult to embrace in the face of self-destructive, self-defeating behavior on the part of the client (Rogers, 1951, pp. 20–25).

The therapist's confidence in the client as the proper architect of the process of therapy—and of his or her life as a whole—logically implies that the therapist need not set goals, give assignments, or direct the process of the relationship. It is this commitment to the agency of the client that is a logical extrapolation from the motivational theory which renders the client-centered approach still radical after all these years.

THE CORE CONDITIONS

For Rogers, the construct of *congruence* refers to a state of wholeness and integration within the therapist. It is a dynamic inner state of being in which the therapist is undistracted by his or her own concerns, and is able to be fully present in the relationship with the client (Baldwin, 1987; Bozarth, 1998; Brodley, 1998). Congruence is a distinctive inner experience as opposed to a behavior, although behavior or communication that issues from the congruent therapist may be labeled "congruent." Congruence is theorized to emerge from the therapist's self-acceptance and positive self-regard (Bozarth, 1998), and from the evolving capacity for self-awareness free from inner censorship (Brodley, In press). A congruent therapist spontaneously conveys to the client the qualities of genuineness and transparency—a willingness to be known. It does not imply self-disclosure, a behavior with which it has been erroneously equated. The client rightly feels him- or herself to be in the presence of a person, not someone enacting a professional role. In fact, while the client-centered therapist *is* a person, he or she is engaging in a practical art and discipline of empathic understanding of the frame of reference of the client. This conscious, disciplined devotion to providing the core conditions in the service of the client may be understood as the enactment of a kind of expertise and as the application of a technique, but to stress this aspect of the practice misses its fundamental character. Peter Schmid describes the practice in the following:

> Person-centered psychotherapy is the practice of an image of the human being which understands the human being as a person and thus encounters him or her personally acknowledging him or her as the Other . . . instead of objectifying him or her by trying to know him or her, to get knowledge over him or her (Schmid, 2001, p. 42).

The essence of client-centered therapy is a relationship between two sovereign human persons in which the therapist's skilled "performance" requires being oneself! It involves the complexity of reflexive awareness of one's being-in-relation with oneself and the client—as Schmid has put it, being an expert at not being an expert.

The second condition is described as the therapist's experience of prizing, nonjudgmental caring, or *unconditional positive regard* toward the client, the client's beliefs, ideas, behaviors, or ways of being. Unconditional positive regard, as Rogers pointed out, is a condition that exists upon a continuum; we are sometimes conditional in our regard for the client, but strive to realize greater and greater acceptance in the relationship. Effective therapy, Rogers asserted, probably would not occur to any significant degree if the therapist were to experience consistently negative feelings or attitudes toward the client. Therapists who are trying to develop themselves in the client-centered approach may first be committed in principle to realizing the condition of unconditional positive regard. The therapist's conscious value as it is lived out with clients gradually leads to spontaneous feelings of warm caring and acceptance of the client, even in the face of beliefs and behavior which the therapist might deplore in other contexts. It is to allow oneself to leave one's ordinary discriminating, dualistic mindset behind in the service of meeting another person and his or her world of meanings.

The third condition is the therapist's experience of *empathic understanding of the client's frame of reference*. Rogers eloquently described this condition in his book *A Way of Being*:

> The way of being with another person which is termed empathic has several facets. It means entering the private, perceptual world of the other and becoming thoroughly at home in it. It involves being sensitive, moment to moment, to the changing felt meanings which flow in the other person, to the fear or rage or tenderness or confusion or whatever, that he/she is experiencing. It means temporarily living his/her life, moving about in it delicately without making judgments, sensing meanings of which he/she is scarcely aware, but not trying to uncover feelings of which the person is totally unaware, since this would be too threatening (Rogers, 1980, p. 142).

Importantly, Rogers did not specify how these core conditions or facilitative attitudes were to be expressed in the therapeutic relationship. Rogers' empathic understanding of the response process (Temaner, 1977) that has been caricatured as merely parroting back—a simplistic technique of "active listening"—was, in fact, a discovery and innovation of great consequence. Shlien asserted that the empathic response (also called "mirroring" or "reflection") had been "unfairly damned" in that it has been portrayed by many as a behavioral technique. Shlien felt that this form of response uttered by the experienced client-centered therapist could be artful and seamless (Rogers, 1986).

There is a crucial distinction between the therapist who instructs him- or herself to repeat back the words of the client *in order to convey to the client that the therapist empathizes and understands,* and the therapist who responds empathically in order to check his or her understanding for him- or herself. In the first case, the therapist has an aim *in addition* to understanding the communication of the client. He or she wishes to imply "You are making sense; I understand what you are saying; I am empathic with you." The second therapist has *no other goals* in the moment other than to grasp the meanings being expressed by the client. The client's experience of being understood by the therapist is a *by-product* of a therapist's sincere effort to grasp the meanings of the client's narrative and his or her relation to his utterances and to express those meanings so as to check their accuracy. You might say that the first therapist, while trying to express understanding of what the client has been saying, is at the same time trying to "spin" his or her response to *achieve a particular effect* in the client. Client-centered therapists, having no goals for clients, also seek no "effects." But, you might ask, if there are no effects, where is the therapy? We would that client-centered therapy, indeed, does have powerful effects, but those effects are the by-products of a relational process that consciously and deliberately strives to minimize influence upon or power over the client (Witty, 2005). Clearly, no therapy is free of influence (Masson, 1988, 1994; Pentony, 1981; Proctor, 2002), but we would maintain that the disciplined attempt to preserve the client's freedom and safety in the therapy relationship creates a distinctive relationship which empowers. The principle which guides the therapist in realizing this relation is that of nondirectiveness.

THE NONDIRECTIVE ATTITUDE

Client-centered therapy is unique in its commitment to principled nondirectiveness (Grant, 1990; Bozarth, 2002; Brodley, 1997; Witty, 2004). The foundation of client-centered practice rests not on method but rather on the therapist's respect for and personal openness to the client as a sovereign being of inexhaustible depth and meaning (Rogers, 1961; Schmid, 2001)

If a therapist directs the client to discuss contents that the therapist believes to be focal to the process, the therapy is not client-centered. If the therapist orchestrates the ways in which clients relate to their concerns or to how they express those concerns, the therapy is process-directive and not client-centered. In this respect, client-centered therapy stands alone within the family of person-centered and humanistic therapies.

In an interview with Michelle Baldwin in 1985, Rogers asserted that the only goals therapists should have are goals for themselves. What he meant was that the only acceptable goals in client-centered therapy relate to the therapist's ability to realize the therapeutic attitudes of congruence, unconditional positive regard, and empathic understanding of the internal frame of reference of the client (Baldwin, 1987).

Rogers' theory of the necessary and sufficient conditions, however, was intended to describe *any type* of therapeutic relation, without regard to therapeutic orientation of the therapist. It is sometimes referred to as the "'integrative' statement of the necessary and sufficient conditions" (Bozarth, 1996a, b). Client-centered therapists do try to realize the attitudinal conditions in their relations to clients; however, they do so from a particular valuational stance of respect for the self-realizing capacities and right to self-determination of their clients. Rogers particularly appreciated Nat Raskin's description of the non-directive attitude which he cited in *Client-Centered Therapy* published in 1951:

> There is [another] level of nondirective counselor response which to the writer represents *the* nondirective attitude. In a sense, it is a goal rather than one which is actually practiced by counselors. But, in the experience of some, it is a highly attainable goal, which . . . changes the nature of the counseling process in a radical way. At this level, counselor participation becomes an active experiencing with the client of the feelings to which he gives expression, the counselor makes a maximum effort to get under the skin of the person with whom he is communicating, he tries to get *within* and to live the attitudes expressed instead of observing them, to catch every nuance of their changing nature; in a word, to absorb himself completely in the attitudes of the other. And in struggling to do this, there is simply no room for any other type of counselor activity or attitude; if he is attempting to live the attitudes of the other, he cannot be diagnosing them, he cannot be thinking of making the process go faster. Because he is another, and not the client, the understanding is not spontaneous but must be acquired, and this through the most intense, continuous and active attention to the feelings of the other, to the exclusion of any other type of attention (Rogers, 1951, p. 29; Raskin, 1947, unpublished manuscript).

Although Rogers did not stress this fundamental attitude in his later writings, he endorsed this stance consistently throughout his long career (Brody, 1991, Brodley and Brody, 1990). Rogers states that in crisis situations or client emergency, even more commitment to a non-directive expression of the attitudes is needed rather than the assertion of the therapist's authority:

> When the situation is most difficult, that's when a client-centered approach is most needed and . . . what is needed there is a deepening of the [therapeutic attitudes] and not trying something more technique-oriented (Rogers & Russell, 2002, p. 258).

Client-centered therapists make a strong distinction between therapies that are, at heart, didactic and therapies that emphasize understanding and valuing the client's personal attitudes, agency, and experiencing. We do not disagree that clients' ideas, beliefs about the world, and themselves are sometimes irrational or distorted. We place our faith in the relationship conditions as a fertile medium in which clients' views of self, others, and the world gradually change in the direction of greater acceptance and greater endorsement of consensual reality. We believe if therapy is a teaching relation—even the most benign and supportive relation—it reinscribes the model of power *over* the client; it reiterates the subordination of client as a receptacle of knowledge from the more powerful and expert figure in authority, the therapist. We would rather express through the consistent, deep attention to grasping the internal frame of reference of the client through empathic understanding, our profound valuing of the subjective reality of the client, including clients who are burdened with disturbances in thinking and emotion. We believe that honoring the client in this way, meeting the client as a whole person, ultimately empowers the person. We observe in the course of client-centered therapy that clients become more authoritative in describing their experiences, in asserting their own ideas, beliefs, and feelings, and in choosing paths of their own forging. This results in greater personal stability and self confidence.

ROGERS' THEORY OF CHANGE

Rogers' presented his theory of the necessary and sufficient conditions for psychotherapeutic personality change in 1957. This seminal contribution to psychotherapy theory has led to scores of studies over the past forty-odd years that have robustly supported the significance of empathy, warmth, and genuineness as aspects of the therapist's presence related to positive outcome in therapy (Patterson, 1984). More recent work by Asay and Lambert supports Rogers' necessary and sufficient conditions. Their research estimates that approximately 30% of the variance in outcome can be attributed to "common factors" which includes the relationship, with 40% relating to client factors such as social learning, health, etc., 15% relating to specific techniques, and 15% reflecting expectancy or hope for the success of therapy (Asay and Lambert, 1999, pp. 23–55). Whether it is described as a "therapeutic alliance" characterized as tasks, bonds, and goals, or more broadly as a relationship, we can be sure that the conditions provided by a caring, genuine therapist who is attempting to understand are pivotal in terms of facilitating therapeutic personality change. Less well acknowledged is the critical role of the client as a "common factor" who actively engages in the relationship, collaborates in the tasks of therapy, and focuses a variety of resources on personal healing and positive change (Tallman & Bohart, 1999).

EXAMPLES OF CLIENT-INITIATED
HOMEWORK

In my practice of client-centered therapy which commenced in 1974, approximately 15% of my clients have initiated homework assignments for themselves in the context of client-centered therapy. Other client-centered therapists who were asked to estimate the percentage of clients who initiate homework have responded with roughly the same percentages. In this section of this chapter I will provide two examples of this self-initiated work by clients. I have selected examples that stand out in my memory due to their distinctiveness or creativity.

"Lourdes"

Lourdes is a 48-year-old woman who emigrated to the U.S. from Honduras upon her marriage to Mark, an American businessman. Her move to the U.S. occurred approximately 20 years ago. Shortly after coming here, Lourdes was accepted to a Master's program to prepare her for work in the Latino/a community here in the U.S. as a counselor.

One of the consequences of her marriage necessitated leaving her aging, widowed mother in Honduras. Because Lourdes is an only child, her leaving for the U.S. left no other family members to care for her mother, although her mother resides with another family in a small apartment attached to their larger home. Her relationship with her mother had been strained and conflicted since puberty when her mother referred to her as a "bad girl" who would become a prostitute unless her mother intervened to prevent it.

In the beginning of therapy, Lourdes expressed gratitude for her mother's efforts at keeping her from a life of dissolution and sin. After a year of therapy, Lourdes began to see her mother's behavior in terms of its profound lack of acceptance of her, and in terms of the emotional violence that had been done to her as a young teenage girl. This was a turning point in the therapy. Lourdes wept bitterly about this inexplicable loss of her mother's love—a love which turned to contempt for her. Convulsed with sobbing in therapy, she said "She stabbed my heart!" For many years, Lourdes had tried in vain to win her mother's love back; she sent money to Honduras every month. She visited loaded with presents. She called every Sunday. Within the therapy, she finally began to accept her mother's hateful, hurtful behavior. She asked me to help her understand her mother's attitudes and behavior. Over time, we pieced together a kind of provisional interpretation of her mother's punitive attitudes which drew from our understanding of religious views of women and sexuality; the conservative attitudes toward women's place and role in Latin America; and, more specifically, her mother's own unhappy relationships with men. This work was necessary because Lourdes did not want to conclude that her mother was a bad, unfeeling person, nor did she want to conclude that there was anything wrong with her behavior during the years her mother had been so punishing.

Lourdes posed to me the question of how she could manage to stay in relation without being continually wounded. She requested my help in devising ways for her to gradually wean herself from this abusive and pain-filled relationship, with the hope that her mother might come to a different understanding of Lourdes as a human being. Over the years, this client requested that I listen to letters she had written to her mother and to comment on them mainly in order that Lourdes not wound her mother in return for all the wounds inflicted in the past. I was asked to help Lourdes prepare for conversations over the phone to help her limit contact if her mother became judgmental. She asked me to review what she had decided she would and would not tolerate on her visits to Honduras. She became capable of limiting her phone calls if her mother started to criticize Lourdes or her husband, and on one trip to Honduras, she actually left a restaurant where she and her mother had gone for a luncheon when her mother insulted her. She had entered a period in which she was not going to take any more abuse. This approach (enacted over a period of 10 years or so) has led to a more harmonious relationship in which her mother has actually begun to express gratitude to her daughter and to praise her many accomplishments. But Lourdes has left her mother behind psychologically and so while she appreciates the positive words, it is too late for her to go back to any real intimacy. Lourdes deeply regrets but accepts this outcome. She has said "My relationship with my mother is what it is, and so be it! It is a great sadness for both of us that she could not accept me as a person!"

Another turning point occurred when she announced that she wanted to work on her own moral development. She had been reading literature about various moral exemplars such as Gandhi and Father Oscar Romero, as well as writers who presented a spiritual vision of human life, including Krishnamurti, and she had become very involved in her own church community. She wanted to work consciously and deliberately on becoming a compassionate, principled person. She enlisted my help in generating tasks that would support this life-long commitment. An example of this occurred recently which may illustrate how these collaborations happen.

Lourdes is a highly intelligent, very attractive, and powerful woman. She has matured and gained confidence in her effectiveness as a counselor, and has taken initiative to educate other helping professionals about Latino a cultures in consultative workshops. As she has worked in community agencies, she has often been supervised by younger, Caucasian men whose knowledge and experience and awareness of Latino culture are no match for her own. She has negotiated these relationships with trepidation, because she does not want to dumb down her own competence and knowledge as a counselor, nor does she want to have conflict with her supervisors.

Lourdes recently requested my help with finding what she terms a "way of compassion" in dealing with the latest of her supervisors who is threatened by her and who is openly hostile to her in agency meetings. First, she asked my opinion about whether I regarded this supervisor's behavior as hostile. With the proviso that I was going on her information only, and obviously had no access to his motivation, I answered tentatively that what she described did indeed seem hostile to me without knowing whether or not he was intending hostility or whether he was even aware of what he had said. She then tried to imagine his vulnerability as a much younger, less experienced supervisor having to deal with someone older, a woman of another race and ethnicity, who had much more experience. In our conversation, we explored the dilemma she faced. Should she behave more deferentially to him? Should she "stroke" his ego in the ways she saw other female counselors doing? Or, should she refuse to treat him as a little boy——which is how she perceived others treating him—— and instead express her true feelings, reactions, and thoughts which had already had the effect of evoking his hostility?

Lourdes expressed the following: "I want to treat him in accordance with my principles—to be compassionate. I also do not want to lose this job; I love the job here. I wonder how to find the way to do both. This is a challenge to my moral development." She asked my opinion which I gave, as I believe in answering clients' questions if I feel that I have an answer of my own to offer. I expressed my belief that colluding with the other staff who were not openly expressing their reactions seemed disrespectful to this supervisor. I also expressed the possibility that if Lourdes took the route of passive compliance, she would feel disappointed in herself and that it would disrupt her personal harmony with herself. She agreed with this and said that she would need to find a way to communicate non-violently in this situation. We spontaneously role-played some responses she might want to make which met the requirements of honesty and respectfulness. She also said that she would increase her meditative practice to enable her to have the necessary self-control to engage with her supervisor non-defensively and from a stance of sincerity and appreciation for him as a person who is doing the best he can. After deciding to go on retreat to have time to meditate, she ended the session saying, "I believe that there are dark forces which may work through us, and my job is to shed light on those dark forces of my own. In that way I can shed more light on him and be open and caring toward him." She explained, "It's not so much of what I say to him or how I say it. It's a matter of transforming my own consciousness in the direction of acceptance."

This example describes an unusual therapy relationship. First, the length of time we have worked together is now approaching 14 years. This has not been continual but with some breaks of several months. She has continued to request more therapy saying that talking with me helps her feel happier with herself because she is more able to live out her values if she expresses what those values are and has the opportunity to map out ways of behaving more consistently.

Second, Lourdes is a client who solicits my reactions, ideas, and views in virtually every session. It is perhaps hard to understand how a non-directive client-centered therapist can justify acceding to these requests because clearly my responses and answers may be highly influential. Although some might say they are directive, I would argue that one's *intention* to be non-directive makes a crucial difference in how clients receive my responses to their requests. When I have asked her directly about the possibility of her taking what may well be flawed counsel from me, she has stated a number of times "Don't worry! I do what I decide is best; I wouldn't do something just because you believe it is a good idea!" Client-centered therapists are not eager to express their thoughts and opinions; there is a willingness to do so when asked, because it accords with a stance of principled non-directiveness (Grant, 1990).

"Harry"

Harry entered therapy in the midst of an emotionally devastating breakup of a long-term relationship. His partner had pushed a note across the kitchen table one morning that said that she was leaving that morning with the dog to move in with a younger man. The fact that both Harry and his partner had been involved in mentoring this younger man at the university at which they both worked made the injury even more painful, as Harry had to face that he had been betrayed by two persons he cares deeply about.

The breakup precipitated a crisis for my client. He acknowledged that for years he had been afflicted with depression, panic attacks, and agoraphobia, and, as a consequence, had come to depend on his partner for almost everything. He could not bring himself to go into a grocery store, do laundry, or travel freely anywhere in the large metropolitan area in which they lived. He understood that this overwhelming dependency had perhaps been gratifying to the partner in the early years of the relationship, but had become more and more burdensome to her as the years passed. His agoraphobia was so intense that a close friend accompanied him to sessions at my office for the first several weeks after the breakup.

At the urging of his family, Harry requested a referral to a psychiatrist for medication. He was prescribed an SSRI, which succeeded in diminishing his overwhelming sense of hopelessness and doom. He gradually became capable of attending our sessions unaccompanied, and I became aware of both his high intelligence and talent, and the depth of his impairment. After several months of weekly sessions, he told me that he had decided to try to work on his agoraphobia so as to enlarge his world and his repertoire of behaviors. He knew that he would either have to make it on his own or return to the small town of his childhood where his family could look after him. He felt that to return to his childhood home would be the end of his life as an adult, independent person.

At this time, Harry's "circle of safety" was small, and he followed the same route to and from work every day. Fortunately, his workplace was an environment in which he was respected and supported. His supervisor had allowed him to take some time off at the worst of the crisis. In the next several weeks he announced that he had located a group for agoraphobics meeting in a church. He attended the group doggedly even though he found it difficult to get there and he was openly skeptical at times about some of the other members and their plans for recovery. However, the normalizing effects of being with other persons who were afflicted with panic disorder and agoraphobia were apparent. He was not alone in this struggle.

Over the next year, he set more goals for himself, to enter a grocery store, to stay alone in his apartment, to travel by himself in his car on a 5 hour road trip to see his mother. All of these initiatives were his own and have gradually led to improvement and a greater sense of personal power. But there were many times where he failed to achieve the goal of shopping or going to an unfamiliar destination. In therapy sessions he would berate himself as a "loser". His despondency was profound. But he has pressed on and has continued to set more goals for himself. He has had difficulty knowing when to allow himself to take a break from the discipline of facing his fears, given that non-agoraphobics may often allow themselves the freedom to decline a challenge.

The point of this case summary is that clients in client-centered therapy sometimes set personal goals and make progress toward fulfilling those goals without any direction by the therapist. We cannot identify with certainty the causal variables involved in his movement toward recovery. Very probably, the therapy, the medication, familial support, support from friends, and his own character were influential in his gradual improvement. It also must be said that the client is not "cured" in any total sense. He still has to overcome inner resistance to traveling to new places and dealing with interpersonal relationships where there is conflict.

MEANS AND ENDS IN THERAPY

In 1970, Tomlinson and Whitney argued that therapeutic outcome criteria necessarily reflect values that practitioners of particular therapy orientations endorse.

This is to say that even the most "objective" statements regarding "good adjustment" are rooted in the theorist's picture of an ideal—of maturation, human development, health, wholeness and the like:

> Therapists typically believe that they know what kind of client behavior is desirable, and though they may not actively strive to develop such behavior, they still evaluate their own efficacy in terms of the degree to which they can observe the presence of that behavior in the client's emergent self.... Thus the measure of outcome must be in terms of what the therapist and his (sic) theory designate as the ideal man (sic), and these considerations are rooted in values, not in objective considerations of adjustment (Tomlinson & Whitney, 1970, pp. 454–455).

The aims of client-centered therapy include strengthening the personal authority of the client as a knower and reliable creator of personal meanings, beliefs, ideas, and whose own inner experiencing can be trusted as a guide for living. Clients in client-centered therapy become more self-assertive, more confident in their own frames of reference, more capable of risk-taking, more open to experiencing, more empathic toward others (Rogers, 1961). These valued ways of being seem to result from the lived value of non-directiveness, which results in a profound respect for the client and for the client's own choices and self-direction. They further argue that the aims of client-centered therapy are consistent with its method.

Within this particular therapeutic paradigm, it should be clear that assigning homework, making interpretations, attempts to influence the client, or any number of "interventions" must be considered contradictory to the aim of trusting the client's own experience as a trustworthy guide. There is one condition, however, under which this contradiction can be avoided; that would be a *request from the client* for homework from the therapist. Most non-directive client-centered therapists are open to questions from clients and do their best to respond with real answers if they have them (contrary to the frequent caricature of the approach as interminably repeating back what the client has said!). So a request for a homework assignment from a client would be accepted and would be responded to with respect for the client's inquiry. The only limit would be the therapist's personal knowledge base in terms of whether or not she or he could recommend a particular homework assignment or set of assignments as potentially helpful in meeting the client's stated aims.

CLIENT-INITIATED EXPERIMENTS
AND HOMEWORK

Because client-centered therapists are willing to answer clients' questions, if clients want concrete suggestions or help with attitudes, beliefs, or problem behaviors, the therapist is open to offering help that he or she deems relevant to the request or to refer the client for adjunctive experiences, education, or other therapy. Had Harry asked specifically for resources that would help him overcome the agoraphobia, I would have readily referred him to a colleague of mine who works from a Cognitive Behavioral framework with problems of panic and agoraphobia. Many clients in client-centered therapy have sought out adjunctive experiences to aid them in reaching personal goals. Included in this list are practices to aid in the management of stress, various types of meditative practice, yoga, more frequent attendance at church, the use of daily affirmations in the context of 12 Step programs, and therapeutic massage. Some clients who are struggling with weight and eating problems and clients with addictions to substances have joined groups such as Overeaters Anonymous, a group dedicated to Fat Acceptance (National Association for Fat Acceptance), structured cognitive behavioral approaches to control bulimia, harm reduction approaches to addiction, and all of the 12 Step programs. Clients have taken up journaling and art therapy to cope with early childhood trauma. A client who was questioning his gender identity utilized his high level of computer expertise to transpose his male face onto female bodies and female faces onto his own scanned image of his male body. The deep acceptance of the therapist seems to allow the client to share these experiments with little fear of not being understood or judged. Because of the therapist's attitude of acceptance of the client whether or not he carries through with proposed experiments, resistance and methods to get the client on task are never an issue. The client does not have to anticipate being remonstrated or even questioned by the therapist about plans she discussed the week before. She is likely in that environment to discuss the fact that she did not follow through and the reasons for aborting the mission.

Barbara Brodley, a master therapist and strong proponent of the client-centered approach in the U.S., provides a session excerpt of one of her clients who initiated homework in order to deal with alcohol use which had become a danger to his life and his marriage (Brodley, in press):

> Client: I've got to admit it, I get drunk and I'm a bastard to her. I've scared the kids. (Pause 10 seconds.) I've got to stop drinking, I'm out of control and I'm killing myself.
> Therapist: Mhm, hmm. It's not only hurting your marriage, your children. You're killing yourself. You're risking your life.
> Client: Yeah, I'm really in danger (pause) and dangerous (pause). I need something besides this [he gestures, referring to the relationship]. I believe I'll cut down or stop, while we're talking. (T: Mhm, hmm) But I lose resolve after a few days. Tension builds up, I start drinking and I'm out of control.
> Therapist: (Mhm, hmm) Talking like this isn't enough to hold you. You loose control.
> Client: Right. (Pause.) I got off cocaine. I stopped killing myself that way. But now I've gotta put some brakes on the drinking! (Pause) I think I need a group, maybe AA, to support me between sessions.
> Therapist: Uhmmm. You need other people who are in this *with you* more than I can be; others who can support you getting control.
> Client: Yeah. I really do. (Pause) I should make some calls for an AA group. (Pause) I'm not sure it'll work for me 'cause I don't like their religion part. (Pause) I guess I'll do that. I'll do that before I see you next.
> Therapist: Mhm, hmm. You've got reservations, and you're not sure it'll help (pause) but you want to try it at least. (C: Yeah) And you want to get to it right away because you feel really desperate. (C: Yeah)

Brodley comments, "The client continues about the risks he takes and his remorse. He starts the next session spontaneously reporting on the action he has taken to get a group."

> Client: I called AA groups, but the one closest to me isn't open to new people now. A couple others were closed or too far away. Anyway, I'm doing something more than talking about it and that's better.

Therapist: Mhm, hmm. It didn't work out yet, but you're doing something, not just talking. (Pause) That feels better.
Client: Yeah. (Pause) I don't know if it'll help, but I want to keep trying until I find one I can get into.

Brodley continues,

In the quoted dialogue, I responded empathically and offered no explicit support, guidance, or approval for the client's plan or for having done what he said he was going to do, or for his intention to continue. Subsequently, the client did join an AA group, got a sponsor and stopped imbibing alcohol while continuing in therapy. His depression and the angry outbursts diminished. He reported that he felt less reactive to annoyances, more tolerant of his children's misbehaviors and petty differences with his wife. Discontinuing his use of alcohol also improved his sleep, his sexual potency and he thought it helped him be more attuned to his wife's needs (Brodley, In press).

Advocates of homework might argue that these gains could have been achieved more quickly with direct assignments, and that the gains might have been more thorough going, but this raises the fundamental question regarding the impact of therapist-initiated projects or goals for clients.

As previously cited, Tomlinson and Whitney argued cogently that means and ends must be consistent within any approach to working with clients. Recognizing that intervention strategies vary in terms degrees of intrusiveness, client-centered practitioners who embrace a non-directive attitude oppose therapists' directing either the process and/or content of therapy. This is because of the belief that the "means" are, in fact, "ends" at a lower level; if the ultimate goal of all therapies is to foster a person who is more autonomous, more free, and more capable of deciding which goals are worthy of pursuit, then the therapy needs to align itself as a practice which is consistent with these goals.

From this point of view, goals set for clients, in the service of which homework assignments are given, may foster dependency at worst or may undermine the client's self-esteem and confidence in his or her own ability to generate meanings and behavior that is more adaptive. For example, asking another person a question has a demand characteristic in that it is difficult not to respond with an answer without violating social norms. But in answering, the client is complying with the therapist. While the therapist's intention may be completely benevolent, the client's experience in answering probably includes an element of compliance.

The evidence for the efficacy of homework has been demonstrated in the work of Kazantzis and Deane (1999). We do not take issue with this claim, given the goals served by the homework: reduction in stress, reduction in anxious or depressed mood, etc. Three categories were identified as not strongly addressed or enhanced by homework; these included "sexual abuse," "learning disorders," and "delusions and hallucinations" (Kazantzis & Deane, 1999, p. 583). From the standpoint of means–ends consistency, homework would appear to be a helpful adjunct to goals of symptom reduction. It is far from clear, however, that unique goals which clients formulate in the course of client-centered therapy such as "a more meaningful life," "living more compassionately," or "restoring dignity" are necessarily enhanced by *therapist-assigned* homework. Some clients may elect to set a course of work or experiments for themselves in the service of precisely such overarching aims: meditation on the suffering of others, taking up a Great Books course, or some other enhancing practice.

Even if we were willing to classify these client-initiated experiments as "homework," they still differ significantly from the homework described in the literature reviewed by Kazantzis and Deane (1999). In these studies, homework related logically to a symptom behavior and was designed by the therapist who tried to achieve high rates of client "compliance" with the assigned work through exploring how confident the client was that he or she would complete the assignment and whether there were any obvious barriers to completion. Even under the best of circumstances with a very benevolent and respectful therapist, the homework is a therapist-initiated intervention in which a client's lack of cooperation may lead the therapist to interpret the "resistance" or to blame the client for faulty motivation. In order to fairly assess comparative outcomes between these cognitive behavioral approaches and non-directive client-centered therapy, there would need to be attention to the discrepancies in what a "good outcome" constitutes, and importantly, who decides when that "good outcome" has been achieved.

SUMMARY

There is no doubt about the efficacy of well-formulated homework assignments in the context of reducing problem behavior (Kazantzis & Deane, 1999). The position of non-directive client-centered therapists critiques the practice in terms of the ethical constraints of nondirectiveness which posit respect for the other person as paramount as opposed to the attainment of behavior change or any other goals not articulated and sought by the client. In the broadest sense certainly some kind of change must occur in order to justify doing therapy, but client-centered therapists place trust in the client as the person who decides whether or not the kind of change produced by psychotherapy is worth the inevitable injuries to self involved in even the most sensitive and carefully nondirective relations.

REFERENCES

Asay, T., & Lambert, M. (1999). The empirical case for the common factors. In M. Hubble, B. Duncan, & S. Miller (Eds.), *The heart and soul of change* (pp. 23–55). Washington, DC: American Psychological Association.

Baldwin, M. (1987). Interview with Carl Rogers on the use of the self in therapy. In M. Baldwin & V. Satir (Eds.), *The use of the self in therapy* (pp. 45–52). New York: Haworth Press.

Bozarth, J. D. (1996a). Client-centered therapy and techniques. In R. Hutterer, G. Pawlowsky, P. F. Schmid, & R. Stipsits (Eds.), *Client-centered and experiential therapy: A paradigm in motion* (pp. 363–368). Frankfurt am Main, Germany: Peter Lang.

Bozarth, J. D. (1996b). The Integrative Statement of Carl R. Rogers. In R. Hutterer, G. Pawlowsky, P. Schmid, & R. Stipsits (Eds.), *Client-centered and experiential psychotherapy: A paradigm in motion* (pp. 25–34). Frankfurt am Main, Germany: Peter Lang.

Bozarth, J. D. (1998). *Person-Centered Therapy: A Revolutionary Paradigm*. Llangarron, Ross-on-Wye, United Kingdom: PCCS Books.

Bozarth, J. D. (2000, March). *Non-directiveness in client-centered therapy: A vexed concept*. Paper presented at the Annual Meeting of the Eastern Psychological Association, Baltimore.

Bozarth, J. D. (2002). Nondirectivity in the person-centered approach: Critique of Kahn's critique. *Journal of Humanistic Psychology, 42,* 78–83.

Bozarth, J. D., & Brodley, B. T. (1991). Actualization: A functional concept in client-centered therapy. In A. Jones & R. Crandall (Eds.), *Handbook of self-actualization* (pp. 45–59). New York: Journal of Social Behavior and Personality, 6.

Brodley, B. T. (1997). The nondirective attitude in client-centered therapy. *The Person-Centered Journal, 4*, 18–30.

Brodley, B. T. (1998). Criteria for making empathic responses in client-centered therapy. *The Person-Centered Journal, 5*, 20–28.

Brodley, B. T. (in press). Client-initiated homework in client-centered therapy. *Journal of Psychotherapy Integration*.

Brodley, B. T., & Brody, A. F. (1990, Summer). *Understanding client-centered therapy through interviews conducted by Carl Rogers*. Paper presented in panel, Fifty years of client-centered therapy: Recent research, presented at the Annual Meeting of the American Psychological Association, Boston.

Brodley, B. T., & Schneider, C. (2001). Unconditional positive regard as communicated through verbal behavior in client-centered therapy. In J. D. Bozarth & P. Wilkins (Eds.), *Unconditional Positive Regard* (Vol. 3, pp. 156–172). Llangarron, Ross-on-Wye, United Kingdom: PCCS Books.

Brody, A. F. (1991). Understanding client-centered therapy through interviews conducted by Carl Rogers. Unpublished master's thesis, Illinois School of Psychology, Chicago.

Goldstein, K. (1939). *The organism*. New York: American Book Company.

Goldstein, K. (1940, 1963). *Human nature in the light of psychopathology*. New York: Schocken.

Grant, B. (1990). Principled and instrumental nondirectiveness in person-centered and client-centered therapy. *Person-Centered Review, 5*, 77–88.

Hutterer, R., Pawlowsky, G., Schmid, P., & Stipsits, R. (Eds.). (1996). *Client-centered and experiential psychotherapy: A paradigm in motion*. Frankfurt am Main, Germany: Peter Lang.

Kazantzis, N., & Deane, F. P. (1999). Psychologists' use of homework assignments in clinical practice. *Professional Psychology: Research and Practice, 30*, 581–585.

Koch, Sigmund. (Series Ed.), & Koch, S. (Vol. Ed.). (1959). *Psychology: A study of a science* (Vol. 3). New York: McGraw-Hill.

Lambert, M. J. (1992). Psychotherapy outcome research: Implications for integrative and eclectic therapists. In J.C. Norcross & M. R. Goldfried. (Eds.), *Handbook of psychotherapy integration* (pp. 94–129). New York: Basic Books.

Lambert, M. J., Shapiro, D. A., & Bergin, A. E. (1986). The effectiveness of psychotherapy. In S. L. Garfield & A. E. Bergin (Eds.), *Handbook of psychotherapy and behavior change* (3rd ed., pp. 157–212). New York: Wiley.

Masson, J. M. (1988, 1994). *Against therapy*. Monroe, Maine: Common Courage Press.

Patterson, C. H. (1984). Empathy, warmth, and genuineness in psychotherapy: A review of reviews. *Psychotherapy, 21*, 431–438.

Pentony, P. (1981). *Models of influence in psychotherapy*. New York: The Free Press.

Proctor, G. (2002). *The dynamics of power in counselling and psychotherapy*. Llangarron Ross-on-Wye, UK: PCCS Books.

Raskin, N. (1947). The nondirective attitude. Unpublished manuscript, Ohio State University, Bowling Green, Ohio.

Rogers, C. R. (1951). *Client-centered Therapy*. Boston: Houghton Mifflin.

Rogers, C. R., & Dymond, R. F. (1954). *Psychotherapy and personality change*. Chicago: University of Chicago Press.

Rogers, C. R. (1957). The necessary and sufficient conditions of therapeutic personality change. *Journal of Consulting Psychology, 21*, 95–103.

Rogers, C. R. (1959). A theory of therapy, personality, and interpersonal relationships as developed in the client-centered framework. In S. Koch (Series Ed.) & S. Koch (Vol. Ed.), *Psychology: A study of a science* (Vol. 3, pp. 184-256). New York: McGraw Hill.

Rogers, C. R. (1961). *On becoming a person*. Boston: Houghton Mifflin.

Rogers, C. R. (1969). *Freedom to learn*. Columbus, Ohio: Charles E. Merrill.

Rogers, C. R. (1970). *Carl Rogers on encounter groups*. New York: Harper and Row.

Rogers, C. R. (1972). *Becoming partners: Marriage and its alternatives*. New York: Dell.

Rogers, C. R. (1980). The foundations of the person-centered approach. In *A way of being* (pp. 113–136). Boston: Houghton Mifflin.

Rogers, C. R. (1980a). Empathic: An unappreciated way of being. In *A way of being* (pp. 137–163). Boston: Houghton Mifflin.

Rogers, C. R. (1986). Reflection of feelings. *Person-Centered Review, 1*, 375–377.

Rogers, C. R. (1986a). Client-centered approach to therapy. In I. L. Kutash & A. Wolf (Eds.), *Psychotherapist's casebook: Theory and technique in practice* (pp. 197–208). San Francisco: Jossey Bass.

Rogers, C. R., & Russell, D. E. (2002). *Carl Rogers the quiet revolutionary*. Roseville, CA: Penmarin Books.

Ryan, R. M., & Deci, E. L. (2000). Self-determination theory and the facilitation of intrinsic motivation, social development, and well-being. *American Psychologist, 55*, 68–78.

Schmid, P. (2001). Comprehension: The art of not knowing. In G. Wyatt (Series Ed.) & S. Haugh & T. Merry (Vol. Eds.), *Rogers' therapeutic conditions: Evolution, theory, and practice* (Vol. 2, pp. 53–71). Llangarron, United Kingdom: PCCS Books. Smith, M. L., & Glass, G. V. (1977). Meta-analysis of psychotherapy outcome studies. *American Psychologist, 32*, 752–760.

Smith, M. L., Glass, G. V., & Miller, T. I. (1980). *The benefits of psychotherapy*. Baltimore: Johns Hopkins University Press.

Tallman, K., & Bohart, A. (1999). The client as a common factor: Clients as self-healers. In M. Hubble, B. Duncan, & S. Miller (Eds.), *The heart and soul of change* (pp. 91–132). Washington, DC: American Psychological Association.

Temaner, B. S. (1977). The empathic understanding response process. Unpublished manuscript, Chicago Counseling and Psychotherapy Center Discussion Papers, Chicago.

Todres, L. (1999). The bodily complexity of truth telling in qualitative research: Some implications of Gendlin's theory. *The Humanistic Psychologist, 27*, 283–300.

Tomlinson, T. M., & Whitney, R. E. (1970). Values and strategy in client-centered therapy. In J. T. Hart & T. M. Tomlinson (Eds.), *New directions in client-centered therapy* (pp. 453–467). Boston: Houghton Mifflin.

Wampold, B. E. (2001). *The great psychotherapy debate*. Mahwah, NJ: Lawrence Erlbaum Associates.

Witty, M. (2004). The difference directiveness makes: The ethics and consequences of guidance in psychotherapy. *The Person-Centered Journal, 11*, 22–32.

Witty, M. (2005). Non-directiveness and the problem of influence. In B.E. Levitt (Ed.), *Embracing Non-Directivity: Reassessing Person-Centered Theory and Practice in the 21st Century* (pp. 228–247). Ross-on-Wye, UK: PCCS Books.

Chapter 3

COGNITIVE THERAPY

Judith S. Beck and Michael A. Tompkins

OVERVIEW OF COGNITIVE THERAPY

Cognitive therapy is an active, directive, time-sensitive, structured, and collaborative psychotherapy. Developed by Aaron T. Beck, M.D., in the early 1960s as a treatment for depression, it has been adapted and found in several hundred studies to be effective for a host of psychiatric disorders including chronic depression, anxiety disorders, substance abuse, eating disorders, and, as an adjunct to medication, bipolar disorder and schizophrenia. Its efficacy has also been demonstrated in the treatment of many medical problems and disorders: hypertension, fibromyalgia, irritable bowel syndrome, and chronic pain, to name a few (Beck, 2005; Butler, Chapman, Forman, & Beck, 2006; Chambless, & Ollendick, 2001).

Cognitive therapy is based on the premise that psychological disorders are associated with the meanings individuals give to events (rather than to the events themselves) and that these meanings are derived from a constellation of core beliefs and assumptions they developed as part of their learning histories (Beck, Rush, Shaw, & Emery, 1979; J. Beck, 1995; DeRubeis, Tang, & Beck, 2001). One central feature of treatment is the identification and modification of key cognitions that lead to negative reactions.

These cognitions include the thoughts that seem to spontaneously arise in individuals' minds (their "automatic thoughts") and their beliefs, their basic understandings of themselves, their worlds, and other people. Specific key cognitions vary from one disorder to the next. When working with clients with panic disorder, for example, it is important to focus on their dysfunctional cognitions about their symptoms, the catastrophic predictions they make when they experience anxiety sensations (Clark, 1986). Key cognitions to target for clients with obsessive–compulsive disorder are not the obsessive thoughts themselves but rather their ideas about having these obsessive thoughts (Clark, 2004). Key cognitions also vary from one individual to the next and treatment is based on the cognitive formulation of the disorder and on the specific conceptualization of the individual client.

Certain elements of treatment characterize therapy. As noted above, first and foremost is that therapists work from a cognitive conceptualization. They understand clients' problems in cognitive terms, i.e., the reason clients react (emotionally, behaviorally, and physiologically) in particular ways is related to the way they interpret their experience. Therapists start conceptualizing clients and their difficulties at the first contact and continue to refine their conceptualization until the client has terminated. This conceptualization guides therapists in helping clients identify important problems and central dysfunctional patterns of thinking and behavior.

A strong therapeutic alliance is another key part of cognitive therapy. Therapists develop this alliance through the use of basic counseling skills (empathy, concern, accurate understanding), through collaboratively making decisions (such as which problems to discuss during a session and what homework to assign), through attending to clients' changes in affect during the session, and through soliciting feedback at the end of sessions (Beck, 1995). Some clients, especially those with Axis II disorders, have highly dysfunctional beliefs about other people and initially view their therapists in a negative way. Their therapists may have to help them respond to their negative cognitions before they are willing to engage in treatment, much less do homework (Beck et al., 2004).

Cognitive therapy sessions are structured. Following a mood check and review of the week (including a review of homework), therapists collaboratively set agendas with clients, focusing on problems important to the client. Clients generally present problems with their relationships, with their mood states, and with managing at home or at work. In the context of discussing a problem, therapists teach clients needed skills, for example, how to evaluate and respond to their dysfunctional cognitions, how to regulate their emotions, and how to modify their behavior. These skills and new understandings are what clients need to practice for homework. Homework may also entail testing ideas that cannot be tested in the therapist's office, as described below. Toward the end of the session, therapists or clients summarize the important points of the session, and, as noted above, the therapist asks the client to provide feedback.

The review of previous homework toward the beginning of each session and the setting of homework toward the end of each session gives direction and structure to the session, and reinforces the message to clients that therapy entails daily active engagement in problem-solving and modification of dysfunctional thinking and behavior (Persons, Davidson, & Tompkins, 2001).

Cognitive therapy is goal-oriented. The therapist's goal is a remission of the client's disorder and prevention of future relapse. Therapists help clients develop specific behavioral goals for themselves, objectives that they will fulfill through their homework at some point in therapy. These goals might include:

- developing consistent habits of daily living (e.g., planning and carrying out a consistent schedule, preparing meals, straightening up the home)
- getting a job or performing better at work (e.g., arriving at work on time, decreasing procrastination, working more steadily throughout the day, speaking more appropriately to the boss)
- improving self-care (regularizing their exercise, sleep, eating, hygiene; taking medication; making and keeping appointments with health care professionals)
- developing and/or improving relationships with family, friends, neighbors, co-workers (initiating contact, conversing, using appropriate assertiveness skills; learning to compromise, negotiate)
- managing better at home (organizing, cleaning, paying bills, doing home repairs)

- refraining from impulsive behavior and deleterious habits (modifying or eliminating overspending, smoking, drug use, self-harm behavior, gambling)
- decreasing avoidance of feared situations (approaching phobic objects and situations, initiating important tasks)
- accepting and coping better with people and situations that cannot be changed (dealing with dysfunctional family-of-origin members, accepting and dealing with limitations or disability)
- accepting and coping better with symptoms (dealing with obsessive thinking, hallucinations)

THE ROLE OF HOMEWORK

Homework plays a central role in helping clients get better and stay better. Clients learn that it is not sufficient merely to discuss problems in session. They need to gain new understandings about themselves, their worlds, and other people, and make small changes in their lives every day. They need to learn new skills (cognitive, behavioral, and emotional) and practice these skills between sessions (Tompkins, 2004). Homework helps clients recover faster and remain well longer (Burns & Auerbach, 1992; Edelman & Chambless, 1993; Kazantizis, Deane & Ronan, 2000; Whisman, 1999). And the use of homework is undoubtedly an important reason for the efficacy of cognitive therapy (Kazantizis et al., 2000; Whisman, 1993).

Homework is not standardized. Therapists and clients collaboratively devise specific assignments as a natural outgrowth of the discussion of problems. When suggesting assignments, therapists are guided by their conceptualization; they are especially cognizant of key cognitions and key behaviors that need to be modified or reinforced. They also consider clients' predilections and capacities, their level of symptomatology, motivation, stage in treatment, and practical factors such as opportunity to complete the task and clients' time and energy constraints. They also consider the nature of the task: its difficulty and time and energy requirements (Tompkins, 2004).

Homework, therefore, differs from one client to another. An important assignment for inactive, depressed clients, for example, is usually to increase specific activities designed to impart a sense of pleasure or mastery. In contrast, an important assignment for anxious clients who are overly busy and stressed is to decrease, delegate, or eliminate specific nonessential activities. Therapists may suggest standard types of homework for an individual client at a given session (e.g., scheduling activities, giving oneself credit, socializing with others, reading therapy notes, engaging in previously avoided activities). Or therapists and clients may create unique homework assignments on the spot.

Homework is set collaboratively. Following the discussion of a problem, therapists may offer suggestions or ask clients what they think might be helpful for them to do during the week. Clients are much more likely to carry out their homework assignments when therapists ensure that the client believes the assignment is doable, beneficial, and relatively easy. It is important for therapists and clients to agree on the frequency and duration of assignments. For some clients, it is also important to specify when to do the assignment and to determine whether they think there will be any psychological or practical obstacles. Following the setting of an assignment, a key question for therapists to ask is, "How likely are you to do this assignment?" (J. Beck, 1995).

When clients do not complete their homework, therapists need to determine whether the difficulty arose due to a practical problem (lack of opportunity, illness, genuine lack of time) and/or interfering cognitions. If the latter is the case, therapists may be able to use standard Socratic questioning to help clients evaluate and respond to these ideas. Some clients who have very long-standing difficulties may have certain ingrained dysfunctional beliefs that make it difficult for them to engage in treatment or do homework: "If I try to do something, I'll fail." "If I focus on my problems, I'll feel worse." "If I start to feel bad, I'll fall apart." More extensive belief modification may be necessary before these clients are willing to carry out assignments between sessions (J. Beck, 2005). Learning to respond to dysfunctional cognitions that interfere with homework completion can provide an important learning experience for clients, as these same kinds of cognitions often interfere with their ability or willingness to engage in other adaptive behaviors as well. As cognitive therapists conduct sessions, they think about clients and their problems in two time frames: "How can I help this client feel better by the end of this session? How can I help this client have a better week?" (J. Beck, 2005). The answer to this second question prompts therapists to think about what clients need to learn in session, how to transfer this learning outside of session, how to have clients practice what they have learned outside of session, and how to facilitate their continued learning outside of session.

Homework helps clients gain confidence in their ability to manage their problems on their own without the assistance of a therapist. Clients who have learned and practiced self-management skills through cognitive therapy homework are more likely to use these skills to ameliorate future downturns in their mood that in the past could have resulted in a full-blown clinical episode (Simons, Murphy, Levine, & Wetzel, 1986), which may explain the lower relapse rates seen in cognitive therapy versus medication for the treatment of depression (Hollon et al., 2005).

Homework has several purposes, including:

- Implementing solutions to problems
- Increasing self-awareness
- Practicing cognitive, behavioral, and emotional skills
- Reinforcing what was learned in session
- Testing ideas
- Preventing relapse

These purposes are described below.

TO IMPLEMENT SOLUTIONS TO PROBLEMS DISCUSSED IN SESSION

A key function of homework is to get clients to solve their real life difficulties, especially helping them function better in various spheres of life, including managing at home and at work, relating better to other people, and taking care of their health. At each session, clients and therapists prioritize clients' problems and discuss them in a problem-solving way.

A schizophrenic client, for example, may be quite disorganized at home. Following an analysis of the problem in session, her homework assignment might be to spend 10 minutes three times a day cleaning the kitchen and/or doing laundry. A solution to a client's angry outbursts toward his partner might be to take "time-outs" when he feels the urge to yell. The therapist of a client who forgets to take her medicine may suggest that she keep a days-of-the-week medicine box in clear sight, set a timer on her watch, and post notes on her bathroom mirror and refrigerator. A depressed client who is spending a great deal of time in front of the television might need his therapist's help to schedule activities throughout the day and evening, including activities that will bring him a sense of both mastery and pleasure.

Activity scheduling is often used to implement solutions to problems discussed in session as it can help solve multiple problems: poor motivation, poor time management, difficulty initiating activities, avoidance, fatigue, anhedonia, and isolation. Committing in session to engaging in specific activities at scheduled times can increase clients' ability to follow through with these activities between sessions.

Activity-scheduling homework can also be used to increase or decrease the frequency of a target behavior. For example, clients who abuse alcohol can schedule specific activities to do at the time when they would ordinarily camp out at their local bar. Clients who are in poor physical shape or who suffer from chronic pain can benefit from scheduling times to increase their exercise level or walking tolerance.

To Increase Self-Awareness

Another important purpose of homework is to help clients make sense of their experience, to understand why they react in certain ways (and what they can subsequently do). When they enter treatment, most clients believe that their emotional or behavioral reactions are directly connected with a certain situation; "Going to stores makes me panicky." "My neighbors are making me so angry." Or they may be mystified by their moods or impulses.

An important goal early in treatment is for clients to start viewing their experience through the cognitive model, grasping that their thoughts are more closely connected to how they feel emotionally (and how they react behaviorally) than they are to situations themselves. ("My prediction that I'll have a panic attack and my image of having a heart attack in the store are what are making me anxious, not the store itself." "My idea, which turns out to be unrealistic, that my neighbors should never make any noise is what is fueling my anger.")

Therapists ask clients to monitor their experience between sessions to identify times when they are feeling worse or behaving in a non-adaptive way. (Or they may ask somaticizers or medical clients to monitor their physiological changes.) They use these emotional, behavioral, and/or physiological changes as a cue to ask themselves what was going through their minds.

Monitoring one's cognitions can provide an "ah hah" experience for clients: "No wonder I felt that way [or did that]." Such understanding can help clients feel more in control and sets the stage for testing and responding to their thoughts. In fact, this self-monitoring process is an essential precursor to a major intervention in cognitive therapy: helping clients learn to evaluate and respond to their dysfunctional thinking in specific situations in order to attain an improved emotional, behavioral, and/or physiological reaction.

Monitoring their experience, rather than reacting to their problems, can also help decrease clients' symptoms (Nelson, 1977). Depressed clients who are asked to record the number of self-critical thoughts they have each hour often experience a decline in the number of these kinds of thoughts (Beck et al., 1979). Similarly, clients who binge eat often find that the frequency of their binges decreases as they monitor their eating behavior. Self-monitoring can also increase the frequency of positive behavior, for example, when couples in distressed relationships keep track of how often they are displaying desirable behaviors toward their partners, or when clients make a check mark every time they take their medication as prescribed.

A final kind of monitoring involves encouraging clients to be aware of doing their therapy homework and giving themselves credit. Doing so gives them confidence that they can do something to affect their mood, behavior, and often their environment.

TO PRACTICE ESSENTIAL SKILLS

To solve their problems and recover from their disorders (and to stay well), clients need to learn cognitive, behavioral, and emotional skills, as described below.

Cognitive Skills

Clients need to use distressing or dysfunctional emotional, behavioral, or physiological cues to identify their maladaptive thinking between sessions. Then they need to respond to these cognitions in a useful way, depending on the nature of their thoughts, their degree of distress, the situation they are in, their stage in treatment, their intellectual capacity, and the nature of their disorder.

Clients may, for example, evaluate the validity and utility of their thoughts, either mentally or through the use of a worksheet such as the Dysfunctional Thought Record (J. Beck, 2006). They may review therapy notes devised in a previous session that contain responses to their thoughts, they may refocus their attention, or, especially as in the case of obsessive thinking or worry, they may accept their thoughts without paying undue attention to them or trying to change them.

Behavioral Skills

In the context of solving problems in session, therapists also teach clients new behavioral skills in session that they are asked to practice and implement between sessions. There are a wide variety of behavioral skills that clients may need to learn. A client with avoidant personality disorder may benefit from practicing conversational or assertiveness skills. An angry client may benefit from doing relaxation exercises. A parent with a child who has oppositional defiant disorder may benefit from practicing setting limits firmly and consistently.

Emotional Skills

A prime goal of cognitive therapy is to help clients reduce negative affect. As mentioned above, depressed clients need to practice responding realistically to their thinking. Clients with generalized anxiety disorder may need, in addition, to learn to distract themselves or refocus their attention. Paradoxically, in order to reduce negative emotions in the long run, some clients benefit from practicing tolerating distressing affect instead of trying to reduce or eliminate it. Clients with panic disorder need to let themselves experience panic attacks so they can learn that their feared catastrophe does not happen (Clark & Ehlers, 1993). Clients with borderline personality disorder may need to let themselves experience high levels of distress so they can see that they do not fall apart (Linehan, 1993). Clients who abuse substances (or engage in other compulsive behaviors such as binge eating, gambling, or hair pulling) need to tolerate negative emotion and urges, often in a graduated fashion, to learn that they can take control of their behavior (Beck et al., 1993).

To Reinforce What Was Learned in Session

Homework allows clients to rehearse new understandings they have gained from treatment. At each session, clients learn new ideas that are important for them to remember. Daily review of these important changes in their thinking (often through reading therapy notes written by the therapist or client) helps clients feel better emotionally and makes it more likely that they will carry out their behavioral homework assignments.

Therapy notes often contain a client's cognitions with robust adaptive responses or behavioral instructions or both. A depressed client, for example, had a three by five card that read, "When I start to feel like a failure, remind myself that I have a real illness called depression, which is making it harder for me to do things right now. When I'm better, I'll be back to my old self. I should give myself a break. I don't consider my brother a failure even though he has depression and doesn't always function too well, either." She had another card that read, "When I'm depressed, the worst thing I can do is stay in bed. Anything else that I do is better. For example, I can call Jane, take a walk, groom the dog, read a magazine, bake bread, or look up websites."

Another assignment that reinforces what the client has learned in session is bibliotherapy. Clients often find therapists' ideas more credible or more convincing when they see them in black-and-white in carefully selected cognitive therapy client pamphlets and books or on the internet. Therapists may also suggest that clients join groups such as Alcoholics Anonymous or Al-Anon to reinforce important learning.

To Test Cognitions

Clients can evaluate many of their cognitions in session. Other cognitions, however, can only be tested between sessions. Some can be tested through self-monitoring. A client who believed that her high anxiety often lasted for entire days was surprised to find that her anxiety fluctuated quite a bit throughout the day. Recognizing this made her feel less vulnerable and more motivated to engage in activities that reduced her distress. A schizophrenic client monitored the intensity of voices in his head when he hummed or listened to a portable music player; he found the voices became less intense, which made him feel more in control of this symptom.

Many other cognitions can be tested through behavioral experiments, planned activities carried out by clients in or between cognitive therapy sessions (Beck et al., 1979; J. Beck, 1995). Their primary purpose is to obtain new information that may help

- to test the validity of the client's existing beliefs about themselves, others, and the world
- to construct and/or test new, more adaptive beliefs, and
- to contribute to the development and verification of the cognitive formulation (Bennett-Levy et al., 2004).

Homework to test assumptions can take many forms, depending on the client's presenting problems and/or the focus of a particular cognitive therapy session. One client had a number of cognitions that could only be tested outside of session:

- I can't get out of bed before noon.
- If I ask my family for help, they'll get hostile.
- If I try to make conversation at the church social, I'll be too tongue-tied to speak.
- If I try to exercise, I'll feel worse.
- If I feel down, the only way I can feel better is by taking a drink.

His therapist framed these cognitions as ideas that could be completely true, completely untrue, or someplace in the middle. First she had to help him to respond to automatic thoughts that interfered with his willingness to put these ideas to the test. When he ultimately agreed to test them for homework, his therapist carefully helped him figure out how to set up the test. He, too, was surprised to find, in almost each case, that his predictions had been largely erroneous.

It is important to recognize that many clients, like the one described above, have interfering cognitions about doing homework. Many of these cognitions can also be tested through behavioral experiments:

- "I'll be too tired."
- "I won't be able to do it."
- "It won't help."
- "I'll end up feeling worse."

It is important for therapists to identify these kinds of cognitions in session so they can help clients learn how to respond to them. One method to do so is to ask clients to imagine that it is time to do a specific activity and to predict how they will be feeling, what they will be thinking, and what they will then do. Therapists also can identify these kinds of automatic thoughts when clients return to session without having completed (and sometimes without having even started) their homework (barring practical obstacles that got in the way). Often an examination of the advantages and disadvantages of doing homework helps motivate clients.

TO PREPARE FOR POTENTIAL RELAPSE

Cognitive therapists begin relapse prevention from the very first session with clients, as they are mindful of what skills clients need to learn and practice at home to get better and stay better. Early in treatment, therapists may be more active in suggesting homework assignments. By the end of treatment, though, clients often design and decide how to implement assignments themselves, so they will be able to "be their own therapist" when treatment has ended (J. Beck, 1995).

It is important for therapists not only to help clients solve problems and evaluate their thinking, for example, but also to teach them how to do these things themselves. When clients have begun to feel somewhat better, are more functional, and are using their cognitive therapy skills outside of session, therapists generally start spacing sessions further apart to give clients the opportunity to do "self-therapy" sessions as part of their homework.

CASE EXAMPLE

When Jerome, a 33-year-old married property assessor, entered treatment, he had just recently been diagnosed with bipolar disorder. He had been moderately depressed for six months. At his first therapy session, he discussed his goals for treatment. His overall goal was to feel better and to avoid future manic and depressive episodes.

In addition, Jerome wanted to improve his relationship with his wife, which had been particularly damaged by his reckless behavior in previous manic episodes. He wanted to be more productive and less argumentative at work; his previous evaluation had been poor and he feared losing his job. He wanted to spend more time with his teenage sons. He also wanted to get his finances in order. These goals became an important focus in treatment and much of his homework ultimately involved taking steps toward achieving them.

Initially, however, his therapist conceptualized that Jerome had some overriding difficulties that needed attention. First, he was taking his psychotropic medication only sporadically. In order to help him become more adherent, his therapist recognized that Jerome needed a three-prong approach to his "homework" of taking medication. In addition to the psychoeducation she provided him in session, she recommended that Jerome read more about bipolar disorder and the importance of medication for homework. She and Jerome discussed what he saw as the pros and cons of taking medication. A second assignment, to read this list daily, helped remind Jerome of how much the potential advantages outweighed the disadvantages. A third assignment, following additional discussion of the topic, was to read a card she helped Jerome compose to motivate him to take medication: "When I don't feel like taking the medicine, remind myself that I really want to make life better for [my wife and sons] and for me. Taking this medication is a sign of strength, not a sign of weakness."

When Jerome returned for his second session, his adherence had markedly improved. His therapist did some practical problem-solving with him (including suggesting that he call his psychiatrist about some side effects he was experiencing) and again helped him respond in writing to other interfering cognitions.

At the second session, Jerome wanted to talk about a problem at work. His boss was pressuring him to finish up some reports that were already significantly overdue. Before his therapist could do problem-solving with him, though, she had to help him respond to his automatic thoughts. "There's nothing I can do about this. He's definitely going to fire me. What's the use of even trying to get the work done?" She used this situation as an opportunity to teach Jerome the cognitive model. He was able to see how his perception of the situation made him feel hopeless. After evaluating his thoughts with his therapist, he concluded that perhaps they would not necessarily turn out to be completely accurate, especially because his boss, up until this point at least, had seemed concerned about Jerome, not angry. They role-played what Jerome could say to his boss without disclosing his illness (because Jerome feared being stigmatized) and decatastrophized his fear that he would be fired on the spot.

For homework, Jerome went ahead and talked to his boss. While their conversation was not wholly positive, they did come up with a plan for Jerome to complete his work and he was able to preserve his job for the time being. The homework assignment demonstrated to Jerome that just because he thought something was true did not necessarily mean it was wholly accurate. From then on, Jerome had an ongoing homework assignment to catch his automatic thoughts when he was feeling distressed or behaving dysfunctionally. Initially he reported these thoughts to his therapist and they collaboratively evaluated them. Fairly soon, his therapist taught him how to evaluate his thoughts himself, which he did as part of his ongoing assignment.

At the second session, Jerome also wanted to discuss how alienated he and his wife were. He was not certain she understood that at least some of his irrational behavior was related to symptoms of bipolar disorder, not to character flaws. They discussed the marital relationship at some length. It seemed apparent that she would not be amenable to coming to a therapy session with him. They then role-played how he could speak to her about his difficulties.

For homework, Jerome told his wife what he had learned about bipolar disorder and offered to show her the psychoeducational materials provided to him by his therapist. At his therapist's suggestion, he took the initiative to plan some pleasurable activities with his wife. (This was another assignment that became ongoing.)

Before Jerome was willing to undertake this discussion with his wife, however, his therapist again had to help him evaluate and respond to his hopeless thoughts: "She won't listen to me. Telling her about bipolar disorder won't do anything. She won't want to do anything fun with me. Nothing will work." Having worked out a problem with his boss, though, Jerome was willing to try. Although this experiment was not a hundred percent successful, Jerome was able to see that he could talk to his wife and change her mind somewhat. A few sessions later, after discussion with his therapist, Jerome began to acknowledge to his wife that his behavior, driven by bipolar disorder, had had a significantly negative effect on her and the family and to relate how sorry he was for his gambling, his excessive irritability, his withdrawal from her and their sons, and his depressive behavior. His declarations did help soften his wife's attitude toward him and she became more amenable to helping him cope with his disorder.

At each session, Jerome discussed with his therapist the homework he had done, the results he had obtained, and the conclusions he had drawn. He continued some of his homework on an ongoing basis; activity scheduling, for example, was an important assignment for Jerome each week, since he initially spent most of his time when he was not at work sleeping, watching television, or surfing the internet. (Later, when he was hypomanic, activity scheduling helped him reduce his activities.)

At each session they also discussed two or three problems and collaboratively devised homework assignments to solve these problems. Some of these assignments tended to be more situation specific, applicable to a specific problem, e.g., how to handle Thanksgiving with his extended family, or what to do about a troublesome neighbor. He continued to do other assignments, including reading his therapy notes, every week.

About three months after the start of treatment, Jerome did indeed lose his job and he became suicidal. His suicidal thoughts became the focus of the next few sessions. Homework included making his gun inaccessible to him (he gave it to a friend), reading therapy notes to address his hopelessness and to remind himself of all the reasons he had for living, enlisting his wife's assistance when he was feeling particularly upset, spending some time with his supportive mother and his friend, being in phone contact with his therapist, and taking active steps to find a new job.

The suicidal crisis passed and Jerome continued to improve. As his depression lifted, his therapist began to direct more discussion toward relapse prevention. What had Jerome learned about depression? What did he understand was important for him to do on a daily basis, whether or not he was depressed (or manic)? How could he get himself to do these things? They made sure the answers to these questions were in therapy notes that Jerome could refer to long after treatment ended. Earlier in treatment, Jerome and his therapist had devised a monitoring form, so he could keep track of changes in his symptoms from day-to-day. They modified a standard form (Sachs, 1996) for bipolar clients, including ratings of his mood, sleep, activity level, eating, thinking, and impulses, among other items. They discussed how he could motivate himself to complete the form in the future, especially when he was feeling relatively euthymic.

Jerome and his therapist also discussed how he could prepare himself for a future depressive episode. He added a few items to his monitoring form to make it more likely that he could pick up some of the more subtle early warning signs of depression. He discussed with his wife what he wanted her to do if she recognized depressive symptoms before he did. He developed a plan in writing of the steps he would need to take to try to avert or reduce the severity of a future episode. His therapist discussed with him how he could remember to refer to this plan, especially because he might not want to be reminded that he probably needed to take special care of himself.

Jerome and his therapist also focused treatment on preventing a manic episode, adding additional early warning signs of mania to his monitoring form. Again, they devised a plan for dealing with mania. They developed responses to hyperpositive thoughts he had had in the past that had led to his getting into difficulties. Gambling had been a particular problem when Jerome had been in a manic state; at one point he had lost over $10,000. Jerome believed that when he was manic he could not control his urge to gamble. Among other interventions, he and his therapist set up a homework assignment to test the belief and clarified an alternative belief, "Using therapy tools can help me curb my impulse."

These tools included the two-person feedback rule and the 48-hour rule (Newman, Leahy, Beck, Reilly-Harrington, & Gyulai, 2002). When Jerome had the urge to gamble (or any strong urge similar to this), he was to experiment with asking at least two people for their opinion. (His therapist helped him see that even CEOs and presidents have advisors.) He was also to wait for 48 hours before engaging in behavior for which he had a strong impulse. He and his therapist made a list of things he could try to do while waiting for the impulse to pass: listening to a therapy tape describing the disadvantages of gambling, doing progressive muscle relaxation, taking slow walks with his wife, sitting down and listening to calming music.

Later, when he did become hypomanic, Jerome managed to complete the experiment and avoid the impulse to gamble. He reported that reading his therapy notes and implementing the 48-hour rule in conjunction with activities to distract himself were the most helpful. These strategies became an important part of the relapse prevention plan that he used once treatment ended.

SUMMARY

Homework plays a central role in cognitive therapy. A significant part of each session is devoted to designing assignments to help clients improve between sessions and to motivating clients to carry out these assignments. Therapists use a cognitive conceptualization of the client to guide treatment, including the development of homework assignments. When difficulties in completing assignments arise (other than those due to practical problems), the therapist again conceptualizes the difficulties in cognitive terms, uncovering and helping clients respond to interfering cognitions. A major thrust in homework is oriented toward relapse prevention: having clients learn skills that they can use long after treatment has ended.

REFERENCES

Beck, A. T. (2005). The current state of cognitive therapy: A forty year retrospective. *Archives of General Psychiatry*, 62:953–959.

Beck, A. T., Freeman, A., Davis, D., Pretzer, J., Fleming, B., Ottaviani, R., Beck, J., Simon, K., Padesky, C., Meyer, J., & Trexler, L. (2004). *Cognitive therapy of personality disorders.* New York: Guilford Press.

Beck, A. T., Rush, J. A., Shaw, B. F., & Emery, G. (1979). *Cognitive therapy for depression.* New York: Guilford Press.

Beck, A. T., Wright, F., Newman, C., & Liese, B. (1993). *Cognitive therapy of substance abuse.* New York: Guilford Press.

Beck, J. (1995). *Cognitive therapy: Basics and beyond.* New York: Guilford Press.

Beck, J. (2006). *Cognitive therapy worksheet packet.* Bala Cynwyd, PA: Beck Institute for Cognitive Therapy and Research.

Beck, J. (2005). *Cognitive therapy for challenging problems: What to do when the basics don't work.* New York: Guilford Press.

Bennett-Levy, J., Butler, G., Fennell, M., Hackmann, A., Meuller, M., & Westbrook, D. (Eds.). (2004). *Oxford guide to behavioural experiments in cognitive therapy.* New York: Oxford University Press.

Burns, D. D., & Auerbach, A. H. (1992). Do self-help assignments enhance recovery from depression? *Psychiatric Annals, 22*:464–469.

Butler, A. C., Chapman, J. E., Forman, E. M., & Beck, A. T. (2006). The empirical status of cognitive-behavioral therapy: A review of meta-analyses. *Clinical Psychology Review, 26,* 17–31.

Chambless, D. L., & Ollendick, T. H. (2001). Empirically supported psychological interventions: Controversies and evidence. *Annu. Rev. Psychol., 52,* 685–716.

Clark D. M. A cognitive model of panic (1986). *Behaviour Research and Therapy,* 24:461–470.

Clark, D. M., & Ehlers, A. (1993). An overview of the cognitive theory and treatment of panic disorder. *Applied and Preventive Psychology*, 2:131–139.

Clark, D. A. *Cognitive-behavioral therapy for OCD* (2004). New York: The Guilford Press.

DeRubeis, R. J., Tang, T. Z., & Beck, A. T. (2001). Cognitive therapy. In K. S. Dobson (Ed.), *Handbook of cognitive-behavioral therapies* (2nd ed.). New York: Guilford Press.

Edelman, R. E., & Chambless, D. L. (1993). Adherence during sessions and homework in cognitive-behavioural group treatment of social phobia. *Behaviour Research and Therapy:33,* 573–577.

Hollon S. D., DeRubeis R. J., Shelton R. C., Amsterdam J. D., Salomon R. M., O'Reardon J. P. et al. (2005). Prevention of relapse following cognitive therapy vs medications in moderate to severe depression. *Arch Gen Psychiatry, 62,* 417–422.

Kazantizis, N., Deane, F. P., & Ronan, K. R. (2000). Homework assignments in cognitive and behavioral therapy: A meta-analysis. *Clinical Psychology: Science and Practice,* 7:189–202.

Linehan, M. (1993) *Cognitive-behavioral treatment of borderline personality disorder.* New York: Guilford Press.

Nelson, R. O. (1977). Methodological issues in assessment via self-monitoring. In J. D. Cone & R. P. Hawkins (Eds.), *Behavioral assessment: New directions in clinical psychology* (pp. 217–240). New York: Brunner/Mazel.

Newman, C. F., Leahy, R. L., Beck, A. T., Reilly-Harrington, N. A., & Gyulai, L. (2002). *Bipolar disorder: A cognitive therapy approach*. Washington, DC: American Psychological Association.

Persons, J. B., Davidson, J., & Tompkins, M. A. (2001). *Essential components of cognitive-behavior therapy for depression*. Washington, DC: American Psychological Association.

Sachs, G. S. (1996). Mood chart (unpublished assessment measure): The Harvard Bipolar Research Program, Massachusetts General Hospital, Boston, MA.

Simons, A. D., Murphy, G. E., Levine, J. L., & Wetzel, R. D. (1986). Cognitive therapy and pharmacotherapy for depression: Sustained improvement over one year. *Archives of General Psychiatry, 43*:43–48.

Tompkins, M. A. (2004). *Using homework in psychotherapy: Strategies, guidelines and forms*. New York: Guilford Press.

Whisman, M. A. (1993). Mediators and moderators of change in cognitive therapy of depression. *Psychological Bulletin, 114*:248–265.

Whisman, M. A. (1999). The importance of the cognitive theory of change in cognitive therapy for depression. *Clinical Psychology: Science and Practice, 6*:300–304.

CHAPTER 4

EMOTION-FOCUSED EXPERIENTIAL THERAPY

Jennifer A. Ellison and Leslie S. Greenberg

Homework has typically been associated with cognitive and behavioural approaches to therapy, yet homework in experiential approaches to therapy, while not typically formalized in theory, is frequently incorporated into experiential practice. Among the Webster's New World Dictionary definitions we find that "homework" has been defined as "study or research in preparation for some project, activity, etc." From this definition one can easily see the intuitive appeal of the use of homework in an experiential approach to treatment. Terminology typically used when introducing homework include "exercises," "experiments," and "activities." The theoretical underpinning of various experiential approaches and homework may be different, but the intent of between-session activities is consistent: to translate in-therapy change into extra-session change by means of homework (Greenberg & Warwar, in press; Mahrer, 1996). Yet, despite increasing clinical interest in maximizing in-session gains through between-session opportunities of carrying forward such gains (particularly given the prevalence of time-limited therapies), the formalization of when to use homework in an experiential approach with clients in the most beneficial way remains lacking in the literature.

EMOTION-FOCUSED THERAPY AND THE EMOTION COACH

In emotion-focused therapy (EFT), Greenberg (2002) has proposed a new integrative framework for experiential approaches incorporating between-session exercises aimed at increasing clients' awareness of how they experience self, other, and the world. EFT incorporates and maximizes in-session moments of change by encouraging the client to carry forward in-session work to between-session and posttreatment opportunities of experiential learning and practice. Particular emphasis is placed upon teaching skills for client contacting, accepting, and utilizing emotional information and resources.

If one considers the definition of homework provided above, EFT is an activity- or task-oriented approach in which the "study or research" is one of self-exploration for the client. The "project" is largely informed by his or her experience in the moment, whether it is within or outside of the formal therapeutic setting. In this sense, between-session activities, or tasks, are well-suited to an emotion-focused approach to therapy in that in-session tasks prepare the client for, and likely increase the probability of, client-initiated activities between sessions as well as self-guided implementation of gain-sustaining activities once treatment has ended. Consequently, implementation of experiential skills or tools that are learned during the acute phase of treatment allows clients to better equip themselves to deal with problems as they arise outside of sessions as well as after treatment has ended.

PRINCIPLES OF EMOTION COACHING

EFT provides an integrative view of the therapist as an "emotion coach" (Greenberg, 2002). A coach is a facilitator who helps motivate people to move from where they are to where they want to be. The agreed upon goals provide the destination. An emotion coach is seen as *following* a client's emotional experience as well as *leading* the client toward deeper experience, while being fully present in the moment with and for the client (Greenberg & Geller, 2001). The dialectic between *acceptance* and *change* (cf. Linehan, 1993) is cultivated by the coach's following and leading stance.

EFT can be seen as operating according to two overarching principles: facilitating a therapeutic relationship and promoting therapeutic work (Greenberg, Rice, & Elliot, 1993). Facilitating a therapeutic relationship works according to three subprinciples: empathic attunement, bonding, and task collaboration. Task collaboration, the third relational principle that is most relevant to homework tasks, emphasizes moment-by-moment and overall collaboration on the agreed upon goals and tasks of therapy. Task collaboration within the therapeutic relationship, as in many other experiential approaches to psychotherapeutic treatment, remains paramount to the therapeutic endeavor. Requesting that the client carry out a homework prescription, while at times sufficient (Goldfried & Davidson, 1976; Kanfer & Grimm, 1980; Mahrer, Nordin, & Miller, 1995; Prochanska & DiClemente, 1982), is not likely to promote the most optimal experiential learning opportunity. Without collaborative task-agreement, compliance, especially with between-session tasks, is unlikely to occur. Furthermore, if the homework exercises do not resonate with the client during treatment, then the likelihood that the client will carry forward such learning practices after therapy is diminished.

The hallmark of the EFT approach is that different tasks are engaged in at different *markers* of different types of emotional processing problems. When using homework, in-session client processing helps to determine the relevance and timing of extra-session suggestions. The presence of in-session markers not only serves as a guide for action within the session, but also provide guidance for client–therapist collaboration on homework tasks. When the task is experienced as contrary to clients' goals, therapists resort to following the moment-by-moment process to become more attuned with their clients' goals. Adopting these principles leads to a style of following and leading clients' moment-by-moment experience as it shifts through and between sessions. For example, homework may be given to consolidate task completion, such as practicing softening of an inner critical voice or contacting healthy emotions during processing of past relationships.

An emotion coach, both in therapy and in designing homework, focuses on developing the clients' strengths, possibilities, and resources and uses language that is prizing and appreciative to help clients move forward by accessing positive emotional resources. The therapist is interested in coaching clients to access and experience internal emotional processes so that they may mobilize internal resources, thereby encouraging not only flexibility in and alternatives of action but also the encourage of the adoption of a new relationship with their "emotional" self.

STAGES OF EMOTION COACHING

Further to the operating principles outlined above, emotion coaching in therapy is based on two phases of *arriving at* and *leaving* emotions (Greenberg, 2002). The underlying idea here is that one cannot leave a place until one has arrived. The first phase, arriving at one's emotions, is guided by identification, awareness, experience, and expression of emotion. Attention toward and allowing of emotion are necessary initial conditions of arriving at an emotion. Here the therapeutic relationship is of primary importance if the interest is in the client tolerating and welcoming his or her emotion in the moment. Offering an in-session atmosphere where the client learns to welcome emotion is also of primary interest in terms of encouraging task completion, whether it is in the context of the session or through homework activity. If the client is not coached to welcome his or her emotional experience and allow it in-session, between-session opportunities for work become limited. Clients in this stage also need to be coached in skills of regulating their emotion in preparedness for situations that may overwhelm them. Emotion regulation becomes particularly important for those clients who enter treatment in an emotionally dysregulated manner, while overcontrolled clients may be served best by learning and practicing expressive skills aimed at experientially opening toward their emotion. Homework, such as noticing one's breathing when anxious or learning to take a time out when too upset, can be given to help people regulate their emotions. Clients also need to be helped to describe their feelings in words in order to aid them in solving their problems. Emotion diaries are used for this purpose. A final aspect of the arriving stage involves helping clients become aware of whether their emotional reactions to a situation are their primary feelings within a situation. *Primary emotions* (Greenberg et al., 1993; Greenberg & Paivio, 1997) are the person's most fundamental and direct initial reactions to a situation, such as being sad at a loss or angry at a violation. Primary feelings are core states in that they are irreducible to any other feeling. If primary feelings are not being accessed, clients must be helped in discovering what their primary feelings are. Homework can be used to help people practice getting to their primary feelings. Examples are provided later in the chapter.

The second phase, leaving an emotion, is guided by utilizing the primary adaptive feelings that have been identified in awareness and transforming the maladaptive feelings. Once the client has been helped to identify and experience a primary emotion, the therapist and client together need to evaluate if the emotion is an adaptive or maladaptive response to the current situation. If the emotion is identified as enhancing to self or other, it is utilized as an informative guide to action. If it is identified as destructive to self or other, it must first be regulated and then replaced or transformed. Once an experience is clearly accepted and recognized as maladaptive, the coach needs to help the client identify the negative voice associated with the maladaptive emotion. The negative voice often is directed inward against the self in the form of a harsh internal critic. While the maladaptive emotion and cognitions associated with the emotion are "alive" in the moment, the client is helped to find and rely on alternative, more adaptive emotional responses and needs. The client needs to be coached to challenge the destructive thoughts associated with their unhealthy emotions from a new stance based on their healthy primary emotions and needs. Here is where primary emotions become particularly useful as informative guides to action. Homework may be designed to address any or all of these differential components in the arriving and leaving phases of treatment in EFT.

FRAMEWORK FOR THE SYSTEMATIC USE OF HOMEWORK IN EFT

Homework is offered in a *non-imposing tentative* manner, as "experiments," "activities," or "exercises" to try, rather than as expert pronouncements of what should be done (Greenberg & Warwar, in press; Greenberg & Watson, 2005). Homework is designed to help consolidate emerging self-organization and change and is highly responsive to the client's state. Homework must fit where the client is in the moment and is never done in a prescribed manner according to an agenda. The relationship is not that of a teacher giving a student homework that must be completed. Rather, homework is offered in the spirit of "try this if you find it relevant and helpful." Homework is given in a spirit of exploration rather than to achieve change. Client empowerment rather than compliance is the goal.

The primary goal of homework in experiential therapy is to encourage the consolidation and completion of in-session changes through extra-session practice after new possibilities have been developed in the session. Equally important is the encouragement of self-initiated experiential practice and learning opportunities that may occur once treatment has ended. It is through a collaborative and co-constructive process that the therapist develops homework to help the client *practice* experiential learning that has emerged in-session. Consequently, emotion coaching in both treatment and homework is based on the basic premise that novel information is best heard and processed by receivers when it is sensitively attuned to their present state. Motivation to engage in homework is a key concern in an experiential approach, where problems are not seen as skill deficits but as affective/motivational problems. Thus, assessment of motivational readiness to do homework is crucial. Any signs of resistance or opposition are taken as motivation in their own right that serve a protective function and are therefore worked within a framework of acceptance. Any signs of opposition are validated and elaborated, and the desire to not do or the anxiety about doing the homework becomes the focus.

Our concern with motivational readiness to do homework means homework suggestions need to be highly situationally relevant to what is emerging in-session. *Hot emotional learning* is facilitated through *hot teaching* when the client is offered homework suggestions while he or she is emotionally aroused that fall within the client's "proximal zone of development" (Vygostsky, 1986). Accordingly, therapist in-session responses or homework suggestions should not be too far ahead of or behind the client's level of experience in the moment. A homework suggestion must always be within the person's capacity to stretch his or her ability to identify, tolerate, experience, or understand what is being suggested. Commitment to homework is also increased if homework is offered when the client's present state is one geared toward high motivation for behavioral change. If the homework is not geared toward the client's present state, the client is unlikely to self-initiate between-session and posttherapy work. The assessment of current emotional states and the provision of forms of guidance that fit momentary emotional states help people mobilize their inner resources and develop a positive sense of self (Greenberg et al., 1993), motivate the person to work toward more adaptive functioning. One of the challenges is to offer homework as a state- and capacity-appropriate scaffold that can support the client in moving toward a new way of being in the world.

Working toward a new way of being in the world is not a process that is fully completed within the time-frame of short-term therapy. Although emotion restructuring is viewed as leading to change in core emotion schemes and therefore to less likelihood of relapse, short-term relapse prevention skills are important. Given that therapy alone does not always change deeply entrenched, learned responses that have developed over a person's lifetime, active engagement in self-work after therapy has ended can be very helpful. This is the period when the client's emotion repertoire will continue to be challenged, changed, and solidified. In our work we have found that an important factor that differentiated those who relapsed from those who maintained gains was the individual's ability after treatment had ended to actively utilize tools that they had developed during treatment. Exercises provided in this chapter offer some of the tools which clients may use to solidify changes that occurred in therapy, after treatment has ended.

In EFT, in-, between-, and post-session tasks are guided by four major empirically supported principles for enhancing emotion processing: (1) increasing awareness of emotion, (2) enhancing emotion regulation, (3) transforming emotion, and (4) reflection on emotion. These principles provide a general guide for understanding different types of in-session and extra-session homework with emotion as well as engagement in relapse prevention activities once treatment has ended. The principles are described below, and examples of the types of homework associated with each are provided (cf. Greenberg, 2002).

EMOTION AWARENESS

Examples of emotion awareness homework are provided below. These homework exercises have been found to be particularly helpful for people who experience minimal emotional awareness, typically through constriction of their emotions. The therapist coaches clients how to become aware of their emotional experiences, hence ensuring client readiness for most, if not all, future in-session emotion work. Once some emotion awareness work has occurred in-session, clients are offered homework as a means of expanding their emotional awareness within their daily lives through between-session opportunities geared toward emotional and experiential awareness (Greenberg, 2002).

Keeping an Emotion Diary

Clients may state that they do not believe they have emotions. They may also find that they are aware that they are experiencing some sort of emotional experience, yet they are unable to describe what it is that they are feeling. Such clients may experience difficulty in getting to their emotions and, consequently, are not accessing valuable information which could direct them toward more adaptive functioning.

Attending to, experiencing, and symbolizing emotional experience are all key aspects of EFT. Recommending that clients keep an emotion diary is helpful early on in therapy, once clients have begun exploring their emotions in-session. As a preface to offering an emotion diary as homework (Greenberg & Warwar, in press), the therapist might say something like, "Emotions are like signals that may get stronger and more intense until they are acknowledged and attended to. If you have a feeling, something has happened even though you may not know what it is. There are certain events that elicit certain emotions. For example, anger may signal violation or being blocked from a goal. Fear signals that your safety is being threatened. Sadness may tell you that you have lost something."

Once the therapist has guided the client toward attending to and acknowledging their emotion, the therapist might say, "Keep an emotion diary by writing down at least 3 emotions you experience during the day. It is helpful to write in your diary as soon after you have experienced the emotion as possible. Describe your experience by addressing some of the following points." A homework sheet with these questions and a place to answer them is provided to the client (Greenberg, 2002).

1. What is your name for the emotion? If you find yourself using only a few words repeatedly, such as frustrated and happy, try and find more emotion words.
2. Did the emotion have a sudden onset or is it a more enduring mood? When did it start?
3. How intense is this emotion (from 1 to 10)? Did it change in intensity?
4. What thoughts are associated with your feeling? Are they about the past, present, or future?
5. What memories are associated with your feeling? Does this feeling make you want to act, or feel like doing something or expressing something? Move closer to or away from something? Make an aggressive move? Make a facial expression?
6. What brought on the emotion or mood? A situation or internal event? Describe the event, and be aware of any shifts in your emotion.
7. Would you describe your feeling as negative or positive? Are you comfortable or uncomfortable having it? What is your attitude towards this feeling? Caring? Ashamed? Do you want it to last longer or go away?
8. Do you have this feeling often? In what kinds of situations does this feeling occur? Similar or different situations?
9. What information is the emotion giving you? Is it telling you something about yourself or a relationship? Is it telling you about your progress toward a goal?
10. What does the emotion need for you or from you? What does it want you to know?
11. Is there anything else you are feeling underneath the emotion?

Identifying your Experience of Different Emotions

Another exercise that may be helpful for clients who, early on, do not appear to focus on their emotion involves identification and differentiation of various emotions.

After the therapist has guided the client through this exercise in-session, the following instructions may be offered as a between-session activity (Greenberg & Warwar, in press).

1. Describe the last time you felt each of the following: angry, sad, fear, shame, and pain. If possible, describe this to another person or an imagined one to help them understand the situation, what you reacted to, what happened in your body, how you felt, and what you did.
2. Consider each emotion and answer the following questions about how you typically experience this emotion: (1) How long does this feeling last? (2) How intense is it from 1 to 10 where ten is very intense? (3) How long does it take for this emotion to occur? (4) Are you quick to experience anger, sadness, fear, and shame? (5) How long does it take for the emotion to leave? (6) How frequently do you experience this emotion? (7) Is this emotion generally helpful or a problem for you?"

Identifying Vulnerable or "At Risk" Periods

An important aspect of relapse prevention involves having clients identify common factors and/or processes that cause them to feel particularly vulnerable to or "at risk" of relapse. Between therapy sessions the therapist may ask clients to pay particular attention to emotional states and negative patterns that lead them to feel as though they may "spiral" back into the emotional state that initially led them to seek treatment. By specifying the process that has led the client to negative emotional states in the past, the client becomes better able to self-engage in the identification of *markers* of vulnerable states, thereby increasing the likelihood that they may also, in turn, activate practices that they have learned which will stop the spiral when their gains are tested following treatment.

EMOTION REGULATION

Teaching clients to develop affect regulation skills to help them cope with overwhelming emotional states is an important aspect of emotion coaching. When clients enter therapy their emotions have often been interrupted or unacknowledged because they may feel painful or overwhelming. As a result, clients may be unaware of how to begin dealing with their emotions that seem painful, confusing, or even outside of their control. Clients' inattention to their emotional aspects of experience or avoidance as a means of controlling their emotions limits their ability to use their emotions as adaptive, informative guides that would help them solve problems of living. The therapist teaches clients emotion regulation skills so that clients begin to experience themselves as capable of attending to, coping with, and tolerating their bodily reactions to their emotions without interrupting them.

Teaching affect regulation skills often occurs as a primary step within an emotion-focused approach to therapy. Further to in-session work, introducing emotion regulation homework is a useful way to accelerate opportunities for future in-session work in that tolerance and welcoming of emotion provides the fertile ground from which preparedness for deeper emotion work occurs. Practicing affect regulation skills in and out of sessions also increases the likelihood that clients will use these skills once therapy has ended given, that they will have mastered skills that provide them with the safety of knowing that they can manage their emotions.

Regulating Breathing

Coaching clients to regulate their breathing is an important aspect of emotion work, particularly in terms of encouraging the client's capacity to self-regulate and self-soothe. Breathing regulation also becomes particularly important when tendencies of emotional under-regulation or over-regulation are present (Greenberg, 2002; Greenberg & Warwar, 2006). People who are under-regulated tend to breathe erratically when they experience heightened emotional distress, and people who are over-regulated tend to attempt to control their emotional experience by holding their breath. With clients who experience difficulty in regulating their breath, the therapist guides them in the session first to attend to their emotional experience and directs them to notice their breathing patterns. The following steps may be offered:

1. Get into a comfortable position. Close your eyes.
2. Relax your body, noticing where you hold tension in your body.
3. As you breathe, focus on your breath. Breath deeply, inhaling through your nose, exhaling through your mouth. As you inhale, let the air fill your stomach, and as you exhale, let your stomach flatten.
4. Let your breathing return to a comfortable and relaxed rhythm.

The initial steps are particularly important because clients may not be aware of how they breathe when they become emotionally aroused. Once clients have attended to the rhythm of their breathing in the moment, the therapist then directs them to engage in deep, diaphragmatic breathing. In doing so, clients begin to feel more relaxed, regulated, and available to working with their emotional experience. After the therapist has coached the client to attend to and regulate their breathing, homework would involve directing clients to notice their breathing patterns in between sessions and engaging in the breathing instructions outlined above.

Safe Place Homework

Establishing a safe place using guided imagery is a useful way to help clients regulate distress associated with overwhelming feelings (Greenberg, 2002). This exercise is typically used when clients experience difficulty regulating their emotional distress in the moment, or when clients need to calm themselves after having experienced a highly emotionally arousing session. This exercise has been found to be particularly important for clients who are dealing with issues of abuse. This exercise is introduced in the session when clients indicate that they are afraid of attending to and experiencing their feelings in therapy and prior to exploration of issues related to traumatic experiences.

For homework, the therapist would ask clients to think of an imaginary or real place in which they feel safe and protected from the world. If clients have difficulty thinking of a place where they feel safe, the first step for homework would be for them to try to imagine a place where they would feel safe. Examples of safe places that clients have used include a mountaintop or a beach.

Once the client has established a safe place, the therapist would guide the client to this place in the session by leading the client through the regulating breathing exercise and then state, "Imagine yourself in your safe place, see your surroundings, the sights and the sounds, notice how peaceful it is there, how relaxed and calm you feel in being there" (Greenberg, 2002).

Once a safe place as been established and imagined in the session, the therapist assigns homework where clients would guide themselves to this place between sessions. This exercise is encouraged not only at times when clients feel dysregulated, but also when they are not experiencing heightened emotional arousal. This helps clients to integrate the safe place into their self-soothing repertoire.

Shifting Out of Emotional States

At times, clients may need to shift out of certain emotions and emotional states. Experiencing a sense of control in shifting emotional states can be particularly useful for clients who are afraid of deeply experiencing their emotions. The experience of being able to get out of an emotion fosters a sense of control for clients who may easily feel out of emotional control. The following exercise (Greenberg, 2002) also provides clients with a further skill that may be utilized when an emotional experience is not completed in the moment and needs to be revisited in the future so that further work may be done.

1. When you are in an emotional state, such as feeling angry or afraid, experience the feeling. Sit with the feeling inside of your body, and name it. Put thoughts to the feeling.
2. Now it is time to shift. Get a clear sense of what you feel before you shift. Put this into words. This will provide a handle you can pick up again later. Tell yourself, "I'll come back to this." Breathe.
3. Shift your focus of attention to the external world. Make contact with external reality. Name what you see. Reach out and touch an object in your view. Breathe again.
4. Now pick something else that you need to pay attention to in your day. Focus on this new task with the knowledge that you can return to your feeling again in the future.

Promoting Self-Empathy

Promoting clients' capacity for self-empathy is important for clients who experience difficulty in welcoming and being compassionate toward their painful feelings. The therapist may guide clients toward openness and interest in their painful feelings by asking them to imagine themselves as a small child who is feeling hurt and is in need of care and attention (Greenberg, 2002; Greenberg & Watson, 2005). In the therapy session, the therapist would ask the client, "What do you imagine it is like for this hurting child? What would you say to comfort her? What does this child need from you to help her? Can you give this to the child?" If clients have difficulty in imagining their own inner child that needs soothing, the therapist may first ask them to imagine a stranger or a child in general before moving clients toward imagining themselves (Greenberg, 2002). Homework would involve the therapist encouraging clients between sessions to imagine this part of the self, their own vulnerable inner child that needs comfort and soothing, hence promoting a stance of care and concern toward the part of the self that experiences painful feelings.

Transforming Emotion with Emotion

One of the most fundamental aspects of promoting emotional change in EFT is the way in which newly emerging emotions are enlisted in the transformation of old emotions. In the therapy session, the therapist directs the client's attention to their emotional experience as it is occurring and evolving in the moment. By doing so, the client becomes aware of their emotional experience that has previously been operating outside of or secondarily to the stagnant emotional response of the past. The therapist helps guide the client toward and through the new emotional experience, facilitating not only the processing of the new information that accompanies the new feelings, but also the valuable information provided by the emerging needs that are related to the new emotions (Greenberg, 2002). For example, if a client is stuck in his anger related to an early childhood experience and is having difficulty working through it, the therapist may direct him to attend to his internal experience so that he may contact where he is emotionally in the moment. Upon having the client focus inward, the therapist may notice the client holding himself and shrinking into the chair. By highlighting the client's action tendency (e.g., covering and retreating), emotional response (e.g., fear), and emerging need (e.g., to protect himself) which have not yet been attended to and acknowledged, the therapist promotes the client's attention toward and openness to new emotional experience. The seeming hold of anger that the client experienced as all-encompassing becomes loosened, freeing him to fully explore the emerging fear and its associated need. Consequently, the client becomes better able to receive the adaptive, self-enhancing information that accompanies the new emotion and the need. In this way, sadness undoes anger (Greenberg, 2002).

Homework is geared toward helping clients activate new experiences that will fuse with and consequently change the form of their old modes of experiencing emotion. Through attention to and synthesis of old and new feelings, people are able to move away from operating according to longstanding patterns that left them feeling stuck and possibly, at times, hopeless and helpless. As a result, people become open to new information facilitated by the new emotion that has previously been outside of their awareness. This is when lasting emotional change becomes possible.

Identifying Underlying Feelings

The following homework is used to help clients attend to and shift from aspects of their experience that have left them feeling emotionally stuck. This exercise is offered to clients as homework which will allow them to identify the emotions that underlie secondary or maladaptive primary feelings. Once the client engages between sessions in the identification of underlying feelings, these other feelings can then be processed in a more differentiated manner in the session with the therapist. The client's openness to opportunities for synthesis of old and new emotions is an important aspect contributing to the final stage of consolidation through reflection. A sheet with the following columns is given as homework (Greenberg, 2002).

1. Describe the situation and your emotional response in which you are stuck.
2. Is this your main feeling?
3. Is the emotion that you are stuck in covering another feeling underneath that is difficult to face?
4. What is this other emotion?

5. What do you need from yourself to help you feel it?
6. Allow yourself to focus on the new feelings and needs.
7. What is this new feeling telling you?

The development of awareness of newly emerging emotions and needs may lead to the client experiencing a sense of hopelessness or helplessness in meeting these needs. Hope and potential for change can often be developed in the moment by coaching the client to attend to and explicate his or her needs. The key to experiential movement and empowerment is to get to the need or want embedded in the new feeling and to feel entitled to the need (Greenberg, 2002). The most important aspect of this exercise is that the clients actively experience their feelings as they check for resonance between their developing emotional state and the different needs that they consider. Accessing and differentiating these newly emerging needs will help the client to move past possible feelings of immobility or ineffectiveness. Hence, growth-enhancing information provided by need explication opens the client to the "I can" of their experience.

Identifying and Receiving Needs

In a situation of concern, identify what you need or want that you think you cannot have now. Answer these statements:

1. What I lost, or my goal that was blocked, was ___, and what I wanted was___. What I can't get now is ___. What I can get now or do is ___.
2. Feel the struggle between the "I can't" and the "I can."
3. Feel what you want or need. Stay in your feeling of wanting until you receive a new view or understanding that can help you achieve what you want. Wait until solutions appear. Your mind will try to come up with solutions if you know your goals and have a definition of the problem.
4. Feel the wanting until it moves you to action.
5. What action will you take? What is your plan? What do you anticipate?

Reflection on goal satisfaction after new action is taken is likely to increase one's sense of mastery and provide further information that will guide future goal-directed behavior. Such mastery experiences become particularly important once treatment has ended given that clients no longer have the therapist to remind them of the importance of accessing and valuing their needs, thereby increasing the importance of self-directed reflection.

Letting Go of Past Relationships

Grief and loss are often emotions that, at times, are experienced as most difficult to overcome. Whether it is experience related to the death of a parent or the end of a marriage, the idea of letting go and moving on may not seem possible to clients. One of the reasons for this is that these emotions are so painful that people often avoid any and all aspects surrounding their pain. When such aspects of experience are avoided, unacknowledged, and denied, the pain unwittingly introjects itself into many other aspects of the client's life, particularly their present relationships with others.

The following homework helps clients acknowledge and face the loss of a loved one in order to move forward (Greenberg, 2002). The therapist instructs the client to write a letter in the first person saying goodbye to the person they have lost. The letter should include the following components:

1. What was the nature of your relationship with the person that you lost?
2. How did you feel about them? What did you love about them? Let yourself feel that.
3. How did they feel about you? For example, "You loved me unconditionally." How did this make you feel about yourself? For example, "I felt very special." What did this mean to you? For example, "It meant that I knew you would be there for me if I needed you."
4. List the things you miss about the person. These are things that you will never have again now that this person is gone. For example, "I miss . . . ." With each thing that you miss, pay attention to how you feel. Let yourself feel the loss of each thing that you miss.
5. Imagine this person sitting in front of you. See his or her face. Say goodbye. What do you want this person to know that would help you move on? What do you need to help you move on?

Supporting Strengths and Resources

Therapeutic focus is typically oriented toward that which is problematic in clients' lives. Client expressions of inner strength and resourcefulness provide ideal opportunities for the introduction of tasks geared toward recognition and consolidation of such strengths and resources. For example, a client entering a session and recounting a positive, self-affirming experience during the week would provide an appropriate opportunity for the therapist to ask the client to specify her strengths in the given situation in that this would optimize the client's consolidation of her internal experience of capability and resilience.

The therapist might ask clients to record strengths and resources as they arise in the session as well as between sessions. Ask them to make this list on a card that they carry with them at all times so that they may add to the list when relevant experiences occur throughout the week. For example, a client may receive a promotion at work and her boss may tell her that they value the diligent effort that she has contributed to a completed project. The client may then add valuable employee and conscientious to her list of strengths. The key to this homework is that the list is made *as the client experiences* their strengths. This exercise may also be useful for clients once they have completed therapy in that it provides a skill or tool that, once implemented, provides further resilience against relapse.

Supporting Positive Emotions

Equally important opportunities to support emotional change occur with positive emotions that foster life-sustaining desire to be close to, to be loved by, or to feel safe with others as well as successful mastery experiences which occur within and between sessions (Greenberg, 2002).

As homework, the therapist might ask clients to consider a time when they experienced pleasurable emotions in relation to another person. For example, after the client has completed the exercise Letting Go of Past Relationships and the homework has been thoroughly explored in-session, the therapist might ask the client to contact and further explore the positive feelings that they experienced within the particular past relationship. The completion of therapeutic work surrounding negative emotions related to the relationship that was once positive and growth enhancing and subsequently accessing those positive aspects of the shared experience between the client and the other person may provide an opportunity for further healing as well as acknowledgment and appreciation of the complexity of emotion experience that often accompanies engaging in interpersonal relationships.

Emotion Restructuring

Maladaptive emotions and the associated beliefs and behavioral reactions that accompany such emotions often occur outside of awareness. These learned responses are often occurring so automatically that the client may experience difficulty in accessing the moment-by-moment processes related to these emotions. Consequently, these emotional responses may seem unreachable in experience, and therefore not open to transformation. The following exercise is one that is meant to be used to help clients identify and restructure maladaptive emotional responses (Greenberg, 2002). It may be thought of as a *meta-exercise* in that it incorporates many of the individual exercises that have been found to assist in the transformation of maladaptive emotions. Accordingly, it is one of the most helpful resources that clients may utilize both during treatment and after treatment has ended. Restructuring maladaptive emotions can be a difficult process, particularly because the responses have become so entrenched within the client's emotion repertoire. It will take time to experience a real change in an unhealthy feeling. Using the following exercise on a regular basis and noting any significant shifts in emotion, beliefs, or meaning will help clients to not only experience change but also witness the change across time when the records are used repeatedly.

1. What is the primary maladaptive feeling in your body? Welcome it. Make sure it is a core maladaptive emotion. There isn't something else more core. How intense is it on a scale of 1 to 10? Do you need to regulate or create distance? If so, how?

2. What are the destructive voices, thoughts, and beliefs in your head? What is the feeling tone of the voices? Contempt? Hostility? Something else? Where does it come from?

3. What is the need in the painful emotions? What do you, or the maladaptive feeling, need to feel better? (For example, in shame I need validation; In fear I need security).

4. What else are you feeling about not having the need met? Identify a healthy emotional response. Give it a voice. Identify what you feel about your need not being met, a person might now feel anger at having been violated or invalidated rather than shame or sadness at having been so abandoned or

unprotected. Imagine a helpful feeling or situation in which you feel that emotion. Enter this feeling or situation.

5. Experience your previously unacknowledged basic need, goal, or concern in your new more primary adaptive emotion. What do you need for yourself? What do you need from others?

6. Bring your adaptive feelings and needs *into contact with* your maladaptive state. Combat your destructive thoughts with your feelings and needs. Integrate your strengths and resources.

Contacting Healthy Emotion

Clients may have difficulty from time to time in engaging adaptive emotion resources in the moment. This is to be expected given that full development of a new emotion repertoire is a fluid process that takes time, energy, and creativity, which may not always be readily available to the client. Clients may be assisted in situations where they experience difficulty in identifying alternative emotional responses that have served them well in the past. Having previously completed emotion restructuring records offers the client concrete process-oriented examples of what has worked for them in the past; therefore, they have a quick reference regarding self-guided resources that may help them solve problematic affective–cognitive states in the present and future. Ask clients to keep a card of alternative emotional responses that have been deemed favorable by the client in-session according to particular situations. For example, when they have felt sad in relation to a particular area of their life, what emotion, when drawn upon and evoked in the moment, brings them energy and a sense of possibility? With time and practice, the new emotional repertoire becomes intuitive, and thereby open to spontaneous engagement by the client. The process of transformation does not end simply because the client completes treatment, and the condition of being an experiencing organism necessitates that new emotional challenges will arise. The key is to provide clients with concrete tools that they may self-initiate when faced with problems of living long after treatment has ended.

Engagement in Self-Care Activities

One of the greatest challenges in relapse prevention is the client's active engagement of tools or skills he or she has learned in therapy, particularly at times of vulnerability (e.g., excessive stress, death of a loved one) when the client may not be able to so readily activate new resources gained within therapy. Remembering to engage in self-care once treatment has ended may be one of the most important prevention-oriented activities that is practiced. One strategy that may be offered in helping clients to remember to engage in self-care is to ensure that the reminder of self-care activity is client-generated and thereby most meaningful to the particular client. For example, if a client is creatively inclined, you could suggest that they make a "self-care bracelet" that they only wear during periods that they have identified as potentially vulnerable ones (e.g., when their world feels chaotic and unpredictable). The identification of vulnerable or "at-risk" period exercise may be incorporated here. In addition to the self-care bracelet, clients could also write a ready-made list which they may refer to regarding self-care activities that have helped them in the past (particularly self-care activities that are stress-situation-specific). The most important aspects of this exercise include the use of the self-care "tool" only at times of vulnerability so that it does not lose its novel purpose of reminding the client to self-care as well as the need for the reminding tool (e.g., bracelet) to be client-generated and thereby self-relevant.

REFLECTING ON EMOTION

Homework exercises which promote reflection offer further opportunities for clients to carry forward in-session emotional change. This final principle is related to the first, emotional awareness, in that it involves making meaning of emotion. In addition to the informational value of emotion awareness, symbolizing emotion in awareness promotes reflection on experience to create new meaning, and this helps people develop new *narratives* to explain their experience (Greenberg & Pascual-Leone, 1997; Pennebaker, 1990; Whelton & Greenberg, 2000). It is the way in which a person explains his or her experience once he or she has become aware of and reflected upon different facets of that experience that allows transformation of previously held convictions and beliefs into new understanding of self, others, and situations.

Research on writing about emotional experience has demonstrated that symbolizing traumatic emotion memories in words helps promote the assimilation of memories into a person's ongoing self-narrative (Van der Kolk & Fisher, 1995). Writing about emotional experience has also been found to produce positive effects on autonomic nervous system activity, immune functioning, and physical and emotional health (Pennebaker, 1990, 1997). Pennebaker (1997) suggests that narrating emotional experiences allows individuals to organize, structure, and ultimately assimilate both their emotional experiences and the situations that elicit their emotional responses. In addition, symbolizing emotional experiences in words allows people to more readily identify and reflect on their emotional patterns and the triggers that tend to engage them in those patterns.

Diarizing an Emotional Memory

Writing about a specific event provides the venue within which clients may consciously begin to understand themselves and their world in the form of a coherent story (Greenberg & Angus, 2004). The therapist might ask the client to write about a past situation about which they continue to experience unresolved emotions. What was the contextual background of the situation? What was their relationship with the other(s) in the situation? How do they view the actions or responses of others? How do they view their own actions or responses? What aspects of the memory remain problematic or puzzling? What emotions did they not want to face in the past situation? What needs were not met? What is the worst of the situation? The therapist may also ask the client to rate on a scale of 1 to 10 the intensity of each of their emotions as they diarize. These self-ratings may then be revisited in the future when clients diarize regarding the same situations. Noting changes in the narrative over time as a result of rewriting the story will further consolidate clients' experiences of making new meaning of that which once seemed unmalleable.

Letter Writing

Having a client write a letter to significant other, not to be sent but as a way of articulating and organizing their experience, may be helpful. In our study of forgiveness, once a good alliance had been established and the client had contacted their hurt and anger as well as gained a sense of entitlement to their unmet needs (Greenberg & Malcolm, 2002), clients wrote a letter to the perpetrator about the impact that the injury had on them. In addition, they wrote a letter back from the perpetrator refusing to accept blame or apologize. The latter was done to highlight that the purpose of treatment was to help the client let go of or resolve the emotional injury, not to have the other person change. This helped clients to articulate in writing the personal meaning of the injury, to help them realize that they were processing how they could resolve the injury, and to help them confront their wish that the other would change (often the other person was deceased or no longer in contact with the client).

Dealing with Overreactions or Surprising Reactions

Overreactions and surprising reactions are common for clients who have disowned and unresolved issues given that factors related to such unresolved issues continue to operate at intrapersonal and interpersonal levels. Clients may be aware that they have overreacted, or that they reacted in a way that was not congruent with the behavior they would have anticipated, yet they may have difficulty understanding why they reacted the way they did. In EFT, rather than *explaining* to the client the reasoning behind his or her reactions, the therapist would help the client make contact with his or her experience and symbolize his or her emotional reactions in words. Only when the emotion has been activated in the moment within the supportive therapeutic environment can in-session and between-session experiential learning and understanding be facilitated. The recommended homework would involve clients identifying aspects of their overreactions as presented, for example, in the following scenario:

1. What is the situation? My partner told me he couldn't see me again because he is working late, again!
2. What is your feeling? Frustration.
3. What is your reaction? I yelled at him, and then I avoided him.
4. In your perception was this an overreaction to the situation? Yes. I don't know why I get so angry? It is so frustrating when he has to work late, but that's no reason for me to yell at him and tell him I don't want to see him at all.
5. What are your physical sensations? Tightness all over and a knot in my chest.
6. Is there a feeling underneath the identified feeling above? Afraid, like I'm not loveable.
7. What does this feeling remind you of? When have you felt this way before? When I was a child, my mother would get angry and tell me that I was in the way all of the time, always under her feet. I felt like I was just a burden and I wasn't good enough for her to love me. When my partner told me that he couldn't see me, the same feeling of not being loveable enough to have around came up.

CASE EXAMPLES OF THE EFT APPROACH
USING HOMEWORK ASSIGNMENTS

Case Example: "John"

"John" was a 43-year-old man who reported in-session that he was unable to experience emotion. He stated that he had not felt an emotion for the past 33 years. He recalled feeling very angry as a child, particularly around the age of 10 to 12. Upon exploration of this period in John's life, it became apparent that his emotion memories of anger were associated with his parents' divorce when he was 10 years old. He learned at this age that expression of his feelings was not "safe" in that his mother would beat him whenever he either overtly or covertly expressed his anger toward her for leaving his father. Consequently, John began interrupting his emotional experience to the extent that he could not recall feeling any emotion since that time in his life, including being unaware of feeling anything when his mother and father died years later. In-session work involved exploration of his interruption of emotion as well as guidance through breathing regulation and the safe-place exercise in the interest of helping John experience his ability to control and tolerate his emotional experience. It was his sense of emotions as "dangerous" and his belief that he did not experience any emotions that became the initial foci in early sessions. John was also coached to become aware of and attend to his bodily felt experience, particularly when his body signaled to him that he was experiencing an emotion. Once John was able to sit with his emotional experience at an internal level and was guided through checking resonance between his bodily felt senses and his emotions at an identification level, he was presented with the exercise of describing an emotion as a between-session activity in the interest of encouraging awareness of his emotional experience that he had constricted for most of his life. John found this exercise to be particularly helpful in that the act of writing allowed him early on to experience as more within his control, hence not as dangerous. He also found that he was able to witness how much he had changed over the period of a few weeks given that he was able to refer to his documented emotional processes early in therapy. He was able to trust that he would be able to regulate his emotion so as not to "lose control," which eventually allowed John to experience openness to the fluidity of his moment-by-moment internal experience as well as appreciation toward the informative value of his emotions.

Case Example: "Sally"

"Sally" was a 21-year-old woman who reported in-session that she knew she needed to work on issues related to her parents, yet she felt unable to begin processing unresolved issues from her childhood. In an earlier session, Sally had expressed feelings of being unloved, unacknowledged, and afraid during her childhood. After Sally's reluctance to enter into this time in her life was validated and explored, the therapist offered Sally reflection homework where she was asked to write about three emotional memories regarding her parents. She was asked to pay attention to her emotional response as she wrote, noting the quality of each emotion as it emerged during the process of writing. She was asked to describe each event, her emotional responses (at the time and in the present), her needs at the time, and what she would like to express to her parents that she was unable to express in the past. Upon diarizing the three events, Sally reported in the following session that she was surprised by her emotional reaction as she was writing about the three memories. Until completing this exercise, she has not realized the extent to which her parents' mistreatment continued to impact upon her as an adult. Her emotional response while writing, in effect, signaled to her the importance of exploring these events from her past at a deeper level in-session with the support of her therapist. She continued to diarize between therapy sessions regarding these three events. In doing so, new meaning of these past events was developed through the newly emerging self-narratives which included Sally's transformation as a scared and devalued girl to an entitled and empowered woman.

CONCLUSION

Homework in EFT is typically used to promote emotion awareness, emotion regulation, transformation of emotion, and reflection on emotion. The main purpose of homework in EFT is to consolidate and reinforce in-session changes through extra-session practice. Homework is offered in a non-imposing, tentative manner rather than as expert pronouncements of what should be done. If clients do not complete homework, this is not seen as non-compliance but as indication of lack of client readiness. Homework is offered in the spirit of "try this if you find it relevant and helpful." Homework is also offered in the spirit of exploration rather than with the sole aim of achieving change. Client empowerment rather than compliance is the goal. Consequently, homework is created in collaboration between the therapist and the client. It is often uniquely devised to fit the client and the circumstance as appropriate. Accordingly, largely client-generated homework development is most likely to fit with the individual's proximal zone of development (Vygostsky, 1986), something that is not too far ahead of the client but can promote a next step or accelerate in-session opportunities for client change. Furthermore, by actively engaging the client in homework development, they become more likely to engage in homework activities once treatment has ended, thereby furthering the likelihood of relapse prevention.

REFERENCES

Goldfried, M., & Davidson, G. (1994). *Clinical behavior therapy* (expanded ed.). New York: Wiley.

Greenberg, L. S. (2002). *Emotion coaching*. Washington, DC: American Psychological Association Press.

Greenberg, L. S., & Angus, L. (2004). The contributions of emotion process to narrative change in psychotherapy: A dialectical constructivist perspective. In L. Angus & J. McLeod (Eds.), *The handbook of narrative and psychotherapy: Practice, theory and research* (pp. 331–350). Thousand Oaks, CA: Sage.

Greenberg, L. S., & Geller, S. (2001). Congruence and therapeutic presence. In G. Wyatt (Ed.), *Rogers' therapeutic conditions: Vol. 1. Congruence* (pp. 131–149). Ross-on-Wye, Herefordshire, UK: PCCS Books.

Greenberg, L. S., & Malcolm, W. (2002). Resolving unfinished business: Relating process to outcome. *Journal of Consulting and Clinical Psychology, 70*, 406–416.

Greenberg, L. S., & Paivio, S. C. (1997). *Working with emotions in psychotherapy*. New York: Guilford Press.

Greenberg, L. S., & Pascual-Leone, J. (1997). Emotion in the creation of personal meaning. In M. J. Power & C. R. Brewin (Eds.), *The transformation of meaning in psychological therapies: Integrating theory and practice* (pp. 157–173). New York: Wiley.

Greenberg, L. S., Rice, L. N., & Elliot, R. (1993). *Facilitating emotional change: The moment-by-moment process*. New York: Guilford Press.

Greenberg, L. S., & Safran, J. D. (1987). *Emotion in psychotherapy: Affect, cognition, and the process of change*. New York: Guilford Press.

Greenberg, L. S., & Warwar, S. (2006). Homework in experiential psychotherapy. *Psychotherapy Integration*.

Greenberg, L. S., & Watson, J. F. (2005). *Emotion-focused therapy of depression*. Washington, DC: American Psychological Association Press.

Kanfer, F. H., & Grimm, L. G. (1980). Managing clinical change: A process model of therapy. *Behavior Modification, 4,* 419–444.

Linehan, M. M. (1993). *Cognitive-behavioral treatment of borderline personality disorder*. New York: Guilford Press.

Mahrer, A. R. (1996). *The complete guide to experiential psychotherapy*. New York: Wiley.

Mahrer, A. R., Nordin, S., & Miller, L. S. (1995). If a client has this kind of problem, prescribe that kind of post-session behavior. *Psychotherapy, 32,* 194–203.

Pennebaker, J. W. (1990). *Opening up: The healing power of confiding in others*. New York: William Morrow.

Pennebaker, J. W. (1997). *Opening up: The healing power of expressing emotions*. New York: Guilford.

Prochaska, J. O., & DiClemente, C. C. (1982). Transtheoretical therapy: Toward a more integrated model of change. *Psychotherapy: Theory, research and practice, 19,* 276–288.

Van de Kolk, B. A., & Fisher, R. E. (1995). Dissociation and the fragmentary nature of traumatic memories: Overview and exploratory study. *Journal of Traumatic Stress, 8,* 505–525.

Vygotsky, L. (1986). *Thought and language*. Cambridge, MA: MIT Press.

Whelton, W. J., & Greenberg, L. S. (2002). The self: A singular multiplicity. In J. Christopher Muran (Ed.), *Self in relation in the psychotherapy process*. Washington, DC: American Psychological Association Press.

Chapter 5

INTERPERSONAL PSYCHOTHERAPY

Jami F. Young and Laura Mufson

OVERVIEW OF INTERPERSONAL PSYCHOTHERAPY

Interpersonal psychotherapy (IPT) is based on the premise that depression occurs in an interpersonal context (Weissman, Markowitz, & Klerman, 2000). Regardless of the etiology, depression affects our relationships and our relationships affect our mood. Numerous studies have established the efficacy of IPT for the treatment of depression in adults (DiMascio et al., 1979; Weissman et al., 1979; Elkin et al., 1989). Based on the success of IPT with adults and the similarities between adolescent and adult presentations of depression (Ryan et al., 1987), IPT has been adapted to treat adolescent depression.

The work of interpersonal psychotherapy for depressed adolescents (IPT-A) targets interpersonal problems that may be causing or contributing to the adolescent's depression. Both the diagnosis and treatment are focused on the individual's interpersonal interactions and how these interactions are affecting the adolescent's depressive symptoms. The goal of treatment is to improve the interpersonal problems and thereby improve the depressive symptoms. Interpersonal problems encountered in adolescent depression generally fall into one of four categories: grief, interpersonal disputes, role transitions, and interpersonal deficits. In the sections that follow, we briefly discuss each problem area. A more detailed discussion of each problem area can be found in the IPT-A manual (Mufson, Dorta, Moreau, & Weissman, 2004).

Grief. The grief problem area is applicable for adolescents with prolonged or delayed grief that results in significant depression symptoms and impairment. In addition, it may also be used for those adolescents experiencing a severe depression during the normal bereavement period. IPT-A is particularly useful for those adolescents who, as a result of the death, have experienced a significant disruption in their support network or who had a conflictual relationship with the deceased. These situations have been identified as risk factors for more complicated bereavement (Clark, Pynoos, & Goebel, 1994). IPT-A helps the adolescent mourn the loss of a loved one, while encouraging the adolescent to develop other relationships that can help fill some of the voids left by the death.

Interpersonal disputes. An interpersonal dispute exists when two people have non-reciprocal expectations about the relationship (Weissman, Markowitz, & Klerman, 2000). Adolescents frequently have disputes with their parents or guardians around issues such as autonomy, money, curfew, and sexuality. In addition to disputes with parents, adolescents may present with disputes within their romantic and peer relationships. The goal of treatment is to help resolve the dispute if possible, and if not, to help the adolescent end the relationship when appropriate or to develop strategies to cope better with the relationship.

Role transitions. Role transitions are changes that occur when progressing from one social role to another. Many role transitions occur as a result of normal developmental shifts in adolescence. Others occur more unexpectedly following a life stressor such as moving to a new town. When an adolescent feels unable to meet the increased responsibilities associated with a role transition, it may result in depression and impairment in interpersonal functioning. Family structural change, following the departure of a parent from the home for various reasons including the separation or divorce of parents, is a subtype of role transitions that may precipitate symptoms of depression. Regardless of the type of role transition, treatment is focused on helping the adolescent develop the skills needed to manage the new role more successfully.

Interpersonal deficits. Interpersonal deficits is the identified problem area when an adolescent does not have adequate social skills to develop and maintain positive relationships with others. Adolescents with this problem area often experience loneliness and decreased self-confidence, which can lead to or exacerbate symptoms of depression. The depression often results in further social withdrawal and isolation, leading to further interpersonal deficits. The goal of treatment is to help the adolescent develop the skills needed to have more satisfying interpersonal relationships and to increase their social support network.

EMPIRICAL SUPPORT FOR IPT-A
ADOLESCENTS

IPT-A was first tested in an open clinical trial. Fourteen 12-to-18 year olds who were referred to a hospital outpatient clinic for depression were treated with IPT-A. Following treatment, adolescents experienced a significant decrease in depressive symptoms and psychological distress, and none of the adolescents met criteria for a DSM-III-R depression diagnosis. Adolescents also demonstrated significant improvement in their general functioning at home and at school (Mufson et al., 1994). These improvements were maintained at 1-year follow-up (Mufson & Fairbanks, 1996).

The next study was a randomized controlled trial comparing IPT-A to clinical monitoring in a sample of clinic-referred depressed adolescents (Mufson, Weissman, Moreau, & Garfinkel, 1999). Forty-eight adolescents diagnosed with major depression were randomized to IPT-A or clinical monitoring. At the end of treatment, IPT-A adolescents reported significantly fewer depressive symptoms than adolescents who received clinical monitoring. Using standards for recovery set forth by the National Collaborative Study for the Treatment of Depression (Elkin et al., 1989), significantly more IPT-A adolescents met recovery criteria as compared to control adolescents. IPT-A also resulted in improved overall social functioning and functioning in the domains of peer and dating relationships, improvements that were significantly greater than in the clinical monitoring condition.

Mufson, Dorta, Wickramaratne, et al. (2004) recently completed an effectiveness study of IPT-A in school-based health clinics in the New York metropolitan area. This randomized controlled trial compared the outcome of IPT-A to treatment as it is usually provided (TAU) in the school-based health clinics. School-based clinicians were randomized to provide either IPT-A or usual care to adolescents diagnosed with Major Depressive Disorder, Dysthymic Disorder, Depression Disorder Not Otherwise Specified or Adjustment Disorder with Depressed Mood. Adolescents treated with IPT-A in comparison to TAU experienced significant reductions in depression symptoms and global impairment and significant improvement in overall and specific domains of social functioning. In addition, as compared with TAU, adolescents treated with IPT-A improved faster and were significantly better by week 8. These findings suggest that community clinicians can be trained to deliver IPT-A effectively and that the results from the efficacy research can be generalized to community-based settings.

A second research group also has conducted studies of IPT for depressed adolescents using a different modification of the adult manual tailored to the Puerto Rican culture. Rosselló and Bernal (1999) compared IPT versus cognitive-behavioral therapy (CBT) versus waitlist for depressed teens. IPT and CBT resulted in a greater reduction in depressive symptoms than the waitlist condition. In addition, IPT was significantly better than the waitlist condition at increasing self-esteem and improving social adaptation.

THE ROLE OF HOMEWORK IN IPT-A

IPT-A is a time-limited treatment, specifically designed as a once weekly, 12-session treatment. IPT-A is divided into three phases: (1) the initial phase, (2) the middle phase, and (3) the termination phase. Because the goal of IPT-A is to change interpersonal relationships that are contributing to or exacerbating the adolescent's depression, homework in IPT-A focuses on changing the adolescent's approach to behavior within the problematic relationship(s).

Homework is considered a natural extension of the work done in the session and is based on the assumption that treatment will be more effective when the adolescent addresses difficulties in outside relationships by practicing skills in between sessions. Furthermore, we believe that homework will increase the likelihood of maintaining treatment gains. In IPT-A, we have characterized homework as interpersonal "work at home" to reflect the fact that these assignments typically follow the interpersonal work conducted in treatment sessions. We have found that calling the activities "work at home" decreases the resistance that may be encountered by adolescents who associate homework with academic assignments. In our experience, the metaphor of an interpersonal experiment is useful for engaging adolescents. Similar to a laboratory experiment where one needs to figure out the right combination of chemicals, these interpersonal experiments will help the adolescent determine the best strategies for dealing with important people or problems in his/her life. These experiments may not succeed at first, but with a few adjustments the adolescent can improve his/her relationships and his/her mood.

Unlike many cognitive behavioral treatments, formal written homework assignments are not given in IPT-A. More typically, the therapist will ask the adolescent, between sessions, to try out a new communication technique or to discuss a particular problem that they have been working on in treatment. The therapist and the adolescent generally design the homework collaboratively so it is individualized for the given adolescent and the phase of treatment. Several assignments may be appropriate in a given situation and it is up to the adolescent and the therapist to decide which assignment will be most fruitful. The majority of the interpersonal "work at home" occurs during the middle phase, although there is some role for homework in all phases of treatment. In the next section, we will discuss the three treatment phases, highlighting the role of "work at home."

INITIAL PHASE

The initial phase of IPT-A typically consists of the first four sessions. During these sessions, the therapist monitors the adolescent's depressive symptoms, educates the adolescent and parents about depression, explains the goals of IPT-A, and conducts the interpersonal inventory to identify an interpersonal problem area that will become the focus of treatment. The interpersonal inventory is an assessment of the adolescent's relationships that identifies the interpersonal issues related to the onset and/or persistence of the adolescent's depression. During the interpersonal inventory, the therapist asks detailed questions about each relationship including positive and negative aspects of the relationship; how the relationship has changed since the adolescent became depressed; and the adolescent's goals for improving the relationship over the course of treatment. While conducting the interpersonal inventory, the therapist also probes for any significant life events that may be related to the depression. The interpersonal inventory typically takes two to three sessions to complete. On the basis of the interpersonal inventory, the therapist helps the adolescent understand the relationship between interpersonal events and his/her depressive symptoms. The therapist identifies common themes or problems in the various relationships, and, together with the adolescent, chooses one of the four interpersonal problem areas that will be the focus of treatment. At the end of the initial phase of treatment, the therapist and adolescent establish a treatment contract. In this contract, the adolescent's role and parents' roles in treatment are specified, the focus of treatment is highlighted, and practical details regarding the treatment are reviewed.

Homework in the Initial Phase

Although there is no formal homework in the initial phase of treatment, the adolescent is encouraged to pay attention to his/her relationships, as well as to changes in his/her mood to help recognize the link between feelings of depression and interpersonal events. This sets the stage for the more formal interpersonal work that begins in the middle phase of treatment. The therapist makes explicit that the adolescent will play an active role in the middle phase of treatment and will be asked to try out new interpersonal techniques in session and outside of treatment. Furthermore, to prepare the parent for the upcoming "work at home," he/she is informed that the adolescent will be practicing new communication techniques and is asked to be open to these attempts. Lastly, the adolescent and parent are informed that the parent might be invited into treatment to work on the identified problem area, as a supplement to the individual work in sessions and the interpersonal "work at home."

Middle Phase

The middle phase of IPT-A consists of sessions five through nine. During this phase of treatment, the therapist and adolescent begin to work directly on the designated problem area. This includes clarifying the interpersonal problem, identifying effective strategies to deal with the problem, and implementing the interventions. Although the specific techniques used in the middle phase of treatment will depend on the identified problem area, certain techniques are used regardless of problem area to clarify the interpersonal problem and identify and practice effective strategies for dealing with the problem. These techniques, communication analysis, decision analysis, and role-playing, which are conducted in the sessions, form the foundation for the "work at home."

Communication analysis is a technique used in the middle phase of treatment to help clarify the interpersonal problem, particularly when the problem involves poor communication. Whenever the adolescent brings in a significant interpersonal event that occurred during the week and was associated with a worsening of mood, it is helpful to get detailed information about the event or conversation such as: How did the discussion start? When did the conversation take place? Where did it happen? What exactly did the adolescent say? What did the person say back? How did that make the adolescent feel? What happened next? Is that the outcome the adolescent wanted? Is that the message the adolescent wanted to send?

Once the therapist has a clear understanding of the communication, he/she can discuss with the adolescent how altering the communication might have led to a different outcome, beginning with any ideas the adolescent may have about what he/she could have done or said differently. Following the identification of more adaptive communication strategies, it is helpful to role-play the communication interaction using these techniques so the adolescent feels more comfortable utilizing the skills and/or strategies in real life. For the role-plays to be most useful, it is important not to simply talk about what it would be like to do something, but to actually act it out. To help engage the adolescent, the therapist can liken the role-play to a play in school. The therapist might say to the adolescent: When you put on a show in school, there are several steps that have to occur before the final performance. First the actors read through the script to get an idea for their lines and the feelings behind them. Then they have several rehearsals prior to the final performance. We are going to do something like that in here. We're going to figure out some new ways of communicating and practice them in here before you try them with others outside the session. The therapist and adolescent can go through what they are going to say before starting the role-play. Then it is helpful to role-play the interaction several times so the adolescent feels comfortable with the new communication strategies.

Following the communication analysis, it is useful to conduct a decision analysis to determine the best course of action for the given problem. Decision analysis in IPT-A closely resembles problem-solving techniques used in other therapies but is focused on addressing interpersonal problems. Decision analysis includes: selecting an interpersonal situation that is problematic, encouraging the adolescent to generate possible solutions to the problem, evaluating the pros and cons of each solution, selecting a solution to try first, and role-playing the interaction needed for the chosen solution. Similar to communication analysis, the adolescent should begin with a manageable problem and then progress to more difficult situations as treatment progresses.

Homework in the Middle Phase

Once the communication analysis, decision analysis, and role-playing are complete, the adolescent is ready for the "work at home." Homework typically involves practicing skills that were the focus of the session. The therapist describes the tasks as interpersonal laboratory experiments that will help the adolescent figure out what techniques will help improve his/her relationships. It is our experience that adolescents find the prospect of an experiment to help solve their problems more palatable than homework. They are told that there is no right or wrong answer. Rather, the experiment will help them explore what may or may not work in that particular interpersonal situation. "Work at home" is not assigned after every session. More typically, an adolescent will be asked to try something at home two or three times during the middle phase of treatment. Examples of interpersonal assignments include talking to a peer at school or having a discussion with a parent about using the phone.

When assigning homework, it is best to start with a topic that is manageable and has a high likelihood of success. For instance, if an adolescent has a difficult time making friends, the first assignment might be asking a friend a question in the hallway, rather than starting a conversation with a peer about why it has been difficult for the adolescent to feel close to people. The discussions and role-plays in session would help prepare the adolescent for this specific assignment. In the case of a role transition following a divorce, the first assignment might be asking the father to spend the day together. Over time, the "work at home" might progress to the adolescent explaining to the father his/her feelings about the parents' divorce. Starting small will generate hope in the adolescent that these interpersonal strategies can successfully facilitate change in their relationships. Prior to assigning the homework, the therapist should talk to the adolescent about any concerns he/she may have about the task, as well as identify potential obstacles to the accomplishment of the task. If the adolescent does not feel ready to complete the work at home, he/she may need additional time in session to discuss and role-play the interaction.

Example: Setting up a "work at home" assignment. Michael is a 14-year-old male whose identified problem area is interpersonal conflict with his mother. Conflict centers on issues of curfew, getting schoolwork done, and Michael being disrespectful. In the middle phase of treatment, Michael discussed his interest in having a later curfew so he could spend more time in the park with his friends. He felt frustrated by his curfew because it prevented him from spending time with his friends. In the past, he came home late resulting in arguments with his mother who worries about him. These arguments made Michael feel guilty and depressed. The therapist asked Michael how his mother felt about his curfew. He stated that she felt his curfew was fair and worried about him being out after dark. However, Michael felt that his mother might be willing to extend his curfew if she knew what friends he was with and where he was. The therapist and Michael conducted a decision analysis about his curfew and came up with different solutions that he might propose to his mom to make his curfew later.

Therapist: Now that we understand your feelings about the curfew and have a sense of your mother's perspective, do you have any ideas about how to resolve this problem?
Michael: My mom should extend my curfew so I can spend more time with my friends.
Therapist: What might be a reasonable amount of time to extend your curfew?
Michael: An hour.

Therapist: Do you think your mom will say yes to an hour? That seems like a lot to ask.

Michael: Probably not. Maybe a half-hour is better.

Therapist: Good compromise. How might we make your mom more comfortable extending your curfew? You said your mom worries about you. Is there anything you might suggest that would make her worry less?

Michael: I could let her know where in the park I will be.

The therapist helped Michael consider how he and his mom might feel about each solution and helped him pick the best course of action. Next she helped Michael outline the specifics of the interaction.

Therapist: How might you start the conversation with your mother?

Michael: I don't know. I guess I could say "Mom, I am unhappy with my curfew."

Therapist: How do you think your mom might respond to that?

Michael: I think she would be okay.

Therapist: Sometimes it helps to show your mom that you understand how she feels. Could you say, "Mom, I know you are concerned about my safety, but I am unhappy with my curfew?"

Michael: Yeah.

Therapist: Okay, what would you say next?

Michael: "Jason and Bill don't have to be home until 7: 00 on weeknights. I was wondering whether I could stay out until 7: 00 as well."

Therapist: How might she respond to this suggestion?

Michael: I think she would say, "I am not Jason and Bill's mom. I'm your mom."

Therapist: So that might not be the best way to ask about changing your curfew. What else could you say?

Michael: "Mom, I was wondering if you would extend my curfew until 7: 00."

Therapist: How might she respond to this suggestion?

Michael: I don't know if she'll agree.

Therapist: What solution might you offer next?

After the discussion, the therapist and Michael role-played the interaction several times. The therapist helped Michael decide on a good time to talk to his mother about the curfew. She also helped him identify potential obstacles to initiating the "work at home."

Therapist: What do you think might get in your way of having this conversation with your mom?

Michael: If I'm nervous, I might not do it tomorrow like I said I would. Or she might be in a really bad mood.

Therapist: What could you do in those situations?

Michael: If she's in a bad mood, I might wait for a different time to talk.

Therapist: And what if you're nervous?

Michael: I can remember how we practiced in here.

Therapist: Good idea. Michael, I want you to try to have this conversation with your mom this week. Next session we'll talk about how it went. Okay? Don't worry if it doesn't work the first time. It will still provide us with information that may help us make it work the next time.

Whenever "work at home" is assigned, in the following session the therapist and adolescent should review the interaction examining possible reasons for its success or failure. This may involve conducting another communication analysis to understand exactly what was said in the interaction. If less adaptive communication techniques were utilized, the work in the session may focus on more role-playing to further practice alternative communication so the adolescent is better prepared for future "work at home" assignments. Even if the conversation was successful, it is important to review the interaction in detail and to link the interpersonal event with any changes in mood or depression symptoms.

Example: Following-up on a "work at home" assignment. Robert is a 17-year-old adolescent whose parents divorced 3 years ago. Robert sees his father infrequently and this upsets him. Robert's father makes promises to see him and take him places, but then doesn't follow through. After discussing this situation in treatment, Robert was able to express his anger and frustration with his father to the therapist. He and the therapist discussed and role-played how he might share his feelings with his father and Robert was given the assignment to have a conversation with his dad.

The following session, Robert reported that he had talked to his dad over the phone. The therapist asked him to tell her about the conversation in detail.

Therapist: When did you have the conversation?
Robert: On Tuesday. My dad called me.
Therapist: Okay, how did you start the conversation?
Robert: I said, "Dad can I talk to you about something?" and he said yes. So I kept going, "When you make plans to do something with me and don't follow through, it makes me feel bad."
Therapist: How do you think your father was feeling when you said that to him?
Robert: He got kind of angry. He said, "What do you mean? I do the best I can. You know I have to work a lot."
Therapist: Robert, how did you feel when your father said that?
Robert: Frustrated.
Therapist: What happened next?
Robert: I was so frustrated that I said, "Never mind," and hung up the phone.
Therapist: How did you feel after that?
Robert: I was mad for the rest of the night.

Following the communication analysis, the therapist praised Robert for initiating the conversation and then asked Robert what he might do differently if he were to have the conversation again. They discussed what Robert might have said after his father's comments that might have led to a different outcome. They also discussed how Robert might have started the conversation with an empathic statement.

Therapist: What might you have said instead of "never mind"?
Robert: I don't know.
Therapist: Maybe you could let him know that you know that he's busy, but you want to spend time with him.
Robert: But he was being a jerk.
Therapist: I know that he didn't respond like you wanted. But when you hung up on him, you felt bad all night. Maybe trying something else would have made you feel better.
Robert: Maybe.
Therapist: Maybe your father felt badly about what you said, so he responded defensively. Next time, you might empathize with his feelings and say, "I know how busy you are but I get disappointed when we don't spend time together. Are there days that might be less pressured for you?"

They continued this conversation, coming up with alternative statements that Robert might use in future conversations with his father. The therapist reminded Robert that working on relationships is not easy and encouraged him to continue to talk to his father about his feelings about their relationship.

During the middle phase of treatment, it is not uncommon for an adolescent to come into session without having completed the between session interpersonal assignment. As is the case with other treatments, it is important for the therapist to ascertain why the adolescent was unable to complete the homework. It may be that the adolescent did not feel ready to have a conversation with the person or didn't know how to initiate the conversation. In this scenario, the therapist would discuss the adolescent's concerns and then would encourage the adolescent to role-play the conversation in session, and if the adolescent was ready, the therapist might assign it as an interpersonal experiment. If the adolescent states that the conversation would not have the desired outcome, it is important to assess whether this assessment is accurate. If the assessment is accurate, the therapist may still encourage the adolescent to try the interpersonal work as practice for future relationships. But work in session would also focus on modifying the adolescent's expectations for that particular relationship.

> Example: "Work at home" resistance. Linda is a 16-year-old female who has interpersonal deficits. She has one friend, Anabel, with whom she spends time, but they are not particularly close. She has always had difficulty opening up to people, but has become increasingly withdrawn since the depression started. Much of the middle phase work has been on improving Linda's interpersonal skills so she can develop new relationships and improve her relationship with Anabel. After several practice runs, Linda was able to role-play starting a conversation with the therapist and asking the therapist to go for pizza after school. Feeling that Linda was ready to try this outside of session, the therapist assigned Linda "work at home" to ask her friend Anabel to have pizza after school. But Linda came back to session the following week without having had the conversation.

> Therapist: Let's talk about what happened.
> Linda: I was going to ask her to have pizza on Tuesday but then I remembered that she plays softball on Tuesdays.
> Therapist: That was an unexpected barrier. Did you get another chance to try?
> Linda: On Thursday, I saw her in the hallway and said hello, but I was so nervous that I forgot what we had practiced saying.
> Therapist: We hadn't anticipated that Anabel might have activities after school. We also could have done a better job of anticipating that you would be nervous. Let's work on some of this stuff so you are more prepared for next time.
> Linda: Okay.
> Therapist: Are there other days that Anabel has activities after school?
> Linda: Tuesday is the only day I know about.
> Therapist: What if you asked Anabel on another day and she said she had plans?
> Linda: I guess I could say, "How about tomorrow?"
> Therapist: That's a great idea.

> The therapist and Linda continued this discussion, addressing the different obstacles to the successful completion of the "work at home" assignment. They then role-played the interaction again several times to decrease Linda's anxiety. By the end of the session, Linda felt ready to try again.

When an adolescent continues to have difficulty initiating homework and the work involves the parents, the therapist may choose to schedule a dyadic session. These sessions serve a number of purposes. First, they give the therapist the chance to talk to the parent about the interpersonal issue and, if necessary, to educate the parent about normal adolescent development. Second, the therapist uses this session to remind the parent that the adolescent is working on ways that he/she communicates with others and to ask the parent to be open to these efforts. Most importantly, these dyadic sessions give the adolescent and parent an important opportunity to improve interpersonal communication with the therapist present as a coach. The focus in these sessions is on the process of communication between the adolescent and the parent(s) rather than on the content. The therapist helps the adolescent and parent to find a manageable topic of discussion and then coaches each participant on what they are saying. For instance, if the adolescent and parent choose to talk about the adolescent's use of the phone and the phone bill, the therapist would make it clear that the point of the exercise is to practice a new way of communicating, rather than finding a solution to the phone. This dyadic work in session opens up the process of communication, which can be continued in future "work at home" assignments.

TERMINATION PHASE

In many ways, the termination phase of IPT-A (sessions 10 through 12) is similar to the termination process of other treatments. The objectives for this phase of treatment include discussing the adolescent's warning symptoms of depression, reviewing strategies that were successful for improving relationships, anticipating potential future situations that may be difficult for the adolescent, and discussing strategies for managing those situations, including the possibility of recurrence of the depression.

Homework in the Termination Phase

It is not uncommon to continue the interpersonal "work at home" assignments in the beginning of the termination phase. For instance, if the discussion in the session has highlighted strategies that have been more difficult for the adolescent, the session might involve a role-play of these strategies followed by a homework assignment to try the strategy during the week. Part of the termination phase work may involve identifying others who can be supportive of the adolescent. In this instance, the therapist might ask the adolescent to initiate a conversation or activity with the identified person as an interpersonal assignment.

Much of the termination phase is focused on the adolescent continuing to use the new skills as a way to handle future interpersonal stressors and to maintain treatment gains. The focus is on the adolescent's progress in the middle phase of treatment both in session and in the "work at home" and on the adolescent's internalization of the interpersonal techniques. In terminating with the parents, the therapist encourages them to help the adolescent continue the increased and improved communication, rather than fall back on old communication patterns.

With both the adolescent and the parents, the therapist emphasizes that the adolescent has the skills needed to continue the interpersonal work outside of treatment. Furthermore, the continued use of these skills will help maintain the improvements in the adolescent's relationships and his/her depressive symptoms and prevent relapse.

DETAILED CASE EXAMPLE

INITIAL PHASE

Jean is a 15-year-old female who reports feeling depressed since she began high school last year. Jean lives with her mother Mrs. M. and older sister Michelle (aged

18). On evaluation, her depression symptoms include depressed mood, irritability, difficulty sleeping, fatigue, poor concentration, and low self-worth. Jean sometimes has thoughts that life isn't worth living, although she denies any thoughts of wanting to hurt herself. Jean has had a difficult time transitioning to high school. Although she did well in middle school, her grades decreased in high school and she has become more socially isolated. Based on a clinical evaluation, Jean was diagnosed with major depression and was referred for IPT-A.

In the first session, the therapist began by reviewing Jean's depression symptoms and confirming the depression diagnosis. Next she met with Jean and her mother to explain the focus and format of IPT-A, educate them about depression, and assign Jean the limited sick role. The therapist explained that, similar to when someone has the flu and cannot do activities as well as normally, people with depression might not function at their normal level. For instance, Jean reported that she isn't doing as well in school. The therapist emphasized that Jean should do as much as she can even if it is not at the level at which she functioned in middle school. In addition, it is important for Mrs. M. to understand that Jean may not do things as well as she would like.

In the remainder of the first session and sessions 2–3, the therapist met with Jean alone to conduct the interpersonal inventory. Jean identified seven people that she wanted to talk about: her mother, her sister Michelle, her aunt, her boyfriend, two close friends, and her father who lives in Florida. She began by talking about her mother with whom she had a close relationship until she began high school. They used to go shopping together and see movies. Jean was able to talk to her mom about certain things, schoolwork and friends, but never spoke much about her feelings. When high school began, Jean felt like her relationship with her mom deteriorated. Her mom is disappointed with her grades in school and "nags" Jean about doing schoolwork. Jean's mom also doesn't approve of Jean having a boyfriend, feeling that she is too young to be dating. They argue about these issues. In these arguments, Jean perceives her mother to be saying, "Why can't you be like your sister?" who Jean thinks her mother favors over her. When these interactions occur, Jean explodes in anger and then withdraws to her room. Jean would like her mother to stop nagging her so much and to accept her for who she is. She would also like to argue less.

Jean describes her relationship with her sister Michelle as "typical" for siblings. They get along pretty well but argue over cleaning their room and using the phone. They mostly spend time together at home after school, but every once in a while will spend a weekend day together. Michelle, who is graduating from high school in a couple of months, tries to help Jean with her schoolwork. Sometimes Jean finds this helpful, but other times she resents her sister for playing this role, particularly because Michelle always seems to do things right. Recently, Jean has become more irritable with Michelle, arguing more about little things. Jean has not been able to talk to Michelle about her depression. She thinks Michelle must know, but they have never discussed it.

Jean describes herself as being very close to her aunt Maria who lives an hour away. Jean goes to her aunt's house whenever she can. They both enjoy painting and often spend time on the weekends painting together. Jean is able to talk to her aunt about her difficulties in school and with her mom. Her aunt encourages her to work things out with her mother. Jean finds talking to her aunt helpful, but has not been able to follow through on her aunt's advice. Jean describes this relationship as very positive, stating she feels better when she is around her aunt.

Jean has been dating her boyfriend, Charlie, for 14 months. They were in 9th grade together but Charlie moved over the summer to a nearby town and now goes to a different high school. Jean reports that this move has been difficult for their relationship. They spend a lot of time on the phone and internet and as a result she spends less time on schoolwork. In addition, Charlie has met a number of new people with whom he spends time and Jean feels left out. Jean's depression symptoms predate Charlie, but she feels like her symptoms have worsened since he switched schools. When she is having a bad day, it feels like an effort to go out with him. Jean describes a similar dynamic with her two girlfriends. She feels better when she is with them, but she finds it easier to withdraw.

Lastly, Jean described her relationship with her father. Her parents divorced when she was 7 years old. For the first 3 years after the divorce, he lived nearby. But then he moved to Florida. Since then, Jean sees her father about two times a year for vacation and speaks to him weekly on the phone. Jean states that she and her father are not particularly close but she is not interested in working on this relationship in treatment.

Based on the interpersonal inventory, the therapist conceptualized the case as an interpersonal role transition. Jean's difficulties began with the transition to high school, where the academic demands increased, she started dating her boyfriend, and her relationship changed with her mother who felt that Jean was too young to be dating. Jean's depression worsened recently following her boyfriend's transfer to a new school. Jean is having a difficult time with all these changes, responding to them by becoming more irritable at home. In addition, she has become increasingly withdrawn from her friends and boyfriend. This withdrawal prevents Jean from getting the support she needs from peers. The therapist outlined the goals of the middle phase of treatment including helping Jean to (1) cope better with her new role, (2) communicate better with her mother about the stresses related to the transition, and (3) get more support from her friends and boyfriend. For homework the therapist asked Jean to pay attention to her relationships in the next few weeks so she could bring in interpersonal events to work on in treatment. Jean agreed.

MIDDLE PHASE

In the middle phase of treatment, Jean and the therapist explored how things had changed since Jean began high school and what Jean could do to feel more comfortable in her new role. The goal was to examine the strategies that Jean was using to adapt to this transition and to identify ones that might be more helpful. It became evident that Jean had not communicated with her family and friends about her difficulty adjusting to high school and the move of her boyfriend. In particular, she felt that her mother had expectations for her that she was unable to meet. Jean tended to keep these feelings inside until she exploded in anger at her mother or sister, which only exacerbated the problem. With her boyfriend and friends, she had become more isolated. Jean and the therapist talked about what her relationships had been like before the transition to high school and how things had changed. They also discussed Jean's relationship with Charlie before and after his move. The remainder of the work involved identifying new skills that were needed to help Jean better cope with high school and the other changes in her life. Because Jean had a difficult time communicating her feelings, much of the work focused on improving her communication skills.

In the remaining sessions of the middle phase, work moved to focusing on the changes in Jean's relationship with her mother. Conflict centered around two areas: Jean's academic difficulties in high school and her relationship with her boyfriend. Jean and the therapist decided to work on the former issue first, because it was less emotionally charged. As they discussed the problem, it became evident that Jean wanted to do well in school, but was finding the work academically difficult. Her mother's disappointment made her more stressed and made her feel like she wasn't good enough. She had never expressed this to her mom and was afraid to do so. The therapist asked Jean how she thought her mother would respond if Jean expressed her feelings to her mother. Jean was not sure but was willing to try. The therapist and Jean spent session 6 first discussing what Jean might say to her mom and how her mom might respond. They then role-played the discussion several times. Although Jean had some difficulty with the role-plays, with feedback from the therapist, she was able to express her feelings. The therapist gave Jean a "work at home" assignment to talk to her mother about her academic difficulties using the techniques practiced in the role-plays. Jean and the therapist also agreed to have mom join them for part of the next session.

Session 7 began with Jean alone to review the homework assignment. Jean had been able to talk to her mother but felt that the conversation did not go as well as she hoped. She explained to her mother that she found the schoolwork challenging but that she was trying as hard as she could. Jean was also able to explain to her mother that when she nagged her about her work, it made Jean more upset and frustrated. Jean's mom was able to hear what Jean had to say, but then proceeded to tell Jean that she wasn't doing well in school because she was spending so much time on the internet and phone talking to Charlie. This led to an argument between Jean and her mother. However, unlike earlier arguments, the two remained calm.

After the therapist had conducted a communication analysis of what had occurred, she asked Jean what she might have done differently to prevent the argument from happening. Jean stated that she could have talked to her mother about finding possible solutions to her academic difficulties but that she was so frustrated she didn't want to "give in." They discussed possible solutions including getting a tutor for certain subjects and limiting the time she was spending on the phone. The therapist and Jean decided to have Jean's mother join them in the session to continue this conversation. The therapist reminded Mrs. M. that Jean was working on communicating her feelings and explained to both Jean and Mrs. M. that the focus of the discussion in session would be on improving the process of their communication.

With encouragement, Jean was able to state that she understands that Mrs. M. thinks she is doing poorly in school because of the time she spends on the phone, but that it is very important to her to stay in touch with Charlie. The therapist praised Jean for expressing her feelings so clearly. Jean reiterated that she wanted to do better in school and suggested some of the possible solutions to her mother. The therapist helped to coach Jean in this interaction and encouraged Mrs. M. to be open to the various solutions. Mrs. M. expressed to Jean that she just wanted the best for her and that she was glad that Jean was trying to do better in school. Based on the discussion, Jean and Mrs. M. agreed on a schedule where Jean completes her homework between 8:00 and 9:00 p.m. and then speaks on the phone and uses the internet until 10:00.

In addition, Jean agreed to talk to her teacher about finding a tutor to help her with certain subjects.

At the end of the discussion, the therapist summarized what had occurred in the discussion, pointing out the positive communication techniques that Jean and her mother had used. Both were able to empathize with how the other was feeling about Jean's academic difficulties. They had come up with some solutions, were able to compromise, and were able to talk calmly to each other. Jean and Mrs. M. agreed that they were able to speak more calmly about Jean's schoolwork than they had in the past. The therapist encouraged Jean and her mother to continue this discussion at home and to consider other potential solutions if the original plan turned out to be unsuccessful. The therapist also emphasized the importance of practicing these new skills to keep them from resorting back to old patterns. Such continued practice is crucial for the prevention of future depressive episodes.

In session 8, the therapist and Jean began talking about Jean's boyfriend and how she could get her mother to feel more positively about their relationship. Jean realized that doing better in school would be the first step, since Mrs. M. blamed Charlie for her academic difficulties. The therapist and Jean also discussed ways for Charlie and Mrs. M. to get to know each other better so Mrs. M. would be more comfortable with Charlie. In the past, Jean had not brought Charlie to the house often and realized that this may be contributing to her mother's discomfort. For "work at home," the therapist encouraged Jean to bring Charlie over to the house. The therapist helped Jean structure the anticipated visit to maximize the likelihood of a success by discussing ways to facilitate discussion between Charlie and her mother.

By session 9, Jean reported that things were much better at home. She was completing her homework as planned and she and her mother were arguing less. Charlie's visit to the house had gone well. Mom had seemed pleased with the visit and did not do anything to embarrass Jean or Charlie. Although the schoolwork was still difficult, Jean felt like her mother wasn't blaming her anymore. Jean's depressive symptoms had improved as well. The therapist and Jean spent session 9 discussing how Jean could start to spend more time with her friends and Charlie, as she had been somewhat withdrawn from them during her depression. Part of this involved discussing and role-playing how Jean could speak to Charlie about the difficult time she was having adjusting to his move to see if they could come up with ideas about how to maintain their relationship. Based on her success with her mother, Jean felt optimistic about communicating to Charlie about her feelings and was willing to try this conversation as a homework assignment.

TERMINATION PHASE

In the remaining three sessions, the therapist and Jean reviewed the work they had done in treatment. The therapist highlighted the skills that Jean had used to communicate with her mother. In addition, the therapist reinforced the link between the improved communication and improvements in Jean's depressive symptoms. The homework served to achieve therapeutic gains and continued work would help maintain gains and prevent relapse. The therapist and Jean discussed how Jean could continue this work once treatment ended; for instance, how Jean might communicate her feelings to her sister and enlist her sister's help with the academic work. Although they had not discussed this relationship much in the treatment, the therapist encouraged Jean to work on this relationship during the remaining sessions and after termination.

During the termination phase, Jean and the therapist discussed Jean's warning signs of depression. Jean identified the main signs as withdrawing from her friends and wanting to stay in bed all day. The therapist stressed the importance of Jean seeking help if these symptoms of depression return. They also discussed future situations that may be difficult for Jean and what interpersonal skills she might use to navigate these situations. For instance, Jean discussed her concerns that the increasing distance with Charlie might put a strain on their relationship. The therapist emphasized the importance of communicating with Charlie about her feelings to maintain her treatment gains. Lastly, they discussed Jean's feelings about ending treatment and evaluated the need for further treatment.

CONCLUSION

IPT-A is a time-limited treatment for adolescent depression with studies supporting its efficacy and effectiveness. The treatment, which is based on the premise that depression occurs in an interpersonal context, works by addressing interpersonal problems that may be causing or contributing to the adolescent's depression. "Work at home" is an extension of the work done in the session and is focused on improving interpersonal communication and problem-solving. The therapist and adolescent collaboratively select homework that is relevant for the identified problem area and is appropriate for the phase of treatment. Although the use of homework in IPT-A has not been empirically tested in a dismantling study, our belief is that treatment will be more effective when the adolescent addresses outside relationships. The goal of the "work at home" is to practice new interpersonal skills so they become part of the adolescent's interpersonal repertoire. This will lead to a decrease in depression. Furthermore, interpersonal "work at home" will increase the likelihood of maintaining treatment gains since these assignments lead to the internalization and generalization of important interpersonal skills. Continued practice once treatment has ended will help maintain treatment gains and help prevent relapse.

REFERENCES

Clark, D., Pynoos, R., & Goebel, A. (1994). Mechanisms and processes of adolescent bereavement. In R. Haggerty (Ed.), *Stress, risk, and resilience in children and adolescents: Processes, mechanisms, and interventions* (pp. 100–145). Cambridge, England: Cambridge University Press.

DiMascio, A., Weissman, M. M., Prusoff, B. A., New, C., Zwilling, M., & Klerman, G. L. (1979). Differential symptom reduction by drugs and psychotherapy in acute depression. *Archives of General Psychiatry, 36,* 450–456.

Elkin, I., Shea, M. T., Watkins, J. T., Imber, S. D., Sotsky, S. M., Collins, J. F., et al. (1989). National Institute of Mental Health Treatment of Depression Collaborative Research Program: General effectiveness of treatments. *Archives of General Psychiatry, 46,* 971–983.

Mufson, L., Dorta, K. P., Moreau, D., & Weissman, M. M. (2004). *Interpersonal psychotherapy for depressed adolescents, 2nd Edition.* New York: Guilford Press.

Mufson, L., Dorta, K. P., Wickramaratne, P., Nomura, Y., Olfson, M., and Weissman, M. M. (2004). A randomized effectiveness trial of interpersonal psychotherapy for depressed adolescents. *Archives of General Psychiatry, 61,* 577–584.

Mufson, L., & Fairbanks, J. (1996). Interpersonal psychotherapy for depressed adolescents: A one-year naturalistic follow-up study. *Journal of the American Academy of Child and Adolescent Psychiatry, 35,* 1145–1155.

Mufson, L., Moreau, D., Weissman, M. M., Wickramaratne, P., Martin J., & Samoilov, A. (1994). The modification of interpersonal psychotherapy with depressed adolescents IPT-A: Phase I and phase II studies. *Journal of the American Academy of Child and Adolescent Psychiatry, 33,* 695–705.

Mufson, L., Weissman, M. M., Moreau, D., & Garfinkel, R. (1999). Efficacy of interpersonal psychotherapy for depressed adolescents. *Archives of General Psychiatry, 56,* 573–579.

Rosselló, J. & Bernal, G. (1999). The efficacy of cognitive-behavioral and interpersonal treatments for depression in Puerto Rican adolescents. *Journal of Consulting and Clinical Psychology, 67,* 734–745.

Ryan, N. D., Puig-Antich, J., Ambrosini, P., Rabinovich, H., Robinson, D., Nelson, B. et al. (1987). The clinical picture of major depression in children and adolescents. *Archives of General Psychiatry, 44,* 854–861.

Weissman, M. M., Prusoff, B. A., DiMascio, A., Neu, C., Goklaney, M., & Klerman, G. L. (1979). The efficacy of drug and psychotherapy in the treatment of acute depressive episodes. *American Journal of Psychiatry, 136,* 555–558.

Weissman, M. M., Markowitz, J. C., & Klerman, G. L. (2000). *Comprehensive guide to interpersonal psychotherapy.* New York: Basic Books.

CHAPTER 6

PSYCHODYNAMIC THERAPY

George Stricker

Psychodynamic psychotherapy is an umbrella term that embraces a wide group of approaches ranging from the classical approach of Sigmund Freud, updated in the form of ego psychology, to the more recent set of relational, interpersonal, and self-psychological approaches (Mitchell, 1988). A basic distinction can be made between a one-person psychology, exemplified by the drive model of the classical works, to the two-person psychology characteristic of the more interpersonal models. There are several threads that tie these two approaches together. One is the emphasis on dynamic unconscious processes, leaving a major task of psychotherapy to be the making of the unconscious conscious, with the expectation that increased awareness will lead to more effective functioning. A second thread is the emphasis on historical determinism, such that today's activities are a function of yesterday's experience, often expressed in unconscious processes, so that a reconstruction of the past can lead to a better understanding of the present, in turn leading to more adaptive and satisfying functioning. This, in turn, also serves a preventive function, as the patient is better able to understand and cope with future difficulties.

As can be imagined, psychodynamic psychotherapy, as I have described it, essentially looks inward, with an emphasis on self-understanding. In one-person approaches there is little attention that is given to the external world except as it reflects on internal processes. In the two-person approach there is a recognition of the patient's relationship to the other, but this also is discussed primarily in terms of the impact of the other on internal processes. In both cases, the approach usually involves long-term work, as the plumbing of the unconscious is not a rapid process.

The evidence for psychodynamic psychotherapy is not as well-developed as the evidence for more time-limited approaches. The construction of sound experimental designs to test long-term therapy is difficult. It would be ethically suspect to withhold treatment for a long period of time, and experimentally inappropriate to compare treatments of markedly different length. However, meta-analyses consistently show that psychotherapy is an effective procedure (e.g., Smith, Glass, & Miller, 1980), but that there is little difference between the effectiveness of the various orientations (Wampold et al., 1997). It also should be noted that the dependent variables typically chosen for psychotherapy research are symptom-related and do not do justice to the myriad processes addressed by psychodynamic psychotherapy.

The particular variant of psychodynamic psychotherapy that I will present in this chapter is referred to as assimilative psychodynamic psychotherapy. It has been presented in great detail elsewhere (Gold & Stricker, 2001; Stricker & Gold, 1996, 2002). Briefly, the psychotherapy initially is conducted in the manner of a traditional relational psychodynamic approach, but techniques drawn from other approaches are assimilated into the treatment as they become relevant. Again, for the purposes of this chapter, the principal technique to be assimilated is homework, a method predominantly rooted in the cognitive-behavioral approach (Beck, Rush, Shaw, & Emery, 1979). In general, there is good evidence for the effectiveness of homework (Kazantzis, Deane, & Ronan, 2000), but little evidence that is specific to the use of homework in psychodynamic psychotherapy.

THE ROLE OF HOMEWORK IN
PSYCHODYNAMIC PSYCHOTHERAPY

Homework refers to out-of-session activities that the patient is asked to engage in by the therapist. These activities and their consequences are then reported and discussed in subsequent sessions. It follows from the description above that there is little specific role for homework in traditional psychodynamic psychotherapy. The psychodynamic therapist is inactive in the classical variant and, although more active in the interpersonal approach, clearly not directive. However, it must be noted that there are many ways in which quasi-homework assignments find their way into even traditional psychodynamic psychotherapy.

Although the focus of psychodynamic psychotherapy is within the patient, and also within the therapist–patient relationship, it is clear that the point of this focus usually is to improve functioning outside the treatment setting. With or without specific direction, the patient is likely to observe the world around him, and even to try new activities, and then to report these observations and activities to the therapist. This feedback process between the consulting room and the outer world is one form of homework, but it often is not stated explicitly by the therapist.

Similarly, there are some activities that the psychodynamic therapist clearly values, such as dream analysis. It is likely that most psychodynamic psychotherapists respond well to dreams when they are spontaneously produced, thereby encouraging further production, and the therapist also even may suggest that future dreams be reported. The patient typically will talk about the difficulty in remembering dreams, and the therapist will respond with a suggestion to keep a pad by the night stand in order to record the dream. This is not described as homework in the literature, but it clearly meets any definition of homework that can be offered, and resembles journaling in form if not in content.

Other than explicit recommendations about such matters as reporting dreams, there are a great many implicit homework assignments in psychodynamic psychotherapy. It is not unusual for a patient to hear a question as a suggestion, so simple inquiries such as "What do you think might have happened if you had ...?" often draw a response such as "Do you think I should....?" If this response is made, the therapist can clarify the difference between an inquiry and a suggestion. However, if the patient simply hears and acts on the "suggestion," a homework assignment inadvertently has been given.

Earlier, the commonalities of psychodynamic psychotherapy were identified as the presence of a dynamic unconscious and historical determinism. In addition, on a more technical level, transference and resistance are seen as integral to the process of psychodynamic psychotherapy. Both of these have specific implications for the incorporation of homework within the treatment.

Transference refers to a specific relationship between the patient and the therapist. The patient often will view the therapist in a manner much as earlier important figures (objects) in the patient's life were seen. If the object either was benign or overpowering, the patient may have a dependent relationship and readily follow any instruction that may be given. In this situation, tacit inquiries will be heard as suggestions, and the suggestions will be followed. I often have patients enter a session by saying that they tried what I suggested in the last session, and I am left wondering what it was that I suggested, as I did not intend to offer a directive. Despite a lack of conscious intention on my part, the patient heard and followed a homework assignment.

Resistance refers to an unconscious process that impedes the development of the psychotherapeutic process. The patient, for reasons that are determined by inner concerns, either does not wish to change or does not easily follow direction. The process of resistance is similar in some ways to the social psychological concept of reactance. The reactant patient values his autonomy and will resist any attempt to impinge on it. For such a patient, a homework assignment, whether explicit or implicit, will be resisted as an attempt to curtail autonomy, and this type of intervention is unlikely to be effective. In this spirit, Beutler (Beutler & Harwood, 2000) recommends that expressive treatments, such as psychodynamic psychotherapy, be used with reactant patients, and more directive treatments, such as cognitive-behavioral therapy, be used for patients who are low on reactance. Thus, the use of explicit homework assignments would be unlikely to be effective with a reactant patient, and might be highly effective with a low reactant patient. Interestingly, it is also likely that the reactant patient might devise his own homework assignments, taking tacit cues from the therapist, but also taking responsibility for the direction of the treatment.

The approach to psychodynamic psychotherapy that will be described in this chapter, as has been noted, is assimilative psychodynamic psychotherapy. A focus is maintained on an expressive, uncovering approach to treatment, with the expectation that doing so will lead to increased awareness and subsequent behavior change. However, there are many instances in which awareness is achieved without behavior change following, and it is in these circumstances that techniques such as homework are assimilated into the treatment. Homework only will be used for a specific purpose and only if the patient is not reactant and is likely to be responsive to it.

Three important points are worth noting in this regard. The first is that the assimilation of a technique from a different approach always requires a seamless integration into the ongoing treatment, so that it is not experienced as jarring and disconnected. In the worst case, the patient will feel that the therapist has changed, that the gently supporting object has become a directive presence, and the homework will not be effective. In the best case, the introduction of the technique will be accomplished in a manner that will connote the caring of the therapist and will be an important aspect of the success of the treatment. This concern and caring may lead to the experience of a corrective emotional experience (Alexander & French, 1946), as the therapist, unlike past authority figures, actually is capable of being concerned about the patient and helpfully responsive to his feelings.

The second important point follows from this and it is that an intervention drawn from one approach takes on different characteristics when used in another. Homework assigned by a cognitive-behavioral psychotherapist fits well with the course of treatment and is one of many directive interventions geared toward the well-being of the patient. However, homework assigned by a psychodynamic psychotherapist represents a departure from the norm, and the patient is likely to respond to it in a manner different from the CBT patient. The more non-directive (not necessarily inactive) therapist now is offering a specific suggestion and, depending on the patient, this can be viewed as an unwelcome intrusion or as a helpful alteration in functioning. Part of clinical skillfulness is in determining which is which, and when a homework assignment will be accepted as constructive rather than rejected as intrusive.

Finally, the last point represents an accommodation of the theory to the success of the foreign intervention. Psychodynamic theory usually views change in a linear fashion, with insight leading to behavior change. However, it is entirely likely that the process of change is cyclical rather than linear, and that insight can lead to behavior change, but behavior change also can lead to insight. The model of personality that underlies this approach (Gold & Stricker, 1993; Stricker & Gold, 1988) is described as the three tier approach. The three tiers are the behavioral, the cognitive-affective, and the unconscious. Each of these interacts with the others, so that intervention at any tier will have an effect in the other tiers. Thus, interventions can be made at any of the tiers, and these include behavioral, cognitive, systemic, and experiential techniques. With this understanding, homework, although it appears incompatible with the general focus of psychodynamic psychotherapy, when used judiciously, can be an important addition to the interventions available to the psychodynamic psychotherapist.

Finally, there is the matter of empirical support. Much as was the case for psychodynamic psychotherapy in general, there is little support for the use of homework in psychodynamic psychotherapy, but a good deal of support for the use of homework in general (Kazantzis et al., 2000) and no indication that the value of the homework is restricted to incorporation in cognitive-behavioral psychotherapy.

In order to illustrate the points made in this brief presentation, I would like to present two separate cases, similar in their use of homework, but very different in the way it was used and the results that followed.

SHARON[1]

Sharon is a woman in her late 20s. When I first saw her, she was about to be married and came because of concerns that were aroused by the wedding. She did not know what to do about her mother, a woman from whom she is estranged and who neglected Sharon early in their relationship, largely because of the mother's drug involvement and possible schizophrenic episodes. Sharon did not want to invite her mother to the wedding, yet felt guilty about this, and about offending her maternal grandmother, who raised her, and who still has warm feelings for her daughter (Sharon's mother). Sharon now has a good relationship with her father, but she also was estranged from him after he divorced her mother and left the family. Her father also had a history of drug and alcohol abuse. Sharon's family of origin was markedly

---

[1] The case of Sharon has been presented previously in a more abbreviated form (Stricker, in press-b).

dysfunctional, neglected her needs, and was thoroughly unresponsive to her. Her grandparents raised her, and she owes much of her current high level of functioning to the contributions they made to her welfare. In contrast with her original family, Sharon's fiancé, Roger, has a family she views as picture perfect, they treat her extremely well, and she would rather deal with this idealized family than the troubled one she came from. She was adamant that she did not want to be embarrassed in front of these people by her unpredictable and dysfunctional mother.

In light of this background, marked by neglect and occasional abuse, Sharon is a remarkably resilient woman. She is quite accomplished, but denial is prominent and she has difficulty in doing anything that might be perceived negatively or as hostile by others. There are occasional bulimic episodes, usually when she feels that she does not measure up to others, and her self-concept is shaky because of the lack of any early mirroring. However, even allowing for the possibility of denial in her report, Roger loves her, is attentive to her needs, and the marriage appears to be a good one.

Sharon was a cooperative and involved patient, she readily related her early experiences, speculated about the impact they might have on her current functioning, and the consequent insecurity and diminished self-regard that resulted from these experiences. She quickly formed a strong attachment to me, seeing me as the father that she had not had in the early years, and as a predictable and caring adult, something that was missing from her upbringing. As a result, she was much attuned to my wishes, trusting of my concern and skill, and therefore quite willing to do anything that might be suggested.

Relatively early in treatment, she was able to see her pattern of needing to be perfect and to satisfy everyone else as being related to her early rejection by both her parents. Her manner of relating to current people, particularly authorities, as though they were figures from her past, was apparent to her. At this point I gave her the homework assignment of trying to recognize this pattern with others as early in her interaction with them as she could, and when she did recognize it, to tell herself that the person was not her parent and that therefore she need not fear being rejected. At the next session, I asked her to report to me whether she was able to identify this pattern, and, if she could, whether she was able to interrupt the process that had, in the past, led to discomfort, hurt feelings, and depression. During the next session Sharon reported, with happiness and pride, that the assignment had worked and she had been very successful in implementing it.

When I asked Sharon to tell me about what happened, she related an event in which her employer, whom she admired, had praised her and she then used this affirmation as motivation and permission to develop a creative program that was very well received. I wondered about the connection between what Sharon did and the homework that I had given her, and she then explained that I had told her to try to find ways to feel better about herself, and she was able to do it in this situation. Needless to say, I did not bother telling her that she had misunderstood the homework assignment, because her way of hearing and interpreting it was a more direct manner of apprehending what indeed was the point of the assignment. We used her interpretation of the homework assignment in response to other events in her life, and she also has handled these better as a result of her self-developed technique. Sharon came to view therapy as a safe zone for her, and she eventually was able to use her safe zone to return to my original assignment and then begin to identify situations in which she was relating to current figures as though they were figures from her past.

However, Sharon's appreciation of the task and her timing of the fulfillment of the homework was more in keeping with her needs and abilities, and she was able to benefit from the assignment by working at her own pace.

Perhaps because Sharon began to feel more confident and better about herself, she left her mother's name off the wedding invitation, made up her mind not to invite her mother to the wedding, and told Roger's family and her grandmother about this resolve. She still felt some twinges of guilt and ambivalence, but she was able to act in a way that she viewed as constructive. It is interesting that my initial inclination, when I heard the presenting problem, was to have Sharon reconcile with her mother, accept the past slights as past, and be able to build a better relationship with her. Sharon knew better, and followed her own path to what she saw as a successful conclusion. This example of allowing a patient to shape the direction of change and define what is helpful in doing so is consistent with a recent movement toward patient-directed psychotherapy (Hubble, Duncan, & Miller, 1999), and was obvious both in Sharon's interpretation of the homework assignment and her decisions regarding her wedding.

The wedding was a great success, Sharon's mother did not come (or attempt to contact her in any way, perhaps justifying Sharon's recognition that the time was not ripe for a renewed relationship), Roger's parents went along with the decision, and Sharon's grandmother, although unhappy, was accepting of this decision and did not try to alter it. Since the wedding, Sharon has enjoyed her relationship with Roger, they now have a small son, and she continues to function in a remarkably adaptive way considering her damaged upbringing.

How did homework contribute to this successful treatment? In two important ways. First, Sharon had the capacity to interpret the assignment in a way that was comfortable for her and then used it to promote her good functioning. Homework provided Sharon with a type of self-surveillance that can be interpreted in psychodynamic terms as the development of an observing ego. Not only did she benefit from the assignment, but she used it, as she reinterpreted it, as a springboard for further growth. To this day, she invokes the assignment when she is faced with a difficult task, using it to gain understanding and control over the situation. This leads to the second benefit of homework. Not only did it help Sharon to master the presenting problem, it also gave her the tools to deal with future situations, thereby serving a preventive as well as a curative function.

SAUL[2]

Saul is a 50-year-old practicing attorney, married for 20 years, and has two sons, 16 and 11. He was in a family firm operated by his father Eli and his older sister until his father retired, and Saul thought that he was then given a very unfavorable division of the firm's assets. He was in a heated battle with Eli (as he refers to his father) over one remaining account and subsequent payments to his father, which Saul did not want to provide because of the unfair division of clients. Saul described himself as depressed, short-tempered, and unmotivated, with some teariness, trouble sleeping, and weight gain. He also thought he was an honest, straightforward man with little pretense, soft and easily taken advantage of, and now being victimized by his father

---

[2] The case of Saul was presented in more detail in another publication (Stricker, 2006).

and sister. Although he initially talked about how he could prevail and how much confidence he had, he had trouble speaking concretely about what his situation was and obviously felt he never had been appreciated, was mistreated and exploited in business by Eli from the beginning, and never was able to extricate himself. He now wanted to change this pattern but was having trouble doing so.

Saul came to treatment at the urging of his wife and, because of his conflicted relationship with his father, was distrustful and wary. I responded to this by listening carefully, speaking gently, only asking necessary questions, and never making any judgments about what he was telling me. Gradually, he seemed to relax slightly, agreed to weekly sessions aimed at helping him with the depression, and said he didn't want to talk about the past (he resented having been in treatment as an adolescent because his parents thought that there was something wrong with him). In the following session, Saul said that he felt very upset and angry after the first session, then felt a fog rolling over him, became too depressed to work, but then the fog finally lifted and he felt better until it was time to come here again. I suggested that the problem may not be depression as much as his difficulty with anger, with his defense against anger being the fog, and the depression then following. This made sense to him, and we spoke about the various ways he has of dealing with anger. Saul left feeling somewhat better, and vowed to do more to take control of his life.

The early portion of treatment followed the structure of traditional exploratory treatment. Saul spontaneously talked about many of his early experiences, despite his initial expression of a wish not to do so. These usually involved his father, and Saul's sense of feeling inadequate and disrespected. The key to the therapy was his experiencing of these events and connections in the context of the therapeutic relationship. In me, he found an older man whom he experienced as understanding, accepting, and prizing of him. This allowed him the freedom to explore his feelings and to experiment with new behaviors.

From the beginning, Saul was very reactive to events around him. If he lost an account, he would assume that Eli would have retained it, and his father did not help by agreeing with that speculation. We discussed how this experience was rooted in his early experiences with his father, and that he was inclined to re-create the early experiences, but did not have to do so if he was aware of the origin.

At this point, with some clarity about dynamic issues, I began to introduce some homework assignments designed to make the dynamic insight more related to his current experience. I first asked him to notice when he was taking things personally, and to try not to do so. Saul felt that he gained immensely by keeping this in mind, and often would pause before responding to someone else when he realized that some slight he had received was not about him, and he could go forward without recalling the deep sense of inadequacy that he carried with him. The second assignment was to notice when he expected people to be what they were not, and to try not to do so. In his dealings with Eli, he constantly found himself disappointed that his father was not more responsive to his feelings and needs, but always expected him to change and become more attentive, and then he felt hurt and rejected when his father behaved as he always had.

The depression that brought Saul to treatment lifted very rapidly, as soon as Saul realized that he could take more responsibility for himself and began to do so. He also dealt more constructively with his father, standing up for himself and not succumbing to the pressure to make a deal that would not be in his best interests. Even when an initial deal fell through because Eli backed out, Saul did not become depressed, but instead recognized that his father had been at fault rather than he, and he was able to move forward in a productive manner. The key here, consistent with his homework, was not to take the deal personally or to expect his father to act in a more supportive manner.

With Saul, as with Sharon, the focus of the homework was not a simple behavioral task but an assignment that was consistent with the dynamic formulations we had reached and fit in seamlessly with the thrust of the treatment. Saul was asked to translate a dynamic recognition into a behavioral one. By noticing his tendency to take things personally, he was able to resist doing so and to overcome some of the debilitating self-doubt that had plagued him. By learning not to expect his father to treat him better, he was able to eliminate some of the bitter disappointments that had interfered with his functioning. As he was able to do these things, he was able to increase the depth of his dynamic self-understanding, thereby furthering the cycle between insight and behavior change that gave rise to the assignment. As Saul learned to do these things in response to direct suggestions, he then began to follow through in new settings even without suggestions from me, and, by doing so, was able to begin to function in a more productive manner. As with Sharon, the preventive aspects of the assignment allowed the extension of an immediate therapeutic gain into a future one.

CONCLUSIONS

In a previous article concerning psychodynamic psychotherapy (Stricker, in press-b), I drew several conclusions, all of which bear repeating here:

Homework should be geared to the individual rather than used automatically as an all-purpose intervention: In both of the cases that have been presented, the homework was keyed to the current concerns of the patient, and to the dynamic issues that were paramount in the treatment. Sharon was asked to notice the repetition of patterns from the past, and Saul was asked to notice when he had unrealistic expectations of others or took slights personally when they were not intended that way. The assignments differed in content, but they both were geared to dynamic issues that were being discussed in treatment, and extended the reach of the treatment into the world of the patient. Homework in psychodynamic psychotherapy may differ from homework in cognitive-behavioral psychotherapy because of this focus on using homework to further dynamic insight rather than to accomplish particular behavioral tasks.

There must be continuity between in-session and out-of-session activity: The assignment asking the patient to notice patterns outside of treatment that are being discussed in treatment provides this extension, and also increases the impact of the treatment. Rather than reserving treatment for a 45 minute period weekly (in Sharon's case, biweekly), it spreads into the fabric of the patient's life, and by doing so, increases the likelihood of therapeutic impact. It also is likely to be of value after therapy has concluded and serve as an insulation against future difficulties.

The possibility of changes in session affecting behavior out of session are enhanced by homework: It is possible that both Sharon and Saul would have come to the realization that the dynamic issues being discussed in treatment were also being played out in their lives. However, by instructing them to attend to these patterns, the process was accelerated. It is particularly noteworthy that Sharon reinterpreted her homework to an assignment that provided her with more continuity between her current concerns, her therapeutic discussions, and her problematic interactions.

Interventions mean different things from different therapists: If Sharon or Saul had been given the assignment by a behavior therapist, it would have been part of a package of directive interventions. It is unlikely, however, that a behavioral therapist would have designed these particular interventions, being related to dynamic issues as they were. The assignments, had they been given by a behaviorist, may well have been effective, but not in the same way. Both patients recognized that the assignments were not to be accomplished for the sake of the assignment, but rather were integrally related to the material of the treatment.

Providing homework can be seen as an active attempt to be helpful and as such can be the basis of a corrective emotional experience: In both cases, the value of the assignment was related to the therapeutic relationship. Both patients perceived me as a benign father figure, something they had been lacking, and a sign of my willingness to go out of my way to do something for them (I was departing from the usual pattern of our treatment) may have been as helpful as the actual assignment. Sharon was better able to relate to her employer because of the model I provided of a caring person (her employer probably was caring as well, but Sharon never recognized that previously). Saul could handle his father's rejection better because he had a situation in which he was not rejected, and used that as a basis for his improved functioning.

Homework places responsibility for change on the patient: Sharon not only carried out the homework by herself, but she reinterpreted it in a manner consistent with her needs. Saul was in the midst of discovering his own capacity to organize and direct his life, and the assignment gave him one more way in which he could do that. In both cases, the value of the homework, per se, was magnified by the experience of doing something in their own interests and being effective in influencing their world. This sense of efficacy can be carried into future situations and will serve a preventive as well as a mutative function.

Successful completion of homework can lead to behavior change, and it also can lead to deeper understanding of the issue of concern: Clearly, both Sharon and Saul changed their behavior as a result of the homework. In addition, and very consistent with the larger goals of assimilative psychodynamic psychotherapy, they had increased awareness of their motives and means of functioning, and these helped to deepen the work they were doing in psychotherapy.

In addition to these conclusions drawn from a previous article, there is one new one that emerged from this presentation:

Successful homework is valuable as a means of dealing with present conflict and for anticipating and preventing future conflict: I already have spelled out the present benefits derived by Sharon and Saul from their homework. In both cases, in addition to coping better with present issues, they learned a tool that helped them to deal with future issues when they recurred. Perhaps the reason why successful treatment often increases in effectiveness after termination is this ability to anticipate and prevent problems that previously would have led to great difficulty.

Finally, and consistent with my recommendations, but supplementary to them, a recent review of the literature (Scheel, Hanson, & Razzhavaikina, 2004) determined that "four conceptually and empirically overlapping predictive factors are important to client acceptability. These are (a) the fit of the recommendation and accompanying rationale with the client's problem formulation and theory of change, (b) the perceived difficulty (i.e., time, effort, complexity) in executing the recommended action, (c) the utilization of client strengths through the recommendation (e.g., proposing an action that requires verbal skill for a verbal client), and (d) the level of social influence the therapist possesses with the client" (p. 47). These recommendations are similar to my recommendation that homework should be geared to the individual, but add the additional factor of the level of social influence of the therapist as a determinant of the likelihood that the homework will be accomplished. The level of social influence is a social psychological way of stating the concept of transference, and it is quite clear within psychodynamic psychotherapy that the nature of the transference will play a large role in directing the course of the treatment.

Thus, we can conclude that an influential psychodynamic therapist, using well-chosen interventions, can add homework to the repertoire of interventions and, by doing so, can increase the likelihood of the success of the treatment and the probability that the preventive functions it serves can add to the long term gains achieved by the patient.

REFERENCES

Alexander, F., & French, T. (1946). *Psychoanalytic therapy*. New York: Ronald Press.

Beck, A. T., Rush, A. J., Shaw, B. F., & Emery, G. (1979). *Cognitive therapy of depression*. New York: Guilford.

Beutler, L. E., & Harwood, T. M. (2000). *Prescriptive psychotherapy: A practical guide to systematic treatment selection*. New York: Oxford University Press.

Gold, J., & Stricker, G. (2001). Relational psychoanalysis as a foundation of assimilative integration. *Journal of Psychotherapy Integration, 11*, 43–58.

Gold, J. R., & Stricker, G. (1993). Psychotherapy integration with personality disorders. In G. Stricker & J. R. Gold (Eds.), *Comprehensive handbook of psychotherapy integration* (pp. 323–336). New York: Plenum.

Hubble, M., Duncan, B., & Miller, S. (1999). *The heart and soul of change*. Washington, DC: American Psychological Association.

Kazantzis, N., Deane, F. P., & Ronan, K. R. (2000). Homework assignments in cognitive and behavioral therapy: A meta-analysis. *Clinical Psychology: Science and Practice, 7*, 581–585.

Mitchell, S. (1988). *Relational concepts in psychoanalysis*. Cambridge, MA: Harvard.

Scheel, M. J., Hanson, W. E., & Razzhavaikina, T. I. (2004). The process of recommending homework in psychotherapy: A review of therapist delivery methods, client acceptability, and factors that affect compliance. *Psychotherapy: Theory, Research, Practice, Training, 41*, 38–55.

Smith, M. L., Glass, G. V., & Miller, T. I. (1980). *The benefits of psychotherapy*. Baltimore, MD: Johns Hopkins University Press.

Stricker, G. (2006). Assimilative psychodynamic psychotherapy integration. In G. Stricker & J. Gold (Eds.), *A casebook in psychotherapy integration* (pp. 53–63). Washington, DC: American Psychological Association.

Stricker, G. Using homework in psychodynamic psychotherapy. *Journal of Psychotherapy Integration*. In press.

Stricker, G., & Gold, J. (1988). A psychodynamic approach to the personality disorders. *Journal of Personality Disorders, 2*, 350–359.

Stricker, G., & Gold, J. R. (1996). Psychotherapy integration: An assimilative, psychodynamic approach. *Clinical Psychology: Science and Practice, 3,* 47–58.

Stricker, G., & Gold, J. R. (2002). An assimilative approach to integrative psychodynamic psychotherapy. In J. Lebow (Ed.), *Integrative/eclectic* (Vol. 4, pp. 295–315). New York: Wiley.

Wampold, B. E., Mondin, G. W., Moody, M., Stich, F., Benson, K., & Ahn, H.-n. (1997). A meta-analysis of outcome studies comparing bona fide psychotherapies: Empirically, "All must have prizes." *Psychological Bulletin, 122,* 203–215.

CHAPTER 7

ACCEPTANCE AND COMMITMENT THERAPY

Michael P. Twohig, Heather M. Pierson, and Steven C. Hayes

Acceptance and Commitment Therapy (Hayes, Strosahl, & Wilson, 1999; the acronym for Acceptance and Commitment Therapy is "ACT," said as a word, not the separate letters) is one of the so-called "third wave" behavioral and cognitive therapies [examples of others include Dialectical Behavior Therapy (Linehan, 1993), Functional Analytic Psychotherapy (Kohlenberg & Tsai, 1991), Integrative Behavioral Couples Therapy (Jacobson & Christensen, 1996), and Mindfulness Based Cognitive Therapy (MBCT; Segal, Williams, & Teasdale, 2002)]. While not abandoning direct or even didactic change strategies, the most unique characteristic of the third wave interventions is the degree of emphasis on contextual and experiential change strategies, including acceptance, defusion, mindfulness, relationship, values, emotional deepening, contact with the present moment, and the like. These characteristics present initial challenges in the use of homework, because first-order change and direct instructional strategies are minimized. Once the experiential nature of these new therapies is acknowledged, however, homework becomes a central part of therapy. As a result, in ACT specifically, a body of supportive materials for doing homework is beginning to appear (e.g., Hayes & Smith, 2005; Heffner & Eifert, 2004). The nature and role of homework in ACT will be the central focus of this chapter. We will begin with a brief description of the ACT approach, followed by a summary of the data in support of it. Then we will show how homework can facilitate acquisition and use of new cognitive, emotional, and behavioral skills.

AN OVERVIEW OF ACT

ACT is not merely a technology for treating abnormal behavior—it is a model for human development linked to a philosophical and theoretical base. ACT argues that human problems stem very dominantly from a behavioral process that impacts all normal human beings: human language and cognition. ACT is linked to its own basic research program into the nature of human language: Relational Frame Theory (RFT; Hayes, Barnes-Holmes, & Roche, 2001). As a result, ACT technology is relatively flexible provided the techniques used are shown to alter theoretical processes specified by the ACT model. Many current therapies only loosely, if at all, use the findings of basic research to inform the technology of the treatment.

Both the underlying philosophy and theory are outlined below. The purpose is to make clear the pre-analytic assumptions of ACT, and its associated basic concepts.

PHILOSOPHICAL ASSUMPTIONS

ACT is based on functional contextualism (Biglan & Hayes, 1996; Hayes, 1993). All forms of contextualism have emerged from pragmatism (Hayes, Hayes, Reese, & Sarbin, 1993), which has several unique features. Truth is based on the workability of analyses, not their point-to-point correspondence within reality. In accord with this philosophical assumption, ACT technology focuses on the function of behavior, not the form of behavior. ACT therapists are relatively disinterested, for example, in whether your thoughts are rational or irrational—what is at issue is whether reactions to thoughts are functional or non-functional. If truth is a matter of workability, then it is critical to specify one's purposes so that it is clear what one is working toward. Goals must be known and stated, but they cannot be justified or evaluated (because doing so requires a measure of workability, and there you are back to the issue of goals). Thus, goals are foundational in contextualism. In ACT, this is also true. Values are considered foundational to therapy because they specify what the client is working toward. Many forms of contextualism (e.g., hermeneutics, dramaturgy, narrative psychology, feminist psychology) seek an appreciation of the participants in a whole event. In contrast, goal of functional contextualism is the prediction-and-influence. Both criteria must be met for something to be considered "true" (thus the hyphens). Because influence is explicitly a goal, functional contextual theories must specify manipulable environmental events that affect concrete actions (Hayes & Brownstein, 1986). Likewise, in ACT any analysis by the client or therapist is "true" only in so far as it specifies how to alter actions that lead in a valued direction.

THEORY OF LANGUAGE AND COGNITION

ACT is based on the idea that human suffering is ubiquitous because of human language. Although language has made living easier and safer, it has also given people the ability to evaluate, judge, and criticize, and this repertoire inevitably leads to self-criticism, emotional avoidance, and to entanglement with cognition. Living without language at this point is not possible or imaginable, so ACT targets recognizing when the use of language is advantageous and when it is not, and teaches skills to put at least some key facets of language under better contextual control.

RFT provides a definition of language as well as evidence for how language causes human suffering. Only a basic introduction is provided here (see Hayes et al., 2001 for a book length treatment). RFT holds that language is possible because of our ability to learn to derive mutual relations among events, regardless of their form. Consider an example using a matching to sample procedure, if a normal adult is trained to select any stimulus (call it "B1") from among an array of B comparisons when first shown a sample A1, and likewise is trained to select C1 given A1 from among a different array, several non-trained relations will be derived. The participant will now select A1 given B1 or A1 given C1 (what in RFT is called a derived relation of *mutual entailment*) and will also select B1 given C1 and vice versa (what in RFT is called a derived relation of *combinatorial entailment*).

These derived relations come under arbitrary contextual control, which enables a wide variety of specific types of relations. People relate things in terms of opposition, comparison (e.g., this is bigger than this), hierarchically (e.g., this is a member or case of this), temporally, causally, and so on based on the specific multiple exemplars that establish contextual control ("C_{rel}" for "relational context") over mutual and combinatorial entailment.

Finally, the functions of any related event can alter the functions of other related events based on the underlying relation between the two and the context that selects a specific function ("C_{func}" for "functional context"). For example, in the sentence "imagine what it tastes like to suck on a juicy lemon" the word "taste" probably serves as a C_{func} for most people, selecting gustatory functions over, say, visual ones. Because the relation between "lemon" and actual lemons is one of similarity or "coordination," some of the gustatory functions of actual lemons are likely to occur (e.g., most readers salivated just a little when reading the sentence, and some actually had their teeth go on edge). This process is called the *transformation of stimulus functions*. The word "transformation" is needed because when complex relations are at play, functions can be actively transformed, not merely transferred. For example, if a young child has three unfamiliar coins presented and is told that A is less than B and B is less than C, and if the child is then given the experience that B can be used to buy candy, A will now be avoided and C will be sought.

These five concepts (mutual and combinatorial entailment, C_{rel}, transformation of stimulus functions, and C_{func}) are the key concepts in RFT. When all five are present, we are said to be dealing with a "relational frame"—a form of learned and arbitrarily applicable relational responding. A substantial body of literature now exists showing that these processes exist and that they can be accounted for by learning history (see Hayes et al., 2001).

Theory of Psychopathology

The theory of psychopathology on which ACT is based emerges directly from RFT. From an ACT perspective, the relational networks necessary for simple verbal problem-solving are argued to be plentiful enough to create psychopathology. Verbal problem solving requires at a minimum three or four relational frames: coordination (e.g., name of events), time or contingency (e.g., what will happen when something is done), comparison (e.g., evaluation of relative impact), and typically hierarchy (e.g., attributes of events). For example "a hard screwdriver is better than my soft finger to pry off this lid and get candy" involves frames of coordination ("finger" = finger), hierarchy ("hard" is an attribute of "screwdriver"), time or contingency (use of screwdriver probably = lid off), and comparison (more likely than with finger).

With these same verbal relations, comes the construction of complex emotions (e.g., depression, anxiety) through frames of coordination; prediction of difficult outcomes through frames of time or contingency (e.g., if I do that I will get anxious); and unhelpful comparisons (e.g., negative comparisons to an unrealistic ideal); among many similar outcomes.

From an ACT perspective, there are two primary unhelpful effects of these verbal relations, despite their enormous utility in problem solving: experiential avoidance and cognitive fusion. Experiential avoidance (Hayes, Wilson, Gifford, Follette, & Strosahl, 1996) is the human tendency to attempt to alter the form, frequency, or situational sensitivity of private events when attempts to do so cause psychological harm. It is one of the more pathological processes known, correlating with virtually every major form of psychopathology (Hayes, Strosahl, Wilson et al., 2004). ACT argues that experiential avoidance flows naturally from very simple forms of human language, relying on the same relational frames as any form of verbal problem solving (e.g., anxiety is bad; if I do x, I won't be anxious; that is good).

Cognitive fusion is the human tendency to allow verbally derived stimulus functions to dominate over all other sources of behavioral regulation. Excessive cognitive fusion is undesirable because it produces unnecessary behavioral rigidity and loss of contact with the present moment. Verbally regulated behavior is notably insensitive to certain variations in natural contingencies (see Hayes, 1989 for a book length review). As verbal functions dominate, subtle aspects of the current environment tend to be missed and new forms of behavior that the environment would support tend not to occur. Said in a more colloquial way, humans begin to live "in their heads."

The most troublesome result of these two processes is psychological inflexibility. Patients become more rigid and less able to persist or change their behavior in the service of their chosen values.

ACT INTERVENTIONS

The underlying philosophy and theory were kept in mind during the development of ACT's technology. Because language is the tool that therapists have in session, they are fighting fire with fire, and as a result, ACT uses metaphors, paradox, and experiential exercises to undermine the ineffective use of language rather than logical, linear, analytic forms of language.

There are six main processes of importance in ACT: acceptance, defusion, self-as-context, focus on the present moment, values, and committed action (see Figure 7.1). Although each will be discussed as a separate component, they are interrelated in many ways and rarely are any of the components dealt with in isolation in any one session. ACT requires a certain amount of flexibility in administration of the treatment consistent with the aim of great behavioral flexibility for the clients. The focus is on what works for the particular client and his or her issues and situation.

The same is true for homework assignments in ACT—they are assigned as appropriate to foster work on these processes. The client almost always leaves the session with a task or homework assignment that targets the process that was being stressed in the session. Sometimes that means practicing an exercise between sessions such as exposure or mindfulness; sometimes that means completing a structured ACT worksheet or section of an ACT workbook (e.g., Hayes & Smith, 2005; Heffner & Eifert, 2004).

Acceptance focuses both on the client giving up an old agenda of controlling and avoiding experiences and replacing it with a willingness to have whatever shows up to be had. Many clients struggle with attempts to get rid of emotions, memories, and/or thoughts, and their struggle has only made their situations worse. In ACT excessive or poorly regulated control efforts are viewed as a problem. An example of an exercise that is used to help the client contact how unworkable attempts at controlling one's private events are is the *Person in the Hole* metaphor (Hayes et al.,

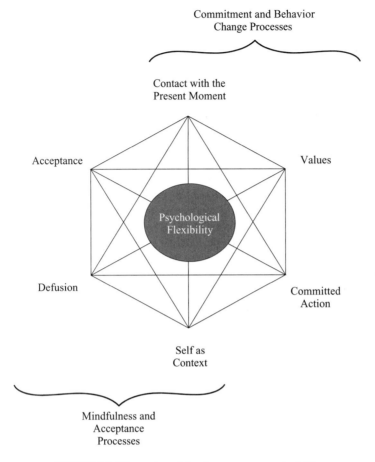

FIGURE 7.1. Illustration of the six core processes in ACT.

1999, pp. 101–104). In this metaphor, the client is told to picture that she has been placed in a field, blindfolded, and told to run around with a sack of tools. She eventually falls in a deep hole (representing her private event that she has been struggling to get rid of) and finds she has only been given a shovel. So she begins to dig (struggling to dig her way out of the hole). She notices as time goes on that this is not working to get her out of the hole, it is getting her deeper in the hole, but she remains committed to digging out of it (the paradox of how struggling with private events can make them stronger). This metaphor is used to point out how the client got where she is without blaming the client. The client's actions make sense in the context of her history. At the end of this metaphor clients are asked to put down the shovel, so that if a new way to approach their problems is discovered they will not be using the old strategies that have only served to make their problems worse.

The other part of acceptance is willingness to have difficult experiences. After a client has identified the struggle to control her problems, an ACT provider helps the client let go of the struggle. One metaphor that is used to illustrate this point is the *Tug-of-War with a Monster* metaphor (Hayes et al., 1999, p. 109). In this particular metaphor, the client is told that her struggle with anxiety, for example, is like being in a tug-of-war with a monster and there is a bottomless pit in-between them. The point here is to highlight the struggle. Then the client is asked what if her job in this metaphor is to drop the rope; drop the struggle. Awareness exercises are also often employed in this stage of treatment. For example, a client is asked to notice physical sensations and emotions and not do anything to change them.

The next component of ACT listed is defusion. Defusion is the component most heavily aimed at undermining the literal content of language. The techniques used for this component show clients that the functions of language are contextually controlled and thus it is possible to have seemingly harmful language occur without it having harmful functions. Part of the goal for this segment is to undermine clients' reason giving, cognitive avoidance, and attachment to rules indicating why one's situation must be the way it is. Clients' adherence to their reasons and rules is a big part of why they are stuck, so during defusion work the therapist works with clients at seeing their reasons as what they are: more words. There are literally scores of ACT defusion techniques but a few examples can be given. One exercise that is often done to illustrate the active part of language is the *Milk, Milk, Milk Exercise* (Hayes et al., 1999, pp. 154–156). The client is asked to say a single concrete noun (the word "milk" is the one traditionally used) and to notice the functions that it can evoke (a taste, a smell, a feeling in the mouth). That word is then repeated rapidly out loud with the therapist, usually for 20–45 seconds. Within half a minute most clients have the experience that the word temporary loses it meaning and its various derived functions disappear (e.g., one is no longer tasting anything) while its direct functions appear, sometimes for the first time ever (one truly notices the strange sound that is produced in saying "milk"). The exercise is then repeated with personally relevant and difficult thoughts (e.g., "stupid" or "mean"). This exercise, which was first described by Titchener nearly 90 years ago (1916, p. 425) quickly reduces both the believability of negative thoughts and their distressing impact (Masuda, Hayes, Sackett, & Twohig, 2004). Another exercise a therapist may use during defusion is to have the client come up with several stories that could also explain how he got to this point in his life, without changing any of the facts in the story. This exercise is used to show the arbitrariness of reasons, and the therapist then brings the focus back to what works for the client instead of what is the "true" story.

Self-as-context is based both on defusion and the acquisition of deictic relational frames such as "here/there" and "I/you." Self-as-context is a sense of perspective—the "I/here/now" from which verbal observations and verbal reports are made. This is the core of what is usually called "pure consciousness." It is a verbally based event that is separate from judgments, evaluations, emotions, decisions, or any other content because it is the context in which verbal humans contact and report about such things, not the things themselves. A metaphor that is used at this point is the *Chessboard Metaphor* (Hayes et al., 1999, pp. 190–192). In this metaphor client's emotions, judgments, evaluations, and so on are compared to black or white chess pieces and the client is asked what part she is in the game. The therapist then suggests that maybe the client is actually the board, holding all the pieces. This metaphor also highlights how the components in ACT are not fully separate. The chessboard metaphor is used to get at acceptance as well as self-as-context in that to hold the pieces is to not struggle with them.

Focus on the present moment is not a discrete intervention component in ACT so much as it is a quality of all ACT sessions. The client is repeatedly brought into rich contact with what is being felt, perceived, or thought in this very moment. Focus on the present moment is seen in the awareness exercise used during acceptance. It is also seen with defusion exercises like the *Leaves on a Stream* exercise (Hayes et al., 1999, pp. 158–162) in which the client is asked to imagine he is sitting on a hill watching leaves pass by on a stream. Then he is asked to put each thought on a leaf and watch it float down the stream noticing when the thoughts pull him into the stream or when his thoughts pull him away from the hill altogether. This is a defusion exercise because when these thoughts are taken literally the natural flow of thoughts is interrupted, but it is also an exercise in contacting the present moment and present experience. Formal mindfulness exercises are also used in this way in ACT protocols.

Together these four processes (acceptance, defusion, self-as-context, present moment) define acceptance and mindfulness processes in ACT. In addition there are behavior change and commitment processes.

One of these is values. The values component is an important part of ACT because it gives the work, both the therapist's and the client's, purpose and meaning, which is necessary in any contextualistic therapy. Having pain without a purpose is useless, and the workability focus in ACT hinges on the client's values. Do the client's old or new strategies work to get him moving toward his values? During values work clients are often asked to journal or write down their values in particular areas such as intimate relationships, family, friendships, work, education, community, and leisure and to rank the importance and current success with each value. Another values exercise is to have the client talk about what she wants engraved on her tombstone when she dies; what does she want her life to stand for and what would be written if someone were to make the epitaph now.

The last component of ACT is committed action, which focuses on building effective patterns of behavior in the service of the client's stated values. Each moment the client has a choice to behave in a way that reflects her values or to do something less in accordance with her values. During committed action the pattern that is built by each choice is examined, so it is clear to the client what her behaviors are in the service of. For example, if the client wants to be about building more social relationships, in a particular moment does the client choose to go to a social gathering or stay home and what kind of pattern of behavior is served with that choice. The aim is to help clients build larger and larger patterns of behavior that are in accordance with who they want to be. These last four processes (self-as-context, present moment, values, committed action) define behavior change and commitment processes in ACT.

EVIDENCE ON ACT

A recent review of ACT (Hayes, Masuda, Bissett, Luoma, & Guerrero, 2004) found ACT outcome research across an unusually broad range of problems, with effectiveness studies and efficacy studies in depression, psychosis, substance use disorders, eating disorders, work-related stress, and other problems. Since that review, additional successful controlled trials have appeared in several other areas such as stigma and burnout (Hayes, Bissett, Roget et al., 2004), smoking (Gifford et al., 2004), and chronic pain (Dahl, Wilson, & Nilsson, 2004; McCracken, Vowles, & Eccleston, 2005). Additionally, the ACT model has begun to be applied to prevention work. A very recent but unpublished study found that a general ACT intervention was effective at

increasing students' abilities to cope with school-related strain over a control condition (Livheim, under submission). ACT educational workshops have been shown to
prevent non-compliance following a diagnosis of type II diabetes (Gregg, 2004), or to
reduce prejudicial attitude toward others (Hayes, Lillis, & Masuda, 2005). The theory
underlying ACT explains this breadth because it is claimed that language itself creates
the problems ACT is tries to solve.

At the level of processes of change, ACT produces an unusually rapid decrease in
the believability (but not necessarily the frequency) of negative thoughts (e.g., Bach &
Hayes, 2002; Zettle & Hayes, 1986), as well as an increase in acceptance (e.g., Gifford
et al., 2004), and these changes are specifically associated with positive ACT outcomes
(e.g., Bach & Hayes, 2002; Bond & Bunce, 2000; Gifford et al., 2004; Hayes, Bissett, Roget
et al., 2004). A review of the ACT process evidence can be found in Hayes, Luoma,
Bond, Masuda and Lillis (2006).

WHEN IS HOMEWORK USED IN ACT?

ACT is a technology grounded in a particular philosophy (functional contextualism) and set of theoretical concepts (RFT and behavioral principles more generally),
and for that reason there is no one-way to do ACT. This is why ACT protocols differ from disorder to disorder, and tend to be functionally written so that they can
be further altered to fit each individual. With the exception of component studies
(e.g., Gutiérrez, Luciano, Rodríguez, & Fink, 2004; Levitt, Brown, Orsillo, & Barlow,
2004; Masuda et al., 2004) almost all ACT protocols contain the core ACT strategies
(defusion, acceptance, contact with the present moment, self-as-context, values, and
behavioral commitment) but they are emphasized to varying degrees depending on
what would be most useful given the clients presentation. For example, the treatment of psychosis stressed cognitive defusion (Bach & Hayes, 2002), whereas the
treatment of individuals at risk for long-term sick leave contained a larger values
component (Dahl, Wilson, & Nilsson, 2004). For that reason, the exact placement and
function of homework varies in ACT manuals and cases. This means for some clients,
formal homework is prescribed only a couple times throughout treatment, and for
others there is homework between every session. It all depends on what would be the
most useful, given the goals of the client and the therapist. With that said, prescribing
homework after each session is commonly the most useful. If homework is broadened
to include systematic attempts to note the relevance of session work to day-to-day
tasks and to apply skills being learned, then homework after each session is nearly
universal.

WHY IS HOMEWORK PRESCRIBED IN ACT?

In the ACT model what is going on is session overlaps with what is going on
in the natural environment and vice versa. This is especially true because human
language itself is the most common ACT target. Behavior shaped through experience
is less rigid than behavior shaped through verbal rules (Hayes, 1989), and direct
exercises and assignments often allow for skills to be shaped and practiced in ways that
are not entirely rule-governed. This is done in session through exercises, metaphors,
paradoxical language, and radically functional talk, and outside of session through
carefully planned homework assignments.

While the client is in session, the therapist has the ability to change the environment and provide opportunities for the client to experience the workability of his or her behavior. When the session is over, the client steps back into the contingencies that are probably helping to maintain the unworkable behavior. This discrepancy in the amount time the client is in session and out in the natural environment puts the therapist at a disadvantage. To some degree this disadvantage is lessened in ACT because the processes being used (e.g., defusion, acceptance) alter the functional environment in and out of session, without necessarily altering the formal environment. Still, homework provides an excellent opportunity to continue to challenge the client's agenda and provide opportunities to shape behavioral flexibility and increase workability without the client having to be in the therapy session.

Consider a client who is struggling with social anxiety. Having the client commit to engaging in something that is anxiety provoking while practicing acceptance and defusion skills can be extremely useful from an ACT perspective. Without such a homework assignment, the client would likely approach his or her day in the usual manner. This small homework assignment can assist the client in behaving differently in situations where the client usually avoids. The homework hopefully produces experiences that are meaningful and lead to greater behavioral flexibility in the presence of situations where the person usually avoids.

Another practical reason homework is important in ACT is because there are restraints placed on what the therapist and client can do in session. For example, it is difficult to create the same struggle that a person with a hoarding problem experiences at home in the therapy session. Therefore, homework is often necessary to provide experiences that will teach the core strategies of ACT in an experiential way. For example, the client might be asked to follow his or her regular routine this week while paying special attention to what one does to reduce urges to hoard. Prior to monitoring this, the client might not be aware of the entire scope of things he or she does to reduce these urges. This would have been a difficult experience to create in session, and was better illustrated through homework.

WHAT IS PRESCRIBED AS HOMEWORK?

The homework that is prescribed in an ACT session usually has to do with core ACT strategies that are being targeted in session. In individual work the content of homework is often linked to specific sessions. If a large amount of the session was spent trying to figure out what the client finds important in life, homework might involve completing a values assessment process. If a large amount of the session was spent on how the client is "buying into his or her thoughts," cognitive defusion exercises might be prescribed in the form of homework.

A more extended example of a defusion assignment might help characterize the approach. The client might be asked to spend ten minutes each day over a period of a week sitting in a comfortable position, with eyes closed, watching his or her thoughts float by on a stream. The client would be asked to pay special attention to when the stream is no longer flowing or the exercise has disappeared, indicating that the client is caught up in his or her thoughts. When he or she notices that has occurred, the client should notice what just happened, step out of that thought and begin again watching his or her thoughts on the stream. This exercise creates experiences that illustrate the difference between experiencing a thought as a thought and taking a thought literally and then experiencing the world from the point of view of that thought. This amounts to a kind of discrimination training, which increases the ability to defuse from thoughts (in this metaphor, letting them float by without attachment), increases the ability to shift from taking a thought literally to just noticing it, and perhaps most importantly, increases the ability to discriminate one mode from another. The ability to see the difference between a thought experienced as "true or false" and a thought experienced as an ongoing relational process can be extremely useful in clinically important situations outside of therapy as the client struggles with thoughts that are functioning as barriers to engaging in valued behaviors. For example, a person diagnosed with social phobia might have the thought "I cannot go to that party because I am too anxious." If that thought is experienced as literally true, the person cannot go to the party until the anxiety is eliminated or diminished. If that thought can be experienced as just a thought, additional options are now available: go to the party while thinking you can't and go to the party while feeling anxious. Going to the party *with* (not in spite of, or in resistance to) difficult thoughts or feelings challenges the client's normal agenda. This in turn increases behavioral flexibility: the ability to persist or change in the service of chosen values *with* your history and the private events it produces.

The structure of homework in ACT is very similar to homework in other types of behavior therapy. Homework is usually prescribed at the end of session, and that same homework is discussed at the beginning of the next session. When the homework is an exercise, it is often useful to practice the homework in session with the client before the session is over. Less time is required if the homework can easily be completed without assistance from the therapist.

Commercial materials in the form of workbooks are beginning to appear to help the ACT clinician with homework exercises. Heffner and Eifert (2004) have published a comprehensive ACT manual for eating disorders that can be used both as a self-help manual and as a homework aid in a course of ACT. Many of the exercises in this manual are generally useful for the ACT clinician and can be modified for specific clinical purposes other than eating disorders. A more general ACT workbook of this kind is also available (Hayes & Smith, 2005) and several additional workbooks, collections of exercises, or collections of ACT stories and metaphors are currently under contract with major publishers, covering areas of anxiety, pain, anger, and depression, among others. Examples of the kinds of exercises these books contain will be given later.

EXAMPLES OF HOMEWORK IN ACT

Many structured homework assignments are provided in the ACT book (Hayes et al., 1999) focused on the six core processes in ACT: acceptance, defusion, self-as-context, contact with the present moment, values, and committed action. Because disorders and clients differ, new exercises and homework are being created on a daily basis worldwide in the ACT community. In addition to the new books appearing, many of these are available at no cost, either through the ACT website (www.contextualpsychology.org) or through the archives of the ACT list serve (see the website above for the link).

The ACT model is specific at the level of targeted processes but open at the level of technology. Over time this is leading to many new methods being created while retaining a core coherence. This process seems likely only to accelerate as the number of people using the approach increases and it is applied to a wider and wider range of disorders and difficulties. The following section provides examples of ACT homework for each of the six core processes.

Acceptance. To orient the client to his or her experience regarding the possible benefits of acceptance over control, the *Clean and Dirty Discomfort Diary* (Hayes et al., 1999, p. 146) can be assigned. The form is completed after situations where the client struggles with thoughts, feelings, or bodily sensations that have been of particular difficulty for the client. For example, a person with a hoarding problem might find some items on sale and have the thought that he or she should purchase a large amount of them because they will not be on sale later. This homework consists of a form that contains the five following questions.

1) What was the experience?
2) What were your immediate reactions in the way of thoughts, feelings, and bodily sensations?
3) What was your level of suffering (1 = low, 100 = high)? [More specific terms for suffering can be used here to fit the client's specific problems.]
4) What did you do about your reactions?
5) What was your new level of suffering (1 = low, 100 = high)?

The client's responses might look something like:

1) "I saw the items were on sale."
2) "I thought I needed them. I would miss out on the sale. I would feel as though I missed out if I did not purchase them. I felt tense, anxious, and an urge to purchase them. I felt uncomfortable."
3) 60.
4) "I bought them so I would not feel this way."
5) 70, "I felt guilty for buying them, and I knew my wife would be upset when I got home."

Often, if the client is accepting of his or her initial reactions one will get responses like to questions 4 and 5:

4) "I did not give into the urge and continued shopping."
5) 30, "I still sort of wanted them, but the feeling was not as bad as I thought, and I was really proud of myself for not giving in, and my wife was pleased with what I purchased."

Willingness homework can start initially with fairly general exercises so that the client can begin to learn what acceptance looks like using non-clinical sensations and emotions. An example is the following (from Hayes & Smith, 2005):

"We are about to see if you are able to use acceptance to increase your ability to sit with uncomfortable emotions. Get a watch and sit somewhere where you won't be disturbed for a minute. We are going to see how long you can hold your breath ... [while doing so] ... we want you to do things such as:

• Notice exactly where the urge to breathe begins and ends in your body. Localize where you feel it.

- See if you can allow that feeling precisely there AND yet to keep on holding your breath. Turn that willingness knob all the way up! Just feel the feeling and do not breathe . . . think of this as a cool opportunity to feel something you rarely feel.
- Notice any thoughts that come up, and gently thank your mind for the thought, without being controlled by that thought. Watch out for sneaky thoughts that can quickly lead to breathing before YOU decide to breathe (e.g., "maybe if you don't breathe you will pass out" etc.). After all, who is in charge of your life? You or your word machine?
- Notice other emotions that may emerge other than the urge to breathe. See if you can make room for those emotions as well.
- Sweep through your body and notice that in addition to the urge to breathe, your body contains other sensations, and continues to function.
- Stay with a commitment to hold your breath as long as you can. As the urge gets stronger, see if you can create the same exact urge but this time one created by you. Everywhere that the first urge was felt (the one you noticed) deliberately put the second one (the exact replica you created).
- Now list a few things you may do during this exercise that will help you get present with your feelings, thoughts, sensations, and urges and yet stay with the purpose of holding your breath. Put down only acceptance strategies, not experiential control or suppression strategies.

Now take a deep breath and hold it as long as you can. When you are finished, write down how long you held it: seconds."

The client is then asked to describe the experience, to note how feelings came and went, to notice thoughts that came up, including particularly "sneaky" thoughts, and finally to link what was just done to the possibility of treating clinically relevant emotions in an accepting way.

Defusion. The functions of defusion exercises in general are to decrease the literal, temporal, and evaluative functions of verbal behavior. There are many instances where looking at the function of ones thought can be more useful than looking at the content of the thought. Reason giving is a specific example where our thoughts promote behavioral inflexibility and maintain unworkable behavior patterns. Humans create reasons for most of our behavior. In instances where we are struggling, reason giving can often be detrimental because we base our behavior on the reasons. In ACT, it is not a question of if the reason is "true" or not; the question is "does following that reason work." *Reasons as Causes Homework* illustrates how difficult it is for humans to not give reasons for our behavior (Hayes et al., 1999, p. 163). In this homework the client is asked to

1) List some of the reasons you are most likely to give to yourself or others for areas in your life that are troublesome. [Space for responding is then provided.]
2) Between now and your next session, try to notice several specific instances where you catch yourself in reason giving mode using reasons like this or others. Write several examples down. Write down how you were feeling in that situation. Then describe how you felt or what you thought when you noticed yourself giving reasons. Bring this in for discussion at your next session. Note whether the reasons you caught yourself using were similar to those listed above.

An example of a response to this form could be as follows:

1) "My parents abused me and did not support me as a child; I never had a good chance."
2) "I was playing with my child and he got upset with me because I didn't know how to play a game properly. I felt like a bad parent, like I should know how to do these things. I blamed my parents for me being incompetent. It made me feel as though I would never be a good parent, like I never had a chance. I noticed I go into this story whenever things go wrong with my children rather than figuring out how to do better. These reasons cause me to give up too quickly."

Assigned mindfulness exercises are commonly used in defusion homework, as well as practice in using a variety of ACT defusion methods with difficult thoughts (e.g., saying the thought extremely slowly; singing the thoughts; saying them in the voice of your least favorite politician; imagining that your negative thoughts were computer pop up ads).

Defusion work is especially important when applied to temporal and evaluative relations, so specific training is sometimes done to help people learn to distinguish descriptive from evaluative talk. For example, Hayes and Smith (2005) have clients distinguish between properties that would disappear if there were no living creatures anywhere in the universe and those that would not. A good wooden table is an example. The woodenness of the table is not dependent on human beings being present (thus, woodenness is a "primary" or descriptive attribute), but its "goodness" is (thus, goodness is a "secondary" or evaluative attribute). As homework, people are asked to list attributes of various objects (movies, trees, and so on) and then to sort these attributes into primary and secondary categories. In the case of a tree, for example, "leaves" are descriptive, but "beautiful" is not. Beautiful describes ones *evaluative reaction* to the tree, not the tree itself. After several examples, clients are then asked to describe the attributes of a recent clinically relevant emotional experience, and to sort these into descriptive and evaluative categories. Defusion techniques are then applied to the latter category (e.g., "I am having the thought that this emotion is too painful").

Self-as-Context

Meditation and mindfulness exercises are the most common forms of homework to help build a transcendent sense of self, but other homework exercises can help set up work on the self. For example, the client could complete the following homework in a journal so that it can easily be discussed at the following session.

1) Specify different time frames in your life (childhood, teens, young adult, adult, etc.).
2) For each time frame, describe yourself during that time (what was occurring in your life, important events, what was your personality like, your thoughts and feelings at that time, what other people thought of you).
3) Write down what was different between these times and what was the same.

This homework should be brought to session and discussed with the therapist. In the discussion the therapist helps the client get back "behind the eyes" of the child that he or she once was. The function of this exercise is to assist the client in seeing that he or she was consciously present at all of these events. Therefore, one thing that is common among these events is the client's sense of self as a place from which experiences occur.

CONTACT WITH THE PRESENT MOMENT

Contact with the present moment exercises are meant to orient clients to the world as they experience it directly, rather than the world as structured by the products of thought. There are a number of exercises that allow the client to contact the present moment. One example is the *Tin Can Monster Exercise* (Hayes et al., 1999, pp. 171–174) that involves mindfully paying attention to the dimensions of experience while contacting emotional experience. When done as homework, typically this exercise is graded, so that the client has little risk of being overwhelmed—that is, it is used with mildly aversive emotional material and only as the client gains ability is it done with more difficult material. When used as homework, it would usually be done in the form of a tape that can be played at home.

The therapist should have the client begin by sitting in a comfortable position with his or her eyes closed. The therapist should help the client focus on the present moment by guiding the client's attention to his or her bodily sensations including one's breathing. The client should pay close attention to the feeling of the air as it comes in and leaves the body. The client should be prompted to bring one's attention back to the present moment when the client gets caught up in his or her thoughts.

Then the client is asked to get in touch with the previously specified feeling or situation (e.g., "how you felt when criticized last week by your spouse"). The client is then asked to notice what comes up in his or her body, emotionally, thoughts, urges to behave overtly, memories, and so on. As each dimension is covered, the client is asked to let go of any struggle with it and just "get present with it." For example, the tape might say:

> "Now I want you to bring into your consciousness the feeling that came up when you were criticized by your spouse last week. And as you do so watch quietly for what your body does. Be like a person in the wild behind a blind watching the wildlife go by: your job is to sit psychologically still and just watch your body. As you do that see if you can find one specific bodily sensation to focus on—if several show up, just come down to one of them. [pause] Now when you get that see if you can notice exactly where that feeling begins and ends. [pause] Imagine that the feeling was colored as if with a coloring pen. See if you can notice the shape it makes in your body. And as you do that, drop any sense of defense or struggle with this simple bodily sensation . . . . If other feelings crowd in, let them know we will get to them later. See if it is possible just to be present with it a little more . . . and then even a little more. [pause] Now I want you to set that reaction aside and get back in touch with the feeling that came up when you were criticized by your spouse last week. And as you do so watch quietly for what your body does. And again see if you can find one specific bodily sensation to focus on—if several show up once more, just come down to one of these to look at. [pause]"

This pattern is repeated at least three times for each dimension. As dimensions change, the specific things said to help the person be present with that domain change. For example, locating bodily sensations makes sense, but with thoughts it might be better to focus on the sound of the words that describes the thought, or the images that they evoke

VALUES

The *Values Assessment Exercise* (Hayes et al., 1999, p. 226) can be used as a guide to help the client clarify his or her values and where one's behavior is inconsistent with one's values. The homework begins by having the client define his or her values in each of the following areas:

1. Marriage/couples/intimate relations
2. Family relations
3. Friendships/social relations
4. Career/employment
5. Education/personal growth & development
6. Recreation/leisure
7. Spirituality
8. Citizenship
9. Health/physical well-being

Next, the client is asked to read and then rate each of the values narratives generated on three different areas. First, the client rates how important the value is on a scale of 1 to 10. Second, the client rates how successfully he or she has been living this value during the past month on a scale of 1 to 10. Third, the client rates the values in order of the importance. This homework has multiple functions. It helps the client define what he or she values and it assists the client in seeing where there are the largest discrepancies between what he or she values in life and how one is behaving.

Another example of an ACT values exercise might be to write out the eulogy one would hope might be given at one's own funeral if one lived his or her life fully from here. In session, this eulogy might actually be read aloud by the client and the emotions it evokes would be processed.

COMMITTED ACTION

This is the area of ACT that will differ the most between disorders and clients. This component of ACT is basically traditional behavior therapy, where nearly any behavior change technique is suitable. The only difference is that the behavior therapy work is done from an ACT perspective. This phase of ACT can include goal setting, guided exposure, skills training, or any of a variety of behavior change methods. When these behavior change strategies are presented to the client, they are done within an ACT framework. For example, a client with social phobia might agree to go for a walk through an area where one's anxiety increases. This homework exercise would be completed as a type of willingness exercise.

ACT AND SELF HELP

ACT is a newer behavior therapy: the first full-length description of the treatment was published in 1999 (Hayes et al., 1999). The availability of self-help books done from an ACT perspective is limited, but it is growing. One available self-help book done from an ACT perspective is focused on the treatment of eating disorders (Heffner & Eifert, 2004). Hayes and Smith (2005) have written a more general self-help book from the ACT perspective. Self-help books on several other topics are under contract or are being negotiated.

Self-help books can be integrated into therapy by working through a published workbook together or using the workbook exercises as a supplement. In the first example, ACT homework can structure therapy itself. ACT-style self-help books are especially experiential; they are full of exercises and assignments. The risk of getting very verbally intertwined with the material and "trying to figure it out" could presumably be higher when acquiring it solely through a written medium. This risk may be decreased if the therapist presented some of the same exercises and then had the client practice them using the book as an aid. For this reason, completing a self-help book with one's therapist might increase its effectiveness, although this will need to be determined empirically. Following a more standardized protocol can be helpful for those who are less familiar with the therapy, which suggests that workbook-based therapy might be more effective than therapy without the workbook.

The other way that self-help material can be added to therapy is by supplementing the material from session with material from self-help books. So far these published self-help books generally follow the same sequencing as most ACT outcome studies or as described in the original ACT book (Hayes et al, 1999). Therefore, clinicians can easily accompany therapy with these books or selected chapters from these books. For example, in an ongoing study on the use of ACT for the self-stigmatizing attitudes of persons in recovery from drug and alcohol abuse (Luoma, Kohlenberg, Bunting, & Hayes, 2005), a client workbook is being used that covers all of the elements of the protocol, with brief descriptions of key concepts that echoed those that would be covered in therapy sessions and exercises that added to those that would be done directly. Clinicians can give clients pertinent chapters from self-help books to assist with core concepts that require additional time. For example, one of the authors recently treated a client for a substance abuse problem and the client was very fused with the belief that he must get rid of his urge to use substances in order to stop using. To aid the material presented in session the client was given two chapters from Hayes and Smith (2005) that focused on decreasing the control agenda and increasing one's willingness to experience the urge to use. This is an example of a situation where the self-help book aided what was presented in therapy.

CLINICAL EXAMPLE

CASE STUDY: HOARDING

Background: The client was a 55-year-old male who worked as a financial planner in a large metropolitan city. His wife of many years recently threatened divorce and told him that his hoarding was getting out-of-control and was receiving more attention than she was. Most of the items that he hoarded pertained to investment opportunities such as newspaper articles, magazines, flyers, and business documents from work. The hoarding involved collecting these items through the house, and as the piles got too large and in the way, they would be moved from the house to the basement, garage, or one of many storage units. He reported that he saved these items as reference for when clients asked him questions, although he admitted that he could never find the item because of the large quantity that he accumulated. He wanted assistance in decreasing his hoarding so that he could save his marriage.

Treatment: The first two sessions focused on his reactions to urges to hoard. We evaluated what he tried to do when the urge to hoard showed up, and how well those strategies worked to decrease the urge. The client could not think of anything that decreased the urge except hoarding, although he was confident there must be a way. To let the client experience the true effectiveness of the control agenda, the client was asked to try every technique he could think of to decrease his urges to hoard as they showed up. He was asked to journal what he tried, how well it worked, and how pleased he was with the outcome. The results of this homework illustrated that the only thing that reduced his urge was hoarding, that it only reduced the urge for a brief period of time, and that he was not pleased with the way hoarding was impacting his life. The homework for the second session involved assessing all the different ways he had tried to reduce his urges to hoard. The natural ways that the client responded to his urges to hoard included: trying to talk himself out of it, rationalizing with himself, distraction from the item, compromising, avoiding, reassuring that he was competent in this area, and hoarding. These two homework assignment plus the work in session decreased the client's attachment to the idea that hoarding was being controlled through controlling the urge. It became evident to the client that he had been working very hard throughout his life to decrease his urge to hoard, but that none of his moves worked in a fundamental way to decrease this feeling.

The idea that attempts at controlling the urge was itself the problem, and that willingness to experience it was a viable alternative, were presented during the third and fourth sessions. The client was given the Clean vs. Dirty Discomfort Diary described in the Acceptance section as homework in the third session. This allowed the client to see that hoarding did not reduce his level of suffering and that not giving into the urge often had surprisingly pleasing effects. After the fourth session he was given the Daily Willingness Diary (Hayes et al., 1999, p. 144) to assess the overall workability of willingness as compared to control. In this homework the client was asked to evaluate 1) how strong his urges to hoard were throughout the day, 2) how much he struggled with them and tried to control them, and then 3) if every day were like today how vital would your life feel? The client was somewhat surprised to see that workability (question 3) correlated more with struggle (question 2) rather than with urges (question 1)—indicating that it was not the content that was hurting as much as the client's reaction to that content. These homework assignments and the work done in session increased the client's willingness to experience the urge more fully without doing anything to decrease it, including hoarding. Significant decreases in hoarding were seen during sessions three and four.

The fifth and sixth session included defusion, self-as-context, and contact with present moment exercises. Homework involved the *Leaves on a Stream* exercise described earlier and a somewhat similar *Awareness of Ones Experience* exercise designed to mindfully notice the breadth of experiences that are available in any one moment. Both of these exercises were practiced once during the session and then given as homework. These exercises promote, defusion, self-as-context, and contact with the present moment. Defusion exercises helped decrease the believability of the client's urges to hoard making acceptance of the urges easier.

The final two sessions (sessions seven and eight) involved values work and behavioral commitment exercises. The client completed the *Values Assessment Exercise*

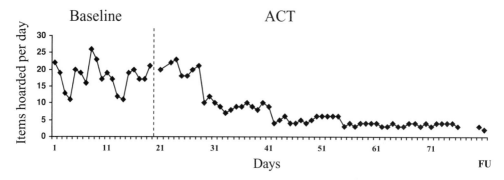

FIGURE 7.2. Daily frequency of compulsions, case example.

described in the Values section. Then, based on his values the client committed to making certain behavioral changes. The Values Assessment Exercise illustrated that his hoarding was getting in the way in many areas that he valued more than hoarding. He committed to a schedule that involved 1) gradually cleaning out one of his storage units, 2) gradually cleaning out his house, and 3) gradually decreasing the amount of items that he brings home per day. For example he committed to taking one truck full of items out of his storage unit every weekend until it was empty, then he would turn do the same with his home, while concurrently decreasing the amount of items that he brings home by one per day per week.

To monitor the affects of the intervention and help focus the client on the treatment, he recorded the number of items hoarded each day. His baseline, posttreatment, and three-month follow-up averages were 18, 7, and 3 items per day respectively (see Figure 7.2). These results were corroborated by similar decreases on the Obsessive Compulsive Inventory (Foa, Kozak, Salkovskis, Coles, & Amir, 1998; 74 pre, 50 post, 23 follow-up); Beck Anxiety Inventory (Beck, Epstein, Brown, & Steer, 1988; 11 pre, 9 post, 4 follow-up); and the Beck Depression Inventory (Beck, 1996; 15 pre, 9 post, 0 follow-up). The client's decreases in hoarding were also associated with decreases on scores on the Acceptance and Action Questionnaire (a general measure of experiential avoidance; Hayes et al., 2004; 28 pre, 17 post, 10 follow-up), and decreases in believability and need to react to the obsession (4 pre, 2 post, 3 follow-up; on a scale of 1 to 5 where 5 indicates a highly believable or a high need to react to the obsession). Additionally, the client rated the intervention as acceptable on the Treatment Evaluation Inventory-Short Form (Kelley, Heffer, Gresham, & Elliot, 1989).

CONCLUSION

ACT is an example of a third wave behavior therapy that saves direct change strategies for overt behaviors and utilizes contextual and experiential methods such as mindfulness and acceptance to address cognitive process that hinder and limit overt behavioral change. The treatment is informed by RFT and is based on the philosophical position of functional contextualism. ACT seeks to undermine the literal grip of language (relational framing) that fosters experiential avoidance, cognitive fusion, and behavioral inflexibility, through the application of six core psychological techniques: acceptance, defusion, contact with the present moment, self-as as-context, values, and commitment to behavior change. Homework can play an integral role in the application of these techniques, by supporting the in-session therapy. Homework can be especially useful because it allows the client to utilize these principles in situations that cannot be created in the therapy sessions, such as public situation for someone who struggles with anxiety. As with most therapies, ACT has its own homework assignments, but therapists often create new techniques to serve the clients needs.

REFERENCES

Bach, P. & Hayes, S. C. (2002). The use of Acceptance and Commitment Therapy to prevent the rehospitalization of psychotic patients: A randomized controlled trial. *Journal of Consulting and Clinical Psychology, 70,* 1129–1139.

Beck, A. T. (1996). *Beck Depression Inventory* (2nd ed.). San Antonio, TX: The Psychological Corporation.

Beck, A. T., Epstein, N. Brown, G., & Steer, R. A. (1988). An inventory for measuring clinical anxiety: Psychometric properties. *Journal of Consulting and Clinical Psychology, 56,* 893–897.

Biglan, A. & Hayes, S. C. (1996). Should the behavioral sciences become more pragmatic? The case for functional contextualism in research on human behavior. *Applied and Preventive Psychology: Current Scientific Perspectives, 5,* 47–57.

Bond, F. W. & Bunce, D. (2003). The role of acceptance and job control in mental health, job satisfaction, and work performance. *Journal of Applied Psychology, 88,* 1057–1067.

Dahl, J., Wilson, K. G., & Nilsson, A. (2004). Acceptance and Commitment Therapy and the treatment of persons at risk for long-term disability resulting from stress and pain symptoms: A preliminary randomized trial. *Behavior Therapy, 35,* 785–802.

Foa, E. B., Kozak, M. J., Salkovskis, P. M., Coles, M. E., & Amir, N. (1998). The validation of a new obsessive-compulsive disorder scale: The obsessive-compulsive inventory. *Psychological Assessment, 10,* 206–214.

Gifford, E. V., Kohlenberg, B. S., Hayes, S. C., Antonuccio, D. O., Piasecki, M. M., Rasmussen-Hall, M. L., et al. (2004). Acceptance theory-based treatment for smoking cessation: An initial trial of Acceptance and Commitment Therapy. *Behavior Therapy, 35,* 689–705.

Gregg, J. (2004). *Development of an acceptance-based treatment for the self-management of diabetes.* Doctoral dissertation, University of Nevada, Reno.

Gutiérrez, O., Luciano, C., Rodríguez, M., & Fink, B. C. (2004). Comparison between an acceptance-based and a cognitive-control-based protocol for coping with pain. *Behavior Therapy, 35,* 767–783.

Hayes, S. C. (Ed.). (1989). *Rule-governed behavior: Cognition, contingencies, and instructional control.* New York: Plenum.

Hayes, S. C. (1993). Analytic goals and the varieties of scientific contextualism. In S. C. Hayes, L. J. Hayes, H. W. Reese, & T. R. Sarbin (Eds.), *Varieties of scientific contextualism* (pp. 11–27). Reno, NV: Context Press.

Hayes, S. C., Barnes-Holmes, D., & Roche, B. (2001) (Eds.), *Relational Frame Theory: A Post-Skinnerian account of human language and cognition.* New York: Plenum Press.

Hayes, S. C., Bissett, R., Roget, N., Padilla, M., Kohlenberg, B. S., Fisher, et al. (2004). The impact of acceptance and commitment training and multicultural training on the stigmatizing attitudes and professional burnout of substance abuse counselors. *Behavior Therapy, 35,* 821–835.

Hayes, S. C. & Brownstein, A. J. (1986). Mentalism, behaviorbehavior relations and a behavior analytic view of the purposes of science. *The Behavior Analyst, 9,* 175–190.

Hayes, S. C., Hayes, L. J., Reese, H. W., & Sarbin, T. R. (Eds.). (1993).*Varieties of scientific contextualism*. Reno, NV: Context Press.

Hayes, S. C., Lillis, J., & Masuda, A. (May 2005). *The struggle against intolerance*. Paper presented at the meeting of the Association for Behavior Analysis, Chicago.

Hayes, S. C., Luoma, J., Bond, F., Masuda, A., & Lillis, J. (2006). Acceptance and Commitment Therapy: Model, processes, and outcomes. *Behaviour Research and Therapy, 44*, 1–25.

Hayes, S. C., Masuda, A., Bissett, R., Luoma, J., & Guerrero, L. F. (2004). DBT, FAP, and ACT: How empirically oriented are the new behavior therapy technologies? *Behavior Therapy, 35*, 35–54.

Hayes, S. C. & Smith, S. (2005). *Get out of your mind and into your life*. Oakland, CA: New Harbinger.

Hayes, S. C., Strosahl, K. & Wilson, K. G. (1999). *Acceptance and Commitment Therapy: An experiential approach to behavior change*. New York: Guilford Press.

Hayes, S. C., Strosahl, K. D., Wilson, K. G., Bissett, R. T., Pistorello, J., Toarmino, et al. (2004). Measuring experiential avoidance: A preliminary test of a working model. *The Psychological Record, 54*, 553–578.

Hayes, S. C., Wilson, K. W., Gifford, E. V., Follette, V. M., & Strosahl, K. (1996). Emotional avoidance and behavioral disorders: A functional dimensional approach to diagnosis and treatment. *Journal of Consulting and Clinical Psychology, 64*, 1152–1168.

Heffner, M. & Eifert, G. H. (2004). *The anorexia workbook: How to accept yourself, heal suffering, and reclaim your life*. Oakland, CA: New Harbinger.

Jacobson, N. S. & Christensen, A. (1996). *Integrative couple therapy: Promoting acceptance and change*. New York, NY: Norton.

Kelly, M. L., Heffer, R. W., Gresham, F. M., & Elliot, S. N. (1989). Development of a modified treatment evaluation inventory. *Journal of Psychopathology and Behavioral Assessment, 11*, 235–247.

Kohlenberg, R. J. & Tsai, M. (1991). *Functional analytic psychotherapy: Creating intense and curative therapeutic relationships*. New York: Plenum.

Livheim, F. (unpublished manuscript). Acceptance and Commitment Therapy in the prevention of school related stress.

Levitt, J. T., Brown, T. A., Orsillo, S. M., & Barlow, D. H. (2004). The effects of acceptance versus suppression of emotion on subjective and psychophysiological response to carbon dioxide challenge in patients with panic disorder. *Behavior Therapy, 35*, 747–766.

Linehan, M. M. (1993). *Cognitive-behavioral treatment of borderline personality disorder*. New York: Guilford.

Luoma, J. B., Kohlenberg, B. S., Bunting, K. & Hayes, S. C. (May 2005). *ACT and self-stigma in substance abuse: A pilot study*. Paper presented at the meeting of the Association for Behavior Analysis, Chicago.

Masuda, A., Hayes, S. C., Sackett, C. F., & Twohig, M. P. (2004). Cognitive defusion and self-relevant negative thoughts: Examining the impact of a ninety year old technique. *Behaviour Research and Therapy, 42*, 477–485.

McCracken, L. M., Vowles, K. E., & Eccleston, C. (2005). Acceptance-based treatment for persons with complex, long-standing chronic pain: A preliminary analysis of treatment outcome in comparison to a waiting phase. *Behaviour Research and Therapy, 43*, 1335–1346.

Segal, Z. V., Williams, J. M. G., & Teasdale, J. D. (2002). *Mindfulness-based cognitive therapy for depression: A new approach to preventing relapse*. New York: Guilford Press.

Titchener, E. B. (1916). *A text-book of psychology*. New York: MacMillan.

Zettle, R. D. & Hayes, S. C. (1986). Dysfunctional control by client verbal behavior: The context of reason giving. *The Analysis of Verbal Behavior, 4*, 30–38.

CHAPTER 8

BRIEF STRATEGIC FAMILY THERAPY

Michael S. Robbins, José Szapocznik, and Gonzalo A. Pérez

Brief Strategic Family Therapy (BSFT) is a research-proven family prevention and treatment approach that was developed and refined over 30 years of clinical and research experience with Hispanic and African American adolescents in Miami (Szapocznik, Hervis, & Schwartz, 2003; Szapocznik & Kurtines, 1989; Szapocznik & Williams, 2000). BSFT has clearly articulated goals (e.g., improvements in family interactions and reduction or prevention of child/adolescent behavior problems) and intervention strategies that are described in a detailed treatment manual (Szapocznik et al., 2003). One important aspect of BSFT is a systematic focus on providing opportunities for families to practice new behaviors and behavior patterns, both in and out of intervention sessions. With respect to the latter, BSFT provides detailed guidelines about how and when to assign homework tasks to facilitate the emergence of new and more adaptive family interactions. The purpose of this chapter is to present the nature of homework assignments in BSFT and the therapist's decision-making process as s/he assigns tasks to family members.

Before discussing homework assignments, however, it is important to understand the context in which homework is being assigned. As such, we begin this chapter with a brief overview of the origins and theoretical underpinnings of BSFT (Section I). In Section II, we present research support for BSFT, anecdotal evidence supporting the importance of homework, and recommendations for future research and developments. Section III presents two case studies of homework in BSFT. Finally, in Section IV, we present the nature of homework in BSFT, including subsections describing the philosophy of assigning tasks, how tasks are assigned, how the nature of tasks evolves over the course of treatment, and common barriers to the successful completion of homework.

SECTION I: THEORETICAL UNDERPINNINGS AND RESEARCH SUPPORT OF BSFT

The origins of BSFT occurred in the early 1970s when the Center for Family Studies (CFS) at the University of Miami (initially the Spanish Family Guidance Center) was formed to address the treatment needs of Hispanic children and adolescents in Miami, Florida. Our first goal at the CFS was to identify and/or develop a culturally appropriate treatment intervention for Hispanic youth with behavior problems. For this we conducted a study comparing the value orientations of the local Hispanic population and the mainstream population [Szapocznik, Scopetta, & King (now Hervis), 1978]. Findings revealed that Hispanics were present-focused, hierarchically oriented, and favored a focus on the family. Because of the primacy on the family, we reviewed the "state of the art" in clinical practice in the early 1970s and were impressed with the fit between our identified Hispanic value orientations or world views and the structural family therapy approach developed by Salvador Minuchin and colleagues at the Philadelphia Child Guidance Center (cf. Minuchin, 1974; Minuchin & Fishman, 1981). Specifically, structural family therapy is present-oriented, respects the population's hierarchical family values, and—similarly—provides a strong rationale for therapists assuming a leadership role with the family. Also, we were struck by the similarities between the clinical population on which structural family therapy was being developed, including large numbers of Puerto Ricans, and our families in Miami. For these reasons, we initially adopted a structural family therapy (Minuchin, 1974; Minuchin & Fishman, 1981; Minuchin, Rosman, & Baker, 1978) approach at the CFS. Over time, we have integrated strategic aspects of family therapy proposed by Haley (1976) and Madanes (1981) into BSFT through a systematic program of clinical research and practice. In its current form, BSFT represents a time-limited family-based intervention that incorporates both structural and strategic elements.

Contextual Focus

BSFT is based on the fundamental assumption that the family is the "bedrock" of child development (Szapocznik & Coatsworth, 1999). That is, the family is viewed as the primary context in which children learn to think, feel, and behave. Family relations are believed to play a pivotal role in shaping child and adolescent development and behavior, and, consequently, are a primary target for prevention and treatment interventions. BSFT recognizes that the family itself is part of a larger social system and—in much the same way as a child is influenced by her/his family—the family is influenced by the larger social system in which it exists (Bronfenbrenner, 1977, 1979, 1986). This includes an understanding of the important influence of peers, school, and the neighborhood on the development of children's behavioral problems. In BSFT, this contextualism also includes a focus on parents' relationships to children's peers, schools, and neighborhoods as well as a focus on the unique relationships that parents have with individuals and systems outside of the family (e.g., work, Alcoholics Anonymous). At the broadest contextual level, BSFT recognizes the role that cultural factors play in the development and maintenance of behavior problems.

BSFT is best articulated around three central constructs: System, Structure/ Patterns of Interactions, and Strategy (Szapocznik & Kurtines, 1989).

System

A system is an organized whole that is comprised of parts that are interdependent or interrelated. A family is a system that is comprised of individuals whose behaviors affect other family members. Because such behaviors have occurred thousands of times over many years, family members become accustomed to the behavior of other family members. These behaviors synergistically work together to organize a family's system.

Structure

A central characteristic of a system is that it is comprised of parts that interact with each other. The set of repetitive patterns of interactions that are idiosyncratic to a family is called the family's structure. A maladaptive family structure is characterized by repetitive family interactions that persist despite the fact that these interactions fail to meet the needs of the family or its individual members. A maladaptive family structure is viewed as an important contributor to the occurrence and maintenance of behavior problems, such as conduct problems and drug abuse. BSFT specifically targets those family structures (e.g., patterns of interaction) that have been shown to be predictors of drug abuse and related antisocial behaviors in the research literature (cf. Szapocznik & Coatsworth, 1999).

Strategy

The third fundamental concept of BSFT, strategy, is defined by interventions that are practical, problem-focused, and planned. Practical interventions are selected for their likelihood to move the family toward desired objectives. Problem-focused interventions are implemented to specifically target patterns of family interactions that are viewed as being directly linked to adolescent problem behaviors. Finally, interventions are planned to maximize the impact of BSFT on the family.

DIMENSIONS OF FAMILY FUNCTIONING ADDRESSED IN BSFT

To diagnose the family's problems, therapists examine family interactions along five interactional dimensions: Organization, Resonance, Developmental Stage, Identified Patienthood, and Conflict Resolution (see Table 8.1).

Organization consists of leadership, hierarchy, and communication flow. Resonance identifies the degree of connectedness among family members, ranging from enmeshment (over involved) to disengagement (under involved). Developmental Stage refers to the degree to which the adolescent is parentified or is infantilized within the family, as well as the degree to which extended family members usurp parental roles and responsibilities (e.g., grandparents undermining parent's rules). Identified Patienthood assesses the degree to which the adolescent's problems are centralized within the family. Conflict Resolution identifies the family's characteristic manner of resolving differences of opinion.

TREATMENT PLANNING IN BSFT

The therapist's assessment on these five dimensions is used to develop a treatment plan that strategically and systematically addresses the repetitive patterns of interactions that are directly linked to the prevention or reduction of the youth's problem behaviors. In addition, the treatment plan strategically addresses problems that are

TABLE 8.1. Dimensions of family and ecological functioning

Organization	Resonance	Developmental stage	Identified patienthood	Conflict resolution
Hierarchy/leadership • One parent is more active than the other. • Child is more powerful than parents. • Lack of collaborative leadership between parents. *Behavior control* • Parents not engaging in effective behavior control when needed / behavior control attempts are ineffective. *Guidance/nurturance* • Parents not nurturing/poor role models. *Spousal subsystem* • Marital relationship is poor. *Sibling Subsystem* • Relationship between siblings is poor. *Triangulation* • Child is stuck in conflict between adults. *Communication flow* • Family members don't communicate directly.	*Enmeshment* • Psychological, emotional, or physical boundaries between family members are very close. *Disengagement* • Psychological, emotional, or physical boundaries between family members are very distant.	*Parenting* • Parent(s) is immature. *Children* • Child is treated or acts too young (e.g., overly restricted, low requirement / opportunity for responsible behavior, no negotiation allowed). • Child is treated or acts too old (e.g., exhibits parent-like behavior or is overloaded with adult tasks). *Extended family* • Extended relative(s) treats parent(s) as child and/or usurps parental role.	*Negativity* • Family members are negative or critical towards the identified patient *Centrality* • The identified patient is almost always the central topic of discussion • Family members are organized around the identified patient and his/her problems *Support* • Family members protect or support the identified patient.	*Denial/avoidance* • Family members deny/avoid conflict. *Diffusion* • Family members jump from conflict to conflict without achieving any depth regarding any particular issue. *Emergence without resolution* • Family engages in an in-depth discussion about a particular issue but is not able to resolve the problem. *Negativity /conflict* • Family interactions are openly critical or hostile

relatively easier to change in early sessions to create positive therapeutic experiences for family members.

Process vs. Content

The distinction between the process of interactions between family members and content of such interactions is absolutely critical to BSFT. Family *process* is represented by the interactions that are linked to the problem symptoms. More specifically, process refers to the flow and patterns of interaction between family members. *Content*, on the other hand, is the actual verbal content or dialogue between family members. Content varies from moment to moment, from circumstance to circumstance, from situation to situation. But process is repetitive, ingrained in the fiber of a family. Because the primary goal of the BSFT therapist is to change maladaptive behavior patterns in the family, the target of her/his interventions is always process, not content. In other words, the focus or BSFT is to change the nature of the interactions that constitute the family's process.

Enactments: The Corner Stone for Assessing and Changing Family Interactions

As noted above, the primary target of assessment and intervention in BSFT is family process. However, obtaining an accurate assessment of family process is essential. Family process is often elusive and difficult to identify because therapists and family members have a tendency to focus more on the content of what family members are saying than on how they are speaking with one another. Sometimes the context of treatment itself can create obstacles for accurately identifying family processes. For example, family members who are active within the family system may become intimidated by the presence of a therapist and remain quiet and passive during treatment. Also, individual family members may attempt to ally with the therapist by sharing "their side of the story" directly with him/her, limiting their interactions with the other members of the family. Considering this, it is essential that the BSFT therapist implement interventions that will elicit the patterns of interaction that are characteristic to the family. This is called *Enactment*.

Enactments refer to family members behaving/interacting in their characteristic manner, that is, as they would naturally behave if the therapist were not present. Very frequently, family members will spontaneously enact (e.g., behave) in their typical way when they fight, interrupt, or criticize one another, etc. Quite often, however, the therapist will need to facilitate family enactments. Facilitating enactments is typically done by systematically redirecting communications to encourage interactions between session participants rather than interactions between session participants and the therapist. By encouraging family members to interact directly with one another, the therapist creates opportunities to (a) assess/diagnose family strengths and weaknesses and (b) create opportunities for the family to practice new behaviors in the session.

Family enactments, then, are a key element of the diagnostic and restructuring process in BSFT, providing essential information for the formulation of an appropriate and potentially successful treatment plan. Interventions designed to promote change in maladaptive behavioral sequences, including in-session tasks and homework tasks, should naturally derive from diagnostic enactments. As we mentioned before, homework tasks in BSFT are always process-focused, and diagnostic enactments allow the therapist to clearly observe the family's process and thus design and assign tasks that are appropriate in terms of (a) the target behaviors they are intended to change and (b) the probability of successful completion by the family.

Restructuring Family Interactions

The ultimate goal in BSFT is to transform maladaptive patterns of family interaction into adaptive patterns that protect or prevent youth from engaging in problem behaviors. Restructuring interventions in BSFT are planned, problem-focused, direction-oriented (i.e., strategic), and practical. Change strategies used include transforming the meaning of interactions through cognitive restructuring interventions called reframes. Reframes are intended to transform negative affect expressed by family members to create a context where more effective family interactions can occur. Other change interventions include: (a) directing, redirecting, or blocking communication, (b) shifting family alliances, (c) placing parents in charge, (d) helping families to develop conflict resolution skills, (e) developing effective behavior management skills, and (f) fostering parenting and parental leadership skills.

Enactments are essential to successful restructuring. BSFT is focused on doing rather than talking about. As such, the therapist introduces new frames or themes (i.e., reframes), coaches family members to behave differently, and pushes an interaction beyond where family members are typically comfortable. All of these strategies are intended to facilitate the emergence new patterns of interaction between family members. Homework builds on this in-session work by providing opportunities for family members to practice and solidify the gains that are made in treatment.

SECTION II: RESEARCH SUPPORT FOR BSFT

A systematic program of research has documented the positive impact of BSFT with behavior problem or "at-risk" children and adolescents, including reductions in conduct problems, association with antisocial peers, and drug use (Santisteban et al., 2003; Szapocznik et al., 1986; Szapocznik et al., 1988). Outcome evidence is important for supporting the usefulness of choosing one therapy approach over another; however, outcomes do not shed light on the mechanisms by which therapy is successful. Below, we review evidence on the efficacy of BSFT in (a) improving family functioning and (b) engaging and retaining adolescents and family members in treatment. Although these research findings do not provide direct evidence documenting the effects of structured tasks, including homework, these studies do provide support (albeit indirect) for the importance of well-planned, structured homework tasks as a vehicle for implementing and consolidating behavioral change in the family.

FAMILY FUNCTIONING

Given the presumed theoretical relationship between improvements in family interactions and the prevention or reduction of behavior problems, we have conducted numerous studies examining the efficacy of BSFT in improving family functioning.

In a study comparing the efficacy of BSFT with a non-family approach with children, (Szapocznik et al., 1989), the SFSR successfully differentiated treatment family interaction outcomes for 69 Hispanic behavior problem 6- to 11-year-old boys that were randomly assigned to one of the three treatment conditions: (a) BSFT, (b) individual psychodynamic child-centered psychotherapy, and (c) a recreational control condition. Although the two treatment conditions were not significantly different in their effect on behavior problems (both outperformed the recreational control), findings revealed a clear distinction between the two treatment modalities in terms of family functioning. In particular, BSFT was significantly more effective than individual child psychodynamic therapy in improving and protecting family functioning at the one-year follow-up. In the individual psychodynamic child therapy condition, a significant deterioration of family functioning was observed at the one-year post-termination follow up, while BSFT cases showed a significant improvement in family functioning at the same assessment time point.

Another study compared BSFT to a group counseling control condition (Santisteban et al., 2002). Compared to the group control condition, BSFT produced increases in adolescent-reported family cohesion and improvements in observer-reported family functioning. Additional analyses revealed that improvements in the BSFT condition were responsible for the family cohesion effect and that deterioration in the group control was responsible for the family functioning effect. This finding is consistent with the prior study (Szapocznik et al., 1989) that showed improvement in family functioning for the BSFT condition and deterioration in family functioning for an individual child psychodynamic control.

An additional study demonstrated that BSFT was associated with significant improvements in family functioning in a drug abuse prevention study. In this study, both adolescents and parents reported significant improvements in parent-adolescent communication as a result of BSFT (Santisteban et al., 1997).

Our research team has also begun to narrow our focus to identify the process of family interactional changes as they occur over the course of treatment (Robbins et al., 2002). Using a rating system that is based on the SFSR, we rated family functioning in treatment sessions for families that showed significant improvements or deteriorations in adolescent conduct problems. Results demonstrated a linear trend of improvement in patterns of family interactions over the course of treatment for successful outcome cases. In contrast, unsuccessful outcome cases showed no improvements or a worsening in repetitive patterns of interactions throughout treatment.

Taken together, these studies provide support for the efficacy of BSFT in improving family functioning. Unfortunately, we have not conducted research studies to identify the precise mechanisms through which BSFT achieves changes in family functioning. Research is needed to examining the assumption that tasks, including homework, are related to these improvements.

ENGAGEMENT AND RETENTION OF FAMILIES

Families with drug-using adolescents are often very difficult to engage in treatment. In light of these difficulties, we designed a series of studies to evaluate the efficacy of specialized engagement procedures in BSFT. Similarly to the research on family interactions, the results of these studies provide evidence of the efficacy of BSFT in engaging and retaining family members; and, as such, provide indirect support for the use of these mechanisms in treatment. Unfortunately, this research does not provide direct evidence that the uses of these in-session and out-of-session tasks are directly responsible for the impressive results reviewed here.

In the first study (Szapocznik et al., 1988), 108 Hispanic families with behavior problem adolescents (who were suspected of, or were observed using drugs) were randomly assigned to one of two conditions: Engagement as Usual (i.e., the control condition) in which client-families were approached in a way that resembled as closely as possible the kind of engagement that usually takes place in outpatient centers, and BSFT-Engagement (i.e., the experimental condition), in which client-families were engaged using specialized engagement techniques. Once engaged into treatment, all youths received BSFT. Results revealed that 93% of the families in the BSFT-Engagement condition were engaged into treatment, compared to 42% of the families in the Engagement as Usual condition. Of the engaged cases, 83% (43) of the BSFT-Engagement condition, vs. 59% of the Engagement as Usual condition, were successfully terminated.

The second study (Santisteban et al., 1996) examining the efficacy of BSFT specialized engagement strategies was a replication of Szapocznik et al. (1988) and it explored factors that might moderate the effectiveness of the engagement intervention under a more stringent criterion for engagement. One hundred and ninety three Cuban Hispanic and non-Cuban Hispanic families were randomly assigned to either BSFT-Engagement (experimental group), BSFT with Engagement as Usual (control group), or group counseling with Engagement as Usual (control group). Engagement as Usual involved no specialized engagement strategies.

In the BSFT-Engagement condition, 81% of the families (42 of 52) were successfully engaged; whereas in the two engagement control conditions combined, 60% (84 of 141) of the families were successfully engaged. The overall rates of this study appear lower than those of the previous study due to the more stringent criteria for engagement. However, when the less stringent criterion for engagement (i.e., attending intake) from the previous Szapocznik et al. (1988) study was used to compare the BSFT-Engagement conditions from both studies, there were no significant differences between the two experimental conditions on the rates of engagement.

The third study (Coatsworth, Santisteban, McBride, & Szapocznik, 2001) tested the ability of BSFT, with the specialized engagement strategies module fully incorporated into the intervention, to engage and retain adolescents and their families, when compared to a community control condition. An important aspect of this study was that the control condition, community control, was not developed and implemented by the investigators. As such, the control intervention (e.g., usual engagement strategies) was less subject to the influence of the investigators. Findings in this study, like in previous studies, showed that BSFT was significantly more successful in engaging cases (43 of 53, or 81%) than the community control (31 of 51, or 61%). Likewise, among those engaged, a higher percentage of BSFT cases (31 of 43, or 71%) was retained in treatment as compared to the community control (13 of 51, or 42%). Additional findings revealed that in the BSFT condition 58% of randomized cases completed treatment (31 out of 53) compared to 25% (13 out of 51) in the community control condition.

SECTION III: NATURE OF HOMEWORK
IN BSFT

PHILOSOPHY OF ASSIGNING HOMEWORK TASKS

As noted above, the main goal of BSFT is to create new family structures. A primary mechanism through which this is accomplished is by creating opportunities in therapy sessions for the family to interact in new ways. During these "in-session tasks," the therapist acts as a coach and guide to facilitate new interactions. However, a fundamental assumption in BSFT is that change is only useful if it is generalized to family interactions outside of the session. For this reason, homework assignments are implemented to build on in-session tasks and provide the family with the opportunity for rehearsing/practicing new behaviors on their own in between therapy sessions. Tasks, inside and outside (i.e., homework) of therapy, are the basic tool for orchestrating/implementing change in BSFT. Specifically, from the first session to the last session, the therapist is explicitly focused on creating opportunities for family members to engage in new behaviors inside the session and then generalize these new behaviors outside of the session.

Tasks, including homework, are always tied to the problematic structures presented by the family. That is, homework is tailored to the unique repetitive interaction patterns of the family and is designed to provide opportunities for the family system to practice new and more adaptive ways of functioning. For example, the therapist may observe that parents do not work together to set up rules and consequences for children's misbehavior. To address this structural problem, the therapist first creates an "in-session task" in which s/he creates and guides a dialogue where the parents come to an agreement about rules. To facilitate the generalization of this collaboration in parenting, a similar task is assigned as a homework assignment (e.g., parents agree to have a 1-hour discussion before the next session to reach an agreement about the consequences they will enforce when a child breaks the new parental rules).

Assigning Homework Tasks

Practicing in the Session

As a general rule, the BSFT therapist must first assign a task to be performed during the session, where the therapist has an opportunity to observe, assist, and facilitate the successful conduct of the task. A task should never be assigned for accomplishment at home before the family has been helped to complete a similar and related task in the therapy session. Once a task has been successfully accomplished within the therapy session, the therapist is ready to ask the family to try that task outside of the therapy session.

As tasks are assigned and negotiated in therapy sessions, the therapist not only monitors how the family is accomplishing the tasks (e.g., parent and adolescent negotiate the rules about the adolescent's curfew), but they are also focused on assessing family skills (e.g., family members' ability to listen and validate the other's perspective) that are being tested during the task. Both the process of completing the task successfully in the session and the skills of family members to complete tasks are weighted when assigning out-of-session homework. However, assessing competence is particularly important for determining if family members have the skills necessary to successfully complete tasks that cannot be performed in the session (e.g., "do a fun activity together, something you would all enjoy"). Family members must demonstrate the capacity/skills required to perform a task successfully in the session before a task is assigned outside of treatment.

Degree of Difficulty: Tailoring Tasks by Phase of Treatment

Therapists strategically select homework tasks to maximize their impact on changing family interactions that are directly linked to the youth's problem behaviors. A fundamental assumption in BSFT is that if a family experiences the successful completion of a homework task, they will be more likely to (a) continue with the new pattern and (b) be successful in changing other aspects of family functioning. In contrast, a family that is unable to successfully complete a task may have more difficulty with tasks as treatment progresses. Thus, at every phase of treatment, therapists make efforts to assign tasks that are *sufficiently doable* at each step of the therapy process.

Early in treatment, as a therapist is joining with family members, the therapist should start with easy tasks. However, over time, the therapist can work up to more difficult tasks by slowly building a foundation of successes with the family. The therapist should not try to accomplish too much in a single leap. The treatment plan should be broken up into specific steps, starting with targeting easier tasks and building to more difficult tasks. Homework tasks mirror the treatment plan. Below, in the section on Examples of Homework Assignments, we discuss specific tasks that we have found to be relatively easy or relatively hard for family members to implement.

Preparing the Family for a Task

The most important part of preparing a family for a task is providing an opportunity to successfully practice the behaviors involved in the task during a therapy session. Beyond practicing in the session, there are a number of other techniques that therapists should use to prepare family members for out-of-session tasks. First, as family members interact in the session, therapists should support them for any positive behaviors or interactions that occur. The therapist should be very clear to family members about the behavior(s) that s/he is supporting and, if possible, punctuate a sequence for family members so they can identify the new behaviors. For example, the therapist can highlight how a family member responded supportively to a negative comment by another family member and describe how this represents a change from how they used to interact.

Second, the therapist should always track family members' investment in behaving in new ways. If a family member appears unmotivated or unwilling to try something new, it is frequently necessary to reframe the behaviors or motivations of other family members to create a new context for family interactions. This strategic use of reframing is often necessary in families in which there is high conflict or a history of poor communication between family members. In either circumstance, family members may be appropriately cautious or pessimistic about trying something new. The therapist must therefore provide a new frame (reframe) to reconnect family members to positive feelings or the hope for something different. In all circumstances, however, therapists should never assign a task that a family member has explicitly (or even implicitly) stated that they are unable or unwilling to do.

Third, the therapist should clearly assign and describe a specific task. A frequent error that therapists make is to assign a very vague or general task to family members (e.g., Tell your mom how you feel, but do it in a way she can hear you better.). This is deadly for family members that have a difficult time keeping interactions organized and focused (e.g., over-involved families or families with a lot of conflict). Therapists should be very specific about what they want the family to accomplish and should work with the family to determine how to carry out the task. Family members' understanding of the task should be confirmed by asking each person to describe what they are going to try and accomplish during the task.

Therapists should never expect the family to accomplish the assigned homework tasks flawlessly. In fact, if the family were skillful enough to successfully accomplish all assigned tasks, they would not need to be in therapy. When tasks are assigned, therapists should always hope for the best, but be prepared for the worst. After all, a task represents a new behavior for the family, an opportunity to interact differently and in more positive ways. With this in mind, therapists can help to prepare family members about the difficulties involved in practicing new behaviors. If a family member is prepared for this difficulty, they are less likely to over-interpret and over-generalize when problems occur, which may help to minimize the potential negative ramifications of this difficulty on the treatment process.

At the beginning of every session (with the exception of session 1), therapists should review the homework assignment from the prior week. A natural tendency is to skip this part or minimize the review because the family often brings in new, urgent problems. Therapists should stay in a leadership role, structuring the session to begin with the review of the homework and ending the session with a new assignment. This type of structure underscores the importance of homework to family members and permits the therapist to prepare the family for the next task.

Handling Difficulties in Completing Homework Tasks

As the family attempts any tasks, including homework, the therapist should assist the family in overcoming obstacles to accomplishing the task. The therapist's job is to review what happened, identify possible causes for the difficulties in completing the task, minimize the impact of these difficulties on the therapeutic process, and design new tasks. In the last step, the therapist starts over and works at overcoming the newly identified obstacles.

The therapist should never be surprised that family members have difficulty accomplishing a homework task. In fact, more often than not, when the family is asked to do practice the new behavior at home, there will be obstacles to overcome before the family is ready to successfully complete the task. Therapists should not become discouraged at this stage. Their mission now is to *identify the obstacle(s)* and then help the family surmount them. Actually, difficulties in doing homework are usually a great source of new and important information regarding the reasons why a family cannot do what is best for them. The most important question in therapy is, "What interactional patterns interfere with the families' ability to carry out the homework task?"

Engaging and Retaining Difficult Families

BSFT includes a specialized engagement strategies module designed to modify these maladaptive interactions and bring the family into treatment. The use of tasks, particularly homework tasks, is an essential component of these engagement strategies. One unique feature of specialized engagement strategies is that they represent the only time in BSFT when homework is recommended when it has not first been assigned in treatment sessions. In fact, many of these specialized engagement strategies occur outside of the office, often prior to the first session.

The *central task* around which the entire process of engagement is orchestrated is having all family members come together to therapy. Detailed examples of tasks used in BSFT specialized engagement strategies can be found elsewhere (Szapocznik, Perez-Vidal, Hervis, Brickman & Kurtines, 1990; Szapocznik & Kurtines, 1989). From our perspective, "resistance" to treatment is viewed as a systemic phenomenon (Szapocznik, Perez-Vidal, Hervis, Brickman & Kurtines, 1990; Szapocznik & Kurtines, 1989). In other words, a family's resistance to engage in treatment is another manifestation of the same maladaptive patterns of interaction that maintain the symptoms in the family. Reducing resistance to treatment, therefore, requires direct intervention to restructure maladaptive patterns much in the same way the BSFT therapist seeks desirable changes in any other aspect of the family's behavior (e.g., analysis of family functioning, joining the family system, reducing negativity, restructuring techniques, etc.).

SECTION IV: CASE STUDIES

Two case studies are provided to illustrate how homework assignments are utilized in BSFT. The first example is a case that was seen for the prevention of drug use, and the second was a case that was seen in therapy for the treatment of problems associated with the adolescent's drug use. The primary difference between the two cases is that the adolescent in the former case was "at risk" for developing serious behavior problems (such as drug use or delinquency), while the adolescent in the latter case was already heavily involved in using drugs and engaging in delinquent behaviors. The BSFT treatment model was implemented in the same way for both cases.

BSFT as a Prevention Intervention: The Case of Richard

Richard is a 12-year-old boy referred for family therapy by his school counselor following several incidents of misbehavior in the classroom and fighting with other students. Richard lives with his mother and father and two younger siblings (10-year-old sister and 8-year-old brother).

Richard's mother initiated the first clinical contact with a telephone call. She expressed concerns about her son's behavior problems at school and acknowledged that she was having similar problems controlling his behavior at home. The therapist scheduled a time to meet with the entire family and explored potential obstacles to the family's participation in treatment. Mother was initially reluctant to involve her husband in treatment, stating that he worked evenings and was not available during times when other family members could meet. She asked if it would be possible for her and her children to meet with the therapist without her husband. The therapist respectfully acknowledged how hard her husband was working and praised her for taking so much responsibility for raising their children, but emphasized the importance of having the entire family present. The therapist suggested to the mother that perhaps she could help her by speaking directly to the father. The mother was still hesitant. The therapist said, "I hear some fears on your part for me to do this. Maybe I can help to reassure you that my only concern is to help your husband see how important it is for us to all work together in helping your son."

Homework Task #1

After additional reframing of the importance of father's participation in treatment, the mother agreed to help the therapist talk to the father directly. The therapist,
paying attention to the family structure (i.e., mother in a centralized family role), asked
the mother to be in charge of arranging contact with her husband. As noted earlier in
our presentation of research, engagement strategies are one of the only times when
homework tasks are implemented before a task has been successfully accomplished
in the session. In this instance, the therapist explored with mother how she planned
to approach her husband to set-up a telephone call with the therapist, supporting
appropriate statements and coaching her to think about other reasons why he should
speak with the therapist. The mother was then given the task of setting up the call
with her husband and the therapist for the following evening.

> As can be seen in this example, homework tasks can occur from the very first contact,
> even prior to a formal therapy session. Also, the nature of homework tasks is tailored
> to the unique problem the family presents. In this case, the mother was in the position
> of protecting the rigid family structure. Szapocznik and Kurtines (1989) provide a more
> detailed description of addressing this type (and other types) of engagement problem(s)
> when working with families of behavior problem youth.

Homework Task #2

During the first session with the family, the therapist observed that mother and
father had very different ideas about what they thought was appropriate parenting.
The most significant disagreements were about (a) defining what qualified as child
misbehavior and (b) implementing consequences for problem behaviors. Although
conflict was minimized, a pattern that was observed in the session followed a consistent sequence: (1) mother would make a statement about a specific problem behavior,
rule, or consequence, (2) father would disagree (often non-verbally by shaking his
head or rolling his eyes), (3) mother and father would stop communicating directly
with one another, and (4) mother would speak directly to Richard about the rules and
consequences for his problem behavior.

The therapist addressed this lack of collaboration in the family's leadership subsystem by noting how both parents are committed to their children and that neither
has given up on doing the best job possible. This reframe helped to shift the parents
from focusing on areas of disagreement to sharing a common goal of helping their
children. The therapist then normalized the observed pattern by letting the parents
know how common it is for parents to have very different ideas about parenting. The
therapist emphasized that the most important aspect of shared parenting was not that
parents always had the same view about how to parent, but that they were able to
discuss these views and negotiate with one another to reach solutions that both found
acceptable.

Immediately following reframing interventions, the therapist asked the mother
and father to share with each other the strength that they have observed in the other's
parenting. The parents actually had very little difficulty identifying a single strength
and—in fact—generated many parenting behaviors that they admired in their partner.
The parents were then given the task of talking with one another about difficulties
they experienced in being parents. Because the parents had demonstrated success in

sharing strengths, the therapist assigned a very non-invasive and minimally challenging task. The focus of the task was to further improve communication in the leadership subsystem. A secondary benefit of the task was to improve their understanding of each other's frustrations and concerns.

> The therapist quickly determined that a lack of collaborative leadership was the most prominent structural problem that needed to be addressed in treatment. In doing so, the first step was to reframe parent behaviors to one another. Highlighting similarities also helped to diffuse some of the frustration that each parent was experiencing. The theme of shared parenting and common goals was used over the course of therapy whenever parents became stuck or fell back into the same pattern of "disagree then disengage" that was observed in the first session. The initial homework task that was assigned was determined by the therapist's assessment. However, only a superficial task was assigned because the therapist wanted to maximize the likelihood that the parents would be able to successfully complete the task. The decision was to start with a small step to encourage a positive connection, rather than force the parents into a negotiation about rules and consequences.

As therapy progressed, the therapist set-up tasks in the session to facilitate more effective parental negotiation and discussion about setting up rules and consequences for behaviors. Homework tasks were assigned and reviewed each week to track the parents' success in generalizing improvements in the session out into the real world. Problems in carrying out homework were directly addressed in treatment and subsequent homework assignments built on these areas. When appropriate, the therapist assigned tasks that involved other family members or the entire family. For example, the parents were asked to discuss the "house rules" about inappropriate language and to develop, with Richard, reasonable consequences for breaking these rules. By the end of treatment, the parents were much more effective in working together to develop rules and consequences for their children's behaviors and presented themselves to their children as allies rather than opponents.

BSFT AS THERAPY: THE CASE OF MARIA

Maria is a 16-year-old girl referred by the juvenile court for the treatment of drug use and delinquent behaviors. Maria lives with her mother and 18-year-old brother.

The therapist received the referral directly from a representative of the juvenile court and initiated the first contact with the family in a telephone call with Maria's mother. During this call, the therapist learned that both Maria and her brother had a history of prior arrests, expulsions from school, and other behavior problems, including drug use. The most recent arrest occurred when Maria was caught breaking into a house with her friends and her older boyfriend to steal electronic equipment. A brief screen conducted at the juvenile detention center revealed a significant drug use problem. The mother agreed to schedule a session for the following day and reported that there would be no obstacles to getting her children to the session.

The first session was characterized by high conflict between all family members. Mother was highly critical of both children, reciting a list of problems that she has with each. Both Maria and her brother were disrespectful and critical of their mother. The therapist systematically attempted to transform the negative exchanges into more positive interactions by reframing relationships in a more positive light (e.g., mother is concerned). One primary focus of the first session was to create a more supportive context where family members were able to acknowledge (if not express) underlying positive feelings about each other. Only after persistent reframing was the therapist able to reduce the overt hostility between family members.

A second goal of the initial session was for the therapist to establish a connection with each family member by validating, reflecting, and accepting the statements made by each person. In doing so, the therapist was explicitly concerned with making sure that each family member viewed that they had something to gain by participating in treatment.

Homework Task #1

The explosive conflict observed in the first session was effectively handled by consistent reframing interventions. However, although family members softened the tone of their interactions, the therapist viewed this as a "cease-fire," rather than a positive reconciliation and reconnection among family members. Based on this fact, the therapist felt that assigning an interactional task would elicit significant conflict and would be very difficult for the family to complete. As such, the therapist decided to assign a task that did not require family members to interact with one another. Instead, each family member was asked to observe her/himself (not other family members) and notice some of the positive things that they do in the home. The therapist provided some examples (e.g., clean up room, cook, drive my sister to school). Each person was asked to bring in at least one positive comment to discuss at the next session.

> The therapist wanted to create an expectation that homework will be assigned every week, but was reluctant to assign a task that was too difficult. Two features of the session were critical in developing the first task: (a) the high level of family conflict and (b) the therapist's success in connecting with each family member. Based on these observations, the therapist assigned a task that focused on positive behaviors, but that did not require family members to interact with each other or to review each other's strengths or weaknesses.

The first few sessions of treatment focused almost exclusively on reconnecting family members to positive feelings they have about one another. After the family demonstrated the ability to share positive feelings with one another in the sessions, the therapist assigned homework tasks that involved minimal risk and that were focused on facilitating a more supportive family context. For example, one task involved having family members share their hopes or dreams for one another and another task asked family members to do something positive for another family member during the week (but do not tell them what it is).

One benefit of reducing family conflict in the mother–daughter dyad was that Maria and her mother were able to engage in thoughtful discussions that did not always end in high conflict. As the tone of family interactions improved, the therapist elicited and guided more focused conversations about friends, drugs, school, and family rules. The therapist maintained an active stance in these discussions, reinvoking themes of family connection and parent support when necessary. However, over time, the therapist was able to back further and further away from these family discussions. Initially, the goal of these conversations was to open up dialogue between the parent and adolescents. Later in treatment, the focus shifted to negotiating (a) how mother could effectively monitor the adolescent behaviors,

(b) what are the family rules about specific behaviors (e.g., drugs, school, friends, curfew), and (c) what are the consequences for breaking these rules. Homework assignments mirrored these goals. Initially, tasks were very open-ended and were only focused on encouraging open dialogues; whereas, later in treatment, tasks were highly specific and focused on particular behaviors, rules, and/or consequences.

CONCLUSIONS

Homework tasks are an essential component of BSFT. Therapists strategically implement tasks to achieve improvements in family interactions that are directly related to the prevention or reduction of adolescent behavior problems. The use of tasks in BSFT is consistent with the model's emphasis on having family members "do" rather than simply "talk about." Tasks are assigned based on the therapist's assessment of family functioning. Early in treatment relatively easier tasks are assigned to foster a sense of success and competence in family members. Later in treatment, tasks tend to be more difficult and complex. In all instances, however, the therapist creates opportunities for family members to practice and demonstrate competence in the task, prior to assigning homework.

ACKNOWLEDGMENTS

This work is supported by funding in part by a grant from the National Institute on Drug Abuse to José Szapocznik, Principal Investigator (1U10DA13720). The authors would like to acknowledge the contributions of Ervin Briones, Syliva Kaminsky, Ruban Roberts, Mercedes Scopetta, Maria Tapia, and Monica Zarate. Please address correspondence to Michael S. Robbins, Center for Family Studies, Department of Psychiatry and Behavioral Sciences, University of Miami School of Medicine, Miami, Florida 33136 (Phone: 305-243-4592; fax: 305-243-4417; email: mrobbins@med.miami.edu).

REFERENCES

Bronfenbrenner, U. (1977). Toward an experimental ecology of human development. *American Psychologist, 32*, 513–531.

Bronfenbrenner, U. (1979). Contexts of child rearing: Problems and prospects. *American Psychologist, 34*, 844–850.

Bronfenbrenner, U. (1986). Ecology of the family as a context for human development: Research perspectives. *Developmental Psychology, 22*, 723–742.

Coatsworth, J. D., Santisteban, D. A., McBride, C. K., & Szapocznik, J. (2001). Brief strategic family therapy versus community control: Engagement, retention, and an exploration of the moderating role of adolescent symptom severity. *Family Process, 40*, 313–332.

Haley, J. (1976). *Problem solving therapy*. San Francisco CA: Jossey-Bass, Publishers.

Madanes, C. (1981). *Strategic family therapy*. San Francisco: Jossey Bass.

Minuchin, S. (1974). *Families and family therapy*. Cambridge, MA: Harvard University Press.

Minuchin, S., & Fishman, H. C. (1981). *Family therapy techniques*. Cambridge: Harvard University Press.

Minuchin, S., Rosman, B. L., & Baker, L. (1978). *Psychosomatic families: Anorexia nervosa in context.* Cambridge: Harvard University Press.

Robbins, M. S., Mitrani, V. B., Zarate, M., Perez, G. A., Coatsworth, J. D., & Szapocznik, J. (2002). Change processes in family therapy with Hispanic adolescents. *Hispanic Journal of Behavioral Sciences, 24*, 505–519.

Santisteban, D. A., Coatsworth, D., Perez-Vidal, A., Kurtines, W. M., Schwartz, S. J., & Szapocznik, J. (2003). The efficacy of brief strategic family therapy in modifying adolescent behavior problems and substance use, *Journal of Family Psychology, 17*, 121–133.

Santisteban, D. A., Coatsworth, J. D., Perez-Vidal, A., Mitrani, V., Jean-Gilles, M., & Szapocznik, J. (1997). Brief structural strategic family therapy with African American and Hispanic high risk youth: A report of outcome. *Journal of Community Psychology, 25*, 453–471.

Santisteban, D. A., Szapocznik, J., Perez-Vidal, A., Kurtines, W. M., Murray, E. J., & LaPerriere, A. (1996). Efficacy of intervention for engaging youth and families into treatment and some variables that may contribute to differential effectiveness. *Journal of Family Psychology, 10,* 35–44.

Szapocznik, J., & Coatsworth, J. D. (1999). An ecodevelopmental framework for organizing the influences on drug abuse: A developmental model of risk and protection. In M. D. Glantz & C. R. Hartel (Eds.), *Drug abuse: Origins and interventions* (pp. 331–366). Washington, DC: American Psychological Association.

Szapocznik, J., Hervis, O. E., & Schwartz, S. (2003). *Brief strategic family therapy for adolescent drug abuse.* Rockford, MD: National Institute on Drug Abuse.

Szapocznik, J., & Kurtines, W. M. (1989). *Breakthroughs in family therapy with drug abusing and problem youth.* New York: Springer Publishing Co.

Szapocznik, J., Kurtines, W. M., Foote, F., Perez-Vidal, A., & Hervis, O. (1986). Conjoint versus one person family therapy: Further evidence for the effectiveness of conducting family therapy through one person. *Journal of Consulting and Clinical Psychology, 54*, 395–397.

Szapocznik, J., Perez-Vidal, A., Hervis, O., Brickman, A. L., & Kurtines, W. (1990). Innovations in *Family therapy: Overcoming resistance to treatment.* In R. A. Wells, & V. A. Gianetti (Eds.), *Handbook of Brief Psychotherapy* (pp. 93–114). New York: Plenum.

Szapocznik, J., Perez-Vidal, A., Brickman, A., Foote, F. H., Santisteban, D. A., Hervis, O. E., & Kurtines, W. M. (1988). Engaging adolescent drug abusers and their families in treatment: A strategic structural systems approach. *Journal of Consulting and Clinical Psychology, 56*, 552–557.

Szapocznik, J., Rio, A. T., Murray, E., Cohen, R., Scopetta, M. A., Rivas-Vasquez, A. et al. (1989). Structural family versus psychodynamic child therapy for problematic Hispanic boys. *Journal of Consulting and Clinical Psychology, 57*, 571–578.

Szapocznik, J., Scopetta, M. A., & King, O. (now Hervis). (1978). Theory and practice in matching treatment to the special characteristics and problems of Cuban immigrants. *Journal of Community Psychology, 6*, 112–122.

Szapocznik, J., & Williams, R. A. (2000). Brief strategic family therapy: Twenty five years of interplay among theory, research and practice in adolescent behavior problems and drug abuse. *Clinical Child and Family Psychology Review, 3*, 117–135.

Chapter 9

PERSONAL CONSTRUCT THERAPY

Robert A. Neimeyer and David A. Winter

Originally formulated by American psychologist George Kelly (1955) and extended by subsequent generations of clinical scientists and practitioners (Neimeyer & Baldwin, 2003; Winter, 1992), personal construct therapy (PCT) has from its inception sought to extend therapy beyond the four walls of the consulting room through the judicious use of between-session assignments. As it has grown as a therapeutic approach, PCT has benefited from convergence with a broad range of other postmodern approaches to psychotherapy that share its emphasis on the active, participatory, and often richly personal ways that clients struggle to construct meaning in their experience, and use this meaning as a guide to action (Neimeyer & Bridges, 2003). The result has been an expanding repertory of classical and innovative methods for fostering client self-awareness and change, and a germinal body of research on their application. Our goal in the present chapter is to introduce the reader to this diversity of methods, offering brief illustrations of a representative selection of time-honored and novel homework strategies. Although space constraints preclude an exhaustive treatment of each, we will also point the interested reader toward "how-to" resources that provide further guidance in the actual application of each method and related therapeutic strategies, and cite research relevant to each method's rationale and therapeutic utility.

PRINCIPLES OF PERSONAL CONSTRUCT THERAPY

In his original exposition of his theory, Kelly used the metaphor of the *person as scientist*, constantly formulating hypotheses about, or constructions of, the world, testing these out, and, if necessary, revising them. In psychological disorders, this process has essentially stalled, the same construction being "used repeatedly in spite of consistent invalidation" (Kelly, 1955, p. 831). Personal construct psychotherapy therefore aims to set in motion once more the process of reconstruction, and again Kelly described it in terms of scientific metaphors. For example:

> We have used the model of scientific methodology in conceptualizing the psychotherapeutic process and the client's reconstruction of life. We believe that the way the scientist learns can be used as a way for the client to learn. We believe that science can be used as a methodological model for persons who do not call themselves scientists. We believe it

can be used as a model for clients who, like scientists, may well seek to reconstrue life. We believe that the therapy room can be a laboratory and the client's community a field project (Kelly, 1955, p. 1067).

To continue the metaphor, the therapist–client relationship may be viewed in the same terms as that between research supervisors and the students they mentor, the former being experts on research methodology and the latter experts on their particular fields of interest. In this model, therapist and client are co-experimenters, and they may together devise homework assignments for the client that can serve as "field experiments." This has clear affinities with a cognitive-behavioral approach, and indeed Kelly (1970) viewed the central feature of such approaches, for example exposure-based treatments for phobic anxiety, as experiments conducted in behavioral terms, with the caveat that the client was "principal investigator" and the client's behavior the independent variable in the design.

Kelly took pains to point out that he was not adopting a narrow construction of scientific methodology, but rather a notion of "creative science" (Kelly, 1955, p. 1067). When applied to therapy, such a notion is consistent with the view of the therapist as being as much an artist as a scientist (Leitner, 2001), or indeed with metaphors of therapy in terms of the telling and rewriting of stories (Neimeyer & Stewart, 2000). Thus, as Kelly's original position has grown and benefited from a vigorous intellectual trade with other constructivist therapies (Neimeyer & Mahoney, 1995; Neimeyer & Raskin, 2000), its working metaphors for therapy have also evolved. As a result, psychotherapy from this perspective might be defined as "the variegated and subtle interchange and negotiation of (inter)personal meanings . . . in the service of articulating, elaborating, and revising those constructions that the client uses to organize her or his experience and action" (R. Neimeyer, 1995, p. 2). It follows that the sort of between-session assignments that characterize constructivist therapy generally and personal construct therapy specifically would be those that advance the goals of making more explicit the often implicit constructions that shape the client's active and emotional engagement with the social world, extending these by "trying on" alternative forms of construing and doing, and reconstructing those aspects of his or her construct system that are no longer working for the client in his or her relevant relationships.

Although features of a personal construct approach to homework overlap those of other approaches to therapy, the central epistemology of constructivism, which focuses on the pragmatic *viability* of human constructions rather than their logical *validity* or truth-value (Mahoney, 1991; R. Neimeyer, 1995), leads to different emphases in the way homework is designed. For this reason we will note such differences after reviewing several common methods used by construct theorists, and providing a clinical vignette illustrating each. In keeping with the broad definition of constructivist psychotherapy offered above, we will group these methods into those concerned with the articulation of personal meanings on the one hand, and their elaboration and extension on the other.

METHODS FOR ARTICULATING PERSONAL MEANINGS

A distinctive aspect of construct theory is its conceptualization of personal meaning systems, which are considered to be constituted by semantic networks of constructs, defined as bipolar dimensions for organizing one's perceptual world and guiding one's actions in it (Kelly, 1955). For example, one client in therapy tended to view nearly every interpersonal context in life in terms of her being *competent vs. incompetent*—to the extent that if she excelled, she felt a (temporary) sense of security, but if she fell short of perfect performance or knowledge in a given domain, she felt anxious, vulnerable, and despondent. Ultimately these reactions were understandable in light of the implications this construct carried for other constructs in her system, including less easily articulated or labeled meanings bearing on her being *lovable vs. unlovable*. Thus, between-session extensions of in-session work often focus on bringing to light these implicit meanings, using any of several methods, two of which will be discussed below. A common thread in these methods is that they blur the line between assessment and intervention, fostering insight, reflection, and often commitment to new action on the part of the client, rather than simply representing methods of evaluation conducted for the strategic benefit of the therapist (Neimeyer, 1993). A second common denominator is that they tend to foster clients' self-exploration of "core role" constructions bearing on their basic sense of identity, often revealing conflicts, impasses, and problematic implications in their meaning systems that tend to perpetuate their symptoms.

LADDERING AND FACILITATIVE QUESTIONS

Laddering was devised by Hinkle (1965) as a "hierarchical technique for eliciting the superordinate constructs of the preferred self hierarchy" (p. 32), and because of its great flexibility in fostering self-exploration, has been widely adopted by subsequent generations of personal construct psychotherapists. Laddering essentially represents a form of recursive questioning, whose aim is to elucidate the higher-order implications of a construct offered by a client or research participant. For example, laddering might proceed from an intriguing, but ambiguous self-description volunteered by a client in psychotherapy ("I've always been a pretty *reticent* person"), or a decisional impasse expressed in a career counseling setting ("I know I should take this *marketing job*, but I just can't seem to make myself do it"). Alternatively, an initial construct might be prompted by offering a respondent a "triadic sort" of elements (e.g., three family members) and inviting him or her to formulate a way in which two are alike and different from the third. In each case, the questioner would elicit the contrast to the initial construction by asking, "What is the opposite of that?" to which the person might respond, for example, by saying the opposite of *reticent* for him is *open about my opinions*. This dimension would then become the first "rung" in the ladder of personal constructs. The investigator would follow by asking the respondent to indicate with which side of this construct the person would *prefer* to be associated (e.g., *reticent*), and then ask "Why?" or "What is the advantage of that?" This ladders up to the next higher-order construct (e.g., "because then I'm *in control of my emotions*"), to which the investigator elicits a further contrast (e.g., *out of control*), another preference, and an associated reason by repeating the cycle of questioning at each new rung. Questioning usually proceeds in this way until the respondent is unable to articulate an answer to the ultimate "why" prompt, or until his or her response represents a simple rewording of the previous construct. The result is typically a multilayered hierarchy of personal meanings, which often conveys something of the superordinate issues or values implied by the more concrete constructs with which the exercise

TABLE 9.1. Facilitative questions used as between-session assignment following laddering interview (Neimeyer et al., 2001)

- What central values are implied by the ideas you align yourself with at the upper end of the ladder? How are these expressed in specific behaviors, traits, or roles you exemplify at the lower end of the ladder?
- Were there points at which you hesitated before assigning a pole preference? What might have been going on for you at that point?
- Who in your life most supports/most resists the preferences you describe?
- Which of these preferences and values are visible/invisible to others? To whom?
- What could be some positive connotations for the non-preferred poles?
- Have there ever been times when you would have placed yourself/your values at the opposite poles of these constructs? What was your life like at that time?

---

began. Once completed, the ladder can then serve as an anchor for self reflection in a between-session assignment, as the client is asked to process its significance in response to any of several facilitative questions (Neimeyer, Anderson & Stockton, 2001) such as those listed in Table 9.1.

An example of laddering was provided by a young college athlete named Tom. Tom's initial complaint had to do with an acutely felt conflict between the world of academic responsibilities and the world of relationships, a problem that cut deeper than simply the typical college difficulties with time management. Indeed, his initial presentation of this issue made it clear that it had at least as much grounding in his relationship to his family values as it had to do with relating to peers. Alerted to the relevance of the family context, I (RAN) suggested that we begin our exploration there, and invited him to consider his mother, his father, and himself, and to tell me some important way in which two were similar and different from the third. Reflecting briefly, Tom volunteered that he and his mother shared a common *work ethic*, whereas his dad showed a *lack of motivation*. I then asked him which he preferred, and he responded without hesitation that he preferred the *work ethic*. Next, I asked him why he preferred this stance, and he replied that it made him more *self-driven and self-reliant*, which he contrasted with *listening too much to others*. Repeating this cycle of questioning (preference–why–contrast–preference), I then learned that being self-driven implied that *he was the one to respond to opportunity or tragedy*, as opposed to *looking to others for a shoulder to cry on or to celebrate with*. Asked for his preference on this construct, however, Tom hesitated visibly, wrinkling his brow. He then stated that, now that he considered it, he actually preferred the latter, thereby reversing his pole preferences on the previous dimensions—a pattern of "crossover conflict" observed in very few non-clinical ladders (Neimeyer, Anderson, and Stockton, 2001).From this point onwards, Tom's preferences were consistently aligned with the "social" rather than "self-determined" poles of his higher-order constructs, as illustrated in Figure 9.1.

Intrigued and somewhat disquieted by the results of his ladder, Tom readily accepted the suggestion that he sift through its implications by journaling in response to any of the facilitative questions listed in Table 9.1. He returned the next session with several pages of thoughtful and often emotional writing, describing the origin of his work ethic in his mother's emphasis on the importance of reaching his goals, though others sometimes gave him "static" about his choices, "even when they weren't on the field for the play." Using similar sports metaphors, Tom went on to analyze his

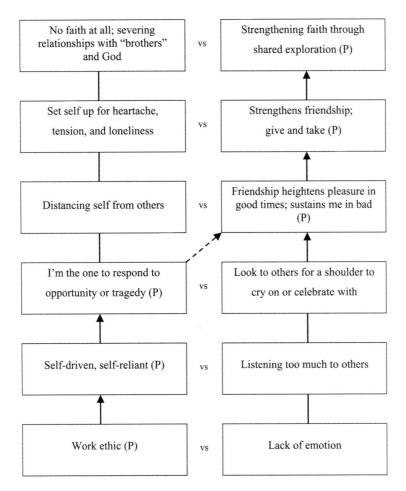

FIGURE 9.1. Personal construct ladder for Tom.
Note: Solid arrows connecting construct poles represent "hard" implications given by respondent in answer to "why" questions; lines represent "soft" or inferred implications. Dashed arrow signals point of crossover conflict. "P" represents respondent's preferred self placement.

ambivalence in what he described as "new ways," achieving important "insights" about how he needed to embrace others in their shared pain as well as happiness, in a manner that ultimately integrated not only the best of his family values, but also those anchored in his faith tradition, as implied by the highest-order constructs elicited by his ladder. Reflecting on the long and slightly tearful pause that had preceded his articulation of the construct at the top of his hierarchy, Tom noted that *strengthening his faith through shared exploration* with others contrasted with a self-interested *severing of his relationship with his "brothers" and with God*, and realized that being able to do the former was "part of his development, of becoming a man." Thus, the laddering interview and the therapeutic homework tethered to it opened, and to a significant extent resolved, the initially vaguely formulated conflicts he felt between achievement and sociality, placing these within a compelling personal context of meaning, faith, and personal development.

Evidence supporting the validity of the laddering method has been provided not only in Hinkle's (1965) original research, but also in a subsequent study of the content and structure of over 100 laddering interviews by Neimeyer and his colleagues (2001). Results generally supported the method's validity. More concrete prompts required more hierarchical levels to converge on core themes, and theoretically more tacit or preverbal superordinate constructs were rated as more difficult to put into words, required longer latency to do so, and were considered more important to respondents than subordinate constructs from the same ladders. Furthermore, a content analysis of the ladders indicated that superordinate constructs more frequently reflected central existential themes of purpose and meaning, whereas subordinate constructs more commonly reflected superficial attitudes and interests. These same authors provided descriptive data on various patterns of laddering structure (e.g., self/preferred-self discrepancy, crossover conflict), and offered several practical recommendations on the use of ladders and their extension into between-session assignments. A randomized trial of cognitive therapy for depression including laddering homework compared to an identical therapy without homework confirms that the former produces greater treatment gains as rated by independent clinicians (Neimeyer & Feixas, 1990).

MIRROR TIME

Mahoney (1991) discussed the use of "mirror time" in constructivist psychotherapy as another technique to enhance clients' self-exploration, which can be used to foster self-confrontation with their body image, to facilitate internal dialogues, or to encourage self-affirmation. As a homework assignment suggested once a trusting therapeutic relationship is established, mirror time involves spending a specified period of time (e.g., 10–15 minutes) before a mirror in a private setting, perhaps accompanied by reflective instrumental music. Depending on the technique's intended focus, the client can be further primed by written questions offered in advance, encouraged to allow her or his attention to range freely, or given a set of guiding instructions (e.g., to pay attention to feelings that arise in the course of the exercise, to allow parts of the self to pose relevant questions and other parts to provide answers, or to shift awareness to different parts of the face or body). Likewise, the feelings and reflections that arise during and after the exercise can be recorded in a free-form journal entry immediately afterward, can be scored on various standardized mood and thought questionnaires, or simply noted for later therapeutic discussion.

An example is provided by Kristen, age 25, who accepted the invitation (by RAN) to spend 30 minutes in front of a mirror guided by the following taped instructions. Ellipses indicate pauses of approximately one minute between questions.

> Gently observe what your attention is first drawn to as you look in the mirror.... Witness what you are thinking, imagining, feeling.... Look deeply into your own eyes.... What do you see? What do you like and dislike as you view this person?... Are there any differences between the person in the mirror and the person you sense yourself to be?... What do you see in this face, this person, which others do not?
>
> Now open your eyes, and pause the tape recorder if you have chosen to use one. Try to capture the flow of feelings, observations, and answers to the above questions while they remain fresh, noting them briefly on paper. Then return to the further instructions below:

Close your eyes for several seconds and take a few slow, relaxing breaths . . . . Set your intentions to be self-aware and self-caring . . . . Then slowly open your eyes, inviting yourself to open to the possibility of seeing yourself in a different way . . . . Speaking aloud, quietly ask yourself the question, "Who are you?" . . . Allow this dialogue to continue in whatever way it does, letting the questioning part of you wait patiently for an answer, as another part formulates a response . . . . What do you most need to ask yourself in this moment of honesty, and what do you most need to hear?

After spending several minutes in such reflections, again note them on paper. Finish by summarizing these in a piece of reflective writing that touches on these themes, beginning with what your attention was drawn toward, and then progressing to the sorts of feelings, thoughts, and possible recognitions or insights stimulated by the exercise.

In response to these instructions, Kristen penned a poignant set of reflections, portions of which follow:

Birthmark below my left eye; no, my right eye. Strange how I am seeing myself opposite from how the world sees me. The freckle on my nose that everyone mistakes for a nose ring. Lots of freckles. Dark circles. Lopsided eyebrows. Wrinkles on my forehead, a new addition. Huge pupils.

I blink and feel the dryness of my contact lenses. I move my jaw to feel its repetitive popping, reminding me of the doctor's words, "mandible worn straight on one side," "permanent damage," and the x-ray on which my cartilage, instead of looking like a thin rainbow stretching in-between this delicate joint, looked like a little misplaced bean. I rub my eye out of habit and press my chapped lips. I try to imagine perfect vision and a perfect temporal mandibular joint. But I find it easier to experience the dull throb and dry eyes. To feel the familiar.

I am in fifth grade. I am 25. I see the fifth grader. I see the young adult. I am beautiful. I am plain. I see both. This is how the world sees me. This is how no one sees me. Not smiling. Not laughing or talking. I open my eyes wide and let air pass under my contact lenses, then, blink and my image blurs.

I like who I see because she knows me. I feel right in her skin. I dislike her because she doesn't have the answers I want. She stares back at me with too many emotions and not enough wisdom. I like her because she's not falling apart and because she sometimes makes people happy. I don't like her because she's unsure.

I see fear behind her look of resolve. This person is scared and still. Quiet and sad. I'm none of those things.

I let myself exist with a number of different possibilities for who I am. Worker, child, daughter, sister, friend, roommate, lover—none of them is how I define myself. I participate in life experiences like . . . a traveler. I am a traveler.

Which makes it strange, then, that when I asked myself, "What do you want from life?" the answer was, "Purpose." This apparent contradiction between who I am and what I want from life was resolved through realizing that I have been traveling through my life experiences in search of my purpose. Even as a child, the question, "What am I here to do?" has been the one driving me. And so I traveled, literally and figuratively, through life. I found my answer working with emotionally troubled girls. I finally felt right in life. I knew why I was here when I worked with those girls . . . . Because I don't want to travel forever.

I ended my time making funny faces in the mirror. This is a favorite pastime of mine, and good therapy for anyone in need of a laugh.

As Kristen's journal illustrates, this deceptively simple method, if offered and accepted in the right spirit, can facilitate deep-going self-reflection that can be productive in itself, or easily integrated into an ongoing therapeutic conversation. Systematic research by Williams, Diehl, and Mahoney (2002) on nearly 100 users of this technique confirms that mirror time can be "strong medicine," producing significant increases in both physiological arousal as assessed by galvanic skin response and in subjective tension during the period of actual mirror use. Interestingly, however, participant ratings of both positive and negative mood states evidenced a significant decrease from pre- to postmirror use, except for two affective states—pride and inspiration—which increased. Such findings are perhaps indicative of a spiking and then subjective dampening of arousal associated with negative and self-critical thoughts during the period of active viewing, especially for women. It is noteworthy that a comparison of participant responses also suggested that "scripting" the mirror time with instructions—rather than leaving the encounter with self unguided—dampened women's self-criticism, and also produced more favorable responses to the exercise as a therapeutic assignment.

METHODS FOR EXTENDING CONSTRUCT SYSTEMS

The differences between objectivist and constructivist epistemology, reflected in an enthusiastic or skeptical response to philosophical realism, respectively, carry important implications for how client meaning systems are approached in psychotherapy (Neimeyer, 1998). From an objectivist perspective, the goal of therapy is to promote improved "reality contact," on the presumption that cognitive distortions sustain troubling emotions and militate against adequate adaptation. From a constructivist view, however, the indefinitely large number of constructions that can be applied viably to life events precludes simple adjudication of their "correctness" on logical or empirical grounds. Equally important, problems are seen as arising at least as much *within* the client's system of meanings and their consensual validation by relevant others as *between* the person's meaning system and a presumed external reality. It follows that homework assignments would be oriented more to the extension of the client's meaning-making into new and hopeful areas than to its correction to meet objective canons of accuracy. The following elaborative and fixed role assignments reflect this orientation.

Elaborating the Contrast to the Symptom

Kelly (1955, p. 366) considered that a symptom can become "the rationale by which one's chaotic experiences are given a measure of structure and meaning." As Fransella (1970) has put it, the symptom is effectively the client's way of life, which will not be relinquished until an equally well-elaborated alternative way of life has been developed. Increasingly, the media attention given to particular symptoms, and websites and support groups devoted to them, provide ready-made, elaborated ways of life that may be attractive for individuals who lack well-defined roles.

Fransella's view was supported by her research on people who stutter, in which she found that stuttering allowed them to anticipate more events than did fluency (Fransella, 1972). Recent research has supported Fransella's pioneering formulations, as persons who stutter have been shown to possess a larger repertoire of constructs for interpreting and anticipating episodes of disfluency than episodes of fluent speech (DiLollo, Manning, & Neimeyer, 2005), and, in direct contrast to fluent speakers, to experience more "cognitive anxiety" in relation to fluency as well (DiLollo, Manning, & Neimeyer, 2003). Fransella (1972) therefore devised a therapeutic approach for such clients in which the focus during sessions was not on stuttering, about which the clients in a sense knew too much already, but on episodes of fluency, however brief, which they experienced during homework assignments. Those clients who were thus able to develop a more meaningful construction of being a fluent speaker showed a decrease in the severity of their stuttering. Extrapolating from this, contemporary constructivist therapists have developed a narrative approach to treatment to help clients identify periods of fluency and construct a new sense of self arising in moments of "resistance" to the dominant problem, ultimately securing social validation for this new and more hopeful identity. In preventive terms, the construction of a secure sense of self without the problem can serve as a hedge against the very high incidence of relapse reported for behavioral therapies for the disorder (DiLollo, Neimeyer, & Manning, 2002).

A similar approach of using homework assignments to elaborate a view of the self without the symptom may, of course, be adopted with other client groups. One illustration concerns the treatment of agoraphobic clients in which graduated exposure to previously avoided situations, much of this in homework assignments, is combined with personal construct group psychotherapy (Winter & Metcalfe, 2005). The first three therapy sessions are conducted in Interpersonal Transaction (IT) groups (Neimeyer, 1988), a specialized format in which dyadic interactions of each group member with every other on a topic provided by the therapist (e.g., advantages and disadvantages of being better able to go out and be more independent) are followed by a plenary discussion. Clients' partners are invited to a further two sessions; and the sixth and final personal construct therapy session is for clients alone. The approach is derived from a research-based personal construct model of agoraphobia that views this symptom as a strategy in which clients constrict their worlds to avoid events, particularly those involving interpersonal conflict, that their construct systems are ill-equipped to predict. This strategy tends to result in the client's interpersonal world being delimited to a partner whose construing is very similar to their own, and who therefore provides a relationship characterized by mutual validation of construing.

The exposure component of treatment effectively involves clients being encouraged to experiment, and to dilate their construing again. The IT group component of the treatment is designed to enable clients to develop patterns of construing that will enhance their capacity to anticipate the events that they will encounter as they become increasingly autonomous. Thus, one session focuses on the elaboration of construing of interpersonal conflict; another on the possible negative implications of going out, which may be serving to maintain clients' agoraphobic symptoms; and another on the elaboration of a viable construction of the self without agoraphobia.

The third IT group session not only draws upon clients' experiences in the exposure sessions but also on a homework assignment of writing a characterization of the self as he or she might be without agoraphobia, a narrative means of fostering an expanded conception of self. For Mandy, the therapist considered that the most important aspect of this exercise was "realizing that even if she lost her symptoms and was able to go out, she had nowhere to go. She acknowledged the need to elaborate the alternatives to being agoraphobic but commented that these sessions were particularly difficult for her albeit worthwhile. Thinking about what she wanted for herself was new to her and the prospect of any sort of change threatening." For June, in the therapist's view, "elaborating self without symptoms was particularly important because, until now, the advantages of being agoraphobic seemed to outweigh the disadvantages. She is starting to think about interests outside the home and family— ways of developing herself and is keen on singing." June herself remarked that, "I found talking about my future, about wanting to join a choral society, very helpful because this is something that is coming back to the surface now, and having an aim in life is really helpful to me. Because up until now I have had nothing to look forward to." Thus, meaning-enhancing interventions were woven through both the therapeutic processing of exposure-based homework, and specialized homework assignments themselves. In a sense, this building of "constructive competencies" can be viewed as a contribution to the goal of relapse prevention, although this is accomplished through expanding one's construct system for engaging life, rather than instigating specific cognitive or behavioral strategies at the first sign of "back-sliding."

This approach has been fully described elsewhere (Winter et al., 2005; Winter and Metcalfe, 2005). Overall, results of a large clinic-based trial support the view that this approach to treatment is well received by clients, and is comparable in effectiveness to the "empirically validated" behavioral approach to the treatment of agoraphobia with which it was compared (Winter, Gournay, Metcalfe, & Rossotti, 2006).

Another client group with whom homework exercises have been used to elaborate a non-symptomatic role consists of those with psychosexual problems. For example, Rodney, whose presenting complaint was that he was unable to ejaculate during intercourse or other sexual activity, had coped with confusion concerning sexuality by constricting his field of awareness to exclude sexual experiences. As he put it, he had "dismissed thinking about it...I didn't really want to confront the subject for the best part of my life." Therefore, an aim of therapy was to elaborate his construing of, and reduce the anxiety caused by, his sexual responses. He was asked to: (1) keep a daily record of the frequency, and degree of pleasure associated with, his sexual urges; (2) complete a repertory grid with sexual situations as elements; and (3) carry out homework tasks (ranging from going to the gym to luxuriating in the bath) to enhance his awareness of pleasurable bodily sensations. The grid, a widely used personal construct technique for articulating and mapping a given domain of meaning (Fransella, Bell, and Bannister, 2004), essentially required Rodney to compare and contrast sexual situations (e.g., masturbation; making a sexual advance) to yield relevant constructs (e.g., *something I am/am not afraid of; associated/not associated with love and togetherness*) on which all situational "elements" in the grid were then rated. A principal components analysis of this matrix of ratings indicated that Rodney construed situations that he "desired to achieve" as associated with fear and avoidance, and masturbation as "tedious." As he said, "I never masturbated to the point of ejaculation and so after a while I just gave it up because it seemed to be more bothersome than enjoyable." It became increasingly apparent that he felt under time pressure in sexual situations, as in various other situations in his life. The following interaction ensued when he was describing his homework experiences in the gym:

> *Therapist (DAW)*: It reminds me a bit of the way in which you talked about masturbation as being something very tedious, wondering how long it's going to go on for. I just

wonder if there's any way in which you can masturbate without time pressure, without necessarily wanting to achieve an orgasm, just purely for pleasure, without necessarily doing it with a goal in mind or an ending of it in mind.

Rodney (R): I ought to try it.

D: In some ways it seems as if you see the sexual situation as one that can go on forever.

R: I always have seen things in life as things with a beginning and an end. I think I actually am scared of other situations that have no ending to them.

In a later session, he related the sense of time pressure to "living in anticipation":

R: I'm constantly living in anticipation of some form or another. . . . Whatever comes, it always seems to be too late, because my anticipation is that I have that image now and it should be fulfilled in a reasonable length of time, but not too long.

His choice of words in this passage is of interest in view of the nature of his sexual problem, since his ejaculations were "too late," occurring not during sexual activity but taking him by surprise, often embarrassingly, some time after this activity.

While I (DAW) negotiated new homework assignments with him, and asked for feedback, this was deliberately done in a somewhat tentative manner. For example:

D: I find it a bit difficult here to keep asking you how things are going sexually because in a way that's again putting performance pressure on you, time pressure, and yet that was one area that we were, originally anyway, going to focus on.

Discussion of these assignments was coupled with exploration of his construing of sexuality, and "time binding" (Kelly, 1955) of some of these constructions, for example an association between sexual responsiveness and manipulation, to the time and events from which they appeared to derive, namely his childhood relationship with his mother. There was also an attempt to develop new constructs orthogonal to those that appeared to underlie his sexual problem. For example:

D: I think it is important that you've had experience of these two contrasting people—an image of someone who seems only to please himself and to be very irresponsible, and at the other extreme the philosophy of pleasing others and not yourself, and sex seems to be one area where it is very necessary to balance those two things. It's all to do with balancing pleasing oneself and pleasing the other person, so in some ways it's not surprising that your problems are focused on that area. And maybe what you have to do is to build up a clearer image of someone who's in the middle—a new personality that isn't at one extreme or the other but, if you like, is at 90 degrees to the two.

Eventually, Rodney reported that he had masturbated to orgasm for the first time, and the positive outcome of therapy extended well beyond the sexual sphere:

D: Do you feel a sense of having broken through a barrier?

R: Yes, I have broken through something, something invisible, which opens for me a whole new way of looking at things, or at least the possibility that in all aspects of life things may not be as stuck as I think they are, unchangeable.

Of course, homework assignments are commonplace in behavioral approaches to sex therapy. However, when used mechanistically they can, paradoxically, exacerbate the very performance anxieties that such approaches view as central to sexual problems (Winter, 1988). As is apparent from the example of Rodney, when such assignments are used in personal construct psychotherapy, this is done in an invitational rather than a prescriptive manner. Not only does this reduce anxiety but it also serves to minimize the guilt that a client may experience when experimenting with some new sexual behavior. For example, Jim, who presented the rare complaint of ejaculating with no sensation of orgasm, construed people who are "able to feel fulfilled sexually" as likely to be "male chauvinist pigs." He resisted the seemingly innocuous fantasies that he required for his own fulfillment because he viewed them as demeaning toward women. We therefore negotiated how he might gradually dilate his field of experience to experiment with these fantasies, agreeing on an initial homework task of buying not a "girlie" magazine or a videotape of hardcore pornography but instead a volume of Japanese prints! He eventually reported being able to experience "more enjoyable ejaculations," and a post-treatment repertory grid revealed that sexual fulfillment no longer carried negative implications for him. The elaboration of more satisfying sexual relationships through homework assignments fostering articulation and negotiation of constructs concerning eroticism, interpersonal bonding, gender identity and reproduction has also been a hallmark of "holonic sex therapy" using constructivist methods (Bridges & Neimeyer, 2003; 2005). Although there is no research evidence for the effectiveness of personal construct sex therapy apart from single case studies (Winter, 2005), such evidence is accumulating for a postmodern approach in this area, consistent with the personal construct perspective (Schorer & LoPiccolo, 1982).

Elaborating the Past

Although the focus in personal construct psychotherapy is more likely to be on the present and the future than on the past, it can occasionally be useful to attempt to elaborate the client's construing of some past experience that has been "suspended" from his or her awareness because it is incompatible with the client's construct system or because its implications are intolerable. Homework exercises can facilitate this process. This was the case with Paul, who I (DAW) first asked to complete an autobiographical self-characterization assignment (Kelly, 1955) between his initial assessment and his first therapy session. Working with clients, therapists can then use a variety of hermeneutic guidelines to assist in the analysis of the protocol (Neimeyer, Ray et al., 2003), and perhaps pave the way for fixed role therapy, which will be explored in more detail in the following section. Paul's (grammatically unaltered) characterization began as follows:

> Where do we start, how about Birth, ok. I was born in Newtown on the 6th. February 1955. I don't remember the birth, perhaps I was too young or maybe I had my eyes closed, I don't know. I went to a nursery, then went on to New Road primary school before going on to the local secondary school where my studies were interrupted by an unforeseen event. I killed my father. I don't really know why, my memory of the event has (sic) doesn't appear full. I was a little screwed up afterwards and probably still am today....

The conclusion of the self-characterization indicated that therapy was a very threatening prospect for him:

> A foreboding has come over me that makes me nervous and distracted just thinking about this and the meeting tomorrow where I will have to talk about my Infamy and try to bring reason to it, where I know it is a painful subject that I can bottle up reasonably well

with the odd histerical alcohol induced breakdown and odd week off due to a lethargic despondency that saps the will to due anything but read and sleep. I guess you need the full monty and replaying that record is not an easy thing to do at the best of times let alone trying to grasp it for reasoning. And it misses a lot.

Elaborating further his difficulties in remembering the reasons for what he termed "the big event," Paul said that he had "encapsulated it and put it on a shelf." Rather than leaping into exposure-based therapy, I made it clear to Paul that it was entirely his choice whether he took the "big event" down from the shelf. We explored this choice using Tschudi's (1977) ABC technique, in which Paul was asked to list the positive and negative implications of taking the event off the shelf and, conversely, of leaving it there. Among the positive implications of taking it off the shelf were that he considered, using a computing metaphor, that it might allow him to develop a "programming patch" rather than to continue to have "faulty reasoning"; and that it would enable him to be more "proactive" as opposed to his present "directionless" life, which he saw as being due to "a big block of bad goo sitting in my brain." After discussing these implications, he said that he knew that he had to take the event off the shelf and to look at it in therapy. I explored with him the sources of support that might be available to him when he did so, and he identified one friend to whom he felt he could turn if necessary. It was apparent that he had considerable difficulties in trusting others, in part due to a belief that if he revealed any aspect of himself to another person this would inexorably lead to the revelation of all aspects, including his killing of his father. He was therefore introduced to the notion of dispersion of trust (Rossotti, 1995), namely, the possibility of placing trust in different people concerning different areas of one's life, and he carried out homework experiments with such behavior.

As a gradual approach to the exploration of the "big event," two repertory grids were completed, one focusing on his construing of significant people, including his father, and the other on his construing of life events, including his father's death. He was also asked to talk about recollections of his childhood prior to the event. Because these recollections were limited, I suggested a homework assignment of discussing his childhood with members of his family. He clearly felt threatened by this assignment, but instead agreed to talk to a childhood friend about his memories of Paul's family. This enabled him to recall incidents in which his father had been violent both toward his mother and toward Paul. His next assignment was to look in the library at newspaper reports of his crime, and finally we agreed that I would obtain the file of his court case as this might help to fill the gaps in his memory of the day of the "big event." The file, which he read at home, did indeed remind him of an incident that had occurred on the fateful day, and that might have been the missing precipitating factor for his actions.

Paul acknowledged that he might never be able to remember perfectly what happened on the day of his father's death. Nevertheless, the elaboration and reliving of the traumatic event in therapy allowed the exploration of issues concerning guilt and enabled him to talk about the event with a friend for the first time. He made major changes in his professional and personal life, suggesting that taking the event off the shelf had indeed allowed him to be more proactive; and a repeat repertory grid indicated that his construing of the "big event" had become more elaborated, and better integrated with his construct system. Such a pattern would be consistent with recent conceptualizations of adaptation to bereavement as entailing assimilation of the loss into one's meaning system or self-narrative (Neimeyer, 2005). The integration of traumatic experiences through construct system elaboration has been shown to mitigate risk of recurrence of posttraumatic symptomatology in survivors of extreme violence (Sewell, 1996).

Experimenting with an Alternative Role

A quintessential technique in personal construct psychotherapy is *fixed-role therapy* (Kelly, 1955), which involves the systematic use of between-session assignments first to articulate the major constructs that frame the client's current identity, and then to extend these through experimentation with an alternative life role. It is noteworthy that this active treatment strategy, first devised by Kelly to promote resilience and personal growth in the urgent context of the Great Depression of the late 1930s, was the first approach to incorporate homework as a core component of psychotherapy.

In this procedure, on the basis of his or her assessment of the client's self-characterization, the therapist drafts a sketch of a role that it might be useful for the client to enact. Kelly (1955) indicated that the following considerations should be taken into account in writing this sketch:

1. The sketch should develop a major theme, and one that involves a basic acceptance of the client rather than an attempt to correct the client's minor faults or "to make a model human being out of him" (Kelly, 1955, p. 369).
2. It should invite the client to experiment with sharply contrasting behavior, although not the complete opposite of the client's current "core role," dislodgment from which could provoke a sense of both threat and guilt. Rather, the constructs that define the new role should be "orthogonal" to the client's major existing construct dimensions, in a sense coaxing him or her in new directions, rather than just reversing the old.
3. It should include constructs that are more permeable (applicable to new events), and therefore conducive to movement, than those in the client's current self-construction.
4. It should present hypotheses that are testable. As is graphically illustrated by Horley's (2005) use of fixed-role therapy in a penal setting, a major factor determining this testability will be the client's environmental constraints.
5. It should include constructs that allow the client to subsume the construing of other people, to see the world through their eyes, this being the basis for those significant relationships with other people that Kelly termed "role relationships."
6. In enacting the sketch, the client will be protected by the make-believe nature of the exercise (G. Neimeyer, 1995). The character portrayed in the sketch should therefore be given a new name, and the sketch should not include direct comparisons with the client. Although doing so is optional, some users have found that the playful use of character names that suggest the essence of the new identity mitigates the threat associated with the role and helps the client remember its key features (see Table 9.2).

Having written the sketch, the therapist carries out an "acceptance check" with the client to determine whether the character depicted is plausible, and not too threatening

TABLE 9.2. Hypothetical fixed role characters and their prominent characteristics

Name	Role description
Andy Vidual	one-of-a-kind, self-enhancing personality
Anna Graham	an intriguing puzzle to others
Anna Lytic	intellectually intense; always looking for deeper meaning
Bobbie Sox	fun-loving and unpretentious
Freida Choose	constructs many alternatives for action
Greg Garious	Mr. Sociability; life-of-the-party
Ira Knee	witty, with a knack for seeing the absurd side of things
Jerry Atric	copes resiliently with losses of aging
Mike Quest	a man with a mission
Otto Kinetic	always on the move
Phil Anthropic	generous to a fault; loves all mankind
Polly Gonn	many-sided personality
Reed Define	likes reframing situations in novel ways
Sally Forth	oriented to an adventurous future
Sharon Sharalike	seeks "give and take" in close relationships
Taylor Made	fits into his "niche" in life perfectly
Wanda A. Round	undirected but happy-go-lucky

to him or her. After any necessary rewriting of the sketch, the client is asked to "become" the new character for two weeks, unbeknownst to friends and associates, while his or her current self is "on vacation." Arrangements are made for frequent meetings with the therapist during this time, these sessions focusing on rehearsal of the role in situations that progress from superficial (meeting new acquaintances as the new character would) to more intimate relationships (making love or praying as the character might). At no time is there an indication that the client will be permanently transformed into the new character and that the old self will not return from vacation. Rather, the aim of fixed-role therapy is to provide "one good rousing, construct-shaking experience" (Kelly, 1955, p. 412), and one that offers the client a period of freedom from being trapped in his or her autobiography, in effect to see the world through a different lens.

Jack was re-referred for therapy for a "long-standing feeling of inadequacy" after an unsuccessful experience of social skills training, during which there had been a marked increase in the severity of his symptoms. Like 80% of a sample of clients attending such groups, a pre-treatment repertory grid indicated that social competence carried some negative implications (Winter, 1987). Thus, for Jack, assertive extraverts were construed, increasingly over the course of social skills training, as demanding and aggressive. Small wonder, then, that, like many other members of these groups, he failed to respond to an approach that involved exercises he viewed as training in aggression. Jack's self-characterization was of someone who had increasingly constricted his concerns around his search for a girl friend, neglecting his other social relationships. It was also apparent that he considered that there was always "a right and wrong opinion," and that he usually believed that he was right and therefore did not bother to consider the views of others who expressed different opinions.

Jack's therapy initially involved "time binding" (Kelly, 1955), in which some of his constructions were tied to the period in childhood from which they appeared to be derived, and attempts to elaborate a construction of himself as a more assertive person (Winter, 1987). As an aid to experimentation with alternative self-constructions,

I (DAW) then prepared the following fixed role of "Jim Nastic" for him to enact, a playfully named character that served as a mnemonic device for the core themes of the sketch.

> Jim Nastic's philosophy of life very much reflects his approach to his favorite sport, tennis: It's not whether a player wins or loses that's important but whether they've played the game to the best of their ability. Whether at work or at play, he believes that if a job is worth doing it's worth doing well, and he brings to everything that he does a certain passion and conviction, which cannot fail to earn your respect. Although you might perhaps think that this would make Jim appear a little too serious and intense, once you get to know him you soon realize that his main concern is to live life to the full and that this includes having fun as well as working hard. Life doesn't always run smoothly for him, of course, but when he has a disappointment he always seems able to learn something from it, and to look to the future rather than brooding on his present or past misfortunes.
>
> One of Jim's greatest strengths at tennis is his ability to anticipate the moves of the other players, be they his opponents or doubles partners. In other areas of his life, he also always tries to see the world through the eyes of the people with whom he comes into contact, perhaps because he has mixed with people from so many different walks of life. His lively curiosity in what makes other people tick is usually reciprocated and leads him, almost before he knows it, into some very rewarding relationships. He also, of course, has his fair share of disagreements with others, but when this happens he always makes an effort to understand the other person's point of view, even though he might not accept it. Because of this, Jim has a reputation both for commitment to those causes that are close to his heart and tolerance of the right of others to hold different opinions.

Let's consider how Kelly's suggestions outlined above were reflected in this role:

1. The major theme of the role, the passion and conviction associated with living life to the full and "playing the game" to the best of one's ability, reframed some of what Jack regarded as impediments to social relationships (such as his intensity) as possible strengths. The role also drew upon some of his acknowledged skills, such as his ability at tennis. It was explicitly not a description of someone whose life was perfect, and acknowledged that Jim's life "doesn't always run smoothly" and that he has "his fair share of disagreements with others," while indicating possible alternative ways of dealing with these.
2. The contrasts involved in the new role were clearly stated (e.g., the importance of winning versus playing the game to the best of one's ability; looking to the future versus brooding on present or past misfortunes). There was a deliberate omission of any constructs regarding relationships with the opposite sex, which were the primary focus of his initial self-characterization, in an attempt to introduce new constructs relatively independent of this area of concern.
3. It was indicated in the role that the new constructs introduced could be applied in a range of situations ("at work or at play").
4. Hypotheses were presented (for example, that "lively curiosity" in others will usually be reciprocated) that were testable in Jack's normal social environment.
5. There was considerable emphasis on trying to see the world through the eyes of others, transferring skills from the tennis court to interpersonal relationships.
6. There was no explicit comparison of Jim with Jack in the sketch.

At the time that the fixed role was being prepared, Jack began to carry out his own experimentation with new constructions and behaviors, which became the focus of therapy sessions. Indeed, when he was eventually given the fixed role sketch, he remarked that "That's me in a nutshell!" He did, however, wish to experiment with how to have a lively curiosity in others without being "nosey"' and in future weeks he carried the role sketch in his pocket, referring to it before entering social situations. At post-treatment assessment, there was a considerable reduction in his symptoms and an indication from the repertory grid that he had reconstrued extraversion and assertiveness so that they no longer carried negative implications for him.

There have been several variations on Kelly's original fixed-role procedure. For example, in some cases the fixed-role sketch has been written by the therapist and client in collaboration (Epting and Nazario, 1987); fixed roles have been adapted for use in the group (Kelly, 1955; Neimeyer, Ray et al., 2003) and couples therapy (Kremsdorf, 1985) settings; and, in "postmodern" renditions of this approach, multiple scripts may be developed and performed to correspond to and highlight different facets of the self (Sewell, Baldwin & Williams, 1998). Moreover, there is also accumulating research evidence of the effectiveness of fixed-role assignments for a host of problems (Beail and Parker, 1991; Karst and Trexler, 1970; Lira et al., 1975; Nagae and Nedate, 2001).

RESISTANCE TO HOMEWORK ASSIGNMENTS

In the above sections we have attempted to suggest the range of constructivist homework assignments, providing illustrations from our own practice. However, the panoply of possibilities devised and described in the personal construct literature is vastly larger than those that could be discussed here, and the interested reader is encouraged to consult other broad overviews of constructivist therapy to appreciate the scope of these procedures (Neimeyer & Bridges, 2003; Neimeyer & Mahoney, 1995; Neimeyer & Raskin, 2000; Winter, 1992; Winter & Viney, 2005). But despite their great diversity, constructivist homework assignments share some common features that tend to distinguish them from modal approaches to cognitive therapy, such as the conspicuous rarity with which constructivists attempt to use homework to reveal "logical errors," "cognitive distortions," or "dysfunctional assumptions" in the client's meaning system or self-narrative. Likewise, assignments are rarely offered in an authoritative or manualized fashion, as great care is taken to follow the client's lead in determining what might be useful, and at what time. These emphases on respecting the integrity of the client's current construct system and according him or her expert status in the therapy relationship are more than mere strategic preferences, but instead reflect the primacy that construct theorists accord to personal meaning, and their general philosophical skepticism about the objectivist assumptions that underpin mainstream rationalist approaches (Neimeyer, 1995; 1998).

The contrasts between constructivist and rationalist therapies are thrown into sharpest relief when considering their approach to the resistant client. That this is the case with clients who resist the completion of homework assignments has been indicated by a comparative process-outcome study of personal construct and cognitive therapies (Winter and Watson, 1999). One of the cognitive therapy clients in this study, Gail, admitted that, rather than diligently complying with a homework assignment of keeping a daily record of negative thoughts, she had retrospectively completed the record chart for the whole week on the night before the session. The therapist responded incredulously and dismissively to this disclosure, and suggested that the client could remind herself to complete the chart in future by sticking it on her bathroom mirror. Gail responded that "in simple terms I haven't done homework since I was 14, 15, 16...and I find it very hard. I was never very good at it then." She went on to suggest that, as well as being threatened by reverting to the role of a schoolgirl failing her homework assignments, she also found the chart a fairly meaningless exercise. The therapist's response was once more to point out the error of her ways:

> You see, I think some of the difficulty...maybe is that you are actually trying to do it 6 days later, which is...a waste of time. I mean, there's actually no point doing it the night before you come to see me...we may as well forget about it.

That the therapist certainly did not forget about it, however, was indicated by the fact that no fewer than 60% of her 247 interventions concerned the client's homework!

Another cognitive-behavioral therapist in this study had given a client, Jilly, homework assignments of wearing gloves and breathing exercises to counter her trichotillomania (Watson and Winter, 2000). After it became apparent that the client was not carrying out these assignments, the following interaction ensued:

> J.: But I can't see how doing all this wearing gloves and breathing and so forth is going to stop me hair pulling, because it won't.
> T: I know about these problems and there's a whole range of things that one needs to do together to get a grip on these problems, because the problem is very difficult and therefore you need a sledgehammer to crack it, it's a very evasive problem and you can't have half-hearted attempts at dealing with it.

Jilly dropped out of therapy after this session.

In contrast to the "heroic" attempts of Gail's and Jilly's therapists to counter their clients' resistance by adopting an approach that might be classified as "ballistic action" (Stiles et al., 1996) is the response of one of the personal construct psychotherapists in the study to a client who failed to complete a homework experiment involving confronting his boss. The therapist took the view that the client had perhaps avoided the confrontation because it was too anxiety-provoking, because his construing of it was not sufficiently elaborated. He therefore asked the client to describe what he would say to the boss, and to anticipate how she would respond. The client was invited to enact the confrontation in the session, and the homework was only mentioned once more. At no point was it indicated that the client's approach to the exercise was wrong. Although we are not implying that all cognitive-behavioral therapists would respond to "compliance failures" in a heavy-handed or authoritarian way, we do believe that the distinctive philosophy of personal construct therapy provides a safeguard against this occurring.

CONCLUSION

In this chapter we have tried to introduce the reader to a range of between-session assignments that are congruent with the spirit and focus of personal construct therapy, which aims to help clients articulate, elaborate, and extend the network of meanings by which they construct a sense of self. We believe that these methods, and the larger repertory of constructivist interventions from which they are drawn, make a useful and empirically informed contribution to the practice of psychotherapy, and invite their broader use by therapists of other traditions.

REFERENCES

Beail, N., & Parker, C. (1991). Group fixed role therapy: a clinical application. *International Journal of Personal Construct Psychology, 4*, 85–96.

Bridges, S. K., & Neimeyer, R. A. (2003). Exploring and negotiating sexual meanings. In Whitman, J. S. & Boyd, C. J. (Eds.), *The therapist's notebook for lesbian, gay, and bisexual clients* (pp. 145–149). New York: Hawthorn Press.

Bridges, S. K., & Neimeyer, R. A. (2005). Sexual holonic mapping: A clinical illustration. *Journal of Constructivist Psychology, 18*, 15–24.

DiLollo, A., Manning, W. H., & Neimeyer, R. A. (2003). Cognitive anxiety as a function of speaker role for fluent speakers and persons who stutter. *Journal of Fluency Disorders, 28*, 167–186.

DiLollo, A., Manning, W. H., & Neimeyer, R. A. (2005). Cognitive complexity as a function of speaker role for adult persons who stutter . *Journal of Constructivist Psychology, 18*, 215–236.

DiLollo, A., Neimeyer, R. A., & Manning, W. H. (2002). A personal construct psychology view of relapse: Indications for a narrative therapy component to stuttering treatment. *Journal of Fluency Disorders, 27*, 19–42.

Epting, F., & Nazario, J., Jr. (1987). Designing a fixed role therapy. In R. A. Neimeyer and G. J. Neimeyer (Eds.), *Personal construct therapy casebook* (pp. 287–289). New York: Springer.

Fransella, F. (1970). Stuttering: not a symptom but a way of life . *British Journal of Communication Disorders, 5*, 22–29.

Fransella, F. (1972). *Personal change and reconstruction*. London: Academic Press.

Fransella, F., Bell, R., & Bannister, D. (2004) *A manual for repertory grid technique* . London: Academic Press.

Hinkle, D. (1965). The change of personal constructs from the viewpoint of a theory of implications. Unpublished dissertation, The Ohio State University, Columbus, OH.

Horley, J. (2005). Issues in forensic psychotherapy. In D. A. Winter and L. L. Viney (Eds.), *Personal construct psychotherapy* . London: Croom Helm.

Karst, T. O., & Trexler, L. D. (1970). Initial study using fixed role and rational-emotive therapy in treating speaking anxiety. *Journal of Consulting and Clinical Psychology, 34*, 360–366.

Kelly, G. A. (1955). *The psychology of personal constructs*. New York: Norton (republished by Routledge, 1991).

Kelly, G. A. (1970) Behaviour is an experiment. In D. Banister (Ed.), *Perspectives in personal construct psychology* (pp. 255–269). London: Academic Press.

Kremsdorf, R. (1985). An extension of fixed-role therapy with a couple. In F. Epting and A. W. Landfield (Eds.), *Anticipating personal construct psychology* (pp. 216–225). Lincoln: University of Nebraska Press.

Leitner, L. M. (2001). Therapeutic artistry: evoking experiential and relational truths. Paper presented at 14th International Congress on Personal Construct Psychology, Wollongong.

Lira, F. T., Nay, W. R., McCullough, J. P., & Etkin, W. (1975). Relative effects of modelling and role playing in the treatment of avoidance behaviours. *Journal of Consulting and Clinical Psychology, 43*, 608–618.

Mahoney, M. J. (1991*). Human change processes*. New York: Basic.

Nagae, N., & Nedate, K. (2001). Comparison of constructive cognitive and rational cognitive psychotherapies for students with social anxiety. *Constructivism in the Human Sciences, 6*, 41–49.

Neimeyer, G. (1995). The challenge of change. In R. A. Neimeyer & M. J. Mahoney (Eds.), *Constructivism in psychotherapy* (pp. 111–126). Washington, DC: American Psychological Association.

Neimeyer, R. (1988). Clinical guidelines for conducting Interpersonal Transaction Groups. *International Journal of Personal Construct Psychology, 1*, 181–190.

Neimeyer, R. A. (1993). Constructivist approaches to the measurement of meaning. In G. Neimeyer (Ed.), *Constructivist assessment* (pp. 58–103). Newbury Park, CA: Sage.

Neimeyer, R. A. (1995). An invitation to constructivist psychotherapies. In R. A. Neimeyer & M. J. Mahoney (Eds.), *Constructivism in psychotherapy* (pp. 1–8). Washington: American Psychological Association.

Neimeyer, R. A. (1998). Cognitive therapy and the narrative trend: A bridge too far? *Journal of Cognitive Psychotherapy, 12*, 57–65.

Neimeyer, R. A. (2005). Growing through grief. In D. Winter & L. Viney (Eds.), *Personal construct psychotherapy*. London: Whurr.

Neimeyer, R. A., Anderson, A., & Stockton, L. (2001). Snakes versus ladders: A validation of laddering technique as a measure of hierarchical structure. *Journal of Constructivist Psychology, 14*, 83–103.

Neimeyer, R. A., & Baldwin, S. (2003). Personal construct psychotherapy and the constructivist horizon. In F. Fransella (Ed.) *International handbook of personal construct psychology* (pp. 247–255). London: Wiley.

Neimeyer, R. A., & Bridges, S. (2003). Postmodern approaches to psychotherapy. In A. Gurman & S. Messer (Eds.), *Essential psychotherapies* (2nd Ed.) (pp. 272–316). New York: Guilford.

Neimeyer, R. A., & Feixas, G. (1990). The role of homework and skill acquisition in the outcome of cognitive therapy for depression. *Behavior Therapy, 21*, 281–292.

Neimeyer, R. A., & Mahoney, M. J. (Eds.) (1995). *Constructivism in psychotherapy*. Washington: American Psychological Association.

Neimeyer, R. A., & Raskin, J. (Eds.) (2000). *Constructions of disorder*. Washington: American Psychological Association.

Neimeyer, R. A., Ray, L., Hardison, H., Raina,, K., Kelly, R., & Krantz, J. (2003). Fixed role in a fishbowl: Consultation-based fixed role therapy as a pedagogical technique. *Journal of Constructivist Psychology, 16*, 243–271.

Neimeyer, R. A., & Stewart, A. E. (2000). Constructivist and narrative psychotherapies. In C. R. Snyder & R. E. Ingram (Eds.), *Handbook of psychotherapy* (pp. 337–357). New York: Wiley.

Rossotti, N. G. (1995). An elaboration on the theme of trust. Paper presented at 11th. International Congress on Personal Construct Psychology, Barcelona.

Schorer, L., & LoPiccolo, J. (1982). Treatment effectiveness for dysfunctions of sexual desire. *Journal of Sex and Marital Therapy, 8*, 179–197.

Sewell, K. W. (1996). Constructional risk factors for a post-traumatic stress response after a mass murder. *Journal of Constructivist Psychology, 9*, 97–107.

Sewell, K. W., Baldwin, C. I., & Williams, A. M. (1998). Multiple self awareness group. *Journal of Constructivist Psychology, 11*, 59–78.

Stiles, W. B., Honos-Webb, L., & Surko, M. (1996). Responsiveness as a challenge to process research. Paper presented at 27th Annual Meeting of Society for Psychotherapy Research, Amelia Island, FL.

Tschudi, F. (1977). Loaded and honest questions. In D. Bannister (Ed.), *New perspectives in personal construct theory*. London: Academic Press.

Watson, S., & Winter, D. A. (2000). What works for whom but shouldn't and what doesn't work for whom but should? A case study of two clients with trichotillomania. *European Journal of Psychotherapy, Counselling and Health, 3*, 245–261.

Williams, A. M., Diehl, N. S., & Mahoney, M. J. (2002). Mirror-time: Empirical findings and implications for a constructivist psychotherapeutic technique. *Journal of Constructivist Psychology, 15*, 21–40.

Winter, D. A. (1987). Personal construct psychotherapy as a radical alternative to social skills training. In R. A. Neimeyer and G. J. Neimeyer (Eds.), *Personal construct therapy casebook* (pp. 107–123). New York: Springer.

Winter, D. A. (1988). Reconstructing an erection and elaborating ejaculation. *International Journal of Personal Construct Psychology, 1,* 81–99.

Winter, D. A. (1992). *Personal construct psychology in clinical practice.* London: Routledge.

Winter, D. A. (2005). Towards a personal construct sex therapy. In D. A. Winter and L. L. Viney (Eds.), *Personal construct psychotherapy.* London: Whurr.

Winter, D., Gournay, K., Metcalfe, C., & Rossotti, N. (2006). Expanding agoraphobics' horizons: An investigation of the effectiveness of a personal construct psychotherapy intervention. *Journal of Constructivist Psychology, 19,* 1–29.

Winter, D. A., & Metcalfe, C. (2005). From constriction to experimentation: A personal construct theory approach to agoraphobia. In D. A. Winter and L. L. Viney (Eds.), *Personal construct psychotherapy.* London: Whurr.

Winter, D. A., & Viney, L. L. (2005). *Personal construct psychotherapy.* London: Whurr.

Winter, D. A., & Watson, S. (1999). Personal construct psychotherapy and the cognitive therapies: Different in theory but can they be differentiated in practice? *Journal of Constructivist Psychology, 12,* 1–22.

Part II

CLIENT POPULATIONS

CHAPTER 10

OLDER ADULTS

Helen M. DeVries

As a population, older adults face an increasing number of stressful life events that are associated with the normal process of aging. Developmental challenges of late adulthood, such as sensory and perceptual losses, loss of significant others, chronic medical and health problems, and changes in work and family roles, may occur in rapid succession or simultaneously, thus complicating the adjustment process. If these developmental demands are not managed successfully, the older adult may be vulnerable for decreased mental and physical well-being.

There is considerable empirical evidence supporting the utility of individual and group cognitive behavioral therapy (CBT) with an older population to treat a variety of mental health disorders (Coon, Rider, Gallagher-Thompson, & Thompson, 1999; DeVries & Coon, 2002; DeVries & Gallagher-Thompson, 2000; Gallagher-Thompson & Steffen, 1994; Gatz, Fiske, Fox, McCallum, & Wetherell, 1998; Teri & McCurry, 2000). The problem-focused approach of CBT, with its emphasis on the development of coping skills, is well suited for helping older adults respond to normal developmental and life-adjustment tasks. In addition, CBT has been shown to be effective in alleviating symptoms of specific psychiatric disorders, especially depression (Gatz et al., 1998).

CBT, therefore, offers an empirically validated model for treating mental health problems associated with the developmental challenges of late-life and is particularly well suited to the needs of older adults. Findings from multiple studies (Coon et al., 1999; Dick, Gallagher-Thompson, Coon, Powers, & Thompson, 1996; Knight, B., 2004; McCarthy, Katz, & Foa, 1991; Rybarczyk, Gallagher-Thompson, Rodman, & Zeiss, 1992; Zeiss & Steffen, 1996) suggest that therapy with the elderly is most helpful if it is (a) not stigmatizing (emphasis on coping skills not psychopathology); (b) structured (so client knows what to expect; (c) time-limited (provides hope that individual will soon see improvement); and (d) goal oriented (has problem-solving focus). CBT meets these criteria. The collaborative and present-focused approach of CBT makes it appealing to an older population.

RECOMMENDED ADAPTATIONS TO CBT FOR
AN OLDER POPULATION

Modifications in the implementation of CBT may be necessary to accommodate physical, sensory, cognitive and personal value changes associated with normal aging. Based on the findings of multiple studies (Knight, 2004; Thompson, Davies, Gallagher, & Krantz, 1986; Zeiss & Steffen, 1996), the following modifications may be needed:

(a) *Slower Pace of Therapy.* Sensory and developmental changes associated with normal aging may require some adjustment to the pace of therapy. Decreased visual and auditory acuity can affect the rate and accuracy of information processing. The therapist should inquire about hearing loss, speak more slowly and clearly. The physical environment should have bright lighting and low background noise. In addition, developmental changes in cognitive processing will impact the older client's ability to absorb and recall new information. Therefore, it would be helpful to present information in several different sensory modalities (e.g., handouts, written feedback) and to have clients frequently repeat major points to ensure they understand new information. Encourage older clients to take notes and write down important information during therapy sessions to improve their capacity to absorb new material. Cognitive screening of an older client to assess level of intellectual functioning will ensure that those with gross deficits (e.g., moderate to severe dementia) are excluded from treatment. Clients with mild cognitive deficits may still benefit from CBT if adjustments are made in method and rate of presenting new material.

(b) *Socialization to Therapy.* Many older adults grew up in a culture that perceived therapy as a treatment for "crazy" people. They may perceive treatment for psychological problems as a shame or embarrassment. Therapists should explore the older client's expectations, stereotypes, and fears about therapy to reassure them and normalize the process.

(c) *Clarification of Therapeutic Process.* Older clients may think of therapy as a passive process, similar to going to a physician to get "fixed." Educating them about the active nature of CBT and the need for their collaborative engagement in the process is vital. Older adults usually don't know what is expected of them in a therapy context, and it is important to "demystify" the process for them. This can be accomplished by explaining the structured format of individual sessions and the use of homework to reinforce and practice skills covered during the therapy sessions, and by emphasizing the importance of completing homework to optimize the effect of therapy. Older clients also may need for the therapist to review the special "rules and conditions" that safeguard therapy and might differ from the normal rules governing social interactions (e.g., confidentiality, limits to confidentiality, etc.).

(d) *Respect for Age and Life Experience Differences.* Most commonly there is an age gap between the therapist and the older adult client. Sensitivity to ways this might impact therapy is important if the therapist wants to develop a strong therapeutic relationship. For example, younger therapists may not understand how the older client's perception of time may shape priorities for therapy. The therapist may want to aim for long-term changes rather than accepting the client's goal for managing the stress of an immediate situation. The therapist's ability to attend to the multiple factors that may be affecting the older adult will enhance the establishment of a therapeutic relationship, foster collaborative goal setting, and facilitate tailoring of treatment to the unique needs of the individual client.

These recommended accommodations may not be necessary for all older clients. Older adults comprise a widely diverse and heterogeneous population. Variations in educational level, physical health, intellectual functioning, interests, life circumstances, and social history are often greater than that found in a younger population. Therefore, it is imperative to obtain a thorough psychological, social, and medical history before beginning therapy.

COMMON BARRIERS TO SUCCESSFUL USE OF HOMEWORK

CBT does not assume that failure to comply with homework assignments is an indication of "resistance" on the part of the client. With older adults, especially, failure to complete homework may be more related to how the homework is explained, assigned, or reinforced than to client resistance. The following are some common therapist errors that create barriers to successful use of homework with older adults:

(a) *Failure to develop a therapeutic relationship.* Successful CBT relies on a strong therapeutic alliance between the therapist and client. Younger therapists may find it a challenge to establish such a relationship with an older client. Lack of cooperation with homework may simply reflect the client's discomfort with the therapist and the therapeutic environment.

(b) *Failure to socialize the client to the expectations for therapy.* CBT requires a collaborative and active involvement on the part of the client. Older adults may expect to be "treated" rather than to actively engage in the therapy process. Socialization of the client into therapy should include a clear indication of the expectations for the client, including the completion of homework assignments as part of the treatment plan.

(c) *Failure to engage the client's commitment to the therapeutic goals.* It is easy for an enthusiastic therapist to assume that her goals for the client are shared by the client. If older adults do not accept or endorse the therapist's goals for treatment, they will be very unlikely to comply with homework assignments.

(d) *Failure to reinforce homework completion and importance during the therapy sessions.* Nothing is more likely to decrease compliance than ignoring the completed assignment when the client comes for the next session. Making homework review and reinforcement a top priority during each session is likely to increase the older adult's compliance with assignments. Also, clients will be more likely to complete homework if the therapist presents a clear rationale for why this assignment is important for achieving therapeutic goals. Do not assume that the client will see the connection between the treatment goal and the homework assignment. Make this explicit for the older client.

(e) *Failure to be specific and clear in assigning homework tasks.* Older adults respond well when they are clear about expectations. If a client is consistently failing to complete assignments or is doing them incorrectly, reexamine how you make the assignment. A vague assignment will frustrate the older adult. Be specific about what they are to do, when they are to do it, and how it is to be done. Provide a written example of the assignment to practice during the session and to take home with them as a reminder.

(f) *Failure to help client problem-solve obstacles to homework completion.* Realistic barriers to homework completion often exist for older adults. For example, daily stressors related to chronic pain, illness, financial worries, sensory deficits, etc. can make it difficult to make homework completion a priority. Work with older clients to find ways to manage these daily stressors so they can engage with homework.

In summary, a collaborative and collegial therapeutic relationship can be developed with older clients by responding to homework non-compliance with a supportive, rather than judgmental, stance. As the therapist works with the client to better understand the reasons why homework was not completed, he/she will actually enhance the client's engagement in the therapeutic process, teach skills in problem solving, and deepen the therapeutic bond. In addition, the therapist will gain a better understanding of the client's world, particularly the resources and constraints that impact functioning. This information enables the therapist to tailor assignments to the realities of the client's world and foster the client's sense of efficacy and competence.

STRATEGIES FOR HOMEWORK WITH
OLDER ADULTS

Several strategies are useful in engaging older adults in homework completion as an essential element of therapy. Based on their research on CBT with older adults, Coon et al. (1999) emphasize the value of consistency in the structure of the therapy session, with review of completed homework and assignment of new homework as a component of every session. Each session should begin with a review of completed homework and end with assignment of new homework. This reinforces the importance of homework and increases the likelihood that the client will complete assignments.

When a client finds it difficult to complete homework, the therapist should work with the client to find ways to overcome the obstacles. Never blame or shame the client. Assume that genuine barriers do exist and that you are working with them to find ways to problem-solve and overcome these difficulties. In addition, it is important to identify any distractions that might interfere with homework completion and to help the client organize specific times and places to get homework completed.

Older adults resist doing things that they don't perceive as meaningful or having a purpose. It is important, therefore, to be clear about how the homework assignment relates to the goals for therapy and to provide a rationale for each assignment. Older adults do not have patience for activities they perceive as "busy work." The therapist must consistently stress how each assignment will help the client achieve therapeutic goals. Coon et al. (1999) also point out that some older adults may have a negative reaction to the term "homework." They suggest using alternate terms, such as "practicing," "working on assignments," and "learning new habits" as more acceptable to some older clients.

TYPES OF HOMEWORK APPROPRIATE FOR OLDER ADULTS

Many of the standard CBT approaches to homework assignments can be used with older adults. If the therapist relates the homework to therapeutic goals, clearly explains the expectations/requirements of the homework, and reinforces client compliance, CBT homework will be effective with older clients. Both cognitively focused and behaviorally focused assignments work well with older adults.

Cognitively-Focused Homework. The core assumption of CBT is that unhelpful thinking patterns contribute to psychological distress. Therefore, therapy aims to identify these unhelpful thinking patterns, challenge or modify them, and replace them with more helpful thinking. Developing the skill to carry out this process is enhanced by having the client practice between sessions. The following techniques, once taught in the therapy session, serve as excellent homework assignments to help clients develop skill and confidence in identifying and challenging negative or unhelpful thinking.

- Three-Column Daily Thought Record (DTR). An effective tool for helping older adults develop skill in identifying unhelpful thinking patterns is the Three-Column DTR. Multiple studies have supported the use of this technique with older clients (Coon et al., 1999; Dick, Gallagher-Thompson, & Thompson, 1996; Gallagher & Thompson, 1981; Gallagher-Thompson & Steffen, 1994; Kemp, Corgiat, & Gill, 1992; Zeiss & Steffen, 1996). Clients are given a sheet that has three columns. Column A (Antecedent) asks the client to identify an event or situation that occurred during the week that was stressful or upsetting. Column B (Belief) asks them to list any automatic thoughts they had in connection with the event. Column C (Consequences) asks them to list all the emotions that they experienced as a result. Once the client understands the process and is able to demonstrate in the session he or she can complete the form for at least one event, the DTR can be assigned as a homework assignment. The rationale is that by recording the stressful events when they occur during the week, the client will be better able to help the therapist understand what kinds of situations lead to negative thinking and negative emotions. It is helpful to ask the client to rate the intensity of the emotional reaction to the event and negative thoughts (most commonly on a scale of 1–10), so that tracking change will be possible as the client learns to intervene and challenge negative or unhelpful thinking. Each week, the session should begin with a review of the client's completed DTR.
- Five-Column Daily Thought Record. Once the client has mastered the basic DTR and has been able to complete these at home for several weeks, introduce the Five-Column DTR. This record adds to the A-B-C of the Three-Column form two more columns. Column D asks the client to replace a particular unhelpful thought from column B with a more helpful way of thinking. Column E asks the

client to re-rate the emotion (on a scale of 1–10) experienced in Column C after challenging the negative thinking. To help clients develop the skills needed to complete the Five-Column DTR, introduce them to some of most common negative thought patterns during the therapy session. These might include: "all or nothing" thinking, name calling, "shoulds," selective (negative) listening, over-interpreting, etc. An excellent description of these and other unhelpful thinking patterns is available in Coon et al. (1999). Recognizing when a particular automatic thought is problematic is an important first step in changing or challenging it. Once the client is able to recognize unhelpful thinking patterns, help her or him generate options of how to challenge them. (See Coon et al., for a more detailed review of this technique). With older clients, it is important to have them write down these definitions or give them the information in writing so they can take the information home for review during the week. Weekly review of completed homework at the beginning of each session serves to reinforce the learning and the likelihood of compliance.

Behaviorally Focused Homework. Another assumption of CBT is that certain behaviors contribute to psychological well-being and should, therefore, be increased. Teaching clients to monitor behavior is critical in helping them understand the relationship between mood and behavior. The implication is that as clients become aware that what they do impacts how they feel, they will be motivated to increase or use behaviors that have a positive impact. Older adults find it empowering to realize that they can have a direct impact on their own psychological well-being by choosing to engage in positive behaviors. Many researchers have found that behaviorally focused interventions are effective with older adults (Coon et al., 1999; DeVries & Coon, 2002; Grant & Casey, 1995; Knight, 2004; Teri & Gallagher-Thompson, 1991; Thompson, 1996; Zeiss & Steffen, 1996). Particularly helpful in fostering positive mood for older adults is increasing and maintaining their engagement in meaningful activities. The following homework assignments use behavioral strategies to encourage older adults to increase mood-enhancing behaviors.

- Daily Mood Rating Form. This homework assignment asks clients to track their mood on a daily basis and to make a link to situations or events that contributed to the mood rating. Clients rate each day's mood on a scale of 1 (very depressed) to 9 (very happy). They then list one or two reasons why they felt that way. The goal is for client's to see the connection between what they do or what happens to them and how they feel. Eventually, this form can be used to track behavioral changes to see their impact on mood. The assumption is that the more pleasant activities or events in the person's day, the better their mood.
- Increase Engagement in Meaningful Activities. It is important in behavioral approaches to increase the frequency with which clients engage in pleasant activities. To help the older client identify the specific activities meaningful for them, have them complete the Older Person's Pleasant Events Scale as a homework assignment. This scale identifies the types of activities that a particular older adult might find meaningful and assesses the frequency of engagement in each type of activity. The scale was adapted for use with older adults (Lewinsohn, Munoz, Youngren, & Zeiss, 1986; Teri & Lewinsohn, 1986) and is more completely described in treatment manuals developed by Dick, Gallagher-Thompson, Coon, Powers, & Thompson (1996), Gallagher-Thompson, Ossinalde, & Thompson

(1996) and Thompson, Gallagher-Thompson, & Dick (1995). If the client completes this scale as a homework assignment, the therapist can score it and use it to help the client target the activities that bring satisfaction and meaning but may be occurring with low frequency. The results are presented in graph form and are easy for older adults to grasp. The data gathered from this exercise help motivate the older client to begin the change process by targeting specific pleasant events to increase as a way to offset negative life events or situations. Therapists can have clients track the frequency of pleasant events and link these to the mood ratings. Coon et al. (1999) recommend a goal of at least four consciously chosen events every day to help maintain positive mood.

- Relaxation Exercises. Many older adults report anxiety or chronic pain as a component of negative mood. Relaxation techniques can help alleviate some of the negative impact of these problems. Teaching older clients progressive relaxation techniques (including deep breathing or guided imagery) helps them develop a coping skill that can be used whenever needed. This skill needs to be practiced and can be part of a homework assignment. Ask clients to rate their level of tension or pain before doing the relaxation exercise. Then ask them to rate their tension or pain after completing the exercise. Have them practice this at home on a daily basis to build skill and confidence in their ability to cope using this technique. Remember to check their monitoring sheets each week when they come for therapy to be sure they are progressing in their ability to use the skill and to reinforce their effort.

Relapse Prevention. CBT aims to develop skills that are sustainable after therapy ends. However, older clients may find it difficult to generalize the skills learned to cope with one type of problem when a new problem occurs. An effective strategy to help clients utilize newly learned skills in novel situations is to have them develop a relapse prevention plan as part of the termination process. Relapse prevention strategies explicitly teach clients to be more competent at generalizing skills to new situations. The relapse prevention plan can include a range of activities from periodic "check-ins" with the therapist to the creation of explicit strategies for responding to potential events or problems that may arise. A particularly effective approach is to have the client anticipate potential situations that might be distressing and threaten their sense of well-being. The client is then asked to generate responses that might be helpful if that situation were to arise. These pretend scenarios can be written down in a notebook that clients take with them at the end of therapy. The expectation is that this exercise reinforces the skills learned by asking the client to anticipate how a particular strategy might be useful in other situations.

CASE STUDIES

CASE EXAMPLE #1

Mrs. L., a 68-year-old retired widow, sought help for depression associated with caring for her 91-year-old frail, but cognitively intact mother. The client stated that since her retirement three years before, she has found herself constantly "on call" for her mother and has had no time for herself. The mother, a Greek immigrant who spoke little English, owned a small apartment complex. She lived in one of the units, assisted by a live-in housekeeper who was present Sunday nights through Friday afternoons. Mrs. L. managed her mother's business and financial matters, did all the grocery shopping, provided needed transportation, and brought her mother to her house every weekend. The client had not had a vacation in several years, had no time for leisure pursuits, and felt hurt and depressed by her mother's constant complaints and apparent lack of appreciation for her caregiving efforts. In therapy, two specific areas of distress were targeted and became goals for treatment. First, Mrs. L. expressed feelings of loss of control and loss of freedom in her personal life. Second, she was finding herself dreading spending long periods of time with her mother because of the constant complaints and criticism heaped on her by the mother. The client described her reaction to these stressors as anger and frustration.

Several CBT strategies were employed to address these areas of distress. Mrs . L . was asked to identify two or three specific activities that she had found pleasant and meaningful that she now believed were out of her control. The client indicated that she enjoyed writing and wished she had more time to devote to this interest but found it difficult to turn down a request from her mother if "all I'm doing is playing with my writing." In exploring why it was so difficult to say no to her mother, Mrs. L. concluded that since there was no external deadline or accountability for her writing, she always felt she had to put her mother's requests ahead of her writing. She was asked to research options for formal writing classes that she could take that would require "output" from her writing on a regular basis. She found a suitable class and enrolled. She then blocked out class time and "homework" time on her schedule and gave this to her mother to help set limits on her availability. The result was that Mrs. L. gained increased control of her time for herself, felt pleasantly surprised by her mother's respect for her schedule, and engaged in an activity that brought her significant satisfaction.

A second goal of treatment was to help Mrs. L. find ways to make her weekend caregiving less aversive. To avoid interacting with her mother, Mrs. L. found herself keeping the television on constantly (which she found annoying), lingering in the kitchen over tasks (which kept her isolated in her own house), and "hiding" from her mother's view. She considered these tactics unpleasant but less aversive than the constant complaints and criticism from her mother. Clearly, a goal for treatment was to increase the number of pleasant interactions between the two. Since Mrs. L. used memories of her childhood as the subject for much of her writing, she was asked to employ her mother as a "resource" for gathering information about those childhood years. This cognitive reframe opened the way for the two to interact around a topic of interest to both of them and cast her mother in a helpful rather than unhelpful role. The assignment was structured by having Mrs. L. record these conversations or take notes for later use. Both mother and daughter enjoyed this exercise and expanded it to include memories of the mother's childhood in Greece. Mrs. L. incorporated many of these stories into her writing and shared these with her mother. Once she began to think of her mother as a resource instead of a burden, she found other ways to enjoy their interactions (e.g., gathering old family recipes, reviewing old family photos, etc.). As a result, she experienced less anger and frustration during her weekends with her mother and began to view her overall caregiving responsibility less negatively.

Finally, Mrs. L. was asked to maintain a mood monitor (DTR) every weekend of her thoughts and feelings when she found herself upset by her mother's criticism and complaints. She discovered that most negative interactions centered on her mother's questions regarding Mrs. L's management of the mother's business (e.g., "Have you taken care of paying the electrician?" "Have you called about the new roof?"). Mrs. L.'s dysfunctional belief was that this indicated that her mother was treating her like a child or was assuming that she was irresponsible ("Of course I took care of these things! Does she think I'm a child?"). Mrs. L. was taught to challenge these thoughts and to generate more helpful ones (e.g., "Mom is feeling really helpless and needs reassurance that everything is under control."). By practicing this new skill, Mrs. L. felt more able to manage the weekends with her mother and maintain a more positive attitude.

Note that homework in this case focused on applying the skills taught in therapy to the real life setting of the client. The homework was tailored to the specific situation of the client (lack of time for meaningful activity, aversive interactions during week-end caregiving, and anger and resentment about mother's perceived criticism). The client's compliance with homework was encouraged by making the demands of the homework assignments relevant to the client's specific concerns and her stated goals for therapy. Older adults are more likely to actively engage in therapy and comply with homework assignments if they have a concrete rationale for how a particular assignment will address their problem and help achieve their goals.

Case Example #2

Mrs. F., a 69-year-old divorced woman, sought therapy for her depressed mood, with complaints of low energy and loss of interest in life. She was living independently in her own home and worked part-time (10 hours per week) for the local Department of Parks and Recreation on their quarterly brochure doing design and layout. She had an art background and reported painting in acrylics as her favorite medium. Mrs. F. reported that she no longer painted because she found it too tiring and painful to carry out the physical aspects of painting on the large canvases that she had used in the past. She also complained that she had no close friends and that her relationship with her children was conflictual, although she considered her youngest daughter to be more supportive than the others. Treatment goals focused on improving the client's mood and sense of well-being by increasing her engagement in personally meaningful activities and by supporting a positive relationship with her youngest daughter.

At first glance, it seemed likely that Mrs. F. would benefit from increasing her so-cial interactions and activities. She was asked to complete the Older Person's Pleasant Events Scale as her first homework assignment to help identify the specific activi-ties that she found personally meaningful. After reviewing the results of the Pleasant Event Scale, the client was able to recognize that some activities that were meaningful to her were happening at low frequency and that other activities that she did not enjoy a great deal were happening at high frequency. What was surprising to the therapist was the clear indication from the results of the assessment measure that Mrs. F. found more pleasure from individual activities than from social activities. Apparently, the two days per week at the part-time job provided adequate levels of social interaction. She liked her colleagues there and did not want to add any more social activities to her week. Based on this finding, the goals of therapy were focused on helping the client explore ways to increase the frequency of enjoyable individual activities.

What seemed most salient for this client was the decrease in the amount of time she spent with her painting. She had completely stopped painting because she no longer had the energy or stamina required to set up or manage the large canvases she had used in the past. Rather than seeking to adapt to a more manageable size canvas, she had simply stopped altogether. In exploring her rationale for not doing smaller scale paintings, the client indicated that she saw no point in painting if she couldn't do it the way she wanted. Challenging this unhelpful thinking pattern became the target of the next phase of treatment.

She was introduced to the common patterns of unhelpful thinking and was taught how to challenge these patterns. She was able to recognize her pattern of "all or nothing" thinking and how that had impacted her engagement in painting. For homework, the client was asked to write out as many challenges as she could to her belief that, "If I can't paint the way I used to paint, I won't paint at all." She was told to envision that she was giving these responses to a friend whom she wanted to help. She was able to generate several challenges to her negative thinking and began to feel hopeful that she might paint again.

The next step was to support her efforts to solve some of the problems/obstacles that she felt had kept her from painting. One of her main concerns was that she had moved to a small apartment and there was no room to set up her painting equipment. In exploring this limitation, she generated the solution of finding a class or workshop for painting that would be available on an on-going basis. She located one that met during the daytime (she didn't like driving at night) and was close to her home. The cost was affordable and so she decided to try it. She was surprised by how much she enjoyed getting back into the painting. And, although she felt some frustration with not painting on a large scale, she was able to challenge this negative thought with the reminder that she was still getting to paint. An unexpected benefit of the painting class was to increase the client's social network to include others with similar interests. While she didn't necessarily want to form deep relationships with these individuals, she enjoyed conversations about painting and art.

The final goal for treatment was to support her relationship with her youngest daughter, whom she perceived to be the most compatible of her children. A weekly mood monitor was given as homework, in which the client recorded a rating for each day's mood and indicated why she felt that way. It became clear when reviewing the homework that her mood dipped on days her daughter didn't phone her. When asked why she didn't call her daughter on those days, she said she didn't want to be a burden to her daughter. This negative belief was challenged and she was able to generate several alternate explanations of why her daughter might not call (had to work late, assumed everything was ok if her mom didn't call). Mrs. F. decided to call her daughter at least twice a week to say hello and see how she was doing. She reported that making the phone calls gave her something to look forward to and helped her feel more in touch with her daughter. She appreciated not feeling as though she had to passively wait for her daughter to call. She indicated that the daughter appreciated her mother's interest and concern for her.

In this case, the homework helped to clarify the issues that needed to be addressed in therapy and provided an action plan to address these issues. The Older Person's Pleasant Event Schedule alerted the therapist to the kinds of activities that were meaningful to the client. Without that assessment, the therapist may have mistakenly tried to convince the client to engage in activities that held no meaning for her. Once the older client understood how much she was missing her painting, she was motivated to engage in finding ways to increase this pleasant event. The mood monitor helped the therapist discover how much the client's mood was impacted by phone calls from her daughter. This realization enabled the therapist to challenge Mrs. F.'s assumptions about why the daughter didn't call and to encourage her to exert more control over this pleasant event (by phoning her daughter). The key to these homework assignments was to tailor them to the specific situation of the client and to provide the client with a rationale for how the assigned activity would help meet therapeutic goals.

CONCLUSION

In conclusion, the use of homework as a component of CBT with older adults can be very effective in supporting the therapeutic process, developing coping skills, and preventing relapse of symptoms. Traditional CBT techniques (thought records, mood monitoring, relapse prevention planning, etc.) are appropriate to use with older clients. To be most effective, homework should be assigned in the context of a strong therapeutic relationship and with a link being established between the goals of therapy and how the homework might help the client achieve those therapeutic goals. Homework should be explained as specifically and clearly as possible, be adapted to the realities of the client's life situation, and when completed, be reinforced. Problem solving around lack of compliance with homework will also increase the likelihood that the client will engage in homework. When these accommodations are in place, older adults will be very likely to comply with and benefit from the homework associated with their therapy.

REFERENCES

Coon, D. W., Rider, K., Gallagher-Thompson, D., & Thompson, L. (1999). Cognitive-behavioral therapy for treatment of late-life distress. In M. Duffy (Ed.), *Handbook of counseling and psychotherapy with older adults* (pp. 487–510). New York: John Wiley & Sons.

DeVries, H. M., & Coon, D. W. (2002). Cognitive/behavioral group therapy with older adults. In F. W. Kaslow & T. Patterson (Eds), *Comprehensive handbook of psychotherapy (Volume 2)*, New York: John Wiley & Sons.

DeVries, H., & Gallagher-Thompson, D. (2000). Assessment and crisis intervention with older adults. In F. Dattilio & A. Freeman (Eds.), *Cognitive-behavioral strategies in crisis intervention* (2nd ed.). New York: The Guilford Press.

Dick, L., Gallagher-Thompson, D., & Thompson, L. (1996). Cognitive behavioral therapy. In R. Woods (Ed.), *Handbook of the clinical psychology of aging* (pp. 509–544). Chichester, England UK: John Wiley & Sons.

Dick, L, Gallagher-Thompson, D., Coon, D., Powers, D., & Thompson, L. W. (1996). *Cognitive-behavioral therapy for late-life depression: A patient's manual*. Palo Alto: VA Palo Alto Health Care System and Stanford University, Stanford, CA.

Gallagher, D., & Thompson, L. (1981). *Depression in the elderly: A behavioral treatment manual*. Los Angeles: University of Southern California Press.

Gallagher-Thompson, D., Ossindale, C., & Thompson, L. (1996). *Coping with caregiving: A class for family caregivers*. Palo Alto, CA: VA Palo Alto Health Care System.

Gallagher-Thompson, D., & Steffen, A. M. (1994). Comparative effects of cognitive-behavioral and brief psychodynamic psychotherapies for depressed family caregivers. *Journal of Consulting and Clinical Psychology, 62*, 543–549.

Gatz, M., Fiske, A, Fox, L. S., McCallum T. J., & Wetherell, J. L. (1998). Empirically validated psychological treatments for older adults. *Journal of Mental Health and Aging, 4,*
9–46.

Grant, R. W., & Casey, D. A. (1995). Adapting cognitive behavioral therapy for the frail elderly.
International Psychogeriatrics, 7, 561–571.

Kemp, B. J., Corgiat, M., & Gill, C. (1992). Effects of brief cognitive-behavioral group psychotherapy with older persons with and without disabling illness. *Behavior Health, and Aging, 2,*
21–28.

Knight, B. (2004). *Psychotherapy with older adults,* 2nd edition. Thousand Oaks: Sage Publications.

Lewinsohn, P., Munoz, R., Youngren, M., & Zeiss, A. *Control your depression.* Englewood Cliffs,
NJ: Prentice-Hall.

McCarthy, P., Katz, I., & Foa, E. (1991). Cognitive-behavioral treatment of anxiety in the elderly:
A proposed model. In C. Salzman & B. Lebowitz (Eds.), *Anxiety in the elderly: Treatment
and research.* New York: Springer Publishing Co.

Rybarczyk, B. Gallagher-Thompson, D., Rodman, J., Zeiss, A., Gantz, F. E., & Yesavage (1992).
Applying cognitive-behavioral psychotherapy to the chronically ill elderly: treatment issues and case illustration. *International Psychogeriatrics, 4,* 127–140.

Teri, L., & Gallagher-Thompson, S. (1991). Cognitive-behavioral interventions for treatment of
depression in Alzheimer's patients. *The Gerontologist, 31,* 413–416.

Teri, L., & Lewinsohn, P. (1986). *Geropsychological assessment and treatment.* New York: Springer.

Teri, L., & McCurry, S. (2000). Psychosocial therapies. In C. E. Coffey & J. L. Cummings (Eds.),
Textbook of geriatric neuropsychiatry, 2nd edition. Washington, DC: American Psychiatric
Press.

Thompson, L. W. (1996). Cognitive-behavioral therapy and treatment for late-life depression.
Journal of Clinical Psychology, 57, 29–37.

Thompson, L. W., Davies, R., Gallagher, D., & Krantz, S. E. (1986). Cognitive therapy with older
adults. *Clinical Gerontologist, 5,* 245–279.

Thompson, L. W., Gallagher-Thompson, D., & Dick, L. P. (1995). *Cognitive-behavioral therapy
for late life depression: A therapist manual.* Palo Alto, CA: Older Adult and Family Center,
Veterans Affairs Health Care System.

Zeiss, A., & Steffen, A. (1996). Behavioral and cognitive-behavioral treatments: An overview
of social learning. In S. Zarit & B. Knight (Eds.), *A guide to psychotherapy and aging: Effective clinical interventions in a life-stage context.* Washington, DC: American Psychological
Association.

Chapter 11

COUPLES

Norman B. Epstein and Donald H. Baucom

Surveys of couple therapists by Geiss and O'Leary (1981) and by Whisman, Dixon, and Johnson (1997) produced very similar findings regarding the types of problems most commonly presented by couples who have sought treatment for their relationships. The problems most frequently encountered in therapy involve the couple's behavioral interactions (e.g., communication problems, power struggles, joint decision making, demonstration of affection), whereas others involve subjective cognitions and emotions (e.g., unrealistic expectations of marriage, lack of loving feelings). Although there is a wide range of theoretical approaches to couple therapy [see Dattilio (1998) for a representative overview], a goal that is shared by practitioners of diverse approaches is the modification of distressed couples' interaction patterns. Behaviorally oriented interventions commonly are used to produce change in partners' subjective experiences within their relationship, as in L'Abate's (1999) use of distance writing assignments to enhance couples' intimacy. Furthermore, based on the demands of large caseloads and the requirements that managed care places on clinicians to provide treatment plans that are short-term and concrete, couple therapists commonly turn to interventions that maximize active client involvement and practice of new behavioral patterns and skills.

In addition to structured interventions designed to alter couple interactions during therapy sessions, homework assignments are a key component of such therapy approaches. In order to meet therapists' needs for guidelines in structuring homework in couple therapy, a number of texts have been published in recent years, such as O'Leary, Heyman, and Jongsma's (1998) *The Couples Psychotherapy Treatment Planner* and Schultheis, O'Hanlon, and O'Hanlon's (1999) *Brief Couples Therapy Homework Planner*. Furthermore, a survey of clinical members of the American Association for Marriage and Family Therapy (Northey, 2002, 2005) indicated that the most commonly used approaches (by a notable margin) were cognitive-behavioral and behavioral therapies, and texts describing these treatments emphasize the importance of homework in maximizing therapeutic effectiveness (Baucom & Epstein, 1990; Epstein & Baucom, 2002; Rathus & Sanderson, 1999). In addition, marriage enrichment and prevention programs such as Markman, Stanley, and Blumberg's (2001) Prevention and Relationship Enhancement Program (PREP) that use cognitive-behavioral methods and homework have proliferated. Consequently, it is important that couple therapists be familiar with the rationale, methods, and potential pitfalls of using structured home-work assignments with their clients.

The aims of this chapter are to describe the purposes of homework in couple therapy, potential barriers to its use with distressed couples, and types of homework assignments used in empirically supported cognitive-behavioral couple therapy. The use of homework is illustrated with case examples.

PURPOSES OF HOMEWORK IN COUPLE THERAPY

Cognitive-behavioral couple therapy (CBCT) shares with other relatively brief approaches, such as strategic therapy (Davidson & Horvath, 1997; Keim, 1999) and solution-focused couple therapy (Hoyt & Berg, 1998), an assumption that marital distress is influenced by the specific patterns of a couple's behavioral interactions. In addition, CBCT targets the meanings that the partners attach to those acts, identifying and modifying inaccurate or inappropriate cognitions. Because couples' interaction patterns and cognitions about their relationships commonly become ingrained or "over-learned" and relatively automatic, cognitive-behavioral therapists assume that therapeutic interventions must be designed to directly induce change and maintain it, both during sessions and in the couple's natural environment (Epstein & Baucom, 2002). Consistent with systems theory concepts, because each individual's responses are elicited by the other's behavior and influenced by the consequences that the partner provides (e.g., reinforcement through attention), it is assumed that the likelihood of change occurring increases when both members of the couple are involved in change efforts. Furthermore, changes in a couple's interactions during therapy sessions cannot be assumed to generalize to their home environment, because the conditions in the two settings may differ substantially. In fact, it is not unusual for a couple to tell their therapist, "We behave better in sessions than at home because you are observing us and you stop us from behaving negatively."

Other common differences between the contexts of therapy sessions and a cou-ple's interactions in daily life that can be best addressed through homework are var-ious aspects of their interpersonal and physical environments (Epstein & Baucom, 2002). Whereas in the therapy room there are minimal distractions, in the real world many factors may impinge on a couple's attempts to interact more constructively. These include interactions with other people (children, phone calls from employers), as well as demands from partners' other roles (e.g., household chores, take-home work projects). Consequently, homework assignments are intended to "export" aspects of therapy into the couple's daily life, imposing structure, allowing couples to practice new skills under real-life conditions and contingencies, and raising clients' aware-ness that they will be reporting their performance to the therapist. The goal is for the couple's positive changes to become increasingly independent of the therapist's presence and interventions, with the couple imposing their own structure on their interactions and monitoring their own behavior. The therapist's weekly review of a couple's homework experiences helps the therapist understand the conditions under which the couple is attempting to institute change in their relationship and guides the therapist and couple in modifying interventions as needed to match the couple's life conditions as well as possible. For example, a couple might report difficulty finding time to engage in intimacy-building homework exercises (e.g., practicing expressive and empathic listening skills; scheduling quiet leisure time together) because they have incompatible shift-work schedules. Consequently, their therapist can explore with them how they have managed to reserve time for therapy each week and help them problem solve about ways to protect even small blocks of time for intimacy each week.

Finally, because distressed couples commonly have sought therapy only after their relationships have deteriorated significantly, they are likely to view themselves as ineffective in solving their problems and hopeless about their future; a negative cognitive set not unlike that existing in depression (Epstein, 1985). Consequently, even if a therapist is able to reduce negative interactions and induce some positive interactions during sessions, the partners' negative appraisals of their relationship may persist as long as the in-session changes fail to generalize to positive change in daily life. Therefore, an important goal of homework is to provide the couple with some concrete evidence that they can implement some desired changes on their own, increasing if only a little at a time their perceived self-efficacy. One of the most important areas in which this shift must take place is in the control of physically and psychologically abusive behavior. Lange, Barends, and van der Ende (1998) note that the treatment of choice for impulse control problems such as intimate partner abuse is self-control training, and they describe the use of brief therapy for aggressive couples that emphasizes homework assignments involving time-outs and structured writing assignments for expressing irritations constructively. Similarly, Heyman and Neidig (1997), Epstein and Baucom (2002), and Holtzworth-Munroe, Meehan, Rehman, and Marshall (2002) describe cognitive-behavioral couple therapy procedures, including homework between sessions (e.g., use of time-outs, anger logs, practice of communication and problem-solving skills), for increasing self-control among abusive partners.

COMMON BARRIERS TO THE SUCCESSFUL USE OF HOMEWORK IN COUPLE THERAPY

Because homework has always been a standard component of cognitive-behavioral therapies (Beck, Rush, Shaw, & Emery, 1979), CBT writers have identified a variety of potential barriers to successful homework and have proposed strategies for overcoming them. Although much of this literature is devoted to individual therapy, most of it also is applicable to couple therapy, and increasingly writers are addressing special challenges in the use of homework with couples.

Tompkins (2003) differentiates task factors, therapist factors, and client factors that can interfere with effective use of homework in cognitive-behavioral therapy and cautions therapists to consider the first two forms before concluding that client noncompliance is due to dysfunctional characteristics of the client. Similarly, Jacobson and Christensen (1996) note that couple therapists commonly attribute homework noncompliance to client resistance when it is likely due to inadequate planning and implementation by therapists. Within Tompkins' (2003) categories, task factors in homework noncompliance involve characteristics of the homework assignment that affect the feasibility of clients carrying them out, such as their clarity and complexity. Thus, the couple described earlier who worked different shifts would be unlikely to complete a homework assignment to spend time each evening catching each other up on their day's experiences. Another homework task that seems bound to fail would be asking a couple who had never practiced problem-solving skills to read a handout on problem-solving steps and to try to practice these new skills at home with a highly conflictual issue.

A couple also may not follow through effectively with a homework task that targets a relatively superficial aspect of their concerns and fails to identify and address broader, more fundamental underlying issues. Epstein and Baucom (2002) differentiate between micro-level behaviors and macro-level patterns and themes in couples' relationships; for example a micro-level interaction in which a wife becomes upset when her husband comes home late from work without calling, versus a broader pattern in which the husband consistently makes decisions that fail to take his wife's needs and preferences into account. If homework assignments are too specific and concrete (for example, simply having the husband call each day to tell his wife when he will be leaving work), one or both partners may view it as trivial, or they may complete it but experience no satisfaction from it. Consequently, a couple therapist needs to collaborate with both partners in identifying the macro-level pattern that is relevant to a core relationship concern (e.g., respect, caring, sharing of power) and plan micro-level homework assignments as ways to begin changing the broader pattern.

As described earlier, one of the rationales for using homework assignments is that they allow couples to introduce new behaviors and cognitive responses under real-life conditions, which may differ significantly from those in therapy sessions. For example, practicing expressive and listening skills in the therapist's office, with no distractions and the therapist present to provide coaching and corrective feedback may be less challenging than practicing on their own at home, with the phone ringing and children interrupting. Thus, homework has an advantage of being realistic, but for just that reason the difficulty level of the task selected may be too high. Consequently, it is important that the therapist interview the couple in detail regarding the conditions that they are likely to encounter at home or in any other *in vivo* setting, so the task can be tailored to those conditions. If homework is to increase clients' sense of self-efficacy and hope for their relationship, it should result in early successes.

Therapist factors that can interfere with homework effectiveness commonly involve the therapist's ability to develop a positive alliance with the couple and to reinforce the clients for compliance with homework that they find challenging and stressful (Tompkins, 2003). Couple therapists face a challenge that therapists who work with individuals do not experience; namely, establishing rapport and trust simultaneously with both members of a couple who each may be attempting to form a coalition with the therapist against the other partner (Epstein & Baucom, 2002). Members of distressed couples typically blame each other for relationship problems and may expend considerable effort trying to convince the therapist that the other person is at fault. Couple therapists must be sensitive in balancing the extent to which they look at and speak with the two members of a couple; in some cases responding empathically to one person's description of his or her distress in the relationship will lead the other person to infer that the therapist is sympathizing and siding with the partner (Epstein & Baucom, 2003). Individuals who do not perceive the couple therapist as understanding their perspectives and at least somewhat supportive of their personal goals for therapy are unlikely to comply with homework assignments.

Epstein and Baucom (2002) describe other therapist characteristics that may act as barriers to clients' engagement in the work of couple therapy, including homework. One such factor is the therapist's failure to motivate the members of a couple to try new ways of behaving and thinking that may at first seem difficult or unlikely to make a difference in their relationship. Given the degree of hopelessness that members of distressed couples commonly experience by the time they seek professional assistance, it is important that the therapist convey some reason for hope that the couple can solve the problems that they face. A number of theoretical orientations to couple therapy (e.g., cognitive-behavioral, strategic, solution-focused) emphasize that the solutions that distressed couples have developed to attempt to solve their relationship problems themselves become problematic. As members of a couple repeatedly turn to the same ineffective solutions, they feel stuck and hopeless. Consequently, it is important that therapists shift partners' focus on ineffective solutions, toward "thinking outside the box" and becoming motivated to try new approaches that have the potential to improve their relationship. Clearly, hopeful motivational messages from a therapist must be realistic, and they must be tied to interventions that have good face validity, or the therapist will quickly lose his or her credibility and members of a couple will lack the motivation to complete homework tasks.

Client factors involve characteristics of the partners that interfere with the likelihood that they will carry out homework tasks. One such factor is distressed partners' common tendency to "stand on ceremony" and refuse to make change efforts before they see the other person making what they consider sufficient efforts first (Epstein & Baucom, 2002). This may reflect an individual's more general tendency to avoid taking personal responsibility for problems in his or her life, or it may be due to the individual perceiving that he or she had invested much more effort into the relationship previously and demanding that the partner behave in a more equitable manner in the future by taking the initiative to work harder now (Epstein & Baucom, 2003). In addition, because homework tasks in couple therapy typically emphasize good will and collaboration, some individuals may avoid participating if they believe that doing so will convey to the partner that the individual has forgiven him or her for past transgressions. Furthermore, in CBCT individuals may avoid homework tasks that involve monitoring and examining the validity or appropriateness of their own cognitions due to a concern that the partner will interpret it as the individual's admission of being irrational and responsible for the couple's problems (Epstein & Baucom, 2002).

Another client characteristic that may be related to "standing on ceremony" or otherwise refusing to participate in homework and other therapeutic efforts is a negative attributional bias toward the partner. Research has indicated that individuals who attribute relationship problems to global, stable, negative characteristics of the partner have low expectancies for progress in therapy, are more dissatisfied with the relationship, and engage in more negative behavior toward the partner during problem-solving discussions (Epstein & Baucom, 2002; Noller, Beach, & Osgarby, 1997). Clinical reports also have identified instances in which an individual discounts the value of a partner's positive behavior during homework tasks by attributing it to negative motives such as an attempt to impress the therapist (Baucom & Epstein, 1990). Although there is no direct empirical evidence that negative attributions are associated with less homework compliance, it seems likely that the other demonstrated manifestations of low motivation and lack of collaborative behavior do not bode well for homework completion.

Differences in two partners' levels of commitment to the relationship and/or to couple therapy also have the potential to affect homework compliance (Epstein & Baucom, 2003). Often one member of a couple is more invested in improving and maintaining the relationship than the other is; the other individual may be ambivalent about the couple staying together or might even be in the process of disengaging from the relationship. In such cases, the more motivated partner is more likely to spend time and effort completing homework tasks, and in some cases an individual's repeated failure to complete homework may be a cue to the therapist that he or she has limited investment in the relationship.

However, sometimes an individual's failure to complete a series of homework assignments may reflect a lack of investment in couple therapy rather than in the relationship. As Tompkins (2003) notes, clients' beliefs about the causes of problems, including relationship problems, vary, as do their beliefs about appropriate ways to treat problems. Couple therapists sometimes hear one member of a couple tell the other, "I don't know why you think we need a stranger, and outsider, to tell us how to solve our problems." Individuals' accurate or distorted beliefs about the characteristics of therapy may conflict with their personal beliefs about ways to deal with relationship problems. Discomfort with working with a therapist may be tied to a belief that a healthy relationship should "come naturally," and that any relationship that requires outside intervention probably should not continue. Alternatively, the individual may hold a standard that "what goes on between a husband and wife is their business only" and that disclosing intimate details of the couple's relationship is inappropriate and even shameful. Some individuals engage in a form of psychological partner abuse that Murphy and Hoover (2001) have labeled "restrictive engulfment," in that they maintain control over the partner through various behaviors that block the partner's access to outside resources, including relationships with other people. Such individuals are unlikely to be motivated to participate in homework and other aspects of couple therapy. Whenever a partner fails to complete homework tasks it is important for the therapist to explore the possibility that he or she perceives that the changes inherent in the tasks will alter the distribution of power or some other aspect of the relationship dynamics that has been to that individual's advantage (Epstein & Baucom, 2003).

Some members of couples have difficulty carrying out homework tasks due to individual psychopathology (e.g., clinical depression, obsessive-compulsive disorder, personality disorders) that must be assessed and taken into account by couple therapists. For example, these is substantial evidence that clinical depression and marital distress co-occur at a rate of approximately 50%, and that the causal process between the two problems often is bi-directional; that is, relationship conflict and distress can contribute to the development of a partner's depression, and in turn an individual's depression symptoms can contribute to problems in the couple relationship (Beach, 2001; Epstein & Baucom, 2002). Once a partner is clinically depressed, he or she may lack the motivation, sense of self-efficacy, and hopefulness needed to sustain homework efforts in couple therapy. Although one therapeutic avenue that can be pursued is individual therapy for the depressed partner, there is empirical evidence that couple therapy can be an effective treatment for depression as long as the depression has been influenced by relationship problems (Beach, 2001). In addition, spouse-assisted therapy for forms of psychopathology, in which the relatively symptom-free individual is educated about depression and coached in playing a supportive role in the treatment of the partner's symptoms, increasingly is a treatment option (Epstein & Baucom, 2002). Thus, individual psychopathology can interfere with an individual's ability to complete homework and actively participate in couple therapy, but it need not preclude conjoint treatment.

Thus, there are numerous possible barriers to successful use of homework in couple therapy, owing to the fact that one is working with two individuals who commonly have different types and levels of motivation for the collaborative efforts that characterize effective couple therapy. The therapist must achieve a balance in establishing positive therapeutic alliances with both partners even as the members of the couple are adversarial with each other. Homework tasks must appear to be equitable, relevant to both partners' goals, consistent with each person's desire to protect himself or herself from further hurt and disappointment by the partner, feasible within the context of the couple's daily life, and designed to demonstrate to the couple that there is hope of relating in a more satisfying manner. Consequently, couple therapists must consider these various pitfalls when designing homework tasks rather than applying them in a routine "textbook" way.

TYPES OF COUPLE THERAPY HOMEWORK ASSIGNMENTS BASED ON THEORETICAL AND EMPIRICAL SUPPORT

Even though homework assignments have long been a standard component of cognitive-behavioral treatments for a wide range of adult problems, research isolating the impacts of homework on treatment outcome has been fairly limited, and the results have been inconsistent (Kazantzis, 2000; Kazantzis, Pachana, & Secker, 2003). Nevertheless, a meta-analysis by Kazantzis, Deane, and Ronan (2000) indicated that CBT treatments that include homework have superior outcome effect sizes than treatments that are limited to interventions within sessions. Unfortunately, empirical research isolating effects of homework in CBT with couples is especially limited, in spite of the fact that the CBCT literature details the use of homework as a core component of treatment (Baucom & Epstein, 1990; Dattilio & Bevilacqua, 2000; Dattilio & Padesky, 1990; Epstein & Baucom, 2002; Jacobson & Christensen, 1996; Rathus & Sanderson, 1999). In fact, although there is a substantial body of empirical support for the overall effectiveness of CBCT in improving the quality of couples' relationships (Baucom, Shoham, Mueser, Daiuto, & Stickle, 1998), outcome studies have not "dismantled" interventions in a manner that would isolate the impacts of homework from the effects of the entire CBCT protocol. Rather, the consistent use of homework tasks with couples has been based on empirically supported social learning principles and the overall effectiveness of active client involvement in the development of relationship skills (Baucom & Epstein, 1990; Jacobson & Margolin, 1979). It is widely assumed by CBCT therapists that couples' dysfunctional behavioral, cognitive, and emotional responses are shaped by learning processes, become ingrained over time, and require extensive and repeated *in vivo* interventions to produce positive change. The learning principle of stimulus control posits that individuals are more likely to enact new responses when cues exist in their environment signaling that those responses are appropriate and desirable (i.e., are likely to be reinforced). Planned homework tasks make use of stimulus control to increase the frequency with which couples enact constructive changes outside the therapy sessions where the therapist provides prompts and reinforcement for such acts. In CBCT, types of homework assignments can be categorized as intended to modify (a) behavior, (b) cognitions, or (c) affect (Epstein & Baucom, 2002). All three types of assignments are typically extensions of interventions initiated within sessions.

HOMEWORK TASKS FOR MODIFYING BEHAVIOR

Epstein and Baucom (2002) differentiate between behavioral interventions involving *guided behavior change* and those involving *development of skills*. Guided behavior change interventions focus on each member of the couple agreeing to enact particular types of constructive behavior that address concerns voiced by the partner or identified as likely to enhance the functioning of the couple. This does not involve teaching the couple any new skills, but rather encouraging them to enact forms of behavior that already are in their repertoires but have been absent. As described above, these guided behavior changes target relatively macro-level patterns and themes that have been identified as contributing to the partners' dissatisfaction with the relationship. For example, if members of a couple have exhibited a low level of mutual emotional support, the guided behavior changes may focus on a variety of supportive acts that they could plan to direct toward each other at home. These planned behavior changes can be specific (e.g., a husband may commit himself to talk with his wife each evening about her experiences of the day) or global (e.g., the members of the couple may agree to find ways to comfort each other when the other person has described feeling stressed). As a stimulus for enacting these forms of behavior at home, the therapist might coach the couple in writing out a brief agreement or contract that they will post on their refrigerator or in some other visible location.

Skills-oriented behavioral interventions involve a standard set of learning principles and procedures intended to remediate deficits in the performance of skills that have been found to be associated with relationship quality, namely, expressive and empathic listening skills and problem-solving skills (Baucom & Epstein, 1990; Epstein & Baucom, 2002; Rathus & Sanderson, 1999). The components of skill-training include *instructions* (oral or written information regarding negative forms of behavior and their disadvantages, as well as constructive skills and their positive impacts on relationships), *modeling* (concrete demonstration of desired behavioral skills, directly by the therapist or by means of videotaped examples), *behavior rehearsal* (the couple practicing the skills, with coaching by the therapist), and *feedback* (specific corrective feedback from the therapist as needed, as well as reinforcement of the partners' successive approximations of desired behaviors). Although the skill-training initially is conducted in the therapist's office, it increasingly is transferred to the couple's daily life by means of homework. Homework tasks may include psychoeducational readings about the skills and their value, watching videotape models of good communication that the couple can emulate, practice of the new skills with increasingly challenging issues (beginning with discussions of benign topics and progressing to conflictual ones), and logs that the partners keep of situations in which they used the skills and what consequences ensued.

In addition to relatively generic communication skills and problem-solving skills, couples may be assisted in developing specific skills that address a particular area of concern in their relationship (Epstein & Baucom, 2002). For example, some couples have deficits in time-management skills, whereas others lack the ability to work as a team in providing structure and discipline for their children. Still others have deficits in assertiveness skills and exhibit aggressive and/or submissive behavior during conflicts. After the therapist provides instructions and modeling of appropriate skills during sessions and the couple has practiced during sessions, homework assignments follow for practicing the skills at home.

HOMEWORK TASKS FOR MODIFYING COGNITIONS AND EMOTIONS

A wide variety of interventions exist for modifying inaccurate or inappropriate cognitions that partners experience regarding each other and their relationship, and the reader is referred to Epstein and Baucom's (2002) text for a detailed description. To a significant degree, these involve components of skill-building previously described for the modification of behavior (instruction, modeling, rehearsal, and feedback). Interventions both within sessions and in homework tasks may emphasize behavior or direct attention to thought processes.

Behavioral interventions intended to modify partners' cognitions are designed to create new information that is inconsistent with the clients' existing views. For example, "behavioral experiments" involve enacting particular conditions and examining whether the consequences match one's existing expectancies. Earlier an example was described of a couple being coached in a guided behavior change homework assignment focused on increasing mutual emotionally supportive behavior. In addition to this being a behavior-change task, it may also be intended to alter one or both partners' belief that the other is selfish and uncaring. As the couple agrees to experiment with providing support for each other at home during the next week, even though some successful instances of supportive behavior may not suddenly modify an individual's negative appraisal and expectancies about his or her partner, these exceptions to the negative perspective may begin to "chip away" at it. Similarly, homework practice of communication and problem-solving skills may be set up as means of reducing partners' hopelessness about their ability to resolve conflicts. Finally, role-taking assignments, in which partners attempt to place themselves in each other's role and talk with each other from the other's perspective, can increase mutual empathy (Epstein & Baucom, 2002).

In the tradition of cognitive therapy (Beck et al., 1979), CBCT interventions designed to modify partners' extreme standards, inappropriate assumptions, negative attributions, inaccurate expectancies, and biased perceptions about each other [see Epstein and Baucom (2002) for a detailed description of these forms of problematic cognitions] also include "cognitive restructuring" techniques. These include a variety of approaches to induce clients to examine information that bears on the validity, logic, or appropriateness of their thinking. Homework tasks may include keeping written logs of upsetting events in the relationship and one's "automatic thoughts" that were associated with emotional distress, identifying types of cognitive distortions in one's thinking, challenging negative attributions regarding a partner's negative behavior by generating possible alternative explanations for it, listing advantages and disadvantages of living according to an extreme or demanding standard for one's partner or relationship, reading psychoeducational materials that counteract unrealistic views of intimate relationships (such as romanticized views of conflict-free relations), and monitoring circular processes in one's couple interactions in order to counteract linear causal thinking and blame of one's partner (Epstein & Baucom, 2002; Rathus & Sanderson, 1999).

Homework tasks also are important means of modifying partners' chronic excessive negative emotional responses to each other, or in other cases increasing partners' awareness and expression of important emotions that have been inhibited (Epstein & Baucom, 2002). Control of dysregulated anger expression in a couple's daily life is more likely to be achieved if the couple practices anger management techniques at home on a regular basis. Homework assignments can include use of time-outs in which the partners explicitly agree to withdraw temporarily from each other when they experience cues of mounting anger and reconvene later when calmer in order to discuss a conflictual issue further, scheduling of specific times to discuss emotions, practice of self-instruction and "cool" self-statements to cope with or accept emotional distress and avoid escalation of conflict, self-soothing behavior such as exercising or listening to relaxing music, and practice of expressive and empathic listening skills to enhance an atmosphere of mutual understanding and respect (Epstein & Baucom, 2002; Rathus & Sanderson, 1999). For those who have inhibited emotions, homework tasks may include using vivid imagery and language to enhance emotional experiences, using expressive and listening skills to encourage monitoring and expression of each person's feelings, and blocking ways in which partners typically have avoided each other and their emotional experiences (Epstein & Baucom, 2002).

In summary, we have provided an overview of interventions for modifying behavior, cognitions, and emotions in distressed couples through homework tasks used to extend and supplement interventions during therapy sessions. All of these homework tasks are intended to firmly establish therapeutic changes within the conditions that couples experience in real-life contexts. Given that partners' behaviors, cognitions, and emotional responses to each other continually interact with each other, homework assignments must be designed with their potential multiple impacts in mind.

THE CASE OF MURRAY AND JUNE

Murray and June are a Caucasian couple, both in their late 30s, married for 12 years, and parents of three children ages 11, 9, and 6, who sought couple therapy due to chronic arguments that had escalated to the point where June threatened to leave Murray. An initial assessment interview with the couple revealed that they had met through their work in the same profession and had married after dating for two years. They both reported that before having children they tended to have minimal conflict and enjoyed engaging in a variety of leisure activities together. Between those activities and their demanding jobs, they were very busy, and neither partner put much time and effort into household upkeep and chores, a pattern for which they seemed to have implicit consensus. Following the birth of their first child, June kept working after taking three months of maternity leave, but after the birth of their second child the couple agreed that June would stay at home with the children for several years and then resume her career.

As the demands of raising two and then three young children mounted, the couple's mutually lax approach to time management and coordination of multiple competing activities increasingly took a toll on the quality of their daily life. The youngest child's asthma added an element of anxiety as well as many visits to doctors, including midnight trips to the hospital emergency room. On the one hand, June became upset that she was burdened with the large majority of household and childrearing tasks (including medical appointments and in-home asthma treatments) while Murray focused his attention on increasing career demands. The tension and conflict between the partners was exacerbated by their poor time-management, priority-setting, and problem-solving skills. For example, weekday mornings tended to be chaotic as the couple attempted to get the three children ready for school as Murray also was preparing to leave for work and they also had to make decisions about plans for dinner and evening activities. They reported consistently feeling rushed and "out of sync with each other," and chronically late for scheduled appointments. They often had arguments during the morning scramble, which continued during phone contacts during the day and typically resulted in residual tension during dinner and afterward. Murray complained to the therapist that June nagged him to become more involved with the children and household responsibilities, whereas he felt that he was "running as fast as I can." In turn, June perceived Murray as preoccupied with his own work priorities, and she made an attribution that this was due to his lack of caring about her.

The therapist's assessment of the couple, through the joint interview, an individual interview with each partner, and observations of their interactions during sessions, led to a case formulation in which the couple's initial mutual attraction, expression of mutual support, and shared positive activities had deteriorated as their style of conducting daily life increasingly became inadequate with the introduction of multiple demands of parenthood and work–family role conflicts. They had poor skills for time management, communication regarding conflicts, and problem-solving, and they had not found new ways to convey caring and emotional support for each other once their earlier pattern of dates and long leisurely talks was no longer feasible. Furthermore, they lacked sufficient anger-management skills, so their frustration with each other often escalated into mutual criticism and even verbal abuse. When the therapist gave the couple feedback about these apparent difficulties in their relationship, they agreed that those should be targets for therapy.

A description of the course of couple therapy with June and Murray is beyond the scope of this chapter, so this summary focuses on the use of homework assignments with the couple. All of the assignments were extensions of cognitive-behavioral interventions during joint therapy sessions. Initially, the therapist and couple focused on improving the couple's expressive and empathic listening skills, to create a more collaborative, respectful, and mutually supportive atmosphere in their interactions. After the therapist described expressive and listening skills and provided each partner with a handout that summarized them, the therapist modeled each type of response and then coached the couple in practicing them in session with relatively low-conflict topics. Their homework involved reviewing the communication guideline handouts at home and practicing the skills each day, taking turns in the roles of expresser and listener. Further practice of communication skills with increasingly contentious topics took place as homework over several subsequent weeks. During the first therapy session the therapist also took some time to introduce the couple to anger-management strategies, again using a handout with instructions, modeling constructive responses, and having each person choose at least one strategy to try at home during the next week (in addition to the use of time-outs that the therapist selected for both of them). The planned homework involving communication skills and anger-management strategies was written on a sheet of paper that the couple would post on their refrigerator as a reminder to practice each day.

As the couple became adept and satisfied with their use of expressive and listening skills, the therapist introduced problem-solving skills during a therapy session and began assigning practice of those skills as homework, similar to what had been done with the communication skills. As a special version of problem-solving, the therapist also coached the couple in brainstorming ways of managing their time better in the mornings, considering advantages and disadvantages of each possible solution, and selecting a mutually acceptable approach to try as homework. A similar approach was used to improve their time management in other situations, such as getting the family ready to visit relatives. Given the couple's longstanding difficulty maintaining adequate structure, their success in carrying out these forms of homework varied from week to week, but a persistent and supportive approach by the therapist helped maintain their efforts, and over the course of four months they made notable improvements in their interaction patterns, which improved their levels of satisfaction with their relationship.

THE CASE OF CONNIE AND JIM

Connie and Jim are an African-American couple in their mid 20s, both employed in managerial positions in large companies and childless at this point by choice, given their goal of making career progress before starting a family. They sought assistance at a university-based couple and family therapy clinic after increasingly intense arguments over a variety of issues erupted into physical violence when Connie grabbed Jim while he was attempting to escape an argument with her and he shoved her into a wall. Both members of the couple reported, on the revised Conflict Tactics Scale (CTS2; Straus, Hamby, Boney-McCoy, & Sugarman, 1996), in the joint interview, and in confidential separate interviews, that this was the first incident of physical violence between them, although the amount and intensity of their verbal aggression toward each other had increased over the past several months. Both partners independently reported feeling safe living with the other and participating in joint couple sessions together, as well as a strong commitment to the relationship, a desire to stop the aggression, and an absence of substance abuse by both partners. Based on the multifaceted assessment of psychological and physical abuse conducted in the clinic, the couple qualified for an ongoing research study comparing the effects of a cognitive-behavioral couple therapy for domestic abuse and treatment as usual at the clinic (a variety of systems-oriented approaches to couple therapy) (Epstein & Werlinich, 2003). Both types of therapy involve an extensive pre-treatment assessment, ten weekly 90-minute sessions, an extensive post-treatment assessment, and a four-month follow-up assessment. After the post-treatment assessment couples are given the option of continuing the same type of therapy for as many additional sessions as they and their therapist deem appropriate to meet their goals. Connie and Jim gave their informed consent to be randomly assigned to one of the two conditions and subsequently began the CBCT treatment.

The CBCT approach included standard cognitive-behavioral components (communication and problem-solving skills training, guidance in monitoring and testing the validity and appropriateness of one's cognitions about the partner and relationship, guided behavior change interventions to increase positive couple interactions).

However, they were supplemented with psychoeducation about forms of psychological and physical abuse and their consequences, anger-management skills training, and sessions focused on recovery from past traumatic experiences associated with abusive behavior within the relationship (Epstein & Werlinich, 2003). For each of these therapy components covered during sessions, the therapist and couple devised homework tasks that provided the couple additional practice of skills and that built on changes initiated during sessions. Thus, after the initial psychoeducation and anger management skills session Connie and Jim took home handouts for (a) reviewing types of abusive behavior and their effects on the individuals and couple relationship, (b) reviewing therapy goals that were discussed during the session and adding any new goals that they desired, and (c) practicing anger management skills at home. Following each expressive and empathic listening communication skills session the couple took home written guidelines for the skills and practiced using them with increasingly challenging topics. Similarly, following sessions devoted to the practice of problem-solving skills, the couple took home handouts describing the problem-solving guidelines and used them several times during the week. Homework tasks following sessions on building positive couple interactions through guided behavior change were tailored to the types of positive patterns that the couple desired; in Connie and Jim's case this involved each person going out of his or her way to share time as a couple engaging in leisure activities that the other person enjoys. Finally, sessions focused on recovery from past relationship trauma were followed by homework involving readings and discussions about conceptions of forgiveness, as well as practice of self-care and partner-nurturing activities.

CONCLUSION

Homework is an important component of many approaches to couple therapy and an integral part of cognitive-behavioral couple therapy. It extends the impact of therapy into the couple's daily life and allows them to implement changes in their relationship under the more complex and challenging conditions of the home environment and other aspects of real life. Feedback that the couples give the therapist about their successes and failures with homework assignments is crucial information about ways that therapeutic interventions need to be tailored to the needs of each couple. The success of homework tasks depends on multiple factors concerning the characteristics of the tasks, how the therapist relates to the members of the couple and presents homework goals and methods, and characteristics of the members of the couple such as their goals for their relationship, attitudes about input from outsiders, degree of motivation to take personal responsibility for relationship problems and their solutions, and their comfort with proposed changes in the relationship. Therapists and couples can use homework as a major resource in achieving progress.

REFERENCES

Baucom, D. H., & Epstein, N. (1990). *Cognitive-behavioral marital therapy*. New York: Brunner/Mazel.

Baucom, D. H., Shoham, V., Mueser, K. T., Daiuto, A. D., & Stickle, T. R. (1998). Empirically supported couples and family therapies for adult problems. *Journal of Consulting and Clinical Psychology, 66*, 53–88.

Beach, S. R. H. (Ed.) (2001). *Marital and family processes in depression: A scientific foundation for clinical practice.* Washington, DC: American Psychological Association.

Beck, A. T., Rush, A. J., Shaw, B. F., & Emery, G. (1979). *Cognitive therapy of depression.* New York: Guilford.

Dattilio, F. M. (1998). *Case studies in couple and family therapy: Systemic and cognitive perspectives.* New York: Guilford.

Dattilio, F. M., & Bevilacqua, L. J. (2000). A cognitive-behavioral approach. In F. M. Dattilio & L. J. Bevilacqua (Eds.), *Comparative treatments for relationship dysfunction* (pp. 137–159). New York: Springer.

Dattilio, F. M., & Padesky, C. A. (1990). *Cognitive therapy with couples.* Sarasota, FL: Professional Resource Exchange.

Davidson, G. N. S., & Horvath, A. O. (1997). Three sessions of brief couples therapy: A clinical trial. *Journal of Family Psychology, 11,* 422–435.

Epstein, N. (1985). Depression and marital dysfunction: Cognitive and behavioral linkages. *International Journal of Mental Health, 13,* 86–104.

Epstein, N. B., & Baucom, D. H. (2002). *Enhanced cognitive-behavioral therapy for couples: A contextual approach.* Washington, DC: American Psychological Association.

Epstein, N. B., & Baucom, D. H. (2003). Couple therapy. In R. L. Leahy (Ed.), *Roadblocks in cognitive-behavioral therapy* (pp. 217–235). New York: Guilford.

Epstein, N. B., & Werlinich, C. A. (2003, October). Challenges of controlled research in a clinical setting. Workshop presented at the annual meeting of the American Association for Marriage and Family Therapy, Long Beach, CA.

Geiss, S. K., & O'Leary, K. D. (1981). Therapist ratings of frequency and severity of marital problems: Implications for research. *Journal of Marital and Family Therapy, 7,* 515–520.

Heyman, R. E., & Neidig, P. H. (1997). Physical aggression couples treatment. In W. K. Halford & H. J. Markman (Eds.), *Clinical handbook of marriage and couples interventions* (pp. 589–617). Chichester, UK: Wiley.

Holtzworth-Munroe, A., Meehan, J. C., Rehman, U., & Marshall, A. D. (2002). Intimate partner violence: An introduction for couple therapists. In A. S. Gurman & N.S. Jacobson (Eds.), *Clinical handbook of couple therapy* (3rd ed., pp. 441–465). New York: Guilford.

Hoyt, M. F., & Berg, I.K. (1998). Solution-focused couple therapy. In F. M. Dattilio (Ed.), *Case studies in couple and family therapy: Systemic and cognitive perspectives* (pp. 203–232). New York: Guilford.

Jacobson, N. S., & Christensen, A. (1996). *Integrative couple therapy: Promoting acceptance and change.* New York: W.W. Norton.

Jacobson, N. S., & Margolin, G. (1979). *Marital therapy: Strategies based on social learning and behavior exchange principles.* New York: Brunner/Mazel.

Kazantzis, N. (2000). Power to detect homework effects in psychotherapy outcome research. *Journal of Consulting and Clinical Psychology, 68,* 166–170.

Kazantzis, N., Deane, F. P., & Ronan, K. R. (2000). Homework assignments in cognitive and behavioral therapy: A meta-analysis. *Clinical Psychology: Science and Practice, 7,* 189–202.

Kazantzis, N., Pachana, N. A., & Secker, D. L. (2003). Cognitive behavioral therapy for older adults: Practical guidelines for the use of homework assignments. *Cognitive and Behavioral Practice, 10,* 324–332.

Keim, J. (1999). Brief strategic marital therapy. In J. M. Donovan (Ed.), *Short-term couple therapy* (pp. 265–290). New York: Guilford.

L'Abate, L. (1999). Increasing intimacy in couples through distance writing and face-to-face approaches. In J. Carlson & L. Sperry (Eds.), *Intimate couple* (pp. 328–340). Philadelphia, PA: Brunner/Mazel.

Lange, A., Barends, E., & van der Ende, J. (1998). Self-control in distressed couples: A pilot study. *Journal of Family Therapy, 20,* 367–382.

Markman, H., Stanley, S., & Blumberg, S. (2001). *Fighting for your marriage: Positive steps for preventing divorce and preserving a lasting love.* (Revised ed.) San Francisco: Jossey-Bass.

Murphy, C. M., & Hoover, S. A. (2001). Measuring emotional abuse in dating relationships as a multifactorial construct. In K.D. O'Leary & R. D. Maiuro (Eds.), *Psychological abuse in violent domestic relations* (pp. 29–46). New York: Springer.

Noller, P., Beach, S., & Osgarby, S. (1997). Cognitive and affective processes in marriage. In W. K. Halford & H. J. Markman (Eds.), *Clinical handbook of marriage and couples interventions* (pp. 44–71). Chichester, UK: Wiley.

Northey, W. F., Jr. (2002). Characteristics and clinical practices of marriage and family therapists: A national survey. *Journal of Marital and Family Therapy, 28,* 487–494.

Northey, W. F., Jr. (2005). Studying marriage and family therapists in the 21st century: Methodological and technological issues. *Journal of Marital and Family Therapy, 31,* 99–105.

O'Leary, K. D., Heyman, R. E., & Jongsma, A. E. (1998). *The couples psychotherapy treatment planner.* New York: Wiley.

Rathus, J. H., & Sanderson, W. C. (1999). *Marital distress: Cognitive behavioral interventions for couples.* Northvale, NJ: Jason Aronson.

Schultheis, G. M., O'Hanlon, B., & O'Hanlon, S. (1999). *Brief couples therapy homework planner.* New York: Wiley.

Straus, M. A., Hamby, S. L., Boney-McCoy, S., & Sugarman, D. B. (1996). The revised Conflict Tactics Scales (CTS2): Development and preliminary psychometric data. *Journal of Family Issues, 17,* 283–316.

Tompkins, M. A. (2003). Effective homework. In R. L. Leahy (Ed.), *Roadblocks in cognitive-behavioral therapy* (pp. 49–66). New York: Guilford.

Whisman, M. A., Dixon, A. E., & Johnson, B. (1997). Therapists' perspectives of couple problems and treatment issues in couple therapy. *Journal of Family Psychology, 11,* 361–366.

CHAPTER 12

FAMILIES

Kathleen Newcomb Rekart and Jay Lebow

Family therapy is now a well-established set of methods for helping with the kinds of problems that bring clients to psychotherapy. Psychotherapy research suggests that the involvement of family members is an essential component in the treatment of several individual disorders and relational difficulties, and has considerable value in the treatment of many others (Sprenkle, 2002). Family therapy represents the most direct means for changing troubled relationships. And when an individual's psychological difficulties are conceptualized and treated in the social context of the family, family members can be helpful in a variety of ways. They can support the client as he or she works toward positive change, can act as a coach or surrogate therapist and reinforce the skills the client is working on in session, and/or can create a family environment that may help prevent relapse.

Research has shown that family therapies can be especially helpful in situations where the person who has the disorder does not recognize the impact of his or her difficulties, is reluctant to seek treatment, or has difficulty completing the treatment protocol without significant social support. In these situations, family therapies can promote participation in and compliance with treatment in many who would not otherwise engage in and follow through with treatment (O'Farrell and Fals-Stewart 2000, 2002; Santisteban et al., 1996). Family therapies have emerged as treatments of choice for major mental illness and adult substance abuse. Similarly, the involvement of family has a well-established effect in the prevention and treatment of child and adolescent disorders (Lebow & Gurman, 1995; Sprenkle, 2002).

When one family member is facing a major mental illness such as schizophrenia, the family environment often becomes chaotic and overly critical, and family relationships easily become characterized by conflict and a lack of empathy and understanding. Family interventions target these interpersonal and environmental factors that can affect the individual's ability to manage his or her illness. When family members understand the nature of the mental illness, they can develop some skills to create optimal conditions for the individual with the disorder. Family treatments for schizophrenia (e.g., Barrowclough & Tarrier, 1992; Falloon et al., 1984; Hogarty et al., 1991; Kuipers et al., 1992; McFarlane, 1990; McFarlane et al., 1995) work with families to promote education about schizophrenia, to create less stressful and more structured home environments, to improve communication, problem solving, and social supports, and to develop strategies for cueing and reinforcing appropriate behaviors (see Glaser et al., 2000; Glynn et al., 1993; Lam, 1991; Morrison & Wixted, 1989; Penn & Mueser, 1996; Nichols & Schwartz, 1998).

In families where there are individuals abusing drugs or alcohol, the other family members are often at a loss for how to handle the situation. From their particular vantage point, family members may be more acutely aware of the scope of the problem than is the individual with the substance abuse problem. Yet they may also adopt coping strategies that serve to enable the individual's problem behavior. Family interventions capitalize on the family's insight into the problem and help family members develop more helpful responses to the individual's self-destructive patterns. For example, several family treatments for adult alcohol abuse focus on helping the family to engage the person with the substance use disorder in treatment, and on training the family to provide positive reinforcement for non-drinking related activities and to not reinforce drinking episodes (Azrin, 1976; O'Farrell, 1993; Rotunda & O'Farrell, 1997; Sisson & Azrin, 1986).

The treatment of child and adolescent disorders, as Kazdin and Weisz (1998) suggest, is often *de facto* family treatment. Family environments, relationships, and interactions that impact the child or adolescent often are the focus of the intervention. For example, parent management training is a treatment strategy employed for a large number of problems including conduct disorder, learning disabilities, medical problems, and ADHD (see Godding et al., 1997; Graziano & Diament, 1992; Kazdin, 2000; Wood & Miller, 2002). Treatments for conduct disorders target parenting effectiveness, parental monitoring, and coercive reinforcement contingencies (Alexander & Parsons, 1973; Patterson, 1986; Scott et al., 2001; Spaccarelli et al., 1992; Webster-Stratton, 1994).

Family treatments for adolescent delinquency (Alexander & Parsons, 1973; Henggeler & Sheidow, 2003; Szapocznik & Williams, 2000) and adolescent substance abuse (Henggeler et al., 2002; Liddle and Dakof, 1995) target family conflict, communication, parenting skills, and problem solving (see also Alexander & Sexton, 2002; Kazdin & Weisz, 1998; Rowe et al., 2002). These approaches typically pair work with the adolescent alone with work with the family and other relevant systems.

In a similar manner, family involvement has been shown to be helpful for child and adolescent anxiety disorders (e.g., Albano & Barlow, 1996; Barrett et al., 1996; Ollendick & King, 1998), depression (e.g., Birmaher et al., 2000; Clarke et al., 1999; Fristad et al., 2003; Goldberg-Arnold et al., 1999; Kaslow et al., 2002; Lewinsohn et al., 1990; Stark et al., 1991), child obesity (e.g., Epstein et al., 1994, 2000; Epstein, 2003), and eating disorders (e.g., Eisler et al., 1997; Geist et al., 2000; Robin et al., 1998). Parenting and family-strengthening programs are effective in preventing many types of adolescent problems [e.g., violent and aggressive behaviors, smoking, teen pregnancy, and school failure; see Kumfer and Alvarado (2003)].

Family therapy is also clearly the treatment of choice for a variety of family relational disorders including difficulties in relationships in nuclear families and extended families surrounding issues such as communication, problem solving, and attachment.

Although there is a wide range of disorders and target behaviors impacted by family therapy, in practice, there are numerous commonalities among the therapeutic techniques employed. Across all disorders, families are attempting to handle difficult situations and build some skills to improve their functioning. Although the specific tasks may differ across the kind of target problem, the same kind of core family processes are ultimately involved, including strengthening communication and problem solving, nurturing attachment, building family structure, and shaping appropriate reinforcement contingencies. Therapist recommended between session task performance, or homework, is one such tool to evoke positive change.

Homework is widely used across theoretical orientations (Dattilio, 2002; Kazantzis and Deane, 1999). Therapists assign homework with the overarching goal that clients incorporate the skills and gains made in therapy into their everyday lives. While there is a dearth of studies of homework in family therapy, there is an obvious ecological fit between family therapy and homework since it is natural to extend the work in sessions to the life family members share outside of therapy. Thus, homework is a widely used component of almost all forms of family therapy (e.g., Birmaher et al., 2000; Carr, 1997; Kolko et al., 2000).

HOMEWORK IN FAMILY THERAPY

Homework provides the individual and family the opportunity to continue the work of the intervention in their home environment (see Dattilio, 2002). There are resources such as workbooks that therapists and families can utilize when formulating out-of-session activities (see L'Abate, 1996, 2004a, b). The most commonly used assignments in family therapy can be classified under the broad headings of psychoeducation, individual assignments, contingency systems, communication practice, affective connecting, family activities, and differentiation.

PSYCHOEDUCATION

The psychoeducation component of homework in family treatment encourages family members to inform themselves more fully about the psychological issues and concepts covered in session (see Lukens & McFarlane, 2004; McFarlane et al., 2003; Murray-Swank & Dixon, 2004). The goals of such assignments are often to provide a greater understanding of the challenges faced in treatment and to build a common vocabulary for discussing issues. Therapists direct the family to purchase reading materials or provide articles or handouts for the family to examine between sessions. Sometimes therapists suggest family members attend an informational session, lecture series, or workshop that is relevant to treatment. Psychoeducation is particular effective in family therapy to help family members comprehend family processes and/or the impact individual disorders have on family relationships. Often these assignments can be used as discussion launchers for the subsequent session.

INDIVIDUAL ASSIGNMENTS

Individual assignments direct each individual to complete given tasks between sessions that work on a variety skills/competencies. These tasks are similar to those that might be in focus in individual therapy, though the exploration of this homework and its meaning in the family therapy context may differ considerably from the individual therapy context. These assignments are personalized to the individual within the larger family system. The goals of such assignments are often to practice skills, to test hypotheses, and to collect data on thoughts, symptoms, and abilities. Assignments may include but are not limited to journal keeping, mood or symptom assessment, behavioral self-monitoring and recording, and/or individualized goal setting. Anger-management and self-control assignments focus individuals on skills crucial for working with others in the context of family treatment. Information garnered from these assignments can help direct treatment to areas of particular concern.

CONTINGENCY SYSTEMS

Homework that focuses on contingency systems instructs family members, especially parents and other caregivers, to set up and maintain a reinforcement plan that works to increase the likelihood that identified individual(s) will engage in desired behaviors. Assignments related to contingency management help structure family interactions to prevent coercive exchanges whereby negative behaviors receive all the family's attention. Token economies or point systems are set up so that the performance of target behaviors earns tokens or points that can be exchanged for other rewarding items or activities. Aspects of these assignments include but are not limited to specifying target behaviors, implementing the contingency plan in the home (e.g., making the point chart or behavior contract, obtaining reinforcers), attending to and reinforcing the targeted behaviors in an appropriate and reliable manner, and finally recording any problems that arise as the ideas discussed in session are put into practice in the home.

COMMUNICATION

Communication practice challenges family members to build upon what they have learned in session about the importance of effective communication and to carry out certain strategies at home. These assignments may include following certain rules for talking to each other, setting aside time to interact, holding a family meeting where people's concerns can be addressed in a constructive manner, and/or developing a structured format for handling problems when they arise. Homework helps the family members continue to identify and modify maladaptive communication patterns outside of session. With work, these effective communication strategies may generalize to the family's everyday interactions, promote better family functioning, and prevent future conflicts and problems.

AFFECTIVE CONNECTING

Beyond communication, other assignments work to build, rebuild, or strengthen family relationships, attachment, and affective bonds (e.g., Liddle & Hogue, 2000). The goal of these assignments is to cultivate positive affect and relationship satisfaction. Family members may be directed to do something nice for another family member, to make a list of family a family member's positive qualities and share it with him or her, and/or to spend time engaging in a mutually pleasant activity with another family member. In this way, the linkages within specific family subsystems are strengthened.

Family Activities

The whole family might be assigned an activity to complete as individuals or as a family. There are several goals advanced by family assignments including collecting information about the family system or strengthening the family structure. For example, the whole family is instructed to reflect how they view family relationship and/or alliances (see Dattilio, 2002). This information helps the therapist capitalize on the strength or focuses on the weaknesses of the family structure to further treatment. For other assignments, the adults in the family are instructed to set boundaries and to engage in operations (e.g., discussions, disagreements) without involving the children. These tasks clarify family roles and can contribute to improvements in family functioning.

Other family tasks involve gathering information about a given problem from multiple sources. Family members collect data and make notes about the quality of family interactions and/or to test a particular hypothesis formulated in session. Sometimes the family is enlisted to monitor each other's progress, to help another member complete his or her homework tasks, to provide encouragement and social support, or to brainstorm ideas for topics to be covered in session. In addition, the family might be directed to engage in activities together as a group to foster a sense that they are a unified front when tackling problems.

Differentiation

Utilizing a quite different kind of assignment, methods of family therapy such as Bowen therapy direct family members to utilize interactions outside of the therapy session as the place to experiment with goals such as becoming more differentiated from other family members. In this context, the therapist acts as coach to help process and shape each individual's ability to find a more successful position vis a vis their own family of origin.

HOMEWORK IN THE CONTEXT OF VARYING TARGETS FOR INTERVENTION

It is clear from this brief discussion that there are numerous ways to supplement in-session work with out-of-session assignments. Within this broad framework, therapists select homework assignments based on the targets of the intervention. While not trying to be exhaustive, we present several examples of how homework is applied to particular targeted presenting problems.

For the family of an individual with a major mental illness like schizophrenia, much of the treatment focuses on supporting the family in developing more effective ways of dealing with the symptoms of the disorder, and this is reflected in the tasks that are assigned for homework (e.g., Mueser et al., 2001). The psychoeducation component of treatment for the family often consists of reading assignments detailing the symptoms and common issues related to schizophrenia (see McFarlane et al., 2003). Family members are also instructed in how to minimize the presence of expressed emotion in ongoing family life, with subsequent follow-up about efforts to achieve this goal. The person with schizophrenia is also often assigned behavioral tasks that a family member may monitor over the course of the week and report back in session. Additionally, when the individual does not follow through with agreed upon tasks, or other problems arise, the family may be directed to have a problem-solving meeting where they work through the problem-solving techniques learned in session (Mueser et al., 2001). Finally, the family may be directed to schedule activities both for themselves and for the individual with schizophrenia in order to decrease the isolation and increase the social supports available in their community (see Glaser et al., 2000).

In behavioral family treatment for adult substance abuse, the targets of the intervention are family functioning both in general and in relation to the individual's drinking behavior. Homework assignments reflect these goals. While the individual with the substance abuse problem has such tasks as committing to sobriety and attending 12-step meetings and submitting to weekly drug tests, family members may be asked to follow certain rules for interacting with each other (e.g., avoiding talking about past drinking episodes or getting divorce) outside of session. Families are frequently encouraged to practice the skills learned in session (e.g., structured listening) and to engage in pleasant activities to enhance the family relationships (see Rotunda and O'Farrell, 1997). In a similar vein, family members of substance abusers who are not in treatment are coached in family sessions in how to create a stable environment in the presence of the substance abuse and how to work with the abuser to obtain help (O'Farrell and Fals-Stewart, 2002).

Family-focused interventions for child and adolescent externalizing problems (oppositional behavior, attention deficits and hyperactivity, aggressive and antisocial behavior, and delinquency) target parenting and parental monitoring, communication, problem solving, family relationships, pro-social behavior, and coping skills. Parents are assigned the tasks of recording the frequency of a child's behaviors, re-enacting a parenting role-play that was practiced in session, attending to and reinforcing "good" behaviors, establishing and maintaining a token economy for the home, contacting the child's teacher and facilitating communication with the school, or scheduling and participating in pleasant parent-child activities (e.g., Prinz and Miller, 1994; Sanders et al., 2000). Homework for the child or adolescent includes recording feelings or the frequency of target behaviors, identifying cognitive distortions, practicing a problem-solving or communication skill learned in session, or substituting pro-social behaviors for aggressive acts in social situations with peers (e.g., Barkley et al., 2001; Hogue et al., 1998).

Family treatments for children and adolescents with internalizing problems (anxiety and depression) focus on symptom reduction and family environment factors that contribute to the exacerbation of the symptoms. Homework assignments for the child or adolescent with anxiety include completing workbook pages, practicing cognitive restructuring techniques, and completing exposures to feared stimuli or situations (e.g., Barrett et al., 1996; Kearney & Alvarez, 2004). Parents of a child with anxiety, are assigned homework related to developing and maintaining a contingency system for the child whereby courageous behaviors prompt social reinforcement and excessively anxious behaviors prompt a reminder to engage in coping skills or might involve adopting new strategies for handling their own anxiety and conflict resolution techniques help parents act as a team when dealing with the child's difficulties (e.g., Barrett et al., 1996; Hudson and Kendall, 2002; Kearney and Alvarez, 2004). Homework for the child or adolescent with depression focuses on completing workbook pages on mood monitoring and depressogenic cognitions (e.g., Clarke et al., 1999). For parents of a child with depression, homework entails practicing problems solving skills and conflict resolution techniques and increasing the frequency of positive family activities (e.g., Clarke et al., 1999; Stark et al., 1991).

Family interventions for other child and adolescent problems such as obesity and other eating disorders promote family behaviors that support the child or adolescent in improving and managing his or her condition. For example, homework for children dealing with obesity centers on making low-calorie food choices, keeping a food journal, and exercising, while family tasks include reinforcing these behavior changes and creating a healthier lifestyle for the family as a whole (e.g., Epstein et al., 1994). Homework for individuals dealing with eating disorders might consist of food diaries, eating a specified diet, and refraining from purging behaviors (e.g., Miller, 2004), while homework for parents might include supporting and reinforcing the child's pro-treatment behaviors, establishing regular family mealtimes, remaining with the child for an hour after eating to prevent purging, and/or practicing conflict resolution techniques to lessen tension in the family (e.g., Robin et al., 1998).

In the context of family relational difficulties, homework typically focuses on communication and connection outside of the context of therapy sessions. This may involve efforts to follow up on assignments between family members who attend sessions or, as in the Bowen method (Bowen, 1966), to do so with other family members who do not attend sessions. Typically, such assignments focus on improving communication, building affective bonds and attachment, and/or becoming less reactive to family anxiety. Minuchin (1974) frequently utilized family tasks to build connection in disconnected family subsystems. Bowen assigned family members tasks of exploring their connections with their own families of origin out of session in order to better differentiate from their early family experiences. In a similar vein in the context of specific presenting difficulties, Liddle and colleagues have made assignments designed to increase parent–child attachment a central part of Multidimensional Family Therapy for adolescent substance abuse (Liddle and Hogue, 2000) Diamond and colleagues (Diamond and Siqueland, 1998) has made such assignments a crucial aspect of their treatment for adolescent depression.

This brief review of the use of homework in family therapy, although not exhaustive, points to how integral homework is in family treatment. The completion of tasks outside of session helps move the therapy forward.

EMPIRICAL FINDINGS

Although there are very few findings that have assessed the value of homework in family therapy, the results of empirical research from individual therapy readily can be extrapolated to the family to point to the increased likelihood of positive outcome in therapy in cases where there was compliance with homework (Kazantzis, 2000). For example, studies of the effects of homework with individuals receiving CBT for depression have shown that treatment with homework was more effective than treatment without (Bryant et al., 1999) and that homework compliance predicts change in symptoms both early and midway through treatment (Addis and Jacboson, 2000). Additionally, individuals who complied more with homework assignments showed significantly greater symptom reduction (Bryant et al., 1999; Burns and Spangler,

2000). Yet achieving this level of compliance is often a challenge—especially in family therapy, given the multiple participants.

BARRIERS TO THE SUCCESSFUL USE
OF HOMEWORK

To some extent, individual and family therapists face some of the same difficulties with homework assignments. Yet other challenges are unique to working in the context of a distressed family system.

By the time a family presents for therapy, the family environment is often characterized by high stress and conflict. Family members involved in treatment may have had little to no experience with psychotherapy and may not know what to expect. To add a level of complexity, each family member may approach treatment with varying levels of motivation and with diverse perspectives on the scope and nature of the problem. Additionally, family therapists are mindful of reports suggesting that close to half of families who seek treatment drop out prematurely (Kazdin, 1996; Wierzbicki and Pekarik, 1993).

Homework compliance is an extension of treatment participation. Thus, several factors affecting involvement in family treatment (see Kazdin, 2000; Kazdin et al., 1997) are particularly relevant to homework completion. In their study of families of children in treatment for externalizing behaviors, Kazdin and colleagues (1997) found stressors and obstacles to coming to treatment, perceptions that the treatment was not relevant to the presenting problem, and a poor relationship between the parent and the therapist were all factors related to families dropping out of treatment. In a similar manner, potential barriers to the successful use of homework in family therapy include treatment engagement, therapeutic alliance, and homework acceptance.

Because homework assignments extend the work of therapy, it is difficult to structure and implement homework assignments for family members who do not attend sessions. Scheduling constraints, childcare issues, perceived low level of need for treatment, lack of motivation for change, and negative perceptions of the therapy process are just a few variables impacting the extent to which family members become engaged in treatment (see Perrino et al., 2001). For example, some research indicates fathers are less likely to agree to agree to participate in child-oriented therapy than are mothers (Duhig et al., 2002). In other cases, children and adolescents may resist treatment (e.g., Szacpocznik et al., 1988). Thus, a major task of the family therapist planning to use homework is promoting session attendance and family involvement in therapy activities.

The family members' relationship with the therapist also impacts successful homework use. The extent to which family members feel the therapist is working hard to help them with their problems impacts the degree to which they integrate his or her recommendations for between-task assignments. Yet, managing the complex interplay of alliances in family treatment is a challenge. For example, a strong alliance between the therapist and a parent might increase the likelihood that the adolescent would be brought to treatment, but might decrease the likelihood that an adolescent would similarly feel a strong alliance and follow through with a homework assignment. Thus, the quality of the therapist's interactions with each family member as well as the systemic implications of these relationships impacts the successful use of homework in therapy.

Another factor influencing homework compliance is the extent to which the family members accept assignments. Of particular import is the family's perception that the homework is reasonable and appropriate given the presenting concerns. Problems with homework compliance arise when tasks are poorly defined or directives are perceived as overwhelming or too difficult to complete given the family structure and level of family functioning. Problems with communication or working as a team and conflictual feelings about change are other examples of issues affecting homework compliance (see Dattilio, 2002).

Frustration, when progress is slower than expected, is another factor that influences task performance. Additionally, clients looking for a speedy solution become disappointed easily when faced with the reality that the real change takes a protracted effort. Thus, the tendency to give up or reject assignments or directives that do not produce immediately results is another potential problem for family therapists using homework.

Families also face the constraints imposed by time and the need for cooperation of all family members in homework. Whereas an individual might be able to complete a homework assignment on his or her own in whatever time they have chosen to allocate, family homework assignments depend on the availability of all family members. In today's busy family, there may be few opportunities to complete collective assignments even when motivation is high.

Individual motivation, either conscious or unconscious, presents yet another possible constraint. Family members may have reasons, in or out of awareness, that assignments may be undesirable. Thus, an individual with a fear of intimacy may avoid collective family assignments designed to build connection. And it often is the involvement of the least motivated family member that blocks the completion of family tasks.

Despite these potential barriers to the successful use of homework in family treatment, most family therapists work to integrate task assignments into therapy. Attention to factors that promote the completion of homework assignments would logically impact treatment success.

STRATEGIES FOR SUCCESSFUL
HOMEWORK USE

While there are several barriers to homework compliance, several techniques can be employed to maximize the effectiveness of homework in family therapy. Strategies that engage family members, that promote positive therapist–family member interactions, and that consider task difficulty in the context of the family system contribute to successful homework use in treatment.

Tactics for increasing family engagement in treatment include inviting important family members to session from the start of treatment. Additionally, discussing the family members' expectations of the treatment helps to promote engagement. Finally, the therapist can employ strategies from structural family therapy (e.g., Minuchin, 1974; Szacpocznik et al., 1988) to "join" with the family in a way that does not challenge the family system and "restructures" aspects of the resistance that prevents family members from attending treatment sessions or completing homework. In this respect, the therapist targets the resistance to homework as a symptom of the family's disorganization utilizing active engagement strategies working within the family system to evoke change.

Therapist behaviors promoting good working relationships with clients also affect homework compliance. Indeed, the extent to which the therapist is a good social reinforcer has been shown to impact homework completion in individual therapy (Mahrer et al., 1994). In addition, a therapist emphasizing the attempt rather than the outcome is in a better position to reinforce all homework-related behaviors. In the face of noncompliance, the therapist must be patient, persistent, and focused on building and maintaining the therapeutic alliance. From a systemic perspective, "joining" with the family allows the therapist to work from within their family structure (e.g., Szacpocznik et al., 1988). From this vantage point, the therapist can make homework recommendations without alienating important family members. Finally, adopting different interaction styles with family members is utilized to bolster the therapeutic alliance with reluctant participants. For example, some research suggests that male clients respond better to structured interactions in session (Carr, 1998), which could be employed as a technique to foster the alliance with fathers in treatment.

The last group of methods that promote effective homework use is focused on making homework assignments acceptable to clients and handling noncompliance. Such efforts before, during, and after task assignment increase the likelihood that a homework assignment will be carried out.

From the start of treatment, the extent to which the therapist discusses the role of homework assignments in therapy, solicits input from the family members, and structures homework that considers the family's expectations and goals impacts homework completion. The early and consistent use of homework affects whether or not family members adopt the stance that homework is important to treatment. Starting off with tasks tailored to the strengths of the family system, focusing homework on areas where there is a high perceived need for change, collaborating with the family to come to an agreement about what the assignments should be, practicing the homework task in session, and giving the family members ample opportunities to ask questions and clarify ambiguities are all important operations to maximize task acceptance.

Post-task, the therapist must follow up with the family and use information obtained from the assignments in treatment planning. Whether or not an assignment went well or was effectively implemented can become the basis for the next assignment. Building on past assignments both in session and when formulating future assignments, emphasizes the importance of between-session tasks. The continuous assessment of homework progress discourages indolence, helps the family avoid setbacks, and allows the therapist to head off potential problems as the family moves beyond the initial acceptance phase of the assignment.

Much of the relevant research on homework acceptance and compliance has been conducted in the context of individual therapy but can be generalized to family treatment. For example, homework assignments must be meaningful to the client and relevant to the treatment goals (e.g., Conoley et al., 1994). Whenever possible, the therapist should make sure the directions for the assignments are in writing to prevent misunderstandings (Cox et al., 1988). Beyond pre-task techniques, the strongest predictor of homework compliance was the therapists' behavior and attention to reviewing the assignments in the subsequent session (Bryant et al., 1999; Worthington,

1986). Indeed, there is a great deal therapists can do to maximize the likelihood clients will follow through with treatment recommendations.

With an awareness of obstacles and an arsenal of strategies, family therapists can structure sessions and interactions to maximize benefits of homework for their clients. Homework assignments are essential ingredients for furthering progress in almost all family therapy. And, whether or not homework assignments are completed, they become dynamic assessment tools providing the therapist with valuable information about the scope of the problem and the extent to which assignments must be scaled back to achieve success with tasks and by extension with treatment. Pinsof (1995) has pointed to how homework assignments are handled number among the key facts available in family assessment; a view that can prove much more useful than family descriptions of their problems. What families do in homework can help identify both family strengths and constraints that maintain family difficulties.

USE OF HOMEWORK IN PREVENTION PROGRAMS

Homework also has an essential role in programs aimed at primary and secondary prevention in families (see Kumpfer and Alvarado, 2003; L'Abate, 1998). Although this chapter is focused on the effective use of homework in the clinical context, the successful implementation of homework in prevention programs follows substantially the same principles. Perhaps the greatest difference lies in the reality that most prevention programs do not engage all members of a family. Homework can only be presented to family members involved in the program, necessitating greater consideration of how family members who are not present respond to the homework.

CASE EXAMPLE: THE WILLIAMS FAMILY

Presenting Problem/Description

Anna Williams, 21, presented to treatment with her son Jake at the urging of Jake's kindergarten teachers because he had been acting out and hitting children at school. The school offered placement in a special needs classroom with more staff, but instead Anna agreed to get him into therapy to help him with his behavior and his self-esteem.

Case Formulation

Anna, a young single mother, had raised Jake under the watchful and critical eye of her own mother, Rose, and largely independently of Jake's father Jim. Anna made all of the parenting decisions often with some unsolicited input from her mother. Jake saw his dad, Jim, on a weekly basis. Anna and Jim's relationship was cordial but not very collaborative. When dealing with Jake, Anna would negotiate and reason with him to try to convince him of the merits of her requests. Often Jake would get his way because Anna would be too worn out to continue the argument. On the other hand, Jim would yell and threaten Jake with unreasonable consequences to gain compliance, which would occasionally escalate into corporeal punishment.

Anna was also being bombarded by input from her mother and extended family about how best to handle Jake, and completely undermining her authority and her sense that she could figure out what was best for him. Her desperate attempts to fix the situation with Jake led her to try any and every suggestion leaving Jake utterly confused about the rules. Rose felt Jake was so out of control that she would no longer provide childcare because the stress was too much for her.

In her search to find the root of Jake's problems, Anna blamed Jim's absence in Jake's life and his lack of financial support for Jake's aggressive behaviors and for her stress. She blamed the teachers and the school for their incompetence. She felt that the school was too understaffed to give Jake the structure he needed to succeed, and she informed the school that she was considering legal action. Finally Anna blamed Rose for continually interjecting her own parenting style and undermining Anna's authority with Jake. It became clear that she was grappling with the realization that her child was having difficulties, failing to see that she might be part of the problem.

COURSE OF TREATMENT

On the basis of the case presentation, the therapist took a parent-management perspective and recommended Anna implement a token economy in the home. By encouraging Anna to give Jake a consistent structure, she could assert herself as the parent and he could begin to learn the rules without them changing every week. For Anna, it was particularly stressful for her to get Jake ready to go to school in the morning and ready for bed at night. As a result he was often upset when he got to school and overtired throughout the day. The morning and night routines were the first targets. In session the therapist brainstormed what successful morning and night routines looked like from Anna's perspective and brainstormed with Jake rewards he would like to receive. For homework Anna agreed to set up a chart with a list of these behaviors, and Jake would get stickers if he successfully engaged in these behaviors that he could trade for a trip to a fast food restaurant.

The next session, the therapist checked about how the chart worked that week, and Anna revealed that Jake behaved better the past week, so she did not want to introduce anything new when he was doing better. She felt that it would be too much for him that week. Anna was praised for thinking about how to best implement the point system and validated her concern that Jake might react negatively to the new system. Yet the therapist persisted and explained that the goal was to get Jake to understand the concept that his good behaviors would be rewarded and also stressed that it was a great opportunity to start the reinforcement when he was doing well so that he would have some opportunities to get reinforced. Together Anna, Jake, and the therapist spent time during session making the chart and breaking down the "going to bed routine" into distinct steps (e.g., washing face with a washcloth, putting toothpaste on a toothbrush, brushing teeth for 2 minutes, going to the bathroom, washing hands, getting into bed). Finally the therapist asked Anna and Jake to bring the chart in next session for review.

Anna and Jake did bring the chart back with five out of seven days filled in. The therapist praised both Anna and Jake effusively for their success! Anna explained that since Jake had been doing better, Rose agreed to watch him on Thursday night and again on Saturday night, but had not completed the chart because Rose felt that adults should not have to bribe children to get them to behave. Anna and Jake reported that things were a lot better at home and Anna noted that Jake was less cranky in the morning because he was getting more sleep at night. The therapist noticed, however, that after one day without the reinforcement, the subsequent day Jake did not get all of the stickers and reflected this observation to Anna. Everyone agreed to invite Rose to the next session to explain how to use Jake's point system. Anna mentioned that Jim should probably come in and learn it too.

The next session both Rose and Jim attended with Anna and Jake. The therapist checked Jake's chart, which was almost all filled out, and took the opportunity to praise Anna and Jake for sticking to the point system for three weeks. Jake had earned his trip to the fast food restaurant and was already thinking of what he wanted to work toward next. In preparation for the next week, the session was spent explaining the point system to Rose and Jim. Jake and Anna role-played how Jake got stickers for following his steps for getting ready for bed, and then both Rose and Jim practiced giving Jake stickers contingent on his good behaviors. Both Rose and Jim were given the opportunity to ask questions, and the therapists tackled Rose's concern about "bribing" children with the reframe of building skills with positive reinforcement. The whole family was assigned contingency management as homework.

The goals for treatment for the Williams family included having Anna establish a level of consistency and structure for Jake that was lacking and helping Jake to learn more appropriate ways of interacting. This example illustrates how the homework assignment gave the family the opportunity to practice the concepts of contingency management at home and showed Anna to break down a complex behavior down into concrete steps to make it more manageable for Jake to comply successfully.

When the homework assignments were not completed, the therapist had the opportunity to hear Anna's concerns about the impact of the assignment on Jake, which might have reflected Anna's anxiety about how changes in her behaviors would affect her relationship with her son. Thus the therapist could explore Anna's ambivalence and offer reassurance. Additionally, the therapist's willingness to make the homework a focus of the session indicated its value as a necessary step to achieving the treatment goals, while the therapist's reinforcement of all pro-homework behavior kept the tone of sessions positive.

Once the Anna accepted the assignment, the therapist remained positive and reinforcing while keeping an eye out for potential problems. One such issue came up when the therapist recognized that an important and influential member of the family, Rose, had not accepted the treatment rationale by her refusal to use the contingency system. The plan to bring Rose into treatment and deal with her concerns directly was an attempt to keep the whole family focused on how best to achieve the treatment goals.

OUTCOME

Homework was successfully implemented in this case and the treatments goals in this case were principally achieved. Jake continued to earn points for his bedtime routine. Anna added other behaviors to his point chart including some chores around the house. Rose quickly became an advocate of the system and used it when she watched Jake. Jim made a chart for Jake at his house, but declined future invitations to come to sessions.

Yet, Jake continued to have some bad days at school. As family therapy progressed, the focus shifted to adding a classroom contingency program.

CASE EXAMPLE: THE KLEIN FAMILY

PRESENTING PROBLEM/DESCRIPTION

The Klein family, Dave, 48, Jess, 42, and William, 14, presented to treatment for William's school refusal and social anxiety. Although his parents reported that William had always been a nervous kid, his anxiety had escalated over the past three months and he was now doing anything he could to avoid school including cutting class and sneaking home while his parents were at work. His grades began to suffer, and he was spending more and more time in his room removed from family and social activities.

CASE FORMULATION

William presented with social anxiety and social withdrawal. A brief interview also revealed that he became nervous and anxious in social settings involving large groups of people—especially unfamiliar people. At school he worried about his clothing and his complexion. In addition he was concerned about the other students judging him negatively in the halls, in the lunchroom, and in his classes. He recognized that his anxieties were impacting his academics and his family relationships, but was at a loss for what to do about it.

Jess and Dave were at a loss to explain their son's behavior since starting high school. They were both graduates of William's high school and were actively involved in school activities. Dave was a star athlete in three sports and a member of the student government. Jess was an honor roll student and played in the orchestra. Both admit they had pictured William following in their footsteps as he enrolled in school this past fall, but had begun to resign themselves to the fact that William's high school experience would be different from their own.

As parents to William, Jess and Dave worked as a team with most issues. However, Jess perceived Dave as particularly insensitive to William's situation while Dave felt Jess coddled William. Dave thought that William would never get over this "phase" if he did not face his fears. Dave advocated taking away William's computer and video games if Williams did not straighten up and "do his job" of attending school. Dave and William had almost daily fights, and Jess felt overwhelmed and unable to bear seeing William so upset. She found herself allowing William to miss school on days when Dave left for work early or was away on business—a fact that increased tension in their marriage.

COURSE OF TREATMENT

On the basis of the case presentation, the therapist focused on William's symptoms in the context of the family system. In addition to William's anxiety, other targets for intervention included Dave and William's interaction patterns and Jess and Dave's marital relationship. The treatment relied heavily on homework to tackle many of these issues.

During the first session, the therapist worked to build some motivation for the between-session tasks by stressing the relevance of homework to the work of therapy. From a brainstorming session focused on things the family felt they wanted to work on in treatment, the therapist was able to give an overview of the kinds of tasks the family would be asked to complete. William mentioned "anxiety and stress," Jess added "family conflict," and Dave mentioned problems with "dishonesty" and "family unity." The therapist then described that the work of therapy would be to develop strategies to achieve their treatment goals that they would be able to implement at home.

The therapist then asked the family to help him collect data about their family and the issues they brought up that they would like to change. Then the therapist gave William a temporary log to keep track of his anxiety level before and after school. Both Dave and Jess were given an article to read on managing anxiety in adolescents. Finally, Dave was to have at least one conversation a day with William that did not mention his anxiety or school refusal.

The second session began with a review of the assignments from last session. William had collected his data about his anxiety before school for five out of seven days in the past week. Both Dave and Jess reported learning a lot from the article they read, and Dave reported that he had tried to engage William in conversations about baseball at least twice in the past week but that William was not very interested. The therapist praised each family member for his or her accomplishments.

During session, the therapist helped the family understand William's anxiety and his avoidance as coping strategy that worked to lessen his anxiety. William and his family were introduced to the concepts of exposure to fear-provoking situations. Both Dave and Jess were taught how to help William identify his anxiety provoking thoughts and work at cognitive restructuring and relaxation in the particularly difficult period of the day before school. Both Jess and Dave practiced encouraging William to work through his thoughts about social rejection through role-plays in session.

The therapist also brainstormed with the family about good conversation topics that they could discuss that did not involve talking about William's anxiety or his grades. William suggested movies, and the family made a plan not only to talk about but also to see a movie over the weekend. In order to understand the family context of William's fear of social evaluation, Jess and Dave were asked to reflect on how their families of origin handled anxiety. The therapist asked them each to write about a time they were really anxious and how their family responded.

The next session, Jess reported that she and William had worked on his thoughts before school every day in the past week. William reported that this work had made him feel slightly less anxious about the school day. Jess and William saw a movie on Friday night, yet Dave could not attend due to work obligations. The therapist had William and Jess re-enact the techniques they used to work on William's thoughts in a role-play, and congratulated them on a job well done.

Both Jess and Dave had completed the family of origin assignment and voluntarily shared what they had written in session. Jess described an event in high school when she was so nervous about an important math test that she was awake all night worrying. Her mother wrote the school a note and allowed her to stay home from school that day. Dave described being "jittery" all day and finding it difficult to sleep the night before big football games. His father told him to "toughen up" and that he should learn to excel under pressure. This led into a discussion about what was positive and negative about the way their family of origin handled anxiety. The exercise helped both Jess and Dave see that they had adopted their parents' strategies in dealing with William.

To build upon and extend the successes from the previous week, the therapist encouraged William to continue working on his thoughts and relaxation techniques. Dave was asked to help William in the morning for two days next week, and Dave agreed. The therapist also asked Dave to accompany William to a movie on Saturday afternoon. Finally the whole family planned to eat dinner out at a restaurant following session.

The goals for treatment for the Klein family included having William learn some strategies for dealing with his social anxiety around school and having his parents learn some strategies for supporting their son without inadvertently maintaining his school avoidance and exacerbating his anxiety. Other goals included improving Dave's capacity to relate to William with warmth and empathy and Jess's ability to engage in behaviors that helped William through his anxiety. This example illustrates how the homework assignment moved the therapy forward. Homework provided Jess and Dave a better understanding of William's condition and contributed to William's symptom improvement. Assignments added information about family of origin issues impacting current parenting behaviors, and bolstered positive feelings by having the family engage in pleasant events.

In order to increase the likelihood of homework compliance, the therapist involved all family members from the beginning of treatment. Sessions were organized around the homework assignments, and the therapist used information obtained from the assignments in treatment. When the homework assignments were not completed, the therapist remained positive but persistent and gave more structured directives for the following week.

OUTCOME

Both William and his family made progress over the course of treatment. Jess and Dave continued to work with William on his social anxiety. As Dave began to play a more active role in helping and supporting William, their relationship improved. William's grades improved and he began to think about joining extracurricular activities. Jess and Dave still reported significant marital problems and continued to work on their relationship in couples' therapy.

SUMMARY AND CONCLUSIONS

Families presenting to treatment hope to learn strategies and skills to improve their functioning. Homework is one essential tool family therapists use to support these strivings. While therapists select homework assignments based on the targets of the intervention, the same kind of core family processes are ultimately involved, such as strengthening communication and problem solving, nurturing attachment, building family structure, and shaping appropriate reinforcement contingencies. Issues related to treatment engagement, therapeutic alliance, homework acceptance, and the vicissitudes of family life are potential barriers to the successful use of homework in family therapy. Finally strategies that engage family members, that promote positive therapist-family member interactions, and that consider task difficulty in the context of the family system contribute to successful homework use in treatment.

REFERENCES

Addis, M. E., & N. S. Jacobson (2000). A closer look at the treatment rationale and homework compliance in cognitive-behavioral therapy for depression. *Cognitive Therapy and Research, 24,* 313–326.

Albano, A. M., & D. H. Barlow (1996). Breaking the vicious cycle: Cognitive-behavioral group treatment for socially anxious youth. Psychosocial treatments for child and adolescent disorders. In Hibbs, E. D. & Jensen, P. S. (eds.), *Empirically based strategies for clinical practice* (pp. 43–62). Washington, DC: American Psychological Association. ,

Alexander, J. F., & B. V. Parsons (1973). Short-term behavioral intervention with delinquent families: Impact on family process and recidivism. *Journal of Abnormal Psychology, 81,* 219–225.

Alexander, J. F., & T. L. Sexton (2002). Functional family therapy: A model for treating high-risk, acting-out youth. In Kaslow, F. W. (ed.), *Comprehensive handbook of psychotherapy: Integrative/eclectic* (Vol. 4, pp. 111–132). New York: Wiley.

Azrin, N. H. (1976). Improvements in the community-reinforcement approach to alcoholism. *Behaviour Research and Therapy, 14,* 339–348.

Barkley, R. A., G. Edwards, G., Laneri, M., Fletcher, K., & Metevia, L. (2001). The efficacy of problem-solving communication training alone, behavior management training alone, and their combination for parent-adolescent conflict in teenagers with ADHD and ODD. *Journal of Consulting and Clinical Psychology, 69,* 926–941.

Barrett, P. M., Dadds, M. R., & Rapee, R. M. (1996). Family treatment of childhood anxiety: A controlled trial. *Journal of Consulting and Clinical Psychology, 64,* 333–342.

Barrowclough, C., & N. Tarrier (1992). *Families of schizophrenic patients: Cognitive behavioural intervention.* London: Chapman and Hall/CRC.

Birmaher, B., Brent, D. A., Kolko, D., Baugher, M., Bridge, J., Holder, D., Iyenger, S., & Ulloa, R.E. (2000). Clinical outcome after short-term psychotherapy for adolescents with major depressive disorder. *Archives of General Psychiatry, 57,* 29–36.

Bowen, M. (1966). The use of family theory in clinical practice. *Comprehensive Psychiatry, 7,* 345–374.

Bryant, M. J., Simons, A. D., & Thase, M. E. (1999). Therapist skill and patient variables in homework compliance: Controlling an uncontrolled variable in cognitive therapy outcome research. *Cognitive Therapy and Research, 23,* 381–399.

Burns, D. D., & Spangler, D. L. (2000). Does psychotherapy homework lead to improvements in depression in cognitive-behavioral therapy or does improvement lead to increased homework compliance? *Journal of Consulting and Clinical Psychology, 68,* 46–56.

Carr, A. (1997). Positive practice in family therapy. *Journal of Marital and Family Therapy, 23,* 271–293.

Carr, A. (1998). The inclusion of fathers in family therapy: A research based perspective. *Contemporary Family Therapy: An International Journal, 20,* 371–383.

Clarke, G. N., Rohde, P., Lewinsohn, P. M., Hops, H., & Seeley, J. R. (1999). Cognitive-behavioral treatment of adolescent depression: Efficacy of acute group treatment and booster sessions. *Journal of the American Academy of Child and Adolescent Psychiatry, 38,* 272–279.

Conoley, C. W., Padula, M. A., Payton, D. S., & Daniels, J. A. (1994). Predictors of client implementation of counselor recommendations: Match with problem, difficulty level, and building on client strengths. *Journal of Counseling Psychology, 41,* 3–7.

Cox, D. J., Tisdelle, D. A., & Culbert, J. P (1988). Increasing adherence to behavioral homework assignments. *Journal of Behavioral Medicine, 11*, 519–522.

Dattilio, F. M. (2002). Homework assignments in couple and family therapy. *Journal of Clinical Psychology, 58*, 535–547.

Diamond, G., & Siqueland, L. (1998). Emotions, attachment and the relational reframe: The first session. *Journal of Systemic Therapies, 17*, 36–50.

Duhig, A. M., Phares, V., & Birkeland, R. W. (2002). Involvement of fathers in therapy: A survey of clinicians. *Professional Psychology: Research and Practice, 33*, 389–395.

Eisler, I., Dare, C., Russell, G. F. M., Szmukler, G., le Grange, D., & Dodge, E. (1997). Family and individual therapy in anorexia nervosa: A 5-year follow-up. *Archives of General Psychiatry, 54*, 1025–1030.

Epstein, L. H. (2003). Development of evidence-based treatments for pediatric obesity. In Kazdin, A.E. (Ed.), *Evidence-based psychotherapies for children and adolescents* (pp. 374–388). New York, NY: Guilford.

Epstein, L. H., Valoski, A., Wing, R. R., & McCurley, J. (1994). Ten-year outcomes of behavioral family-based treatment for childhood obesity. *Health Psychology, 13*, 373–383.

Epstein, L. H., Paluch, R. A., Gordy, C. C., Saelens, B. E., & Ernst, M. M. (2000). Problem solving in the treatment of childhood obesity. *Journal of Consulting and Clinical Psychology, 68*, 717–721.

Falloon, I. R. H., Boyd, J. L., & McGill, C. W. (1984). *Family care of schizophrenia: A problem-solving approach to the treatment of mental illness.* New York: Guilford.

Fristad, M. A., Goldberg-Arnold, J. S., & Gavazzi, S. M. (2003). Multi-family psychoeducation groups in the treatment of children with mood disorders. *Journal of Marital and Family Therapy, 29*, 491–504.

Geist, R., Heinmaa, M., Stephens, D., Davis, R., & Katzman, D. K. (2000). Comparison of family therapy and family group psychoeducation in adolescents with anorexia nervosa. *Canadian Journal of Psychiatry, 45*, 173–178.

Glaser, N. M., Kazantzis, N., Deane, F. P., & Oades, L. G. (2000). Critical issues in using homework assignments within cognitive-behavioral therapy for schizophrenia. *Journal of Rational-Emotive and Cognitive Behavior Therapy, 18*, 247–261.

Glynn, S. M., Pugh, R., & Rose, G. (1993). Benefits of relatives' attendance at a workshop on schizophrenia at a state hospital. *Psychosocial Rehabilitation Journal, 16*, 95–101.

Godding, V., Kruth, M., & Jamart, J. (1997). Joint consultation for high-risk asthmatic children and their families, with pediatrician and child psychiatrist as co-therapists: Model and evaluation. *Family Process, 36*, 265–280.

Goldberg-Arnold, J. S., Fristad, M. A., & Gavazzi, S. M. (1999). Family psychoeducation: Giving caregivers what they want and need. *Family Relations: Interdisciplinary Journal of Applied Family Studies, 48*, 411–417.

Graziano, A. M. & Diament, D. M. (1992). Parent behavioral training: An examination of the paradigm. *Behavior Modification, 16*, 3–38.

Henggeler, S. W., Clingempeel, W., Brondino, M. J., & Pickrel, S. G. (2002). Four-year follow-up of multisystemic therapy with substance-abusing and substance-dependent juvenile offenders. *Journal of the American Academy of Child and Adolescent Psychiatry, 41*, 868–874.

Henggeler, S. W., & Sheidow, A. J. (2003). Conduct disorder and delinquency. *Journal of Marital and Family Therapy, 29*, 505–522.

Hogarty, G. E., Anderson, C. M., Reiss, D. J., Kornblith, S. J., Greenwald, D. P., Ulrich, R. F. et al. (1991). Family psychoeducational, social skills training and maintenance chemotherapy in the aftercare treatment of schizophrenia. II: Two year effects of a controlled study on relapse and adjustment. *Archives of General Psychiatry, 48*, 340–347.

Hogue, A., Liddle, H. A., Rowe, C., Turner, R. M., Dakof, G. A., & LaPann, K. (1998). Treatment adherence and differentiation in individual versus family therapy for adolescent substance abuse. *Journal of Counseling Psychology, 45*, 104–114.

Hudson, J. L., & Kendall, P. C. (2002). Showing you can do it: Homework in therapy for children and adolescents with anxiety disorders. *Journal of Clinical Psychology, 58,* 525–534.

Kaslow, N. J., Baskin, M. L., & Wyckoff, S. C. (2002). A biopsychosocial treatment approach for depressed children and adolescents. In Kaslow, F. W. (Ed.), *Comprehensive handbook of psychotherapy: Integrative/eclectic* (Vol. 4, pp. 31–57). New York: Wiley.

Kazantzis, N. (2000). Power to detect homework effects in psychotherapy outcome research. *Journal of Consulting and Clinical Psychology, 68,* 166–170.

Kazantzis, N., & Deane, F. P. (1999). Psychologists' use of homework assignments in clinical practice. *Professional Psychology: Research and Practice, 30,* 581–585.

Kazdin, A. E. (1996). Dropping out of child psychotherapy: Issues for research and implications for practice. *Clinical Child Psychology and Psychiatry, 1,* 133–156.

Kazdin, A. E. (2000). Perceived barriers to treatment participation and treatment acceptability among antisocial children and their families. *Journal of Child and Family Studies, 9,* 157–174.

Kazdin, A. E., Holland, L., & Crowley, M. (1997). Family experience of barriers to treatment and premature termination from child therapy. *Journal of Consulting and Clinical Psychology, 65,* 453–463.

Kazdin, A. E., & Weisz, J. R. (1998). Identifying and developing empirically supported child and adolescent treatments. *Journal of Consulting and Clinical Psychology, 66,* 19–36.

Kearney, C. A., & Alvarez, K. M. (2004). Manualized treatment for school-refusal behavior in youth. In L. L'Abate, (Ed.), *Using workbooks in mental health: Resources in prevention, and rehabilitation for clinicians and researchers* (pp. 283–299). New York : Haworth.

Kolko, D. J., Brent, D. A., Baugher, M., Bridge, J., & Birmaher, B. (2000). Cognitive and family therapies for adolescent depression: Treatment specificity, mediation, and moderation. *Journal of Consulting and Clinical Psychology, 68,* 603–614.

Kumpfer, K. L., & Alvarado, R. (2003). Family-strengthening for the prevention of youth problem behaviors. *American Psychologist, 58,* 457–465.

Kuipers, E., Leff, J., & Lam, D. (1992). *Family work for schizophrenia. A practical guide.* London: Gaskell.

L'Abate, L. (1996). *Workbooks for better living.* (http://www.mentalhealthhelp.com).

L'Abate, L. (1998). Discovery of the family: From the inside to the outside. *American Journal of Family Therapy, 26,* 265–280.

L'Abate, L. (2004a). *A guide to self-help workbooks for clinicians and researchers.* New York: Haworth.

L'Abate, L. (Ed.) (2004b). *Using workbooks in mental health: Resources in prevention, psychotherapy, and rehabilitation for clinicians and researchers.* New York: Haworth.

Lam, D.H. (1991). Psychosocial family intervention in schizophrenia: a review of empirical studies. *Psychological Medicine, 21,* 423–441.

Lebow, J. L., & Gurman, A. S. (1995). Research assessing couple and family therapy. *Annual Review of Psychology, 46,* 27–57.

Lewinsohn, P. M., Clarke, G. N., Hops, H., & Andrews, J. A. (1990). Cognitive-behavioral treatment for depressed adolescents. *Behavior Therapy, 21,* 385–401.

Liddle, H. A., & Hogue, A. (2000). A family-based, developmental-ecological preventive intervention for high-risk adolescents. *Journal of Marital and Family Therapy, 26,* 265–279.

Liddle, H. A., & Dakof, G. A. (1995). Efficacy of family therapy for drug abuse: Promising but not definitive. *Journal of Marital and Family Therapy, 21,* 511–543.

Lukens, E. P. & McFarlane, W. R. (2004). Psychoeducation as evidence-based practice: Considerations for practice, research, and policy. *Brief Treatment & Crisis Intervention, 4,* 205–225.

Mahrer, A. R., Gagnon, R., Fairweather, D. R., Boulet, D. B., et al. (1994). Client commitment and resolve to carry out postsession behaviors. *Journal of Counseling Psychology, 41,* 407–414.

McFarlane, W. R. (1990). Multiple family groups and the treatment of schizophrenia. In M. I. Hertz, S. J. Keith and J. P. Docherty (eds) *Handbook of schizophrenia, volume 4: Psychosocial treatment of schizophrenia* (pp. 167–189). Amsterdam: Elsevier Science Publishers.

McFarlane, W. R., Link, B., Dushay, R., Marchal, J., & Crilly, J. (1995). Psychoeducational multiple family groups: Four-year relapse outcome in schizophrenia. *Family Process, 34*, 127–
144.

McFarlane, W. R., Dixon, L., Lukens, E. & Lucksted, A. (2003). Family psychoeducation and
schizophrenia: A review of the literature. *Journal of Marital and Family Therapy, 29*, 223–245.

Miller, K. J. (2004). A review of workbooks and related literature on eating disorders. In L'Abate,
L. (Ed.), *Using workbooks in mental health: Resources in prevention, and rehabilitation for clinicians and researchers* (pp. 301–326). New York: Haworth.

Minuchin, S. (1974). *Families and family therapy.* Cambridge, MA: Harvard U. Press,

Morrison, R. L., & Wixted, J. T. (1989). Social skills training. In A. S. Bellack, (Ed.), *A Clinical
guide for the treatment of schizophrenia* (pp. 237–261). New York: Plenum.

Mueser, K. T., Sengupta, A., Schooler, N. R., Bellack, A. S., Xie, H., Glick, I. D., & Keith, S. J.
(2001). Family treatment and medication dosage reduction in schizophrenia: Effects on
patient social functioning, family attitudes, and burden.*Journal of Consulting and Clinical
Psychology, 69*, 3–12.

Murray-Swank, A.B., & Dixon, L. (2004). Family psychoeducation as an evidence-based practice. *CNS Spectrums, 9*, 905–912.

Nichols, M. P., & Schwartz, R. C. (1998). *Family therapy: Concepts and methods* 4th ed. Needham
Heights, MA: Allyn and Bacon,.

O'Farrell, T. J. (1993). A behavioral marital therapy couples group program for alcoholics and
their spouses. In O'Farrell, T. J. (Ed.), *Treating alcohol problems: Marital and family interventions*
(pp. 170–209). New York: Guilford.

O'Farrell, T. J., & Fals-Stewart, W. (2000). Behavioral couples therapy for alcoholism and drug
abuse. *Behavior Therapist, 23*, 49–54, 70.

O'Farrell, T. J., & Fals-Stewart, W. (2002). Alcohol abuse. In D. H. Sprenkle (Ed.), *Effectiveness
research in marriage and family therapy* (pp. 123–161). Alexandria, VA: American Association
for Marriage and Family Therapy.

Ollendick, T. H., & King, N. J. (1998). Empirically supported treatments for children with phobic
and anxiety disorders: Current status. *Journal of Clinical Child Psychology, 27*, 156–167.

Patterson, G. R. (1986). Performance models for antisocial boys. *American Psychologist, 41*, 432–
444.

Penn, D. L. & Mueser, K. T. (1996). Research update on the psychosocial treatment of schizophrenia. *American Journal of Psychiatry, 153*, 607–617.

Perrino, T., Coatsworth, J., Briones, E., Pantin, H., & Szapocznik, J. (2001). Initial engagement in
parent-centered preventive interventions: A family systems perspective. *Journal of Primary
Prevention, 22*, 21–44.

Pinsof, W. M. (1995). *Integrative problem-centered therapy: A synthesis of family, individual, and
biological therapies.* New York: Basic Books.

Prinz, R. J., & Miller, G. E. (1994). Family-based treatment for childhood antisocial behavior:
Experimental influences on dropout and engagement. *Journal of Consulting and Clinical
Psychology, 62*, 645–650.

Robin, A. L., Gilroy, M., & Dennis, A. B. (1998). Treatment of eating disorders in children and
adolescents. *Clinical Psychology Review, 18*, 421–446.

Rotunda, R. J., & O'Farrell, T. J. (1997). Marital and family therapy of alcohol use disorders:
Bridging the gap between research and practice. *Professional Psychology: Research and Practice, 28*, 246–252.

Rowe, C. L., Liddle, H. A., McClintic, K., & Quille, T. J. (2002). Integrative treatment develop-
ment: Multidimensional family therapy for adolescent substance abuse. In F. W. Kaslow &
J. Lebow (eds.), *Comprehensive handbook of psychotherapy: Integrative/eclectic* (pp. 133–161).
New York: Wiley.

Sanders, M. R., Markie-Dadds, C., Tully, L. A., & Bor, W. (2000). The triple P-positive parenting program: A comparison of enhanced, standard, and self-directed behavioral family

intervention for parents of children with early onset conduct problems. *Journal of Consulting and Clinical Psychology, 68,* 624–640.

Santisteban, D. A., Szapocznik, J., Perez-Vidal, A., Kurtines, W. M., Murray, E. J., & LaPerriere, A. (1996). Efficacy of intervention for engaging youth and families into treatment and some variables that may contribute to differential effectiveness. *Journal of Family Psychology, 10,* 35–44.

Scott, S., Spender, Q., Doolan, M., Jacobs, B., & Aspland, H. (2001). Multicentre controlled trial of parenting groups for childhood antisocial behaviour in clinical practice. *British Medical Journal, 323,* 194.

Sisson, R. W. & Azrin, N. H. (1986). Family member involvement to initiate and promote treatment of problem drinkers. *Journal of Behaviour Therapy and Experimental Psychiatry, 17,* 15–21.

Spaccarelli, S., Cotler, S., & Penman, D. (1992). Problem-solving skills training as a supplement to behavioral parent training. *Cognitive Therapy and Research, 16,* 1–17.

Sprenkle, D. H. (Ed.). (2002). *Effectiveness research in marriage and family therapy.* Alexandria, VA: American Association for Marriage and Family Therapy.

Stark, K. D., Rouse, L. W., & Livingston, R. (1991). Treatment of depression during childhood and adolescence: Cognitive-behavioral procedures for the individual and family. In P.C. Kendall, (ed.), *Child and adolescent therapy: Cognitive-behavioral procedures* (pp. 165–206). New York: Guilford.

Szapocznik, J., Perez-Vidal, A., Brickman, A. L., Foote, F. H., Santisteban, D., Hervis, O., et al. (1988). Engaging adolescent drug abusers and their families in treatment: A strategic structural systems approach. *Journal of Consulting and Clinical Psychology, 56,* 552–557.

Szapocznik, J., & Williams, R. A. (2000). Brief strategic family therapy: Twenty-five years of interplay among theory, research and practice in adolescent behavior problems and drug abuse. *Clinical Child and Family Psychology Review, 3:* 117–134.

Webster-Stratton, C. (1994). Advancing videotape parent training: A comparison study. *Journal of Consulting and Clinical Psychology, 62,* 583–593.

Wierzbicki, M., & Pekarik, G. (1993). A meta-analysis of psychotherapy dropout. *Professional Psychology: Research and Practice, 24,* 190–195.

Wood, B. L., and Miller, B. D. (2002). A biopsychosocial approach to child health. In F. W. Kaslow, (ed.), *Comprehensive handbook of psychotherapy: Integrative/eclectic* (Vol. 4, pp. 59–80). New York: .

Worthington, E. L. (1986). Client compliance with homework directives during counseling. *Journal of Counseling Psychology, 33,* 124–130.

Part III

SPECIFIC PROBLEMS

CHAPTER 13

BORDERLINE PERSONALITY DISORDER

Noam Lindenboim, Alex L. Chapman, and Marsha M. Linehan

The primary purpose of this chapter is to elucidate the role of therapy homework in the context of an empirically supported treatment for borderline personality disorder—Dialectical Behavior Therapy (DBT; Linehan, 1993a). Borderline personality disorder (BPD) is a disorder of emotion dysregulation, and patients who meet criteria for BPD often present with myriad life difficulties and comorbid disorders. According to the biosocial theory on which DBT is based, individuals with BPD have fundamental deficits in the skills necessary to regulate emotions, but they also have difficulties in a variety of other skill domains, including interpersonal skills, attention, distress tolerance, and self-management. Consequently, the acquisition and strengthening of behavioral skills is a fundamental goal of DBT. Along with behavioral skills training, generalization strategies, and other interventions in DBT, homework assignments constitute one of the means to achieve this goal. This chapter includes a description of BPD and Linehan's biosocial theory, an overview of DBT, and a discussion of the role of homework in DBT in achieving treatment goals and prevention of relapse. In addition, we discuss some of the unique barriers to implementing homework assignments with BPD patients and DBT strategies used to overcome these barriers.

BIOSOCIAL THEORY OF BORDERLINE PERSONALITY DISORDER

The *Diagnostic and Statistical Manual of Mental Disorders, 4th Edition* (DSM-IV; American Psychiatric Association, 1994) defined borderline personality disorder (BPD) as "...a pervasive pattern of instability of interpersonal relationships, self-image, and affects, and marked impulsivity beginning by early adulthood and present in a variety of contexts" (p. 650). Defining features of BPD include efforts to avoid abandonment, unstable interpersonal relations, identity, and affect, impulsive, self-damaging behavior, suicidal and/or parasuicidal behavior, problems with anger, and paranoia or dissociation in response to major stressors (American Psychiatric Association, 1994).

According to Linehan's (1993a) biosocial theory, BPD is a pervasive dysfunction of the emotion regulation system caused by the transaction of biology/temperament and environmental factors. The primary biological factor is *emotion vulnerability*, which consists of quick, strong, and long-lasting emotional reactions. The environmental factor consists of an *invalidating rearing environment,* characterized by a deficit in the environmental support necessary to help the emotionally vulnerable child learn how to regulate emotions. The invalidating environment punishes, ignores, dismisses, or trivializes the child's emotional experience, in addition to oversimplifying the ease of problem solving. The invalidating environment also may involve abuse (physical, sexual, emotional), and may consist of caregivers who become emotionally dysregulated when their child experiences strong emotional arousal. In a systemic interplay, the child's emotional temperament and the invalidating environment transact (mutually influence each other). Emotion vulnerability pulls for invalidating behavior when the caregivers are unable to regulate their own emotions; do not understand why the child is so upset; or lack the requisite skills to sooth, coach, or help the child manage overwhelming affect. Similarly, the invalidating environment amplifies emotion vulnerability, reinstating the very conditions that trigger invalidating behavior, and so on. Eventually, the child learns that emotions are frightening and is left bereft of the skills required to manage emotions, resulting in *emotion dysregulation.*

Emotion dysregulation broadly involves difficulty up or down-regulating emotional arousal, along with an inability to direct attention away from emotional stimuli. Many of the behavioral problems commonly seen among borderline individuals (e.g., substance abuse, suicide attempts, self-injurious behaviors, and eating disorders) result from emotional dysregulation, or function to regulate emotions. For instance, self-injury may be an outcome of the impaired problem-solving, cognition, or information processing associated with intense emotional arousal (Chapman, Gratz, & Brown, 2006), or a strategy to reduce unwanted or intolerable emotions. The biosocial theory of BPD takes a systemic view of emotions and emotion dysregulation. Emotions are considered full-system responses, encompassing environmental triggers for emotional arousal, cognition, perception and interpretations, physiological changes and brain activity, emotion-expressive tendencies, and actions; consequently, dysregulation in the emotional system leads to dysregulation in a variety of other areas.

Dialectical Behavior Therapy: Overview of the Treatment and the Research

DBT is an empirically supported cognitive-behavioral treatment for BPD. Initially developed to treat highly suicidal women, DBT evolved into a treatment for BPD, primarily due to the prevalence and severity of suicidal behaviors in individuals who meet criteria for. The first randomized controlled trial (RCT) was conducted by Linehan and colleagues (Linehan, Armstrong, Suarez, Allmon, & Heard, 1991; Linehan, Heard, & Armstrong, 1993; Linehan, Tutek, Heard, & Armstrong, 1994) and compared DBT with a control condition that consisted of treatment for BPD as it usually occurs in the community (treatment-as-usual, or TAU). The results indicated that patients in DBT had greater reductions in the frequency and medical risk of parasuicidal behavior, anger, and the use of emergency and inpatient treatment services, along with a considerable advantage in terms of service costs. DBT patients also had greater increases in global and social adjustment (Linehan et al., 1991). Since this study was published, seven RCTs across four separate research groups have evaluated DBT or DBT-oriented treatments of BPD (Koons et al., 2001; Linehan et al., 1999, 2002, 2006; Turner, 2000; van den Bosch et al., 2002; Verheul et al., 2003). The outcome data indicate the superiority of DBT, when compared with TAU and other control conditions, particularly in the reduction of suicidal and self-injurious behaviors, as well as illicit drug use (Linehan et al., 1999, 2002). Following the criteria set forth by Chambless and Hollon (1998), DBT meets criteria for an *efficacious and specific* treatment, in that multiple studies from different sites and with different investigators have demonstrated the efficacy of DBT in comparison to several active control conditions.

DBT is a comprehensive, cognitive-behavioral treatment with theoretical roots in behavioral science, dialectical philosophy, and Zen practice. Most often associated with Marxist socioeconomic principles, *dialectical philosophy* posits that reality is constantly changing in response to tension that exists between polar opposites, most commonly referred to as "thesis" and "antithesis." Both thesis and antithesis are incomplete and insufficient on their own, but when synthesized, they form a more complete, coherent whole. The process of dialectics involves the emergence and synthesis of thesis and antithesis; the synthesis itself constitutes the next thesis, the contradictions inherent in which produce yet another antithesis, and so on.

When applied to the treatment of BPD, the most central tension or dialectic in DBT is that of acceptance and change (Chapman & Linehan, 2005; Linehan, 1993a; Robins & Chapman, 2004). DBT began as an application of well-grounded standard behavioral and cognitive therapy procedures that had garnered empirical support for other disorders (i.e., problem solving, skills training, exposure, contingency management). However, Linehan (1993a) quickly discovered that patients reacted negatively to a treatment focused purely on behavioral or cognitive change. Indeed, this treatment may have mirrored the message given by the invalidating environment that BPD patients would not be so "pathological" if they would just change their thinking and behavior. On the other hand, a purely acceptance-based approach may invalidate the seriousness of the clients' problems and the need to make changes. In a dialectical fashion, an emphasis on change (thesis) pulled for acceptance (antithesis), and an emphasis on acceptance pulled for change, resulting in a treatment that actively involves the *synthesis* of acceptance *and* change strategies.

THE FUNCTIONS AND MODES OF DBT

As a comprehensive treatment, DBT addresses five important functions: (a) improving *motivation to change* behavior and to work toward developing a life-worth-living; (b) *increasing behavioral capabilities*, particularly in terms of skills needed to regulate emotions, but also in the areas of interpersonal, distress tolerance, mindfulness, and general self-management skills; (c) ensuring that new skills and capabilities *generalize* to the patient's natural environment; (d) *structuring the environment* in a manner that leads to reinforcement for functional, life-enhancing behaviors and punishment or extinction of dysfunctional behaviors; and (e) enhancing the skill and motivation of therapists who treat BPD patients.

DBT is structured in a manner that addresses each of these functions. In its standard form, DBT consists of individual therapy, group skills training, phone consultations, a therapist consultation team, as well ancillary treatments as needed (e.g. pharmacotherapy, case management). *Individual therapy* focuses on reducing dysfunctional behaviors and enhancing motivation to change. Individual therapy also includes several interventions designed to generalize behavioral skills to the patient's natural environment, most notably homework assignments, the use of an audiotape recording of each session listened to by patients between sessions, and coaching on the use of skillful behavior, both in session and via telephone or email consultation. Group-based *skills training* focuses on building and generalizing capabilities through the teaching and practice of skills designed to help BPD patients regulate emotions (*emotion regulation skills*); tolerate distress and manage crises without making the situation worse (*distress tolerance skills*); mindfully participate in the present moment and regulate attention (*mindfulness skills*); and skillfully navigate interpersonal relationships (*interpersonal effectiveness skills*). Finally, the *therapist consultation team* consists of a micro-level "community" of individuals who treat BPD patients (Chapman & Linehan, in press; Linehan, 1993a). The team essentially applies DBT interventions to therapists in order to provide the support, training, practice, and feedback required to enhance motivation and promote effective therapy. The goal of helping the BPD patient establish a life worth living binds together all of these modes of treatment.

The Role of Therapy Homework in DBT

Homework assignments in DBT serve several functions. Because DBT is based on the premise that patients with BPD have deficits in skills, one of the most important functions of homework is to facilitate the acquisition and strengthening of those skills. In both skills training and individual therapy, homework often is used to assess patients' skill levels, introduce patients to new skills, facilitate their practice of skills, and to provide an opportunity for the therapist to give feedback, coaching, reinforcement, and didactic information on the patient's use of skills in daily life.

Once skills are acquired, patients must be able to apply them with ease and expertise in a variety of contexts; consequently, another function of homework in DBT is to help the patient *generalize* treatment gains to his or her natural environment. According to Skinner, generalization occurs when "... the control acquired by a stimulus is shared by other stimuli with common properties" (Skinner, 1953, p. 134). Indeed, one of the most important functions of DBT is to ensure that the ability of the therapist and therapy team to elicit and reinforce effective behavior somehow transfers to the patient's natural environment. Homework assignments allow the patient to try out new skills and determine whether they work outside of the therapy context. The therapist provides coaching and feedback to ensure that therapy leads to effective behavior in the patient's day-to-day life.

Homework is used in DBT in a manner consistent with the empirical literature on efficacious treatments, and with the principles that apply to the effective learning and strengthening of behaviors. Most the skills taught in DBT came from behavioral treatments found to be efficacious with other populations, or from basic research in the areas of emotion, personality, and social psychology. For example, the skill of "opposite action" in the emotion regulation module involves reducing emotional sensitivity and intensity through exposure to an emotion-eliciting event and acting in a manner opposite to the action tendency associated with the emotion. This skill is based historically on the principle of *reciprocal inhibition* (Wolpe, 1954) and draws from exposure therapy, a treatment that is efficacious in the treatment of anxiety disorders, such as post-traumatic stress disorder (Foa & Kozak, 1986), obsessive-compulsive disorder (Franklin et al., 2000), and panic disorder (Barlow, 1988).

The content of homework assignments in DBT is geared toward ameliorating skill deficits considered central to the biosocial theory's conceptualization of BPD patients (Linehan, 1993a,b). Homework assignments to enhance *emotion regulation* skills might involve assignments designed to reduce vulnerability to negative emotions; increase the likelihood of experiencing positive emotions; increase mindfulness and acceptance of emotions; and hone the ability to continue with goal-directed behavior despite fluctuating moods. To enhance *distress tolerance* skills, assignments aim to enhance the ability of patients to tolerate crises without worsening the situation, through distraction, self-soothing, awareness, and acceptance of reality. In the *interpersonal effectiveness* module, homework assignments focus on having clients practice clarifying their goals in interpersonal situations, figuring out how strongly to assert their wishes, and acting appropriately assertive, in a manner that enhances self-respect, goal attainment, and relationship functioning. Finally, *mindfulness* assignments are almost entirely experiential, with the goals of helping patients practice the skills of observing, describing, and participating effectively in the current moment, without judgment, and while focusing on one thing at a time.

Types of Homework Assignments in DBT

There are essentially four types of homework assignments in DBT: (a) *discrete* homework assignments, (b) *self-monitoring* homework assignments, (c) *skills practice* assignments, and (d) *conditional* homework assignments. *Discrete* homework assignments involve the explicit assignment of a discrete task, sometimes for a specified period (e.g., practice eating mindfully three times a week for the next week). This type of assignment is a regular component of the skills training group, and occurs less frequently in individual therapy.

In skills training, there is a formalized system of homework handouts and assignments designed to help patients learn and practice new behavioral skills. Each of the four primary skill modules has a set of homework sheets, and typically, patients are asked to complete one or more of the homework sheets each week. For instance, in the emotion regulation skills module, some of the homework sheets involve sections on which the patients note which emotions they had over the past week, the prompting events or triggers of the emotions, their bodily sensations of emotion, the action urges associated with the emotions, and their behaviors. This particular assignment is designed to help patients increase their awareness of emotions, the factors that prompt them, and the action urges and behaviors associated with them. Patients fill out their homework sheets, and each week the first half of the skills training session focuses on homework review. Skills trainers and patients enter into a dialogue about which skills were practiced and difficulties understanding or implementing new skills. Skills trainers use a variety of behavioral strategies to strengthen skill acquisition and homework completion, including shaping, positive reinforcement, didactics on particular skills, and coaching on the effective use of skills. Often, discrete homework assignments are used to consolidate the learning of a particular skill, provide a structured opportunity to try these skills, and to increase the likelihood that the skill behavior will be in the patient's behavioral repertoire to draw upon when needed.

A second type of homework assignment in DBT is the *self-monitoring* homework assignment. Self-monitoring assignments involve having patients monitor various behaviors on an ongoing basis, typically daily. In skills training, patients are asked to track the practice of each skill across all skill modules on a self-monitoring form called the *diary card*. Each week, the patients circle which skills they practiced on each day of the week. They also note the extent to which they tried to use skills and how helpful the skills were, using a scale that ranges from 0 (did not try skills) to 7 (skills were executed automatically and were helpful). Ultimately, the goal is to shape the patients toward increasing ease of skill use, such that they eventually use the skills as automatically as shifting gears while driving a car.

Similar to the skills group, a *self-monitoring* assignment in individual DBT involves filling out a self-monitoring *diary card* on an ongoing basis. In individual therapy, the patient keeps track of a variety of behaviors, most typically including the following: (a) emotional and physical misery, (b) urges to engage in self-injury, suicidal, or drug use behavior, (c) drug and alcohol use, (d) prescription drug use and misuse, (e) lying, (f) self-reinforcement for functional behaviors, among other behavioral targets that are ideographically determined to be relevant behavioral targets for the patient.

In individual therapy, this self-monitoring homework assignment is integral to the organization of session time. The therapist uses the information provided on the diary card to organize the session according to the most important treatment targets, following a standard hierarchy of targets. At the top of the hierarchy is *life-threatening behavior*, including suicidal crisis behavior, suicide attempts, ideation, and urges, as well as non-suicidal but deliberate self-injury and other potentially life-threatening behaviors. The next item on the hierarchy is *therapy-interfering behavior*, such as missing sessions, lying, aggressive behavior toward the therapist, lack of engagement or commitment to therapy, or lack of compliance with homework in either skills training or individual therapy. Next are the *quality-of-life interfering behaviors*, (i.e. any behavior that directly hinders the effective implementation of treatment) including problems associated with DSM-IV Axis I disorders, problems in living (finances, housing, etc.), or other difficulties that threaten quality of life. The last two items on the hierarchy include behavioral skills, and secondary behavioral targets, or "dialectical dilemmas" (discussed later in this chapter). Essential to individual therapy, this ongoing self-monitoring assignment is the primary "source of data" on the high priority targets of treatment, as well as the primary tool used to organize the focus of each session.

There is some evidence that the daily monitoring of behaviors may have therapeutic benefits that extend beyond the purposes noted above. For instance, some studies have indicated that there is very little concordance between reports on behaviors that are tracked weekly and reports on behaviors that are tracked on a daily basis (Smith et al., 1999), suggesting that daily self-monitoring may increase the accuracy of the clinical information on which the therapist bases his or her interventions. In addition, the findings of one of our studies suggested that time spent monitoring a target behavior may enhance recall of behavior that occurs between sessions. In a randomized clinical trial that evaluated the efficacy of DBT in comparison to a control treatment for women who met criteria for opioid dependence and BPD, participants in the DBT condition evidenced a strong association between their reports of drug use and the data on drug use collected via urinalysis ($r = 0.72$, $p < 0.02$). In the control condition, which did not involve daily self-monitoring, this correlation was very small ($r = 0.02$), and non-significant (Linehan et al., 2002). Indeed, some researchers have suggested that improvement in the specificity of patients' autobiographical memory may underlie some of the treatment effects of DBT (see Lynch et al., 2006, for a detailed discussion of the mechanisms of change in DBT).

The third type of homework assignment involves *skills practice* assignments that encourage the *continual practice* of skills. This type of homework assignment is designed primarily to strengthen skills, with the ultimate goal of helping the patient develop skills that are so over-learned that they are emitted effortlessly in every situation in which they are needed, particularly in crises. Indeed, learning and strengthening skills requires time and repeated practice under conditions that support new learning. Patients with BPD often present with stormy lives characterized by chaos, overwhelming stressors, and repeated crises; thus, it is particularly important for them to practice skills during the periods of calm that occur between crises. Because patients with BPD experience quick, strong, and long-lasting emotional responses and have difficulty regulating their emotions, attempting to learn new skills can become untenable in the midst of a crisis. Indeed, some studies have indicated that cognition and information processing are disrupted and tend to narrow under conditions of intense emotional arousal, resulting in difficulties with effortful cognitive processes and problem solving (Gellatly & Meyer, 1992). Essentially, learning a new skill in a time of crisis is akin to running marathons while having pneumonia, or learning a Bach toccata with a pinched nerve in the back. Therefore, the goal of ongoing practice homework assignments is to help the patient become such an expert in new skillful behavior that he or she can effectively handle even the most challenging situation.

Lastly, the fourth type of homework assignment is the *conditional* type. This type of homework assignment most commonly occurs in individual therapy. In fact, aside from the self-monitoring assignments, individual therapists tend to use conditional homework assignments much more often than other types of homework assignments. DBT is a principle-driven treatment that requires the flexible application of treatment interventions in a manner that most effectively targets each patient's problems. Using the self-monitoring *diary card*, the patient comes into each session with a list of potential behaviors on which to focus. The therapist typically spends the most time on high priority behaviors, and the approach follows a problem-solving model. After highlighting high-priority behaviors (i.e., "Oh, I see that you cut yourself on Thursday"), a detailed chain analysis is conducted. The chain analysis consists of a detailed discussion of the events surrounding a single instance of dysfunctional behavior, with the goal of determining, in minute detail, the events that set up conditions for the behavior to occur (vulnerability factors or establishing operations), the prompting events or triggers for the behavior, and the consequences of the behavior. Either after or during the chain analysis, the therapist and patient generate solutions (often involving the use of specific skills) that will make the behavior less likely to occur under similar conditions in the future, or that solve the ongoing problems that led to the behavior in the first place. These solutions are agreed upon, and the patient may be given a *conditional* homework assignment that involves implementing the solutions the next time a similar situation is encountered.

For example, one of the authors of this chapter had a patient who struggled with intense, episodic suicidal ideation, most commonly in response to feeling overwhelmed with stressors related to work demands and familial conflict. This patient believed that suicide would provide an escape from emotional pain. After a detailed chain analysis, the therapist generated a solution that involved having the patient ask herself, "What do I want right now? Do I want to be dead, or do I want to escape or find peace?" As it turned out, the patient actually wanted peace, but could not think of any way to attain it other than suicide. The homework assignment was for the patient to use specific self-statements ("I don't want to be dead. I just want peace. What skills can I use now to get peace?") whenever she had suicidal ideation. This is an example of a *conditional* homework assignment, because (a) it was assigned in response (contingent on) to the occurrence of a problem behavior (suicidal ideation), and (b) the instruction was for the patient to use the strategy in a manner contingent on the occurrence of suicidal ideation.

Other conditional homework assignments involve the application of if–then rules for the patient. For instance, the client may be encouraged to use crisis survival or distress tolerance skills whenever he or she is in a crisis. Another example might involve the use of a chain analysis by the client. Sometimes, clients are instructed to complete a chain analysis form after the occurrence of a specific type of behavior, such as a self-injury act. In sum, DBT includes many types of homework assignments that involve having the patient engage in new behaviors outside the therapy room, but only a fraction of this work fits traditional model of discrete homework assignments.

HOMEWORK AND RELAPSE PREVENTION

In DBT, homework plays a key role in preventing the relapse of dysfunctional behaviors. Indeed, as a skills-training approach, homework in DBT aims to hone the very skills that patients need to enhance quality of life and prevent the relapse of behaviors that threaten quality of life. In addition, homework can be used specifically to reduce the likelihood that certain behaviors will occur again in the future. For instance, when a crisis has occurred, the therapist often uses conditional homework assignments to help the patient find a way to reduce the likelihood that a similar crisis will recur. For instance, the therapist might urge the patient to engage in imaginal rehearsal of effective coping behaviors that he or she could use next time a similar situation arises. If people in his or her natural environment reinforce the patient's crisis behaviors, the therapist might assign the patient the task of restructuring the environment to prevent the reinforcement of crisis behaviors. For example, one of the authors of this chapter had a patient who frequently engaged in rage behavior at her parents' home (throwing things, breaking things, yelling, screaming). Over time, it became apparent that the parents often became very solicitous, warm, and soothing after the rage attacks (possibly, reinforcing rage behavior). In order to prevent the relapse of rage behavior, the therapist assigned the patient the task of educating her parents on reinforcement and asking them to stop being warm and supportive when she has "rage attacks."

Relapse prevention fundamentally is a task that involves enhancing the *generalization* of treatment gains, and homework in DBT can enhance generalization in several ways. For instance, homework assignments may facilitate generalization by bringing the therapist into the patient's natural environment. The therapy setting often constitutes a context in which dysfunctional behaviors are extinguished (Lynch et al., 2006) and effective behaviors are reinforced. Research on extinction has indicated that the re-emergence of extinguished responses (e.g., the relapse of cutting or drug use) may occur in new settings or at times in the future, because people essentially fail to re-trieve the memory that the behavior has extinguished [the *memory of extinction* (Bouton, 1993; Bouton & Brooks, 1993)]. Homework assignments therefore may constitute ex-tinction "reminders" (essentially, reminders of therapy) that reduce the re-emergence of dysfunctional behavior in settings outside the therapy room. Similarly, the mere existence of homework assignments may bring the therapist to the patient's natural environment, serving as a reminder of effective behaviors learned in treatment.

COMMON BARRIERS TO THE EFFECTIVE USE OF HOMEWORK WITH BPD PATIENTS

There are several barriers to the effective use of homework with BPD patients. Many of the barriers are similar to those encountered with other clinical populations, such as a mismatch between the homework assignment and the treatment targets, unclear instructions on the homework assignment, poor motivation, and difficulty remembering or executing homework assignments. For the following section, we focus on barriers that we have found to be unique to BPD patients, and that are consistent with the biosocial theory underlying DBT. These barriers include emotion dysregulation, dialectical dilemmas, and motivational problems.

EMOTION DYSREGULATION

According to the biosocial theory of BPD, many of the behavioral problems of BPD patients are caused by a fundamental deficit in the ability to regulate emotions, combined with a susceptibility to quick, intense, and long-lasting emotions. Indeed, individuals with BPD have considerable difficulty with many of the tasks involved in regulating emotions, such as modulating physiological arousal, diverting attention from emotional stimuli, inhibiting impulsive behavior, and organizing behavior to achieve external, non-mood dependent goals [see Gottman and Levenson (1986), for a review of the key tasks involved with emotion regulation]. In turn, the therapist may view and target many of the barriers to the successful use of homework in DBT as emotion-regulation problems. In this way, problems with the completion of homework assignments are conceptualized in a similar manner as other behavioral problems, and in many cases, represent a microcosm of the myriad life difficulties experienced by BPD patients.

There are several problems related to emotion dysregulation that may interfere with the successful implementation of homework assignments in DBT. The patient may have difficulty completing homework assignments primarily because of deficits in the skills necessary to regulate intense emotional arousal. Indeed, intense, dysreg-ulated arousal can make it exceedingly difficult to pay attention, process information, and remember the point of any given homework assignment. Patients also often report that they were overwhelmed with other tasks and stressors and could not manage "one more thing." Other patients may have difficulty with completing a homework as-signment (particularly, the self-monitoring type of assignment), because it forces them to look inward and think about their problems. In many cases, these patients may ex-perience shame when they attend to their life difficulties; avoiding homework is a way to avoid shame. An additional problem may emerge when the patient attempts to complete a homework assignment under conditions of high emotional arousal. Indeed, patients often report that they tried to complete their homework but were "too upset" to do it.

BPD patients often engage in mood-dependent behavior and have difficulty inhibiting this behavior in the service of long-term goals. They experience intense and often-changing moods that prompt urges to engage in a variety of behaviors. For instance, the most common urge associated with anxiety is to escape or avoid the anxiety-provoking situation. The action urges associated with shame compel people to hide those aspects of themselves or their behavior of which they are ashamed. At least at the beginning of treatment, BPD patients often have difficulty inhibiting the action urges associated with a variety of emotions. Homework often requires that patients inhibit mood-dependent behavior in the service of long-term goals (e.g., to learn a new skill); thus, BPD patients who have difficulty inhibiting mood-dependent behavior also tend to struggle with homework.

DIALECTICAL DILEMMAS

Consistent with the dialectical philosophy underlying DBT, some of the barriers to the successful implementation of homework in DBT involve failures to synthesize dialectical tensions. While developing DBT, Linehan (1993a) identified several distinct patterns of phenomena that appeared to be interfering with applying behavioral therapy techniques with BPD patients. Linehan classified these into three "dialectical dilemmas," (a) *emotion vulnerability* vs. *self-invalidation*, (b) *active passivity* vs. *apparent competence*, and (c) *unrelenting crises* vs. *inhibited grieving*. Reflecting the patient's dysregulated emotional system, these patterns typically involve vacillation between extreme poles of thought and action, without integration or synthesis. Thesis and antithesis move back and forth as if on a "teeter-totter," never forming an integrated whole or moving toward a synthesis representing more effective behavioral patterns.

The first dialectical dilemma involves vacillation between extreme *emotion vulnerability* and *self-invalidation*. Emotional vulnerability in this context refers to the experience of vulnerability by the patient. Essentially, the patient experiences him/herself as fragile, crazy, intensely vulnerable, and as being completely controlled by the environment. The patient may believe that it is impossible to do what the therapist expects, and may feel angry at the therapist for assigning homework, because the therapist expects too much. Alternatively, clients sometimes feel angry when the homework assignment is perceived as "too simple to solve problems of this magnitude." On the other pole of the dialectic, self-invalidation involves invalidation of the individual's own affective experiences, looking to others for accurate reflections of reality, oversimplifying the ease of solving life's problems, and inhibition of emotional experiences and expression. In this case, the patient may underestimate the difficulty of the homework task and then actively engage in self-punishment, criticism, or invalidation when he or she encounters difficulty completing the task.

Another dialectical behavior pattern involves the dialectic of *active passivity* versus *apparent competence*. At times, the individual demonstrates the competency to effectively solve problems with very little help, but in other contexts, appears to completely lack this same competency. The patient who exhibits apparent competence often appears to have competencies and capabilities that actually are not present; thus, the therapist may unknowingly assign homework tasks that are overly difficult, resulting in failure experiences for the patient. The therapist also might assume that the patient is capable of completing the task but is not motivated or working hard enough. In this case, the therapist may fail to notice or address skill deficits that are interfering with the completion of homework assignments.

At the other side of the dialectic is *active passivity*, where the BPD patient approaches problems passively and helplessly, and enlists individuals in his or her environment to come up with solutions to life problems. In this case, the therapist may underestimate the patient's capabilities and avoid assigning homework, do all the "therapy work" for the patient, or assign overly easy tasks that have little impact on therapeutic progress.

Finally, the third dialectical behavior pattern involves *unrelenting crisis* versus *inhibited grieving*. Unrelenting crisis refers to the clinical observation that the lives of BPD patients often involve constant turmoil, stress, and disaster. These factors can undermine homework practice in several ways. For instance, patient and therapist may be caught in a cycle of constantly managing crises and "putting out fires" that allows little room to focus on the strengthening of skills. Indeed, this is partly why the DBT skills group (with its focus on building skills) occurs separately from the individual therapy sessions. Unrelenting crisis also may involve a chaotic interpersonal environment, consisting of individuals who essentially punish skillful behavior. For instance, the authors of this chapter have had patients who go out to their home environments to practice a new interpersonal skill, only to be told, "That psychology mumbo jumbo won't work on me!" When the patient's natural environment punishes newly learned behaviors or fails to reinforce therapeutic progress, homework can be extremely challenging.

At the other end of the dialectic, BPD patients often avoid or inhibit the experience and expression of painful emotions in response to stressful life events (*inhibited grieving*). Most notably, BPD patients may inhibit the natural grieving response to a life filled with tragedy and crisis. Inhibited grieving also broadly involves experiential avoidance, or attempts to avoid, escape, or suppress unwanted emotions, thoughts, or physical sensations (Hayes et al., 1996). With patients who tend to avoid their problems, assigning homework that encourages them to focus on and tackle their problems head-on can be a daunting task.

Motivational Problems

Although motivational problems may underlie problems with homework in many clinical populations, DBT conceptualizes motivation from a behavioral perspective, essentially proposing that sufficient motivation to change is present when the contingencies of reinforcement support behavior change. However, BPD is a disorder of emotion dysregulation, in which motivation to change behavior often waxes and wanes in response to changing moods or emotions. Indeed, for patients who repeatedly self-injure, attempt suicide, and are in toxic interpersonal environments characterized by abuse, behavior change can be as painful as trying to scale a mountain of hot coal with one's bare hands and feet. Under these conditions, it is exceptionally difficult to maintain a consistent motivation to change. Indeed, we have often found that consistent low or unstable motivation to complete homework assignments is caused or exacerbated by many of the factors discussed above (i.e., emotion dysregulation, dialectical dilemmas, lack of reinforcement for new behavior).

STRATEGIES TO OVERCOME BARRIERS TO
EFFECTIVE HOMEWORK IN DBT

In DBT, problems with homework often fall into the category of *therapy interfering behaviors* and are managed in a manner that is similar to other behavioral targets. For most behavioral targets in DBT, the chain analysis serves as the springboard from which the therapist implements a variety of treatment interventions. As discussed previously, the chain analysis in DBT is a method used to evaluate, in minute detail, the circumstances surrounding a particular problem behavior. The chain analysis primarily occurs in individual DBT, although at times, group skills trainers may conduct brief chain analyses of problems in completing homework. When a patient does not complete a homework assignment, the therapist often conducts a chain analysis to determine what has interfered with the completion of homework. The therapist works to help the patient clearly define the problem that led to difficulty with homework, fluidly moving back and forth between assessment of problems and interventions to solve these problems. Because the chain analysis is primarily a change-based strategy, it often is important for the therapist to weave acceptance-based strategies in order to facilitate the patient's engagement in the process, and to enhance the patient's amenability and motivation to change. For instance, in many cases, therapy-interfering behavior is perfectly understandable, given the presence of emotion dysregulation, chaotic interpersonal environments, and other factors; thus, the therapist may use validation strategies to convey that dysfunctional behavior is understandable; at the same time, it *must* change [see Linehan (1997) and Koerner & Linehan (2003) for a detailed discussion of validation in DBT].

A clear and detailed assessment of the problems that led to difficulties with homework can point the therapist and patient in the direction of useful solutions. Chain analysis is not *always* conducted when a patient has problems with homework; however, at the very least, it is important for the therapist to ask useful questions that facilitate effective problem solving. The therapist may inquire whether the patient took in or encoded information about the assignment in the first place (e.g., Did the patient hear the assignment? Was the patient paying attention while homework was being assigned?). Another question a therapist might ask is whether the assignment was encoded but somehow not retrieved at the appropriate time (e.g., Did the thought of doing the homework ever enter the patient's mind in between sessions?). In addition, the therapist might inquire as to whether the patient knew how to do the assignment, was able to find and understand the instructions, or whether there were obstacles to doing the homework (e.g., emotions dysregulation, willfulness, lethargy, other people). A critical point here is that BPD patients often feel ashamed and expect to be judged for not completing assigned tasks. It is essential for the therapist to approach homework difficulties in a non-judgmental manner, as problems to be solved.

Based on an assessment of what got in the way of completing the homework, the therapist might use a variety of strategies to help the patient. If the problem appears to be one of emotion dysregulation, the therapist might help the patient practice regulating emotions in session, reduce factors that create vulnerability to overwhelming emotions (e.g., insomnia, mismanagement of physical illness), or conduct exposure interventions to reduce the patient's sensitivity to emotional stimuli. If the problem is related to dialectical dilemmas, the therapist would help the patient find some way to synthesize these behavioral patterns. For instance, if the phenomenon of *apparent competence* led the therapist to give an overly difficult homework assignment, the therapist might help the patient more accurately express his or her capabilities. Indeed, if the problem is that *unrelenting crises* got in the way of the homework, the therapist might help the patient reduce chaos or crises, or if this is not possible, intervene directly in the environment on behalf of the patient.

In addition, several other strategies may be helpful, depending on the reason for homework difficulties. For instance, the therapist and patient may use contingency management strategies, by setting up a system of reinforcement for homework completion. The therapist also may manage contingencies in the therapeutic relationship, by expressing mild disappointment when homework is not completed, and praise and enthusiasm when it is completed. If the problem was one of low motivation, the therapist might use a variety of strategies geared toward enhancing the patient's commitment. For instance, the therapist might "sell commitment" by connecting the homework assignment with the patient's goals (e.g., "This skill is going to help you attain a life worth living!"); work with the patient to devise the pros and cons of completing homework. Even when motivation is not the problem interfering with homework, the therapist often seeks a renewed commitment to do the homework, and follows this up with troubleshooting aimed at coming up with back-up plans to circumvent additional barriers to completing the agreed upon assignment.

RESEARCH ON HOMEWORK IN DBT

To date, two studies have addressed homework in DBT. Lindenboim et al. (2005) found that suicidal BPD participants in a year-long standard DBT treatment, on average, practiced at least one skill on more than 60% of the days in treatment. Summing over the 19 skills represented, sample mean for the treatment year was upwards of 4 skills practiced a day. Miller et al. (2000) examined client perceptions of the usefulness of the DBT skills as part of a quasi-experimental treatment study of DBT with suicidal adolescents with BPD features. On a 5-point scale ranging from (1) not at all helpful to (5) extremely helpful, mean client ratings of the 19 specific skills ranged from 3.00 to 4.27 indicating moderate to high overall perceived utility and acceptability of DBT skills in that sample. Although this second study was not directly focused on homework implementation, the finding that patients tended to experience homework assignments as acceptable and useful indirectly supported the use of homework in DBT.

CASE ILLUSTRATIONS

The following section involves two case examples designed to illustrate the role of homework assignments in DBT. Each case example consists of a description and DBT-based conceptualization of the case, followed by a discussion of the types of homework assignments used in treatment, the barriers to successful implementation of homework, and strategies used to overcome these barriers.

CASE EXAMPLE I

Case Description and Conceptualization

Tory was a 28-year-old single Caucasian female referred for treatment following hospitalization for a suicide attempt. She reported a history of sexual and physical abuse by her father and, at the time of intake, she met criteria for BPD, PTSD, Bulimia Nervosa, and Social Phobia. Tory had attempted suicide on three occasions in her life (mainly via overdosing) and cut herself about twice a week, without suicidal intent. In addition, Tory reported several impulsive, mood-driven behaviors, including binge-eating and excessive drinking. She also reported *emotion dysregulation*, consisting of periodic, intense mood changes, difficulty regulating her emotions, and problems with excessive and inappropriate shame. Tory also noted that she often had difficulty thinking or believed that others were watching or scrutinizing her, particularly when she was very anxious. Finally, Tory reported that she often felt as if she were an empty "void."

Homework Assignments

Tory entered standard DBT treatment, consisting of individual therapy, skills training, and phone consultation as needed. Individual therapy targeted reducing or stopping self-harm behavior, suicidal ideation, and disordered eating. Homework assignments consisted of self-monitoring via the *DBT diary card*, completing chain-analysis worksheets whenever she engaged in cutting or binge eating behaviors, as well as tasks that exposed her to avoided social cues. All of the patients in Tory's skills group were suicidal women with BPD. Homework in group largely followed Linehan's manual (1993b), and included worksheets and exercises in all four modules *mindfulness, interpersonal effectiveness, emotion regulation,* and *distress tolerance*. Many of the homework assignments were of the *discrete* type, which typically accompany each individual skill module, but the group leaders also worked with Tory to develop individualized *skills practice* homework assignments that were tailored to her problems. These assignments consisted of building mastery experiences, acting in a manner opposite to the action urges associated with shame and anxiety ("opposite action"), and assignments designed to reduce perfectionism.

Barriers to Homework Implementation

The primary barriers to homework with Tory included emotion dysregulation and the dialectical dilemma of *emotion vulnerability* versus *self-invalidation*. Tory was very courteous and pleasant but appeared anxious and uncomfortable in the group. Tory's group cohort had developed a culture of dedication, hard work, and home-work completion; however, it quickly became evident that Tory was struggling in the group, both in the didactic portion and in the homework practice. In terms of emotion dysregulation, Tory appeared flustered and anxious especially during the homework review, a portion of the group time during which the group leaders focus on one patient at a time and discuss homework. When she became anxious, and she usually said whatever was necessary to get the attention of the group away from her as quickly as possible. Consequently, it was difficult for the group leaders to provide her with the time, attention, and feedback she needed to benefit from the homework assignments. In terms of the dialectical dilemma of *emotion vulnerability* versus *self-invalidation*, Tory often reported extreme emotional instability and attributed her difficulty completing homework to problems that were beyond her control. (e.g., being too emotional). On the other end of the polarity, Tory would invalidate her own experience, by downplaying and oversimplifying challenges in her life and the difficulty of the material (e.g., stating "I am too dumb").

Strategies Used to Overcome Barriers

The skills training and individual therapists used several strategies to overcome these barriers to effective homework implementation with Tory. First, in order to help Tory reduce her level of anxiety about being the focus of attention in group, the skills trainers encourage her to practice relaxation and mindfulness exercises during group. The individual therapist worked with Tory to expose her to anxiety provoking social cues, which subsequently led to a reduction in her anxiety during group. Although Tory continued to struggle with some homework assignments, once her anxiety and avoidance behavior had reduced, it was much easier for the therapists assess these difficulties and help her find solutions to overcome them. To reduce self-invalidation, the therapists highlighted her use of unrealistic self-expectations (perfectionism) and judgments and actively encouraged her to reframe and re-phrase these self-statements. The therapists also modeled ways to do this, by using validation strategies to convey understanding of how difficult the homework assignments were, as well as self-disclosure of their own struggles in trying to practice the skills. Finally, earlier in treatment, the therapists worked on stimulus controls strategies to help Tory avoid situations in which she was likely to experience shame (the most frequent precipitant for the binge episodes); however, later on, Tory began to implement homework that involved exposure to shame-eliciting situations, along with response prevention.

CASE EXAMPLE II

Case Description and Conceptualization

Wendi was a 38-year-old divorced Caucasian woman, unemployed, who came to treatment following a recent suicide attempt prompted by a relationship break-up. She met criteria for BPD, as well as severe recurrent Major Depressive Disorder, Panic Disorder, and alcohol abuse. She demonstrated *emotion dysregulation*, in that she had considerable difficulty with intense shame, as well as a pattern of intense, widely fluctuating moods. She also had considerable difficulty establishing a sense of identity and setting life goals. For instance, she reported a pattern of changing jobs, careers, and religious orientations, along with confusion about who she is as a person. Wendy had a history of recurrent suicide attempts and considerable difficulty regulating impulsive behavior when she was emotionally aroused. Finally, Wendi also reported the tendency to dissociate whenever she was overwhelmed by stressors at work, school, or in her relationship with her ex-partner.

Homework Assignments

As with Tory, Wendy received standard DBT, including skills training, individual therapy, and as-needed telephone consultation. The first few weeks of treatment involved obtaining and strengthening a commitment to stop all suicidal behaviors. Many of the homework assignments during this period were of the *conditional* type. For instance, Wendi's individual therapist taught her some of the distress tolerance skills and instructed her to use these strategies whenever she experienced the urge to harm herself. Wendi had notable success with these strategies, and had stopped all overt suicidal behavior within the first few weeks of treatment. The individual therapist also worked with Wendi to develop a treatment plan focused on increasing her ability to regulate emotions, reducing the occurrence of distressing situations or crises, and adding some structure and pleasant activity to her life. In addition, Wendi received *discrete* and ongoing *skills practice* homework assignments during skills training, in order to enhance her skills acquisition.

Barriers to Homework Implementation

The first barrier to homework completion was related to the problem of *emotion vulnerability*. Wendi had established rapport very quickly with her individual therapist, but found the skills trainers to be "difficult." She regularly complained to her primary therapist that the "skills trainers push her too much," that "they don't understand what she's going through" and that she "can't do all these skills." Wendi often did not fill out the skills or the behavioral targets on the *diary card*, and did not practice her skills in a consistent manner. Perhaps due in part to these difficulties with homework, Wendi did not appear to be benefiting from treatment, after her initial drop in suicidal behavior. In fact, she frequently communicated to her individual therapist that treatment was "not helping."

Strategies to Overcome Barriers

Initially, the individual therapist made use of chain analyses and contingency management strategies to help Wendi complete and benefit from her homework. When Wendi came to session without her homework done, the individual therapist would have her fill out her self-monitoring *diary card* in session, without extending the session length. Essentially, Wendi had to complete her homework before arriving in order to have a normal-length session. The therapist also used chain analyses to determine what seemed to be getting in the way of homework completion. Based on these analyses, the therapist reduced the number and difficulty of the homework assignments; reinforced small steps toward more skillful behavior (i.e., *shaping*), coached Wendi on using stimulus control strategies to help her remember her homework assignments, and used heavy doses of "cheerleading", communicating faith in Wendi's ability to complete the homework assignments.

Despite these interventions, Wendi did not seem to be improving in treatment, and by her account, was not practicing skills or completing her homework consistently. In fact, during one session, Wendi stated that "the skills were not all that helpful, and all the therapist ever has to offer are skills, or for her to do x or to do y," and that she thinks she needs something different. The therapist highlighted the pattern that Wendi seems to need and wants help, but that she is not putting effort into therapy, and is consistently telling the therapist that treatment is not working. Using the dialectical strategy of *extending* the seriousness or implication of Wendi's communications, the therapist suggested to Wendi that they consider the possibility that the therapy is not working, and that a different therapist might be more helpful. The therapist emphatically stated that she would consider it unethical to knowingly conduct ineffective therapy. As it turns out, this was the "magic" intervention for Wendi. She completely changed her demeanor. She told the therapist that therapy has been helpful (even skills training) and that she has been doing more work than she has been reporting, primarily because she was terrified of communicating that she was getting better. As it turns out, Wendi was afraid that, if people believed she was improving, they would stop helping her and increase their expectations of her. The therapist validated her fear, (based on a long history of these kinds of experiences) and came up with a solution to this problem that involved changing the contingencies of treatment. The solution was to agree that Wendi could continue to see her therapist as long as she was improving in therapy. Subsequently, Wendi's progress improved, as did the accuracy of her reports about her progress, and she consistently completed her homework assignments.

SUMMARY

DBT is a comprehensive, multi-modal cognitive behavioral treatment that is firmly embedded in a dialectical philosophy. The biosocial theory of BPD posits that patients with BPD suffer from a fundamental dysfunction of the emotion regulation system, characterized by both motivational and skill deficits. Several different types of homework assignments are used in DBT to ameliorate skills deficits and facilitate the targeting of behavior by the therapist. Some of the homework assignments are instrumental to the process of targeting and working toward high priority goals (e.g., self-monitoring *DBT diary cards*), while other homework assignments are more directly focused on having the patient hone particular skills (e.g., *skills practice* assignments). Homework in DBT is used in a variety of ways to enhance skill acquisition, strengthening, and generalization among BPD patients.

In many ways, DBT was built from the "bottom up" to address problems with implementing standard therapy procedures with multi-problem patients. Along these lines, therapy with BPD patients often involves many barriers to homework implementation. Much of the focus of individual therapy in DBT is geared toward preventing or ameliorating problems that serve as barriers to developing a life worth living, through the synthesis of acceptance and change strategies. Barriers to homework implementation are treated as therapy-interfering behaviors, and the therapist tackles these problems in a similar manner as other behavioral difficulties, based firmly in a DBT case conceptualization, behavioral principles, and common therapeutic sense. The underlying assumption is that the most caring thing a therapist can do is to help patients change in ways that bring them closer to their own ultimate goals. In terms of research on homework, some encouraging evidence supports the acceptability of homework in DBT. In addition, contrary to clinical lore, evidence suggests that suicidal BPD patients do, indeed, practice their skills and do their homework. We hope that this chapter provides guidance on the important role of homework in DBT that will encourage clinicians to use this therapeutic tool in a manner that enhances the lives of BPD patients.

REFERENCES

Aitken, R. (1982). *Taking the path of zen*. San Francisco: North Point Press.
American Psychiatric Association (1994). *Diagnostic and statistical manual of mental disorders: DSM-IV*. Washington, DC: American Psychiatric Association.
Barlow, D. H. (1988). *Anxiety and its disorders: The nature and treatment of anxiety and panic*. New York: Guilford.

Bouton, M. E. (1993). Context, Time, and Memory Retrieval in the Interference Paradigms of Pavlovian Learning. *Psychological Bulletin, 114*, 80–99.

Bouton, M. E., & Brooks, D. C. (1993). Time and Context Effects on Performance in A Pavlovian Discrimination Reversal. *Journal of Experimental Psychology-Animal Behavior Processes, 19*, 165–179.

Chambless, D. L., & Hollon, S. D. (1998). Defining empirically supported therapies. *Journal of Consulting and Clinical Psychology, 66*, 7–18.

Chapman, A. L., Gratz, K. L., & Brown, M. Z. (2006). Solving the puzzle of deliberate self-harm: The experiential avoidance model. *Behaviour Research and Therapy, 44*, 371–394.

Chapman, A. L., & Linehan, M. M. (2005). *Dialectical behavior therapy for borderline personality disorder*. In M. Zanarini (Ed.), *Borderline Personality Disorder* (pp. 211–242). Florida: Taylor & Francis.

Foa, E. B., & Kozak, M. J. (1986). Emotional processing of fear: Exposure to corrective information. *Psychological Bulletin, 99*, 20–35.

Franklin, M. E., Abramowitz, J. S., Kozak, M. J., Levitt, J. T., & Foa, E. B. (2000). Effectiveness of exposure and ritual prevention for obsessive- compulsive disorder: Randomized compared with nonrandomized samples. *Journal of Consulting and Clinical Psychology, 68*, 594–602.

Gellatly, I. R., & Meyer, J. P. (1992). The effects of goal difficulty on physiological arousal, cognition, and task-performance. *Journal of Applied Psychology, 77*, 694–704.

Gottman, J. M., & Levenson, R. W. (1986). Assessing the role of emotion in marriage. *Behavioral Assessment, 8*, 31–48.

Hayes, S. C., Wilson, K. G., Gifford, E. V., Follette, V. M., & Strosahl, K. (1996). Experiential avoidance and behavioral disorders: A functional dimensional approach to diagnosis and treatment. *Journal of Consulting and Clinical Psychology, 64*, 1152–1168.

Koerner, K., & Linehan, M. M. (2003). Validation principles and strategies. In W. O. O'Donohue, J. D. Fisher, & S. C. Hayes (Eds.), *Cognitive behavior therapy* (pp. 229–237). New Jersey: Wiley.

Koons, C. R., Robins, C. J., Tweed, J. L., Lynch, T. R., Gonzalez, A. M., Morse, J. Q. et al. (2001). Efficacy of dialectical behavior therapy in women veterans with borderline personality disorder. *Behavior Therapy, 32*, 371–390.

Lindenboim, N., Comtois, K. A., & Linehan, M. M. (2005). Skills practice in dialectical behavior therapy for suicidal borderline women. (Manuscript submitted for publication).

Linehan, M. M. (1993a). *Cognitive-behavioral treatment of borderline personality disorder*. New York: Guilford.

Linehan M. M. (1993b). *Skills training manual for treating borderline personality disorder*. New York: Guilford.

Linehan, M. M. (1997). Validation and psychotherapy. In A. C. Bohart & L. S. Greenberg (Eds.), *Empathy reconsidered: New directions in psychotherapy* (pp. 353–392). Washington, DC: American Psychological Association.

Linehan, M. M., Armstrong, H. E., Suarez, A., Allmon, D., & Heard, H. L. (1991). Cognitive-behavioral treatment of chronically parasuicidal borderline patients. *Archives of General Psychiatry, 48*, 1060–1064.

Linehan, M. M., Comtois, K. A., Murray, A. M., Brown, M. Z., Gallop, R. J., Heard, H. L. et al. (2006). Two-year randomized controlled trial and follow-up of dialectical behavior therapy vs. therapy by experts for suicidal behaviors and borderline personality disorder, *Archives of general psychiatry, 63*, 757–768.

Linehan, M. M., Dimeff, L. A., Reynolds, S. K., Comtois, K., Shaw-Welch, S., Heagerty, P. et al. (2002). Dialectical behavior therapy versus comprehensive validation plus 12 step for the treatment of opioid dependent women meeting criteria for borderline personality disorder. *Drug and Alcohol Dependence, 67*, 13–26.

Linehan, M. M., Heard, H. L., & Armstrong, H. E. (1993). Naturalistic follow-up of a behavioral treatment for chronically parasuicidal borderline patients. *Archives of General Psychiatry, 50,* 971–974.

Linehan, M. M., Schmidt, H., III, Dimeff, L. A., Craft, J. C., Kanter, J., & Comtois, K. A. (1999). Dialectical behavior therapy for patients with borderline personality disorder and drug-dependence. *American Journal of Addiction, 8,* 279–292.

Linehan, M. M., Tutek, D. A., Heard, H. L., & Armstrong, H. E. (1994). Interpersonal outcome of cognitive behavioral treatment for chronically suicidal borderline patients. *American Journal of Psychiatry, 151,* 1771–1776.

Lynch, T. R., Chapman, A. L., Rosenthal, M. Z., Kuo, J. R., & Linehan, M. M. (2006). Mechanisms of change in dialectical behavior therapy: Theoretical and empirical observations. *Journal of Clinical Psychology, 62,* 459–480.

Miller, A. L., Wyman, S. E., Huppert, J. D., Glassman, S. L., & Rathus, J. H. (2000). Analysis of behavioral skills utilized by suicidal adolescents receiving dialectical behavior therapy. *Cognitive & Behavioral Practice, 7,* 183–187.

Robins, C. J., & Chapman, A. L. (2004). Dialectical behavior therapy: Current status, recent developments, and future directions. *Journal of Personality Disorders, 18,* 73–89.

Skinner, B. F. (1953). *Science and human behavior.* New York: Macmillan.

Smith, R. E., Leffingwell, T. R., & Ptacek, J. T. (1999). Can people remember how they coped? Factors associated with discordance between same-day and retrospective reports. *Journal of Personality and Social Psychology, 76,* 1050–1061.

Turner, R. M. (2000). Naturalistic evaluation of dialectical behavioral therapy-oriented treatment for borderline personality disorder. *Cognitive and Behavioral Practice 7,* 413–419.

van den Bosch, L. M. C., Verheul, R., Schippers, G. M., & Van den Brink, W. (2002). Dialectical behavior therapy of borderline patients with and without substance use problems. Implementation and long-term effects. *Addictive Behaviors, 27,* 911–923.

Verheul, R., van den Bosch, L. M. C., Koeter, M. W. J., de Ridder, M. A. J., Stijnen, T., & van den, B. W. (2003). Dialectical behaviour therapy for women with borderline personality disorder: 12-month, randomised clinical trial in The Netherlands. *British Journal of Psychiatry, 182,* 135–140.

Wolpe, J. (1954). Reciprocal inhibition as the main basis of psychotherapeutic effects. *Archives of Neurology and Psychiatry, 72,* 205–276.

Chapter 14

CHRONIC DEPRESSION

Lawrence P. Riso and Michael E. Thase

While once of limited interest to the field, chronic depression is now recognized as a major public health problem (Howland, 1993). Not only is chronic depression common, representing 19% of all depressed patients (Keller & Hanks, 1995) and 6% in the community (Kessler et al., 1994), but it is also associated with considerable psychosocial impairment (Howland, 1993), and is extremely challenging to treat (Akiskal, 1997). Response rates to both pharmacotherapy and psychotherapeutic are considerably below that for nonchronic depression (Howland, 1991; Markowitz, 1995; Thase et al., 1994). Recent evidence suggests combination treatments of medication and psychotherapy may be the helpful (Keller et al., 2000). Psychotherapeutic approaches continue to grapple with ways to improve therapeutic outcomes for this extremely difficult population. In this chapter, we focus specifically on the use of homework assignments in cognitive-behavioral therapy with chronically depressed patients. We begin with a definition of chronic depression, followed by barriers to the successful use of homework with this group, and then offer suggestions for good homework assignments. We conclude with two case examples of chronic patients that illustrate some difficulties and successes in the use of homework during therapy. Since the approach to homework with chronically depressed patients is not qualitatively different than that for nonchronic patients, we only discuss the aspect of homework that deserve special attention. We discuss homework within the context of both cognitive therapy and the Cognitive Behavioral Analysis System of Psychotherapy (CBASP), which was specifically designed to treat chronic depression.

DEFINITION OF CHRONIC DEPRESSION

Chronic depression does not exist as a DSM-IV diagnosis or even a DSM-IV subtype of depression. Rather, the term is generally used to refer to any DSM-IV depressive disorder with a duration of two years or longer. This would include dysthymic disorder defined as depressed mood with low-grade symptoms for two years or longer, along with the co-occurrence of dysthymic disorder with a major depressive disorder [known as "double-depression" (Keller & Shapiro, 1982)]. Major depressive disorder can also have a chronic course (i.e., major depressive disorder, chronic type) if the full criteria are met for at least two years. Some research also regards recurrent episodes of major depressive disorder in which there is no remission between episodes as a form of chronic depression (Keller et al., 2000). Finally, chronic depression may also include a major depressive episode which has partially remitted, but continues for over two years.

ADDRESSING BARRIERS TO THE
SUCCESSFUL USE OF HOMEWORK

Thase et al. (1994) examined the efficacy of cognitive behavioral therapy (CBT) for chronic versus nonchronic depression. These authors found that CBT was slower-acting and less efficacious for chronically depressed patients. Chronic patients seemed to have difficulty "grasping or embracing the collaborative-empirical or self-help aspects of CBT" (p. 212), and the authors suggested the need for a modified CBT approach for this group. Below we have identified five features of chronic depression that present barriers to the successful use of homework during treatment. These barriers include hopelessness/helplessness, avoidance (cognitive, emotional, and behavioral), and hypohedonia. As already mentioned, these aspects of chronic depression are not *qualitatively* different from nonchronic depression; however, they deserve special attention when implementing homework in therapy.

Hopelessness/Helplessness

Although defined as depressed mood for two years or longer, chronically depressed patients have endured many years or even a lifetime of depression. Often times chronic patients declare, "I've been depressed as long as I can remember" or "deep down, I'm always depressed and unhappy." Having undergone several failed trials of antidepressant medication is common along with years of psychotherapy. As Moore and Garland (2003) described, the hallmark of chronic depression is a chronic cognitive triad of low self-esteem, hopelessness, and helplessness.

Chronic depression is marked by particularly negative dysfunctional explanatory style contributing to their hopelessness (McCullough et al., 1994; Riso et al., 2003). Negative events are attributed to personal shortcomings that have broad implications for life (internal and global causes) rather than to specific situational determinants. Thus, a negative interpersonal interaction is attributed to being an unlovable person who is destined to a life of solitude and loneliness, rather than to a clash of personalities or a misunderstanding. McCullough (2000) described chronic patients as helpless and passive with an external locus of control and a global style of thinking. Thus, chronic patients believe that bad things "just happen" to them and there is not a thing they can do about it. Operating at a "preoperational" (or prelogical) level of interpersonal awareness, they are unable to causally link the thoughts and behaviors they bring into a situation with the negative outcomes that follow (McCullough, 2000).

Hopelessness and helplessness present the most severe obstacles to the successful implementation of homework assignments in therapy. After so much time and unhelpful treatment, it is a lot to expect patients to enter therapy with a fresh new attitude and hope that *this time*, things will be different. For instance, they may interpret suggestions to re-engage with their environment as asking for the impossible. They may passively avoid attempts at collaboratively deriving homework assignments and may believe that the therapist's suggestions are pointless. Remaining mindful of this backdrop of hopelessness when formulating homework is critical. Selling the benefits of homework too strongly can lead clients to feel deeply misunderstood. Respect and validation for the chronic patient's skepticism is essential. However, at the same time, the therapist must persevere with a "wait and see" attitude.

Helplessness will also sabotage the cognitive therapist's ideal of collaboratively arriving at homework tasks. Asking patients, "so, what do you think would be a good task for you to try for this week?" will tend to be met with a shrug or a blank stare. Worse yet, they can interpret this as another instance of their ineptness and begin to withdraw from therapy. On the other hand, because chronic patients are already passive, taking on too much responsibility for crafting homework week after week will foster even greater passivity, withdrawal, and disengagement. One approach to this "see-saw" dilemma is to make use of the interpersonal theory of Donald Kiesler (1983, 1996) (see McCullough, for more on implementing this approach). The circumplex depicts interpersonal interactions along the superordinate dimensions of control (dominance versus submission) and affiliation (hostility versus friendliness). Dominance and submission are *reciprocal* (or complementary) interpersonal tendencies. Thus, exhibiting one will elicit the opposite (dominance pulls for, and submission pulls for dominance). Hostility and friendliness are *corresponding* interpersonal tendencies. Exhibiting either tendency will elicit the same (friendliness pulls friendliness, and hostility pulls hostility). Within this model, chronic patients can be expected to have a hostile submission posture. It is critical to remain aware that this will elicit a hostile dominant posture from the therapist. With the aid of Kiesler's interpersonal model, therapists can also more carefully monitor how directive or dominant they are in sessions so as not to inadvertently elicit submission and unassertiveness from patients. Therapists can strategically vary their behavior from a friendly dominant posture (e.g., "Let's take a look at how you behaved in this situation"), which helps to impose structure, to a friendly passive posture (e.g., "I'm not exactly sure what we can do about this situation"), which helps to elicit problem solving. The therapist can also more readily recognize and respond to potentially damaging interpersonal interactions throughout treatment. For instance, the model helps therapists guard against a tendency to respond to a hostile response from patients with more hostility.

AVOIDANCE (COGNITIVE, AFFECTIVE, AND BEHAVIORAL)

A cardinal feature of chronic depression is avoidance. Chronically depressed patients exhibit high rates of comorbid avoidant personality disorder (Pepper et al., 1995), high levels of overvigilance schemas (Riso et al., 2003), and elevated levels of a harm avoidant temperament (Hellerstein et al., 2001). They may be afraid to explore key cognitions and problematic behaviors, which manifests itself in session as jumping from topic to topic. Often there is emotional avoidance as well. Patients may describe having "no feelings" or glibly relate disturbing experiences with little outward sign of emotional upset. Behaviorally, they may avoid social contacts for fear of rejection and humiliation. Attempts to engage them with their environment may be viewed as holding little potential for improving their mood, and considerable potential for causing pain, disappointment, and embarrassment.

Avoidance presents a considerable impediment when assigning homework, particularly homework that is directed as increasing activity level and taking social risks. Therefore, before therapists jump to action-oriented interventions, one strategy is to first address the patient's readiness for change (Prochaska, DiClemente, & Norcross, 1992). For instance, chronic patients may be aware of their difficulties and recognize the need to make changes, but may simply not be prepared to take on the challenge (i.e., be in the "contemplation" vs. "action" phase). Their mere presence in therapy should never be taken as de facto evidence that they are ready to make changes in their lives. The wish of a chronic patient is often to somehow rid them of their depression without having to confront their avoidance of people, situations, thoughts, and emotions. Other patients will be in therapy because they have become so severely isolated, that the therapy is their only regular social contact.

Patients who are in the contemplation phase need to be allowed to explore their ambivalence about change and the advantages and disadvantages of continuing their pattern of avoidance. We have used a metaphor of a hiker who has just had a painful fall into narrow cave opening. He falls halfway into the cave and is afraid to move, lest he fall even farther and hurt himself even more. He works with a guide up above to brace himself and make tiny movements that would present minimal risk, but might help him get out of the predicament. Thus, patients need to be gently questioned about the possible advantages of making changes.

Early in therapy, only homework with a very high likelihood of success should be attempted. While this is good general practice when assigning homework for any condition, the issue of successful homework early in therapy is especially critical when dealing with the chronically depressed patient. Avoidance of the topic of homework assignments and failure to complete them can severely disrupt the use of this essential component of treatment. Thus, great care should be taken to follow-up on homework and empathy and exploration should follow when patients are not able to follow through. Dealing with patients with years of well-practiced avoidance makes it all too easy to collude with their anxiety and avoidance and get shaped into deemphasizing homework and failing to follow-up when homework is not completed.

HYPOHEDONIA

Loss of interest (or "hypohedonia" when chronic) among the most common symptoms of chronic depression (Keller et al., 1995) along with a lowered temperamental capacity for reward (Hellerstein et al., 2001). Consequently, chronically depressed individuals have persistent difficulty in initiating behaviors that could bring about reward or pleasure. Thus, even after working through a patient's helplessness, hopelessness, and avoidance to actually complete a homework assignment, they may fail to have the intended positive mood shift. The failure of the homework to produce a mood shift is potentially hazardous for further undermining motivation for homework and reaffirming the belief that there is no hope for the future. However, it is critical to emphasize for hypohedonic patients that the goal of homework for the early part of therapy is not to alter mood. Rather, it is to alter behavior with the expectation that mood changes will follow. In other words, mood change often lags behind behavioral change. As mood shifts begin to occur, they are likely to be small and incremental. The therapist needs to carefully tune into even small changes in mood and make certain that they are not dismissed by patients as insignificant. Small shifts can be critical pieces of evidence for patients that their chronic depression can in fact be shaken and so therapists need to respond enthusiastically when this occurs.

GOOD COGNITIVE THERAPY HOMEWORK ASSIGNMENTS FOR CHRONIC DEPRESSION

MOOD MONITORING

When asked about their patterns of mood fluctuations, many chronic patients will say there are none. All they can recall is a steady unwavering depressed mood unaffected by external events. However, even chronically depressed patients experience fluctuations in their mood. Their belief in a "flat line" of depressed mood is likely an example of *all-or-nothing thinking*. Even chronically depressed patients experience some level of reactivity. Homework is necessary to help patients understand the more subtle nuances of their moods and discover that periods of relative good mood do exist, however fleeting. Once this is established, therapy can focus on understanding not only what circumstances are mood lifting, but, also those that tend to deepen depression. Simply monitoring mood on a 1 to 10 scale regularly will help demonstrate the finer gradations in their mood state and even teach them something about which activities and situations are associated with positive shifts.

ACTIVITY SCHEDULING

Cognitive therapy for depression will often start with activity scheduling. For chronic patients, activity scheduling has the potential to bring a degree of early symptom relief that can be critical for patients with low expectations for therapy and an impoverished sense of self-efficacy. If too much time elapses before the chronic patient sees some improvement, their hopelessness can be reinforced and they may see little use in continuing. However, as we mentioned above, positive mood shifts of any significance sometimes will not occur in response to activity scheduling early in therapy and may lag behind changes in behavior. Thus, for the first 2–3 weeks, the patient may need to deemphasize changes in mood and focus instead on changing the behaviors that are expected, at some point, to begin to lift their depression. Early in treatment, changes in how the patient uses their time should be an end in and of itself. If they are actually able to make behavioral changes, this should be acknowledged a considerable accomplishment, regardless of whether or not there is a shift in mood.

CORE BELIEF WORKSHEETS

Overgeneralized negative themes (i.e., early maladaptive schemas or core beliefs[1]) may be particularly important to address in chronic depression. Maladaptive core beliefs are more prominent in chronic depression compared to nonchronic groups, even when taking into account differences in personality disorder symptoms (Riso

---

[1] The terms "schema" and "core belief" both refer to thematic cognitive material and they are used interchangeably in this chapter. However, others use the term "schema" to refers to implicit cognitive structure or the interconnectedness among cognitive elements and the term "core belief" to refer to the consciously available content of a schema (Clark & Beck, 1999).

Old core belief: _____

How much do you believe the old core belief right now? (0-100)
    *What's the most you've believed it this week? (0-100)
    *What's the least you've believed it this week? (0-100)

New belief: _____

How much do you believe the new belief right now? (0-100) _____

Evidence that contradicts old core belief and supports new belief	Evidence that supports old core belief with reframe

FIGURE 14.1. Core Belief Worksheet.

et al., 2003). Examples of such beliefs include defectiveness, abandonment, mistrust, and unlovability. These core themes are stable and specific over time and so can reasonably be used as the basis for the case conceptualization (Riso et al., in press). The core belief worksheet (CBW; Beck, 1995; see Figure 14.1) can be extremely useful in session and also for homework to help patients shift to more functional and balanced beliefs. In session, the therapist and patient will identify a central core belief and formulate an alternative more-balanced view. Evidence that supports the old core belief with a reframe is placed in the right-hand column and evidence that contradicts the old core belief and supports the new belief is placed in the left-hand column. After gaining some proficiency with this technique in session, it can then be used as a homework. Assigning the CBW for homework can be extremely useful in undoing a damaging core belief as patients obtain practice fighting their distorted schema-consistent processing of events. By completing the CBW for homework week after week, patients will be regularly forced to scan the environment for evidence that is inconsistent with their maladaptive beliefs, rather than only attending to evidence that supports the old belief. Simply completing the sheet in session is not adequate to undo this automatic tendency. An example of the CBW in practice is provided in the first case example later in this chapter.

BEHAVIORAL EXPERIMENTS DESIGNED TO EVALUATE CORE BELIEFS

Behavioral experiments are often used to demonstrate the link between thoughts and emotions, between mood and activity, and to demonstrate the distorted nature of automatic thoughts and underlying assumption. In therapy with chronically depressed patients, behavioral experiments can be especially useful in examining core beliefs. Behavioral experiments about core beliefs can be done concurrently with the CBW. One patient with a core belief that he was "weak" believed that his wife could not respect him if he ever self-disclosed feelings of insecurity in their relationship. After making negative predictions about the outcome, he was pleasantly surprised by the positive interaction with his wife feelings of closeness and intimacy that resulted.

CBASP Homework—the Coping Survey
Questionnaire

CBASP was developed by McCullough (2000) specifically to treat individuals with chronic depression. The therapy assumes that chronicity of depression is related to repeated stressful or unsatisfactory interpersonal interactions. Over time, repeated negative interactions with others leads to further erosion in social facility and greater entrenchment of depression in a self-perpetuating cycle. Chronic patients develop negative expectations for themselves and others in relationships and negative global interpretations of social interactions. Ultimately, they become utterly hopeless about their ability to attain what they desire in social interactions. They enter interpersonal situations with no thoughts about what they would like to see happen, but rather the belief that "nothing I do makes the slightest bit of difference."

The primary therapeutic exercise in CBASP is the Coping Survey Questionnaire (CSQ; see Figure 14.2). In completing the five steps of the CSQ, patients learn to succinctly and "objectively" describe a stressful interpersonal situation and to identify and remediate unproductive interpretations and behaviors. An equally important step of the CSQ is learning to formulate realistic and attainable desired outcomes (Step 5). In completing the exercise, patients are forced to consider the functional relationship between what they put into situations and what they get out of them. In other words, chronic patients learn that they tend to produce their stressful and unsatisfactory interpersonal outcomes, and so they have the power to change outcomes that are closer to what they would want. In CBASP, the patient brings in one CSQ to therapy for review that was completed for homework the previous week. The entire session is then devoted to reviewing the CSQ, an exercise known as "situational analysis."

CASE EXAMPLE 1

John is a 38-year-old married father of two boys, ages 4 and 10. He has an undergraduate degree in business and works in human resources for a large corporation. His presenting problems included depression and excessive anxiety when giving presentations required for his job. Further assessment revealed that he had met DSM-IV criteria for dysthymic disorder since early adulthood and had features of social anxiety disorder. In addition to social anxiety giving presentations as work, he felt anxious around co-workers, rarely interacted with them, and ate lunch alone every day. He felt too anxious to engage in casual conversation with people he met when going to the store or traveling for business. Although he found his work dull and uninteresting, he stuck with it anyway, fearing that he was not capable of much else. He ended up marrying his college girlfriend, but literally lost contact with every friend he had had in college. Although he functioned relatively well in his marriage, his life consisted of a job that made him anxious, social isolation outside of his immediate family, and few hobbies or activities.

A developmental history revealed that John was overweight as a child and came from a highly critical family. He described his mother as a very "mannerly" woman who constantly criticized him for the way he spoke and the way he presented himself to others. She would frequently correct his grammar and the things he said, often

COPING SURVEY QUESTIONNAIRE

Patient:_____   **Therapist:**_____

Date of Situational Event:_____   **Date of Therapy Session:**_____

Instructions: Select one problematical event that has happened to you during the past week and describe it using the format below. Please try to fill out <u>all</u> parts of the questionnaire. Your therapist will assist you in reviewing this situational analysis during your next therapy session.

Situational Area: Spouse/Partner__ Children__ Extended Family__ Work/School__ Social__

Step-1. Describe *what* happened:

Step-2. Describe your *interpretation* of what happened (How did you read the situation?):

    1.

    2.

    3.

Step-3. Describe what you *did* during the situation (e.g., What you said/how you said it):

Step-4. Describe how the event came out for you (Actual Outcome):

Step-5. Describe how you *wanted* the event to come out for you (Desired Outcome):

Step-6. Was the Desired Outcome achieved? YES___ NO ___

FIGURE 14.2. Coping Survey Questionnaire.

making him feel publicly humiliated and embarrassed. When he began to withdraw socially as a child, his mother would criticize him for not saying enough (e.g., "why don't you say something?") when they were around others. His father was described as an intimidating person who always needed to be right. His father would repeatedly shoot down John's opinions and had to win every argument. While John was a bright individual and did well at school, his parents actually expressed disappointment and embarrassment at his decision to pursue work in human resources.

John's days were filled with self-doubt, anxiety around others, and a core belief that he was incompetent. In his words, he was a "loser." He kept to himself, was reluctant to interact with others, became extremely nervous during presentations at work and was extremely indecisive. He spent much of his time worrying about work and dreading parties and social gatherings. He was very anxious when at work and attempted to compensate for his core belief of incompetence by either avoiding his work and procrastinating, or by being excessively perfectionistic with his work. He labored long hours to attempt to produce perfect reports, although this led to frantic last minute efforts and reports that, ironically, were replete with embarrassing errors made in haste. This pattern was particularly problematic for his work presentations. The preparation would occupy a tremendous amount of energy and time to the exclusion of spending time with his family, doing exercise, and doing other activities. He would become so consumed with the fear of looking incompetent that his depression would worsen for the weeks leading up to a presentation.

CBW: One of the primary interventions used in treatment was the CBW. After completing a CBW in session using historical information, it was then used as a homework throughout the treatment. John was to gather evidence that supported the old core belief with reframe (right side), or gather evidence that contradicted the old belief and supported the new one (left side). He was able to see the destructive effects of this belief on his life and was quite compliant with the task. However, he had considerable difficult disputing, or reframing, his old core belief (right side of CBW):

John: Well, for evidence that supports the old belief, I wrote, "I'm in a job that I don't enjoy and I've undersold myself."

Therapist: What's the reframe?

John: I don't know. I can come up with one.

Therapist: Well, is your job at least *gainful* employment?

John: Yeah.

Therapist: And you've been telling me that you are actually pretty good at it. Is that true?

John: Yes, that's true.

Therapist: What about as a reframe, "I'm in a job that I don't enjoy and I may have undersold myself, *but*, it's steady and gainful employment and I'm quite competent at it. Does present help shift in your core belief?

John: Yeah . . . that helps.

Therapist: What else did you have difficulty reframing?

John: I also wrote that people think I have a nowhere job. I couldn't reframe this one either.

Therapist: How do you know people think this?

John: I don't really *know* it, but people give me a funny look when I tell them what I do. I guess it's possible that they just don't know what I'm talking about.

Therapist: Can you put this into a reframe?

John: I guess I could say, "people think that I have a nowhere job, *but*, maybe they just don't understand my job.

With the therapist's assistance, John was able to fight through his schema-consistent processing and develop excellent reframes. However, John continued to report the negative impact of his core belief.

> John: I see what you are trying to do with the core belief worksheet. I know at some level that my belief of incompetence really isn't true, but that doesn't mean it doesn't still get to me when I'm out there. You know what I mean?
> Therapist: Yeah, I think so. You can see logically when you are here with me that there is little evidence so support your core belief of incompetence; however, it still has the power to effect you after our sessions.
> John: That's exactly right.
> Therapist: Changing a core belief and the way it affects your mood and behavior can be like turning a battleship around. It can really take time. What do you think about continuing the CBWs for homework over the next three weeks and then re-evaluating at that point? We'll go over them together each week in session.
> John: I can try it.
> Theraspist: Good. Be sure and rate how much you believe the old core belief from 0 to 100 each time you do it.

After several weeks, ratings of how strongly he held the old core believe gradually declined from 79 to 60. While the change was modest, it demonstrated two important things that were highlighted in therapy. First, it demonstrated the plasticity in his core belief of incompetence. That is, factors other than his actual level of competence were affecting his belief which implicated a role for selective and biased processing of information. Second, while the belief did not go down to 0, there was movement. Therefore, further progress was possible. The therapist highlighted these points made in therapy to gain leverage in persuading the patient to continue with this homework. Over the next several months, the patient was actually able to archive a substantial body of evidence that refuted the old belief and was consistent with the more balanced belief of "I'm at least as competent as most people." This evidence included meetings that went well at work and others respected what he had to say, completing several hours of tasks, getting caught up on bills, interacting well with his children, and honest and open interactions with his wife.

Progress can be slow with the CBW as patients learn to gradually undo their tendency to scan the environment for schema-consistent information and they may have their doubts about it along the way. A therapeutic stance that is up-beat, optimistic, and persevering can be essential to get this exercise to be successful.

Behavioral Experiments

John completed a series of behavioral experiments aimed at evaluating the core belief that he was incompetent and that other people would see him as a "loser." The behavioral experiments began with simple interactions with strangers. Instead of avoiding the elevator if someone else was in it, he made a point to take the elevator and forced himself to make conversation. He made a point to say *something*, even if just small talk, to the receptionist at work and to co-workers he would pass in the hallways and in the parking garage. As these interactions began to disconfirm his predictions of negative outcomes, therapy focused on more difficult experiments for homework. He experimented with expressing more of his opinions during meetings at work, struck up conversations with people at social functions, and worked getting to the gym more often for his workouts. For nearly every single one of these behavioral experiments, people responded well to John and he was able to accomplish a great deal more than what he predicted. While his core belief of incompetence was still with him, through the course of therapy, it was much less prone to getting activated and he gained some skill at keeping it under control.

Following his success with interpersonal interactions, the behavioral experiments began to focus on his perfectionism. In therapy, he and the therapist worked out a time schedule for completing tasks at work and behavioral experiments tested whether or not this time schedule was in fact possible. He also experimented with turning in work that, in his eyes, was short of perfection. Adhering to a timeline was a particularly important behavioral experiment for his work presentations in order to contain the preparation. Over time, John discovered that his compensatory strategies of perfectionism or avoidance were counterproductive. He learned that he could give a competent and organized presentation without the attendant disruption in his life and worsening of his depressive symptoms.

John's homework focused mainly on re-evaluating his negative core beliefs, his avoidance of social interactions, and his avoidance and perfectionism with tasks at work. After extensive use of homework over several months of therapy, John built up a database of evidence that counteracted his negative core belief ("I'm a loser") and gradually gained greater acceptance of his alternative belief ("At the very least, I'm competent"). He became more spontaneous in his interactions with others, more willing to self-disclose, and more willing to make himself vulnerable to others. This allowed him to establish greater connectness with his co-workers, his family, and his neighbors. His depressed symptoms faded considerably and he was in remission of his dysthymic disorder by his ninth month of therapy.

CASE EXAMPLE 2 (CBASP)

Judy is 39-year-old and a mother of two boys, ages 7 and 14. She had a history of major depressive episodes in her teens and early adulthood. After her divorce, which was three years before admission, her mood gradually deteriorated and she developed dysthymic disorder. She was given primary custody of her two boys and felt scared, overwhelmed, and depressed related to multiple stressors she encountered in trying to maintain her household as a single parent. One particularly salient stressor was her eldest son's behavioral problems, which created difficulties at home and at school.

A developmental history regarding significant figures in her life was completed during the first two sessions (known as the "significant other history" in CBASP). She described a fairly positive relationship with her mother who she said was generally caring, although did not respond well when Judy came to her with a problem. She was told to just accept problems and that "this is just the way things are." Her father was described as a critical man. She often felt that, in his eyes, everything she did was wrong. There was no negotiating with him when there were disagreements and she got the message that women were "stupid" and do not know how make decisions. From these experiences, she developed several key hypotheses about herself and relationships:

"If I complain, I'll be criticized or ignored."
"If I withhold how I feel, I'm in control."
"If I try to do something on my own, I will fail."

Combined with her current stressors, these ideas left her feeling hopeless about the future and feeling helpless about her ability to make changes in her life.

One CSQ was completed for homework each week and reviewed in the following session. The CSQ homework was designed help her to develop new skills and demonstrate that her efforts can in fact make a difference. One of her early CSQs appears in Figure 14.3. In this situation, Judy's ex-husband wanted to buy the kids an extra computer so they could play computer games at home. She did not want this computer, did not have much room for it, and did not want her children to be playing more computer games at home. The CSQ revealed her belief that she had no ability or right to make decisions for her children. This was remediated in session with the therapist to the more accurate interpretation that she was actually capable of making a decision and did have the right to take control. After an in-depth review of the CSQ homework, the patient and therapist did several role-plays to sharpen Judy's skills in asserting her opinion. Thus, the course of therapy involved her completing the CSQ for homework, reviewing it in session, and then role playing the situation for the remainder of the session.

The CSQ in Figure 14.4, completed later in therapy, needed very little remediation and demonstrates how Judy is gaining increased confidence, skill and control. She gradually learned that if she does not need to blame herself, she can be extremely effective.

SUMMARY

While using homework assignments in cognitive therapy with chronic depression is not qualitatively different from using homework with acute depression, a number of factors require special emphasis including their helpless/hopelessness, avoidance, and hypohedonia. The homework that can be particularly useful includes mood monitoring, activity scheduling, CBWs, and behavioral experiments. The CBW is a particularly important component of treatment for several reasons. Previous research suggests that maladaptive core beliefs are particularly important in chronic depression. Moreover, conceptualizing chronic patients in terms of generalized maladaptive core beliefs helps to organize a large number of complaints under a coherent theme. Change at the level of generalized belief structures is likely to be important for meaningful and lasting improvement for chronic depression.

In CBASP a standard homework is used every session, the CSQ. This feature alone has several advantages in that in keeps the course and focus of therapy highly structured and presents a tremendous amount of repetition to aid learning and skill acquisition. The CSQ form helps patients define situations, focus on their desired outcomes, and examine the functional relationship between what they bring to the

COPING SURVEY QUESTIONNAIRE

Patient:_____   **Therapist:**_____

Date of Situational Event:_____   **Date of Therapy Session:**_____

Instructions: Select one problematical event that has happened to you during the past week and describe it using the format below. Please try to fill out all parts of the questionnaire. Your therapist will assist you in reviewing this situational analysis during your next therapy session.

Situational Area: Spouse/Partner__ Children_X_ Extended Family__ Work/School__ Social__

Step-1. Describe *what* happened:
In a family therapy session, Joey complained to the therapist that I would not let his father buy him a computer for Christmas. We both expressed our feelings on the topic, and we both got very frustrated. The issue was left open-ended I went home and was very upset with myself.

Step-2. Describe your *interpretation* of what happened (How did you read the situation?):

   1. ~~Kurt is making me out to be the bad guy and putting the kids in the middle of our disagreement.~~
➔ It is important for me to maintain boundaries when it involves Kurt's influence in our home.

   2. ~~I have no right to stop Kurt from doing this.~~
➔ I have primary custody of the kids and I must make decision based upon what I think is best for our home.

   3. ~~I'm incapable of making a decision~~.
➔ I'm capable of making a good decision.

Step-3. Describe what you *did* during the situation (e.g., What you said/how you said it):
~~I became enraged with Keith's request, defensive, and was unable to clearly justify the reasons for my decision.~~
➔ You have a computer at home for school and it even has several games. We do not need another computer. I'm sorry, but it's my decision.

Step-4. Describe how the event came out for you (Actual Outcome):
The decision was left open which was extremely stressful for me.

Step-5. Describe how you *wanted* the event to come out for you (Desired Outcome):
To calmly and decisively present the rationale for my decision and not allow Kurt to buy the computer. I did not want to leave it open.

Step-6. Was the Desired Outcome achieved? YES___   NO _X_

FIGURE 14.3. Example of Coping Survey Questionnaire for case example-II. The parts that were remediated in session appear in strikethrough print.

COPING SURVEY QUESTIONNAIRE

Patient:_____   **Therapist:**_____

Date of Situational Event:_____   **Date of Therapy Session:**_____

Instructions: Select one problematical event that has happened to you during the past week and describe it using the format below. Please try to fill out all parts of the questionnaire. Your therapist will assist you in reviewing this situational analysis during your next therapy session.

Situational Area: Spouse/Partner__ Children_X_ Extended Family__ Work/School__ Social__

Step-1. Describe *what* happened:
The boys were in the living watching TV when Ben began to cry. He came into the kitchen to show me a small cut on his face.

Step-2. Describe your *interpretation* of what happened (How did you read the situation?):

   1. The boys were annoying each other and a fight broke out.

   2. I can get my point across if I remain calm.

   3. I really let this escalate and get out of control.
→ This really says nothing about me!

Step-3. Describe what you *did* during the situation (e.g., What you said/how you said it):
I took Ben into the kitchen and washed his face. I asked each of them what happened. Without yelling, I told them that they both played a part in this incident and how dangerous their fighting can get.

Step-4. Describe how the event came out for you (Actual Outcome):
Good. I maintained composure, told them what I thought, and Keith said he was sorry for what he did.

Step-5. Describe how you *wanted* the event to come out for you (Desired Outcome):
Exactly the way it did. To calmly take control and firmly tell them they both played a role.

Step-6. Was the Desired Outcome achieved? YES_X_ NO ___

FIGURE 14.4. Example of Coping Survey Questionnaire for case example II. The part that were remediated in session appear in strikethrough print.

situation and the outcomes that result. As clients begin to see that there actions have social consequences and that they have the power to influence these outcomes, their mood begins to improve.

   Use of the CSQ should be confined to treatment under the CBASP model. Effective use of the CSQ is a skill that takes weeks or months to master and so it should not be used as an occasional technique within cognitive therapy. Whether the use of the

CSQ within CBASP or more standard cognitive therapy techniques are more effective awaits further data.

REFERENCES

Akiskal, H. S. (1997). Overview of chronic depressions and their clinical management. In H. S. Akiskal, G. B. Cassano (Eds.), *Dysthymia and the spectrum of chronic depressions*. New York: Guilford.

Beck, J. S. (1995). *Cognitive therapy: Basics and beyond*. New York: Guilford Press.

Clark, D. A., & Beck, A. T. (1999). *Scientific foundations of cognitive theory and therapy of depression*. New York: John Wiley & Sons.

Hellerstein, D. J., Little, S. A. S., Samstag, L. W., Wallner, L. W., Batchelder, S., Muran, J. C., et al. (2001). Combined medication and group psychotherapy in dysthymia: A randomized prospective outcome study. *Journal of Psychotherapy Practice & Research, 10*, 93–102.

Howland, R. H. (1991). Pharmacotherapy of dysthymia: A review. *Journal of Clinical Psychopharmacology, 11*, 83–92.

Howland, R. H. (1993). Health status, health care utilization and medical comorbidity in dysthymia. *International Journal of Psychiatry Medicine, 23*, 211–238.

Keller, M. B., Klien, D. N., Hirshfeld, R. M. A., Kocsis, J. H., McCullough, J. P., Miller, I. et al. (1995). Results of the DSM-IV mood disorders field trial. *American Journal of Psychiatry, 152*, 843–849.

Keller, M. B., McCullough, J. P., Klein, D. N., Arnow, B., Dunner, D. L., Gelenberg, A. J., et al. (2000). A comparison of nefazodone, the cognitive behavioral-analysis system of psychotherapy, and their combination for the treatment of chronic depression. *The New England Journal of Medicine, 342*, 1462–1470.

Keller, M. B. & Hanks, D. L. (1995). Course and natural history of chronic depression. In J. H. Kocsis & D. N. Klein (Eds.). *Diagnosis and treatment of chronic depression* (pp. 58–72). New York: Guilford.

Keller, M. B., & Shapiro, R. W. (1982). Double depression: Superimposition of acute depressive episodes on chronic depressive disorders. *American Journal of Psychiatry, 139*, 438–442.

Kessler, R. C., McGonagle, K. A., Zhao, S., Nelson, C. B., Hughes, M., Eshleman, S., et al. (1994). Lifetime and 12-month prevalence of DSM-III-R psychiatric disorders in the United States: Results from the National Comorbidity Survey. *Archives of General Psychiatry, 51*, 8–19.

Kiesler, D. J. (1983). The 1982 Interpersonal Circle: A taxonomy for complementarity in human transactions. *Psychological Review, 90*, 185–214.

Kiesler, D. J. (1996). *Contemporary interpersonal theory and research: Personality, psychopathology, and psychotherapy*. New York: Wiley.

Markowitz, J. C. (1995). Psychotherapy of dysthymic disorder. In J. H. Kocsis & D. N. Klein (Eds.). *Diagnosis and treatment of chronic depression* (pp. 58–72). New York: Guilford.

McCullough, J. P. (2000). *Treatment for chronic depression: Cognitive behavioral analysis system of psychotherapy*. New York: Guilford.

McCullough, J. P., McCune, K. J., Kaye, A. L., Braith, J. A., Friend, R., Roberts, W. C., et al. (1994). Comparison of a community dysthymia sample at screening with a matched group of nondepressed community controls. *Journal of Nervous and Mental Disease, 182*, 402–407.

Moore, R. G., & Garland, A. (2003). Cognitive therapy for chronic and persistent depression. West Sussex, England: Wiley.

Pepper, C. M., Klein, D. N., Anderson, R. L., Riso, L. P., Ouimette, P. C., & Lizardi, H. (1995). DSM-III-R Axis II comorbidity in dysthymia and major depression. *American Journal of Psychiatry, 152*, 239–247.

Prochaska, J., DiClemente, C. C., & Norcross, J. C. (1992). In search of how people change: Applications to addictive behaviors. *American Psychologist, 47,* 1102–1114.

Riso, L. P., du Toit, P. L., Blandino, J. A., Penna, S., Dacey, S., Duin, J. S., et al. (2003). Cognitive aspects of chronic depression. *Journal of Abnormal Psychology, 112,* 72–80.

Riso, L. P., Froman, S. E., Raouf, M., Penna, S., & Blandino, J. A. (in press). Long-term stability of maladaptive schemas in depressed outpatients. *Cognitive Therapy and Research.*

Thase, M. E., Reynolds, C. F. III., Frank, E., Simons, A. D., Garamoni, G. G., McGeary, J., et al. (1994). Response to cognitive behavior therapy in chronic depression. *Journal of Psychotherapy Practice and Research, 3,* 204–214.

CHAPTER 15

CHRONIC PAIN

Malcolm H. Johnson

The primary purposes of acute pain and the reason it is noxious are to interrupt ongoing activity in order to warn the sufferer of tissue damage, to discourage movement that might exacerbate injury or prevent healing, and to teach the organism to avoid the pain-producing circumstances. Therefore, it is no wonder that when pain persists to become chronic, many sufferers tend to continue to reduce activities to avoid pain and to look to others for physical treatments such as medications or procedures to resolve the physical injury they assume still exists, rather than expecting their own efforts to provide resolution. Furthermore, chronic pain sufferers that do attempt to self-manage their pain tend to use passive strategies such as resting, taking medication and using hot/cold packs that are associated with higher levels of pain-related disability (Blyth, March, Nicholas, and Cousins, 2005).

In fact, the evidence increasingly shows that self-management approaches based on components of cognitive-behavior therapy, including those that are incorporated into multidisciplinary pain management programs, offer the best prospect of return to satisfactory functioning for the chronic pain sufferer (Morley, Eccleston, & Williams., 1999), and that maintained or increased activity is often part of the rehabilitation process (Von Korff et al., 2005).

However, in spite of this evidence for treatment success in the short term, the treatment of chronic pain patients is plagued by relatively high relapse rates (Turk & Rudy, 1991), with a major contribution to relapse being failure to generalize behaviors learned during treatment to the environment outside the treatment setting or to maintain behaviors following treatment. The potential for the effective use of homework to improve generalization and maintenance is clear in spite of the dearth of direct evidence for the efficacy of homework in chronic pain treatment. The few studies that have assessed the usefulness of homework for chronic pain treatment have mostly looked at single modes of treatment, such as relaxation training for treating chronic headache (e.g., Blanchard et al., 1991). For the most part the findings of these studies

Note: Sections of this chapter are adapted from Johnson, M. H., & Kazantzis, N, (2004), Cognitive behavioral therapy for chronic pain: Strategies for the successful use of homework assignments. *Journal of Rational-Emotive and Cognitive-Behavioral Therapy, 22*(3), 189–218. © 2004 Springer Science + Business Media, Inc.

have been equivocal, although several have shown a trend for homework to make a useful contribution.

Although there is not much firm evidence for the efficacy of homework for psychological treatment of chronic pain, for many of the most significant components such as relaxation and exercise/reactivation, home practice, following initial in-session instruction and coaching, *is* the treatment. Thus, for chronic pain treatment, whether one considers the encouragement to complete treatment activities outside the treatment setting as homework or the treatment itself, the encouragement and awareness of strategies to maximize the prospect of patients maintaining treatment activities is an essential part of effective treatment.

This chapter will first present two cases to highlight some of the issues presented by the chronic pain patient. Some of the components of chronic pain treatment and the homework that might be incorporated into them will then be reviewed. Finally, some of the barriers to homework in chronic pain and strategies to manage them will be discussed.

CASE ONE: JOSEPHINE

Josephine is a 43-year-old woman who has experienced pain for almost three years. She has been referred to a pain treatment center by her employer and the employer's compensation agency. The problem commenced shortly after she obtained a new job. She applied for this position as her husband was forced to close down the family bricklaying business following an injury. This left the family short of income and struggling to pay the mortgage.

Josephine had not worked outside of the family business since before her three children were born, about 18 years ago. She was very apprehensive about starting the job and unfortunately received a position that one of the existing workers in the organization had hoped to receive. This meant that relationships with her co-workers were strained from the start. The position involved enrolling telephone callers on a database, using the telephone and computer at the same time. The organization had set hourly and daily targets for this new enterprise but because of the newness of the position had not set up the telephone system with headsets. For the first three months Josephine was using a telephone hand piece tucked into her shoulder while typing. She continued the work without informing her employer about the pain that she was experiencing because she hoped the pain would go away. She was also concerned that, if she took time off work, she would lose the job, particularly as the other workers appeared keen that she fail. Over the time that she continued working with the pain, she became less and less able to carry out her normal household activities, feeling that all she was able to do was to rest in order that she could go to work the next day.

Eventually, after about four months, she complained about the pain and the company provided a telephonist's headset and arranged an ergonomic assessment of her workstation. The ergonomist was critical of the workplace provided and changed her seat position and keyboard. Unfortunately, this did not relieve the pain and she was able to continue work for only another month or so. Over the next few months the pain spread from her shoulder and neck to both forearms, her other shoulder, and lower back. She previously had low back pain when she was pregnant with her last two children.

For some time after the onset of the pain Josephine self-medicated with non-steroidal anti-inflammatory drugs, and did not seek medical attention. Because she did not seek medical attention early, the information that the compensation agency and the employer have about the early stages of her problem is limited and they have required her to attend multiple medical consultations to attempt to ascertain the cause of her pain. She finds the examinations very anxiety-provoking.

At this stage Josephine appears mildly depressed and is spending much of her time either in bed or watching television. Any activity causes her considerable discomfort and she believes that movement and activity, as well as being painful, contributes to the spread of her pain. She believes that her employer is responsible for her current plight and that she has a serious physical problem. She was referred to a physical therapist and found that the movements and exercises that he encouraged made her pain much worse and the deep muscle relaxation training he suggested caused increased spasms of pain in her arms. Her husband has started working again but is receiving less remuneration so the family continues to be dependent upon the compensation payments that Josephine receives.

All physical examinations indicate that there are no structural problems that contribute to her pain and she has received a diagnosis of fibromyalgia from a consultant rheumatologist.

FORMULATION

Fibromyalgia is a diagnosis applied to presentations of widespread musculo-skeletal pain. Although the condition has been widely researched, there is little conclusive information about its cause although it seems to be associated with altered central processing of pain and other perceptual information. The pattern of onset is often similar to that of Josephine, who initially appears to have suffered from a relatively focused pain condition. Josephine's early response to her pain was perturbed by the stressful circumstances that she was in both at work and at home and this probably contributed to the maintenance and spread of her pain. Patients with fibromyalgia appear to benefit from most of the treatment components discussed below. Lifestyle changes and gentle exercise and stretching appear to be particularly important (Okifuji, & Turk, 1999).

Josephine's experience of her condition and her beliefs about it constitute major barriers to her rehabilitation. She is convinced her pain signals a serious physical problem set off by the difficult conditions in which she worked until a headset was provided. She is angry and resentful because her employer has failed to arrange effective treatment and also because they appear suspicious about the validity of her pain and have required her to attend several medical assessments. Josephine's pain has not responded to the various treatments that she has tried and she believes activity contributes to her condition becoming worse. Her circumstances continue to be stressful.

CASE TWO: BETSY

Betsy is a 49-year-old woman who has been diagnosed with complex regional pain syndrome (type 1) (CRPS) in her right hand. The CRPS followed a minor surgical procedure to Betsy's hand just over 12 months ago. It came on about two weeks after the surgery. Betsy went back to the surgeon complaining about the sensitivity in her hand and that it seemed more swollen now than immediately following the procedure. The surgeon indicated there was little that he was able to do. She felt dismissed and was reluctant to go back. Instead she took anti-inflammatory drugs and eventually went to an acupuncturist. Neither of these treatments was effective and Betsy finds the only thing she is able to do is to completely protect her hand as almost any use of it or contact with it causes a substantial increase in her pain. The hand and wrist are swollen and blue looking and are often cold to the touch. She has been asked to see me by her medical practitioner who is concerned that Betsy seems to have given up trying to help herself.

Betsy is married with an eight year old son who suffers Down's syndrome and a 22-year-old daughter who lives in the house next door with her own 2-year-old child. Betsy's daughter is very supportive of her and provides considerable help with household activities. Betsy's husband is less understanding; he tells her to "get her act together" and "stop blobbing around" and thinks she is using the pain as a way to avoid managing their son. Apparently, he has an alcohol problem and is quite unreliable leaving her to feel that she is required to manage her son by herself.

FORMULATION

Betsy's pain condition, CRPS, is a condition that occasionally follows a relatively minor injury, usually to a limb. Pain is disproportionate to the initial injury and is accompanied by changes to blood flow. CRPS is often associated with swelling, color changes, and temperature changes as well as disuse of the affected limb. Patients with CRPS benefit from programs that assist them to use the affected limb as well as other components of psychological treatment for pain. Analgesic medications and nerve blocks are also helpful for CRPS (Wilson, Stanton-Hicks, & Harden, 2005).

The observable physical changes that have accompanied the pain in Betsy's hand have increased her conviction that some serious damage has occurred. Additionally, in common with Josephine, she believes that someone else is responsible for the problem and her surgeon's less than sympathetic response to her complaint has caused her to feel angry with him. Betsy has stopped using her hand because of the pain, and she has interpreted the pain increases that occur when she tries to do something as evidence that she is damaging herself. While protecting her hand allows a short-term reduction of pain, it is likely to increase her disability long-term through disuse. Betsy's life is complicated by her son's intellectual disability and her husband's lack of support and skepticism regarding the impact of her pain condition.

These cases illustrate several of the most challenging aspects of chronic pain. The beliefs and concerns of both patients are likely to substantially decrease the prospect that they will initially engage in psychological treatment let alone complete homework. These beliefs will be discussed in the barriers to homework section below. First however, the components of psychological treatment and suitable homework will be canvassed.

TREATMENT COMPONENTS, COMMENTS, AND APPROPRIATE HOMEWORK

RELAXATION TRAINING

Sometimes called the aspirin of psychological treatment, relaxation training is also a cornerstone in the psychotherapeutic treatment of chronic pain. There is considerable evidence for its efficacy (Jessup & Gallegos, 1994; NIH Technology Assessment Panel on Integration of Behavioral and Relaxation Approaches into the Treatment of Chronic Pain and Insomnia, 1996). To explain relaxation training to patients it can be pointed out that muscle tension causes pain, and that our bodies respond to pain by guarding and bracing the painful area, thereby substantially increasing the pain experienced and potentially establishing a vicious cycle (Dolce & Raczynski, 1985). Even in cases of neuropathic pain or where there is clearly a physical process causing the pain, one can point out to patients that, while the pathological pain might not readily be controlled by relaxation, the secondary pain that results from reactive muscular activity can. I have found this rationale for relaxation acceptable even for patients with pain resulting from cancer. Relaxation training might be a useful opening gambit to introduce psychological interventions and homework to both Josephine and Betsy and perhaps overcome their likely skepticism about the efficacy of psychological interventions. Because both women's lives are stressful, relaxation training can initially be presented as a way of coping with the stress related consequences of pain. There are a multitude of instructions for training relaxation and meditation (e.g., Catalano & Hardin, 1996) and most practitioners will have a preferred technique. However, it is important that the strategy used is suitable for the patient's problem. For example, when Josephine was instructed in relaxation she experienced increases in her pain. Deep muscle relaxation or other techniques that require muscle tension as well as relaxation might cause increased pain for some patients. In session rehearsal to assess response is essential.

OTHER FACTORS TO TAKE INTO ACCOUNT

Many people with anxiety problems experience increases in anxiety when they try to relax (Braith, McCullough, & Bush, 1988; Heide & Borkovec, 1983, 1984). When initial relaxation training is carried out in a treatment session these people might not report the increase in anxiety, as they might not be sure what to expect, or the warnings often presented before relaxation training, that people do not always benefit from relaxation straight away, might cause them to believe their increased anxiety is normal. Certainly, if they are experiencing increased anxiety, they will be unlikely to persist or adhere to homework. It is important therefore to monitor the response in early treatment and homework sessions. Several authors (e.g., Goldfried & Davidson, 1976) suggest levels of relaxation should be monitored before and after each relaxation session. This will indicate whether the client is relaxing or becoming more anxious. If the pain sufferer is not improving in their ability to relax or is becoming more anxious, alternate relaxation/meditation techniques such as autogenic training (Schultz & Luthe, 1959), mindfulness meditation (Kabat-Zinn, 1990), or attentional training (Papageorgiou & Wells, 1998; Wells, 1990) can be trialed. According to Arena and Blanchard (1996), patients should be warned not to sit or stand too quickly because of the risk of orthostatic hypertension and, if provided with a relaxation tape or CD (generally a good idea), patients should be encouraged to alternate using the tape with relaxing without it, so they do not become dependent on the tape. Patients should be encouraged to practice relaxation at least daily. However, as with most homework, it is more important that it is set at an attainable level.

Activity Scheduling, Graduated Exposure, and Pacing

There are a number of reasons that the levels of activity of pain patients might be important. As both Josephine and Betsy illustrate, pain patients frequently reduce activity levels, sometimes through fear they will cause damage or reinjure themselves and sometimes just because it hurts. Other patients adopt patterns of activity that alternate between doing lots, typically when they are feeling better or when they are stressed, this activity then increases their pain level and they drastically reduce activity levels for a period. This 'boom and bust' pattern of activity is generally thought to be quite counterproductive and learning strategies for appropriate activity-rest cycling (Gil Ross, & Keefe, 1988) is important for patients that exhibit this pattern (see also Keefe, Beaupre, & Gil, 1996).

Reactivation appears to be an important component of chronic musculo-skeletal pain treatment. It serves to counter the effects of disuse and may counter the neuroplastic pain amplifying processes that contribute to pain chronicity (Verbunt et al., 2004). For pain sufferers who are highly fearful of pain, movement, or activity, it is the increase in activity that is likely to be the most challenging component of chronic pain treatment. Homework injunctions that take into account this fear will be most successful. Vlaeyen et al. (2001) have described a successful program in which fearful pain sufferers are exposed to a personalized, graduated hierarchy of activities. This process facilitates management of the pain-related fear during the program of reactivation. In order to integrate these considerations into reactivation homework, it will clearly be important to monitor and account for the fear of pain and activity, possibly using the psychometric instruments mentioned below. Then carefully design the homework to assist the patient to overcome their fear, perhaps using behavioral experiments as described by Vlaeyen et al. (2004). Occasionally, patients will interpret instructions to reactivate or exercise as permission to do as much as they wish in spite of the pain. These patients will need to be instructed to limit their activities.

Pain Control Strategies

There are a number of strategies commonly taught during pain management that appear to involve diversion of attention from the painful experience. Indeed, distraction is one of the strategies most frequently used by pain patients. Distraction analgesia has been argued to be a function of a limited capacity to process information (Kahneman, 1973; McCaul & Malott, 1984). It is suggested that attending to one source of input, or occupying the capacity of the information-processing system with one type of activity, prevents the allocation of capacity to painful input, and pain perception is thus reduced. While distraction has been shown to be effective in experimental pain and acute clinical pain, there is little evidence for its effectiveness with chronic pain, and several assessments of coping skills used by chronic pain patients found use of distraction associated with higher pain, despite its ability to increase pain tolerance in the short term (Johnson & Petrie, 1997). Johnson and Petrie suggested that patients might use distraction to persist with activities beyond their abilities and thus reinjure themselves. It seems that homework involving distraction strategies should include limits to its use. When patients are prescribed distraction, they should be provided with limiting information for activities they carry out when distracted in the same way as prescribing exercise, and encouraged to use time rather than pain as a guide (Gil et al., 1988). When selecting a distraction strategy, it is important to tailor it to the interests of the patient. For example, if a patient who hated math is asked to do math problems in their head, adherence is likely to be low. Morley, Biggs, & Shapiro (2004) have recently published a useful guide to attentional training.

SELF-MONITORING

Self-monitoring of appropriate cognitive and behavioral responses has always been a component of psychological treatment for chronic pain (e.g., White, 2001). Self-monitoring has the potential to reveal the relationships between responses and also provides an indication of symptom changes throughout the course of treatment. In pain treatment a number of targets have been monitored, including pain levels, activity (exercise, uptime), mood, and medication intake. However, self-monitoring of pain levels has the potential to be a two-edged sword. On the one hand, monitoring may demonstrate the relationships (or lack of relationship) between pain levels and other variables such as mood and activity (Follick, Ahern, & Laser-Wolston, 1984; Linton, 1985). As demonstrated by Fordyce et al. (1981), diary records of pain levels have also shown that medication use and health care consumption are not necessarily related to pain. Evidence indicates that self-monitoring can provide valid and reliable information about pain and activity (Affleck Tennen, Urrows, & Higgins, 1991; Follick et al., 1984). Thus, monitoring records can be important ammunition to persuade patients that changing activity levels, and medication use is not as risky as they might believe.

On the other hand, the process of self-monitoring pain, which requires the pain sufferer to attend to their pain on a regular basis in order to report, has two deleterious potential outcomes. Firstly, in much chronic pain rehabilitation the goals of treatment are less focused on pain control and more on reducing disability and improving mood. For the pain sufferer that continues to believe their salvation lies in stopping the pain, suggesting they monitor pain levels might serve to maintain pain as their central focus. Secondly, in acute pain, attending to pain increases pain experience (Levine, Gordon, Smith, & Fields, 1982) and in chronic pain, attention to pain is associated with increased distress, disability, and health care utilization independent of pain intensity (McCracken, 1997). Thus, the immediate effect of monitoring pain levels might be increased reporting of pain. The longer-term effect might be that this iatrogenic hypervigilance influences the cycle described by Vlaeyen and Linton (2000), producing, over time, reductions in activity and increases in pain related disability and distress. Von Baeyer (1994) examined the reactive effects of daily monitoring pain and found that monitoring did not increase subjective reports of patients' low back pain and distress over the eight days of the study. This study might indicate that self-monitoring of pain levels is not problematic, but the short period of relatively infrequent monitoring and the lack of longer follow-up suggest that this study does not counter the cautions mentioned above.

It appears that the most useful information from self-monitoring of pain levels is derived during the assessment phase. This period tends to be relatively brief. Until more evidence is available, it would appear prudent to restrict self-monitoring of pain levels to this phase and if self-monitoring is intended to be an extended process, either through treatment or continued following treatment, other relevant responses should be selected.

GOAL SETTING

The use of goal setting in treatment for pain has often been in conjunction with home practice of treatment components such as graded activation/exercise, relaxation, etc. (e.g., Johansson, Dahl, Jannert, Melin, & Andersson, 1998; Peck, 1982). However, goal setting may have additional contributions to chronic pain management. The lives of many chronic pain patients have been dominated by pain and their attempts to control it. As in the case of Josephine, many of their social, recreational, and occupational endeavors have been limited or terminated by pain and she and Betsy both appear to be "waiting to get better" so they are able to resume their premorbid existence rather than having adjusted their goals and activities. Most clinicians working with pain patients have observed similar patients and noticed that this does not bode well for their rehabilitation. Supporting these observations, there is an increasing body of evidence that argues that acceptance of their condition among chronic pain patients predicts better long-term outcomes (McCracken & Eccleston, 2003). For example, Schmitz, Saile, and Nilges (1996) have shown that chronic pain sufferers who are more flexible in adjusting their personal goals experience less effect of pain and disability on their mood and improved impact of coping strategies on disability. Thus, encouraging patients to set goals in other areas of their lives serves to reorient patients away from pain and to motivate them to commence activities and rebuild their lives, potentially improving their mood and disability.

Sternbach (1987) suggests patients formulate goals in work, social activity, and recreational areas of their lives and that the goals should be specific. Nicholas, Molloy, Tonkin, & Beeston (2000) argue that people should select goals that are relevant, realistic, and achievable. I would add that goals should be broken down into steps and the size of the steps adjusted so that the patient's confidence estimate that they will achieve the step is high. Patients can also be encouraged to use self-control or self-reinforcement strategies (see Watson & Tharp, 2002) to enhance the chances that the homework and the goals will be achieved.

BARRIERS TO HOMEWORK

Josephine and Betsy illustrate the various beliefs and attitudes that pain patients might have that will prove significant barriers to their engaging in any self-help treatments including those that rely on home practice. As mentioned, many pain sufferers will perceive their problem to be caused by a physical injury that either has not recovered, or has not been effectively identified and are likely to be skeptical about the efficacy of psychological interventions. Furthermore, they might be fearful that engaging in the interventions will cause increased pain or exacerbate their injury. Therefore, in order to engage in psychological treatment in the first instance or to adhere to homework prescriptions, a rationale for both psychological treatment and homework suited to the client's understanding of the nature of their problem, their expectations of treatment, and the nature of the homework to be suggested is a prerequisite.

The assessment process should clarify the patient's understanding of their problem and also prior medical evaluation should provide information regarding the nature of the pain problem. The latter is particularly important as patients with musculoskeletal pain problems such as fibromyalgia and chronic low back pain may respond to different aspects of therapy to patients with difficult neuropathic pain conditions such as phantom limb pain or chronic pain conditions that are the result of pathological conditions such as rheumatoid arthritis.

The Psychological Assessment

It is apparent from the cases described above that if the clinician is not aware of any of several elements of the client's history, and fails to attend to the emotions, beliefs, and concerns of the client, the prospect of successful engagement in a self-management program and completion of homework will be severely compromised. In order to maximize adherence to homework, several specific aspects of the client's beliefs about their pain need to be considered in the context of a full psychological assessment. For the questionnaires suggested below, the response to individual items may be as informative as total scale scores.

1. As mentioned, the extent to which pain sufferers believe the pain results from an unhealed injury or undetected physical cause or pathological process is likely to indicate whether they accept that psychological interventions will be helpful. Instruments such as the West Haven-Yale Multidimensional Pain Inventory (now called the MPI, Kerns, Turks, & Rudy, 1985), the Survey of Pain Attitudes (Jensen, Turner, Romano, & Lawler, 1994), or the Revised Illness Perceptions Questionnaire (Moss-Morris et al., 2002) all provide information about perceptions of cause. If pain sufferers believe their pain is caused by some as-yet unidentified pathology, they may still be amenable to psychological interventions and homework if it is presented as intending to ameliorate the consequences of the pain. So an explanation such as:

> "Chronic pain can make your life incredibly stressful. You know, problems with the mortgage, and so on. Learning some relaxation skills will often help control the stress, and sometimes, because it can reduce pain producing muscle tension, it can also reduce pain. One thing about relaxation it takes a while to learn to do it right and the more you practice it the better you seem to get."

2. Adherence to homework that includes increasing physical activity or activation will be impacted by the extent to which movement causes their pain to increase, particularly if pain sufferers are fearful of movement and activity or believe that such movements and activities might be harmful to them. Clearly, if movement hurts, they will require a good rationale to encourage them to increase their activity. Fear of movement/activity has been shown to predict disability among chronic low back pain sufferers (Crombez, Vlaeyen, Heuts, & Lysens, 1999). Both Josephine and Betsy above have experienced increases in pain when they have tried to do things. Because they believe they might be increasing damage, they are fearful of and have substantially reduced their levels of movement and activity. This will leave them vulnerable to

the disuse effects described by Bortz (1984). Instruments such as the Tampa scale for Kinesiophobia (Kori, Miller, & Todd, 1990) and the Pain Anxiety Symptom Scale (PASS, McCracken, Zayfert, & Gross, 1992) have been shown to effectively measure fear of pain (McCracken, Gross, & Eccleston, 2002).

3. There is also considerable evidence to suggest that patients vary in the extent that they believe that rehabilitation is dependent upon their own rather than others' actions. Some patients believe that someone else is responsible for the pain as illustrated by both cases. Clearly, the pain sufferer that believes that their rehabilitation is in others' hands, or that it is someone else's responsibility to cure them, will be less inclined to adhere to suggestions that they engage in actions themselves to improve their condition without these beliefs being specifically addressed. Instruments that assess the perception of responsibility include the MPI, the Survey of Pain Attitudes, and the Pain Stages of Change Questionnaire (Kerns, Rosenberg, Jamison, Caudill, & Haythorthwaite, 1997).

4. Finally, it is important to be aware that the path to chronicity for pain sufferers is often littered with failed treatment and self-help attempts. Often patient's short-term experience of increased or unchanged pain is sufficient to deter them from continuing a particular treatment effort even though the long-term outcome of the treatment might have been improved function and quality of life. These failures impact on the extent that patients believe they might be able carry out tasks to change their condition even if they believe that their rehabilitation is in their own hands. The Pain Self Efficacy Questionnaire (Nicholas, 1994), which assesses pain patient's beliefs that they can carry out a range of activities in spite of their pain, should provide an indication of their perception of the extent that they can participate in their own rehabilitation. This questionnaire has been shown to predict outcomes of treatment for chronic pain patients (Strong, Westbury, Smith McKenzie, & Ryan, 2002).

Managing Beliefs

The goals of psychological treatment for chronic pain are often different than patients expect. While the clinician might anticipate helping the patient to reduce disability, improve mood and improve general quality of life, the patient often believes that stopping the pain is the only way their life can improve. Turk and Meichenbaum (1994) have described a process of education and goal negotiation they call a "collaborative reconceptualization of the patient's views of pain" to deal with these initial difficulties (Turk & Meichenbaum, 1994, p. 1339). The next section offers some suggestions for achieving this.

Beliefs about the cause and current maintainers of their pain. People expect that pain signals tissue damage or a risk of tissue damage because almost invariably in acute pain it does. A useful first step in having chronic pain sufferers accept that pain might not automatically mean tissue damage is to point out that people can have tissue damage without experiencing pain, for example, when people are injured during sporting activities or in war zones. Most individuals will be aware of cases where people continued with activities apparently unaware of the extent of the injuries they had. This allows the clinician to explain a little about the gate control system (Melzack & Wall, 1965), and that pain signals are altered at a spinal level. To communicate the effect such neural plasticity can have, analogies are often useful.

"You can imagine that there is an amplifier in the pain transmission system, so if you are in danger or are really stressed the amplifier turns the pain down so you can deal with the problem. Unfortunately, we now understand that sometimes when pain stays around for a period of time the amplifier seems to get turned up and you have much more pain than can be explained by the injury, which might well have healed. Of course you are not aware that this is happening and are likely to believe that you have an injury that hasn't healed properly and you are going to be careful to make sure that you don't make the pain worse and stop doing things in order to allow the injury to heal, all of which is probably unhelpful because it allows the process to continue and also because you stop doing things you enjoy it can make you feel miserable and as you aren't getting better it can make you anxious and worried."

Another analogy that can be useful is the telephone exchange.

" Imagine the telephone rings, you answer it and there's no-one there, so you check the phone and find it's working ok, then you will probably look at the telephone wires, again they seem ok but the phone keeps ringing. Finally you realize that the problem is in the telephone exchange. Chronic pain is a bit the same. You have pain from a your back say, so you will expect your back to have the problem, you go to have it checked out, like answering the phone and then having the phone checked because it keeps ringing. Then you check the muscles and tendons of the back, like the telephone wires and poles. But if the problem is in the exchange, the brain, nothing you do in these areas will have any impact. This doesn't mean that you are imagining the pain, that it isn't real, or that you are mad, it's just that the pain part of the central nervous system can make the phone ring even when there's no-one there."

As with the amplifier analogy it is important to help the patient understand the effect of these nervous system changes behaviorally in terms of activity and mood effects and this can lead into discussion about the fear related reductions in activity.

"We know that one of the reasons we have pain in the normal course of events is to cause us to stop moving the injured part of the body so it can heal. Of course, when the pain continues, it must seem like you have to continue to limit your movement and activity. As well as this, if you are worried about the pain continuing and that this might mean a continued injury you are going to be apprehensive about doing further damage, perhaps even permanent damage. Unfortunately, your pain-related reductions in movement and activity then produce changes in your muscles and even over time in, your bones, that can make you vulnerable to increased pain when you try to do things again. One of the things that we have only recently realized is that resuming movement and activity is also an important component of healing. That's why they get people out of bed after surgery and give them physical therapy."

Managing fear of movement/activity/pain. In order to encourage patients to reactivate or engage in a program that involves exercise the first step will be to have them believe that they can do so without causing themselves damage, although they should be warned that their pain might well increase. They will therefore need to accept that pain and damage are no longer related, perhaps using one of the explanations above. As one of the founders of psychological treatment of chronic pain, Bill Fordyce would say "hurt doesn't equal harm." Some additional suggestions for addressing the specific worries patients might have are provided by Balderson, Lin, & Von Korff (2004).

Encouraging homework. To encourage homework a straightforward explanation of the reasons for it is best:

"We know that often when people have relapses after treatment it is because they haven't continued to do the things that have been helpful for them. Home practice does two things. First, it lets you try these exercises while you are still coming along for treatment, and we can make sure that you are doing them in the right way for you and if there are any problems, either with the exercises or with practical stuff like finding a time and place to do them, we can hopefully help you work it out. Second, it starts you off fitting the exercises into your life so they can be part of your normal day. Then there is a much better chance that you'll keep doing them and retain the benefit when the treatment ends."

OTHER BARRIERS

ADHERENCE AND MOOD

There is a wealth of evidence that demonstrates the elevated risk of mood problems among chronic pain sufferers with some studies suggesting as many as 80% suffer mood disorders (Sinel, Deardorff, & Goldstein, 1996). The effects of depression on motivation, energy, and self-efficacy as well as the evidence that mood impacts on self-management in a variety of medical conditions such as cardiac disease and diabetes (Bennett, 2000), suggest that additional care is required with the depressed patient to be sure that proposed homework is at a level that the patient considers achievable. In some instances it might be necessary to assist the patient with their mood prior to commencing any pain-focused therapy. It is certainly better to ensure initial success by proposing homework that the patient is 100% sure they will be able to complete, rather than having to deal with the fallout from failed homework.

What's in a Name

Epidemiological studies show that chronic pain is associated with lower levels of educational achievement (e.g., Blyth et al., 2001). Clinical experience suggests that the term "homework" might be associated with unsuccessful school performance and is therefore unlikely to enhance compliance (Kazantzis & Lampropoulos, 2002). Alternative terms that might be better accepted are "home practice" or "self-management exercises."

What Will Happen if I Seem Better?

As illustrated by the case of Josephine, many patients experiencing chronic benign pain will have experienced the skepticism of others. They may have been told that there does not appear to be sufficient injury to explain the pain they are experiencing and they may have received hints that others are not persuaded of the validity of their pain. Morley, Doyle, & Beese (2000) report that 60% of their chronic pain sample indicated they had experienced negative social consequences including disbelief after disclosing their pain. Clinical observation indicates that some patients might exaggerate their pain behaviors in an attempt to convince others of the reality of their pain, and then struggle to engage in therapeutic activity that might belie the "my pain is real" impression that they wish to create. Allied to this issue is the concern that many patients may have about the effect of recovery on their compensation status. The behavior of the compensation agency, sometimes requiring repeated physical assessments to demonstrate the validity of the disability as illustrated by the case of Josephine, will have conveyed the enthusiasm of the agency to encourage the pain sufferer back to employment and perhaps some skepticism regarding the validity of their pain. Under these circumstances, the pain sufferer might be concerned that indications of improvement, particularly demonstrated by completion of exercise or activity types of homework rather than after a medical intervention, might cause the compensation agency to prematurely limit their eligibility or pressure them to return to the workforce. Because of the anxiety engendered by these concerns, many chronic pain sufferers, like Josephine and Betsy, will be alert for any suggestion that the clinician doubts the reality of their pain. Being referred to a psychosocial practitioner will accentuate their vigilance. Therefore, it is important that the clinician acknowledges the validity of the pain, assuages any suspicions the patient has, and explains how pain might continue although the physical injury has healed (see above) before proposing a self management regime. Additionally, the patient might be reassured by a letter sent by the clinician to the employer or compensation agency that provides a context for the activity or exercise based homework proposed.

Attention and Concentration

Finally, the attentional demands of chronic pain potentially distract the pain patient and impact on their information processing ability (Grigsby, Rosenberg, & Busenbark, 1995). Many chronic pain patients report impaired cognitive functioning (McCracken & Iverson, 2001). This is probably best overcome by documenting the homework proposed in sufficient detail in the manner mentioned elsewhere in this volume so that the patient can successfully complete it.

REFERENCES

Affleck, G., Tennen, H., Urrows, S., & Higgins, P. (1991). Individual differences in the day-to-day experience of chronic pain: A prospective study of rheumatoid arthritis patients. *Health Psychology, 10*, 419–426.

Arena, J. G., & Blanchard, E. B. (1996) Biofeedback and relaxation therapy for chronic pain disorders. In R. J Gatchel & D. C Turk (Eds.), *Psychological approaches to pain management: A practitioner's handbook* (pp. 179–230). New York: Guilford.

Balderson, B. H. K., Lin, E. H. B., & Von Korff, M. (2004). The management of pain-related fear in primary care. In G. J. G. Asmundson, J. W. S. Vlaeyen, and G. Crombez (Eds.), *Understanding and treating fear of pain.* Oxford, England: Oxford University Press.

Bennett, P. (2000). *Introduction to clinical health psychology.* Buckingham, UK: Open University Press.

Blanchard, E. B., Nicholson, N. L., Taylor, A. E., Steffek, B. D., Radnitz, C. L., & Appelbaum, K. A. (1991). The role of regular home practice in the relaxation treatment of tension headache. *Journal of Consulting Clinical Psychology, 59*, 467–470.

Blyth, F. M., March, L. M., Brnabic, A. J., Jorm, L. R., Williamson, M., & Cousins, M. J. (2001). Chronic pain in Australia: A prevalence study. *Pain, 89*, 127–134.

Blyth, F. M., March, L. M., Nicholas, M. K., & Cousins, M. J. (2005). Self-management of chronic pain: a population based study. *Pain, 113*, 285–292.

Bortz, W. M. 2nd. (1984). The disuse syndrome. *Western Journal of Medicine, 141*, 691–694

Braith, J A., McCullough, J. P., Bush, J. P. (1988). Relaxation-induced anxiety in a subclinical sample of chronically anxious subjects. *Journal of Behavior Therapy and Experimental Psychiatry, 19*: 193–198.

Catalano, E. M., & Hardin, K. N. (1996). *The Chronic Pain Control Workbook* (2nd ed.). Oakland, CA: New Harbinger.

Crombez, G., Vlaeyen, J. W. S., Heuts, P. H. T. G., & Lysens, R. (1999). Fear of pain is more disabling than pain itself. Evidence on the role of pain-related fear in chronic back pain disability. *Pain, 80*, 329–340.

Dolce, J., & Raczynski, J. (1985). Neuromuscular activity and electromyography in painful backs: Psychological and biomechanical models in assessment and treatment. *Psychological Bulletin, 97*, 502–520.

Follick, M. M., Ahern, D. K., & Laser-Wolston, N. (1984). Evaluation of a daily activity diary for chronic pain patients. *Pain, 19*, 373–382.

Fordyce, W., McMahon, R., Rainwater, G., Jackins, S., Questad, K., Murphy, T. et al. (1981). Pain complaint-exercise performance relationship in chronic pain. *Pain, 10*, 311–321.

Gil, K. M., Ross, S. L., & Keefe, F. J. (1988). Behavioral treatment of chronic pain: Four pain management protocols. In R. D. France & K. R. R. Krishnan (Eds.), *Chronic pain* (pp. 317–413). Washington, DC: American Psychiatric Press.

Grigsby, J., Rosenberg, N. L., & Busenbark, B. (1995). Chronic pain is associated with deficits in information processing. *Perceptual and Motor Skills, 81*, 403–410.

Goldfried, M. R., and Davison, G. C. (1976). *Clinical behavior therapy.* New York: Holt, Rinehart and Winston.

Heide, F. J., & Borkovec, T. D. (1983). Relaxation induced anxiety: Paradoxical anxiety enhancement due to relaxation training. *Journal of Consulting and Clinical Psychology, 51*, 171–182.

Heide, F. J., & Borkovec, T. D. (1984). Relaxation induced anxiety: Mechanisms and theoretical implications. *Behavior Research and Therapy, 22*, 1–12.

Jensen, M. P., Turner, J. A., Romano, J. M., & Lawler, B. K. (1994). Relationship of pain specific beliefs to chronic pain adjustment. *Pain, 57*, 301–309.

Jessup, B. A., & Gallegos, X. (1994). Relaxation and biofeedback. In P. D. Wall & R. Melzack (Eds.), *Textbook of pain* (3rd ed., pp. 1321–1336). New York: Churchill Livingstone.

Johnson, M. H., & Petrie, S. M. (1997). The effects of distraction on exercise and cold pressor tolerance for chronic low back pain sufferers. *Pain, 69*, 43–48.

Johansson, C., Dahl, J., Jannert, M., Melin, L., & Andersson, G. (1998). Effects of a cognitive-behavioral pain-management program. *Behavior Research and Therapy, 36*, 915–930.

Kabat-Zinn, J. (1990) *Full catastrophe living: Using the wisdom of your body and mind to face stress pain and illness.* New York: Dell Publishing.

Kahneman, D. (1973). *Attention and Effort.* Englewood Cliffs, NJ: Prentice-Hall.

Kazantzis, N., & Lampropoulos, G. K. (2002). Reflecting on homework in psychotherapy: What can we conclude from research and experience. *JCLP/In session: Psychotherapy in Practice, 58*, 577–585.

Keefe, F. J., Beaupre, P. M., & Gil, K. M. (1996) Group therapy for patients with chronic pain. In Gatchel, R. J., & Turk D. C. (Eds.), *Psychological approaches to pain management: A practitioner's handbook* (pp. 259–282). New York: Guilford.

Kerns, R. D., Rosenberg, R., Jamison, R. N., Caudill, M. A., & Haythorthwaite, J. (1997). Readiness to adopt a self-management approach to chronic pain: the pain stages of change questionnaire (PSCQ). *Pain, 72*, 227–234.

Kerns, R. D., Turk, D. C., & Rudy, T. E. (1985) The West Haven-Yale Multidimensional Pain Inventory (WHYMPI). *Pain, 23*, 345–356.

Kori, S. H., Miller, R. P., & Todd, D. D. (1990). Kinesiophobia: A new view of chronic pain behavior. *Pain Management, Jan/Feb*, 35–43.

Levine, J. D., Gordon, N. C., Smith, R., & Fields, H. L. (1982). Post-operative pain: Effect of extent of injury and attention. *Brain Research, 234*, 500–504.

Linton, S. (1985). The relationship between activity and chronic back pain. *Pain, 21,* 289–294.

McCaul, K. D., & Malott, J. M. (1984). Distraction and coping with pain. *Psychological. Bulletin, 95,* 516–533.

McCracken, L. M. (1997). Attention to pain in persons with chronic pain: A behavioral analysis. *Behavior Therapy, 28,* 271–284.

McCracken, L. M., & Eccleston, C. (2003). Coping or acceptance: What to do about chronic pain? *Pain, 105,* 197–204

McCracken, L. M., Gross, R. T., & Eccleston, C. (2002). Multimethod assessment of treatment process in chronic low back pain: Comparison of reported pain-related anxiety with directly measured physical capacity. *Behaviour Research and Therapy, 40,* 585–594.

McCracken, L. M., & Iverson, G. L. (2001). Predicting complaints of impaired cognitive functioning in patients with chronic pain. *Journal of Pain and Symptom Management, 21,* 392–396.

McCracken, L. M., Zayfert, C., & Gross, R. T. (1992). The pain anxiety symptoms scale: Development and validation of a scale to measure fear of pain. *Pain, 50,* 67–73.

Melzack, R., & Wall, P. D. (1965). Pain mechanisms: A new theory. *Science, 150,* 971–979.

Morley, S., Doyle, K., and Beese, A. (2000). Talking to others about pain: Suffering in silence. In M. Devor, M. C. Robotham, & Z. Wiesenfeld-Hallin (Eds.), *Progress in pain research and management: Vol. 16. Proceedings of the 9th World Congress on Pain* (pp. 1123–1129). Seattle, WA: IASP Press.

Morley, S., Biggs, J., & Shapiro, D. (2004). *Attention management in chronic pain: A treatment manual.* http://www.leeds.ac.uk/medicine/psychiatry/attman/introduction.htm.text]

Morley, S., Eccleston, C., & Williams, A. (1999). Systematic review and meta-analysis of randomized controlled trials of cognitive behavior therapy and behavior therapy for chronic pain in adults, excluding headache. *Pain, 80,* 1–14.

Moss-Morris, R., Weinman, J., Petrie, K. J., Horne, R., Cameron, L. D., & Buick, D. (2002) The Revised Illness Perceptions Questionnaire (IPQ-R). *Psychology and Health, 17,* 1–16.

Nicholas, M. K. (1994). Pain Self Efficacy Questionnaire (PSEQ): preliminary report. University of Sydney Pain Management and Research Centre, St. Leonards.

Nicholas, M., Molloy, A., Tonkin. L., & Beeston, L. (2000). *Manage your pain.* Sydney: ABC Books.

NIH Technology Assessment Panel (1996). Integration of behavioral and relaxation approaches into the treatment of chronic pain and insomnia. *Journal of the American Medical Association, 276,* 313–318.

Okifuji, A., & Turk, D. C. (1999). Fibromyalgia: Search for mechanisms and effective treatments. In R. J Gatchel & D. C Turk (Eds), *Psychosocial factors in pain* (pp. 227–246). New York: Guilford.

Papageorgiou, C., & Wells, A. (1998). Effects of attention training on hypochondriasis: a brief case series. *Psychological Medicine, 28,* 193 –200.

Peck, C. (1982). *Controlling chronic pain.* Sydney: Fontana.

Schmitz, U., Saile, H., & Nilges, P. (1996). Coping with chronic pain: Flexible goal adjustment as an interactive buffer against pain related distress. *Pain, 67,* 41–51.

Schultz, J. H., & Luthe, W. (1959). *Autogenic training: A psychophysiologic approach to psychotherapy.* New York: Grune and Stratton.

Sinel M. S, Deardorff W. W, & Goldstein T. B. (1996) *Win the battle against back pain: An integrated mind-body approach.* New York: Bantam-Doubleday-Dell.

Sternbach, R. A. (1987). *Mastering pain: A twelve step program for coping with chronic pain.* New York: Ballantine.

Strong, J., Westbury, K., Smith, G., McKenzie, I., & Ryan, W. (2002) Treatment outcome in individuals with chronic pain: Is the Pain Stages of Change Questionnaire a useful tool? *Pain, 97,* 65–73.

Turk, D. C., & Meichenbaum, D. (1994). A cognitive-behavioral approach to pain management. In P. D. Wall & R. Melzack (Eds.), *Textbook of pain.* (3rd ed., pp. 1337–1349). New York: Churchill Livingstone.

Turk, D. C., & Rudy, T. E. (1991). Neglected topics in the treatment of chronic pain patients-relapse, non-compliance, and adherence enhancement. *Pain, 44*, 5–28.

Verbunt, J. A., Seelen, H. A., & Vlaeyen, J. W. S. (2004). Disuse and physical deconditioning in chronic low back pain. In: Asmundson, G. J. G., Vlaeyen, J. W. S. and Crombez, G. (Eds.), *Understanding and treating fear of pain*. Oxford, UK: Oxford University Press.

Vlaeyen, J. W. S., de Jong, J., Geilen, M., Heuts, P. H. T. G., & Van Breukelen, G. (2001). Graded exposure in vivo in the treatment of pain related fear: A replicated single-case experimental design in four patients with chronic low back pain. *Behaviour Research and Therapy, 39*, 151–166.

Vlaeyen, J. W. S., de Jong, J., Leeuw, M., & Crombez, G. (2004). Fear reduction in chronic pain: Graded exposure *in vivo* with behavioral experiments. In G. J. G. Asmundson, J. W. S. Vlaeyen, & G. Crombez (Eds.), *Understanding and treating fear of pain*. Oxford, UK: Oxford University Press.

Vlaeyen, J. W. S., & Linton, S. J. (2000). Fear-avoidance and its consequences in chronic musculoskeletal pain: A state of the art. *Pain, 85* 317–332.

Von Baeyer, C. L. (1994). Reactive effects of measurement of pain. *Clinical Journal of Pain, 10*, 18–21.

Von Korff, M., Balderson, B. H. K., Saunders, K., Miglioretti, D. L., Lin, E. H. B., Berry, S. et al. (2005) A trial of an activating intervention for chronic back pain in primary care and physical therapy settings. *Pain, 113*, 323–330.

Watson, D. L., & Tharp, R. G. (2002). *Self-directed behavior: Self modification for personal adjustment*. Belmont, CA: Wadsworth.

Wells, A. A. (1990). Panic disorder in association with relaxation induced anxiety: An attentional training approach to treatment. *Behavior Therapy, 21*, 273–280.

White, C. A. (2001). *Cognitive behavior therapy for chronic medical problems: A guide to assessment and treatment in practice*. Chichester: Wiley.

Wilson, P. R., Stanton-Hicks, M., & Harden, R. N. (2005). *CRPS: Current diagnosis and therapy*. Seattle: IASP Press.

Chapter 16

EATING DISORDERS

Tanya R. Schlam and G. Terence Wilson

Homework assignments play a central role in cognitive-behavioral therapy (CBT) in general, and in CBT for eating disorders in particular. The *Diagnostic and Statistical Manual of Mental Disorders* (*DSM-IV-TR*; American Psychiatric Association, 2000) defines two main eating disorder diagnoses, anorexia nervosa (AN) and bulimia nervosa (BN), and also includes a third, eating disorder not otherwise specified (EDNOS).

TYPES OF EATING DISORDERS

Individuals with AN weigh significantly less than normal for their height, yet are terrified of weight gain. There are two subtypes of AN: (1) individuals with the binge eating/purging subtype who binge and/or purge regularly, and (2) individuals with the restricting subtype who do not.

Individuals with BN are often normal or low normal weight but are excessively concerned about their weight and shape. They frequently binge eat and subsequently, in an attempt to control their weight or shape, use compensatory behaviors such as vomiting, misusing laxatives, fasting, or exercising excessively.

EDNOS is the most common eating disorder diagnosis found in clinical practice (Fairburn & Bohn, 2005). The EDNOS category includes many who meet all but one of the criteria for a diagnosis of AN or BN. The EDNOS category also includes one provisional diagnosis, binge eating disorder (BED). The majority of individuals with BED tend to be overweight or obese (Striegel-Moore et al., 2001). They binge eat at least two days a week but do not engage in compensatory behaviors.

TREATMENT

Manual-based CBT consists of roughly 20 sessions over a 16–20 week period (Fairburn, Marcus, & Wilson, 1993), and is widely viewed as the most effective treatment for BN (Whittal, Agras, & Gould, 1999; Wilson & Fairburn, 2002). In the most rigorous and comprehensive evaluation of the research evidence to date, the National Institute for Clinical Excellence (NICE, 2004) in the United Kingdom concluded that CBT is the treatment of choice for adults with BN. This recommendation was given the highest possible methodological grade. It is the first time NICE has recommended a psychological therapy as the initial treatment of choice for a mental disorder (Wilson & Shafran, 2005). The recommendation is in essence a mandate for clinicians in England and Wales to practice evidence-based treatment and to use CBT to treat BN. The NICE guidelines reflect the strength of the numerous randomized controlled trials (RCTs) demonstrating the efficacy of CBT for BN. In short, CBT has been shown to be a more effective treatment for BN than antidepressant medication and other psychological therapies with which it has been compared.

CBT for BED has been shown to be superior to antidepressant medication (Grilo, Masheb, Brownell, & Wilson, 2004; Ricca et al., 2001), but it has not been shown to be superior to other psychological treatments such as interpersonal psychotherapy (IPT) or superior to behavioral weight loss treatment (Wilfley, Wilson, & Agras, 2003; Wilson, 2005; Wonderlich, de Zwaan, Mitchell, Peterson, & Crow, 2003). Nevertheless, based on the quality of the research, the NICE (2004) guidelines stipulate that adults with BED who require outpatient treatment should be offered CBT for BED.

The NICE (2004) guidelines recommend that "as a possible first step" patients with BN or BED follow an empirically supported self-help program, perhaps with some guidance from a healthcare professional. One of the main self-help programs that has been evaluated and received some support for the treatment of BN and BED is a book based on cognitive behavioral principles, *Overcoming Binge Eating* (Fairburn, 1995). A pure self-help program is, in a sense, nothing more than an extensive, self-administered homework assignment. Guided self-help (GSH), in which a therapist typically meets briefly (20–30 minutes) and infrequently (4–10 times) with the patient, also largely focuses and depends on the completion of homework.

One study, using a sample of BED patients, compared GSH to pure self-help using the Fairburn (1995) book and found that a higher percentage of patients in GSH (68%) than in pure self-help (6%) followed the complete self-help program (Carter & Fairburn, 1998). At the end of treatment, there was a trend for more GSH than pure self-help patients to have ceased binge eating, but this trend disappeared at follow-up. Another study, using a sample composed primarily but not exclusively of BED patients, found that GSH was superior to unguided self-help using the Fairburn (1995) book in reducing binge eating (Loeb, Wilson, Gilbert, & Labouvie, 2000). A third study with a sample of BN and BED patients found that four sessions of GSH using the Fairburn (1995) book outperformed a waitlist control condition but unguided self-help did not (Palmer, Birchall, McGrain, & Sullivan, 2002). Together these findings underline the importance of therapist contact and raise the possibility that the techniques GSH therapists employ improve homework, and therefore treatment, adherence.

In contrast to BN and BED, there has been a paucity of controlled treatment research on AN (Agras et al., 2004), and CBT for AN remains, for the most part, untested (Wilson, 2005). Nevertheless, AN and BN share a number of characteristics, and CBT adapted for AN may prove useful (Vitousek, 2002). An initial study has found CBT to be a promising treatment for preventing relapse in adult AN patients once they successfully complete inpatient therapy (Pike, Walsh, Vitousek, Wilson, & Bauer, 2003).

In a recently augmented version of CBT for eating disorders, patients' specific eating disorder diagnosis is disregarded (Fairburn, Cooper, & Shafran, 2003). In this treatment, patients with AN, who are suitable for outpatient treatment, receive a longer version of essentially the same core cognitive behavioral treatment that patients with other eating disorders receive; all patients subsequently receive specific treatment modules individualized to their particular case. A trial of this transdiagnostic CBT for eating disorders is currently underway, and preliminary results appear promising (Fairburn, 2004). Nevertheless, given the current lack of evidence for the treatment of AN, this chapter will focus on the treatment of BN and BED, although much of the content will be relevant to AN. In the remainder of this chapter, we describe homework assignments in CBT for BN and BED, detail ways of enhancing homework adherence, and present two case studies.

HOMEWORK ASSIGNMENTS IN CBT
FOR BN AND BED

The empirical support of CBT for eating disorders described earlier is supplied by studies using manual-based CBT for BN and BED (Fairburn et al., 1993; Wilson, Fairburn, & Agras, 1997). Most components of this theory-driven treatment involve homework assignments, and the assignments are cumulative. The major components of manual-based CBT for BN and BED (Fairburn et al., 1993) requiring specific homework assignments are as follows: self-monitoring food intake; weekly weighing; changing eating habits and reducing dietary restraint; problem-solving; reducing body-checking and body-avoidance behaviors; and relapse prevention training. These components will now be described in more detail.

In the first session, patients are asked to begin monitoring their food intake daily, writing down what and where they eat as soon as possible after the fact on the provided monitoring forms. These forms include space for patients to record any times they binge or employ compensatory behaviors. There is also space for patients to write down relevant comments about the circumstances surrounding their eating, such as "I just had a fight with my mother," "I just drank two martinis," or "I just weighed myself and feel fat and disgusting."

The therapist explains to patients that detailed monitoring will help them identify what triggers binge eating and purging for them. This use of self-monitoring to identify the antecedents, details, and consequences of the problematic behavior is common to CBT interventions for a range of different clinical disorders. When a patient returns with completed monitoring records, the therapist works with the patient to conduct an individualized behavioral analysis and establish under what precise circumstances this patient tends to binge. They also work together to establish situational variability and determine why under different conditions the patient did not binge. As treatment progresses, self-monitoring allows both therapist and patient to keep track of the patient's progress and to note which interventions are particularly associated with decreased binge eating for this patient.

Self-monitoring food intake has been shown to decrease binge eating in the absence of any other intervention (Latner & Wilson, 2002). For patients, knowing that they must record what they eat may help them to decrease the extent to which they binge eat or eat "on automatic pilot." Indeed, in the Latner and Wilson (2002) study, 27.8% of the women with BED ceased binge eating completely during the period in which they self-monitored (Latner & Wilson, 2002). This reactivity of self-monitoring has been found for a range of behaviors; for example, self-monitoring has been found to decrease the monitored behavior in cigarette smoking (i.e., Abrams &

Wilson, 1979) and in obesity (i.e., Green, 1978). Self-monitoring is thus a powerful homework assignment and intervention in its own right.

In addition to being asked to start monitoring in session one, patients are also asked to weigh themselves once and only once a week on the same day each week. The therapist explains to patients that it is not helpful for them to either never weigh themselves or to weigh themselves multiple times a day, two extremes that many eating disorder patients alternate between. Instead, the rationale behind weighing once a week is that it is important for patients to keep track of any significant changes to their weight that may occur during treatment. Daily shifts in weight are not informative in this respect, but trends across several weeks are. In addition, frequent weighing reinforces patients' obsession with their weight which, according to the cognitive model of what maintains binge eating, can lead to rigid dieting and subsequent binge eating (Fairburn et al., 1993, p. 369).

In session one, patients are also asked to begin reading the book *Overcoming Binge Eating* (Fairburn, 1995) and to focus particularly on reading step one of the self-help manual in the back of the book. The therapist recommends that patients write in the book, placing check marks next to relevant passages, x marks next to sections that do not apply, question marks next to sections they have questions about, and asterisks next to sections they would like to discuss with the therapist (C. G. Fairburn, personal communication, September 27, 2002).

If patients return the next week having successfully monitored for 6 or 7 days, they are asked to continue monitoring and, in addition, to begin reducing their dietary restraint. Patients are asked to change their pattern of eating so that they plan each day the times they will eat three meals and two to three snacks, ensuring that they eat something every 3 to 4 hours. If patients are engaging in compensatory behaviors, they are asked to stop. The combination of monitoring food intake and eating regularly tends to decrease or eliminate binge eating, making it easier for patients to stop compensatory behaviors.

Later on in treatment, the therapist encourages patients, in addition to no longer skipping meals, to eliminate the two other forms of dieting (not eating enough calories and not eating specific "forbidden foods"). Patients are given a homework assignment to develop a list of foods they forbid themselves to eat such as chocolate or ice cream. Gradually, patients then experiment with eating such "forbidden foods" in planned, controlled situations. Patients ultimately may decide they do not want to eat formerly "forbidden foods" regularly. Nevertheless, eliminating the identification of certain foods as "forbidden" can decrease the likelihood that eating such a food will trigger a binge. Patients are also encouraged to expose themselves to other situations involving food that they may have been avoiding, such as eating in front of others or eating foods of unknown caloric content.

There is some empirical evidence to support the importance of decreasing dietary restraint. Reduction of dietary restraint has been found to be a mediator of treatment outcome in CBT for BN (Wilson, Fairburn, Agras, Walsh, & Kraemer, 2002); BN patients therefore need to decrease the extent to which they attempt to restrict the amount of food they consume.

The therapist also encourages patients to practice stimulus control while they eat so that, for example, they only eat in one or two places in their home; they sit down while they eat; they serve themselves a portion and put the rest of the food away; and they refrain from eating while watching television. Patients are also advised not to bring into the house foods that tend to trigger binge eating for them.

Once patients are successfully planning regular meals, they are encouraged to engage in distracting, pleasurable alternative activities (such as calling a friend or going for a walk) when they feel the urge to binge. As a homework assignment, patients develop a list of alternative activities and the list is then discussed and modified, if need be, in session. The therapist also teaches patients how to problem-solve formally, and patients are asked to do so regularly both in and out of session.

Patients' intense concerns about their shape and weight, which seem to play a central role in the maintenance of the disorder, can be addressed using both cognitive and behavioral techniques (Fairburn et al., 1993). In session, the therapist and patients can engage in cognitive restructuring of problematic thoughts such as "I cannot be happy at my current weight" (reported by a woman of normal weight). The therapist and the patient can together list the evidence for and against this thought and then draw a reasoned conclusion, such as: "I am not happy at my current weight right now, but that does not mean that I can never be happy at this weight. Indeed, last Saturday I felt happy most of the day and I weighed the same as I do now."

It can sometimes be particularly helpful to employ a functional focus with patients and help them examine the consequences of having a certain belief. For example, the therapist can ask: "What are the positive and negative consequences of believing that you cannot be happy at your current weight?" Patients can then be asked to challenge other problematic thoughts for homework.

Patients can also be asked to complete a behavioral homework assignment involving exposure to previously avoided situations, such as wearing a bathing suit or looking in a full length mirror. Similarly, patients can be asked to eliminate body checking behaviors, such as pinching or measuring certain parts of their body to see how large they are.

Finally, for homework patients develop a written relapse prevention plan incorporating the treatment strategies that they have found particularly helpful. The therapist reviews this plan and offers suggestions. Relapse prevention gives patients strategies they can use to cope with future problems should they arise after therapy ends. The relapse prevention plan generally involves reinstituting prior homework assignments (such as monitoring food intake and eating regularly). It seems logical that the more diligently patients have completed their homework, and thus made behavioral changes and developed new eating habits, the easier it will be for them to reinstate such changes when needed and prevent relapse.

CBT for BN typically achieves much of its effect during the early therapy sessions (Wilson et al., 1999; Wilson et al., 2002). This rapid response to treatment that some patients experience and that bodes well for their final treatment response (Wilson et al., 1999) may well be attributable at least in part to their homework completion (Wilson & Vitousek, 1999; Wilson et al., 2002), particularly the early behavioral assignments to monitor intake and subsequently plan regular times to eat.

STRATEGIES TO ENCOURAGE HOMEWORK COMPLETION

The majority of patients with AN and many patients with BN are ambivalent about, and frequently resistant to, changing their eating behaviors. These patients' ambivalence about changing can prevent them from completing therapy homework assignments. CBT assumes that as part of the treatment the therapist needs to address motivation and help increase patients' commitment to change (O'Leary & Wilson, 1987; Vitousek, Watson, & Wilson, 1998; Wilson & Schlam, 2004; Wilson et al., 1997). Properly administered CBT involves a number of strategies designed to increase patients' motivation to complete their homework and to change.

1. Build a strong therapeutic alliance (Wilson & Vitousek, 1999). If patients like their therapist, want to please their therapist, and find praise from their therapist reinforcing, they may be more likely to complete homework assignments. Similarly, if patients feel their therapist understands, respects, and can help them, they may be more likely to complete anxiety-provoking homework assignments. The therapist can demonstrate understanding by expressing empathy with patients and validating how frightening change can be (Vitousek et al., 1998). The therapist can also help foster a collaborative rather than antagonistic relationship by using a Socratic style of questioning to help patients examine their assumptions and come to new conclusions (Vitousek et al., 1998). Finally, if patients begin to see positive results from the treatment, this progress may further strengthen the therapeutic alliance (Wilson et al., 1999) and contribute to future homework adherence. Symptom improvement may thus enhance the therapeutic alliance which in turn may lead to further symptom improvement and so on creating a "positive feedback loop" and an "upward spiral" of recovery (Tang & DeRubeis, 1999, pp. 901–902).

2. Provide a rationale for each homework assignment. When patients understand the purpose behind an assignment and that completing the homework will help them achieve their goals, they may be more likely to comply. Similarly, once patients find that completing a homework assignment such as self-monitoring has helped them, they may be more likely to try future homework assignments. The therapist can remind patients of their previous success while following the program by referring to a summary sheet or graph of the patients' progress.

3. Work collaboratively with patients in designing homework assignments. Although the manual describes detailed homework assignments, the manual is also intended to be tailored to each individual patient. Particularly when patients are having trouble completing certain homework assignments, the therapist should work collaboratively with the patients to design homework assignments they are willing to complete. Thus, patients who balk at weighing themselves only once a week because they usually weigh themselves daily might decide with the therapist that they will first experiment with weighing themselves three times a week.

4. Check that patients understand the homework assignment. A common reason patients give for not completing the homework is that they did not understand exactly what they were supposed to do.

5. Put the homework assignment in writing and provide forms where applicable. Providing patients with written homework instructions helps ensure that patients understand the assignment and do not forget to complete it. Giving patients neatly typed forms to fill out may help make the assignment seem more legitimate, structured, and important. Such forms can also make the assignment clearer and less time consuming to complete.

6. Give patients a book to read and reference. In CBT for BN and BED, patients are asked to read the book *Overcoming Binge Eating* (Fairburn, 1995). The book contains quotations from people with eating disorders and cites research studies, serving to further legitimize the treatment. Patients who feel ambivalent about making behavioral

changes may still be willing to read the book, which can serve as a motivational tool. The book includes a self-help manual that patients can refer to during and following treatment, should it be needed for relapse prevention. The book contains detailed instructions on how to problem solve and how to self-monitor and also includes a sample food record for patients to use as a model.

7. Encourage patients to start monitoring immediately after the first session. Since early response to treatment is associated with positive outcomes (Wilson et al., 1999), the therapist should try to facilitate an early response. The therapist can build on the momentum of the first session by encouraging patients to start monitoring food intake immediately following the session (C. G. Fairburn, personal communication, September 27, 2002).

8. Ask patients if they can think of anything that might prevent them from doing the homework assignment (Tompkins, 2004, p. 164) and problem solve together any obstacles the patients describe (Wilson & Vitousek, 1999). Addressing in advance any reasons patients can think of for not completing the homework may increase adherence.

9. Ask how likely the patients think it is that they will complete the assignment and have them rate the likelihood from 0 to 100% (Tompkins, 2004, p. 41). If patients state that they think it is very likely they will complete an assignment, it may create a self-fulfilling prophesy and increase homework adherence.

10. Work collaboratively with patients to agree upon a specific day and time for home-work completion when relevant (Tompkins, 2004, p. 29). For example, the therapist should ask patients whether they prefer to plan the times of the day's meals and snacks in the morning or the night before. Similarly patients can pick in session the day of the week on which they will weigh themselves. If patients are in guided self-help, they can make appointments with themselves at specific times to hold bi-weekly review sessions.

11. Review the homework at the start of every session. Reviewing the homework first and in detail communicates to patients that their homework is important. The review also gives the therapist a chance to praise and reinforce patients for completing the homework. In the early sessions of CBT, the therapist reviews patients' food mon-itoring records in detail and points out patterns that need changing. The therapist can reinforce the monitoring by showing patients how helpful detailed monitoring records are in determining specific antecedents to binges. In later sessions, the thera-pist continues to review the monitoring records and also may go over patients' lists of alternative activities or review their problem solving sheets.

In GSH, the therapist generally reviews only one or two days of monitoring, but the therapist also reviews with clients and records on a summary sheet the number of "good days" they had that week. The definition of a "good day" changes as patients progress through the self-help program, but it essentially means the number of days on which patients completed their homework. By monitoring homework completion, the therapist may encourage patients to complete the homework more consistently and thoroughly (Springer & Reddy, 2004). Early on in GSH, the therapist may look through patients' copies of *Overcoming Binge Eating* to check that they have marked the pages up and to answer any questions about the book they may have.

12. Graph patients' progress in terms of number of binges, purges, or "good days" a week. Including patients' weight on the graph can allow patients to see, as is generally the case, that even if they stop purging they generally do not gain much, if any, weight.

Patients can also inspect a graph of the number of "good days" (days on which they completed their homework) and the number of binges they had that week to see if they are negatively correlated. Seeing that completing their homework decreases or eliminates their binge eating can be powerfully reinforcing.

13. Reinforce patients with praise for completing their homework. Even if the homework is not entirely complete, the therapist can reinforce patients for what they have completed, thus encouraging successive approximations of thorough homework (Wilson & Vitousek, 1999). The therapist should also reinforce patients for any progress they have made.

BARRIERS TO THE SUCCESSFUL USE OF HOMEWORK

THERAPIST ISSUES

There are several ways that therapists may unwittingly decrease the likelihood that their patients will successfully complete homework assignments.

1. Therapists may run out of time in session and hurriedly assign the homework in the last few minutes of the session, giving patients the impression that the homework is not important. The therapist instead needs to structure the 50 minute session, setting an agenda so that patients understand that the first 10–15 minutes of the session will be devoted to reviewing the monitoring records and other homework and the final 10 minutes will be devoted to assigning the next week's homework. It is crucial that the therapist take the time to explain the homework assignments thoroughly and ensure patients understand what they are supposed to do. Either the therapist or the patients should write down the assignment so patients have a copy they can refer to at home.
2. Therapists may assume that a particular assignment is self-explanatory and not bother to demonstrate for patients exactly how to use a specific form. It is generally helpful, however, for the therapist to model for patients how to use the form. Even in a brief 25 minute GSH session, taking 5 minutes to demonstrate exactly how to monitor or plan meal times and how straightforward it is can be well worth the time. Demonstration can be particularly important when working with older adults who may find homework instructions without demonstrations difficult to follow.
3. Therapists new to CBT may anticipate that they will have difficulties convincing their patients to monitor what they eat every day (Wilson & Vitousek, 1999). In fact, if the rationale for monitoring food intake is presented clearly and patients are asked to anticipate any potential problems with monitoring in advance, the majority of patients will return the following week having monitored diligently for 6 or 7 days.

Therapists who anticipate non-compliance with homework assignments may create a self-fulfilling prophecy. Such therapists may unwittingly give their patients clues through their use of language that they do not expect their patients to complete the homework. For example, a therapist may tentatively ask a patient, "Did you manage to get to any of the homework?" When the patient replies, "No," the therapist may quickly reassure the patient, "Oh, that's all right."

In fact it is not all right if patients fail to complete the homework since their eating disorder is unlikely to resolve if they do not make the behavioral changes completing the homework requires. Instead of reassuring patients who have not done their homework, the therapist can respond by seeming surprised or perplexed that patients would not want to complete homework that can help them recover from their eating disorder (Fairburn et al., 1993, pp. 371–372). Therapists can also use an analogy and ask patients if they would expect a medication to work if they did not take it (C. G. Fairburn, personal communication, September 27, 2002).

4. A final common mistake is for the therapist to not review the homework at the beginning of the session or to not review the homework at all. A variation on this mistake occurs when the therapist turns the homework review into therapy and shifts the focus away from the homework prematurely. When patients arrive at session upset or with a story from the week to share, it can be easy to get sidetracked and postpone or forget to thoroughly review the homework. Reviewing the past week's self-monitoring sheets, however, should generally be the first thing a therapist does in session after inquiring briefly as to how the patient is doing.

If patients are upset about an event during the week, the therapist can ask whether they need to discuss the event immediately or whether they can put discussing the event on their weekly agenda and first review the homework. Information gleaned from reviewing the homework and the self-monitoring sheets allows the therapist and patient to set an appropriate agenda for the session (Fairburn et al., 1993). In those rare instances when patients are in crisis, the therapist may decide to forgo the agenda entirely and deal with the problem at hand. Generally, even patients who have had a difficult week are eager to focus specifically on the details of their eating disorder and the ways in which their stress has affected their eating.

Patient Issues

Patients who experience a great deal of fear about changing their eating behaviors or who lack motivation to change may have trouble completing their homework assignments. Although it may be tempting for the therapist to blame such patients for being non-compliant with the homework and to write such patients off, CBT has an arsenal of techniques designed to increase readiness to change (Vitousek et al., 1998). Some common patient issues that can interfere with homework completion are listed below.

1. The fear of weight gain can stop patients from completing homework assignments and changing their eating habits. This fear of gaining weight or becoming fat is a diagnostic criterion for AN and is also common in BN. Intense fear of weight gain can lead patients to be afraid to complete many of the homework assignments, including weighing themselves only once a week, eating regular meals with normal quantities of food, and ceasing to purge.

One technique that may help normal-weight BN patients with this problem is for the therapist to first validate their feeling that making changes that might affect their weight is scary. The therapist then blends empathy with firmness (Wilson, 1996) by suggesting to the patients that it would be worthwhile to experiment with completing the homework assignment and see whether it does, in fact, affect their weight. For example, some patients may be reluctant to stop weighing daily for fear that they will gain weight. Such patients can be encouraged to use a behavioral experiment to test this belief by not weighing themselves for a week and seeing at the end of that week whether they have gained a significant amount of weight. AN patients, on the other hand, actually do need to gain weight, and with these patients the focus needs to be more on the pros and cons of maintaining the status quo versus choosing to gain weight and recover.

2. Sometimes patients have low motivation to change which negatively affects the amount of homework they complete. There are a number of strategies in CBT that can be employed to try to increase patient motivation at any point during treatment that it becomes necessary (Vitousek et al., 1998; Wilson & Schlam, 2004). One helpful technique to use in session is to have patients list first the cons and then the pros of completing a particular homework assignment, such as eating regular planned meals.

3. Sometimes patients claim they do not have time to monitor their food intake or complete other homework assignments. It is true that self-monitoring can be somewhat time-consuming and tedious and patients must be motivated to complete it. If patients return to the second session of CBT without having monitored their food intake over the past week, it generally suggests that the patients' motivation for treatment needs to be strengthened.

When patients have difficulty monitoring, the therapist should try to determine exactly what the difficulty is. Sometimes patients prefer to use a notebook or a palm pilot to monitor, and these adaptations can work well. Occasionally, when patients cannot seem to monitor fully, we have suggested they try monitoring only their binges or only the times they eat and not what they eat. If patients lack the motivation to monitor fully, however, they may be more likely to drop out of treatment. Even if such patients remain in therapy, self-monitoring is a central part of treatment and diluting the intervention may dilute treatment effectiveness (Wilson & Vitousek, 1999). If patients completely refuse to self-monitor, a therapist may choose not to use CBT to treat such patients since self-monitoring is so central to this treatment. In such cases, interpersonal therapy or medication may be more appropriate.

4. Sometimes patients do not monitor their binges because they are embarrassed and do not want to think about what they have eaten. The therapist can anticipate this problem in advance and state in the first session that sometimes people feel embarrassed about monitoring exactly what they eat. The therapist can then inquire whether the patients feel embarrassed and explain that there is no need to feel embarrassed, since the therapist has seen the monitoring records of many binge eaters and will not judge them (C. G. Fairburn, personal communication, September 27, 2002).

Some patients may find it difficult to monitor because they do not want to become aware of the extent of their problem. The therapist should explain that a more detailed awareness of the problem can give patients motivation and insight into precisely what needs to be changed. For example, a patient's food records may make it clear that the patient is not eating enough food during the day and is binging at night.

5. Patients sometimes see doing homework as an all-or-nothing proposition. If they cannot complete every element of the homework perfectly, then they decide not to do any homework at all. For example, if such patients forget to monitor in the morning, then they may not monitor for the rest of the day. Similarly, if such patients binge early in the day, they may decide that the rest of the day is ruined and fail to monitor either the binge or anything else they eat that day.

When such patients binge eat and feel that treatment is not going well, they may at least temporarily stop monitoring, stop planning meal times, and stop completing homework altogether (Wilson & Vitousek, 1999). The therapist needs to explain to such patients that seeing homework completion in such an all-or-nothing way is not helpful. The therapist can recommend that patients try to return to following the program as soon as possible after a binge. The therapist can also point out that while it makes sense that patients might want to avoid writing down and focusing on the content of their binges, consistent monitoring, particularly on difficult days, can help them determine precisely what precedes the binges and how best to intervene. The therapist can also reassure the patients that progress can be uneven and that sometimes two steps forward are followed by one step back.

6. A common excuse patients give for not completing homework is that it was a very stressful week. Although the therapist should of course sympathize with patients who are going through a difficult period, for many patients every week is a stressful week and stress is not an appropriate reason to avoid homework assignments. The therapist can ask patients to consider whether completing the homework will ultimately increase or decrease the amount of stress in their life. Completing homework assignments can give patients a sense of control over their behavior and can help decrease, rather than increase, stress.

TWO CASE STUDIES

The following case studies have been modified from the originals to remove or disguise any identifying personal information.

GUIDED SELF-HELP FOR A MAN WITH BED

James was a 63-year-old divorced teacher with a body mass index (BMI) of 34 placing him in the obese range. When James sought treatment, he met criteria for BED and was binge eating at night approximately six times a week. James was not eating regular meals during the day, and he suffered from chronic pain in his right ankle and foot that caused him to have difficulty sleeping at night. Pain medication sometimes helped dull the pain, but James's doctor did not want to increase his pain medication any further, and it frequently remained difficult for James to sleep. His therapist hypothesized that the combination of dietary restriction during the day and difficulty sleeping at night due to pain were contributing to James's binge eating pattern. James received 10 sessions of GSH over a period of 4 months. The first session lasted 45 minutes and the remaining sessions lasted 25 minutes.

In session two, James brought in completed food monitoring forms for the prior seven days and the therapist went over the forms with him in detail. Since beginning to monitor, James had had three binges that week rather than his usual average of six. The therapist praised James for completing the forms and pointed out that the monitoring revealed a general pattern of skipping breakfast, having a light lunch, and overeating or binging at night.

The therapist also pointed out several ways that James could improve on his homework. The therapist recommended that James include more detail on his monitoring forms about the amount of food eaten, without writing down the exact amount or caloric content. Thus instead of writing simply that he ate peanuts, James would write that he ate a large handful of peanuts. The therapist explained that having more information on the quantity of food consumed would help them examine James's eating patterns in greater detail. Upon questioning, it became clear that James was not always monitoring right after he ate, and his therapist encouraged him to monitor as soon as possible after eating to increase the accuracy of the food records. James also was not noting on the forms whether he was reading or watching television while he ate. The therapist explained that such information could help them examine whether, as is common, James tended to overeat when he engaged in other activities while eating.

James reported that he was having difficulty with the homework assignment to weigh himself weekly and that in fact he had weighed himself daily. The therapist went over with James the rationale for weighing only once a week (that small daily fluctuations in weight are not particularly informative and can be unnecessarily upsetting, and that staying so focused on the number on the scale can encourage excessive preoccupation with food and weight). James agreed that he would move the scale to a closet in the basement where he would not see it and where he would need to make a special trip down the stairs on his hurt ankle to weigh himself. As the time for the session was almost over, the therapist quickly explained that since James had done such a good job monitoring, he was ready to move on to step two and that he should begin to plan to eat three regular meals and two to three snacks, ensuring that he eats every 3 to 4 hours.

When James returned for session three, he again reported having had three binges over the week, two while watching television. The therapist therefore encouraged James to experiment with not eating while watching television. James had succeeded in weighing himself only once that week, and his therapist praised him and asked him whether he had found weighing less frequently helpful, which he had.

James had had less success with the rest of the homework assignment. James's monitoring forms showed that although he had monitored what he ate, he had not planned any times to eat. When the therapist asked James why he had not planned times, it became clear that James had misunderstood the directions and thought that he needed to plan what foods he would eat rather than just to plan the times he would eat. James had found the prospect of planning exactly what he would eat overwhelming and thus did not try. In session, the therapist helped James plan the times he would eat for the remainder of that day and the following day, showing him exactly how to do so. Now that this misunderstanding was resolved, James succeeded in completing the full homework assignment for session four.

In session four, James reported having had two binges late at night when he could not sleep. The therapist discussed with James that since the guideline is to eat every 3 to 4 hours, if he is up until 3:00 am due to his pain, it is completely appropriate for him to feel hungry and to eat something. This information helped James to reframe the fact that he felt hungry and ate late at night and helped him to feel less upset by his behavior. James began to realize that he could eat a planned snack late at night and it did not have to turn into a binge. The therapist also reminded James to practice stimulus control and to stop bringing foods he tended to binge on, such as ice cream, into the house. Finally, the therapist gave James a homework assignment to bring in a list of alternative activities he could engage in when he felt the urge to binge.

At this point in GSH treatment, James and his therapist began to meet every other week over 3 months. James returned for session five having had only one binge during each of the past 2 weeks. It seemed that not having sweet "binge foods" in the house helped James to decrease his binge frequency. James did not forbid himself from ever eating cake or candy, but he tried to eat them only outside of the house and in limited quantities.

James had completed his homework to create a list of alternative activities but the list included tedious items such as washing dishes and paying bills. In session, the therapist and James brainstormed to find engaging, pleasurable alternative activities that James could do late at night when he was in pain. Popular alternative activities that generally work well for patients such as calling or visiting a friend were not feasible so late at night. James offered that he enjoyed taking a shower and listening to music. The therapist recommended that James try these activities but observed that listening to music might not be a distracting enough alternative activity. The therapist then introduced problem solving and asked James to practice problem solving at home.

When James returned for session six he reported that he had not binged at all over the prior 2 weeks. He explained that engaging in alternative activities helped him. In addition to using alternative activities, James had monitored and planned times to eat, but he had not completed the homework assignment to problem solve. Therefore, in session, the therapist and James chose a relevant problem (how to handle eating at a buffet) and briefly problem solved in session. The solutions they came up with included having a snack a couple of hours before the buffet, not drinking too much alcohol when eating from the buffet, surveying the entire buffet before selecting which foods to eat, and making sure to sit down while eating. James and his therapist chose another problem, his tendency to buy "binge foods" if they were on sale, wrote it down on a piece of paper, and James agreed to practice solving the problem at home and bring the sheet back to go over in session.

Over the next 2 weeks, James had just two binges and both occurred late at night when he was in pain. For the final 6 weeks of treatment, James succeeded in eliminating his binge eating completely, an accomplishment he attributed to using alternative activities, eating regularly, and not bringing "binge foods" (even if they were on sale) into the house. James's therapist pointed out that much of James's progress was due to his hard work both inside and outside of session.

During the final months of treatment, James did occasionally miss a few days of food monitoring. While developing a written plan for relapse prevention, James expressed that he would like to experiment with no longer monitoring, but he agreed that if his problem with binge eating returned then he would begin monitoring again. His therapist alerted him that if he were to relapse, he might not remember that he had a written plan. Together they problem solved how James could remember to use the plan if he noticed signs of relapse. At the end of treatment, James felt pleased that he had stopped binging and had lost 10 pounds. Eight months after treatment ended he had regained some of the weight but he remained binge free.

CBT for a Woman with BN and a History of AN

Caitlin was a 21-year-old junior in college who completed 20 weekly sessions of CBT. She had been hospitalized for AN in high school, but she currently met criteria for BN and binged and purged approximately five times a week. Her BMI of 20 placed her in the low range of normal, but she was determined not to gain a pound over her current weight of 115, and she thought longingly of the time when she weighed 100 pounds and her BMI was 17 (well below normal). She readily admitted that she wished she could be anorexic again but, as sometimes happens to patients with a history of AN, she found she could no longer starve herself.

Instead, Caitlin found herself barely eating during the day, but binge eating late at night. Caitlin attempted to eat nothing during the day except perhaps a small salad and a diet Coke. She had a strict rule that she could not eat more than 900 calories a day, and she did her best to follow this rule. At night, however, hunger would wake her up, and she would binge on ice cream or whatever food was in the refrigerator and subsequently purge. Using the CBT model of what maintains BN, the therapist hypothesized that if Caitlin could begin to eat regular meals and snacks throughout the day, she would feel less hungry and she could succeed in breaking her cycle of binging and purging at night.

In session one, Caitlin described the history of her eating disorder and the therapist told her about the treatment. The therapist then asked Caitlin whether she would begin reading the book *Overcoming Binge Eating* (Fairburn, 1995) for homework and whether she would monitor her food intake and when she purged. This first homework assignment was intentionally not too threatening or challenging. Like many patients with a history of AN, Caitlin felt resistant to changing her eating habits and would have likely felt ambivalent about the rationale that monitoring could help her recover from her eating disorder. The therapist therefore presented to her that monitoring and weighing once a week would allow her to experiment and keep track of how any changes she made to her eating behavior affected her binging and weight (Wilson & Vitousek, 1999). Caitlin agreed to complete the homework assignments and to start monitoring that evening.

Caitlin returned to session two having read most of the book and having monitored every day over the past week. Her records showed that she had binged and purged four times that week. Caitlin's therapist asked her what she made of the research presented in the book *Overcoming Binge Eating* (Fairburn, 1995) showing that, on average, even if a person vomits after binging, over 50% of the calories from the food are still absorbed. As sometimes occurs, Caitlin remained convinced that, despite what the book said, she was able to purge more thoroughly than others and to rid herself of essentially all the calories she had consumed.

Her therapist socratically questioned this conviction by asking Caitlin why she did not lose weight since, if she excluded the calories from the binges which she later purged, she was essentially consuming no calories at all. Caitlin said that she had wondered about this herself and found it frustrating that she could not lose weight. Grudgingly, Caitlin admitted that perhaps some of the calories she consumed during her binges were absorbed before she purged, but she still insisted that much less than 50% of the calories were absorbed.

In session three, Caitlin had continued to monitor and reported that she had decreased the number of times she binged and purged to three times that week. She spoke wistfully of the days when she had weighed 100 pounds and spoke of wanting to redouble her efforts to diet so she could return to that low weight. Together with her therapist, Caitlin discussed the pros and cons of her weighing 100 pounds. Caitlin explained that one pro was that she had felt happier with her appearance at that weight and that she had felt happier in general. Upon questioning, Caitlin agreed that one con was that she had needed to purge daily to maintain that weight. Another con was that even when she weighed 100 pounds, she had still wanted to lose more weight. Her therapist then suggested as a hypothesis that Caitlin might not be able to return to weighing 100 pounds, but that she seemed willing to destroy her psychological health in the process of trying to reach that weight. Her therapist further suggested that a possible goal for Caitlin could be to be able to one day say: "I wish I could lose some weight, but it's not the end of the world if I can't."

Her therapist then introduced the homework assignment of planning regular times to eat meals and snacks, an assignment Caitlin found terrifying because of her fear of weight gain. Her therapist explained that instead of binging on foods at night, Caitlin could spread the calories out throughout the day and that weight gain was unlikely. Her therapist encouraged Caitlin to experiment with eating regular meals by pointing out that she could always go back to what she was currently doing. Caitlin responded that it was impossible for her to imagine eating three meals a day, but she reluctantly agreed to try to eat two meals a day during the coming week.

In session four, Caitlin reported that she had succeeded in planning and eating two meals on 3 days, but the rest of the days she had eaten only dinner. Her lunches were very small (half a lettuce sandwich or a cup of soup), but her therapist still praised her progress. Examination of her monitoring records revealed that her three binges and purges that week had been on days when she had skipped lunch, although there was one day where she skipped lunch and did not binge. Nevertheless, the pattern generally provided evidence that eating more regularly might help Caitlin to stop binging. For homework, the therapist asked Caitlin to make a list of the pros and cons of eating three meals and two snacks a day.

Caitlin returned to session five with a list that included mostly cons and only one pro. The cons of eating regularly included: (1) I will gain weight and become fat, and (2) not eating all day makes me feel strong and in control. Her only pro was that her eating problem would continue unless she changed. With the help of questions from her therapist, Caitlin added some more pros to the list including that eating regularly should help her (1) stop binging, (2) stop feeling hungry and thinking about food constantly, and (3) be able to meet a friend for lunch. Her therapist also pointed out that the practice of binging and purging are generally associated with weight gain (something Caitlin desperately wanted to avoid).

Caitlin responded that she understood rationally the problem with not eating all day, but that she felt better about herself when she did not eat. Her therapist validated her feelings, but blended this empathy with firmness (Wilson, 1996) by saying: "I understand that you're anxious about eating three meals a day, but if you want to overcome this problem, you're going to have to eat regularly. It's essential. It's a prescription. When you feel like you shouldn't eat a meal, that's the eating disorder speaking. It's going to feel strange at first because you're not used to eating regularly. It will be scary, but I think you can do it. You probably won't gain weight. It's worth trying. After all, is what you're currently doing working?"

In session six, Caitlin reported that she had succeeded in eating three meals one day that week. Over the next several sessions, Caitlin and her therapist continued to discuss the pros and cons of eating regularly. Her therapist continued to present Caitlin with evidence that the problem was not going to go away on its own. Caitlin gradually began to eat more regularly but she continued to try to limit her intake to 900 calories a day.

While looking at Caitlin's food records one week, her therapist commented: "You have to eat enough during the day to be satisfied. If you're really hungry at night, what is that telling you?" Caitlin admitted that perhaps she was not eating enough during the day. Her therapist reinforced her by saying: "It certainly looks that way from your records. If you were serving lunch to a friend, would you think half a lettuce sandwich was enough food? Eating enough during the day is not negotiable. To the extent that you haven't eaten enough during the day, it increases the likelihood you'll binge at night."

Caitlin and her therapist agreed to engage in collaborative empiricism to test some of Caitlin's core beliefs. Caitlin monitored her weight and what and when she ate in order to test her belief that if she ate three fairly substantial meals and two snacks a day she would gain weight. Caitlin also agreed to test her belief that if she did not purge she would gain weight.

Although her portion sizes continued to be modest, Caitlin was able to begin eating more regular meals and snacks. She also succeeded in being less strict about her 900 calorie a day limit. Amazingly to her, her weight did not go up when she ate more regularly. (This phenomenon is actually more the rule than the exception.) For the final month of treatment, Caitlin was able to eat three meals daily and she did not binge or purge at all.

Caitlin's final homework assignment was to develop a written relapse prevention plan, describing the progress she had made and how she could maintain it, what she had learned, and what she still needed to accomplish. Caitlin wrote that she had learned that regular eating did not have to mean overeating and that she enjoyed being less hungry during the day. She realized that she continued to need to focus on eating regularly, eating large enough portions, and fighting her eating-disordered thoughts that she needed to diet and lose weight. Although her recovery was not yet complete, Caitlin felt proud that she had succeeded in reaching the point where she could say, and more or less believe, "I wish I could lose weight, but it's not the end of the world if I can't. In fact, it is probably healthier if I don't try to lose weight."

CONCLUSION

As these two case studies illustrate, homework is absolutely essential to the effective use of CBT in the treatment of eating disorders and in the prevention of relapse. Adherence to homework assignments, including difficult assignments that provoke anxiety, is best achieved in the context of a strong relationship in which clients understand the rationale for the assignment and are able to articulate in their own words how the assignment may help them. Research should help develop ever more effective homework assignments and ever more effective means of enhancing adherence to help patients recover and stay well.

REFERENCES

Abrams, D. B., & Wilson, G. T. (1979). Self-monitoring and reactivity in the modification of cigarette smoking. *Journal of Consulting and Clinical Psychology, 47,* 243–251.

Agras, W. S., Brandt, H. A., Bulik, C. M., Dolan-Sewell, R., Fairburn, C. G., Halmi, K. A., et al. (2004). Report of the National Institutes of Health workshop on overcoming barriers to treatment research in anorexia nervosa. *International Journal of Eating Disorders, 35,* 509–521.

American Psychiatric Association. (2000). *Diagnostic and statistical manual of mental disorders* (4th ed., text revision). Washington, DC: American Psychiatry Association.

Carter, J. C., & Fairburn, C. G. (1998). Cognitive-behavioral self-help for binge eating disorder: A controlled effectiveness study. *Journal of Consulting and Clinical Psychology, 66,* 616–623.

Fairburn, C. G. (1995). *Overcoming binge eating*. New York: Guilford.

Fairburn, C. G. (2004, April). *The relationship between treatment research and clinical practice*. Paper presented at the International Conference on Eating Disorders, Academy for Eating Disorders, Orlando, FL.

Fairburn, C. G., & Bohn, K. (2005). Eating disorder NOS (EDNOS): An example of the troublesome "not otherwise specified" (NOS) category in DSM-IV. *Behaviour Research and Therapy, 43*, 691–701.

Fairburn, C. G., Cooper, Z., & Shafran, R. (2003). Cognitive behaviour therapy for eating disorders: A "transdiagnostic" theory and treatment. *Behaviour Research and Therapy, 41*, 509–528.

Fairburn, C. G., Marcus, M. D., & Wilson, G. T. (1993). Cognitive-behavioural therapy for binge eating and bulimia nervosa: A comprehensive treatment manual. In C. G. Fairburn & G. T. Wilson (Eds.), *Binge eating: Nature, assessment and treatment* (pp. 361–404). New York: Guilford.

Green, I. (1978). Temporal and stimulus factors in self-monitoring by obese persons. *Behavior Therapy, 9*, 328–341.

Grilo, C. M., Masheb, R. M., Brownell, K. D., & Wilson, G. T. (2004, August). *Outcome predictors for the treatment of binge eating disorder*. Paper presented at the annual convention of the American Psychological Association, Honolulu, HI.

Latner, J. D., & Wilson, G. T. (2002). Self-monitoring and the assessment of binge eating. *Behavior Therapy, 33*, 465–477.

Loeb, K. L., Wilson, G. T., Gilbert, J. S., & Labouvie, E. (2000). Guided and unguided self-help for binge eating. *Behaviour Research and Therapy, 38*, 259–272.

National Institute for Clinical Excellence. (2004). *Eating disorders—Core interventions in the treatment and management of anorexia nervosa, bulimia nervosa and related eating disorders*. NICE Clinical Guideline No. 9. London: NICE. Retrieved January 28, 2004, from http://www.nice.org.uk.

O'Leary, K. D., & Wilson, G. T. (1987). *Behavior therapy: Application and outcome* (2nd ed.). Englewood Cliffs, NJ: Prentice-Hall.

Palmer, R. L., Birchall, H., McGrain, L., & Sullivan, V. (2002). Self-help for bulimic disorders: A randomised controlled trial comparing minimal guidance with face-to-face or telephone guidance. *British Journal of Psychiatry, 181*, 230–235.

Pike, K. M., Walsh, B. T., Vitousek, K., Wilson, G. T., & Bauer, J. (2003). Cognitive behavior therapy in the posthospitalization treatment of anorexia nervosa. *American Journal of Psychiatry, 160*, 2046–2049.

Ricca, V., Mannucci, E., Mezzani, B., Moretti, S., Di Bernardo, M., Bertelli, M., et al. (2001). Fluoxetine and fluvoxamine combined with individual cognitive-behaviour therapy in binge eating disorder: A one-year follow-up study. *Psychotherapy and Psychosomatics, 70*, 298–306.

Springer, C., & Reddy, L. (2004). Measuring adherence in behavior therapy: Opportunities for practice and research. *The Behavior Therapist, 27*, 99–101.

Striegel-Moore, R. H., Cachelin, F. M., Dohm, F. A., Pike, K. M., Wilfley, D. E., & Fairburn, C. G. (2001). Comparison of binge eating disorder and bulimia nervosa in a community sample. *International Journal of Eating Disorders, 29*, 157–165.

Tang, T. Z., & DeRubeis, R. J. (1999). Sudden gains and critical sessions in cognitive-behavioral therapy for depression. *Journal of Consulting and Clinical Psychology, 67*, 894–904.

Tompkins, M. A. (2004). *Using homework in psychotherapy: Strategies, guidelines, and forms*. New York: Guilford.

Vitousek, K. B. (2002). Cognitive-behavioral therapy for anorexia nervosa. In C. G. Fairburn & K. D. Brownell (Eds.), *Eating disorders and obesity: A comprehensive handbook* (pp. 308–313). New York: Guilford.

Vitousek, K. B., Watson, S., & Wilson, G. T. (1998). Enhancing motivation for change in treatment-resistant eating disorders. *Clinical Psychology Review, 18*, 391–420.

Whittal, M. L., Agras, W. S., & Gould, R. A. (1999). Bulimia nervosa: A meta-analysis of psychosocial and pharmacological treatments. *Behavior Therapy, 30*, 117–135.

Wilfley, D. E., Wilson, G. T., & Agras, W. S. (2003). The clinical significance of binge eating disorder. *International Journal of Eating Disorders, 34*, S96–S106.

Wilson, G. T. (1996). Acceptance and change in the treatment of eating disorders and obesity. *Behavior Therapy, 27*, 417–439.

Wilson, G. T. (2005). Psychological treatment of eating disorders. *Annual Review of Clinical Psychology, 1*, 439–465.

Wilson, G. T., & Fairburn, C. G. (2002). Eating disorders. In P. E. Nathan & J. M. Gorman (Eds.), *A guide to treatments that work* (2nd ed., pp. 559–592). New York: Oxford University Press.

Wilson, G. T., Fairburn, C. G., & Agras, W. S. (1997). Cognitive-behavioral therapy for bulimia nervosa. In D. M. Garner & P. E. Garfinkel (Eds.), *Handbook of treatment for eating disorders* (pp. 67–93). New York: Guilford.

Wilson, G. T., Fairburn, C. G., Agras, W. S., Walsh, B. T., & Kraemer, H. (2002). Cognitive-behavioral therapy for bulimia nervosa: Time course and mechanisms of change. *Journal of Consulting and Clinical Psychology, 70*, 267–274.

Wilson, G. T., Loeb, K. L., Walsh, B. T., Labouvie, E., Petkova, E., Liu, X., et al. (1999). Psychological versus pharmacological treatments of bulimia nervosa: Predictors and processes of change. *Journal of Consulting and Clinical Psychology, 67*, 451–459.

Wilson, G. T., & Schlam, T. R. (2004). The transtheoretical model and motivational interviewing in the treatment of eating and weight disorders. *Clinical Psychology Review, 24*, 361–378.

Wilson, G. T., & Shafran, R. (2005). Eating disorders guidelines from NICE. *Lancet, 365*, 79–81.

Wilson, G. T., & Vitousek, K. M. (1999). Self-monitoring in the assessment of eating disorders. *Psychological Assessment, 11*, 480–489.

Wonderlich, S. A., de Zwaan, M., Mitchell, J. E., Peterson, C., & Crow, S. (2003). Psychological and dietary treatments of binge eating disorder: Conceptual implications. *International Journal of Eating Disorders, 34*, S58–S73.

CHAPTER 17

LOW SELF-ESTEEM

Melanie J. V. Fennell

Low self-esteem (reflected in negative thoughts and statements about the self) is a theme common to a range of clinical problems and diagnostic categories. It may be: an aspect of current symptomatology (for example, in depression); a consequence of other difficulties (for example, a response to changes in functioning following trauma, or a product of the erosion of self-confidence that often accompanies chronic anxiety); or an enduring vulnerability factor for a range of problems (for example, depression, self-harm, eating disorders and social anxiety). In the latter case, unless tackled in its own right, low self-esteem can create continuing vulnerability to emotional disorder (Fennell, 1998).

This chapter starts from the premise that the essence of low self-esteem is a negative perspective on the self, reflected in central beliefs that could be articulated as follows: "I am . . . [negative descriptor]." That is, self-esteem is at root a cognitive phenomenon—though its expression is many-faceted, coloring not only thinking but also emotions, body state and behavior. A cognitive-behavioral approach is described, that aims to undermine low self-esteem and to create a more accepting, kindly perspective.

This work can sometimes be done within the context of focused, short-term cognitive therapy. For example, it is often an integral part of working with depression and social anxiety, especially in the later, preventive phases of treatment where attention turns to formulating and testing alternatives to unhelpful assumptions and beliefs. However, when self-esteem has been damaged by consistent, highly aversive early experiences, and when the negative view is experienced as *fact* rather than learned opinion (Fennell, 2004), then even *entertaining* the idea that there might be another way of viewing the self can seem a remote possibility. In this case, treatment is likely to take longer, and a broader range of interventions may be required. In either case, as Beck et al. (1979) emphasized, homework is not an optional extra, but "an *integral, vital component* of treatment" (p. 272), which provides clients with opportunities to see how low self-esteem constricts their daily lives, and ensures that new learning moves beyond the consulting room into the real world and that new perspectives are independently tested through direct personal experience in real-life situations. This maximizes the chances that emotional transformation will accompany changes in cognition and behavior (Bennett-Levy, Butler, Fennell, Hackamn , Mueller, & West brook, 2004).

The chapter outlines a cognitive model of low self-esteem and a coherent program of cognitive-behavioral interventions that follows logically from it [both have been most fully elaborated in a text written for the general public (Fennell, 1999; Fennell, 2006)]. The program combines the tried-and-tested methods of classical, short-term cognitive therapy with more recent developments emerging from work with enduring or recurrent psychological problems and personality disorders (e.g., Beck, Freeman, Davis, et al., 2003; Padesky, 1994; Young, Klosko, & Weishaar, 2003). The role of homework is explored in relation to each element of the program, and points are illustrated throughout with reference to the story of a person with low self-esteem who was treated with cognitive therapy—"Iris" (not her real name).[1]

Case illustration: Iris came for help in her late 30s, describing a longstanding history of recurrent depression, anxiety and lack of assertiveness. She had recently experienced significant changes at work: her boss, whom she liked and respected, had been replaced by a new boss with an abrasive management style. In addition, she was facing challenging professional examinations, on which further promotion depended. For reasons related to availability of work, she was temporarily separated from her husband, and their 15 year old son was living with him. Her most pressing treatment goal was to stop panicking about the exams, and this was the focus of the first three weekly sessions. In the longer term, she wanted to feel better about herself; these broader issues would become a focus once the immediate pressure of the exams was over. This took a further 15 sessions, spread over 9 months. At first sessions were fortnightly, then monthly. This limited contact meant that homework was absolutely crucial to progress; without it, the time available for Iris to work on her longstanding difficulties would have been inadequate. Fortunately, her Rules for Living operated in her favor: her high standards meant that she wanted to do well in therapy, and she was concerned to please her therapist. As things progressed, her interest in self-discovery, and the beneficial effects of changes she made, took over as prime motivators.

A COGNITIVE MODEL OF LOW SELF-ESTEEM

DEVELOPMENT OF LOW SELF-ESTEEM

The model outlined in (Figure 17.1) is an elaboration of Beck's original model of emotional disorder (Beck, 1976).

It suggests that, on the basis of experience (interacting with "wired in factors" such as temperament and genetic heritage), people form fundamental conclusions about themselves (the "Bottom Line")—core beliefs, in cognitive terms. When experience is negative, so correspondingly the Bottom Line is also negative. Although the Bottom Line is commonly a product of early experience, an initially positive sense of self can be shaken or undermined by events at any stage in life, for example trauma (Janoff-Bulman, 1992) or less dramatic changes involving the loss of aspects of the person on which (often implicitly) self-worth has been predicated (e.g., ageing, retirement

---

[1] Details have been changed so as to protect the client's identity.

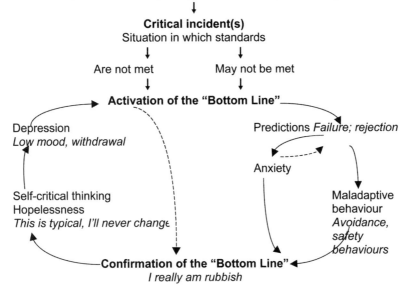

(Early) experience
Wired in factors
Lack of praise or validation, lack of interest, 'odd one out' in family
Loss, rejection, neglect, bereavement. Emotional/physical/sexual abuse
Father's emotional abuse; mother's preoccupation and failure to protect
↓
"Bottom Line" (core or basic beliefs)
Global negative self-judgement
(Assessment of worth/value as a person)
I am rubbish
↓
"Rules for Living" (specific dysfunctional assumptions)
"Escape clauses," standards against which worth can be measured
I must do everything to please others, or I will be punished
If I do not perform to the highest possible standard, I will be rejected
↓
Critical incident(s)
Situation in which standards
↓   ↓
Are not met   May not be met
↓   ↓
Activation of the "Bottom Line"

Depression   Predictions *Failure; rejection*
Low mood, withdrawal

                                              Anxiety

Self-critical thinking   Maladaptive
Hopelessness   behaviour
This is typical, I'll never change   *Avoidance,*
                                                          safety
                                                          behaviours
Confirmation of the "Bottom Line"
I really am rubbish

FIGURE 17.1. A cognitive model of low self-esteem. [Adapted with permission from: Fennell, M. J. V. (1997). Low self-esteem: A cognitive perspective. *Behavioural & Cognitive Psychotherapy, 25*, 1–25]

or redundancy, loss of strength and physical fitness, chronic ill health, bereavement, disability).

The model suggests that, assuming the Bottom Line to be true, people develop specific conditional dysfunctional assumptions ("Rules for Living"; Fennell, 1999). These operating principles allow people (more or less) to function in the world and (more or less) to feel comfortable about themselves. The rules create a structure for measuring worth on a day-to-day basis. They also function as "escape clauses," in that activation of the system can be avoided so long as their terms are met (e.g., "I am basically rubbish, but *so long as* I succeed in pleasing others/perform to a high standard, then I'm OK"). If however circumstances arise which mean that, as the person sees it, the rules *may be broken* (there is some element of uncertainty) or definitely *have been broken* (there is no doubt), then the system is activated and problems arise. The model suggests that, if there is uncertainty, people will tend to follow an anxious path; if, on the other hand, there is no doubt, then their experience will be closer to depression.

Activation of the system can occur at a relatively minor level on a day-to-day basis. However, if the Bottom Line is sufficiently convincing and powerful, and the Rules for Living sufficiently stringent, then activation can pave the way to episodes of anxiety and depression of clinical intensity and to enduring misery.

Case illustration: Iris was the oldest of four children. Her father worked extremely long hours, and was often away. At home, he was silent and withdrawn, or would suddenly explode in rage, shouting abuse and sometimes physically violent. After these explosions, he would storm out of the house, roaring that the family was a bunch of no-hopers and that he was leaving for good. It was impossible to guess what triggered these outbursts. Iris's mother tried her hardest to provide a loving counterbalance to her husband's behavior, but was often tired, nervous, irritable and preoccupied. Following her mother's example, Iris tried desperately to find a way to please her father, appease his wrath and protect the family (for example, by being tidy, helpful and quiet, and by working hard at school). Sometimes she seemed to succeed for a while, but in the long run the situation continued unchanged. As nothing she did made a difference, she concluded it must be her fault—there must be something wrong with her.

Iris's Bottom Line was: "I am rubbish" (i.e., something superfluous, with no inherent value). She believed this 100% when distressed, and 80% when feeling well. Her attempts to keep the peace crystallized into two Rules for Living: "I must do everything to please others," and "I must always perform to the highest possible standard." Failure to meet these requirements would reveal what rubbish she was, and would inevitably lead to criticism, punishment and rejection. The consequence was a more or less constant sense of vulnerability: she could never be sure that she would not unwittingly offend, and her need to perform perfectly at all times created relentless stress.

MAINTENANCE OF LOW SELF-ESTEEM

When the Rules May Be Broken (Uncertainty)

The sense that rules crucial to the maintenance of self-esteem *may be broken* brings the system on line, stimulating doubts and anxious predictions (Iris: "She'll put me down in front of everyone," "What if I get it wrong?"). Anxious predictions are accompanied by physiological symptoms of anxiety (Iris: diarrhea, tension to the point of pain, racing heart), which may in themselves become a focus for further predictions (Iris: "If people see what a state I'm in, they'll think I can't do this job," "I must be ill"). Predictions also provoke a range of maladaptive behaviors, including: outright avoidance (Iris: avoidance of expressing opinions, avoidance of challenges); "safety seeking behaviors" (Salkovskis, 1991), designed to improve the situation but in fact preventing old perspectives from being updated and sometimes making things worse (Iris: offering to help people even if she had too much to do herself, over-preparing work assignments); self-medication (Iris: tranquillizers, occasional alcohol); and genuine inhibitions in performance (Iris: clumsiness, mind going blank), which the person attributes to their own failings rather than seeing them as understandable (and trivial) consequences of fear. Even if all goes well, contrary to prediction, this information is unlikely to lead to a radical rethink of the old perspective. Rather, people with well established low self-esteem characteristically discount positive outcomes as a product of chance or of the precautions they took—exceptions to the rule.

The end result is a sense that the old view of the self has been confirmed (Iris: "This just proves what rubbish I am"). The sense of confirmation may be followed or accompanied by a stream of self-critical thinking, colored by hopelessness (Iris: "Stupid, stupid. This is you, Iris—this is it, for you"). Depression follows, varying from transient periods of low mood to full-blown episodes of clinical intensity. The circle closes: depression implies anticipation of negative outcomes and further negative thinking about experience and about the self (Beck et al., 1979, p. 11).

Case illustration: We can now see why Iris's current situation was causing her such difficulties: her new boss's critical stance and the forthcoming exams impacted on both Rules for Living at once. The resulting sequence was beautifully illuminated by an incident she recorded for homework between the first and second sessions of treatment.

She had been required to present a set of accounts to her boss and colleagues. She was afraid that she would make crucial errors and be unable to present her findings coherently. She stayed up most of the night before working on her report and, when it came to the presentation, her anxiety was so high that she felt positively ill and found it hard to focus on what she was saying. Later, she was convinced that everyone thought she was rubbish—and she agreed with them. In fact, her colleagues congratulated her on doing a good job under difficult circumstances. Iris discounted this ("They're just being kind—relieved it wasn't them in the hot seat"). She felt that her Bottom Line had once again been confirmed, and her mood plummeted.

When the Rules Have Been Broken (No Doubt)

In contrast, when the perception is that the rules *have been broken*, the person may pursue the path indicated by the long dotted line, heading straight for the sense that negative ideas about the self have been confirmed, and thus into depression.

Case illustration: In the same week, Iris recorded another situation which she was convinced proved the truth of her Bottom Line. Her son came to stay for the weekend, and was rude and uncommunicative. He spent most of the time in his bedroom, playing on his computer. Iris felt devastated: his behavior must be entirely her fault— they would never have a good relationship. Once again her mood plummeted.

Oscillation

In clinical practice, where pure anxiety and depression are rare, clinicians may well find that clients oscillate between the two paths, depending on circumstances. Thus, clients may first be encountered when seriously depressed and withdrawn and, as they recover, start to encounter situations that arouse anxiety. The temptation at this point is to retreat. The model, however, allows therapist and client to predict oscillation, and to prepare for and deal with it. That is, a strength of the model is that it crosses diagnostic boundaries and integrates anxiety and depression within a unitary framework, with reference to higher order cognitive factors (assumptions, beliefs) common to both.

Case material: Iris experienced oscillation after her son's visit. For a while, she found it hard to function at all. She spent hours in bed, not answering the phone, ruminating and feeling hopeless. After two days, she began to realize that cutting herself off was making her feel even worse—it would be better to contact people again and return to work. But the prospect was terrifying: Could she cope? What would people think? For some time she oscillated between anxiously trying to convince herself that all would be well, and a powerful urge to shut the door and hide from the world. Luckily a good friend called round and insisted on taking her out. She was able to tell him all about what had happened and, with his encouragement, got herself moving again.

COGNITIVE THERAPY FOR LOW SELF-ESTEEM

A SUMMARY OF TREATMENT INTERVENTIONS

The sequence of interventions suggested by the model above is summarized in Table 17.1.

The interventions are designed to fulfill two complementary functions: (1) weakening and undermining the old Bottom Line and Rules for Living, and the patterns of thinking, feeling and behavior that they generate; and, (2) establishing and strengthening more helpful and constructive alternatives. All the interventions target

TABLE 17.1. Cognitive therapy for low self-esteem: Summary of interventions

Assessment	Delineating presenting problems Identifying the Bottom Line Assessing the extent and severity of its impact
Conceptualisation	Developing a shared understanding of problem development and maintenance Encouraging metacognitive awareness ("A thought is not a fact")
Working with symptoms	Using cognitive-behavioral methods to work directly with symptoms of anxiety and depression (e.g., applied relaxation, graded task assignment, activity scheduling, time-management, etc.)
Working with negative automatic thoughts	Correcting biases in perception (directing attention to qualities, assets, strengths and skills) Correcting biases in interpretation (questioning and testing anxious predictions, eliminating safety behaviors, questioning self-critical thoughts, cost-benefit analysis of self-critical thinking)
Reformulating Rules for Living	Identifying more realistic and helpful assumptions and testing them out in practice
Undermining the Bottom Line	Correcting biases in perception (search for counter-evidence, positive data log, establishing an alternative self-representation—self-acceptance, balanced view—and experimenting with operating from it) Correcting biases in interpretation (reinterpreting the "evidence"; continua; piecharts)
Working with formative experiences	Historical test (finding new meanings, reinterpreting "supporting evidence," searching for counter-evidence) Examining childhood memories, reliving, imagery work
Creating a blueprint for the future	Summarizing learning, identifying ongoing targets for independent work, action planning, preparing for setbacks, agreeing follow-up arrangements

cognitive biases (schema maintenance processes) that contribute to the persistence of the problem: attentional biases which favor information that confirms existing perspectives while screening out information that contradicts them; interpretational biases that distort incoming information so that it appears to confirm old perspectives ("logical errors," attributional style); and consequent biases in memory (encoding and retrieval).

A Suggested Order of Events

As a rule of thumb, therapists are recommended to proceed in the order indicated in the table, i.e., to work first with presenting problems and specific maintaining processes, and only subsequently to address broader, more abstract concerns (Rules for Living, the Bottom Line). A focused approach to specific maintaining factors, using classical cognitive-behavioral methods, encourages engagement, fosters hope, and demonstrates that changes, however small, can be made. The significance of these to the bigger picture can be highlighted through guided discovery, for example: "What does this observation tell us about how helpful your rules for living are?," "What are the implications of this experiment for your overall view of yourself?"

Case material: Iris's decision to work on her approach to the forthcoming examinations in the first three sessions of therapy is a successful example of this strategy. She began to feel that she could make a difference, and this (she later said) gave her the courage to work on her negative sense of herself. At the same time, her careful observation of everyday events provided valuable information about background beliefs and assumptions, while the work she did on questioning and testing specific predictions prepared the ground for acquiring a broad range of cognitive-behavioral skills.

However, it is not always possible to proceed at the level of specific maintenance processes, in that the power of the Bottom Line and associated negative beliefs about others (e.g., "No one can be trusted") and the future (e.g., "Change is impossible. This is who I am") can make working on key issues appear impossibly difficult to clients. In this case, therapists may do better initially to work on strengthening the therapeutic alliance, while introducing measures that encourage clients gradually to see their beliefs for what they are—ideas acquired through experience, and therefore understandable and perhaps extremely powerful, but nonetheless not necessarily true or helpful (Fennell, 2004). Such "metacognitive awareness" [awareness of cognitions as events in the mind, rather than as reflections of objective truth or of the self (Teasdale, Moore, Hayhurst, Pope, Williams, & Segal, 2002)] creates a space, however limited and fragile, in which specific cognitive behavioral interventions can begin to promote change.

THE ROLE OF HOMEWORK IN TREATING LOW SELF-ESTEEM

As explained above, the model and the program of possible interventions incorporate ideas and methods from well-established, evidence-based protocols for anxiety and depression, as well as from work with more challenging, long-term clients. For this reason, in devising homework assignments, clinicians can fruitfully draw on classic cognitive therapy texts (e.g., Beck et al., 1979; Beck et al., 1985; Beck, 1995; Beck et al., 2003; Young et al., 2003), as well as on a range of chapters in this volume (e.g., Chapters 5, and 18).

Homework is central to work at each stage of cognitive therapy for low self-esteem, first as a means of developing day-to-day awareness of the system in operation (self-observation), and then as a forum for experimenting with new ways of thinking and acting and exploring their impact on emotion and on sense of self. In this section, we shall consider how homework can enhance each element of therapy in turn, illustrating points with examples from Iris's experience.

ASSESSMENT

Assessment, through standard questionnaires (e.g., the Rosenberg Self-Esteem Scale; Rosenberg, 1965) and/or through clinical interview, begins the process of mapping the territory of low self-esteem. It covers: the nature, onset and course of presenting problems; the client's goals for therapy; information (if accessible) about underlying assumptions and beliefs, their intensity and impact; and information about the client's current circumstances. Sometime clients can provide a full picture of what troubles them, its context, and how they would like things to change, but not necessarily. Where information is lacking (for example because, in the calm of the consulting room, the client finds it hard to identify the precise nature of cognitions active in more troubling situations), homework can be used to flesh out the picture with specific detail. If assessment is spread over two sessions, between-session monitoring of thoughts, emotions, body sensations and behavior can provide graphic detail about responses in problem situations (just as Iris's records of presenting the accounts and the weekend with her son illuminated both anxious and depressive maintaining processes). This emphasis on self-investigation communicates an attitude of curiosity to the client ("Just how *does* this system work?"), as well as introducing the idea that cognitive therapy is a collaborative venture, where both parties contribute their expertise. The therapist may be the expert on cognitive therapy (at least at this stage), but clients are the experts on their own lives. Other possible homework assignments include listening to a tape of the session (in order to reflect on its content and identify misunderstandings) and reading educational material about cognitive therapy and about low self-esteem (or, if appropriate, specific prominent aspects of the vicious circle such as anxiety or depression). Useful self-help texts include: Butler and Hope (1995), Fennell (1999), Greenberger and Padesky (1995), McKay and Fanning (1992).

Case material: The records Iris kept after the first session highlighted how anticipatory predictions drove her anxiety up and how her attempt to save the situation (overworking) actually made it more difficult for her to perform well. She was struck by how quickly and completely she shut out feedback that contradicted her own perception that she was rubbish ("I don't give myself a chance, do I?").

CONCEPTUALIZATION

Developing Shared Understanding of Problem Development
and Maintenance

Assessment and self-monitoring create a foundation for a cognitive formulation of the case (Persons, 1989), which explains what created vulnerability to experiencing difficulty at *some* point (early experience, consequent beliefs and assumptions), what triggered difficulty at *this* point (activating circumstances), and what is keeping the problem going (maintenance processes). The flowchart in Figure 17.1 provides a possible framework for formulation (the material in italics relates to Iris's case).

In its entirety, the flowchart is complex and therapists would be wise to begin with no more information than the client can readily absorb—for example, a simple vicious circle explaining the reciprocal relationship between low mood and negative thinking (Iris: "Once your mood dips, all you can see is what you hate about yourself—and then you feel even worse"), or illustrating how safety behaviors prevent disconfirmation of negative predictions (Iris: "Trying so hard to do well wears me out, and I don't even know if I need to"). The full conceptualization can be built up over a number of sessions as further information comes to light. This transparent, shared process engages the client in detective work which helps to reveal the logic inherent in what may seem confusing patterns of thought and behavior (Iris: "Ah, so *that's* what's going on"). Homework once again provides an invaluable source of information to disconfirm or validate hypotheses about problem development and maintenance, and gather more information about areas which may not initially be clear. If the client has a copy of the formulation (whatever its stage of development), then s/he can check it out against real life experience and evaluate its accuracy and usefulness.

Case material: Iris and her therapist both kept copies of the formulation flowchart. Iris used it as a way to understand specific upsetting incidents. For example, when her son next came to stay, the formulation helped her to notice her instant reaction that his behavior must be her fault and her consequent dip in mood, and to consider that there might be other reasons for how he was (in fact, he was missing her badly but felt it would be disloyal to his father to say so).

Encouraging Metacognitive Awareness

Formulation in itself can communicate an important message: "Given your experiences, it makes sense that you should think about yourself (others, the world) in this way, but these ideas are just that—learned opinions, not objective truth." Clients need not believe this message whole-heartedly—indeed, it would be surprising if they did, especially if their difficulties are highly distressing and disabling. However, engaging actively in therapy depends on being open to accepting the message, however tentatively, as (at least) a workable hypothesis which can be tested out in treatment. The rationale for cognitive therapy ("Ideas, even powerful ones, are hypotheses which can be questioned and checked out through experience") provides a framework for the specific interventions outlined in Table 17.1. Homework can be used to drive this message home, for example, by helping clients to delineate and monitor the particular biases in perception and interpretation which maintain their low self-esteem, observing in everyday situations how they shut out and distort information that might contradict old perspectives (Padesky, 1993, 1994; Fennell, 1999, p. 43).

Case material: Iris looked out for examples of times when incidents relating to her high standards occurred. She recorded her immediate thoughts, feelings and behavior when: (a) she felt she *had* performed to criterion; (b) she felt she had *not* performed to criterion; and (c) she was unclear whether she had performed to criterion or not. Her task was to work out what impact her reactions had on her central belief ("I am rubbish"). She noticed that: (a) when she performed to criterion, her immediate re-action was: "Well, I made it that time, but next time…" or "Now they'll expect everything I do to be this good." She felt pressurized and anxious, and had a strong urge to run away; (b) when she did not perform to criterion, her reaction was: "This is absolutely typical, nothing I do is good enough, how can I ever expect to get any-where, I really am rubbish, etc., etc., etc.," and she felt more and more depressed, again with an urge to run away; and (c) when it was unclear whether she had per-formed to criterion or not, her reaction was always to assume the worst and feel just as bad. These observations taught her that it really did not matter what happened—any outcome could be used to reinforce and strengthen her negative view. Recognizing this self-defeating pattern helped Iris sometimes to respond in a different way: "Aha! There's my perfectionism trap again." This created a small space in which to choose whether to operate in the old way, or to experiment with something new. She also no-ticed the same kind of pattern in relation to pleasing people: she would twist whatever happened until it fitted her central idea of herself.

Working with Symptoms

These methods are included because, during therapy for low self-esteem, clients may meet criteria for emotional disorders (depression, anxiety) which require treat-ment in their own right. It is important that they be integrated with the overall program for low self-esteem; indeed, they can be used to find out more about and to question and test the thinking that fuels low self-esteem.

Case material: Following an argument with her husband and a setback at work, Iris experienced a period of intense depression. The therapist introduced her to estab-lished cognitive behavioral interventions designed to improve mood and undermine depressive thinking. Monitoring (and then scheduling) activities for homework were used as behavioral experiments to investigate and counter negative thoughts (e.g., "I can't do anything," "I won't enjoy it," "There's no point"). These highly specific, practical interventions helped Iris and her therapist to refine their understanding of how her ideas about herself pulled her down and paralyzed her when things did not work out as she wished ("I really am rubbish—no good to anyone") and how her rules drew her even further into low mood (for example, she tended to avoid activities that she did not think she could carry out to her usual standard, and felt unjustified in taking time for relaxation and pleasure). Iris's homework records provided detailed, hot-from-the-press information about her thoughts, feelings and behavior, as well as offering opportunities to challenge and test prevailing views and investigate new alternatives (e.g., "May be I can do a little, if I plan it carefully," "Even if I don't enjoy it, it could be better than sitting in this chair feeling miserable," "The point is to find out what happens if I do"). Once her mood had lifted, it was possible to return to an explicit focus on self-esteem, and depression management skills became part of Iris's "blueprint for the future" (see below).

Working with Negative Automatic Thoughts

Homework is crucial to acquiring the skills to respond constructively to distress-ing thoughts and emotions as they occur in real life. When treating low self-esteem, the prime points of leverage for this work are anxious predictions and self-critical thoughts. Through therapist coaching and independent practice, clients learn to fol-low a systematic process of inquiry, which readers will find described in classic texts, such as: Beck et al., 1979; Beck et al., 1985; Beck, 1995; Greenberger and Padesky, 1995; Hawton et al., 1989. The insight acquired through day-to-day self-observation is used as a basis for change (questioning old ways of thinking and testing new ones). Behav-ioral experiments (both within and between sessions) are particularly valuable here, in that they provide direct experiential evidence that (for instance) anxious predictions are untrue, or that it is possible to treat oneself in a kinder and more accepting way (see Fennell and Jenkins, 2004 for a range of examples). In addition, it may be help-ful for clients to investigate for themselves the benefits and drawbacks of self-critical thinking as they are played out in everyday life.

Case material: Iris used classic cognitive behavioral methods routinely between sessions to identify, question and test unhelpful thoughts. Early in treatment, for example, she and her therapist questioned her panicky thought that it would be absolutely catastrophic to fail her exams—a disaster which would prove what rubbish she was, and from which her career would never recover. Close investigation revealed that in fact it was common (almost expected) to fail these particular exams first time round, as the bar was set so high, and that she would have opportunities to take them again. She used this discussion as a basis for an experiment: to ask colleagues about their experiences. She discovered that two people she respected had passed only on the second or third attempt. The experiment helped her to adopt a less frantic approach to the exams: a key thing was to be in good shape to take them, and it was clear that overworking and missing sleep would not achieve this. She shifted the balance of her day, making sure that she had time to unwind and ensuring that she ate properly and went to bed at a reasonable hour.

Later in therapy, it emerged that Iris believed that self-criticism was essential to producing high quality work and that without it she would become a lazy slob. It did not occur to her that doing well can be a pleasure in itself, and that driving herself might be redundant and even counter-productive. She agreed to investigate this idea for homework, noting the real impact of criticism (whether it came from herself or from other people), observing the effects of criticism on other people (for example, in the office), and doing a small survey of people she respected (she asked them what they thought were the pros and cons of being highly self-critical). She was surprised to discover just how negative the impact of criticism was: it actually created anxiety, sapped motivation and induced paralysis. She was then willing to explore the idea that treating herself with kindness and compassion might be more productive (Gilbert, 2005)—and in fact recognized that this was how she treated others. She began to plan relaxing and pleasurable activities for herself "whether I deserve it or not," and to answer the critical voice in her head from a more accepting and tolerant stance. At the same time, with her therapist, she worked to counter the bias towards accepting anything that confirmed her belief about herself and ignoring or rejecting anything that contradicted it by identifying positive qualities in herself (e.g., funny, persistent, intelligent), and recording these for homework as they expressed themselves on an everyday basis (e.g., making a friend laugh, sticking at mastering a new computer program even though it was hard, and finally understanding it). This technique, "positive data logging" (Padesky, 1994), not only redirects attentional focus in daily life, but also helps to establish and strengthen a more positive and kindly Bottom Line (see section "**Undermining the Bottom Line**" below.)

Reformulating Rules for Living
(Dysfunctional Assumptions)

Once clients can successfully identify and answer situation-specific negative automatic thoughts, treatment moves on to investigate and change higher level cognitive structures, starting with Rules for Living (dysfunctional assumptions). Modifying these broader, cross-situational operating principles is likely to extend over a number of sessions. In-session work with the therapist is boosted by independent homework assignments investigating the nature and impact of the assumptions (which before therapy may never have been put into words), exploring their origins and defining how they might now be redundant or anachronistic, questioning how congruent their demands are with the reality of human frailty, examining their pros and cons, formulating more realistic alternatives, and testing these out through systematic behavioral experiments (see Fennell, 1999, Chapter 7; Mooney and Padesky, 2000).

Case material: Iris decided first to work on her need to please others for fear of rejection. This work proceeded across three sessions, with intervening homework assignments (questioning the old rule, formulating a new rule and road-testing it). The rule's origins were clear (her mother's example and urgent wish to avoid her father's wrath). However, reflection and discussion suggested that it was impossible to please everyone, and that trying to do so created strain, exhaustion and ultimately resentment. Iris formulated an alternative: "It's OK to put myself into the equation." By this she meant that she wished to continue to do things for others (altruism was one of her values), but that she needed a more balanced approach which would allow her at the same time to meet her own needs. Behavioral experiments followed, e.g., saying "no" to requests for help, and asking for support when she needed it instead of struggling on alone. Iris predicted that if she behaved in this new way she would be attacked and rejected; in fact she was unable to detect any difference in others' reactions. Once the new system was in place, she used the same process to challenge her stringent standards.

Undermining the Bottom Line

Modifying central beliefs about the self may also be time-consuming, though changes here are facilitated by previous work on negative thoughts, especially if (as suggested above) the implications of this work for broader beliefs are made explicit. It is often helpful to employ a complementary fusion of methods designed to weaken the old system and methods intended to establish and strengthen more positive alternatives (e.g., positive data logging, see above). Readers will find ideas on how to modify core beliefs detailed in a range of cognitive therapy texts (e.g., Padesky, 1994; Beck, 1995; Fennell, 1999; Beck et al., 2003; Young et al., 2003). As with dysfunctional assumptions, in-session work is carried forward via associated homework assignments. However, therapists should be aware that working with the old Bottom Line can be distressing. For this reason, they may choose at least initially to do much of the work in the relative safety of the consulting room, and/or to weight what they do towards identifying, elaborating and operating from a new positive alternative rather than focusing on the old, negative system (Padesky, 2005).

Case material: In the context of a therapy review, Iris and her therapist summarized all the interventions described above and explored their impact on her global sense of herself. Iris realized that things had changed. She felt more entitled to consider her own needs, and less driven constantly to push herself. She was now noticing positive aspects of herself without needing to write them down, and was broadly able to treat herself with the same care and consideration that she gave to others. Her belief in "I am rubbish" now stood at 40% when distressed, and 20% when she was feeling well. For homework, she reflected on the question: "If you were not rubbish, what would you like to be?" Her answer was: "I am a normal human being with normal human strengths and weaknesses. I do not need to prove myself to anyone." She believed this new idea 80% when bearing in mind all the work, which she had accomplished over therapy, and 45% when the old system was active. She and her therapist agreed that, over the final weeks of therapy, she would continue to build on the skills she had acquired within the context of balancing out these two perspectives against one another. Using what she had learned, which point of view made better sense? And how could she consistently act in accordance with the new, kinder perspective? It was at this point that an important vulnerability factor emerged: the continuing toxic power of the past.

Working with Formative Experiences

Cognitive therapy, like behavior therapy, has tended to emphasize the importance of working with maintaining factors rather than delving into the past. Sometimes however the past is an appropriate focus, for example because clients feel the need to make sense of how they came to be the way they are, because much of the "evidence" supporting the Bottom Line (and associated beliefs about others, the world and future) is located in the past, or because the past intrudes in the form of highly emotional (even traumatic) memories, flashbacks and the like. In this case, it can be helpful to investigate formative experiences in order to determine and question the meanings that clients have attached to them (for example, blaming themselves for childhood maltreatment), to search for experiences that might counter the negative perspective on the self, and sometimes to engage in directly transforming images and memories or in formal trauma work (reliving; Ehlers and Clark, 2000). Again, this work (though potentially healing) can be profoundly distressing, for example if it requires clients to confront events and relationships that were intensely and consistently aversive, and if clients have used cognitive and emotional avoidance to deal with them. Thus again it may be wise initially to confine much of the work to therapy sessions, proceeding to homework assignments (e.g., repeated reliving, reviewing evidence from the past, consulting others who were there at the time) only once the client is confident of managing associated emotions. At this point, it may be helpful to ensure that clients have means of soothing and grounding themselves if homework investigations prove intensely painful to implement. It should be noted that this level of distress and difficulty is not inevitable; when formative events have been less consistent or aversive, and if prior work on thoughts and assumptions has produced substantial change, the work can be done relatively quickly and without excessive distress.

Case material: Iris was still unable to think about her childhood without pain. When her old beliefs were activated, she was troubled by intensely distressing intrusive memories of incidents involving her father (this happened, for example, when her husband used a certain tone of voice to criticize her). She felt that she would be unable wholly to accept her new sense of self unless she exorcised these ghosts. She and her therapist agreed to engage in a historical review, dividing her life into 10 year chunks and, in each, identifying the experiences that she saw as "evidence" supporting the idea that she was rubbish, questioning the meaning she had attached to these experiences, and searching for experiences that did not fit. This was towards the end of therapy, when the gap between sessions was 2–4 weeks, so Iris did much of this work on her own, with the therapist being used as a relatively objective sounding board and source of possible new meanings. With great courage, Iris faced the past, finding the first 10 years particularly difficult, because of her father's behavior. Through independent reflection and in-session discussion, and by talking to her siblings (both parents were dead), she moved painfully towards a new understanding: her father's behavior was a reflection of his own very serious problems, not of something wrong with her. She realized that her mother's preoccupation and irritability came from fear and exhaustion, not lack of love. She was unable to think of any counter-evidence on her own, but used a therapy session to identify experiences that she had ignored or discounted, with her therapist's help (for example, happy times with her mother, a grandmother who had loved her, a teacher who had praised and valued her). These were further elaborated and added to for homework. Her conclusion was that she had been a normal, bright little girl who had done everything she could to make things better in the family, and that her failure to do so reflected an insoluble problem, not any shortcomings in herself. She completed most of the work on the remaining two decades of her life on her own, the therapist having the homework task of reading what she had written and commenting on it. At the end of this process, her belief in her old view never exceeded 15% and her belief in the new perspective had increased to a steady 95%.

CREATING A BLUEPRINT FOR THE FUTURE

Before ending treatment, it is helpful to ensure that new learning is summarized and consolidated in the form of a 'therapy blueprint' (Fennell, 1999, Chapter 9). This allows clients to reflect on the process of therapy and to think ahead, identifying how to build on changes they have made, and preparing for possible setbacks (it is arguable that old systems of thinking and behaving are never, as it were, "deleted from the hard disk," and can be resurrected by appropriate environmental circumstances). The "blueprint" is ideally a collaborative effort between client and therapist, but the main work can helpfully be done as homework by both. The client's summary can be guided by a framework of questions (e.g., "How did your problems develop? What kept them going?" "What did you learn in therapy (ideas, methods)? How will you carry that forward?," "What might lead to a setback for you? How would you know you were having a setback? What would you do about it?"). The therapist's homework can be to review session notes (s/he may, for example, have a record of successful interventions used early in therapy which the client has now forgotten).

Case material: Iris's used the questions listed above to draft a blueprint for homework. She and her therapist discussed it as their penultimate session, and a final homework assignment was to fine-tune it. The blueprint summarized the information encapsulated in her formulation, tracing the origins of her difficulties and what had maintained them. She listed interventions that had been particularly useful, and identified areas on which she still wished to work (for example, her relationship with her husband). She made a careful note of signs that would tell her that the old system was active (for example, physical tension, wanting to retreat to bed), and worked out what to do when this happened (stand back, work out what is going on, use what you know).

PRACTICAL ISSUES

The sequence described above implies a relatively smooth progress through therapy. Naturally this is not always the case, and the final section of the chapter identifies some of the practical, clinical issues that can arise when incorporating homework assignments into work with low self-esteem.

ATTENDING TO THE THERAPEUTIC RELATIONSHIP

Low self-esteem can impact on the therapeutic relationship in many ways. Some clients try to please their therapists by being excessively subservient and apologetic, some find it hard to trust the therapist or believe in his/her good will, some are consumed by infectious hopelessness, some are so exquisitely sensitive to signs of disapproval or rejection that the therapist walks on eggshells, some find it hard to engage in therapy because they cannot believe they deserve the therapist's time—and so forth. This chapter has focused on specific, technical cognitive therapy skills that can enhance self-esteem. However, it will be clear that attention must be paid to emerging process issues, and therapists will need to respond sensitively and flexibly when these arise.

TAKING ACCOUNT OF THE CLIENT'S ENVIRONMENT

It is hard to develop self-esteem if your environment confirms your negative sense of self. If you are subject to relentless adversity, it may seem that this reflects some defect in you. If you are in an abusive, critical or neglectful relationship, it is hard to feel worthwhile. Even people who are well-intentioned may unwittingly feed into low self-esteem (as when, for example, a depressed person's family takes over their responsibilities, intending to help but in fact confirming their sense of uselessness). Therapists should remember that self-esteem is not entirely intrapsychic, but rather a product of the interaction between cognition and environment.

UNDERSTANDING THE STATUS OF NEGATIVE
STATEMENTS ABOUT THE SELF

If people are depressed, they will almost inevitably make derogatory comments about themselves. However these may or may not reflect enduring low self-esteem. In some cases, negative self-statements may be an aspect of the current problem or a consequence of other problems, and resolve if these are appropriately treated. While it is necessary to address chronic low self-esteem if it is present, it is also important not to assume a need for long-term, in-depth therapy unless there is clear evidence that this is warranted. Caution is wise, given the relative paucity at the time of writing of an evidence base for such treatment (James, 2001), compared to the substantial weight of evidence demonstrating the effectiveness of focused, short-term cognitive therapy with both anxiety and depression.

Incorporating Experiential Learning Methods

Most readers can probably remember times when clients have said to them: "I see what you mean, but I don't feel any different." This disjunction between intellectual understanding and emotional transformation sometimes results from relying on verbal techniques in isolation from direct experiential learning (e.g., role play, imagery work, behavioral experiments). Working with more enactive methods provides clients with fully rounded, emotional and sensory experiences which are much more difficult to discount (Bennett-Levy et al., 2004). As Iris said, "Once you've done it for yourself, you can't get away from it."

Modulating Anxiety Levels

When using experiential methods, it is important to recognize that engaging in feared and avoided situations, dropping safety behaviors, and confronting images and memories can be frightening. This needs to be taken into account so that experiments are risky enough to provide opportunities for new learning, but not so risky that they seem unmanageable. In- session experiments often prompt clients to move farther and faster than they might be able to do alone (because the therapist is present to coach, reassure and encourage). This puts real-life homework assignments within reach that might otherwise have been avoided.

Linking the General and the Specific

Early, specific interventions at the level of thoughts and behavior need explicitly to be linked with higher order concerns (the Bottom Line, Rules for Living). Otherwise they may appear trivial to the client, undermining the motivation to complete homework assignments. Equally, when working with the Bottom Line and with Rules for Living, it is important that new ideas are not left at a high level of abstraction, but are "nailed down" by experimenting with specific, practical, everyday changes in thinking and behavior. Again, guided discovery is the key, with questions like: "What are the implications of this new idea for what you do on a day-to-day basis?" "How will you put this into practice today?" "How will you operate differently in that situation next time it comes up?" "What are the practical implications of that?" In-session planning and rehearsal can then maximize the chances that changes in higher order cognitions do not remain purely theoretical, but are translated into specific experiences in real life.

CONCLUSION

This chapter has outlined a cognitive model of low self-esteem and a cognitive-behavioral treatment program based upon it. It has considered the value of independent self-help assignments (homework) at each stage in therapy, and concluded by identifying practical issues that need to be taken into account when working to enhance self-esteem.

Our overall aim in working with clients who do not value themselves is to help them to create more realistic and flexible standards for themselves, and to establish a stance that acknowledges inevitable human weakness and frailty without condemning it, and without losing a fundamental underlying sense of self-acceptance. Homework is central to this endeavor, because it means that new learning escapes the confines of the consulting room and finds opportunities to flourish in the real world.

REFERENCES

Beck, A. T. (1976). *Cognitive therapy and the emotional disorders.* New York: International Universities Press.

Beck, A. T., Emery, G., & Greenberg, R. L. (1985). *Anxiety disorders and phobias: A cognitive perspective.* New York: Basic Books.

Beck, A. T., Freeman, A., Davis, D. D., & Associates. (2003). *Cognitive therapy of personality disorders* (2nd ed.). New York: Guilford.

Beck, A. T., Rush, A. J., Shaw, B. F., & Emery, G. (1979). *Cognitive therapy of depression.* New York: Guilford.

Beck, J. S. (1995). *Cognitive therapy: Basics and beyond.* New York: Guildford.

Bennett-Levy, J., Butler, G., Fennell, M. J. V., Hackmann, A., Mueller, M., & Westbrook, D. (2004). *The Oxford guide to behavioural experiments in cognitive therapy.* Oxford: Oxford University Press.

Butler, G., & Hope, T. (1995). *Manage your mind: The mental fitness guide.* Oxford: Oxford University Press.

Ehlers, A., & Clark, D. M. (2000). A cognitive model of post-traumatic stress disorder. *Behaviour Research and Therapy, 38,* 319–345.

Fennell, M. J. V. (1997). Low self-esteem: A cognitive perspective. *Behavioural and Cognitive Psychotherapy, 25,* 1–25

Fennell, M. J. V. (1998). Low self-esteem. In N. Tarrier, A. Wells, & G. Haddock (Eds.), *Treating complex cases: The cognitive behavioural therapy approach.* Chichester UK: Wiley.

Fennell, M. J. V. (1999). *Overcoming low self-esteem.* London: Constable Robinson.

Fennell, M. J. V. (2004). Depression, low self-esteem and mindfulness. *Behaviour Research and Therapy, 42,* 1053–1067

Fennell, M. J. V. (2006). Overcoming low self-esteem self-help course. Constable Robinson, London.

Fennell, M. J. V. (Accepted for publication). Low self-esteem. In Hawton, K., Salkovskis, P. M., Kirk, J., & Clark, D. M. (Eds.), *Cognitive behaviour therapy for psychiatric problems* (2nd ed.). Oxford: Oxford University Press.

Fennell, M. J. V., & Jenkins, H. (2004). Low self-esteem. In Bennett-Levy, J., Butler, G., Fennell, M. J. V., Hackmann, A., Mueller, M., & Westbrook, D. (Eds.), *The Oxford guide to behavioural experiments in cognitive therapy.* Oxford: Oxford University Press.

Gilbert, P. (Ed.). (2005). *Compassion.* London: Routledge.

Greenberger, D., & Padesky, C. A. (1995). *Mind over mood: A cognitive therapy treatment manual for clients.* New York: Guilford.

Hawton, K., Salkovskis, P. M., Kirk, J., & Clark, D. M. (Eds.). (1989). Cognitive behaviour therapy for psychiatric problems: A practical guide. Oxford: Oxford University Press.

James, I. A. (2001). Schema therapy: The next generation, but should it carry a health warning? *Behavioural and Cognitive Psychotherapy, 29,* 401–407

Janoff-Bulman, R. (1992). *Shattered assumptions: Towards a new psychology of trauma.* New York: Free Press.

McKay, M., & Fanning, P. (1992). *Self-esteem* (2nd ed.). Oakland, CA: New Harbinger.

Mooney, K., & Padesky, C. A. (2000). Applying client creativity to recurrent problems: Constructing possibilities and tolerating doubt. *Journal of Cognitive Psychotherapy, 14*, 149–161.

Padesky, C. A. (1993). Schema as self-prejudice. *International Cognitive Psychotherapy Newletter, 5/6*, 16–17.

Padesky, C. A. (1994). Schema change processes in cognitive therapy. *Clinical Psychology and Psychotherapy, 1*, 267–278

Padesky, C. A. (2005). *Constructing a new self: A cognitive therapy approach to personality disorders.* Workshop presentation, May, London UK.

Persons, J. B. (1989). *Cognitive therapy in practice: A case formulation approach.* San Francisco: Norton.

Rosenberg, M. (1965). *Society and the adolescent self-image.* Princeton NJ: Princeton University Press.

Salkovskis, P. M. (1991). The importance of behaviour in the maintenance of anxiety and panic: A cognitive account. *Behavioural Psychotherapy, 19*, 6–19.

Teasdale, J. D., Moore, R. G., Hayhurst, H., Pope, M., Williams, S., & Segal, Z. V. (2002) Metacognitive awareness and prevention of relapse in depression: Empirical evidence. J. *Consulting and Clinical Psychology, 70*, 275–287.

Young, J. E., Klosko, J. S., & Weishaar, M. E. (2003). *Schema therapy: A practitioner's guide.* New York: Guilford.

CHAPTER 18

OBSESSIONS AND COMPULSIONS

David A. Clark

Obsessive compulsive disorder (OCD) is an anxiety disorder characterized by the persistent and repeated occurrence of obsessions and/or compulsions of sufficient severity as to be time-consuming or to cause marked distress or impairment (DSM-IV-TR; APA, 2000). Obsessions are repetitive and intrusive thoughts, images, or impulses that are subjectively unwanted and unacceptable or even abhorrent, are difficult to control even though subjectively resisted, and generally produce considerable distress (Rachman, 1985). At some point during the course of the disorder the individual recognizes that the obsession is excessive, unreasonable, or even senseless.

Compulsions are repetitive, stereotypic behaviors or mental acts (rituals) that are usually performed in response to an obsession in order to reduce distress or to prevent some imagined negative consequence associated with the obsession (APA, 2000). Compulsions usually involve an intense urge to carry out the ritual so the person feels a loss of control over the response (Rachman & Hodgson, 1980). Individuals with OCD might try to resist carrying out the compulsion but they eventually give into the overpowering urge to perform the ritual.

The lifetime prevalence of OCD is between 1% and 2% in the general population. There may be a slightly greater preponderance of women with OCD and the onset of the disorder typically occurs in adolescence and young adulthood. OCD is a chronic disorder in which the majority of individuals show a waxing and waning of symptoms over many years. It has a low spontaneous remission rate and there is evidence that episodes are triggered by stressful experiences or critical incidents. Like other anxiety disorders, OCD can have a significant detrimental impact on educational and occupational advancement, social functioning and family/marital satisfaction (for review and further discussion of the disorder, see Antony, Downie, & Swinson, 1998; Clark, 2004; Rachman & Hodgson, 1980; Rasmussen & Eisen, 1998).

This chapter focuses on the use of homework assignments within a cognitive-behavioral approach to understanding the persistence and treatment of obsessions and compulsions. I begin with a brief description of the cognitive-behavioral model of OCD followed by discussion of its treatment protocol and empirical research on the role of homework. Common barriers or difficulties encountered in assigning homework to individuals with OCD are considered. This is followed by discussion and illustration of specific homework exercises that have been used in treatment of OCD. The chapter concludes with a case study that demonstrates the role of homework assignments in alleviating obsessive and compulsive symptoms.

COGNITIVE-BEHAVIORAL MODEL OF OCD

In the late 1960s a highly effective behavioral intervention for OCD was developed called *exposure and response prevention* (ERP). The individual with OCD is systematically exposed to successively more distressing situations that trigger the anxious obsession while at the same time being prevented from relieving the anxiety via performance of a compulsive response. Exposure to obsession-relevant situations must be prolonged (60–90 minutes), repeated frequently, and conducted in a graduated fashion. Prevention of the compulsive response throughout the exposure session is critical and the sessions should not cease until there is a significant reduction in anxiety (Kozak & Foa, 1997; Steketee, 1993, 1999). A very important part of the treatment regimen is the assignment of daily ERP sessions that the client completes between therapy sessions.

Despite a very high post-treatment response rate of approximately 80% among treatment completers (Foa & Kozak, 1996), problems became apparent with a strictly behavioral theory and treatment of OCD. There were certain aspects of the phenomenology of obsessions and compulsions that the behavioral model could not explain, and ERP proved less effective as a direct treatment of obsessional ruminations. In addition, a significant number of people with OCD refuse to accept ERP and residual OC symptoms often remain even after a successful course of ERP (for further discussion see Clark, 2004; Foa, Steketee, Grayson, & Doppelt, 1983; Rachman, 1983).

Discontent with a strictly behavioral approach to OCD led to the proposal that the infusion of a more cognitive orientation into the behavioral model and treatment of OCD might enhance our understanding and therapeutic response to the disorder. Beginning with Salkovskis (1985, 1989, 1999) and then later Freeston (Freeston, Rhéaume & Ladouceur, 1996), Rachman (1997, 1998, 2003), and Clark (Clark, 2004; Clark & Purdon, 1993), a new cognitive-behavioral perspective and treatment of OCD emerged. Figure 18.1 illustrates the general framework of the CBT formulation. Although researchers differ on which appraisal process or set of beliefs is critical in the pathogenesis of obsessions and compulsions, the different theories adhere to this general outline.

The various CB theories of OCD all consider three general processes critical to the pathogenesis of the obsession. First, there is the occurrence of an unwanted intrusive thought, image, or impulse that may be entirely uncharacteristic of the type of thought you would normally experience (i.e., an ego-dystonic intrusive thought). CB theorists posit that the natural occurrence of unwanted intrusive thoughts is the source of clinical obsessions. Whether an unwanted intrusive thought (e.g., "did I lock the door?," "I wonder if I could be contaminated by touching this dirty phone?," or "was I completely honest when I recalled that incident to a friend?") turns into a distressing obsession or simply fades from conscious awareness depends on how it is appraised. If this second component in the process involves the faulty appraisal that the intrusive thought is personally significant because it portends some possible dire consequence

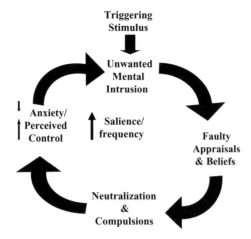

FIGURE 18.1. The cognitive-behavioral model of OCD.

for one's self or others, then the thought will be treated as an internal threat to one's well-being (Rachman, 2003). A faulty appraisal of significance will then lead to a third process critical in the escalation of the obsession. The individual will feel compelled to engage in some compulsive act or other strategy that is intended to neutralize the anxiety and ensure that the dreaded outcome associated with the obsession does not occur. Although the compulsion or neutralization response restores a sense of control over the unwanted intrusive thought or obsession and reduces anxiety, the overall effect is to increase the frequency and salience of the intrusive thought. The more frequent and distressing the intrusive thought the greater the likelihood that it will be misinterpreted as a highly significant and threatening phenomenon (Clark, 2004).

   A number of faulty appraisal and belief domains have been identified that together can transform a benign ego-dystonic intrusive thought into a clinical obsession. Table 18.1 presents a definition and clinical example of each of the appraisal or belief domains (for further discussion see Clark, 2004; Freeston et al., 1996; Obsessive Compulsive Cognitions Working Group, 1997; Taylor, 2002).

COGNITIVE-BEHAVIORAL TREATMENT
OF OCD

   Cognitive-behavioral therapy (CBT) for OCD is based on the cognitive-behavioral model previously described. The faulty appraisals listed in Table 18.1 as well as the dysfunctional neutralization and compulsive responses used to control the obsession and its associated distress are targeted for change. The goal of treatment is to modify the faulty appraisals and beliefs so that the obsession is no longer considered a significant, personal threat but rather a benign intrusive thought that can be safely ignored. To achieve this "de-catastrophizing" of the obsession, cognitive and behavioral strategies are utilized within the session and as between-session homework assignments. In fact, the most potent intervention tool used in CBT for OCD is still exposure and response prevention. However ERP is often modified and delivered differently in CBT so that it becomes an effective means of achieving cognitive change.

TABLE 18.1. Definition and examples of key appraisal and belief domains of OCD

Appraisal/ belief	Definition	Clinical example
Overestimated threat	To exaggerate the severity and/or probability of an imagined highly negative outcome or consequence.	"If I shake a stranger's hand, then I will contract a fatal disease."
Thought-action fusion (TAF)	To assume that thinking about a negative event increases the likelihood that the event will occur (TAF- Likelihood), or having "bad" thoughts is morally equivalent to "bad" deeds (TAF-Moral).	"If I have unwanted intrusive thoughts of a loved one in a car accident, she/he is more likely to have an accident." (TAF-Likelihood) "Having thoughts of molesting a child is as repugnant as actually doing it." (TAF-Moral)
Inflated responsibility	To believe that one is able to produce or prevent a negative outcome that could have a real or imagined consequence on the self or others. Therefore the person believes he or she must take every conceivable precaution to ensure that the feared consequence never occurs.	"If I see a piece of glass on the road, I must pick it up. If I didn't, it would be my fault if a car ran over the glass and had an accident."
Overimportance of thought	To assume that the repeated occurrence of an unwanted thought implies that it must be very important or significant.	"Because I keep having these upsetting impulses to stab my children wherever I handle a knife, it must mean that I have latent violent tendencies."
Control of thoughts	To believe it is possible and highly desirable to have near perfect control over unwanted distressing intrusive thoughts.	"If I don't get better control over these obsessions, I will become overwhelmed with anxiety".
Intolerance of uncertainty	To believe that it is critical to achieve almost absolute certainty in thought or action to maximize predictability and control, and minimize ambiguity and novelty.	"I need to be certain that I am completely forgiven of any sin that I have committed."
Perfectionism	To believe that one must strive for the one best response to each problem and that even minor mistakes and inaccuracies must be avoided because they will lead to serious consequences.	"I must ensure there is not even a speck of dirt in my room that could lead to contamination."

There are six goals associated with a CBT approach to obsessions and compulsions: (a) normalize the obsession, (b) identify the client's unique appraisal pattern, (c) reduce the significance of the obsession, (d) eliminate compulsions and other forms of neutralization, (e) relinquish mental control efforts, and (f) modify faulty core beliefs. To achieve these goals the client first must be educated into the cognitive-behavioral model of OCD. The client learns that most people have unwanted intrusive thoughts of dirt/contamination, doubt, uncontrolled aggression/violence, unacceptable sexual acts, and the like. It is imperative that clients shift their focus from trying to control the obsession to an engagement in the therapeutic process of changing their faulty beliefs and appraisals. The only way they can begin to do this is to understand that the reason they have highly persistent and distressing obsessions instead of occasional "normal" unwanted intrusions is that they misinterpret the obsession as a personally significant threat which they must control. They then engage in futile compulsive rituals and other neutralization strategies which over time only intensifies the obsession. Thus in addition to adopting more functional appraisals and beliefs about the insignificant and benign nature of the obsession, the client learns that the most effective response is to "do nothing."

Education into the CBT model, identification and modification of faulty appraisals and beliefs, elimination of compulsions and other control efforts, and the adoption of a benign, "full acceptance" view of the obsession are achieved through a number of intervention strategies. Deliberately provoking the obsession and instructing the client to maintain concentrated attention on the unwanted thought and its associated interpretation, while at the same time preventing a compulsive or neutralization response, is the main intervention strategy. This is ERP with a "cognitive twist." Through repeated exposure to the obsession and challenging the faulty appraisals and beliefs, the client learns to adopt a more benign interpretation of the obsession. Control responses that previously seemed so necessary are now viewed as counterproductive. In addition to ERP, more standard cognitive restructuring (i.e., evidence gathering, down-arrow technique, identifying cognitive errors, challenging dysfunctional beliefs) is used to directly modify faulty appraisals and obsession-related beliefs. Self-monitoring and behavioral experiments are assigned in order to test-out the veracity of dysfunctional interpretations and alternative, more functional appraisals and beliefs. All of these interventions are used in the therapy session or they can be assigned as between-session homework exercises.

There is strong empirical support for the effectiveness of ERP both as a therapist-directed within-session intervention and as between-session homework assignments (e.g, Abramowitz, 1997; Eddy, Dutra, Bradley, & Westen, 2004; Foa, Franklin, & Kozak, 1998; Stanley & Turner, 1995). It would appear that self-directed exposure can be just as effective as more intense therapist-directed ERP (see discussion by Foa et al., 1998; Stanley & Turner, 1995). However, exposure and response prevention are allows assigned as daily homework in any clinical trial of behavioral treatment of OCD no matter how intense and prolonged the within-session ERP (e.g., Abramowitz, Foa, & Franklin, 2003; Franklin, Abramowitz, Bux, Zoellner, & Feeny, 2002; Kozak, Liebowitz, & Foa, 2000). For example Franklin et al. (2002) noted that in addition to 15 two-hour ERP treatment sessions, clients were assigned another two hours of daily exposure homework. So it is practically impossible to disentangle the effectiveness of ERP as a homework assignment versus its utilization within the therapy session. Admittedly it would make little sense to offer behavioral treatment for OCD without also directing the client to engage in ERP between-sessions in order to ensure generalization of treatment gains to naturalistic settings that trigger obsessional symptoms.

There is some clinical and empirical evidence that lack of motivation or commitment to follow ERP instructions either as within-session exercises or as homework assignments can result in poor treatment response (see Foa et al., 1983; Rachman & Shafran, 2000; Steketee & Shapiro, 1995). A recent clinical outcome study that compared ERP and CBT found that high homework compliance was associated with lower post-treatment OCD symptoms in both treatment conditions (Whittal, Thordarson, &

McLean, 2005). This finding is consistent with the more general view that homework compliance is an important factor in facilitating treatment effectiveness for various emotional disorders (Burns & Spangler, 2000; Kazantzis, Deane & Ronan, 2000).

Outcome studies indicate that cognitive therapy is equally or slightly more effective than ERP in the treatment of OCD (Van Oppen et al., 1995; de Haan et al., 1997; Whittal et al., 2005), although this conclusion has not always been supported (McLean et al., 2001). However, there is no evidence that adding cognitive interventions to ERP improves treatment effectiveness (for review see Clark, 2004). Yet, it would appear that homework compliance may be equally important whether the assignment involves ERP or a behavioral challenge of faulty appraisals and beliefs. As well, relapse prevention programs for OCD teach clients to continue using ERP and cognitive restructuring to reduce risk of relapse (Emmelkamp, Kloek, & Blaauw, 1992; Hiss, Foa, & Kozak, 1994). Although there are no published empirical data on whether poor homework compliance increases the risk of relapse in OCD, it would be a safe assumption given the known importance of homework in promoting effective treatment of the acute phase of the disorder.

PROBLEMS ENCOUNTERED IN ASSIGNING HOMEWORK

In CBT for obsessions and compulsions homework assignments are important for ensuring the generalization of treatment effects beyond the therapist's office and for modifying faulty obsession-related appraisals and beliefs through behavioral experiments and other data gathering exercises. Abramowitz, Franklin, and Cahill (2003) emphasize that the person with OCD must go beyond the completion of "programmed" ERP homework exercises and incorporate exposure and ritual prevention into their everyday life (what they term "lifestyle exposure"). It is likely that those who practice "lifestyle exposure" will experience better treatment maintenance and less risk of relapse. However, for homework assignments to be successful and incorporated into one's everyday life, the client must first understand the rationale for the assignment, become fully engaged in the between-session task, and accurately evaluate the outcome of the assignment. Unfortunately there are a number of factors that can undermine the effectiveness of homework in treatment of OCD.

HIGH LEVELS OF ANXIETY OR DEPRESSION

There is empirical evidence that mild to moderate levels of depression may not interfere with the effectiveness of ERP. However, OCD clients with a severe comorbid depressive disorder may not respond as quickly or as completely to a trial of ERP (Foa et al., 1983; Stanley & Turner, 1995; Steketee & Shapiro, 1995). On the other hand, there is no empirical evidence that high levels of pretreatment anxiety are predictive of poorer outcome. However, clinical experience suggests that depression and anxiety can interfere with compliance to homework. The severely depressed OCD client will suffer from fatigue, low motivation, and possibly a generalized negative expectancy about the success of treatment.

A highly anxious or fearful client may be very resistant to exposing himself or herself to what may be perceived as overwhelming levels of anxiety that would occur during the exposure exercise. Clients often develop a strong aversion to and avoidance of anxious feelings and so may not be convinced there is "long-term gain for short-term pain" by engaging in ERP, especially outside the perceived safety of the therapist's office. There are three responses open to the therapist. First, ensure that the client fully understands the nature of OCD, the treatment rationale, and the importance of ERP. Second, it may be necessary to breakdown the exposure hierarchy to smaller incremental steps and spend a longer time exposing the client to milder anxiety situations. Although this extends the length of treatment, it ensures that the reluctant client experiences some success earlier in treatment. And third, any dysfunctional thoughts and beliefs about doing homework assignments should be identified and targeted for therapeutic change using the same cognitive restructuring and behavioral experimentation strategies that are employed to deal with the cognitive basis of obsessions and compulsions.

PERFECTIONISM AND INTOLERANCE OF UNCERTAINTY

As noted in Table 18.1, perfectionism and intolerance of uncertainty are belief domains that characterize OCD (Obsessive Compulsive Cognitions Working Group, 1997, 2003). Both appraisal and belief domains can undermine compliance with homework assignments. The OCD client with strong perfectionistic tendencies might hold unrealistic standards of what constitutes completion of a homework task. For example, I have had clients with OCD who had great difficulty completing questionnaires or engaging in self-monitoring because they were afraid that they would provide inaccurate or incomplete information that would then jeopardize the treatment process. For the perfectionistic person we often see an example of "all-or-nothing" thinking; "if I can't do the task perfectly, it is better that I not do it at all."

A number of researchers have noted that intolerance of uncertainty plays a central role in OCD (Abramowitz et al., 2003; Grayson, 1999). Grayson (1999) suggested that the high anxiety seen in OCD may be due to individuals' attempts to be 100% certain that they are not in danger or that they have prevented the possibility of some threat from occurring to another person. The quest for certainty is often in response to excessive doubt about whether or not a possible negative outcome has been prevented (Rachman, 2002). Thus, intolerance of uncertainty can undermine homework assignments when the client is unwilling to take some risk (or tolerate some doubt) or to suspend their quest for certainty even during performance of the homework task. For example, a client with checking compulsions might be asked to leave the house without checking that the lights are turned off or that the door is locked. This would require that the client be willing to tolerate thoughts and feelings of uncertainty that he or she had locked the door and turned off the lights for some time after completing the task. Once again, if the client refuses the homework assignment, the task could be broken down so that it is "less risky," but in all likelihood the therapist will need to use cognitive restructuring to deal directly with the intolerance of uncertainty and perfectionism beliefs. The goal is to teach the client to become more comfortable with an acceptable level of uncertainty and a "less than perfect" performance (Abramowitz et al., 2003).

MODIFYING OBSESSIONAL CONTENT

A homework assignment can actually be counterproductive if formulated incorrectly. A number of CBT writers have warned that therapists should not try to directly modify obsessional content (Salkovskis, 1985, 1989; Whittal & McLean, 1999; see also discussion in Clark, 2004). Let me illustrate this point with an example. You are treating a person who has persistent and distressing obsessions of committing a violent act against older persons. For instance, while walking along a street, your client has intrusive images and impulses of tripping any elderly person he sees walking with the assistance of a cane. In response to these distressing impulses your client avoids public places where he might see elderly people and he repeatedly offers prayers of penitence whenever he has the violent impulse.

It would be particularly counter-therapeutic to set as a homework assignment an evidence-gathering exercise in which the client recorded information for or against the belief that he is highly unlikely to carry out his aggressive impulse. Such an exercise is an example of trying to directly modify the obsessional content; in this case, that the client is a violent person who might violently attack a frail elderly victim. The homework assignment will fail because it merely becomes another means of obtaining reassurance. Another reason the exercise will fail is that the person with OCD already knows the obsession is illogical, even senseless. Thus, it would be useless to try and convince the person he is not violent; he already knows this but worries incessantly about the "what if."

A much more effective homework assignment is to ask the client to record evidence that "this is a dangerous impulse that must be controlled" versus "this is a benign feeling that I can just ignore." Notice that the homework assignment now targets the dysfunctional beliefs about control that are integral to the persistence of the obsession. The objective of the exercise now becomes a test of whether the client's appraisal of the obsession is faulty or not, as opposed to trying to convince the person he is not violent. It is likely that clients will give-up on homework assignments that inadvertently target their obsessional content because they will find such exercises ineffective at best and a reinforcement of their obsessional concerns at worse.

REASSURANCE SEEKING AND NEUTRALIZATION EFFECTS

Individuals with OCD will often seek reassurance from therapists, family members, and friends as a means to allay their fears and obsessional concerns. However, the provision of reassurance is futile and counterproductive because it will only increase the salience of the obsession and focus attention on the obsessional content rather than the faulty appraisals and beliefs (Abramowitz et al., 2003; Freeston & Ladouceur, 1999; Salkovskis, 1985; Whittal & McLean, 1999). When individuals compulsively seek reassurance or generate a memory of reassurance ("My mother said I was not getting sick"), they are engaging in a form of neutralization which in the long-term fuels the obsession.

A homework assignment could fail because the client turns it into a reassurance-seeking venture or engages in subtle neutralization. As an example, let's take a client with a somatic obsession who is plagued by the persistent question "Am I getting sick and in risk of vomiting?" In order to challenge the client's faulty overimportance appraisal of the obsession, she is asked to record information on how friends and family evaluate an intrusive thought like "am I getting sick?" The point of the exercise is to contrast how the client attaches great importance to the thought of getting sick whereas other people attach less importance and therefore experience the thought less often. However, the client uses the exercise as an opportunity to gather more information on the signs and symptoms of "getting sick." The assignment becomes counterproductive if the data gathering exercise encourages her to also ask people whether she looks sick. Instead of testing out her appraisal of overimportance, she could end up engaging in even more reassurance seeking behavior. In this case the homework assignment has promoted more reassurance seeking which will lead to more frequent and distressing somatic obsessions.

Another way in which the homework assignment could fail is if the client used the information she gathered to directly neutralize her distress about getting sick. She could do this by habitually reassuring herself that she did not have the symptoms of sickness that friends and family reported in the data gathering exercise. Whether by reinforcing reassurance seeking from others or by becoming a neutralization response, the client could report back to the therapist that she feels more distress and has a greater problem with fear of getting sick after the homework assignment. It is very important that the therapist assess the functional aspects of a homework assignment and ensure that reassurance seeking or neutralization have not crept into the assignment.

Abstract, Vague or "Far Future" Fears

Morrison and Westbrook (2004) in their chapter on cognitive-behavioral homework assignments for OCD note that one of the difficulties in devising homework assignments may be that the OCD client has difficulty describing his or her fears because of prolonged avoidance or rapid use of neutralization. In other instances, the obsessional fear may be quite vague or general such as concerns that "the anxiety will be intolerable and will remain elevated forever," or a fearful feeling that something bad will happen but the client is unable to be more specific about the "something." Some clients with OCD have obsessional fears that deal with "far future" negative consequences such as contracting a disease that does not appear until many years after the initial contamination or the fear of being eternally punished by God. In each of these cases it is important that the therapist design homework assignments that target the faulty appraisals of the unwanted obsession ("how the person makes this intrusive thought personally important") rather than struggle with trying to define the specific nature of the obsessional fear.

Low Expectations

There is some evidence that negative outcome expectancy for behavioral treatment of OCD might be associated with poorer response, although too few studies have reported expectancy data to arrive at a firm conclusion (see review by Steketee & Shapiro, 1995). It is even less certain whether a positive expectancy would enhance treatment response. As stated previously, compliance with homework does appear to predict better outcome with behavior therapy for OCD, and it is likely that positive expectancy predicts compliance (Steketee & Shapiro, 1995). Clinical impression suggests that clients who do not expect to derive any positive benefit from a homework assignment rarely put enough time or effort in the exercise to obtain any positive benefit. The deleterious impact of low expectancy will be particularly pronounced in clients who are especially fearful about engaging in exposure.

It is important that the therapist determine the cognitive basis to the low expectancy and to target these negative expectancies and beliefs in the therapy session. For example the client with OCD may believe that exposure and response prevention cannot be effective because OCD is a brain disorder, or that exposure will elicit an overwhelming amount of anxiety, or that the exposure exercise involves unnecessary risk. Whatever the underlying cause of homework noncompliance and low expectancy, it is important that these beliefs be addressed in therapy before any between-session ERP exercises are attempted.

COGNITIVE AND BEHAVIORAL HOMEWORK EXERCISES FOR OCD

As noted previously, CBT homework exercises are designed to challenge the faulty appraisals and beliefs of the obsession, to reinforce more adaptive evaluations of the obsession, and to encourage cessation of compulsions or neutralizing activities. Most of the homework assignments are based on exposure and response prevention but are modified into actual behavioral experiments that test out the faulty appraisals and beliefs of OCD. This section describes a representative homework assignment that can be used to restructure each of the faulty appraisals and beliefs specified in the cognitive behavioral model of OCD (see Table 18.1 above). For a more extensive discussion of homework assignments for CBT of OCD see Clark (2004), Freeston and Ladouceur (1999), Rachman (2003), Morrison & Westbrook, (2004), Salkovskis (1999), Salkovskis and Warwick (1988), and Whittal and McLean (1999).

OVERESTIMATED THREAT

The most effective homework assignments for overestimated threat appraisals are based on ERP. After constructing a hierarchy of situations that trigger a fearful obsession and arranging the situations from least distressing to most distressing, the CBT therapist begins with a moderately distressing situation, exposes the client to that situation for an extended period of time, and encourages the client to refrain from all compulsions or other neutralization strategies. For homework, clients repeatedly expose themselves on a daily basis to the situation and other moderately distressing situations, at the same time refraining from any form of compulsion or neutralization.

In subsequent sessions more difficult situations in the hierarchy are targeted for ERP, with an accompanying homework assignment designed to reinforce the gains made in the therapy session. In order to use the ERP homework exercise to challenge faulty overestimated threat appraisals, the therapist first identifies what is so threatening about the target situation. Clients then record their threat appraisals at the time of the ERP exercise and then the actual outcome of the homework task. The therapist then uses these data as evidence that challenges the clients' automatic tendency to overestimate the threat associated with the target situation. With repeated ERP experience, clients learn to challenge their initial overestimated threat evaluations of obsessional concerns and to counter these with more appropriate evaluations of risk and threat that match the actual outcomes that the client has experienced during the homework assignments.

Thought-Action Fusion (TAF)

To address the faulty belief that merely thinking an obsessional thought or impulse, such as "stabbing my child with a kitchen knife," increases the likelihood that you would actually murder your child (TAF- Likelihood bias), the CBT therapist can assign homework that involves a gradual increase in "cognitive risk." For example, the client could be asked to interact with her child in the kitchen with the knives hidden in a closed drawer. She would record the frequency of the "stabbing obsession," her anxiety level and desire to commit the violent act. Next she would interact with the child while the drawer remains open, again recording frequency of the obsession, anxiety and desire to act on the obsession. The next assignment could be interacting with her child while the knife is on the counter, and so on until she is able to use the knife for preparing food while her child is in the kitchen.

By collecting rating data in successively more difficult situations, the client learns three important lessons that can be used to counter the TAF-Likelihood bias. First, despite an initial increase in the "stabbing obsession" and a corresponding spike in anxiety, the desire or urge to commit the violent act remains low. This is contrary to the TAF-Likelihood belief that the more you have an obsession, the greater the likelihood that you will act on it. Second, obsession frequency and anxiety level decrease significantly the longer the client stays in the obsession-relevant situation. And third, there is not the slightest behavioral evidence that her child was put at increased risk even though she had the obsession. Although this type of homework assignment is critical for treating obsessions characterized by TAF-Likelihood appraisals, it is important that the therapist first conduct a thorough assessment in order to verify that the client has no history of aggression or criminal assault.

Inflated Responsibility

ERP homework assignments can be modified to target the inflated responsibility appraisals that are particularly evident in checking compulsions. A type of "responsibility gradient" can be built into the ERP exercises so that clients become more aware of the negative effects of faulty inflated responsibility evaluations. For example, a man with a checking compulsion could be asked to leave the house for work before his spouse and have her turn-off all appliances, light switches, and lock the door. He will sit in the car, wait for her, and record whether he had the obsession "did I turn everything off and lock the house?" In addition, he completes ratings of perceived level of responsibility, anxiety and urge to check. In the next assignment the client is asked to turn everything off in the house and lock the door accompanied by his spouse. Again ratings are made immediately upon getting into the car. In a third homework exercise the client turns everything off and locks the door while his spouse stands at the front door of the house. This continues in successive steps until the client turns everything off and locks the door while his spouse waits in the car.

In reviewing the successive homework assignments, the CBT therapist focuses on the relationship between the client's increased ratings of responsibility, and heightened levels of anxiety and urge to check. As responsibility for locking the house shifts from the spouse to the client, intensity of the obsession, anxiety level, and urge to check all increase. The objective of these exercises is to highlight the effects of excessive perceived responsibility on anxiety and urge to check. The therapist uses this homework to help shift the client from viewing the urge to check as a reasonable response to a realistic doubt (i.e., "did I lock the door?"), to understanding that the urge to check is a futile response to deflate an excessive sense of personal responsibility for preventing an imagined negative consequence (i.e., "I've left the house wide open, we'll be robbed, and it will be all my fault for being so careless").

OVERIMPORTANCE OF THOUGHT

A good homework assignment for this appraisal was described by Whittal and McLean (2002). Clients are first asked to estimate the number of times in a week they see an innocuous sign such as advertisements of "house for sale." The therapist records the estimated number. Clients are then given the assignment to count and record the number of "for sale" signs spotted in a one week period. The following week clients are instructed to cease counting "for sale" signs but simply record the number of times they inadvertently spot a "for sale" sign. The usual finding is that clients continue to record many more "for sale" signs even when they are no longer purposefully counting. The therapist can use this homework experience to show clients that once a person's attention is directed toward a stimulus, there is an automatic increase in its frequency, even when one is no longer purposely trying to attend to the stimulus. This exercise directly challenges the overimportance appraisal in which a person believes that if a thought occurs frequently it must be important or significant. The homework demonstrates that any thought, even an entirely neutral one like "for sale" signs, can become frequent if given attentional priority. Instead of assuming that the elevated frequency of the obsession means it must be important, the exercise supports an alternative view; that the obsession is frequent because it is given attentional priority.

CONTROL OF THOUGHTS

The "alternate thought suppression" homework assignment can be used to deal with the belief that one must attempt to gain greater control over the obsession (for more details see Clark, 2004; Morrison & Westbrook, 2004; Rachman, 2003). Clients are instructed to exert exceptionally strong effort and determination to intentionally suppress any semblance of the obsession on particular days of the week (i.e., Monday, Wednesday, Friday, and Sunday). On alternate days (i.e., Tuesday, Thursday, and Saturday) clients are asked to just let the obsessions come and go in their mind without intentionally trying to suppress the thought. A record is kept on the daily frequency of the obsession and anxiety level. After two or three weeks the therapist can plot the frequency and anxiety data on a graph so that the client can visually compare the effects of intentional suppression on frequency of the obsession and level of anxiety. Two outcomes are possible; either there is no difference between suppression and no suppression days in frequency (or anxiety) of the obsession, or the no-suppression days are associated with a lower frequency (anxiety) of the obsession. In either case the therapist now has data indicating that there is little benefit to continued efforts to control the obsession. In fact, the entire effort may be counterproductive, leading to a paradoxical increase in the frequency of the unwanted intrusive thought and level of anxiousness.

Intolerance of Uncertainty

Rachman (2003) describes the use of minisurveys that can be usefully applied to deal with the belief that the most effective way to deal with doubt is to be absolutely certain about an action or outcome. To illustrate, a client has persistent obsessional doubts about whether she completed a variety of daily tasks correctly such as locked doors, turned off appliances, mailed envelopes, collected all the mail, understood everything she read, etc. To be certain that these tasks were performed correctly, she engaged in checking and repeating rituals. In one homework assignment the client is asked to list a number of tasks that are associated with persistent doubts. Beside each task is a rating scale from 0 "not at all certain/considerable doubt," 50 "half certain/half doubt," to 100 "absolute certainty/not the slightest possibility of doubt." The client is asked to survey a number of family members and close friends by collecting their certainty ratings on the various daily tasks listed on her homework sheet. Individuals are instructed to assign a number between 0 and 100 that reflects their estimated level of certainty that various daily tasks were always completed.

In a second homework assignment the client is asked to rate her level of certainty with a variety of nonobsessional tasks or concerns. There are a number of observations that can be drawn from these exercises that can be used to challenge intolerance of uncertainty. First, it will be clear from the minisurvey that absolute certainty is rarely, if ever, attained and yet most people can live comfortably with at least some degree of doubt. In fact, the client may find that people often forget whether they did ordinary daily tasks like lock the door before leaving for work, or turned every light off in the house. And second, the client learns that she often tolerates uncertainty in her performance of nonobsessional tasks (i.e., can't recall whether she put the box of paperclips back in the drawer at the office). The point of these exercises is for clients to learn that absolute certainty is not only unattainable but unnecessary in order to live a safe and productive life.

Perfectionism

A cost/benefit homework assignment can be very helpful in dealing with the belief that there is a single perfect response to particular situations and that mistakes must be avoided at all cost. Clients are asked to identify a number of tasks they frequently perform at home or work (e.g., wash dishes, respond to email, read a book, schedule meetings, prepare reports, etc.). Beside each task they estimate how perfectly they perform each task from 0 "not at all perfect" to 100 "absolutely perfect." Together with the therapist, the client writes down some ways that each task could be performed more perfectly (i.e., how one could increase the perfection rating by 10 or 20 points). The client then selects a few tasks and in the next week tries to perform these tasks more perfectly by following the procedures worked out with the therapist. A record is kept on how perfectly the task was actually done, and the costs and benefits associated with devoting extra time and effort to "more perfect performance." At the next session the CBT therapist can use these data to discuss with the client the costs and benefits of striving for perfection in ordinary routine daily tasks. The homework assignment can be very helpful in challenging the belief that perfection is always a worthy goal and that any deviation from this goal is to be avoided at all costs.

CASE ILLUSTRATION OF OBSESSIONAL RUMINATION

PRESENTING PROBLEM AND CLIENT DESCRIPTION

Jane was a 22-year-old woman, in a common-law relationship, who had returned to university after several interruptions in her educational pursuits. Jane was the youngest of four siblings and her parents' divorce when she was 14 years old left Jane and her mother on their own. The economic strain that ensued as well as the break-up of the family was a precipitating event in Jane's life. Shortly afterwards she developed considerable anxiousness, worry, and guilt over doubts about her sexual orientation, or that she was sexually aroused by violence and would lose control. Secondary problems included increased conflict with her mother, emergence of depressive symptoms, and a period of two–three years in which she abused alcohol.

Jane's scores on a number of self-report symptom measures were as follows; Beck Depression Inventory: 17, Beck Anxiety Inventory: 20, Penn State Worry Questionnaire: 78, Maudsley Obsessive-Compulsive Inventory Total Score: 23, and the 60-item Padua Inventory Total Score: 129. On the Padua subscales she scored 46 on Impaired Mental Control, 36 on Contamination, 28 on Checking Behaviors, and 3 on Urges and Worries of Losing Control over Motor Behavior. These scores indicate a mild to moderate level of depressive symptoms and general anxiousness. However, her scores on the Penn State Worry Questionnaire and OCD measures were substantially elevated even by clinical norms. Further analysis of the Padua Inventory revealed very high scores on all subscales except Urges and Worries of Losing Control over Motor Behavior which was within the normal range. The psychometric data, then, clearly support a primary treatment focus on obsessive-compulsive symptoms.

CASE CONCEPTUALIZATION

Based on clinical interviews with Jane and collaborated by independent interviews with her mother the primary Axis I diagnosis was Obsessive Compulsive Disorder. A few weeks after the break-up of her family, she did exhibit some signs of depression that would be consistent with a comorbid Adjustment Disorder with Depressed Mood. Her elevated worry focused almost entirely on her obsessional concerns so she did not meet criteria for Generalized Anxiety Disorder. An Axis II disorder was not apparent although she did exhibit some symptoms of borderline personality disorder such as emotional vacillation, strained interpersonal relationships, and some impulse control issues like a brief period of abusing alcohol, sexual promiscuity, heightened activity, and extravagant shopping. The initial onset of OCD occurred when she was 14 years old and for much of the next 8 years she struggled with OCD symptoms that waxed and waned in intensity. It was evident that these symptoms were causing significant personal distress and intermittently impaired Jane's ability to study to the point where she had to interrupt her education on more than one occasion.

In offering a formulation for this case, I shall follow a format for CBT case conceptualization of OCD described in Clark (2004). There were three contributing factors or critical experiences that may have triggered the emergence of OCD. The parent's divorce and the loss of the family home were important general stressors. In addition, one of Jane's sister's announced to the family that she was lesbian and Jane subsequently began to recall an incident of childhood masturbation with a friend when she was 8 years old that caused her to feel tremendous guilt. In addition to the immediate critical incidents, there were a number of distal factors that placed Jane at higher risk for OCD. There was a strong family history of depression, anxiety, and alcoholism in her father's family and her mother also suffered from depression. In addition, another sibling was diagnosed with OCD and successfully treated with fluoxetine.

Jane presented with a subtype of OCD classified as "pure" obsessional rumination without overt compulsive rituals. She had persistent and very disturbing doubts over control of her sexual impulses and whether she might commit violent sexual acts against others. Her obsessional ruminations included "Am I sexually aroused by women which would mean that I am a lesbian?," "Am I sexually aroused by violence and therefore capable of raping an innocent person?," "As an 8 year old girl, did I masturbate because I was sexually aroused after tying up my friend in a pretend game of kidnapper?," and "Could I lose control and molest an innocent child?" Jane also had a mild secondary obsession about germ contamination and would check toilet seats several times and repeatedly wash her hands. Her primary response to the sex and violent obsessions was to repeatedly seek reassurance from her common-law husband and mother that she was not a lesbian, a possible child molester, or had been sexually aroused by "violence" when she was a child. She also tried to suppress the obsessions directly, distract herself, or reassure herself that the obsessional concerns were irrational and not likely to happen. Unfortunately all of these responses were ineffective and she spent much of the day greatly distressed over persistent worries about loss of control over these apparent sexual impulses.

Jane felt significant anxiety and guilt whenever she had the sex and violence obsessions. She exhibited a number of faulty appraisals such as (a) "I must be a 100% certain that I would never act in a 'perverted' way" (intolerance of uncertainty), (b) "If I can't control these unwanted sexual intrusive thoughts and feelings, what's to say I won't lose control of my behavior and become violent" (control of thoughts), (c) "The more I have these unwanted obsessions about sex and violence, the greater the likelihood that I'll 'snap' and actually commit these crimes" (TAF- Likelihood), (d) "I might be having these uncontrollable sex and violent obsessions because unconsciously I am a potential child molester or rapist" (threat overestimation), (e) "This memory of having masturbated as a child after tying up my friend must be important and significant in some way because the memory is so persistent, distressing and uncontrollable" (overimportance of thoughts), and (f) "Because I 'lost control' of my sexual impulses when a child and masturbated means that I have to maintain strict control over my sexual impulses and feelings as an adult in order to prevent myself from losing control again and harming someone" (elements of inflated responsibility, control of thoughts, and overestimated threat appraisals). Jane's misinterpretation of these unwanted sex and violence thoughts can be traced to various underlying core beliefs that she is a bad, terrible, and immoral person who is prone to perversion and who is quite mentally weak. She believed that underneath her façade of conscientiousness and control was a raging, "perverted" evil person who enjoyed harming innocent and defenseless individuals. If she did not maintain strict control over unwanted sexual thoughts and feelings, this evil person might emerge in the form of a rapist or child molester.

In response to the sex and violence obsessions, Jane's main compulsion was to seek reassurance from others that she was "normal" and that she would not harm anyone. She engaged in self-reassurance by spending hours analyzing her thoughts and feelings to determine if she really was sexually aroused by violence, children, or naked women. She erroneously believed that these mental control efforts were critical to preventing herself from losing control and harming others. She assumed that her inability to control the obsessions meant that she might also lose control of her sexual impulses. Thus, successful mental control became a type of test of her moral character. Her core belief was that she had less mental control than most people and that the key to overcoming her anxiety was to improve her ability to control the unwanted thoughts and feelings.

Imaginal Exposure Assignment

The first half of Jane's course of CBT dealt with her persistent obsessional rumination about whether she had engaged in childhood masturbation because she was aroused by imagined violence with her friend (i.e., play in which she tied up her friend and pretended to be her kidnapper). This was interpreted as a highly significant, threatening memory because it was her only experience that supported her obsessional doubt about her possible propensity to sexual deviance and violence. Her faulty appraisals of threat, control, importance of thoughts, and responsibility were first targeted with cognitive restructuring exercises conducted both within the session and assigned as homework. Evidence was gathered on the normality of childhood masturbation, and that childhood sexual feelings are not a predictor of adult sexuality. We also gathered evidence of any other indication in her adolescence or early adulthood that she might be a "latent rapist or child molester," and compared the emotional and mental state of someone "worried she might be sexually violent" versus a person who "engaged in violent sexual behavior." We also worked on the possibility that her memory of the childhood incident may be inaccurate and distorted; that after all these years, is she sure that she was sexually aroused by a specific imagined act of aggression against her friend?

Interestingly, the cognitive restructuring had little impact on the frequency or intensity of the obsessional doubt. It became clear that a key faulty appraisal had been missed in our therapy sessions. After many years of not thinking about the childhood masturbation incident, Jane suddenly developed this disturbing memory and became convinced that dwelling on such sex and violence thinking might actually increase the chances that she would actually engage in such disgusting behavior (i.e., TAF- Likelihood). To deal with this aspect of her obsessional concerns, the following homework assignment was developed. Jane agreed to spend at least 20 minutes each day dwelling on the thought "I am aroused by violence and so might be a rapist." She was asked to record her anxiety level before and after each exposure session, the intensity of her urge to engage in violent behavior, and any associated fearful thoughts. A week later Jane returned to therapy reporting a dramatic reduction in the frequency and intensity of her "violence obsessions" for that week. More importantly she discovered that purposefully thinking about being a rapist did not intensify the urge to become violent; on the contrary, the frequency of the obsession and her level of anxiety actually declined appreciably. The imaginal exposure homework, then, proved to be a more direct challenge to Jane's faulty appraisal of the obsessions and served to "de-catastrophize" the significance of the thoughts and memories.

Behavioral Experiment Assignment

Although the imaginal exposure assignments were initially very effective, after many months Jane reported a resurgence of her obsessional doubts about sex and violence. Re-assessment revealed that she was now using the exposure as a type of neutralization strategy; whenever she had the sex and violence obsessions, she immediately engaged in exposure in order to eliminate the obsession. Clearly what was needed was a more direct behavioral experiment that would convincingly show Jane that her problem was not that she was a "latent rapist" who needed more control over her thoughts but rather that she misinterpreted the "rapist thoughts" as a highly significant threatening occurrence because she was so pacifist, nonviolent in her nature that she found such thinking highly repugnant.

To test out these two competing beliefs "I have sex and violence obsessions because I have an underlying propensity to lose control and become violent as evidenced by past childhood experiences" versus "I have sex and violence obsessions because I am overly sensitive to this type of thinking due to a highly conscientious, moralistic, and nonviolent nature." Jane agreed to conduct the following homework behavioral experiment. In the next week, she was to engage in sexuality activity with her common-law husband when it was clear that he was somewhat reluctant and then when he was fully accepting of the idea. She was to rate her level of enjoyment and sexual arousal on occasions when he was reluctant to have sex versus times when he clearly wanted to engage in intimate sexual behavior.

Jane missed the next scheduled session but subsequently returned and it was clear that the homework assignment was a turning point in her treatment. She reported that she was unable to be persuasive, let alone force, her spouse to have sex against his will. She discovered that when her spouse rebuffed her sexual advances, she was "put off" by this rather than sexually aroused by his resistance. Jane also reported that her highest levels of sexual satisfaction occurred when the couple engaged in mutually desired sexual intimacy. We then contrasted her experiences with the probable thoughts and feelings of someone sexually aroused by power and aggression. She was able to accept that the outcome from the behavioral experiment confirmed that she was a sensitive non-violent person who was abhorred rather than aroused by acts of aggression and domination of another person.

Course of Treatment

Jane had 52 sessions of individual CBT for her obsessions and compulsions that spanned a seven-year period. Most of the CBT sessions were offered in two 12–18 month time intervals that were separated by a three-year period of no treatment contact. A follow-up session was provided approximately two years after treatment termination. In addition, Jane had two psychiatric consults and at various times throughout her treatment was prescribed bupropion, clonazepam, valproic acid, and then finally fluoxetine. However, by her own admission as well as independent psychiatric evaluation, the remission of OCD symptoms was due primarily to the CBT, with pharmacotherapy providing some reduction in general anxiousness and intermittent periods of heightened activity. At last contact Jane was continuing to experience an almost complete remission of her violence and sex obsessions; she had completed her educational training and moved to another Canadian city to begin a new life.

CONCLUSION

OCD is a chronic and potentially debilitating anxiety disorder that can be particularly challenging to treat because of its heterogeneous and idiosyncratic symptom presentation. Although the behavioral treatment known as exposure and response prevention is the most effective psychological intervention for the disorder, a more cognitive understanding and treatment of obsessions and compulsions offers new insights and treatment possibilities for those who have not shown a satisfactory response to ERP. This chapter presented the new CBT approach to OCD. Homework assignments were described that target dysfunctional OCD beliefs of overestimated threat, thought-action fusion, inflated responsibility, overimportance of thought, control, intolerance of uncertainty and perfectionism. Various complications were noted that can arise when assigning homework to obsessional clients. The chapter concluded with a case illustration of the use of homework in CBT for obsessional ruminations. A consistent message throughout this chapter is that homework assignments are critical to the effectiveness of ERP or CBT in reducing obsessions and compulsions, maintaining treatment gains, and preventing relapse.

REFERENCES

Abramowitz, J. S. (1997). Effectiveness of psychological and pharmacological treatments for obsessive-compulsive disorder: A quantitative review. *Journal of Consulting and Clinical Psychology, 65*, 44–52.

Abramowitz, J. S., Foa, E. B., & Franklin, M. E. (2003). Exposure and ritual prevention for obsessive-compulsive disorder: Effects of intensive versus twice-weekly sessions. *Journal of Consulting and Clinical Psychology, 71*, 394–398.

Abramowitz, J. S., Franklin, M. E., & Cahill, S. P. (2003). Approaches to common obstacles in the exposure-based treatment of obsessive-compulsive disorder. *Cognitive and Behavioral Practice, 10*, 14–22.

American Psychiatric Association (2000). *Diagnostic and statistical manual of mental disorders (4th Edition, Text Revision).DSM-IV-TR*. Washington, DC: American Psychiatric Association.

Antony, M. M., Downie, F., & Swinson, R. P. (1998). Diagnostic issues and epidemiology in obsessive-compulsive disorder. In R. P. Swinson, M. M. Antony, S. Rachman, & M. A. Richter (Eds.), *Obsessive-compulsive disorder: Theory, research and treatment* (pp. 3–32). New York: Guilford.

Burns, D. D., & Spangler, D. L. (2000). Does psychotherapy homework lead to improvements in depression in cognitive-behavioral therapy or does improvement lead to increased homework compliance? *Journal of Consulting and Clinical Psychology, 68*, 46–56.

Clark, D. A. (2004). *Cognitive-behavioral therapy for OCD*. New York: Guilford Press.

Clark, D. A., & Purdon, C. L. (1993). New perspectives for a cognitive theory of obsessions. *Australian Psychologist, 28*, 161–167.

de Haan, E., van Oppen, P., van Balkom, A. J. L. M., Spinhoven, P., Hoogduin, K. A. L., & van Dyck, R. (1997). Prediction of outcome and early vs. late improvement in OCD patients treated with cognitive behaviour therapy and pharmacotherapy. *Acta Psychiatria Scandinavia, 96*, 354–361.

Eddy, K. T., Dutra, L., Bradley, R., & Westen, D. (2004). A multidimensional meta-analysis of psychotherapy and pharmacotherapy for obsessive-compulsive disorder. *Clinical Psychology Review, 24*, 1011–1030.

Emmelkamp, P. M. G., Kloek, J., & Blaauw, E. (1992). Obsessive-compulsive disorders. In Wilson, P. H. (Ed.), *Principles and practice of relapse prevention* (pp. 213–234). New York: Guilford.

Foa, E. B., Franklin, M. E., & Kozak, M. J. (1998). Psychosocial treatments for obsessive-compulsive disorder: Literature review. In R. P. Swinson, M. M. Antony, S. Rachman, & M. A. Richter (Eds.), *Obsessive-compulsive disorder: Theory, research and treatment* (pp. 258–276). New York: Guilford.

Foa, E. B., & Kozak, M. J. (1996). Psychological treatment for obsessive-compulsive disorder. In M. R. Mavissakalian & R. F. Prien (Eds.), *Long-term treatments of anxiety disorders* (pp. 285–309). Washington, DC: American Psychiatric Press.

Foa, E. B., Steketee, G., Grayson, J. B., & Doppelt, H. G. (1983). Treatment of obsessive-compulsives: When do we fail? In E. B. Foa & P. M. G. Emmelkamp (Eds.), *Failures in behavior therapy* (pp. 10–34). New York: Wiley.

Franklin, M. E., Abramowitz, J. S., Bux, D. A., Zoellner, L. A., & Feeny, N. C. (2002). Cognitive-behavioral therapy with and without medication in the treatment of obsessive-compulsive disorder. *Professional Psychology: Research and Practice, 33*, 162–168.

Freeston, M. H., & Ladouceur, R. (1999). Exposure and response prevention for obsessional thoughts. *Cognitive and Behavioral Practice, 6*, 362–383.

Freeston, M. H., Rhéaume, J., & Ladouceur, R. (1996). Correcting faulty appraisals of obsessional thoughts. *Behaviour Research and Therapy, 34*, 433–446.

Grayson, J. B. (1999). Series response: Compliance and understanding OCD. *Cognitive and Behavioral Practice, 6*, 415–421.

Hiss, H., Foa, E. B., & Kozak, M. J. (1994). Relapse prevention program for treatment of obsessive-compulsive disorder. *Journal of Consulting and Clinical Psychology, 62*, 801–808.

Kazantzis, N., Deane, F. P., & Ronan, K. R. (2000). Homework assignments in cognitive and behavioral therapy: A meta-analysis. *Clinical Psychology: Science & Practice, 7*, 189–202.

Kozak, M. J., & Foa, E. B. (1997). *Mastery of obsessive-compulsive disorder: A cognitive-behavioral approach. Therapist guide.* San Antonio: TX: Graywind Publications.

Kozak, M. J., Liebowitz, M. R., & Foa, E. B. (2000). Cognitive behavior therapy and pharmacotherapy for obsessive-compulsive disorder: The NIMH-Sponsored Collaborative Study. In W. K. Goodman, M. V. Rudorfor, & J. D. Maser (Eds.), *Obsessive-compulsive disorder: Contemporary issues in treatment* (pp. 501–530). Mahweh, NJ: Lawrence Erlbaum Associates.

McLean, P. D., Whittal, M. L., Sochting, I., Koch, W. J., Paterson, R., Thordarson, D. S., et al. (2001). Cognitive versus behavior therapy in the group treatment of obsessive-compulsive disorder. *Journal of Consulting and Clinical Psychology, 69*, 205–214.

Morrison, N., & Westbrook, D. (2004). Obsessive-compulsive disorder. In J. Bennett-Levy, G. Bulter, M. Fennell, A. Hackmann, M. Mueller, & D. Westbrook (Eds.), *Oxford guide to behavioural experiments in cognitive therapy* (pp. 101–118). Oxford: Oxford University Press.

Obsessive Compulsive Cognitions Working Group (1997). Cognitive assessment of obsessive-compulsive disorder. *Behaviour Research and Therapy, 35*, 667–681.

Obsessive Compulsive Cognitions Working Group (2003). Psychometric validation of the obsessive beliefs questionnaire and the interpretation of intrusions inventory: Part I, *Behaviour Research and Therapy, 41*, 863–878.

Rachman, S. J. (1983). Obstacles to the successful treatment of obsessions. In E. B. Foa & P. M. G. Emmelkamp (Ed.), *Failures in behavior therapy* (pp. 35–57). New York: Wiley.

Rachman, S. J. (1985). An overview of clinical and research issues in obsessional-compulsive disorders. In M. Mavissakalian, S. M. Turner & L. Michelson (Eds.), *Obsessive-compulsive disorder: Psychological and pharmacological treatment* (pp. 1–47). New York: Plenum.

Rachman, S. J. (1997). A cognitive theory of obsessions. *Behaviour Research and Therapy, 35*, 793–802.

Rachman, S. J. (1998). A cognitive theory of obsessions: Elaborations. *Behaviour Research and Therapy, 36*, 385–401.

Rachman, S. J. (2002). A cognitive theory of compulsive checking. *Behaviour Research and Therapy, 40*, 625–639.

Rachman, S. J. (2003). *The treatment of obsessions*. Oxford: Oxford University Press.

Rachman, S. J. & Hodgson, R. J. (1980). *Obsessions and compulsions*. Englewood Cliffs, NJ: Prentice-Hall.

Rachman, S., & Shafran, R. (2000). The mechanisms of behavioral treatment and the problem of therapeutic failures. In W. K. Goodman, M. V. Rudorfor, & J. D. Maser (Eds.), *Obsessive-compulsive disorder: Contemporary issues in treatment* (pp. 533–549). Mahwah, NJ: Lawrence Erlbaum Associates.

Rasmussen, S. A., & Eisen, J. L. (1998). The epidemiology and clinical features of obsessive-compulsive disorder. In M. A. Jenike & W. E. Minichiello (Eds.), *Obsessive-compulsive disorders: Practical management* (pp. 12–43). St. Louis, MO: Mosby.

Salkovskis, P. M. (1985). Obsessional-compulsive problems: A cognitive-behavioural analysis. *Behaviour Research and Therapy, 23*, 571–583.

Salkovskis, P. M. (1989). Cognitive-behavioural factors and the persistence of intrusive thoughts in obsessional problems. *Behaviour Research and Therapy, 27*, 677–682.

Salkovskis, P. M. (1999). Understanding and treating obsessive-compulsive disorder. *Behaviour Research and Therapy, 37*, S29–S52.

Salkovskis, P. M., & Warwick, H. M. C. (1988). Cognitive therapy of obsessive-compulsive disorder. In C. Perris, I. M. Blackburn, & H. Perris (Eds.), *Cognitive psychotherapy: Theory and Practice* (pp. 376–395). Berlin: Springer-Verlag.

Stanley, M. A., & Turner, S. M. (1995). Current status of pharmacological and behavioral treatment of obsessive-compulsive disorder. *Behavior Therapy, 26*, 163–186.

Steketee, G. S. (1993). *Treatment of obsessive compulsive disorder*. New York: Guilford.

Steketee, G. (1999). *Overcoming obsessive-compulsive disorder: A behavioral and cognitive protocol for the treatment of OCD*. Oakland, CA: New Harbinger.

Steketee, G., & Shapiro, L. J. (1995). Predicting behavioral treatment outcome for agoraphobia and obsessive compulsive disorder. *Clinical Psychology Review, 15*, 317–346.

Taylor, S. (2002) Cognition in obsessive-compulsive disorder: An overview. In R. O. Frost & G. Steketee (Eds). *Cognitive approaches to obsessions and compulsions: Theory, assessment and treatment* (pp. 1–12). Oxford: Elsevier.

van Oppen, P., de Haan, E., van Balkom, A. J. L. M., Spinhoven, P., Hoogduin, K., & van Dyck, R. (1995). Cognitive therapy and exposure *in vivo* in the treatment of obsessive compulsive disorder. *Behaviour Research and Therapy, 33*, 379–390.

Whittal, M. L., & McLean, P. D. (1999). CBT for OCD: The rationale, protocol, and challenges. *Cognitive and Behavioral Practice, 6*, 383–396.

Whittal, M. L., & McLean, P. D. (2002). Group cognitive behavioral therapy for obsessive compulsive disorder. In R. O. Frost & G. Steketee (Eds.), *Cognitive approaches to obsessions and compulsions: Theory, assessment, and treatment* (pp. 417–433). Amsterdam: Elsevier Science.

Whittal, M. L., Thordarson, D. S., & Mclean, P. D. (2005). Treatment of obsessive-compulsive disorder: Cognitive behavior therapy vs. exposure and response prevention. *Behaviour Research and Therapy, 43*, 1559–1576.

Chapter 19

PSYCHOSIS

Hazel Dunn and Anthony P. Morrison

Psychosis is a relatively common condition that can lead to prejudice, stigma, and even social exclusion. It can be costly to the individual, carers, and mental health services as well as the wider health care system and to society as a whole. While there are significant financial costs associated with psychosis, which can be readily measured, it is the personal cost to the individual of the physical and psychological consequences of the diagnosis that are most immediately obvious rather than the experience of psychosis itself.

Daily life can change dramatically; employment, income, social functioning, and relationships may be affected; and there may be a loss of expectations, leading to grief for the life that could or should have been, and appraisals of shame and entrapment are also common (Birchwood, 2003). Prognosis has been pessimistic but there is now a shift in interest and expectations for the treatment of this condition. Interested stakeholders are demanding more optimistic theoretical models and more acceptable methods of treatment that empower individuals .(Department of Health, 2001).

PSYCHOSIS AND PSYCHOTHERAPY

Within the developments in cognitive therapy over the past two decades its application to psychosis has arguably attracted the greatest attention as clients, carers, and service providers look for effective, acceptable treatments that offer a long lasting effect and reduce the chances or impact of relapse.

In the field of psychotherapy it is held that a "cognitive revolution" (Mahoney, 1974) has taken place. Until recently, the growth of cognitive models and therapies was largely confined to the emotional disorders, to the point where today CBT is commonly judged to be a first line treatment in a range of emotional disorders (Salkovskis, 2004). Very little attention was given to any psychological treatment of schizophrenia, and it has been suggested that the flawed concept of schizophrenia itself was responsible for the paucity of interest and research in this area (Bellack, 1986; Bentall, 1990; Chadwick, Birchwood, & Trower, 1996). Traditionally, it was believed that psychotic symptoms or experiences were vastly different from normal experiences, impervious to counter-argument or the impact of experience, and therefore unresponsive to psychological therapies in general (Jaspers, 1913/1963).

It was the advent of new cognitive psychological models of positive psychotic symptoms (Bentall, Kinderman, & Kaney, 1994; Chadwick & Birchwood, 1994; Garety, Kuipers, Fowler, Freeman, & Bebbington, 2001; Morrison, 2001), focusing on persistent delusions and hallucinations, which brought attention from researchers and clinicians. That focus has changed over a decade to extend to others who have related diagnoses and experiences, and target outcomes other than symptom reduction (Garety, Fowler, & Kuipers, 2000). The main aim of CT for people with psychosis is to reduce their distress and improve their quality of life (Morrison, Renton, Dunn, Williams, & Bentall, 2003).

There is widespread recognition that cognitive-behavioral treatments that are provided as an adjunct to medication can be successful in reducing distress and disability in people with psychosis. Numerous randomized controlled trials have now been conducted that demonstrate the efficacy of CBT for people with psychosis (Kuipers et al., 1997; Sensky et al., 2000; Tarrier et al., 1998; Turkington, Kingdon, & Turner, 2002). In addition, there have been several meta-analyses that conclude that CBT for people with psychosis is effective and should be provided routinely (Gould, Mueser, Bolton, Mays, & Goff, 2001; Pilling et al., 2002; Rector & Beck, 2001). In addition, cognitive therapy has also been shown to reduce transition to psychosis in those at high-risk (Morrison et al., 2004). On the basis of such evidence, it would seem reasonable to suggest that all patients experiencing distress associated with psychotic experiences should be offered access to CBT, as recommended in recent treatment guidelines for schizophrenia.(National Institute for Clinical Excellence, 2003). The remainder of this chapter will outline an approach to the use of homework assignments in the delivery of cognitive therapy.

HOMEWORK IN COGNITIVE THERAPY

Homework assignments carried out between clinical sessions are an essential part of cognitive therapy and, in theory, are accorded a causal role in effecting outcome. Beck et al. (1979) describe homework as "an integral, vital component of treatment" (p. 272) and recommend that homework assignments should be utilized throughout therapy, but especially in the earlier phases with depressed patients, to "improve level of functioning, counteract obsessive thinking, change attitudes, and give a feeling of gratification" (p. 141). This can be achieved by providing the person with opportunities to collect information, test dysfunctional beliefs, and practice new skills.

Homework largely aims to gather information and give the patient the opportunity to put into practice concepts or techniques learned in the therapy session. Homework tasks are collaboratively devised with an explicit rationale identified to increase compliance, and should be linked to achieving a goal or goals. The tasks should not be too difficult but not so easy that they have no meaning, and ideally they should meet the criteria for being specific, measurable, achievable, relevant and time limited (SMART), as defined under the problem orientation of therapy.

Homework, in a generic form, reinforces the learning process, and in cognitive therapy individuals experiment with more realistic and effective ways of thinking and behaving. Reflecting on the results of these experiments the person defines what has been learned and can refine and put into operation further experiments to either consolidate new beliefs and behaviors or expand on them. Homework tasks are devised to help the client make progress towards identified goals; therefore, they must be relevant and achievable. If there is doubt about the appropriateness of a specific homework task then the client and therapist must consider whether it meets these two criteria.

It is only by experiencing emotions and behaving in different ways that patients can collect new evidence to use in the re-appraisal of delusional beliefs (Morrison, 1998). Delusional beliefs will rarely change following intellectual challenging alone (Chadwick et al., 1996), and are more likely to be strengthened rather than weakened if the patient perceives the therapist's stance as confrontational (Milton, Patwa, & Hafner, 1978).

Kazantzis, Deane, and Ronan (2000) reviewed the available empirical evidence and concluded that patients who receive CBT that includes homework assignments improve at least 60% more than those who receive treatment without homework tasks (although the studies reviewed did not include patients with a diagnosis of schizophrenia, it is likely that similar principles will apply in CBT for psychosis). It must be remembered that the undertaking of homework is not restricted to the client, in the collaborative alliance there are many occasions when the therapist will be active between sessions, but there are no studies reporting the effect of therapist homework tasks on client outcome.

Types of Homework

Homework is any activity, agreed in the therapy session, which is undertaken prior to the next session. This activity falls into the broad categories of information gathering, hypothesis testing, and the continued practice of newly gained skills. The categories are not mutually exclusive ad any combination may be used at any one time to help the client achieve their goals.

Information Gathering

The commonest form of recorded information gathering in therapy is the completion of questionnaires. They may be validated global questionnaires useful for assessment purposes and monitoring change, such as the Beck Depression Inventory (Beck, Ward, Mendelson, Mock, & Erbaugh, 1961) to assess depressive symptomatology or the Peters Delusions Inventory (Peters, Joseph, & Garety, 1999) to assess unusual ideas and beliefs; scales that are perceived to be clinically useful and provide information that may contribute to the case formulation, for example the Meta-Cognitions Questionnaire (Cartwright-Hatton & Wells, 1997) or the Beliefs about Paranoia Scale (Morrison et al., 2005); or idiosyncratic scales devised locally for a specific purpose. Clients who experience psychosis and seek treatment invariably experience distressing emotional states, which should be assessed using routine measures developed for adult populations.

Visual analog scales, where the person is asked to indicate their response to a question on a horizontal line, with anchor points at each end, are frequently used, as is asking the person to indicate their response on a scale of 0 to 10 or 0 to 100. These data can give both factual and attitudinal information. These types of data can be useful in many ways, for example, to assess the severity of symptoms, and current functioning level, to aid the establishment of a diagnosis, to act as a baseline from which to measure change in therapy, and to highlight areas of concern that need action (e.g., risk of self-harm).

Often the relationship between two or more variables can be explored. For example, John, who experienced auditory hallucinations and persecutory delusions, kept a diary of the frequency, intensity, and duration of both his positive symptoms and his alcohol use. Asking the person to write down an outline longitudinal description of the development of their problems and identify factors that maintain them is a common homework task. Activity records or schedules, where the person records their activity at hourly intervals during the day, can be used to establish patterns of behavior and identify periods of inactivity. When combined with the assessment of mastery and pleasure, it is possible to assess the emotional component of activities the person engages in. Beck et al. (1979) describe using a client daily record of activity to obtain objective data about a depressed client's level of functioning as opposed to the biased and inaccurate account from the client when asked to estimate functioning. This can be particularly useful for people with psychosis who are experiencing negative symptoms such as avolition, apathy, anhedonia and social withdrawal.

The use of thought records is central to cognitive therapy and the person begins by identifying thoughts, emotions, and behavior in a situation and then uses this information as a basis to generate alternative ways of thinking or behaving (Beck et al., 1979). Exercises that ask the person to collect information that aids the process of decision making may also be employed. A cost–benefit analysis is a comparison of the advantages and disadvantages of taking specific decisions, as are surveys that are undertaken to gain information from population samples to broaden the person's knowledge base, for example, asking people who use cannabis what effects it has on mood and thinking.

Morrison et al. (2003) describe the use of diaries and idiosyncratic recording forms to collect information on the relationship between auditory hallucinations and high levels of distress and arousal for psychotic clients. Probably the most common form of information gathering on the client's part, overall, is that of reading about the presenting problem and the therapy. This helps the person develop insight, normalize their experiences, develop an understanding of what therapy may entail and allows them to make informed choices throughout therapy.

It is usually assumed that the homework tasks described above involve reading and writing but it is possible for those with sight impairments and literacy problems to use other methods of gaining and recording information such as the use of audio taping. The audio taping of clinical sessions is commonplace, giving the person a factual record of the session to aid memory and understanding, and clients are encouraged to listen to tapes of sessions for homework.

Hypothesis Testing

Following assessment and the establishment of a problem list the next step in cognitive therapy is usually the development of a goals list for the person. The next step after this is to identify a hypothesis about the cause of the problem (the formulation will be central to this process) and then test out this hypothesis.

Designing a test should be a collaborative effort between client and therapist, with the therapist shaping the homework while the client adapts it to their own situation. An example of this can be seen in a test of the hypothesis of a person who experiences panic disorder and believes that during a panic attack they will faint. The test will be to induce a panic attack in the person, and get them to stop using any "safety behaviors" (over or covert behaviors that the person uses to prevent fainting from happening), thereby putting them in a position where their hypothesis, or prediction, will be confirmed. Similar tests can be used with people with psychosis who often experience panic attacks or catastrophic beliefs about such experiences being indicative of an impending relapse (Gumley, White, & Power, 1999). Similarly, such tests can be utilized in relation to voice hearers; for example, asking someone to bring on their voices and try out different strategies in order to challenge beliefs about power and control over voices (Chadwick et al., 1996) Although such tests are often done in session, they can also be used as homework (Burns, Adams, & Anastopolous, 1985). This test helps the person realize the inaccuracy of their hypothesis. If it is carried out in session the therapist will ask the client what sense they make of the result and help them to work out why the hypothesis was wrong and to develop a modified hypothesis. The modified hypothesis can then be tested, evaluated and then accepted, rejected or refined.

Some hypothesis testing is done in session, some independently, and some are done in session and then practiced independently for homework but still within the cycle of test, evaluate, reject or refine. This contributes to the emotional processing that is believed to occur when new information is incorporated into existing memory structures (Foa & Kozak, 1986).

For example, Mandy, who experienced persecutory delusions, believed the presenters on a television program were conducting conversations with her. Normally she would say things such as "yes, that's right" or "I agree entirely" but, for homework, to test out if the presenters were listening to her, she argued with them and noted their responses.

Before hypothesis testing takes place in reality, it may be necessary for some clients to rehearse required behavior out of the real situation or in imagination. If the homework is to behave differently in a feared social interaction the person may find contemplation of the task in reality too anxiety provoking, and may need to observe modeled behavior and engage in substantial rehearsal.

Practice/Maintenance/Relapse Prevention

Once the client has had the opportunity to develop more helpful or adaptive ways of thinking or behaving, these new skills must be put into practice as soon as possible and repeated until they become part of the person's repertoire of available problem-solving strategies. They should not be identified and stored away as an emergency strategy; rather, they are "kept sharp" by regular use and help the person maintain the gains made in therapy.

When the stage of relapse prevention or management is addressed, a "blueprint" of the person's relapse signature is recorded and strategies to monitor signs of relapse and limit its' impact are identified. This can be considered ongoing homework and, if the person is offered follow up or booster sessions, may be evaluated, accepted or rejected, or refined. Scott (2002) describes the use of daily mood graphs to identify fluctuations in quality and severity of mood shifts for a client with bipolar disorder and, within a defined management plan, take appropriate action.

EFFECTS OF COMPLIANCE AND
NON-COMPLIANCE

The completion of appropriate homework tasks in cognitive therapy is significantly correlated with outcome in affective disorders (Beck et al., 1979; Burns & Spangler, 2000; Addis & Jacobson, 2000; Garland & Scott, 2002). Homework facilitates the generalization of learning from therapy sessions into everyday life and promotes the independent practice of acquired skills. If the client is active between therapy sessions, then longer-lasting change effects are observed and there is a greater likelihood of the ongoing application of those skills (Beck et al., 1979). Clearly, clients who complete homework tasks are likely to remain in therapy and have better outcomes than those who do not (Kazantzis et al., 2000). Those clients who are less active between sessions make less progress and may drop out of therapy or there may be early termination by the therapist if the client is perceived to have low suitability for the therapy.

CLIENT MOTIVATION

Homework compliance, for all clients in CBT, is influenced by both client and therapist variables (Bryant, Simons, & Thases, 1999). Client variables such as depression, motivation to resolve symptoms, hopefulness, beliefs about self-efficacy, ability to problem solve, thoughts about homework tasks, and a wish to please the therapist may increase compliance with homework. The overall skill of the therapist, ability to explain the rationale for and possible gains for homework, ability to predict or recognize possible obstacles, and the positive reinforcement given on completion may affect the client's compliance. These two sets of variables will have an impact on the client's cognitions relating to the generic concept of undertaking homework, the use of homework in therapy, and specific assignments, as will the client's previous experiences of homework in any setting. Studying therapist behaviors in relation to homework, Worthington (1986) found that discussion of the previous session's agreed homework and the exploration of clients' attitudes about the current assignment predicted subsequent compliance.

Therapists cannot directly motivate clients, but they can help create the circumstances or environment in which the client will be motivated to be active. If the goals of therapy meet the specific, measurable, achievable, relevant criteria, then appropriate, collaboratively designed homework assignments, based on goal acquisition, client capacity and stage of therapy are more likely to be completed.

Client Resistance

Resistance to homework may reflect covert resistance to cognitive therapy itself. Clients who continue to attend therapy sessions may be assumed to be engaged with the therapy and therefore motivated to be active, but this may not always be the case. Some clients who continue to attend sessions but are not active between them may be returning for the non-specific aspects of the therapy, the warmth and empathy of the therapist in a non-judgmental, collaborative relationship may be a positive reinforcer. Alternatively, there may be a negative reinforcement factor in that clients fear the consequences of non-attendance, either from other professionals or family, or they may be troubled by the thought of unilaterally ending therapy.

INCREASING HOMEWORK TASK COMPLETION

Burns and Nolen-Hoeksema (1991) suggest that uncooperative clients may need a more persuasive introduction to cognitive therapy than the more compliant ones. If the client is truly engaged with the therapy but resists completing meaningful homework assignments, then a number of factors may be important (Bryant et al., 1999). Meaningful homework is rarely easy to complete; at the very least it takes up time, usually requires some effort on the part of the individual, and sometimes may cause some distress by the nature of the material it generates or focuses on. Even the word "homework" itself can trigger a negative reaction; some people have unpleasant memories of homework relating to school or other institutions, some may have experiences of failure and negative consequences relating to homework, others may fear that the work will be "marked" by the therapist, and they may not be "doing it right" or that their results may not be "good enough."

The content of some homework assignments may cause distress for some clients, who may use avoidance to deal with sensitive issues. Encouraging the person to focus on such issues without being explicit about the rationale, process and possible gains will not enhance compliance. When the issue of resistance is addressed in therapy and the client is asked to identify reasons for reluctance or avoidance, it may not be possible for them to be honest with the therapist. If there is a good therapeutic alliance and the client is confident of their concerns being understood and accepted, then it may be possible to make progress in overcoming them.

If the client is not totally in agreement with the goals of therapy or has other goals which are a priority, for them, then he or she is unlikely to undertake home-work designed to achieve them (Shelton & Levy, 1981). Similarly if the homework is assigned by the therapist and not collaboratively decided, compliance may be compromised.

All these factors have significance for clients with emotional disorders, and for those with psychosis the therapist should pay even greater attention to them and have strategies to reduce the likelihood or impact of these problems rather than trying to deal with them after they have surfaced. Individuals who fail to continue in treatment with CBT for psychosis appear either not to have accepted or understood the treatment rationale or the possible benefits/outcome (Tarrier et al., 1998). Kuipers et al. (1998) found a good outcome (18 months after baseline) in cognitive therapy for psychosis was strongly predicted by the degree of the individual's cognitive flexibility relating to delusions.

CLIENTS' EXPERIENCES

There has long been a general perception that people with psychosis are difficult to engage in therapy and cannot or will not undertake homework tasks. This view is changing and there is a shift toward identifying meaningful homework tasks as indicated by the formulation of the client's problems.

In a recent study (Dunn, Morrison, & Bentall, 2002) explored the experiences of homework in CBT, for clients with psychosis. The clients readily identified reasons why they did, or did not do, homework between therapy sessions, and the following themes were reported as having the greatest influence on the completion of agreed tasks.

Motivation was the most cited factor, followed by **memory**, **difficulty** and **rationale**. Other factors included **perceived benefits of therapy**, **insight**, **effort**, and **relevance of assignments to problems**.

HELPFUL STRATEGIES

The present findings suggest that increasing homework compliance in clients might be achieved through a number of therapist behaviors. To help a client remember to do the homework, it may be useful to make sure they take away written or audio-taped instructions of the what, where, when, and how of the assignment. This should only be done after the acceptance of the rationale for the task (the why) has been established. Having a written rationale for the homework will remind the client of how it will contribute to achieving goals (drawn from the problems and goals list) and emphasize relevance. Similarly, ensuring that the selection of homework tasks is done collaboratively and in relation to the session content should maximize the chances of it being relevant (if a patient sets their own homework, it should be easier for them to remember the why, what, when, etc.). Supplying the client with pre-printed formats for data collection, e.g., activity scheduling and diaries and a good quality file, or folder, in which to keep handouts, past homework, current homework instructions, and rationale could have a number of positive effects on homework compliance. Everything needed to complete the homework would be in one place; files and folders are more difficult to lose or overlook than single sheets of paper; seeing the file or folder would serve as a prompt to undertake homework, and seeing past homework may reinforce compliance with current tasks. Utilizing the clients existing strategies for remembering important tasks in their lives would be appropriate; they may use a diary or calendar; may have a diary or task reminder facility on their computer, or perhaps rely on family members to prompt them to do things. If the client has regular contact with other mental health professionals, they could be used as co-therapists and prompts for homework completion.

People who experience psychotic symptoms may be as able to undertake home-work tasks as well as those with any other psychological disorder (Glaser, Kazantzis, Deane, & Oade, 2000), and the important points for therapists to address are as follows:

1. The therapist should ensure there is a clear link between sessions and goals.
2. The therapist should give a clear rationale given for the homework.
3. Gains must be explicitly highlighted.
4. The therapist should identify possible obstacles and problem-solve them collaboratively.
5. The therapist should give written instructions and rationale to the client.
6. The therapist and client should agree on meaningful tasks that are achievable.

CASE EXAMPLE

Michael had a two year history of paranoid and persecutory delusions. He witnessed and experienced physical violence for most of his childhood, and used violence himself both for protection and to establish his status in a social group that rewarded aggression and violence. He began to use illicit drugs at the age of 14 and was involved in crime to finance these habits, moving from petty criminal acts to burglary and robbery. He recently served four years in a high security prison for a violent offence, having previously served a series of shorter sentences over the past eight years. Michael's world was structured and experienced through violence and his rule for survival was "hit first, later hit second and third—don't ask questions."

While in the high security prison Michael was encouraged, by another prisoner who became something of a father figure to him, to evaluate his life and think about what he wanted other than a future either spent in prison or an early violent death.

On release, two years ago, he determined to "go straight" and resumed his relationship with a previous partner and they had a son together. Michael stayed away from his usual acquaintances and their locations, refused requests to become involved in crime (he was highly sought after for his considerable skills), and stopped using drugs. He wanted to be a better partner and father, and "have a future."

These changes in behavior resulted in a very different lifestyle for him, one he had previously not known, and while he was in a stable caring relationship with a son he adored, he had no friends, no money, no employment, and no status.

Michael reported that symptoms started on withdrawal from drugs 18 months ago; he was restless, agitated, irritable, and not sleeping well. At the same time he was being pestered and taunted, and sometimes threatened, by previous acquaintances for refusing their requests. He isolated himself at home to avoid certain people and drug use and therefore had time on his hands with little to do. He had no hobbies, no family contacts, and no friends who were not involved in crime. His delusional beliefs were that he would be murdered by a group of unspecified people, but that they would kidnap him and beat him to death. He had not done anything, he believed, to warrant such retribution but he was convinced he was being observed and followed by these people, or their associates, and that it was simply a matter of time before he was "bundled into a white van and systematically beaten to death by the group."

As the treating therapist my initial thoughts on hearing the referral details centered on his suitability for therapy. Michael, in fact, engaged very well with both the therapist and the therapy; after refusing to take the medication prescribed by the psychiatrist, he was open to considering a different approach to understanding and managing his symptoms. We quickly established a problem list that included not only positive symptoms but also relationship and quality-of-life issues. The problems were reframed as goals that were broken down into short, medium and long-term categories.

Empowerment

The formulation highlighted a number of factors, described above, that contributed to the development and maintenance of psychotic symptoms, and the first homework completed by the client was a time line indicating where he had lived, who with, and what he had gained and/or learned from each period in his life. Michael suggested this task after a discussion about why and how he had reached the circumstances he now found himself in. He wanted to know "who was to blame," "what he should have done differently," and, most importantly, "how he could stop it happening again."

Michael "dealt in facts" and always needed to "know exactly what is going on," and we used this to establish the significant experiences leading up to the present. I resisted the temptation to apply his need for facts to the assumptions he was making in relation to delusional beliefs, preferring to leave that to a later stage for homework.

It seemed experiences of homework had been negative for Michael; he was not interested in any of the subjects taught in school, he had no respect for the teachers, and he learned that there were no unwanted consequences for not doing the work. In fact he was rather proud of not submitting one piece of work in his senior school.

We turned his experiences around and looked at what would motivate him to complete tasks between sessions; this took the majority of a therapy session and broadened out to identify what were the motivating factors for any of Michael's behaviors. It was Michael who made those connections and not the therapist. I was careful not be directive, he had experienced enough of that and it did not work, because I wanted him to be responsible for what he was going to do. Most of his life has been directed and shaped by others and I wanted therapy to empower him to make choices and take responsibility.

DATA COLLECTION

Michael had drawn out a broad time line and more detail of the time just prior to the emergence of psychotic symptoms was added, as were the even finer details of the maintenance cycles for mood and positive symptoms. This completed the comprehensive formulation that incorporated all the relevant experiences that had contributed to the development and maintenance of his problems and it was the basis from which we explored, puzzled over, and eventually normalized, his current situation.

At this stage, however, it was important for Michael to establish "exactly what is going on" in relation to being watched and followed. He could not say what the facts were but that he "felt it was going on." Of course he currently either did not look at people he suspected, or very occasionally, gave them "menacing stares" which startled them and caused them to drop any eye contact initially but then give recurrent glances.

Michael's tasks were to note where and when he thought he was being watched or followed; write down a description of the person/people doing it; and note what it was they were specifically doing that lead to his conclusions about them. He also kept a record of his mood state before, during, and after these episodes.

HYPOTHESIS GENERATION

The initial formulation with the specific data relating to Michael's paranoid delusions gave us a rich map to reflect on. How he got there, what had happened along they way, how long it took, where he thought he was, where he might be, where he wanted to be, how to get there, how long it would take, how he would know when he had there, who was going with him; all these questions and answers were the basis for our hypothesis generation.

Of course I had my own ideas about this, but that is all they were. What did I know about the world Michael inhabited? My role was to be an objective perspective that helped suggest other possible interpretations of his experiences. Not to tell him he was wrong in his conclusions but to put forward the idea that he may not have got it exactly right, and the only way we could know that was to generate some hypotheses and test them out. Michael's hypotheses were there in the formulation, the alternatives were yet to be added.

Acknowledgment of how distressing these experiences were for him and the feedback that it must be taking considerable effort and even bravery to start and "look the enemy in the face" were an integral part of sessions. It was important for Michael that I understood how difficult it was for him to engage in these exercises and that I did not belittle his fears.

The specific information he collected for homework lead to the following conclusions

- He could not be certain that people were observing or following him.
- His suspicious/paranoid thoughts were worse when he was anxious or angry or depressed.
- When he looked a people, without staring, they did not appear to be doing anything suspicious at all.
- Nothing bad had ever happened to him since becoming paranoid.

Michael was helped to reach these conclusions by the use of gentle questioning that encouraged him to think more broadly about possible explanations for specific incidents. Examples of questions are:

- What did you make of that?
- What else did they do?
- How did that make you feel?
- Is there any relationship between your mood and your thoughts?
- Are there any other explanations?
- What sense would a friend or relative make of this?

So if what he thought was true may not be, what other explanations could there be? Again, the gentle questioning helped him to generate the following possibilities:

1. He was completely mad.
2. The criminals who were "out to get him" were so clever that even he could not spot what they were up to.
3. The criminals were trying to drive him mad by making him distressed.
4. Maybe it was not really happening.

We looked at each of these statements and considered which looked like the most likely, not the most frightening, or compelling, or believable.

1. Well we checked his presentation against common beliefs about what constitutes madness and that did not appear to be the case.
2. Really clever people could observe and follow him without his being aware, but they had had two years in which to act on their observations. How much more did they need to know about him?
3. If they wanted to drive him mad it was not working, and would violent criminals spend that amount of time and energy to that effect?
4. "Maybe it was not really happening" was true.

Then what could be happening?

Again, using gentle questioning, Michael was encouraged to return to the formulation and look at a more compassionate, psychological explanation for his experiences.

By doing so we were able to develop a formulation that incorporated a bio-psycho-social interpretation of his situation. Michael himself said "it seems like I got it wrong big time, but when I look at it now what other sense could I have made of it at the time," "at least now I think I can see where I got it wrong and how from then on in it just had a life of its own."

His hypothesis suggested that anxiety and fear had triggered paranoid thoughts and that his own actions had served to maintain them. "If you think paranoid well then you act paranoid, don't you?"

Hypothesis Testing

This hypothesis need to be tested and Michael decided that he would work on his mood states by doing activities that he found relaxing before going outside of his home and monitor the number and intensity of paranoid thoughts he had. When he experienced a paranoid thought, he would establish the evidence for and against it and thereby come up with an accurate thought. If the hypothesis was correct, then the resulting change in mood would lower the number and intensity of the paranoid thoughts.

He also decided that he "just better settle, once and for all, if there really was any danger." So instead of only going out when it was most safe or with others or avoiding certain places, he planned to drop all his safety behaviors and behave in an opposite way, even to the point of seeking out white vans and loitering nearby them.

Michael quickly learned that his moods did indeed precipitate negative thoughts and that altering thinking improved his mood and reduced the incidence and severity of those once distressing and compelling thoughts.

Relapse Prevention/Management

Near the end of therapy a final formulation was described that incorporated what he had learned and changed about his problems. His homework in the relapse management phase was to complete another time line, but this one was to be prospective. This took the form of identifying possible obstacles or pitfalls he may encounter in life and how to avoid or problem solve them, how to look after himself both physically and psychologically, and how to measure his progress regularly.

Practical Strategies Employed in Therapy

Homework in therapy is not unlike any other type of homework and the following strategies work strategies were used by Michael, and other clients, not increase the likelihood of tasks being completed:

- The client used a folder to store all the paper documents generated in therapy.
- Explicit instructions for homework tasks were written down by the client.
- The rationale for the homework and the expected gains were also written down and kept by the client.

- Possible obstacles for the completion of tasks were generated, written down, and strategies to overcome them were devised.
- The client's partner was used to prompt his undertaking of tasks, and specific times in the week were set aside for them to be completed.

At the end of therapy Michael was largely free of paranoid thoughts, although he occasionally experienced them when he was stressed by everyday life events. He had started to "reinvent himself as a new man" and was becoming the father and partner he wanted to be. He had plans to re-train as either a mechanic or builder and was optimistic that he would not return to his previous lifestyle.

CONCLUSION

Homework is an integral part of cognitive therapy for psychosis, and it is, therefore, important to ensure that patients (and therapists) are aware of the need for work to be conducted between sessions. Homework should be agreed collaboratively between therapist and patient, and can involve collecting information, experimenting or practising skills. There are many factors that can increase the likelihood of a patient attempting their homework, such as motivation, addressing memory problems, ensuring an appropriate level of difficulty and the relevance of assignments to problems and providing a coherent rationale. It is also important to allocate sufficient time and effort to addressing such factors within therapy sessions.

REFERENCES

Addis, M. E., & Jacobson, N. S. (2000). A closer look at the treatment rationale and homework compliance in cognitive-behavioural therapy for depression. *Cognitive Therapy and Research, 24*, 313–326.

Beck, A. T., Ward, C. H., Mendelson, M., Mock, J., & Erbaugh, J. (1961). An inventory for measuring depression. *Archives of General Psychiatry, 41*, 53–63.

Beck, A. T., Rush, J. A., Shaw, B. F., & Emery, G. (1979). *Cognitive therapy of depression: A treatment manual*. New York: Guilford.

Bellack, A. S. (1986). Schizophrenia: Behaviour therapy's forgotten child. *Behaviour Therapy, 17*, 199–214.

Bentall, R. P. (1990). The syndromes and symptoms of psychosis: Or why you can't play twenty questions with the concept of schizophrenia and hope to win. In R. P. Bentall (Ed.), *Reconstructing schizophrenia*. London: Routledge.

Bentall, R. P., Kinderman, P., & Kaney, S. (1994). The self, attributional processes and abnormal beliefs: Towards a model of persecutory delusions. *Behaviour Research and Therapy, 32*, 331–341.

Birchwood, M. (2003). Pathways to emotional dysfunction in first-episode psychosis. *British Journal of Psychiatry, 182*, 373–375.

Bryant, M. J., Simons, A. D., & Thase, M. E. (1999). Therapist skill and patient variables in homework compliance: Controlling and uncontrolled variable in cognitive therapy outcome research. *Cognitive Therapy and Research, 23*, 381–399.

Burns, D. D., & Nolen-Hoeksema, S. (1991). Coping styles, homework compliance, and the effectiveness of cognitive-behavioral therapy. *Journal of Consulting and Clinical Psychology, 59*, 305–311.

Burns, D. D., Adams, R. L., & Anastopolous, A. D. (1985). The role of self-help assignments in the treatment of depression. In E. E. Beckham & W. R. Leber (Eds.), *Handbook of depression treatment, assessment, and research*. Homewood, IL: Dorsey Press.

Burns, D. D., & Spangler, D. L. (2000). Does psychotherapy homework lead to improvements in depression in cognitive therapy or does improvement lead to increased homework compliance? *Journal of Consulting and Clinical Psychology, 68*, 46–56.

Cartwright-Hatton, S., & Wells, A. (1997). Beliefs about worry and intrusions: The metacognitions questionnaire and its correlates. *Journal of Anxiety Disorders, 11*, 279–296.

Chadwick, P., & Birchwood, M. (1994). The omnipotence of voices: A cognitive approach to auditory hallucinations. *British Journal of Psychiatry, 164*, 190–201.

Chadwick, P. D., Birchwood, M. J., & Trower, P. (1996). *Cognitive therapy for delusions, voices and paranoia*. Chichester: Wiley.

Department of Health. (2001). *The mental health policy implementation guide*. London: HMSO.

Dunn, H., Morrison, A. P., & Bentall, R. P. (2002). Patients' experiences of homework tasks in cognitive behavioural therapy for psychosis: A qualitative analysis. *Clinical Psychology and Psychotherapy, 9*, 361–369.

Foa, E. B., & Kozak, M. J. (1986). Emotional processing of fear: Exposure to corrective information. *Psychological Bulletin, 99*, 20–35.

Garety, P. A., Kuipers, E., Fowler, D., Freeman, D., & Bebbington, P. E. (2001). A cognitive model of the positive symptoms of psychosis. *Psychological Medicine, 31*, 189–195.

Garety, P. A., Fowler, D., & Kuipers, E. (2000). Cognitive-behavioural therapy for medication resistant symptoms. *Schizophrenia Bulletin, 26*, 73–86.

Garland, A., & Scott, J. (2002). Using homework in therapy for depression. *Journal of Clinical Psychology, 58*, 489–498.

Glaser, N. M., Kazantzis, N., Deane, F. P., & Oades, L. G. (2000). Critical issues in using homework assignments within cognitive-behavioural therapy for schizophrenia. *Journal of Rational-Emotive & Cognitive Behavior Therapy, 18*, 247–261

Gould, R. A., Mueser, K. T., Bolton, E., Mays, V., & Goff, D. (2001). Cognitive therapy for psychosis in schizophrenia: An effect size analysis. *Schizophrenia Research, 48*, 335–342.

Gumley, A., White, C. A., & Power, K. (1999). An interacting cognitive subsystems model of relapse and the course of psychosis. *Clinical Psychology and Psychotherapy, 6*, 261–278.

Jaspers, K. (1913/1963). *General psychopathology* (trans. J. Hoenig & M. W. Hamilton, 1959). Manchester: University Press.

Kazantzis, N., Deane, F. P., & Ronan, K. R. (2000). Homework assignments in cognitive and behavioural therapy: A meta-analysis. *Clinical Psychology: Science and Practice. 7*, 189–202.

Kuipers, E., Garety, P., Fowler, D., Dunn, G., Bebbington, P., Freeman, D., et al. (1997). The London-East Anglia randomised controlled trial of cognitive-behaviour therapy for psychosis I: Effects of the treatment phase. *British Journal of Psychiatry, 171*, 319–327.

Kuipers, E., Fowler, D., Garety, P., Chisholm, D., Freeman, D., Dunn, G., et al. (1998). London-East Anglia randomised control trial of cognitive-behavioural therapy (CBT) for psychosis: III. Follow-up and economic evaluation at 18 months. *British Journal of Psychiatry, 173*, 61–68.

Mahoney, M. J. (1974). *Cognition and behaviour modification*. Cambridge, MA: Ballinger.

Milton, F., Patwa, V. K., & Hafner, R. J. (1978). Confrontation versus belief modification in persistently deluded patients. *British Journal of Medical Psychology, 51*, 387–401.

Morrison, A. P. (1998) Cognitive behaviour therapy for psychotic symptoms. In N. Tarrier, A. Wells & G. Haddock (Eds.), *Treating complex cases: A cognitive behaviour therapy approach*. Chichester: Wiley.

Morrison, A. P. (2001). The interpretation of intrusions in psychosis: An integrative cognitive approach to hallucinations and delusions. *Behavioural and Cognitive Psychotherapy, 29*, 257–276.

Morrison, A. P., French, P., Walford, L., Lewis, S. W., Kilcommons, A., Green, J., et al. (2004). A randomised controlled trial of cognitive therapy for the prevention of psychosis in people at ultra-high risk. *British Journal of Psychiatry, 185*, 291–297.

Morrison, A. P., Gumley, A. I., Schwannauer, M., Campbell, M., Gleeson, A., Griffin, E., et al. (2005). The beliefs about paranoia scale: Preliminary validation of a metacognitive approach to conceptualising paranoia. *Behavioural and Cognitive Psychotherapy, 33*, 153–164.

Morrison, A. P., Renton, J. C., Dunn, H., Williams, S., & Bentall, R. P. (2003). *Cognitive therapy for psychosis: A formulation-based approach*. London: Psychology Press.

National Institute for Clinical Excellence. (2003). *Schizophrenia: core interventions in the treatment and management of schizophrenia in primary and secondary care*. UK: NICE.

Peters, E. R., Joseph, S. A., & Garety, P. A. (1999). Measurement of delusional ideation in the normal population: Introducing the PDI (Peters et al. Delusions Inventory). *Schizophrenia Bulletin, 25*, 553–576.

Pilling, S., Bebbington, P. E., Kuipers, E., Garety, P. A., Geddes, J., Orbach, G., et al. (2002). Psychological treatments in schizophrenia: I. Meta-analysis of family intervention and cognitive behaviour therapy. *Psychological Medicine, 32*, 763–782.

Rector, N., & Beck, A. T. (2001). Cognitive behavioral therapy for schizophrenia: An empirical review. *Journal of Nervous and Mental Disease, 189*, 278–287.

Salkovskis, P. M. (2004). A NICE year for CBT and a CBT year for NICE. *Behavioural and Cognitive Psychotherapy, 32*, 129–130.

Scott, J. (2002). Cognitive therapy for clients with bipolar disorder. In A. P. Morrison (Ed.), *A casebook of cognitive therapy for psychosis*, Hove: Brunner-Routledge.

Sensky, T., Turkington, D., Kingdon, D., Scott, J. L., Scott, J., Siddle, R., et al. (2000). A randomized controlled trial of cognitive-behavioral therapy for persistent symptoms inschizophrenia resistant to medication. *Archives of General Psychiatry, 57*, 165–172.

Shelton, J. L., & Levy, R. L. (1981). *Behavioral assignments and treatment_compliance: A handbook of clinical strategies*. Champaign, IL: Research Press.

Tarrier, N., Yusupoff, L., Kinner, C., McCarthy, E., Gladhill, A., Haddock, G., et al. (1998). A randomized controlled trial of intense cognitive behaviour therapy for chronic schizophrenia. *British Medical Journal, 317*, 303–307.

Turkington, D., Kingdon, D., & Turner, T. (2002). Effectiveness of a brief cognitive-behavioural therapy intervention in the treatment of schizophrenia. *British Journal of Psychiatry, 180*, 523–527.

Worthington, E. L. Jr. (1986). Client compliance with homework directives during counselling. *Journal of Counselling Psychology, 33*, 124–130.

CHAPTER 20

SEXUAL DYSFUNCTION

Nancy Gambescia and Gerald Weeks

A BRIEF HISTORICAL PERSPECTIVE

The landmark publication of Masters and Johnson, *Human Sexual Response*, gave the field of sex therapy its major impetus in 1966. A detailed explanation of the physiology of the human sexual response cycle was offered for the first time. *Human Sexual Inadequacy* (1970), their second volume, rendered the original comprehensive account of what have become the major sexual dysfunctions and their treatments. Although the important stage of sexual desire was not included in either volume, many dysfunctions involving arousal, orgasm, and pain were described. A fundamental element of the treatment program stipulated by Masters and Johnson (1970) was the use of behavioral assignments to be performed by the couple in the privacy of their home. In fact, Masters and Johnson (1970) were one of the earliest to introduce the concept of homework as standard treatment protocol for sexual dysfunctions. Diagnostic terms and therapies have undergone revision and expansion over the years; however, homework exercises continue to be essential to the treatment of sexual dysfunctions.

Interestingly, their 1970 text did not contain any reference citations in the body. Instead, an extensive bibliography or "referral index" was incorporated at the end of the book (Masters & Johnson, 1970, p. 393). Hence, it is difficult to tell which of the cited references influenced the authors' thinking on a specific topic, particularly with respect to treatment formulation or the use of homework. Nonetheless, the therapeutic approach taken by Masters and Johnson (1970) can unquestionably be described as behavioral. In general, sexual problems were considered a result of situational or environmental factors such as faulty learning, lack of education, misinformation, negative sexual attitudes, lack of sexual experience, or unfortunate occurrences. The psychotherapeutic treatment proposed by Masters and Johnson (1970) addressed these etiologic factors through a series of systematic homework assignments that augmented the clinical work.

Just one year after the publication of *Human Sexual Inadequacy* (Masters & Johnson, 1970), Lazarus (1971) released a behavior therapy text that included a chapter on overcoming sexual inadequacy. Incremental homework assignments were recommended to reduce sexual anxiety, increase sexual performance, and enhance sexual pleasure. Other behavioral treatment approaches included correcting misconceptions, desensitization, assertiveness training, and aversion training. Many of these approaches or techniques involved the prescription for completing homework three times per week (Lazarus, 1971). Graduated homework assignments were also used by Wolpe in treating sexual problems as early as 1958 (Wolpe, 1958).

The next most influential work in sex therapy was published by Helen S. Kaplan in 1974. Her text, *The New Sex Therapy*, was similar to that of Masters and Johnson (1970); the mainstay of her approach was behavioral and the major innovation to sex therapy was a unique combination of physical homework exercises with psychotherapy (Kaplan, 1974). Her therapeutic method involved incremental behavioral homework assignments while working within a psychodynamic model. Although Kaplan (1974) recognized the importance of resolving relational conflict, the text does not demonstrate the use of this approach. In fact, she suggested that the therapist "bypass" deeper intrapsychic as well as marital problems in order to focus on the behavioral interventions and homework. Psychodynamic exploration of the individual was performed but only when the behavioral treatment was insufficient to treat the symptoms.

In a later publication, Kaplan (1979) supplemented the work of Masters and Johnson (1966, 1970) by recognizing that sexual desire was as a prerequisite for the physiological processes of arousal and orgasm. She revised the sexual response cycle by adding the psychological stage of desire at the beginning. Also, she reorganized the sexual response cycle into a triphasic model including the stages of desire, arousal, and orgasm (Kaplan, 1979). Today, hypoactive sexual desire is recognized as the most common sexual disorder (see Weeks & Gambescia, 2002).

THEORETICAL FOUNDATIONS

Each of the different approaches to managing sexual dysfunctions has a theoretical foundation that determines the techniques used in treating sexual problems. In the introductory chapter of the first *Handbook of Sex Therapy*, the theoretical foundations in various sex therapy treatment approaches were compared and contrasted (LoPiccolo & LoPiccolo, 1978). In all, seven elements were common to most sex therapy treatment approaches. The first element, mutual responsibility, is noteworthy because it emphasizes the use of homework as a mainstay in the treatment of sexual dysfunctions. Moreover, the role of the non-symptomatic partner in homework assignments is described. In order to carry out the homework, the dysfunctional partner needed to have a partner who functioned as the co-therapist at home. The notion of mutual responsibility is also significant because it represented a rudimentary approximation to what is now considered a systems approach to sex therapy. A systems approach recognizes the reciprocal nature of sexual dysfunctions; the symptom bearer is not the only person to sustain and continue the problem. The partner is an important participant in creating, maintaining, and treating the sexual dysfunction. The couple, not the individual, is the identified patient (Weeks & Hof, 1987).

The second common element in various sex therapy approaches described by LoPiccolo and LoPiccolo (1978) was about information and education. A good deal of sexual dysfunction could be traced to a lack of information or misinformation. Thus, the therapist educates and listens for misinformation in the session, and prescribes educational assignments for the couple to learn at home. The third element was attitudinal change. Negative attitudes that have been internalized from the family, including past negative sexual experiences, contribute to dysfunction. The therapist would correct these attitudes in the sessions and have the clients mentally rehearse the new beliefs at home. Again, homework exercises were a mainstay. Eliminating performance anxiety was the fourth element. Specific sexual activities and incremental homework assignments having a desensitizing effect were used. The fifth element, increasing communication and effective sexual technique, helped the couple to verbalize their sexual desires in the session and outside of the office during the assignments. The therapist would also educate the couple about sexual techniques and have them practice at home. The sixth component was called changing destructive life-styles and sex roles. This element generally had less to do with sex and more to do with the balance of power and responsibility within the couple's relationship. The final theoretical foundation, prescribed change, was the hallmark of sex therapy (LoPiccolo & LoPiccolo, 1978). This element reflected the application of successive approximations to achieve successful resolution of sexual difficulties. The in vivo desensitization occurred through homework assignments.

Annon (1976) developed another popular behavioral model of sex therapy known as PLISSIT. The use of homework assignments was an important component of this approach. The P represents permission-giving. Clients are encouraged to openly discuss and try new sexual and sensual behaviors at home. LI refers to limited information. The therapist provides information and education, including reading assignments that are conducted outside of the session and later reviewed with the therapist. SS stands for specific suggestions or assignments to be carried out at home. IT or intensive therapy occurs only if the preceding steps have failed. This part of the model is much less standardized and clear but appears to involve psychodynamic rather than behavioral approaches.

Some of the more recent texts in sex therapy, while highly regarded and detailed, have not added significantly to the theoretical foundations described above (Leiblum and Rosen, 2000). For example, Wincze and Carey (1991) use the same behaviorally oriented principles and techniques, including homework assignments. Weeks and Hof, in 1987, published the first book that expanded the range of earlier theoretical foundations. The authors and contributors to *Integrating Sex and Marital Therapy* (Weeks & Hof, 1987) argued that sex and marital therapy were inseparable. This text had the effect of producing a paradigm shift in sex therapy; the systemic concept that both partners are part of the problem or the continuation of the problem was finally being understood. Moreover, homework assignments were still viewed as an essential part of therapy although homework achieved a new meaning. The behavioral assignments were given to the couple as a couple. In the past, only one partner was receiving therapy with the partner's help.

Woody (1992) extended this line of thinking in a text about integrative systems therapy for sexual problems. Later, Weeks (1989, 1994) refined the integrative systems approach to the assessment and treatment of sexual and relational problems. Three areas of risk factors were considered: the individual partner, interactional issues, and intergenerational components of the problem. Behavioral, cognitive, and affective aspects of the sexual difficulty are addressed. This intersystemic theoretical approach was implemented in two texts on sex therapy dealing with erectile dysfunction and hypoactive sexual desire (Weeks & Gambescia, 2000, 2002). Both texts utilized systemic homework assignments during which each partner derives pleasure from the assignment while changing the dynamics of their relationship.

Treatment of relational risk factors constitutes an integral component of intersystemic sex therapy because the sexual symptom becomes imbedded in a complicated web of dyadic interactions. Particular attention is focused on each partner's view of the predicament and how it is systemically maintained. The therapist also evaluates the couple's contracts, styles of communication, conflict resolution mode, and capacity for intimacy.

The exclusive topic of the theoretical foundations of sex research and therapy was addressed in 1988 through the publication of a special issue of *The Journal of Sex Research*. Wiederman's (1998) review concluded that sex therapists need to take a multivariate view of sexual problems. This view would include the biogenic and psychogenic factors in sexual dysfunction as well as the interactive nature of a number of different models. We believe the intersystem approach implemented by Weeks and Hof (1987) and Weeks and Gambescia (2000, 2002) for treating sexual problems fulfills Wiederman's (1998) recommendation.

THE ROLE OF HOMEWORK IN TREATING SEXUAL DYSFUNCTIONS

The therapist treating sexual dysfunctions must play a directive role in session and beyond the therapy hour through the judicious use of assignments to be performed at home. Behavioral homework continues to provide the most direct and effective means of treating relational and sexual problems (Sheldon & Ackerman, 1974; L'Abate, 1986; Andolfi, 1980; Warburton and Alexander, 1985; Weeks and Treat, 2001). Moreover, homework and the couple's continued use of behavioral exercises are associated with relapse prevention of sexual dysfunctions (McCarthy, 1993).

FACILITATING HOMEWORK ASSIGNMENTS

Couples entering treatment for sexual difficulties are often fatigued by the chronic effects of the sexual dysfunction and express skepticism that the treatment can work. Frequently they have attempted to resolve the problem on their own and have failed. Typically, they have worries about the process of therapy, particularly the use of homework. The therapist must allow each partner to discuss his or her concerns. It is important to normalize their fears through explaining, for instance, that pessimism and skepticism often result from thwarted attempts to correct the situation on their own.

A critical factor in promoting successful completion of homework assignments is to recognize that one or both partners may be ambivalent, tenuous, or unequally committed to the treatment or to their investment in the relationship. Ultimately, commitment is an important factor in overcoming skepticism and pessimism and preventing relapse. Committed partners encourage each other when feeling hopeless, progress is slow, or the issues become painful and the tendency is to give up. The couple must work together, make their relationship a priority, want to solve this problem together, and reinforce each other for being responsible (McCarthy, 1997).

For many, the term homework connotes forced behavior and causes automatic resistance to the idea. It is prudent to allow opportunities to discuss reactions to the concept of homework and/or to construct alternate labels such as "tasks" or "exercises." The alliance between therapist and partners is a decisive feature in supporting compliance. Clients must view themselves as a part of a team rather than feeling coerced or controlled by the therapist. Generally, compliance is enhanced when the therapist explains the rationale for a prescription and when the partners are included in planning the assignments to be performed at home. The couple must clearly understand the relationship between the problems and goals of treatment. Unambiguous, concise, explicit instructions are more likely to promote successful completion of tasks (Strong & Claiborn, 1982). When the assignments are not completed or if the couple has a problem with any part of the task, the partners will be more likely to discuss what part of the task was difficult. Ultimately, understanding the benefits of homework assignments will promote commitment to the long-term goals of treatment. Thus, there are considerable preventative benefits to explaining cognitive interventions and behavioral assignments in the early stages of treatment (McCarthy, 2004).

RESPONSIBILITY FOR SEXUAL PLEASURE

The cognitive behavioral homework is designed to help the partners to recognize that they have control over their feelings and behavior. This objective can be accomplished through assignments that promote responsibility for sensual and sexual enjoyment. Many of our clients feel powerless with respect to owning and controlling their sexual feelings. They believe that sexual gratification is something that happens to them. Therapists must teach that sexual desire and satisfaction are created, fostered, practiced, and nurtured by the self and the partner (Weeks & Gambescia, 2002). Responsibility for one's sexual satisfaction is also encouraged through psychoeducational and cognitive methods that employ sexual fantasy to prime the psyche into a sexual state. At times, each partner must take responsibility by proactively thinking and fantasizing about sensual and sexual material. This process is often fostered through reading assignments, guided imagery, and cognitive restructuring. Additionally, the prescription for solo sexual stimulation is often used in some of the advanced homework assignments. For example, the treatment of anorgasmia, erectile dysfunction, and vaginismus often incorporates solo exploratory exercises initially, while the partner is later integrated into treatment. We discovered that the following questions can be given to the couple as homework and followed up in subsequent sessions.

- What does sexuality mean for you?
- In what ways are you a sexual/sensual being?
- In what ways do others think you are a sexual being?
- What do you like most/least about being sexual?
- What does it mean to experience sexual pleasure?
- What is good about experiencing sexual pleasure?
- What are some of the negative consequences of experiencing sexual pleasure?
- How do you feel about letting yourself feel any kind of pleasure or enjoyment?
- Which senses allow you to feel pleasure?
- Would someone in you family be upset if they knew how much pleasure you got out of life?

The Essential Components of Homework

The therapist plays an active role in recommending homework that will provide opportunities to practice and incorporate newly acquired behaviors. In this manner, homework extends the learning experience from the office to the home, augmenting the overall therapeutic benefits. Typically, sex therapy homework assignments contain four basic components: psychoeducation, bibliotherapy, communication skills, and the physical assignments.

Through psychoeducation, the therapist corrects as much misinformation as possible about sexuality in general, and about each partner's beliefs and ideas about their difficulty. The therapist must be vigilant about the effects of sexual mythology on the belief system of each partner since sexual myths underlie sexual problems and perpetuate relationship discord. Homework assignments (cognitive, behavioral, informational, etc.) reinforce the skills that are learned in session, thereby reducing anxiety and promoting sexual functioning.

As the therapist discovers areas of misinformation, there are opportunities to recommend specific readings that will provide correct information. Thus, bibliotherapy is an important component of psychoeducation and homework in general. Of course, the timing of this sort of homework recommendation is critical. It is also prudent to pace the bibliotherapy in order to insure that the material is discussed by the couple, reviewed in session, and understood. In the beginning of treatment, we often recommend books dealing with broad areas of sexual intimacy. Later, specialized recommendations are made regarding a narrow subject area specific to the sexual problem. Some of the wide-ranging texts we recommend are as follows:

Barbach, L. (1982). *For each other: Sharing sexual intimacy*. New York: Doubleday.

Comfort, A. (1994). *The new joy of sex*. New York: Crown.

Friday, N. (1998c). *My secret garden: Women's sexual fantasies*. New York: Pocket Books.

Friday, N. (1998b). *Men in love*. New York: Dell Publishing Co.

Zilbergeld, B. (1992). *The new male sexuality*. New York: Bantam.

Communication training is an essential part of any psychotherapy, but it is critical to the treatment of sexual problems. During the therapy session, effective communication techniques such as "I" statements and active listening are modeled and promoted. The partners are encouraged to make clear requests of each other and to share feelings. In addition, they are taught to communicate systemically, attending to the reciprocal and interlocking patterns of relating. Obstacles to effective communication are also noted and corrected. Clear, concise, positive rather than destructive communication patterns are correlated with marital longevity (Gottman, 1994). The couple is encouraged to practice communication skills outside of the session through homework assignments and bibliotherapy. Gottman and Silver's (1999) text is useful and popular among our clients since it clearly demonstrates patterns of adaptive communication and warns against the pitfalls of destructive, negative interactions. The ability to communicate sexual wishes, desires, and concerns will promote long-term positive results and preclude relapse of sexual problems.

Sensate Focus, a term first coined by Masters and Johnson (1970), constitutes a significant portion of the physical homework. The foremost objective of sensate focus is for each partner to become more aware of his or her own physical sensations. Also, because couples with sexual dysfunctions gradually avoid physical and sexual contact over time, the homework enables them to slowly reconnect in ways that are mutually satisfying (McCarthy, 1997). Thus, sensate focus homework serves to interrupt the cycle of avoidance of physical intimacy. The emphasis is on feeling sensual rather than sexual sensations, therefore, the homework exercises do not demand any particular performance. Sensate focus homework increases the sense of cohesion, love, caring, commitment, cooperation, and intimacy between partners. The couple may have entered therapy thinking that just one partner had a problem. Gradually, they can appreciate how the problem has impacted their relationship and how their relationship may have contributed to the difficulty. Working together as a team, with each partner taking responsibility for their part, is a powerful message regarding the strength of their relationship.

Proscribing Intercourse

Kaplan (1979) used the phrase pleasuring exercises to describe the reciprocal nature of the homework tasks; each partner gives and then receives sensual pleasure. The exercises are also incremental; small steps are taken in order to ensure success. Each step desensitizes the couple to sexual anxiety. Once the therapist assesses that the couple is ready to do homework exercises involving physical contact with each other, sensate focus can be implemented. Initially, the therapist describes the purposes of the physical homework with the partners. The progressive, non-sexual, and non-demanding nature of sensate focus is stressed. The couple must comprehend that numerous homework trials are necessary and that physical intimacy is reintroduced in small, safe, graduated increments.

The first prescription is for the couple to avoid intercourse and any activity that is sexual. The rationale for not attempting intercourse is usually self-evident; however, some need to be told that this proscription helps to create a non-demand environment that removes performance pressure and promotes relaxation. The couple must be given an opportunity to discuss how they feel about this prohibition, although most report a sense of relief. The therapist then works with the couple to devise homework exercises that involve incremental, reciprocal, sensual touch. Each step is tailored to the specific needs of the partners.

Creating a Sensual Environment

Initially, the couple is helped to take responsibility for creating an environment that is private, relaxing, and free from interruptions. We usually recommend a location outside of the bedroom, if possible. This involves planning ahead and selecting convenient times that are sufficient and unhurried, yet not too long. We emphasize that time together in a relaxed manner is the priority. Although it is intuitively obvious to the therapist that any distractions should be eliminated, it is essential to explain that telephones, beepers, cell phones, and televisions are to be removed during the homework exercises. The couple is instructed to create an environment that appeals to the senses. We often suggest pleasant music, massage oil, scented candles, comfortable temperature, comforters, etc. The use of recreational drugs is prohibited. Sometimes couples ask if it is acceptable to drink wine, and, while we do not recommend it, a small amount can promote relaxation, if desired. Next, we explain that there is a giver and a receiver for each exercise. Sometimes we flip a coin to determine who is to be the first giver, in an effort to remove anxiety about initiation. We have found it useful to have the giver also set the environment such as choosing the location and music. The couple alternates responsibility for "taking charge" of the environment.

IMPLEMENTING THE PHYSICAL HOMEWORK ASSIGNMENTS

The couple and therapist discuss a starting point for the non-demand sensual pleasuring, whether clothing is to be worn, and the specific activity that will be performed. It must be clear from the beginning that the degree and type of physical contact is under the control of the therapist; however, the couple may help in designing some of the incremental steps. For instance, we often begin by asking the partners to describe the kinds of touching that they find to be mutually enjoyable, such as cuddling or holding hands. Determine the style of touch that has been historically positive for the couple and avoid areas that have been problematic in the past. One couple was very uncomfortable with the idea of facial massage. For them it was too threatening and generated too much anxiety. This couple started with holding hands while walking and progressed to hand massage. In general, the therapist can help the couple get started by suggesting various kinds of touch involving the hands, feet, scalp, and the face. Explain that the massage is sensual and loving and not therapeutic such as a massage that one would seek from a professional.

The therapist is obliged to structure the exercises to fit the couple rather than try to fit the couple to the exercises. We recommend a progressive series of many small steps; each assignment is built upon the successes achieved in the previous attempt. The therapist provides the general structure and facilitates feedback from the couple about the activities that were successful and what they wish to do next. The feedback from each task serves as the foundation for the next exercise.

Because intercourse is proscribed, partners can appreciate sensual touch as an end in itself rather than as a means to an end. Sensual activity that is not goal oriented promotes an unhurried, relaxed, experience. Prior to treatment, many couples developed a perfunctory routine that eliminated sensual touch or foreplay, especially for the partner with the sexual dysfunction. We work with the couple to discuss and plan what kind of sensual touch they would like to include in the physical homework.

NON-DEMAND SENSUAL PLEASURING

The partners are instructed to notice what they are feeling on a moment-to-moment basis. Also, they are encouraged to discuss what was good about each experience in order to generate as many positive interactions as possible. Gottman (1994) has empirically shown that couples having happy stable relationships are those who experience the most positive interactions. These positive interactions promote confidence that the couple is moving in the right direction, competence about what they have done, and a good feeling about the relationship in general. The next directive, verbalizing what is needed in order to keep the feelings pleasurable, is considerably more difficult for many clients because they do not wish to appear selfish. This task requires a significant amount of encouragement, praise, and patience in getting started. Eventually, the therapeutic directive is to explore what kinds of sensual pleasuring the other person would like, promoting an awareness of the other's sensual needs. In addition, the couple is supported to be experimental and creative, thereby expanding the repertoire of intimate sensual behaviors.

Typically, the couple begins each therapy session by reporting about the progress of the completed homework exercises. In general, we are interested in what the couple enjoyed best and least, if the exercises went smoothly, and if there were any problems for either partner. In contemplating the next assignment, the therapist considers the hierarchy and the importance of small steps in order to ensure success. The couple is asked what they would like to do next in the way of touching. Determine if they have chosen an incremental progression that could promote closeness and reduce anxiety.

During the initial trials, the giver chooses the type of touch; however, the receiver quickly becomes an active participant directing the giver. If the giver or receiver becomes aroused, then he or she can enjoy the feelings but do nothing beyond what was previously planned. The partners should concentrate on what is feeling good. The receiver is not to worry about the giver but to focus on the self when on the receiving end. This sounds like an easy exercise to do, but we have found that couples need a lot of practice before everything begins to flow, especially the communication.

The therapist suggests that the couple directly attempt to create positive anticipation for sensual pleasuring by thinking positive thoughts, remembering past pleasant experiences together, and saying positive and affectionate things to each other during the day. Have them take note of any negative thoughts or feelings that occur during the exercise and to write them down later so they can be discussed in the next session. We recommend that the couple complete the exercise three times between sessions.

Sensual Pleasuring Involving Erotic Stimulation

The couple continues the non-genital sensual pleasuring until both are comfortably able to give each other a full body non-genital massage. This process can take from one to several weeks, depending on the steps set up in the hierarchy and the severity of the sexual problem. The therapist should never push the couple or accelerate the pace because the couple is getting impatient. Go at a pace likely to produce pleasurable experiences and success.

Gradually, genital stimulation is introduced. The goal of mutual sensual pleasuring continues to be emphasized by the therapist. The prohibition against intercourse is still in effect. However, the scope of the sensate focus exercises expands, allowing the partners to experience genital sensations in an anxiety-free environment. There should be no pressure to feel desire or to perform. Hopefully, the genital stimulation will produce some physical sexual arousal accompanied by feelings of desire although this goal is never stated.

When genital touch is introduced, the directions presented earlier are repeated. The couple is instructed to start with non-erotic sensual touching and to gradually move to breast and genital stimulation. This part of the experience is exploratory. The goal is to discover which body areas are most sensitive to sexual stimulation and to experiment with trying different ways of being touched. Remind the partners to focus on the pleasurable sensations, and to interrupt any negative cognition that may emerge. This time each partner is advised to let the genital sensations build to whatever level is desirable. The longing and arousal that accompany genital and breast stimulation may facilitate having an orgasm, but is not necessary. An orgasm is a pleasurable activity and when it can be easily achieved may have a positive effect on lowering anxiety.

Transitioning to Intercourse

The physical homework gradually evolves to include intercourse. The act of coitus, like the other forms of sensual touch, must also be non-demanding in and of itself. The couple is reminded that if a partner does not want to have intercourse, they should be free of the demand. Hopefully, the prior sensate focus exercises have taught the couple to expand their sexual repertoire allowing them to experience sex in a variety of ways. Intercourse is just one way of having sex; it is not the ultimate goal of sex. Non-demand intercourse by definition does not require any particular type of performance, thus, if intercourse is desired without orgasm, it should be acceptable.

The therapist must recognize that transitioning to intercourse may be difficult because of unrealistic expectations associated with it. Many couples believe that intercourse alone is the ultimate goal or expression of their sexuality and that unwavering sexual desire and arousal are necessary preconditions or something must be wrong. Moreover, there is a common expectation that the partners should feel a consistent synchronous desire for intercourse. These expectations are impractical and can create anxiety about not feeling enough desire or arousal for intercourse. The therapist helps the couple to accept that if a partner does not wish to have intercourse, it is fine. The couple can do something else that is pleasurable and sensual. If the couple decides to have intercourse, instruct them to focus on the sensations, positive thoughts, fantasies, and other techniques that have helped to make the experience pleasurable. Remind them that sometimes they will feel more desire and excitement, sometimes less. Repeat that the partners should not worry about what they feel. Rather, they can enjoy the fact that they are doing something that brings them closer and builds positive experiences.

HOMEWORK ASSIGNMENTS FOR SPECIFIC SEXUAL PROBLEMS

Sensual touching that is incremental and non-demanding is fundamental to sexual enjoyment. Sensate focus homework exercises continue to be a central component in the treatment of sexual dysfunctions. Additional assignments are widely used in conjunction with sensate focus for specific sexual dysfunctions. Because clinical practice tends to pave the way for research, disparities exist between commonly used treatments and actual rates of effectiveness (Heiman & Metson, 1997). In this section, homework assignments used to treat specific sexual dysfunctions are reviewed. Nonetheless, many of the commonly used prescriptions have not yet achieved a level of empirical efficacy.

DESIRE PHASE DISORDERS

Sexual desire can be conceptualized as an emotional willingness, interest, appetite, or motivation to engage in sexual activity. Sexual fantasies are the key feature of sexual desire. Hypoactive sexual desire (HSD) is marked by an absence or deficiency in sexual fantasies as well as a lack of interest in sexual activity. The psychiatric condition, HSD, causes personal or relational distress and is not a consequence of organic pathology or medication effects (APA, 1994). In general, individuals with HSD fantasize less, masturbate less, and often avoid sexual activity with a partner more than those with a healthy sexual appetite. The incidence of HSD varies according to the population studied; however, it appears to be considerably more common in women. According to Laumann, Gagnon, Michael, and Michaels (1994), 15% of men and 33% of women in an American non-clinical study reported a lack of sexual desire.

Heiman and Meston (1997) published a review of the research on empirically validated treatments for sexual dysfunctions and found that there were no controlled studies to demonstrate the effective treatment of HSD. Most of the sex therapy literature on HSD focuses on cognitive-behavioral treatment techniques that typically arise from clinically based models (Beck, 1992; Kaplan, 1979; Leiblum & Rosen, 1988; LoPiccolo & Friedman, 1988; Masters & Johnson, 1970; Winzce & Carey, 1991). Weeks and Gambescia (2002) described a systematic and comprehensive approach to treating HSD that involved the use of a myriad of techniques. Typically several etiological factors are linked together in a complex fashion and each HSD case must be considered within a unique context. We believe that psychotherapy that is to be effective with this type of intricate problem must be based on the Intersystem Approach described earlier (Weeks, 1987; Weeks & Hof, 1987; Weeks, 1995). Homework assignments, therefore, address individual, relational, and intergenerational issues related to the person's lack of sexual desire. For instance, homework for the individual partner(s) includes prescriptions regarding physical exercise, guided imagery, gradual exposure to sexual material, directed masturbation, and exposure to fantasy through bibliotherapy or selected visual materials (Bright, 2000; Friday, 1998a; Martin, 1997). Homework for the couple includes sensate focus, communicating sensual and sexual wishes and needs, and conflict resolution exercises (Barbach, 1995). Additionally, the continued use of these types of homework assignments will promote compliance and prevent relapse of the sexual symptoms, particularly with desire phase disorders (McCarthy, 1999). The couple is also directed to explore intergenerational messages regarding sexual intimacy, pleasure, and entitlement to sexual satisfaction (Hof & Berman, 1986).

Betty and Mark, in their mid-30s, sought treatment for her lack of sexual desire which began five years earlier, after the birth of their first child. The couple had delayed getting treatment until Betty had lost all desire and Mark was frustrated and angry, insisting that something be done. Using an intersystemic approach, it was apparent that the couple had difficulties in all of the three major areas. Betty had gradually become depressed over the growing emotional distance in their relationship. She had started taking Paxil, a SSRI antidepressant, and after a few weeks Betty had difficulty having orgasm. She believed that her lack of desire was a consequence of orgasm difficulty. Thus, Betty was advised to see her psychiatrist to switch to another medication, reduce the dose, or otherwise address the medication dilemma. Moreover, Betty had considerable resentment and anger toward Mark for not helping with the childcare. Mark was an ambitious man who spent every minute he could working. He believed that his contribution to the family was solely financial. Betty also noted that her marriage was turning out just like her parent's. She described her father as a life-long workaholic and her mother as chronically disappointed. To make matters worse, the couple had been avoiding any physical contact for several months.

The marital problems were addressed with weekly conjoint sessions focusing on each partner's expectations and the impact of Mark's behavior on Betty and her sexual desire. In addition, the couple was started on incremental homework when the resentment subsided. First, they were given assignments to be more positive and affectionate with each other and to have a "date" night each week. Then, they began the sensate focus exercises. Over a period of several months, many of the issues were addressed in session and through the use of homework. Eventually, the couple reported considerably more marital satisfaction and they enjoyed sex again.

AROUSAL PHASE DISORDERS

The next stage of the sexual response cycle involves the continuation of sexual desire in addition to numerous physiological responses, both genital and extragenital. As the blood supply to the genitals increases, erection take place in the male and the swelling/lubrication response occurs in the female.

Male erectile disorder is the persistent or recurrent inability to attain or to maintain an adequate erection until completion of the sexual activity causing marked personal or relational distress (APA, 1994). The incidence of erectile dysfunction (ED) increases with age, affecting 52% of men between 40 and 70 (Feldman et al. 1994). The individual with ED often suffers from low self-esteem, anxiety, and depression as a result of the ED (Althof, 2002). Frequently, this sexual dysfunction adversely affects sexual satisfaction in partners (Chevret et al., 2004); therefore, cognitive-behavioral homework assignments for the couple are essential. These assignments include sex education, communication training, nongenital pleasuring, and sensate focus exercises. Treatment for ED often incorporates the use of medications and devices in addition to psychological therapies. Typical homework for the man with ED entails cognitive techniques such as thought stopping and thought substitution as well as guided masturbation incorporating the stop–start technique. Intergenerational homework promotes discussion of learned sexual scripts, constructing sexual genograms, and bibliotherapy to correct sexual myths (Hof & Berman, 1986; Zilbergeld, 1992; DeMaria, Weeks, & Hof, 1999; Milstein & Slowinski, 1999). Behavioral homework, such as the couple's continued use of sensual and erotic scenarios, is fundamental to successful treatment and relapse prevention (McCarthy, 2001). Thus, intersystemic treatment of erectile dysfunction is a comprehensive bio-psycho-social approach which stresses the importance of homework and relapse prevention. For a more detailed discussion of the intersystemic treatment of erectile dysfunction, see Weeks and Gambescia (2000).

A 26-year-old man was referred by his urologist for treatment of situational ED. He was involved in his first serious committed relationship and he was fearful that his girlfriend would leave him if he could not correct the sexual problem. It appeared that he would think self-defeating thoughts each time they had sexual relations such as "I know I am going to lose my erection" or "she will leave me" or "I cannot function like a man." After an intersystemic assessment, he was educated about the sexual response cycle and given a reading assignment of Zilbergeld's (1992) *Male Sexuality*. Cognitive-behavioral psychotherapy addressed the negative cognitions and promoted relaxation. The physical homework involved guided masturbation that facilitated control over his erections. He was instructed to intentionally lose his erection and regain it each time before having an orgasm. Finally, with much encouragement from the therapist, his girlfriend attended a few sessions and the couple frankly discussed their concerns and plans for the future. Sensate focus exercises were performed success-fully at home. The male client kept in touch with the therapist reporting that they were engaged and continued to enjoy sexual relations 18 months post treatment.

With female sexual arousal disorder (FSAD), the desire for sexual intimacy is present yet there is a persistent or recurrent inability to attain or to maintain sexual arousal until completion of the sexual activity (APA, 1994). Sexual arousal is a com-plicated phenomenon for women (Basson, 2000, 2002). Often, organic factors such as menopause or diminished vaginal lubrication contribute to the subjective lack of arousal (Padma-Nathan, Brown, Fendel, Salem, Yeager, & Harning, 2003). However, relationship and other contextual concerns can interfere with sexual arousal as well (Basson, 2002; Rosen & Beck, 1988). Although the reported prevalence of FSAD is roughly 15% of the general population, there is little empirical evidence about effec-tive psychotherapy for this disorder (Laumann, Paik, & Rosen, 1999). Nonetheless, the same intersystemic homework assignments recommended for HSD are often em-ployed for women with inhibited sexual arousal. The woman is encouraged to explore her body and examine cognitions that may interfere with sexual pleasure. The couple's homework includes the practice of sensual awareness, genital self-exploration, sen-sate focus, and coital alignment to facilitate clitoral stimulation during coitus (Pierce, 2000).

ORGASM PHASE DISORDERS

The third phase of the sexual response cycle involves orgasm. Female orgasmic disorder is the persistent or recurrent delay in or absence of orgasm following normal sexual desire and excitement phases. The woman's age, sexual experience, and ade-quacy of sexual stimulation must be considered (APA, 1994). The reported incidence of anorgasmia in American women is 24% (Laumann et al., 1994). Homework assign-ments typically involve psychoeducation, particularly bibliotherapy (Barbach, 1975, 1982; Heiman & LoPiccolo, 1988). The woman is directed to explore her own body us-ing a mirror and to note the occurrences of negative cognitions. Thought stopping and restructuring are then practiced. Self-sensual exploration and guided masturbation with the use of a vibrator have been most successful in treating female orgasm disor-der (Heiman & Meston, 1997). Anorgasmic women often have difficulty expressing their sexual needs to a partner in order to receive adequate sexual stimulation (Kelly, Strassberg, & Turner, 2004). Consequently, it is important to incorporate the partner into treatment and to use homework assignments, such as sensate focus, to enhance verbal and nonverbal communication.

Inhibited orgasm is rare in men. It is the persistent or recurrent delay in, or absence of, orgasm following the stages of sexual desire and arousal. The clinician must take into account the person's age and the quality of physical and emotional stimulation during sexual activity (APA, 1994). As with some of the other sexual dysfunctions, there is no recognized effective treatment for inhibited orgasm in men. Nonetheless, the authors have had success using the treatment techniques suggested by Apfelbaum (2000) in which delayed ejaculation is viewed as a desire phase disorder with concomitant performance pressures. Homework assignments include cognitive-behavioral exercises that recognize that the man's sustained erections are not neces-sarily an index of sexual desire or erotic arousal. Guided masturbation and eventual partner involvement are common.

364 GAMBESCIA AND WEEKS

Premature Ejaculation (PE), also referred to as rapid ejaculation, is a very common orgasm phase disorder, particularly in younger men. The reported incidence is approximately 29% although other estimates vary considerably (Laumann, Paik, and Rosen, 1999; Laumann et al., 1994). PE is the persistent or recurrent ejaculation with minimal sexual stimulation before, on, or shortly after penetration or before the person or the partner wishes it (APA, 1994). PE is correlated with anxiety, embarrassment, depression, lack of confidence, and relationship discord (Symonds, Roblin, Hart, & Althofs, 2003). Treatment approaches and homework assignments are associated with short-term success rates of approximately 50%; conversely, relapse is common according to Symonds et al. (2003). Medications are sometimes used in the more severe cases of PE although psychological treatments are used more commonly. Homework assignments vary according to the specific presentation but in general focus on psychoeducation about the physiology of the sexual response cycle, recognition of ejaculatory inevitability, and ejaculatory control (Polonsky, 2000). The stop-start technique (Masters & Johnson, 1970) and bibliotherapy (Metz & McCarthy, 2003) are recommended for the individual client. Partner cooperation is encouraged, thus, homework exercises for the couple involve the generic cognitive-behavioral techniques described earlier such as sensate focus.

SEXUAL PAIN DISORDERS

Dyspareunia is a nonspecific term that describes recurrent, persistent painful coitus. Psychogenic dyspareunia is rare in men. In women, however, it is more common (10–15%) and can be caused by a multitude of organic, psychogenic, and mixed factors, requiring medical as well as psychological intervention to determine the origin and appropriate treatment (Laumann, et al., 1994).

Vaginismus is the recurrent, persistent involuntary spasm of the musculature of the outer third of the vagina that prevents sexual intercourse (APA, 1994). In some cases, vaginismus is the result of organic factors causing genital pain and resulting spasm. In other instances, there is no known organic etiology. In severe cases, women with this condition are unable to use a tampon, undergo a pelvic examination, or participate in sexual intercourse. The incidence of vaginismus is unknown but 15% of women attending sex therapy clinics report this problem (Spector & Carey, 1990). Presumably, some women experience vaginismus due to attempting intercourse in the absence of sexual desire or arousal; however, others report enjoyment of sexual activity, and can experience orgasm with noncoital sexual stimulation. Regardless, many women with vaginismus are emotional distressed, anxious, fearful of penetration, and view themselves as abnormal (Tugrul & Kabakci, 1997).

Despite its prevalence, there are no empirical studies investigating treatment efficacy comparing different modalities (Heiman & Meston, 1997). The standard treatment involves a cognitive-behavioral approach including in vivo desensitization homework with therapeutic processing. Gradual insertion, by the woman, of objects (such as dilators) of increasing size into the vagina in a controlled setting is very effective (Heiman & Meston, 1999). We have found that many women drop out of treatment for vaginismus unless they are told at the outset that the exercises should never involve any pain and that they are in control of the process when they are at home. Kegel homework exercises are often prescribed in order for the woman to gain control over tensing and relaxing the pubococcygeus muscles surrounding the opening of the vagina. Systematic desensitization (Leiblum, 2000) and bibliotherapy (Katz & Tabisel, 2002; Goodwin & Agronin, 1997) are also beneficial provided the woman's motivation for treatment is to increase her sexual repertoire, not simply to become pregnant. Eventually, the partner is included in the insertion training homework with the woman's guidance. Finally, sensate focus and guided coitus under conditions of the woman's control are accomplished through a series of homework exercises.

At the urging of her husband and gynecologist, a 35-year-old woman requested treatment of an unconsummated marriage of eight years. She took pleasure in sexual relations with her husband on a regular basis and was able to experience orgasm through non-coital stimulation. The couple did not struggle with marital discord; in fact they enjoyed and respected each other. He was cooperative, pleasant, and attended sessions as needed. She was mildly anxious in some situations but did not fulfill the diagnostic criteria for a psychiatric diagnosis. Her chief complaint was that she feared penetration of any sort including the use of a tampon or gynecological examination. She was from an Italian Catholic family of origin. Although there was no history of sexual abuse or latent incest, sexual information was never discussed in the home. Somehow, the client learned to be guilty and fearful about coitus. Her husband, while from a similar background, was more relaxed about the notion of sexual pleasure. Often, the couple joked about her inability to "erase the old tapes"; she could not give up faulty beliefs about sexuality that prevented her from enjoying intercourse.

Initially, the woman was given a book about sexuality to read at home and share with her husband. In session, she was educated about the anatomy and physiology of the genito-urinary system and sexual myths were corrected as they arose. She performed many genital self-examinations at home with the use of a hand mirror and reported numerous negative cognitions about her genitals. Thought stopping and thought substitution were often utilized to help her to become more accepting of her body. Kegel exercises and the eventual insertion of graduated dilators were performed at home. This process took several months as she continued to require encouragement, information, and reassurance. The in vivo desensitization, relaxation exercises, and cognitive behavioral therapy were augmented by sensate focus exercises. Eventually her husband helped to insert the dilators into her vagina under her guidance and control. Also, he enjoyed participating in the physical homework. Intercourse was finally successful, using a female superior position under her control. She laughed about how she could have been so afraid of something that did not hurt at all. The couple checks in periodically and continues to enjoy coitus five years post-treatment.

CONCLUSION

Homework assignments continue to be the most effective way of optimizing therapeutic gains in the treatment of sexual dysfunctions. Some of the treatments for sexual dysfunctions, including the use of homework, have been scientifically supported. Other treatments have been used with varying degrees of reported efficacy but have not been empirically validated. Nonetheless, sex therapy homework typically involves a combination of psychoeducation, bibliotherapy, communication skills, and physical exercises. In all cases, homework requires collaboration, judicious preparation, and careful timing in order to promote compliance and prevent relapse. The authors have found that homework that is intersystemic is most comprehensive since it addresses individual factors, relational problems, and internalized messages from the partners' families of origin.

REFERENCES

Althof, S. E. (2002). Quality of life and erectile dysfunction. *Urology*, 59, 803–810.

American Psychiatric Association. (1994). *Diagnostic and statistical manual of mental disorders* (4th ed.). Washington, DC: APA.

Andolfi, M. (1980). *Family therapy: An interactional approach*. New York: Plenum.

Annon, J. (1976). The PLISSIT model: A proposed conceptual scheme for the behavioral treatment of sexual problems. *Journal of Sex Education and Therapy, 2*, 1–15.

Apfelbaum, B. (2000). Retarded ejaculation: A much misunderstood syndrome. In Leiblum, S. & Rosen, R. (Eds.), *Principles and practice of sex therapy* (3rd ed.). New York: Guilford.

Barbach L. (1975). *For yourself: The fulfillment of female sexuality*. New York: Anchor.

Barbach, L. (1982). *For each other: Sharing sexual intimacy*. New York: Doubleday.

Barbach, L. (Ed). (1995). *Erotic interludes: Tales told by women*. New York: Plume/Penguin.

Basson, R. (2000). The female sexual response: A different model. *Journal of Sex & Marital Therapy, 26*, 51–65.

Basson, R. (2002). Are our definition of women's desire, arousal and sexual pain disorders too broad and our definition of orgasmic disorder too narrow? *Journal of Sex & Marital Therapy, 28*, 289–300.

Beck, J. G. (1992). Behavioral approaches to sexual dysfunction. In Turner, S., Calhoun, K., & Adams, H. (Eds.), *Handbook of clinical behavior therapy* (2nd ed). New York: Wiley.

Bright, S. (Ed). (2000). *Best American erotica 2000*. New York: Touchstone.

Chevret, M. Jaudinot E., Sullivan K., Marrel A., et al. (2004). Impact of erectile dysfunction (ED) on sexual life of female partners: Assessment with the index of sexual life (ISL) questionnaire. *Journal of Sex and Marital Therapy, 30*:157–172.

Comfort, A. (1994). *The new joy of sex: A gourmet guide to lovemaking in the nineties*. New York: Crown Publishing.

DeMaria, R., Weeks, G., & Hof, L. (1999). *Focused genograms: Intergenerational assessment of individuals, couples, and families*. Philadelphia: Brunner/Mazel.

Feldman, H. A., Goldstein, I., Hatzichristou, D. G., Krane, R. J., & McKinlay, J. B. (1994). Impotence and its medical and psychological correlates: results of the Massachusetts Male Aging Study. *Journal of Urology. 151*, 54–61.

Friday, N. (1998a). *Forbidden flowers: More women's sexual fantasies*. New York: Pocket.

Friday, N. (1998b). *Men in love*. New York: Dell.

Friday, N. (1998c). *My secret garden: Women's sexual fantasies*. New York.

Goodwin, A. J., & Agronin, M. (1997). *A woman's guide to overcoming sexual fear and pain*. Oakland, CA: New Harbinger.

Gottman, J. (1994). *What predicts divorce: The relationship between marital processes and marital outcomes*. Hillsdale, NJ: Lawrence Erlbaum Associates.

Gottman, J., & Silver, N. (1999). *The seven principles for making marriage work: A practical guide from the country's foremost relationship expert*. New York: Three Rivers.

Heiman, J., & LoPiccolo, J. (1988). *Becoming orgasmic: A sexual and personal growth program for women*. New York: Simon & Schuster.

Heiman, J. R., & Meston, C. M. (1997). Empirically validated treatment for sexual dysfunction. *Annual Review of Sex Research, 8*, 148–194.

Hof, L., & Berman, E. (1986). The sexual genogram. *Journal of Marital and Family Therapy, 12*, 39–47.

Katz, D., & Tabisel, R. L. (2002). *Private pain: Understanding vaginismus and dyspareunia*. Plainview, NY: Katz-Tabi Publications.

Kaplan, H. (1974). *The new sex therapy.* New York: Brunner/Mazel.

Kaplan, H. (1979). *Disorders of sexual desire and other new concepts and techniques in sex therapy.* New York: Brunner/Mazel.

Kelly, M. P., Strassberg, D., & Turner, C. (2004). Communication and associated relationship issues in female anorgasmia. *Journal of Sex and Marital Therapy, 30,* 263–276.

L'Abate, L. (1986). *Systematic family therapy*. New York: Brunner/Mazel.

Laumann, E., Gagnon, J. H., Michael, R., & Michaels, S. (1994). *The social organization of sexuality.* Chicago: University of Chicago.

Laumann, E., Paik, A., & Rosen, R. (1999). Sexual dysfunction in the United States. *Journal of the American Medical Association, 281,* 537–544.

Lazarus, A. (1971). *Behavior therapy and beyond*. New York: McGraw-Hill.

Leiblum, S., & Rosen, R. (1988). *Sexual desire disorders*. New York: Guilford.

Leiblum, S., (2000). Vaginismus: A most perplexing problem. In S. Leiblum, & R. Rosen (Eds.), *Principles and practice of sex therapy* (3rd ed.) (pp. 181–202). New York: Guilford.

LoPiccolo, J., & LoPiccolo, L. (Eds.) (1978). *Handbook of sex therapy*. New York: Plenum.

LoPiccolo, J., & Friedman, J. (1988). Broad-spectrum treatment of low sexual desire: Integration of cognitive, behavioral, and systemic therapy. In S. Leiblum and R. Rosen (Eds.), *Sexual desire disorders* (pp. 107–144), New York: Guilford.

Martin, R. (Ed). (1997). *Dark eros: Black erotic writings*. New York: St. Martin.

Masters, W. H., & Johnson, V. (1966). *Human sexual response*. Boston: Little, Brown.

Masters, W. H., & Johnson, V. (1970). *Human sexual inadequacy*. Boston: Little, Brown.

McCarthy, B. (1993). Relapse prevention strategies and techniques in sex therapy. *Journal of Sex & Marital Therapy, 19,* 142–146.

McCarthy, B. (1997). Chronic sexual dysfunction: Assessment, Intervention, and realistic expectations. *Journal of Sex Education and Therapy, 22,* 51–56.

McCarthy, B. (1999). Relapse prevention strategies and techniques for inhibited sexual desire. *Journal of Sex & Marital Therapy, 25,* 297–304.

McCarthy, B. (2001). Relapse prevention strategies and techniques with erectile dysfunction. *Journal of Sex & Marital Therapy, 27,* 1–8.

McCarthy, B. (2004). Primary prevention and secondary intervention with sexual problems and dysfunction. *Journal of Family Psychotherapy, 15,* 15–25.

Metz, M. E., & McCarthy, B. W. (2003). *Coping with premature ejaculation: How to overcome PE, please your partner and have great sex*. Oakland, CA: New Harbinger.

Milstein, R., & Slowinski, J. (1999). *The sexual male: Problems and solutions*. New York: Norton.

Padma-Nathan, H., Brown, C., Fendl, J., Salem, S., Yeager, J., & Harning, R. (2003). Efficacy and safety of topical alprostadil cream for the treatment of female sexual arousal disorder: A double-blind, multicenter, randomized, and placebo-controlled clinical trial. *Journal of Sex and marital Therapy, 29,* 329–344.

Pierce, A. P. (2000). The coital alignment technique: An overview of studies. *Journal of Sex and Marital Therapy, 26,* 257–268.

Polonsky, D. (2000). Premature ejaculation. In Leiblum, S. & Rosen, R. (Eds.), *Principles and practice of sex therapy* (3rd ed.). New York: Guilford.

Rosen, R. C., & Beck, J. G. (1988). *Patterns of sexual arousal: Psychophysiological processes and clinical applications*. New York: Guilford.

Sheldon, J., & Ackerman, J. (1974). *Homework in counseling and psychotherapy*. Springfield, IL: Charles C. Thomas.

Spector, I. P., & Carey, M. P. (1990). Incidence and prevalence of the sexual dysfunctions: A critical review of the empirical literature. *Archives of Sexual Behavior, 19,* 389–408.

Strong, S., & Claiborn, C. (1982). *Change through interaction: Social psychological processes of counseling and psychotherapy*. New York: Wiley.

Symonds, T., Roblin, D., Hart, K., & Althof, S. (2003). How does premature ejaculation impact a man's life? *Journal of Sex and Marital Therapy, 29,* 361–370.

Tugrul, C., & Kabakci, E. (1997). Vaginismus and its correlates. *Sexual and Marital Therapy, 12,* 23–34.

Warburton, J., & Alexander, J. (1985). The family therapist: What does one do? In L. L'abate (Ed.), *The handbook of family psychology and therapy, Vol.11.* (pp. 1318–1343). Homewood, Il:Dorsey.

Weeks, G. R. (1987). Systemic treatment of inhibited sexual desire. In G. Weeks & L. Hof (Eds.), *Integrating sex and marital therapy: A clinical guide* (pp.183–201). New York: Brunner/Mazel.

Weeks. G. R. (Ed.) (1989). *Treating couples: The intersystem model of the Marriage Council of Philadelphia.* New York: Brunner/Mazel.

Weeks, G. R. (1994). The intersystem model: An integrative approach to treatment. In G. Weeks & L. Hof (Eds.), *The marital-relationship therapy casebook: Theory and application of the intersystem model* (pp. 3–34). New York: Brunner/Mazel.

Weeks, G. R. (1995). Inhibited sexual desire. In G. Weeks & L. Hof (Eds.), *Integrative solutions: Treating common problems in couples therapy* (pp. 215–252). New York: Brunner/Mazel.

Weeks, G. R., & Hof, L. (Eds.) (1987). *Integrating sex and marital therapy: A clinical guide.* New York: Brunner/Mazel.

Weeks, G., & Gambescia, N. (2000). *Erectile dysfunction: Integrating couple therapy, sex therapy, and medical treatment.* New York: W. W. Norton.

Weeks, G., & Treat, S. (2001). *Couples in treatment: Techniques and approaches for effective practice* (2nd ed). Philadelphia: Brunner-Routledge.

Weeks, G., & Gambescia, N. (2002). *Hypoactive sexual desire: Integrating sex and couple therapy.* New York: W. W. Norton.

Wiederman, M. (1998). The state of theory in sex therapy. *The Journal of Sex Research, 34.* 167–174.

Wincze, J. P., & Carey, M. P. (1991). *Sexual dysfunction.* New York: Guilford.

Wolpe, J. (1958). *Psychotherapy by reciprocal inhibition.* Stanford, CA: Stanford University Press.

Woody, J. D. (1992). *Treating sexual distress: Integrative systems therapy.* Newbury Park, CA: Sage.

Zilbergeld, B. (1992). *The new male sexuality.* New York: Bantam.

CHAPTER 21

SUBSTANCE ABUSE

Timothy R. Apodaca and Peter M. Monti

An implicit goal of all psychological treatment is for clients to generalize gains made in therapy to their lives outside of treatment, and the use of between-session assignments (homework) is a logical way to help accomplish this goal. More than 30 treatment-outcome studies have examined the effects of homework assignments in psychotherapy, and a recent meta-analysis reached two main conclusions: psychotherapy involving homework assignments yields greater treatment outcomes than psychotherapy without homework; and homework compliance significantly predicts treatment outcome (Kazantis, Deane, & Ronan, 2002).

Over the past 20 years, substance abuse treatment has evolved to embrace more cognitive-behavioral approaches, and accordingly, has placed a greater emphasis on between-session assignments to enhance treatment effectiveness. In addition, changes in managed care have significantly reduced overall length and intensity of substance abuse treatment, further increasing the importance of homework assignments as a means to help clients more quickly learn and assimilate new skills from treatment. *Finally, because it often serves to raise awareness of circumstances associated with the abuse of alcohol or drugs, homework is particularly useful in the prevention of subsequent substance use following treatment.* This chapter will present several of the most widely used and empirically supported substance abuse treatments, and describe the use of homework within each treatment modality. Next, common barriers to homework compliance in substance abuse treatment will be discussed, followed by two case examples.

EMPIRICALLY SUPPORTED STRATEGIES FOR THE EFFECTIVE USE OF HOMEWORK

The following section will focus on several empirically supported models of treatment, including theoretical basis for homework within each model, and specific examples of types of homework utilized in each model. Note that some types of homework are used in multiple models. As such, these will be mentioned within the context of each model they are a part of, but will only be described initially.

Relapse Prevention

Relapse prevention is a type of cognitive-behavioral therapy that was origi-nally developed for the treatment of drinking problems, and has also been adapted for use with cocaine treatment. The strategies used in relapse prevention treatment are based on the theory that learning processes play a critical role in the develop-ment of maladaptive behavioral patterns such as substance abuse. These strategies are designed to facilitate abstinence and to provide assistance for clients who ex-perience relapse. Relapse prevention focuses on three distinct areas: anticipating and preventing relapses from occurring; coping effectively with a relapse (should one occur) in order to minimize negative consequences and to learn from the ex-perience; reducing global health risks and achieving lifestyle balance (Dimeff & Marlatt, 1995). Rather than viewing relapse as a dichotomy ("I'm sober or I've failed"), relapse prevention treatment presents relapse as a transitional process in which an initial slip or lapse may or may not return to pretreatment levels of use.

Relapse prevention treatment often begins with self-monitoring of substance use if the client is still actively using, or to monitor cravings if the client is abstinent. *Self-monitoring*, (described more fully in the section on Behavioral Self Control Training) is used to throughout relapse prevention treatment in order to identify high-risk situations (see Figure 21.1). Dimeff and Marlatt (1995) suggest having clients write a brief *autobiographical sketch* at the outset of relapse prevention treatment in order to capture self-image as both a drinker, and as an abstainer. These self-portraits are used to assist the counselor in understanding the client's motivation for changing substance use behavior, and to help identify potential barriers that might come up in the course of treatment.

Day	Time	Hours	Place	Who with	Other activities	Cost	Consequences	Standard drinks
Monday	12-1 pm 5-11 pm	7	Gill's Tavern	Paul	None	$28	Argument with wife	9
Tuesday	8-10 pm	2	Home	Family	Watching a movie	$4	None	4
Thursday	6-8 pm	2	Restaurant	Wife, Bill, Sue	Eating dinner	$6	None	3
Friday	12-1 pm 5-11 pm	7	Gill's Tavern	Paul, Mike	None	$32	Boss yelled at me, hangover	10
Sunday	3-7 pm	4	Home	Family	Cooking on grill	$6	None	3
Monday	8-11 pm	3	Bernie's Club	Tom, John	Playing pool	$15	None	5
Wednesday	9-11 pm	2	Home	Wife	Watching TV	$6	None	4
Friday	4-11 pm	7	Red Rock Bar	Mike, Tom, Paul	None	$35	Argument with Tom, hangover	11
Saturday	3-9 pm	6	Paul's house	Paul, Mike	Watching game	$10	None	6

FIGURE 21.1. Self-monitoring (example from Case Study #2).

Next, clients are asked to complete the *Inventory of Drinking Situations* (Annis, 1982; Annis, Graham, & Davis, 1987). This 100-item self-report questionnaire provides a profile of situations in which the client drank heavily in the past year. Categories included are: unpleasant emotions, physical discomfort, pleasant emotions, testing control over alcohol, urges and temptations to drink, conflict with others, pressure from others to drink, and pleasant times with others. These categories were derived from research showing that relapses often occurred in the context of such situations. The most common situational factors that have been identified as precipitating relapse to substance use are: negative emotional states, interpersonal conflict, and social pressure—these three account for approximately 75% of relapses (Cummings, Gordon, & Marlatt, 1980; Marlatt & Gordon, 1985). Once the client completes the Inventory of Drinking Situations, the relapse prevention counselor can use the information to construct a hierarchy of high-risk drinking situations specific to each client. The client is then taught coping strategies such as avoiding drinking cues such as people or places, engaging in activities such as hobbies or exercise, and substituting nonalcoholic drinks (Dimeff & Marlatt, 1995).

Once a client has stopped drinking, it is very common for him or her to experience significant urges and cravings. Homework in the form of a *craving diary* is used to assist the client in learning to manage such urges and cravings. The client is asked to track every craving or urge, and to make note of its severity and duration. Similar to a drinking diary, the craving diary is used by the client to self-monitor between sessions in order to identify urges and cravings in the moment. This is thought to be important so that the client can more successfully label and detach from the urge in order to "watch it come and go" rather than succumb to it. Clients are instructed to write on an index card any coping instructions learned in treatment, and to carry the card as a reminder between sessions.

Next, relapse prevention treatment focuses on increasing the client's awareness of thoughts and feelings, with a particular focus on anxiety, anger, or depression (because these negative states are highly associated with relapse to substance use). The client's ability to increase awareness of these states is facilitated by another homework assignment: keeping a *daily record of negative thoughts and feelings* for a period of two weeks (Dimeff & Marlatt, 1995), followed by the presentation of specific cognitive and behavioral coping strategies such as replacing negative thoughts, distraction, and relaxation training.

The final stage of relapse prevention treatment involves addressing global lifestyle management, with the belief that lifestyle imbalance can produce an ongoing sense of deprivation that serves to build up stress and increase the risk of relapse. Marlatt and Gordon (1980) have described the concept of a "should–wants ratio" to illustrate that addictive behavior can be an attempt to compensate for a sense of deprivation. Following this concept, a type of homework in relapse prevention treatment is to have clients *self-monitor all activities* for several weekdays and one typical weekend. The client is instructed to record the event and assign a numerical value to the event using a nine-point scale, with pure "should" on one end and a pure "want" on the other end of the scale. (see Figure 21.2). The client can then calculate a daily score by adding up the daily total and dividing that score by the number of events. This type of numeric can be useful in guiding the client to explore ideas to incorporate more healthy "wants" in his or her life to achieve lifestyle balance. *Completion of homework assignments serves a critical role in helping clients to maintain therapeutic gains and to prevent relapse.*

Activity   Rating

Drink coffee, read newspaper   1 2 3 4 5 6 7 8 (9)
                                  should   want

Replace headlamp bulb in car   (1) 2 3 4 5 6 7 8 9
                                  should   want

Drive kids to school   1 2 3 4 (5) 6 7 8 9
                                  should   want

Work   1 2 3 (4) 5 6 7 8 9
                                  should   want

Lunch with a friend   1 2 3 4 5 6 (7) 8 9
                                  should   want

Take out trash, recycling   (1) 2 3 4 5 6 7 8 9
                                  should   want

Pay bills   (1) 2 3 4 5 6 7 8 9
                                  should   want

Fix dinner   1 2 (3) 4 5 6 7 8 9
                                  should   want

Clean up kitchen   1 (2) 3 4 5 6 7 8 9
                                  should   want

Help kids with homework   1 2 3 4 5 6 (7) 8 9
                                  should   want

Fold laundry   1 (2) 3 4 5 6 7 8 9
                                  should   want

Conversation with spouse   1 2 3 4 5 6 7 8 (9)
                                  should   want

Prepare for tomorrow's work   1 2 (3) 4 5 6 7 8 9
                                  should   want

Bedtime reading   1 2 3 4 5 6 (7) 8 9
                                  should   want

FIGURE 21.2. Activity scale of wants and needs (sample).

COPING SKILLS TRAINING AND CUE EXPOSURE TREATMENT

Coping skills training (CST) is derived from both classical learning theory models and social learning theory models of the relationship between alcohol-related cues and relapse (Monti, Kadden, Rohsenow, Cooney, & Abrams, 2002). The underlying conceptualization is that the substance abuse client lacks important coping skills for daily living, such as an inability to regulate positive and negative mood states, and difficulty coping with social and interpersonal situations (Monti & Rohsenow, 2003).

Triggers	Thoughts	Feelings	Behavior	Short-Term Consequences	Long-Term Consequences
People Alone or with husband Places At home Events Baby crying Holidays Call from Mom	"I'm lonely." "I wish I had more family and friends near by." "I just want a break." "This is so hard."	Loneliness Sadness Anger Resentment	Drink - Wine - Gin & tonic - Usually six to nine drinks	Feel relaxed Don't think about problems as much Calmer Less anxious Feel warm	Husband upset Feel like a bad mother Shame/guilt Gaining weight Don't get out, just stay at home more Problems still there

FIGURE 21.3. Functional analysis (example from case study #1).

Empirical evidence supports the use of CST across several substances, including alcohol (Monti et al., 2001), tobacco (Abrams et al., 1992) and cocaine (Monti, Rohsenow, Michalec, Martin, & Abrams, 1997).

CST is based in part on a *functional analysis* approach that involves analyzing the antecedent and consequent events surrounding any episode of alcohol or drug use, and developing a set of alternative cognitive and behavioral coping skills to reduce the risk of use when facing similar situations (Monti et al., 1997). *Thus, this homework assignment can be helpful in preventing future substance use.* Clients are taught to create and use functional analysis to identify situations that are likely to lead to substance use, including situational factors and cognitive and emotional responses to situations. Clients are then taught alternative thoughts, feelings, and behaviors to employ in the same situation. Each functional analysis identifies: a trigger situation, thoughts and feelings in response to the situation, behavior (substance use), and positive and negative short-term and long-term consequences (see Figure 21.3).

CST then provides a variety of treatment modules in two broad areas, communication skills training and cognitive behavioral mood management training. If the client is being seen in individual treatment, then the selection of treatment modules may be linked to the client's individual functional analysis. If CST is being delivered in a group format with rolling admissions, the treatment modules would likely be standardized. Monti and Rohsenow (2003) have described and rank-ordered in importance the treatment modules as follows. For communication skills training: (1) Drink Refusal Skills, (2) Giving and Receiving Positive Feedback, (3) Giving Constructive Criticism, (4) Receiving Criticism about Drinking/Drug Use, (5) Listening Skills, (6) Conversation Skills, (7) Developing Social Support Networks, and (8) Resolving Relationship Problems. Additional communication skills modules include: Nonverbal Communication, Introduction to Assertiveness, Refusing Requests, and Receiving Criticism in General.

Regarding the mood management training component of CST, Monti and Rohsenow (2003) rank-order the modules in order of importance as: (1) Managing Urges to Drink, (2) Problem Solving, (3) Increasing Pleasant Activities, (4) Managing Negative Thinking, (5) Anger Management, (6) Seemingly Irrelevant Decisions, and (7) Planning for Emergencies. For example, the Managing Negative Thinking module can be used to introduce cognitive restructuring for modifying thoughts and affect in response to the trigger situation. Alternative behaviors to gain some of the desired positive consequences can also be explored in the Increasing Pleasant Activities module. While a full discussion of the numerous treatment modules that comprise CST is beyond the scope of this chapter, the interested reader is referred to Monti and colleagues (2002) for a full clinical description of the approach and each treatment module.

A client must develop a strong and realistic sense of confidence regarding his or her ability to successfully cope with stressful situations without drinking. This type of confidence develops over time, and is strongly aided by *practicing new coping behaviors in the natural environment*. Hence, the prescription of specific behavioral tasks between sessions is an important component of CST. Monti and colleagues (2002) propose that such homework is a powerful and necessary adjunct to coping skills and cue exposure treatment, and provide preplanned homework exercises for each session of their skills training program. Many of the homework assignments require that the client try in a real-life situation what he or she has already role-played during a treatment session. The homework assignment may also require that the client record certain facts concerning the practice (the specific behavior, the response the behavior evoked, and evaluation of performance).

Behavioral homework assignments can also be tied to specific treatment goals of the client. For example, if a client reported that drinking served an important social function, a behavioral assignment might be to have the client investigate alternative environments for socializing, such as meeting friends for coffee or going to a movie. If a client has reported smoking marijuana as a way to reduce stress, he or she may be encouraged to try exercise, yoga, or meditation in-between sessions as homework, and then report back on the result the following session. If a client has reported that drinking provides an important way of socializing, then his or her homework might be to try joining a new club, sports team, or church; or to attend a self-help meeting such as Alcoholics Anonymous or Narcotics Anonymous.

Exposure to substance-use cues has become a new core element in CST interventions (Monti et al., 2002). Learning theory suggests that repeated exposure to a cue while preventing the drinking or drug use response should result in habituation or even extinction of the conditioned response. Furthermore, the practice of applying coping skills in the presence of alcohol cues should increase both the effectiveness of these skills when the cues occur, as well as the substance abuse client's self-efficacy (Monti et al., 2002). In cue exposure treatment, the client holds and smells his or her favorite alcoholic beverage in the presence of the counselor, and is asked to monitor and report on the strength of any urges to drink. In addition, imagery can be used to generate mood states that have commonly preceded drinking for the client (Cooney, Litt, Morse, Bauer, & Gaupp, 1997). Urge-specific coping skills are then introduced. These include: delay, thinking of negative consequences of drinking, thinking of positive consequences of sobriety, alternative food or drink, alternative behaviors (Monti et al., 2002). Over the course of about six sessions the client is exposed to his or her favorite beverage and taught to utilize these coping skills as a way of coping with urges, and to experience how the urges decline with time and through the use of the new skills. While some researchers have assigned exposure homework to clients (e.g., Blakey & Baker, 1980), this is not generally recommended. Rather than encourage practice of exposure outside of sessions, it is preferable to encourage practice of the use of the new coping tools.

BEHAVIORAL SELF-CONTROL TRAINING (BCST)

Therapist-Directed BCST

Behavioral self-control training (BCST) was originally designed to assist heavy drinkers to moderate their level of drinking, and is primarily used for early-stage problem drinkers rather than individuals with a diagnosis of Alcohol Dependence. BCST typically involves eight steps: setting limits on number of drinks per day, self-monitoring of drinking behaviors, changing the rate of drinking, practicing assertiveness in refusing drinks, setting up a reward system for achievement of goals, learning about antecedents to heavy drinking, learning new coping skills, and relapse prevention (Hester, 2003). Research has shown that BCST can be either therapist-directed (Miller, Taylor, & West, 1980) or delivered using computer software (Hester & Delaney, 1997). BCST has also been shown to be effective without a therapist among drinkers who are seeking treatment, through the use of a self-help manual. Self-directed BCST will be considered in the following section.

Homework plays a central role in BCST, starting with the use of *self-monitoring*. Clients are generally given blank self-monitoring cards to fill out with each drink consumed, and asked to record information such as day, time, number of hours spent drinking, place, who the client was with, any other activities engaged in, cost of drinking, consequences, and total number of standard drinks. Self-monitoring cards are designed to help clients begin to identify patterns of drinking, and heavy drinking in particular (see Figure 21.1).

After monitoring drinking for a period of time, the client then examines the "drinking diary" to look for patterns to identify high-risk drinking situations. Some common themes tend to be: drinking with certain "drinking buddies," starting drinking earlier in the day, and drinking quickly. Clients are then encouraged to set a limit on total number of drinks per day and drinks per week. This must be a substantial reduction from what he or she is currently drinking. The client is then taught a number of *behavioral strategies* for cutting down, such as sipping (rather than gulping) drinks, alternating non-alcoholic drinks with alcoholic drinks, as well as engaging in other activities along with drinking (such as eating, playing cards or darts). Many clients in BCST may feel uncomfortable in refusing drinks, so assertiveness training and drink refusal skills are often taught, as in coping skills training.

BCST also makes use of *reward systems for success*, encouraging clients to develop tangible, individually meaningful rewards for meeting drinking goals (Hester, 2003). For example, if a client meets his or her goal of reducing the number of drinks per week from 18 to six, a reward might be the purchase of a book or a trip to the movies. The point is that the reward should be chosen by the client in order for it to have reinforcing value for meeting a drinking goal. These reward systems are implemented between-sessions, and can be considered a type of homework. Further coping skills and behavioral strategies for reducing drinking are provided for the duration of BCST, and treatment generally includes some components of relapse prevention as described above. Because BCST is often used with clients who have moderation as a treatment goal (as opposed to abstinence), relapse prevention efforts can be directed at preventing a relapse to heavy, problematic drinking.

Self-Directed BCST (Bibliotherapy)

Bibliotherapy—the provision of self-help materials to guide behavior change—will be considered as a special form of behavioral self-control training (BCST). Bibliotherapy essentially takes the treatment manual that a therapist would use in BCST and gives it to the client. Several such books have been published (e.g., Miller & Muñoz, 2005; Sanchez-Craig, 1993; Sobell & Sobell, 1993) and tested in a large number of research studies. The first report on the usefulness of bibliotherapy for problem drinking was an unexpected finding. Miller (1978) designed a study to test the relative effectiveness of aversive counterconditioning (AC), therapist-directed behavioral self-control training (BSCT), and a controlled drinking composite (CD) in order to treat self-referred and court-referred clients. Individuals in all three groups decreased their drinking, and there were no significant treatment differences between groups. At the end of treatment a subset of clients were randomly chosen to either receive or not receive a self-help manual (based on BSCT) designed to help maintain treatment gains. By 3-month follow-up, those who had received the manual showed significantly lower weekly consumption and lower peak blood alcohol concentration than those who had not received the manual. At the 3-month follow-up, the remainder of the clients were given the manual. By 12-month follow-up, all groups showed comparable, significant improvement, including the AC group that had been least improved at 3-month follow-up.

Subsequent studies by Miller and colleagues yielded further support for the efficacy of a BSCT-based self-help manual in the absence of formal treatment, for self-referred problem drinkers (Miller, Gribskov, & Mortell, 1981; Miller & Taylor, 1980; Miller, Taylor, & West, 1980), with evidence that improvements lasted up to eight years (Miller, Leckman, Delaney, & Tinkcom, 1992). A variety of other researchers have also found moderate reductions in drinking with the use of bibliotherapy among self-referred problem drinkers. In a Scottish study, Heather and colleagues (1986) recruited problem drinkers through newspaper advertisements, and mailed either a self-help manual (created by the authors, and based on behavioral principles) or an informational booklet (as a control group). The group that received the behaviorally based self-help manual showed a significantly greater reduction in drinking at 6-month follow-up than the group that received the informational booklet. The reductions in drinking observed at 6 months persisted through a 1-year follow-up (Heather, Robertson, MacPherson, Allsop, & Fulton, 1987). Each of the above studies provided a self-help manual in the context of 1–2 sessions with a counselor. In the first of two Scottish studies, Heather and colleagues asked whether receiving a self-help manual alone (with no therapist contact) would be beneficial (Heather, Whitton & Robertson, 1986) They recruited problem drinkers through newspaper advertisements, and sent via mail either a self-help manual (based on behavioral principles) or an informational booklet (as a control group). The manual group showed a significantly greater reduction in drinking at 6-month follow-up. Unexpectedly, participants in both groups sought formal treatment after receiving their materials, including 40% of those classified as high consumers (more than 100 units/week), compared with 19% of those classified as low consumers (less than 100 units/week). Reductions in drinking observed at 6 months were still evident at 1-year follow-up (Heather, Robertson, MacPherson, Allsop, & Fulton, 1980).

In an attempt to identify the "active ingredients" of bibliotherapy, Spivak, Sanchez-Craig, and Davila (1994) conducted a study comparing specific behavioral advice versus general information. Participants recruited by newspaper ads received a 15-minute session in which they were given one of three different types of materials. One group received a 30-page manual, with a cognitive-behavioral step-by-step approach to achieve abstinence or moderate drinking (similar to BCST). A second group of participants was given a two-page brochure that summarized the information from the longer manual. Finally, a third group was given a package of more general informational materials about the effects of alcohol and hazardous drinking. Fewer heavy drinking days were reported at 12 months for those receiving specific advice (manual and brochure condition) compared with nonspecific advice (general information). The authors concluded that specific behavioral methods were critical in order to successfully maintain drinking reductions.

A recent study by Cunningham and colleagues (2001) found that a short (16-page) booklet resulted in significantly lower levels of client drinking six months later (compared with those who did not receive the booklet). The short booklet provided to clients by these researchers contained many elements from BSCT, including: self-monitoring (drinking diary), a decisional balance exercise, setting a drinking goal, specific behavioral strategies to reduce or quit drinking, as well as a list of further community resources.

In sum, self-directed BCST—homework without therapy—has been shown to be of benefit among self-referred problem drinkers. It should be noted, however, that studies examining the use of bibliotherapy with heavy drinkers identified through screening (those who are not seeking alcohol treatment) have produced less encouraging results. [For a complete review of bibliotherapy for alcohol problems, see Apodaca and Miller (2003)].

HOMEWORK IN COUPLES AND FAMILY TREATMENT FOR SUBSTANCE ABUSE

CRA/CRAFT

The Community Reinforcement Approach (CRA) is a broad spectrum behavioral treatment approach that attempts to bring about change in a wide range of life areas (e.g., family, work, social/recreational) in order to treat substance use disorders (Meyers & Smith, 1995). Because of the importance given to significant others (SOs) in the client's life, CRA will be considered along with couples treatment in the following section. CRA attempts to rearrange environmental contingencies such that non-use is more rewarding than substance use, thus blending operant conditioning with a social systems approach to use a substance abuse client's entire community to bring about lifestyle change.

One way in which significant others are involved in CRA homework is through the use of disulfiram (Antabuse), a medication to deter the use of alcohol. Disulfiram causes a client to become ill upon consuming alcohol, and has been shown to be effective for clients who have experienced numerous treatment failures. However, the utility of disulfiram is limited by a client's willingness to take it as prescribed (Fuller & Roth, 1979). Hence, CRA seeks to enlist the support of a spouse or other significant person in the client's life to enhance medication compliance through a *medication contract*. This is designed to be done in a supportive, rather than a punitive, fashion. The couple agrees to have the SO monitor the taking of the medication, and decides upon a certain time of day when this will occur when the couple is usually together, such as breakfast or bedtime. The SO is instructed to give a supportive statement, such as "I really appreciate that you are taking the disulfiram. I care about you, and I'm glad that you are trying to stop drinking." The client takes the medication, and then thanks the SO for his or her supportiveness. Because the medication is designed to be taken every day, this is a form of behavioral homework that must be done daily on the part of both the SO and the client. CRA also makes use of Functional Analysis, as described earlier.

A variation on CRA called CRAFT (Community Reinforcement Approach and Family Training) has been described as a method that utilizes a significant other to engage a substance abuser into treatment. In CRAFT, a counselor works directly with a concerned SO, and trains him or her to positively reinforce sober behavior and withhold reinforcement for substance using behavior with the goal of getting the drug-abusing SO to enter treatment. These methods are discussed and role-played during therapy sessions, and then carried out as a form of homework between sessions by the SO. This approach has been successful with alcohol as well as other types substance abuse (Smith, Meyers, & Miller, 2001).

Behavioral Marital Therapy

Behavioral marital therapy (BMT) seeks to both bring about changes in drinking and to improve marriage and family relationships that have likely been damaged by drinking (O'Farrell & Fals-Stewart, 2003). BMT usually takes place over the course of 10–20 highly structured therapy sessions, each of which includes a review of homework from the previous session, introduction of new material, and assigning of new homework. One of the first homework assignments given is a *Daily Sobriety Contract*, which includes the client's intention to not drink or use drugs that day, along with a spousal expression of support. The spouse also records performance of the daily contract on a calendar given to him or her by the counselor. Other things which can be recorded on the Sobriety Contract include attendance of 12-step meetings or completion of urine drug screens. If warranted, the use of disulfiram, similar to that described above as a component of CRA, can also be added to the sobriety contract (O'Farrell & Fals-Stewart, 2000).

A type of homework specific to the spouse in the context of BMT is alcohol-focused spouse involvement, developed by McCrady and colleagues (1986). This method teaches specific skills to help the spouse reinforce abstinence in the drinking partner, and includes issues such as decreasing behaviors that trigger drinking, allowing the drinker to experience naturally occurring adverse consequences of drinking, responding to help the drinker in drink refusal situations, and to assertively discuss concerns about drinking-related situations. These are all skills that can be practiced in the course of treatment, and then practiced as a form of homework between sessions.

Name: <u>Bill</u>   Name of Partner: <u>Susan</u>

Day   Date   Pleasing Behavior

Day	Date	Pleasing Behavior
Monday	8/5	Made my favorite dinner.
Tuesday	8/6	Told me she appreciated me.
Wednesday	8/7	Rubbed my shoulders when I had a bad headache.
Thursday	8/9	Was patient with my grumpy morning mood.
Friday	8/10	Told me she loved me.
Saturday	8/11	Got up with the kids so I could sleep in.
Sunday	8/12	Encouraged me to go for a walk when I needed some time alone.

FIGURE 21.4. Catch your partner doing something nice (sample).

There is substantial overlap between these techniques and those used in CRAFT, described above.

Once the client has begun to abstain from drinking, BMT begins to focus on improving marital and family relationships. The family may lack communication skills and mutual positive feelings, which if not addressed, may trigger a relapse to drinking (O'Farrell & Fals-Stewart, 2003). The general sequence of learning these new skills involves therapist instruction and modeling, couple practice and role-play during session, assignment and review of homework. In order to *increase pleasing behaviors* between the couple, O'Farrell (1995) has described an exercise that utilizes a worksheet entitled, "Catch Your Partner Doing Something Nice" (see Figure 21.4). This encourages each partner to notice any caring behaviors that occur throughout each day or each week. These items are then read during the next session and each spouse practices acknowledging caring behaviors from the other partner. An additional assignment can include planning a "Caring Day," wherein each partner plans ahead to surprise their spouse with a day when they do special things to show they care. Finally, couples are guided in planning and doing shared rewarding activities. This can be started by assigning homework wherein each spouse makes a list of possible activities that involves both partners, and may also involve children or other adults. Couples are then encouraged to select one of the activities and try it before the next session. Communication skills training and problem-solving skills training are incorporated in the treatment to assist partners in negotiation and compromise (O'Farrell & Fals-Stewart, 2003). *Increasing pleasant interactions is designed to help prevent a return to drinking.*

McCrady and colleagues (1996) have described other ways in which a significant other can be utilized in treatment. In addition to having clients self-record attendance at self-help groups such as Alcoholics Anonymous, behavioral marital therapy sometimes has the SO record estimates of client drinking, along with attendance at Alanon by the SO and AA by the client.

OVERVIEW OF COMMON BARRIERS

While little has been written about barriers to homework compliance specific to the field of substance abuse, studies from other areas of psychotherapy are informative in considering this issue. Detweiler and Whisman (1999) have described therapist factors, task factors, and client factors that may affect homework compliance. Therapist factors include issues such as unrealistic goal setting by the therapist, and a lack of positive reinforcement for homework completion. Specific therapist behaviors—confronting and teaching—have been found to be significantly related to client noncompliance (Scheel, Hanson, & Razzhavaikina, 2004). Task factors would include issues such as a mismatch between client's abilities and difficulty of the assignment, while client factors include characteristics such as age, gender, and lack of commitment by the client (Detweiler & Whisman, 1999). Higher levels of client motivation for treatment are associated with greater homework compliance (Helbig & Fehm, 2004).

Monti and colleagues (2002) have offered a number of suggestions to address these factors in order to foster homework compliance in substance abuse treatment. First, the term "homework" should be avoided, as it may have negative connotations for some clients (between-session assignments can be referred to as "practice exercises" instead). Additionally, the rationale and potential benefit to the client should be presented along with a clear description of what is expected. Clients can be asked to identify potential barriers in completing the assignment, and ways to overcome the barriers can be generated by both client and therapist. To further increase the likelihood the assignment is completed, the therapist should ask the client to identify a specific day and time to complete the homework assignment. Finally, therapists should review the homework from the previous session at the beginning of each new session in order to build the expectation that homework is an important part of treatment. Praise should be offered to all approximations to homework compliance in order to reinforce the behavior. Annis and Davis (1991) have suggested that in the early phases of treatment, it is critical that homework be designed for the client to build confidence. In other words, assigning homework tasks that are easily accomplished early on and slowly get more difficult in the course of treatment can boost a client's sense of self-efficacy to continue and may enhance the likelihood of later homework compliance.

Client motivation is a significant consideration in substance abuse treatment in general, and should be considered regarding homework compliance. An important conceptual framework for understanding client motivation and noncompliance with homework is the transtheoretical model of change developed by Prochaska and DiClimente (1986), which proposes that individuals pass through a series of stages when making a change in addictive behavior. There are six proposed stages: precontemplation, contemplation, preparation, action, relapse, and maintenance. Individuals in the precontemplation stage are unaware of a problem with their behavior and report no intention to change. The contemplation stage is marked by an awareness that a problem exists along with thoughts about making a change. The preparation stage includes individuals who are ready to change in both attitude and behavior, and may have begun small steps to change the behavior. In the action stage, an individual is actively modifying or change behavior, and is ready to learn new skills. The relapse stage involves a temporary return to substance use, while the maintenance stage is characterized by a sustaining of changes that have been accomplished and continued use of behavior change strategies.

Most homework assignments used in substance abuse treatment are designed for an individual in the action stage. However, if a client is in precontemplation or contemplation, an action-oriented homework assignment would not be a good match to client stage, and would have a higher likelihood of noncompliance (Connors, Donovan, & DiClemente, 2001). This can be addressed through the use of motivational interviewing, which is a client-centered, directive method for enhancing intrinsic motivation to change by exploring and resolving ambivalence (Miller & Rollnick, 2002). Motivational interviewing (MI) has as a central assumption that ambivalence about substance use and change is normal, and utilizes both therapeutic techniques and an overall therapeutic style to assist clients resolve ambivalence and increase motivation for change. Specific techniques include the use of open questions, affirmations, reflective listening, and summaries with the primary goal of highlighting the discrepancy between a client's goals or values and substance use behavior. In addition to these techniques, MI emphasizes a therapeutic style that is best characterized as one that respects client autonomy, is a collaboration between client and clinician, and is characterized by the clinician eliciting a client's internal motivation for change rather than seeking to "impose" motivation from external sources (Miller & Rollnick, 2002). A large body of literature supports the utility of motivational interviewing for substance use disorders (Burke, Menchola, & Arkowitz, 2003; Dunn, Deroo, & Rivara, 2001).

CASE STUDIES

In order to illustrate how different types of homework can be utilized in substance abuse treatment, two case studies will be presented. The first case represents a patient who received treatment using the Coping Skills Training model presented above. The second case study illustrates the use of homework through a Behavioral Self-Control Training approach, augmented by the use of Motivational Interviewing.

CASE STUDY #1

Kathy was a 26-year-old married woman who presented for treatment at a day hospital program at a private psychiatric facility. She sought treatment at the urging of her family, following a steady increase in her drinking over the course of the prior year. The treatment program was based on group-delivered Coping Skills Training, described earlier, and was augmented by daily individual sessions with a therapist. The group treatment included sessions on: functional analysis, problem solving, developing social support networks, assertiveness training, drink refusal skills, managing negative thinking, increasing pleasant activities, anger management, and relapse prevention.

On her first day in the program, Kathy met with her individual therapist and provided some background. Approximately a year and a half prior to treatment, Kathy had relocated to a different part of the country as a result of her husband's job. She reported that within the past year, she had given birth to her first child, and had found the combination of a move to a different part of the country and adjustment to parenthood to be quite stressful. Kathy had been abstinent throughout her pregnancy, and reported being a social drinker prior to that. However, since the birth of her daughter, her drinking had steadily increased to the point where she was drinking six to nine drinks daily upon admission to the treatment program. At the end of the first day's individual session, Kathy was asked to complete a functional analysis as homework.

At the beginning of the following day, Kathy met with her individual therapist and was asked about the homework. She reported that she had been unable to complete it, due to the fact that from the moment she arrived home she was busy with childcare responsibilities. Because many of the components of the day treatment program were linked to the functional analysis, her therapist asked if she would be willing to complete it in the context of a group session later in the day, and she agreed. With the assistance of the group leader, Kathy completed the functional analysis on a dry-erase board used in the group therapy sessions (see Figure 21.3). This exercise was enlightening for Kathy, as it revealed some of the internal processes that preceded her decision to drink. In particular, she struggled with feelings of loneliness, sadness, and anger resulting from her family's recent move. She identified thoughts that led her to drink as a way of alleviating the emotional discomfort that she was feeling. Within the context of the coping skills training she was receiving, this homework assignment highlighted areas to be targeted in her treatment. Treatment modules on anger management, managing negative thinking, and increasing pleasant activities would be important for her to achieve abstinence.

In her next individual session, Kathy and her therapist discussed ideas about how to meet her needs of relaxation and socialization without drinking. The therapist encouraged Kathy to increase the pleasant activities in her life not associated with drinking, according to guidelines from Monti and colleagues (2002). The main idea for these activities was that they do not depend on others, and have some physical, mental, or spiritual value for the client. Ideally, 30–60 minutes are set aside each day for these pleasant activities in order to achieve a balance between "wants" and "shoulds," with the idea that the more fun things a person has to do, the less he or she will miss alcohol or use alcohol to create fun. For homework, her therapist asked her to complete the "Increasing Pleasant Activities" worksheet at home (see Figure 21.5), and to bring those ideas the next day. She brought in a list of ideas, including: starting to take a yoga class or exercise class, joining a book club, and going out to dinner or dancing with her husband. Upon exploring which of these she might like to try first, Kathy expressed hesitation about approaching her husband about these activities. She was concerned that he would not want to leave their young daughter with a babysitter. Reminding Kathy of the assertiveness training skills presented in a group session earlier in the week, the therapist engaged her in a role-play activity designed to give her practice at discussing the issue with her husband. After the role-play, her confidence was somewhat higher, and she agreed to speak to her husband that evening as a behavioral homework assignment. The next day she reported that the conversation had gone well, and that her husband had been more than willing to help find a babysitter in order for the two of them to go out more often, and had encouraged her to take a yoga class in the evening after he came home from work when he could take care of their child. She also decided to start walking several times a week, and to begin meeting a friend for coffee once a week.

Finally, Kathy reported that she had missed out on going to church since she and her husband had moved, but that she had neglected to look for a new church

Write down your own personal "menu" of pleasant activities that are not associated with substance use.

Reading _____

Walking _____

Seeing movies _____

Going out dancing with husband _____

Going out to dinner _____

Yoga _____

Having coffee with a friend _____

Attending church _____

Listening to music _____

Talking on the phone _____

Now, schedule 30–60 minutes of "personal time" every day to engage in these activities. Set aside the time, but do not decide on the activity until the time comes. Select the activity from the menu above.

	Appointments for personal time	After your personal time, record the activity you decided to do
Monday	9:30–10:00 a.m.	walking
Tuesday	9:30–10:00 a.m.	walking
Wednesday	6:30–8:00 p.m.	yoga class
Thursday	2:00–3:00 p.m.	reading
Friday	9:30–10:00 a.m.	walking
Saturday	3:00–4:00 p.m.	coffee with friend
Sunday	10:00–11:30 a.m.	attending church

FIGURE 21.5. Increasing pleasant activities (example from case study #1).

because of the baby and the stress of relocating. She decided she and her husband would try out a new church each Sunday as a pleasant activity, and a way to reconnect spiritually and seek a larger community. After successfully completing the five-day partial hospital treatment program, Kathy was referred to an outpatient therapist who continued to follow her progress.

CASE STUDY #2

Alex was a 38-year-old male referred to outpatient treatment following an incident where he showed up at his construction job intoxicated. He reported drinking most days, but not every day, averaging about five or six drinks per day. He also tended to drink more heavily on the weekends (8–12 drinks) when socializing with friends. He was uncertain about entering treatment, voicing several times during his initial interview, "I'm not an alcoholic." The therapist utilized motivational interviewing techniques (Miller & Rollnick, 2002) to assist Alex in exploring his ambivalence, rather than confronting any resistance head-on. Alex was invited to explore the pros and cons of his alcohol use. This type of decisional balance exercise is derived from

	My drinking as it is now	**Cutting down or quitting drinking**
Benefits of:	Tastes good Have fun with friends Relaxing	Fewer problems with boss More control over my life Get more support from family Health might improve Probably save money
Costs of:	Kind of expensive Might lose job Family continue to worry/complain Keep having money problems Could get DUI	Feel left out at parties May get bored No way to "unwind"

FIGURE 21.6. Decisional balance (example from case study #2).

the work of Janis and Mann (1977), who viewed decision-making as a rational process that involves weighing the positive aspects and negative aspects of any behavior. After some initial surprise that his substance abuse counselor was asking him about "the good things" about drinking, Alex identified that he enjoyed the taste of beer, and that drinking was a relaxing way for him to unwind and have fun with friends. When asked about the "not-so-good" things about his current drinking, Alex mentioned several, including the financial cost, being at risk for losing his job, fear of getting arrested for driving under the influence, and some conflict with his family. Next, Alex was invited to consider the potential costs and benefits of making a change in his drinking, either cutting down how much he drank, or quitting altogether. He said that changing his drinking would likely have a number of benefits, including fewer problems with his boss, getting more support from his family, possibly improving his health, saving some money, and generally feeling a bit more in control over his life. Alex also mentioned a number of concerns, or potential "costs" of making a change, including concern about feeling left out at parties if he didn't drink, and a fear that he would be bored with no way to relax or unwind (see Figure 21.6).

Note: A decisional balance exercise can also be completed as homework between sessions: When a client completes this exercise, he or she may be surprised by the number and strength of the perceived pros and cons, where more positive benefits of behavior change paired with more negative costs of continued substance use is associated with greater readiness to change behavior. More negative costs of behavior change and more positive benefits of continued substance use is associated with less willingness to consider change (Connors, Donovan, & DiClemente, 2001). When completed between sessions by the client, this exercise can serve to alert the therapist whether attention should be given to enhancing client motivation for change.

Continuing to use motivational interviewing strategies, the counselor next asked Alex about his goals for himself. He stated his short-term goals were to improve his situation at work and improve his relationship with his wife. His longer-term goals were to purchase a house for his family, and to eventually start his own contracting company. Next, the counselor asked Alex how his current level of drinking fit in with those goals, to which Alex stated, "It doesn't." At that point Alex decided it was time to make a change in his drinking. He said that he would like to cut down, but not quit drinking completely, so the counselor proceeded with behavioral self-control training. For homework at the end of his first session, Alex was asked to monitor and record his drinking for two weeks (see Figure 21.1).

At the next session, the counselor and Alex reviewed the drinking diary, and together identified several circumstances common to the times when his drinking caused problems. First, on days when he drank any alcohol with his lunch, he tended to drink too much that day. Second, he tended to not be doing any activity other than drinking. Finally, Alex noticed that his drinking often caused problems when he was drinking with his friend Paul. There were also several circumstances when Alex seemed to be able to drink and not experience problems: when he began drinking later in the evening, when he was not with Paul, and when he was doing some activity in addition to drinking. After setting a daily maximum of four drinks, Alex was given the choice to pick which homework assignment to try for a week: avoid drinking with Paul at all for one week, wait to begin drinking until after 7:00 p.m. on all drinking days, or engaging in some form of additional activity each time he drank. Alex thought it would be difficult to avoid Paul without angering his friend, so he chose the second two strategies for homework.

The following week, Alex reported that he had been able to engage in activities each time he drank by choosing to go somewhere he could play pool with friends rather than going to the tavern where there was nothing to do besides drink. He was mostly successful at waiting to begin drinking until after 7:00 p.m., with the exception of a Sunday afternoon when he drank during the afternoon while watching a football game. In addition, Alex reported that he had only drank with his friend Paul one time during the week, and that he had ended up drinking more than he wanted to (eight drinks), and had woken up with a hangover the next day. Despite being at the pool hall that night, Alex had found it difficult to resist heavy drinking, because Paul had bought several rounds of "shots" to go along with the beer they had been drinking. Alex decided to try going a week not drinking with Paul at all, stating he was disappointed that he had gone over his daily limit on that occasion.

Alex's treatment proceeded with the therapist teaching a number of behavior strategies to avoid heavy drinking, including sipping his drinks, and alternating non-alcoholic drinks with alcoholic drinks (e.g., having a soft drink in-between beers). In the course of eight weeks of outpatient Behavioral Self-Control Training, Alex began to notice that he felt better physically as he was drinking less, which encouraged him to cut down further by choosing to have more non-drinking nights each week. His situation with his boss began to improve as Alex began showing up on time clear-headed each day, and had no further incidents of coming back to work after drinking at lunchtime. By the time he left treatment, Alex was drinking about three nights each week, with a maximum daily limit of four drinks, and a maximum weekly limit of twelve drinks.

SUMMARY

The general literature on psychotherapy has shown that involving homework assignments yields greater treatment outcomes than psychotherapy without homework (Kazantis, Deane, & Ronan, 2002). Within the more specialized field of substance abuse treatment, factors such as a decrease in the average number of treatment sessions, along with an increase in the use of cognitive-behavioral approaches, have resulted in the prominent use of homework as a critical aspect of many substance abuse treatment modalities. This chapter has reviewed the use of homework *both to enhance treatment gains and to prevent relapse* in the context of several of the most empirically supported substance abuse treatments, including relapse prevention, coping skills training, behavioral self-control training, and couples/family therapy.

Perhaps the most common barrier to homework compliance in substance abuse treatment is client motivation. Fortunately, the past 15 years have witnessed the development and widespread implementation of motivational interviewing, which is both a counseling style and a set of techniques designed to assist clients in resolving ambivalence about treatment and enhance motivation. While motivational interviewing is certainly not the answer to all issues regarding homework compliance, it does provide a powerful tool by which clinicians can deal with this common problem.

In sum, homework is a powerful adjunct to substance abuse treatment, and offers the distinct advantage of allowing clients to practice newly acquired skills in real-life problem situations. This type of real-world practice increases the likelihood that behaviors learned in treatment will more effectively generalize to clients' everyday lives.

Acknowledgments

Preparation of this chapter was supported in part by grant T32-AA007459 from the National Institute on Alcohol Abuse and Alcoholism. The authors wish to thank Tracey Rocha for her assistance with the literature review for this chapter.

REFERENCES

Abrams, D. B., Rohsenow, D. J., Niara, R. S., Pedraza, M., Longabaugh, R., Beattie, M., et al. (1992). Smoking and treatment outcome for alcoholics: Effects on coping skills, urge to drink, and drinking rates. *Behavior Therapy, 23*, 283–297.

Annis, H. M. (1982). *Inventory of drinking situations (IDS-100).* Toronto, Canada: Addiction Research Foundation of Ontario.

Annis, H., & Davis, C. S. (1991). Relapse prevention. *Alcohol Health & Research World, 15*, 204–213.

Annis, H. M., Graham, J. M., & Davis, D. S. (1987). *Inventory of drinking situations (IDS) user's guide.* Toronto, Canada: Addiction Research Foundation of Ontario.

Apodaca, T. R., & Miller, W. R. (2003). A meta-analysis of the effectiveness of bibliotherapy for alcohol problems. *Journal of Clinical Psychology, 59*, 289–304.

Blakey, R., & Baker, R. (1980). An exposure approach to alcohol abuse. *Behaviour Research and Therapy, 18*, 319–325.

Burke, B. L., Arkowitz, H., & Menchola, M. (2003). The efficacy of motivational interviewing: A meta-analysis of controlled clinical trials. *Journal of Consulting and Clinical Psychology, 71*, 843–861.

Connors, G. J., Donovan, D. M., & DiClemente, C. C. (2001). *Substance abuse treatment and the stages of change: Selecting and planning interventions.* New York: Guilford.

Cooney, N. L., Litt, M. D., Morse, P. A., Bauer, L. O., & Gaupp, L. (1997). Alcohol cue reactivity, negative mood reactivity, and relapse in treated alcoholic men. *Journal of Abnormal Psychology, 106*, 243–250.

Cummings, C., Gordon, J. R., & Marlatt, G. A. (1980). Relapse: Strategies of prevention and prediction. In W. R. Miller (Ed.), *The addictive behaviors* (pp. 291–321). Oxford, England: Pergamon.

Cunningham, J. A., Sdao-Jarvie, K., Koski-Jannes, A., & Breslin, F. C. (2001). Using self-help materials to motivate change at assessment for alcohol treatment. *Journal of Substance Abuse Treatment, 20,* 301–304.

Detweiler, J. B. and Whisman, M. A. (1999). The role of homework assignments in cognitive therapy for depression: Potential methods for enhancing adherence. *Clinical Psychology: Science and Practice, 6,* 267–282.

Dimeff, L. A., & Marlatt, G. A. (1995). Relapse prevention. In R. K. Hester and W. R. Miller (Eds.), *Handbook of alcoholism treatment approaches: Effective alternatives* (2nd ed.) (pp. 188–212). Boston: Allyn and Bacon.

Dunn, C., Deroo, L., & Rivara, F. P. (2001). The use of brief interventions adapted from motivational interviewing across behavioral domains: A systematic review. *Addiction, 96,* 1725–1742.

Fuller, R. K., & Roth, H. P. (1979). Disulfiram for the treatment of alcoholism. An evaluation in 128 men. *Annals of Internal Medicine, 90,* 901–904.

Heather, N., Robertson, I., MacPherson, B., Allsop, S., & Fulton, A. (1987). Effectiveness of a controlled drinking self-help manual: One-year follow-up results. *British Journal of Clinical Psychology, 26,* 279–287.

Heather, N., Whitton, B., & Robertson, I. (1986). Evaluation of a self-help manual for media-recruited problem drinkers: Six month follow-up results. *British Journal of Clinical Psychology, 25,* 19–34.

Helbig, S. and Fehm, L. (2004) Problems with homework in CBT: Rare exception or rather frequent? *Behavioural and Cognitive Psychotherapy, 32,* 291–301.

Hester, R. K. (2003). Behavioral self-control training. In R. K. Hester and W. R. Miller (Eds.), *Handbook of alcoholism treatment approaches: Effective alternatives* (3rd ed.) (pp. 152–164). Boston: Allyn and Bacon.

Hester, R. K., & Delaney, H. D. (1997). Behavioral Self-Control Program for Windows: Results of a controlled clinical trail. *Journal of Consulting and Clinical Psychology, 65,* 686–693.

Janis, I. L., & Mann, L. (1997). *Decision making: A psychological analysis of conflict, choice, and commitment.* New York: Free Press.

Kazantis, N., Deane, F. P., & Ronan, K. R. (2000). Homework assignments in cognitive and behavioral therapy: A meta-analysis. *Clinical Psychology: Science and Practice, 7,* 189–202.

Marlatt, G. A. & Gordon, J. R. (1985). *Relapse prevention.* New York: Guilford.

Marlatt, G. A., & Gordon, J. R. (1980). Relapse prevention: Future directions. In M. Gossop (Ed.), *Relapse and addictive behavior.* London: Tavistock/Routledge.

McCrady, B. S., Noel, N. E., Abrams, D. B., Stout, R. L., Nelson, H. F., & Hay, W. N. (1986). Comparative effectiveness of three types of spouse involvement in outpatient behavioral alcoholism treatment. *Journal of Studies on Alcohol, 47,* 459–467.

McCrady, B. S., Epstein, E. E., Hirsch, L. S. (1996). Issues in the implementation of randomized clinical trial that includes alcoholics anonymous: studying AA-related behaviors during treatment. *Journal of Studies on Alcohol, 57,* 604–612.

Meyers, R. J., & Smith, J. E. (1995). *Clinical guide to alcohol treatment: The community reinforcement approach.* New York: Guilford.

Miller, W. R. (1978). Behavioral treatment of problem drinkers: A comparative outcome study of three controlled drinking therapies. *Journal of Consulting and Clinical Psychology, 46,* 74–86.

Miller, W. R., Gribskov, C. J., & Mortell, R. L. (1981). Effectiveness of a self-control manual for problem drinkers with and without therapist contact. *International Journal of the Addictions, 16,* 1247–1254.

Miller, W. R., Leckman, A. L., Delaney, H. D., & Tinkcom, M. (1992). Long-term follow-up of behavioral self-control training. *Journal of Studies on Alcohol, 53*, 249–261.

Miller, W. R., & Muñoz, R. F. (2005). *Controlling your drinking: Tools to make moderation work for you.* New York: Guilford.

Miller, W. R., & Rollnick, S. (2002). *Motivational Interviewing: Preparing people for change.* New York: Guilford.

Miller, W. R., & Taylor, C. A. (1980). Relative effectiveness of bibliotherapy, individual and group self-control training in the treatment of problem drinkers. *Addictive Behaviors, 5*, 13–24.

Miller, W. R., Taylor, C. A., & West, J. C. (1980). Focused versus broad-spectrum behavior therapy for problem drinkers. *Journal of Consulting and Clinical Psychology, 48*, 590–601.

Monti, P. M., Kadden, R. M., Rohsenow, D. J., Cooney, N. L., & Abrams, D. B. (2002). *Treating alcohol dependence: A coping skills training guide* (2nd ed.). New York: Guilford.

Monti, P. M, & Rohsenow, D. J. (2003). Coping skills training and cue exposure treatment. In R. K. Hester and W. R. Miller (Eds.), *Handbook of alcoholism treatment approaches: Effective alternatives* (3rd ed.) (pp. 152–164). Boston: Allyn and Bacon.

Monti, P. M., Rohsenow, D. J., Swift, R. M., Gulliver, S. B., Colby, S. M., Mueller, T. I. et al. (2001). Naltrexone and cue exposure with coping and communications skills training for alcoholics: Treatment process and one-year outcomes. *Alcoholism: Clinical and Experimental Research, 25*, 1634–1647.

Monti, P. M., Rohsenow, D. J., Michalec, E., Martin, R. A., & Abrams, D. B. (1997). Brief coping skills treatment for cocaine abuse: Substance use outcomes at 3 months. *Addiction, 92*, 1717–1728.

O'Farrell, T. J. (1995). Marital and family therapy. In R. K. Hester and W. R. Miller (Eds.), *Handbook of alcoholism treatment approaches: Effective alternatives* (2nd ed.) (pp. 195–220). Boston: Allyn and Bacon.

O'Farrell, T. J., & Fals-Stewart, W. (2003). Marital and family therapy. In R. K. Hester and W. R. Miller (Eds.) *Handbook of alcoholism treatment approaches: Effective Alternatives* (3rd ed.) (pp. 188–212). Boston: Allyn and Bacon.

O'Farrell, T. J., & Fals-Stewart, W. (2000). Behavioral couples therapy for alcoholism and drug abuse. *Journal of Substance Abuse Treatment, 18*, 51–54.

Prochaska, J. O., & DiClemente, C. C. (1986). Towards a comprehensive model of change. In W. R. Miller & N. Heather (Eds.), *Treating addictive behaviors: Processes of change.* (pp. 3–27). New York: Plenum.

Sanchez-Craig, M. (1993). *Saying when: How to quit drinking or cut down.* Toronto: Addiction Research Foundation.

Scheel, M. J., Hanson, W. E., & Razzhavaikina, T. I. (2004). The process of recommending homework in psychotherapy: A review of therapist delivery methods, client acceptability, and factors that affect compliance. *Psychotherapy: Theory, Research Practice, Training, 41*, 38–55.

Smith, J. E., Meyers, M. S., & Miller, W. R. (2001). The community reinforcement approach to the treatment of substance use disorders. *The American Journal on Addictions, 10*, 51–59.

Sobell, M. B., & Sobell, L. C. (1993). *Problem drinkers: Guided self-change treatment.* New York: Guilford.

Spivak, K., Sanchez-Craig, M., & Davila, R. (1994). Assisting problem drinkers to change on their own: Effect of specific and non-specific advice. *Addiction, 89*, 1135–1142.

CHAPTER 22

TRAUMATIC BRAIN INJURY

Janet M. Leathem and Muriel Christianson

Approximately 250 per 100,000 of the population sustain traumatic brain injury (TBI) annually (Cassidy et al., 2004), making it the most commonly occurring neurological condition. Of these 102 per 100,000 are hospitalised (Chesnut, Carney, Maynard, Patterson, Mann, & Helfand, 1998). Because of advances in trauma care these individuals are surviving injuries that would previously have been fatal (Klimczak, Donovick, & Burright, 1997). Young people, particularly males (who outnumber females two or three to one), are more likely to sustain TBI often in relation to motor vehicle accidents, especially where alcohol has been involved (Hillier, Hiller & Metzer, 1997) and those in lower socioeconomic, educational, and ethnic minority groups are also overly represented (ACC, 2004; Cassidy et al., 2004, Hillier, et al, 1997, Sosin., Sniezek, & Thurman, 1996). These people are typically at the beginning of their working lives often with young families. The need for effective rehabilitation assumes major importance if these individuals are to return to school and jobs, to resume their places in the family unit and to maintain an acceptable quality of life as soon as possible. This need has only recently been recognised and has led to a rapid growth in the rehabilitation industry.

The effects of TBI which include impairment of physical skills and cognitive ability as well as changes to emotional and interpersonal functioning (Karol, 2003) combine to make rehabilitation in this client group extremely challenging. Decreased ability to initiate responses, shallow self-awareness and impaired judgement, impulsivity and social disinhibition, verbal and physical aggression, childish behavior, impact most on the ability to function in society (Hoofien, Gilboa, Vakil, & Donovick, 2001; Lezak, 1987; Thomsen, 1984). Less obvious cognitive impairments, including difficulties with attention, memory, thinking speed, and executive functions, can severely limit the range of a person's activities, but are generally easier to deal with, while physical deficits are easiest to understand and accept (Hillier & Metzer, 1997).

Because brain function is exceedingly complex, brain injury and recovery are also complex (Rao & Lyketsos, 2002). Many resume normal functioning quite quickly while others, especially those who have sustained severe TBI may continue to have on-going effects that respond much more slowly to rehabilitation or that last indefinitely (Gray, 2000). The bottom line is that rehabilitation can help people adjust to these difficulties (Johnstone & Stonnington, 2001) but best practice guidelines suggest that positive outcomes will only result when therapy is directed at specific rather than general goals, when therapy has a practical focus and applies directly to the individual's real world and when therapy aims are reinforced to compensate for memory impairments (Chestnut et al, 1998). Homework, involving the application of therapy to everyday life is a critical component in the rehabilitation of this client group.

This chapter will outline some special considerations relating to neuropsychological implications following TBI. These include adjusting therapy where necessary to maximise its application to the groups most likely to sustain TBI, tailoring therapy to the specific individual deficits and needs, undertaking therapy in the face of co-morbid TBI related difficulties, and delivering therapy that is reinforced by homework and skill practice. The chapter will conclude with two cases studies that illustrate some of the points made.

SPECIAL CONSIDERATIONS RELATING TO REHABILITATION FOLLOWING TBI

Lack of Awareness and Denial

The first barrier to rehabilitation after brain injury occurs when the person who has sustained TBI lacks awareness of their impairments. This presents as unconcern, not recognising that they have difficulties at all, absent or deficient monitoring of behavior and impaired self-regulation, all of which is associated with frontal lobe damage (Butler & Satz, 1988; Prigatano & O'Brien, 1991, Sherer, Boake, Levin, Silver, Ringholz, & High, 1998). Without awareness of their deficits those with difficulties arising from TBI may not see the reason for being in treatment at all. Accordingly development of the capacity for self-observation may itself be the first goal of psychotherapy after TBI (Cicerone & Fraser, 2000). Insight is likely to slowly develop, when the reality of their difficulties becomes obvious often through a series of "a-ha" episodes (Dirette, 2002) occurring when a functional task is attempted but the outcome a significant and perhaps painful failure, e.g., being told repeatedly that they cannot work full-time, trying it then finding that fatigue makes it impossible. Homework tasks that help to develop awareness can be set up in the form of safe behavioral experiments that pair knowledge about the difficulty and practical experience of the consequences of that difficulty.

In some cases, however, the lack of awareness is not due to organic damage, but to psychological denial, i.e., an emotional reaction and protective response in the face of increasing recognition of disability and emotional distress (Cicerone, 1989). It is important to differentiate between the two. Both groups may demonstrate a resistance to engage in rehabilitation, but those in denial are more likely to acknowledge their physical symptoms and deny any cognitive or functional disability or acknowledge problems with memory but not with thinking or personality (Cicerone, 1989). Gradually exposing a person with TBI to different scenarios, particularly community-based and real-life activities (Cicerone, 1989), and discussing how successful these have been can help to increase awareness and lessen denial. When it is not interfering with maximal functioning or participation in rehabilitation, denial is not necessarily harmful as it may permit the pacing of recovery following trauma by reducing excessive amounts of anxiety and depression (Janoff-Bulman & Timko, 1987). However, in the end awareness is necessary for engagement in rehabilitation activities (Andersson,

Gundersen, & Finset, 1999; Prigatano & Ben-Yishay, 1999) for without awareness, the individual is unlikely to engage in therapy.

BEHAVIORAL AND EMOTIONAL CHANGES

Damage to frontal and temporal regions is also associated with other emotional changes (Kwentus, Hart, Peck, & Kornstein, 1985) such as reduced impulse control, increased or decreased activation, or excitability (Lucas, 1998). Comments and conversation will appear blunt and tangential, making conversation difficult to follow especially in a social setting. Actions will seem unpredictable, illogical, and lack apparent consideration for the feelings of others and may be aggressive and confrontational, both physically and verbally. Reduced control may also manifest as inappropriate or excessive laughing or crying (Burton & Volpe, 1988; Dunlop et al., 1991). Again intervention should involve both discussion and practical demonstration and aim at increasing awareness and training in strategies for compensating for the specific difficulty and the intervention should be applied and monitored in the everyday setting. Family members may be involved.

Apathy or the impairment of initiating and carrying out behavioral tasks (Marin, 1990) is often mistaken for laziness or thoughtlessness by those close to the person with TBI (e.g., when an opportunity to assist with a household chore is missed). It is important to assist carers and family to understand that failure to *think* of helping is not the same as unwillingness to help. Talking about the problem on its own is unlikely to result in change. Instituting systems for use in everyday setting that cue behavior is likely to result in real change, e.g., pre-programmed cell phones, pagers, alarms and computers, phone messages, lists of activities to be performed left in prominent/consistent places.

These difficulties may be exacerbated by reactive factors, e.g., the frustration caused by inability to function as before (Demark & Gemeinhardt, 2002). Depression, and anxiety are prevalent at higher rates after TBI than is reported in the general population (Deb, Lyons, Koutzoukis, Ali, & McCarthy, 1999; Fann, Burington, Leonetti, Jaffe, Katon, & Thompson, 2004; Fann, Katon, Uomoto, & Esselman, 1995; NIH Consensus Conference, 1999; Seel, Kreutzer, Rosenthal, Hammond, Corrigan, & Black, 2003) particularly when there is prolonged or repeated difficulty in resuming former work and social activities (Cicerone, 1989), or a lack of acceptance of disability (Hoofien et al., 2001). Depression, as applied to brain-injured patients, typically includes feelings of worthlessness, helplessness, guilt, loss of interest in work and family activities, and decreased libido accompanied by symptoms of exhaustion, poor concentration, anger or irritability, and intrusive negative thoughts. Those who develop depression are more likely to be minorities, unemployed, and receiving low incomes (Seel et al., 2003). After repeated failures in coping with the environment, many simply withdraw to where they feel safer but which lessens social contact with others (Prigatano, Fordyce, Zeiner, Roueche, Pepping, & Wood, 1986). A number of anxiety disorders have been observed in individuals who have experienced TBI and are often due to impairment of the ability to understand or adapt to external and internal stimuli. As a result, they are less able to regulate anxiety or to use it as a signal to alert themselves to potential problems. Caution is warranted in diagnosing post-TBI mood disorders, as a number of symptoms, such as changes in sleep, appetite, or libido, fatigue, and need to check things (as a necessary adaptation to memory impairment) could be secondary to the injury itself and mask as psychopathology (Butler & Satz, 1988; Leathem & Babbage, 2000; Rao & Lyketsos, 2002).

Some people find it impossible to cope with environmental demands that they previously could have handled with ease. They become overwhelmed emotionally and experience what Prigatano (1992) calls a "catastrophic reaction." Expressions of catastrophic reaction may range from explosive externalisation—screaming, swearing, lashing out, throwing things—to more internalised reaction such as passive withdrawal, regressive behavior, hostility to others, sullen behavior, and/or neglect of self-cares (Miller, 1991). It can be difficult to anticipate which environmental events will trigger this reaction and often the angry outbursts may appear unprovoked. Generalized irritability is reported by 30–64% of those with TBI and family members after TBI, with higher figures reported after severe TBI (Alderman, 2003).

Cognition

Difficulty with cognitive functions such as attention, memory, information processing speed, visual–spatial abilities, language, and executive skills has significant impact on delivery of rehabilitation services. Memory disturbances are the best known and among the most frustrating of the cognitive disturbances that may follow TBI and occur after mild, moderate, and severe brain injury (Klimczak et al., 1997). Difficulties can be experienced in the processes of attention, encoding items into memory, consolidating information in memory, and retrieving information from memory (Skeel & Edwards, 2001). These difficulties interact to make intervention more challenging and rehabilitation must be designed to allow for this. Thorough assessment of ability across the various domains of function is imperative not only in order to anticipate how impairments may interact, but to compensate for them and to identify areas of strength that may assist rehabilitation. For example, in order to remember something to work on it out of session, the individual must attend to it in the first place, i.e., sustain attention for the duration of the session, be able to focus on the task at hand without being distracted, be able to consider and process information (working memory), encode, store and then be able to retrieve the learned material. Further, they have to process material at a standard rate and think abstractly. These components are essential to the rehabilitation/psychotherapy process yet are the very areas that are compromised after TBI. Failure to consider all areas of weakness may result in a seemingly productive therapy session being promptly forgotten due to co-existing memory difficulties. When during therapy and between-session activities are not practised there is no consolidation of the gains made. This may equally apply to homework in physical therapy, cognitive, speech language, or psychological therapy. None of it will be undertaken at home or out of session if details as to the when, why and how and even that it was to be done, are forgotten. Homework compliance can be enhanced by ensuring that sufficient time is allowed for at the end of each session in order to discuss appropriate between session activities, to check for any potential obstacles that may arise and find ways to address these. Having a folder in which to keep session notes, reading materials and homework summaries can help to compensate for impaired memory and organisational skills that may get in the way of homework compliance.

The executive functions (those capacities that enable a person to engage in independent purposive behavior) may also be reduced after TBI due to damage to structures in the frontal lobes (Lezak, 1995). These capacities include planning, initiation, maintaining, and monitoring behavior, judgement as well as the ability to engage in abstract thought (Lezak, 1987). In those with disturbances in initiation and abstract reasoning, the cognitive steps to carry out complex action may be absent or markedly impaired. When given instructions from another person, they may do what they are told in a very concrete and literal manner. They may not understand the subtleties of humour or sarcasm. They may show pronounced preservative errors, in that, once engaged in an activity, they may find it difficult to inhibit or change that activity (Prigatano et al., 1986).

Impairment of attention and memory coupled with inflexibility in thinking and acting; slow and inefficient processing of information; difficulty with learning; and poorly organised behavior and verbal expression interact to seriously compromise cognitive functioning (Szekeres, Ylvisaker, & Cohen, 1987).

PHYSICAL

Sensory, motor, and autonomic function may be compromised following TBI. Long-term neurological sequelae may include a variety of movement disorders, dizziness, fatigue, headaches, pain, decreased libido, hypersensitivity to noise, sleep disorders seizures and seizures (NIH Consensus Conference, 1999). Complicated neural networks involving the eyes, optic nerves and cerebral cortex work together to process and integrate visual input. Survivors of TBI commonly complain of double and blurred vision, sensitivity to light, trouble judging distance and difficulties with the perception, processing, and interpretation of visual-spatial stimuli (Shaw, 2001).

While physical disabilities following TBI typically stabilise with time they may continue to restrict the range of future vocational opportunities. Intervention needs to be adapted to allow for mobility, balance and co-ordination, ambulation, vision, visual perceptual issues, and overall strength and endurance (Ninomiya, Ashley, Raney, & Krych, 1995), otherwise improvements will not occur in the real world.

CO-MORBIDITY OF COGNITIVE, EMOTIONAL & OTHER DIFFICULTIES

Those who sustain traumatic brain injury often sustain damage not only to multiple parts of the brain compromising many areas of brain function but damage to other parts of the body as well. In such cases, adjustment has to be made to the way that intervention is delivered, to accommodate changes in mobility, dexterity, visual acuity, taste, smell, communication and to co-morbid physical difficulties, e.g., headaches, pain, tinnitus, seizures and blurred vision in addition to changes in cognitive and emotional function (Englander et al., 2003).

THE SIGNIFICANCE OF PRE-EXISTING CONDITIONS

Some who have sustained TBI have experienced pre-existing psychological difficulties. These may make adjustment to the changes associated with the injury more difficult and are typically exacerbated by post injury biological changes and psychosocial environmental factors (Deb et al., 1999; Klimczak et al., 1997; Lewis, 1991; Rao & Lyketsos, 2002). Many survivors of TBI have histories of substance abuse and difficulties with interpersonal relationships and these are associated with poorer post-injury adaptation as measured by employment and independent living status (Bogner et al., 2001; MacMillian, Hart, Martelli, & Zasler, 2002). In New Zealand, for example 43% of young Mäori (aged 15–24 years) and 32% of non-Mäori youth are likely to be hazardous drinkers (Grigg & Macrae, 2000). After injury, these issues combined with dysfunction resulting from the trauma can lead to verbal or physical aggression, generalised anger, and an inability to abstain from substance abuse (Delmonico, Hanley-Peterson, & Englander, 1998). In short, sustaining TBI rarely improves on previous function and consideration of this is important in goal setting, i.e., expectations should not exceed prior levels of function.

In summary, there is a complex interaction among the variables that influence the recovery from brain injury. These variables include level of awareness, physical, cognitive outcomes, adjustment to changes, co-morbidity, and premorbid characteristics (Prigatano, 1988, 1992). Homework tasks for those with TBI should be: tailored to the individual, achievable, practical, and presented with a clear instructions and rationale.

INTERVENTIONS FOR PSYCHOLOGICAL
DIFFICULTIES AFTER TBI PSYCHOTHERAPY

There is general agreement that psychotherapy has a role in helping people to cope with consequences of TBI especially the depression and loss of self-esteem associated with the changes and losses (Cicerone & Fraser, 2000; NIH Consensus Conference, 1999, Prigatano, 1986, Szekeres et al., 1987). Treatment can help those with TBI to accept their current level of function, to challenge and modify distorted, dysfunctional, extreme and/or unrealistic thoughts and beliefs and to foster empowerment, self-sufficiency and independency (Sohlberg & Mateer, 2001).

As there are few controlled studies specifically aimed at demonstrating the efficacy of psychological interventions after TBI (Leber & Jenkins, 1996) there is a reliance on information from similar illnesses (e.g., stroke, anxiety or major depressive disorder), a practice that has limitations as the conditions differ in terms of physiology (Hurley & Taber, 2002).

Cognitive-behavioral techniques are used extensively in rehabilitation after TBI because they are relatively structured and directive, and easily adapted to accommodate the cognitive and wide range of other difficulties associated with TBI (Cicerone, 1989; Ponsford, 1995). Adaptations may include simple homework tasks such as: providing session summaries (to help maintain continuity between sessions in spite of memory problems), practicing relaxation exercises and completing activity schedules (to gauge participation levels and assist with awareness). More demanding tasks can include completing thought record sheets (which need to be practised in session and presented in a very simple concrete form) and practicing decision-making and problem solving skills. Homework tasks that are more specific to TBI can include reading information on the various outcomes that may follow TBI, practicing compensatory techniques for particular cognitive impairments (e.g. using a memory diary, cues for maintaining attention), or using alternative forms of expression to illustrate the meaning of the injury (Prigatano, 1991). Practicing skills helps with learning. Manchester and Wood (2001) note that new responses need to be acquired procedurally, consolidated through practice and then employed in appropriate situations.

Treatment of anxiety disorders involves cognitive techniques that focus on awareness of triggers and environmental control, pace and structure their activities, and provide assistance with adjustment to altered functions and roles. Treatment of irritability, substance abuse and sexual dysfunction have been successfully treated with cognitive therapy, social support, education and development of interpersonal skills (Alderman, 2001, 2003; Delmonico et al., 1998; Dombrowski, Petrick, & Strauss, 2000).

While standard interventions for treating anxiety, depression, irritability and obsessive disorders can be used with those with TBI, they should be modified in a way that is empathic with the person's specific cognitive deficits. Thus, communications should be less complex, more down to earth, and geared to helping them identify specific deficits and develop strategies to compensate for lost functions (Epstein & Ursano, 1994). Furthermore, most therapeutic headway will be made, if clinicians take time to understand the true nature of the changes and losses that have taken place in the inner and outer worlds of their clients with TBI (Epstein & Ursano, 1994; Prigatano, 1988).

Administration of sedating medication is an appealing option in the management of aggression as the risks imposed by this behavior are substantially and rapidly reduced. However, while sedation may sometimes be appropriate as an emergency measure, it will not target the factors underlying irritability and aggression necessary for long term improvement (Alderman, 2003).

Rehabilitation success can be enhanced by collaboration with the client and family members or other support persons in the client's life (Sohlberg & Mateer, 2001) although there is a lack of scientifically sound research on the effectiveness of various types of family involvement (Oddy & Herbert, 2003). With the agreement of the person who has sustained the TBI It is suggested that families can be involved with (1) interviewing processes; (2) identifying and prioritizing goals; and (3) monitoring change and revisiting goals. As therapy progresses, families can also assist with identifying problematic situations, encouraging the client with therapy tasks, and in developing concrete support plans for any difficulties that may arise after conclusion of therapy. As appropriate, families can assist with reporting on client progress and providing feedback for the therapist. Family members may be able to help with homework, by providing reassurance, assisting with organisation, and providing prompts when memory is an issue.

COGNITIVE REHABILITATION

The evidence for efficacy of treatment for cognitive difficulties is also limited (National Institute on Clinical Excellence, 2003). Cognitive rehabilitation is widely used both to aid the recovery of normal functioning where possible, as well as to provide compensatory strategies to minimise the negative impact of the symptoms that persist. There are four main approaches: restoration of function; attempting to teach skills to reduce the impact of the deficits resulting from the TBI; adapting tasks or the environment to aid performance of tasks; and finally using behavioral approaches such as feedback and reinforcement to support the learning of skills and strategies. There are many case reports demonstrating a wide range of techniques, stimulation, human effort and ingenuity in the literature, most based on clinical experience and observation of what works (National Institute on Clinical Excellence, 2003).

In the end the components of neuropsychological rehabilitation include a mix of psychotherapy, cognitive rehabilitation, the establishment of a therapeutic environment with an team of rehabilitation professionals, education, and working alliance with family and a protected work trial (Prigatano, 1992). In general, intervention/s should be based on comprehensive and integrated assessment undertaken by a range of rehabilitation professionals. Interventions should be tailor made for the particular needs of the client, may be innovative, will probably target several different domains of impairment and utilise methods of therapy that have been scientifically proven as useful in similar client groups (due to limited evidence based research with groups with TBI). Because of a high frequency of cognitive difficulties, interventions should be targeted to specific everyday needs, applied and rehearsed in everyday settings and richly reinforced by family members.

CASE STUDY 1

Four years earlier MN, a 51-year-old livestock agent had fallen asleep at the wheel of a car resulting in an accident in which he sustained a severe brain injury as evidenced by an initial Glasgow Coma Scale of 6, post-traumatic amnesia of 3 months, and retrograde amnesia of more than 24 hours. Post-traumatic headaches, slowing of information processing speed, and difficulties with memory and fatigue prevented his return to work and were still a problem 4 years post accident. Higher executive function was intact. The difficulties as formally assessed corresponded to those reported in his everyday life.

MN presented as a pleasant person somewhat apologetic (for not returning to full-time work) who experienced some word finding difficulties. Emotionally, he felt "detached, like a spectator," had difficulty handling arguments with people he knew well, and did not deal with criticism as readily as before the accident. He put part of this down to continuing to feel guilty for causing the accident. He was not clinically depressed.

He lived in a rural setting with his son aged 15, who attended high school by bus. His wife had died in an asthma attack two years prior to the accident. MN drove a 50 minute round trip to part-time work (3 half-days per week) as a picture framer in a large town. He enjoyed the work and found the older owner of the business very supportive and easy to work with. MN's tendency to tire easily was apparently the major barrier preventing him from return to full-time employment. Increased fatigue invariably increased his memory difficulties and tendency to irritability. He would then become short-tempered with his son. He had a keen interest in exotic fish and had large tanks at home. There had been some difficulty with remembering feeding and breeding timetables.

The results of the neuropsychological assessment were discussed with MN who fully understood the nature of his neuropsychological deficits when these were discussed with him and was keen to engage in further rehabilitation. In recognition of his information processing speed and verbal memory difficulties, the results were discussed slowly and illustrated on a white board. Time was available for questions and MN was encouraged to write the results down. These were kept in a plastic sleeve that was clipped into a specific section in a small ring bound folder that he could take home to remind himself of the outcomes and would later be used to assist with remembering other important information.

INTERVENTIONS

In consultation with MN, areas were targeted for intervention in the following order: prospective memory (relating to general household tasks, caring for his son and managing the fish); fatigue and headaches; issues concerning irritability and motivation. Baselines were obtained for frequency of forgetting, frequency and intensity of headaches and irritability, context and time of fatigue. His son assisted with recording.

To assist with prospective memory a small folder was set up as suggested by Sohlberg and Mateer (2001). It contained a calendar section in which all future appointments, events, meetings, and important dates relating to, for example, work, son, son's school activities, fish, bill payments, car, health, and rehabilitation were marked. Another section with disposible pages listed only the things that he needed to remember to do *today*. This was important as he became irritated when he forgot something on one of his trips to town and would have to wait or make a special trip. A work section contained verbal information given to him by his employer. (He was able to remember tasks and procedures that he was shown visually.) Separate sections were also set up for Fish and Rehabilitation. The specific details of what each section of the folder was for, and how it was to be used was written on the back of the divider separating the current section from the one proceeding. Again as suggested by Sohlberg and Mateer (2001), follow up ensured that MN was using the folder in the correct manner (he was contacted by phone at preset times every two days).

The problem of forgetting whether or not and which fish he had fed was to some extent overcome by placing a clipboard with a pen attached to tanks. He practiced with his son's oversight not walking away from a tank without checking off what he had done on the clipboard. He found that this in itself was sufficient, i.e., he rarely found himself wondering afterwards whether or not the fish had been fed. The daily, weekly, and monthly program relating to the fish was kept in a separate section of the folder. Consumables to be replaced were entered into the calendar section for later entry to the things-to-do today section.

Fatigue and pain management was dealt with by a combination of behavior therapy and cognitive-behavior therapy (CBT). He was taught relaxation exercises, which were recorded when they were first presented to him and encouraged to practice them at home with the aid of a tape. Initial reminders to do the exercises were entered into the calendar section of his folder.

MN was seen in five individual sessions of CBT focused on helping him to stop from letting fatigue and the accident dictate his life for him. He realized that most of his activities and decisions are made around fatigue. For example, he declined being involved with many activities because he was or thought he would be too tired. This was exacerbated by living in the country and being concerned about driving while tired, especially since this had been the cause of the original accident. Methods for dealing with fatigue were covered. Incorrect attributions about living in the country, e.g., that it would make it more difficult for some of his son's undesirable friends to visit were challenged (they visited anyway) and he was challenged to think about whether he kept fatigue as a problem to stop himself having to face the future.

At the end of each therapy session the important points were reviewed and recorded along with any between-session "homework" requirements. These notes were dated and either kept folded in a plastic insert in the "Rehabilitation" section of the folder or clipped in as separate pages. Reminders to do the homework were entered into the calendar section at the same time as the date of the next appointment. The "homework" was reviewed at the beginning of the following session.

This case illustrates the way therapy was geared to MN's specific strengths and weaknesses. The interventions for fatigue, pain and motivation were the same as for non-brain injured populations with add-ons to compensate for other TBI related problems. This involved a different approach to therapy *sessions* (deal with concepts slowly due to information processing speed problems; write main points on white board and client writes summary at the end of the session and reminders in calendar section of folder to compensate for verbal learning and memory difficulties) therapy *homework* (reminders to do between session homework; access to review of previous session/s through notes in folder) and *evaluation* of therapy (review of episodes of forgetting from tank clipboards, discussing changes in psychometric measures).

CASE STUDY 2

RR, a 25-year-old laborer of Mäori descent, sustained severe brain damage in an assault during a bar room brawl 18 months earlier. He was admitted with multiple facial and head bruises and a deep laceration to right hand. He was drowsy on admission with a Glasgow Coma Scale score of 6/15 compromised by high alcohol levels. CT scan revealed a basal skull fracture and bilateral bleeding in the frontal lobes. He had sustained concussions, two and three years previously, while playing rugby. RR left school at 15 years without qualification, worked 2 years as a farm hand, 4 years in the sawmill, and had been unemployed for several years between. He had been the lead singer in a local band also playing the guitar and played representative rugby.

Seen 18 months after the assault, RR presented in bare feet, casually dressed in torn jeans and beanie. There was obvious facial scarring especially around his right eye and mild right hemiparesis. He was somewhat tangential in responding to enquiry often straying from the topic, then requesting that the original question be repeated. He experienced headaches, general slowing, difficulty walking (keeping his balance), loss of dexterity in both hands, more on the right, reduced concentration, and double vision. He reported considerable difficulty both in initiating and in maintaining conversations and often felt anxious and nervous when around new people and in unfamiliar social situations. As a result, he tended to avoid such situations or rely on the support of a trusted companion. Additionally, he felt less flexible when called upon to adjust to unexpected changes and did not recognise when he had said something to upset someone else.

RR lived with his brother and sister-in-law, his own relationship having disintegrated due to his irritability in the months after the accident. He had not returned to work and no longer drove the car. He could no longer play the guitar due to damage to his right hand. He was no longer singing in the band due to deterioration of his voice caused by damage to his vocal cords from the tracheotomy tube while in intensive care. He was advised against playing rugby on safety grounds. He spent his days watching TV, resting, and sometimes going for a walk. He managed his own finances (used an ATM card and paid his outgoings on time).

Neuropsychological assessment revealed difficulties with cognitive function across the board but slightly more with domains of function that are vulnerable to brain injury (e.g., information processing speed and higher executive function). It was considered highly probable that RR's pre-accident IQ was low average especially on language-based subtests. RR was able to remember appointments and important tasks.

INTERVENTIONS

Formulation of the case included recognition of the influence of frontal lobe difficulties: reduced impulse control and information processing speed, some limitations in his awareness of his difficulties, irritability as well as physical injuries: including motor slowing, double vision. These changes had lead to severe significant losses: job, recreation, sport, relationship, and, consequently, his self-esteem on issues concerning awareness, anger, socialization, grief, and loss.

RR received a set of interventions targeted toward reduction in his levels of social anxiety and avoidance, feedback, and advice regarding his interpersonal communication style, as well as addressing the underlying issues of low self-esteem. The therapeutic approach was cognitive behavioral and incorporated strategies such as provision of psychoeducational material, relaxation techniques, thought recording, video work, activity scheduling and behavioral experiments. Baseline measures were taken to allow treatment efficacy to be ascertained.

Taking into account RR's learning difficulties, more sessions were scheduled that normally might be expected and clear and basic language used. A life skills coach was involved at various stages of the treatment process in order to provide some continuity between sessions and once therapy has been completed. RR attended all appointments and engaged enthusiastically in the therapeutic process. He practiced a basic relaxation technique and used it on a daily basis at home. He was reliable in thought recording and practicing tasks set up after feedback around his interpersonal communication style and practice at initiating and maintaining conversation from the video work.

The interventions in this case were the same as for non-brain injured populations with add-ons to compensate for other TBI related problems and were focused on issues of grief and loss, substance use, social avoidance, irritability, and inflexibility of thinking. The approach to therapy *sessions* (deal with concepts slowly due to information processing speed problems; using simple language, using basic language, entering his phenomenological world), therapy *homework* and *evaluation* of therapy (review: thought, mood, and irritability diary; activity record; change in video-taped role play; and report of life skills coach)

REFERENCES

Accident Rehabilitation and Compensation Corporation. (2004). *ACC injury statistics*. Wellington: ACC Statistical Publications.

Alderman, N. (2001). Managing challenging behaviour. In R. L. Wood & T. M. McMillan (Eds.), *Neurobehavioural disability and social handicap following traumatic brain injury* (pp. 175–207). Hove: Psychology Press Ltd.

Alderman, N. (2003). Contemporary approaches to the management of irritability and aggression following traumatic brain injury. *Neuropsychological Rehabilitation, 13*, 211–240.

Andersson, S., Gundersen, P. M., & Finset, A. (1999). Emotional activation during therapeutic interaction in traumatic brain injury: Effect of apathy, self-awareness and implcations for rehabilitation. *Brain Injury, 13*, 393–404.

Bogner, J. A., Corrigan, J. D., Mysiw, W. J., Clinchot, D., & Fugate, L. (2001). A comparison of substance abuse and violence in the prediction of long-term rehabilitation outcomes after traumatic brain injury. *Archives of Physical Medicine and Rehabilitation, 82*, 571–577.

Burton, L. A., & Volpe, B. T. (1988). Sex differences in emotional status of traumatically brain-injured patients. *Journal of Neurological Rehabilitation, 2*, 151–57.

Butler, R. W., & Satz, P. (1988). Individual psychotherapy with head-injured adults: Clinical notes for the practitioner. *Professional Psychology: Research and Practice, 19*, 536–541.

Cassidy, J. D., Carroll, L. J., Peloso, P. M., Borg, J., van Holst, H., Holm, L., et al. (2004). Incidence, risk factors and prevention of mild traumatic brain injury: Results of the who collaborating centre task force on mild traumatic brain injury. *Journal of Rehabilitation Medicine, 43*, 28–60.

Chesnut, R. M., Carney, N., Maynard, H., Patterson, P., Mann, N. C., & Helfand, M. (1998). *Evidence report on rehabilitation of persons with traumatic brain injury.* Oregon: Oregon Health Sciences University Evidence-based practice center.

Cicerone, K. D. (1989). Psychotherapeutic interventions with traumatically brain-injured patients. *Rehabilitation Psychology, 34*, 105–114.

Cicerone, K. D., & Fraser, R. T. (2000). Counseling interactions. In R. T. Fraser & D. C. Clemmons (Eds.), *Traumatic brain injury rehabilitation: Practical, vocational, neuropsychological, and psychotherapy interventions.* Boca Raton, Florida: CRC press Inc.

Deb, S., Lyons, I., Koutzoukis, C., Ali, I., & McCarthy, G. (1999). Rate of psychiatric illness 1 year after traumatic brain injury. *American Journal of Psychiatry, 156*, 374–378.

Delmonico, R. L., Hanley-Peterson, P., & Englander, J. (1998). Group psychotherapy for persons with traumatic brain injury: Management of frustration and substance abuse. *Journal of Head Trauma Rehabilitation, 13*, 10–22.

Demark, J., & Gemeinhardt, M. (2002). Anger and its management for survivors of acquired brain injury. *Brain Injury, 16*, 91–108.

Dirette, D. (2002). The development of awareness and the use of compensatory strategies for cognitive deficits. *Brain Injury, 16*, 861–871.

Dombrowski, L. K., Petrick, J. D., & Strauss, D. (2000). Rehabilitation treatment of sexuality issues due to acquired brain injury. *Rehabilitation Psychology, 45*, 299–309.

Dunlop, T. W., Udvarhelyi, G. B., Stedem, A. F., O'Connor, J. M. C., Isaacs, M. L., Puig, J. G., et al. (1991). Comparison of patients with and without emotional/behavioural deterioration during the first year after traumatic brain injury. *The Journal of Neuropsychiatry and Clinical Neurosciences, 3*, 150–156.

Englander, J., Bushnik, T., Duong, T. T., Cifu, D. X., Zafonte, R., Wright, J., et al. (2003). Analyzing risk factors for late posttraumatic seizures: A prospective, multicenter investigation. *Archives of Physical Medicine and Rehabilitation, 84*, 365–373.

Epstein, R. S., & Ursano, R. J. (1994). Anxiety disorders. In J. M. Silver, S. C. Yudofsky & R. E. Hales (Eds.), *Neuropsychiatry of traumatic brain injury* (pp. 285–312). Washington DC: American Psychiatric Press, Inc.

Fann, J. R., Burington, B., Leonetti, A., Jaffe, K., Katon, W. J., & Thompson, R. S. (2004). Psychiatric illness following traumatic brain injury in an adult health maintenance organization population. *Archives of General Psychiatry, 61*, 53–61.

Fann, J. R., Katon, W. J., Uomoto, J. M., & Esselman, P. C. (1995). Psychiatric disorders and functional disability in outpatients with traumatic brain injuries. *American Journal of Psychiatry, 152,* 1493–1499.

Gray, D. S. (2000). Slow-to-recover severe traumatic brain injury: A review of outcomes and rehabilitation effectiveness. *Brain Injury, 14,* 1003–1014.

Grigg, M., & Macrae, B. (2000). Monitoring and evaluation, tikanga oranga hauora 4. In T. P. K. Social Development Directorate, Wellington (Ed.).

Hillier, S. L., Hillier, J. E. & Metzer, (1997). Epidemiology of traumatic brain injury in South Australia. *Brain Injury, 11,* 649–659

Hillier, S. L., & Metzer, J. (1997). Awareness and perceptions of outcomes after traumatic brain injury. *Brain Injury, 11,* 525–536.

Hoofien, D., Gilboa, A., Vakil, E., & Donovick, P. J. (2001). Traumatic brain injury (TBI) 10–20 years later: A comprehensive outcome study of psychiatric symptomatology, cognitive abilities and psychosocial functioning. *Brain Injury, 15,* 189–209.

Hurley, R. A., & Taber, K. H. (2002). Emotional disturbances following traumatic brain injury. *Current Treatment Options in Neurology, 4,* 59–75.

Janoff-Bulman, R., & Timko, C. (1987). Coping with traumatic events: The role of denial in light of peoples assumptive worlds. In C. R. Snyder & C. E. Ford (Eds.), *Coping with negative life events: Clinical and social perspectives.* (pp. 131–160). New York: Plenum Press.

Johnstone B., & Stonnington, H. H (Eds.). (2001). *Rehabilitation of neuropsychological disorders: A practical guide for rehabilitation professionals.* Philadelphia: Psychology Press.

Karol, R. L. (2003). *Neuropsychosocial intervention: The practical treatment of severe behavioral dyscontrol after acquired brain injury.* Florida: CRC press.

Klimczak, N. J., Donovick, P. J., & Burright, R. G. (1997). Psychotherapy with the brain injured adult. *Psychotherapy in Private Practice, 16,* 33–44.

Kwentus, J. A., Hart, R. P., Peck, E. T., & Kornstein, S. (1985). Psychiatric implications of closed head trauma. *Psychosomatics, 26,* 8–17.

Leathem, J. M., & Babbage, D. (2000). Affective disorders after traumatic brain injury: Cautions in the use of the scl-90-r after traumatic brain injury. *Journal of Head Trauma Rehabilitation, 15,* 1246–1255.

Leber, W. R., & Jenkins, M. R. (1996). Psychotherapy with clients who have brain injury and their families. In R. L. Adams, O. A. Parsons, J. L. Culbertson, & S. J. Jenkins (Eds.), *Neuropsychology for clinical practice: Etiology, assessment and treatment of common neurological disorders* (pp. 489–505). Washington DC: American Psychological Association.

Lewis, L. (1991). Role of psychological factors in disordered awareness. In G. P. Prigatano & D. L. Schacter (Eds.), *Awareness of deficit after brain injury: Clinical and theoretical issues* (pp. 223–239). Oxford: Oxford University Press.

Lezak, M. D. (1987). Relationships between personality disorders, social disorders, social disturbances, and physical disability following traumatic brain injury. *Journal of Head Trauma Rehabilitation, 2,* 57–69.

Lezak, M. D. (1995). *Neuropsychological assessment* (3rd ed.). New York: Oxford University Press.

Lucas, J. A. (1998). Traumatic brain injury and post-concussive syndrome. In P. J. Snyder & P. D. Nussbaum (Eds.), *Clinical neuropsychology. A pocket handbook for assessment.* New York: American Psychological Association.

MacMillan, P. J., Hart, R. P., Martelli, M. F., & Zasler, N. D. (2002). Pre-injury status and adaptation following traumatic brain injury. *Brain Injury, 16,* 41–49.

Manchester, D., & Wood, R. L. (2001). Applying cognitive therapy in neurobehavioural rehabilitation. In R. L. Wood, & T. M. McMillan (Eds.), *Neurobehavioural disability and social handicap following traumatic brain injury* (pp. 157–174). Hove: Psychology Press Ltd.

Marin, R. S. (1990). Differential diagnosis and classification of apathy. *American Journal of Psychiatry, 147,* 22–30.

Miller, L. (1991). Psychotherapy of the brain-injured patient: Principles and practices. *Cognitive Rehabilitation*, 24–30.

National Institute on Clinical Excellence. (2003). *Head injury: Triage, assessment, investigation and early management of head injury in infants, children and adults*. London: National Collaborating Centre for Acute Care.

NIH Consensus Conference. (1999). *Consensus conference: NIH consensus conference: Rehabilitation of persons with traumatic brain injury, jama*. Paper presented at the Rehabilitation of Persons with Traumatic Brain Injury.

Ninomiya, J., Ashley, M. J., Raney, M. L., & Krych, D. K. (1995). Vocational rehabilitation. In M. J. Ashley & D. K. Krych (Eds.), *Traumatic brain injury rehabilitation* (pp. 367–389). Boca Raton: CRC Press.

Oddy, M., & Herbert, C. (2003). Intervention with families following brain injury: Evidence-based practice. *Neuropsychological Rehabilitation*, *13*, 259–273.

Ponsford, J. (1995). Dealing with the impact of traumatic brain injury on psychological adjustment and relationships. In J. Ponsford, S. Sloan, & P. Snow (Eds.), *Traumatic brain injury. Rehabilitation for everyday adaptive living* (pp. 231–264). Hove: Psychology Press Ltd.

Prigatano, G. P. (1986). Psychotherapy after brain injury. In G. P. Prigatano, D. J. Fordyce, H. K. Zeiner, J. R. Roueche, M. Pepping & B. Wood (Eds.), *Neuropsychological rehabilitation after brain injury* (pp. 67–95). Baltimore, MD: The John Hopkins University Press.

Prigatano, G. P. (1988). Emotion and motivation in recovery and adaption after brain damage. In S. Finger, T. E. Levere, C. R. Almli & D. G. Stein (Eds.), *Brain injury and recovery: Theoretical and controversial issues* (pp. 335–350). New York: Plenum Press.

Prigatano, G. P. (1991). Disordered mind, wounded soul: The emerging role of psychotherapy in rehabilitation after brain injury. *Journal of Head Trauma Rehabilitation*, *6*, 1–10.

Prigatano, G. P. (1992). Personality disturbances associated with traumatic brain injury. *Journal of Consulting and Clinical Psychology*, *60*, 360–368.

Prigatano, G. P., & Ben-Yishay, Y. (1999). Psychotherapy and psychotherapeutic interventions in brain injury rehabilitation. In M. Rosenthal, E. R. Griffiths, J. S. Kreutzer, & B. Pentland (Eds.), *Rehabilitation of the adult and child with traumatic brain injury* (3rd ed.) (pp. 271–283). Philadelphia: F.A. Davis Company.

Prigatano, G. P., Fordyce, D. J., Zeiner, H. K., Roueche, J. R., Pepping, M., & Wood, B. (1986). *Neuropsychological rehabilitation after brain injury*. Baltimore MD: The John Hopkins University Press.

Prigatano, G. P., & O'Brien, K. P. (1991). Awareness of deficit in patients with frontal and parietal lesions: Two case reports. *Barrow Neurological Institute Quarterly*, *7*, 17–23.

Rao, V., & Lyketsos, C. G. (2002). Psychiatric aspects of traumatic brain injury. *The Psychiatric Clinics of North America*, *25*, 43–69.

Seel, R. T., Kreutzer, J. S., Rosenthal, M., Hammond, F. M., Corrigan, J., & Black, K. (2003). Depression after traumatic brain injury: A national institute on disability and rehabilitation research model systems multicentre investigation. *Archives of Physical Medicine and Rehabilitation*, *84*, 177–184.

Shaw, J. (2001). The assessment and rehabilitation of visual-spatial disorders. In H. Johnstone & H. H. Stonnington (Eds.), *Rehabilitation of neuropsychogical disorders: A practical guide for rehabilitation professionals* (pp. 125–160). Philadelphia: Psychology Press.

Sherer, M., Boake, C., Levin, E., Silver, B. V., Ringholz, G., & High, W. M. (1998). Characteristics of impaired awareness after traumatic brain injury. *Journal of the Neuropsychological Society*, *4*, 380–387.

Skeel, R. L., & Edwards, S. (2001). The assessment and rehabilitation of memory impairments. In H. Johnstone & H. H. Stonnington (Eds.), *Rehabilitation of neuropsychological disorders: A practical guide for rehabilitation professionals* (pp. 53–85). Philadelphia: Psychology Press.

Sohlberg, M. M., & Mateer, C. A. (2001). *Cognitive rehabilitation. An integrative neuropsychological approach*. New York: Guilford.

Sosin, D. M., Sniezek, J. F., & Thurman, D. J. (1996). Incidence of mild and moderate brain injury in the United States, 1991. *Brain Injury, 10,* 47–54.

Szekeres, S. F., Ylvisaker, M., & Cohen, S. B. (1987). A framework for cognitive rehabilitation therapy. In M. Ylvisaker & E. M. R. Gobble (Eds.), *Community re-entry for head injured adults* (pp. 87–136). Boston: Little, Brown and Company (Inc).

Thomsen, I. V. (1984). Late outcome of very severe blunt head trauma: A 10–15 year second follow-up. *Journal of Neurology, Neurosurgery, and Psychiatry, 47,* 260–268.

Part IV

DIRECTIONS FOR RESEARCH, PRACTICE, AND PREVENTION

CHAPTER 23

DIRECTIONS FOR RESEARCH ON HOMEWORK

Michael J. Lambert, S. Cory Harmon, and Karstin Slade

A CRITICAL APPRAISAL OF EMPIRICAL FOUNDATIONS

Psychotherapy is the most widely researched and well established mental health treatment available to patients today. Over 5000 studies have been conducted on various forms of psychotherapy and their contributors to effective outcomes (e.g., Lambert, 2004; Lambert & Ogles, 2004; Roth & Fonagy, 2005). Such research has established both the cost effectiveness of these psychotherapy procedures and identified patient, therapist, and procedural characteristics that are likely to result in optimal effects. The use of homework in psychotherapy is one method by which therapists have sought to strengthen and reinforce the benefits of psychotherapy. As is evident in the current text, homework is viewed as an important factor in effecting positive change across a broad range of disorders and within a variety of treatment orientations. Following a review of psychotherapy treatment efficacy, this chapter will detail the role of homework in psychotherapy and its relationship to outcome. Additionally, the current state of the research evidence, homework compliance, and suggestions for future research will be considered. Despite being overly broad and therefore imprecise, we consider "homework" in the current context as any out of office activity directed by a therapist and intended to have a therapeutic effect if undertaken by a client during the course of psychotherapy. We turn now to a brief overview of psychotherapy outcome.

Hundreds of studies have now been conducted on the effects of psychotherapy, including research on psychodynamic, humanistic, behavioral, cognitive, and variations and combinations of these approaches. Reviews of this research, both qualitative and quantitative, have shown that about 75% of those who enter treatment show some benefit, with 40% to 60% of patients experiencing full recovery in carefully controlled research trials lasting approximately 14 weeks (Lambert & Ogles, 2004). Psychotherapy of various orientations and formats has been found to be effective across a variety of patient disorders. The extent and richness of this finding extends over five decades of research, thousands of treated individuals, hundreds of settings, and multiple cultures.

The breadth of empirical results clearly demonstrates that the treatments reduce distressing symptoms, resolve interpersonal problems, restore work performance, and improve quality of life for the majority of individuals seeking treatment. This finding generalizes across a wide range of disorders with the exception of severe biologically based disturbances, such as bipolar disorder and the schizophrenias, where the impact of psychological treatments is secondary to psychoactive medications, but still important for improving and maintaining patient functioning. Across disorders there is variability, such that some disorders (e.g., phobias, panic) yield to treatment more easily than others (e.g., obsessive compulsive disorder), and some require longer and more intense interventions. The severity of initial disturbance experienced by the individual is the best predictor of both final treatment response and the amount of psychotherapy necessary for recovery. In general, 50% of patients experience improvement following 8 sessions of treatment and recovery following 20 sessions (Anderson & Lambert, 2001). Given the extreme burden of illness that accompanies psychological disorders (e.g., depression) and the significant impact such disorders have on work (lost productivity) and family functioning, psychological treatments have rather remarkable consequences and efficiency. In addition, psychological interventions reduce the costs associated with the treatment of physical disorders and significantly offset medical cost (Chiles, Lambert, & Hatch, 1999).

Because the general efficacy of psychological treatments is well established in relation to both no treatment and placebo interventions, a great deal of interest and energy over the last three decades has been focused on identifying the ingredients of effective treatments. This research has often taken the form of randomized clinical trials that attempt to explain outcome as a function of theory-driven psychotherapies offered to carefully selected patients who are classified based on the diagnosis of a specific disorder that is presumed to yield to the specific treatment. Such research has opened up the possibility that "best practices" based on patient diagnosis can be identified and offered, resulting in the maximization of patient benefit.

Such a possibility is not without its problems. For example, the authors of DSM-IV acknowledge that a diagnosis does not necessarily inform treatment. In their introductory chapter, they caution clinicians about the limits of the diagnostic system: "Making a DSM-IV diagnosis is only the first step in a comprehensive evaluation. To formulate an adequate treatment plan, the clinician will invariably require considerable information about the person being evaluated beyond that required to make a DSM-IV diagnosis" (American Psychiatric Association, 1994, p. xxv). Despite this warning, the randomized clinical trial research paradigm, which is intended to inform clinical practice, assigns participants to treatments based on their DSM-IV diagnoses.

Although diagnosis is important in some circumstances, it does not merit the research and clinical weight in psychological disturbances that it may warrant in other medical conditions. While physical disease models link physiological processes with pathology, psychological diagnoses are descriptive, with only a few clear links to etiology. In contrast to a diagnosis model, psychotherapeutic practice tends to be organized around modality (individual, group, couple, family), patient age (adult, adolescent, child) and theoretical approach (cognitive-behavioral, psychodynamic-interpersonal, humanistic-experiential).

Organizing practice around non-diagnostic traits does not mean therapists ignore patients' symptoms. On the contrary, it is because psychotherapeutic treatment must vary far more *within* diagnostic groups than between them. Issues of personality, intelligence, age, gender, race, culture, education, socioeconomic status, circumstance of presentation, family composition, living arrangements, social support, prior therapy, psychological mindedness, motivation, initial level of severity, and many other factors have very large impacts on what therapists actually do. Essentially, every patient gets a different treatment, as therapists respond to these many factors. In other words, knowing the diagnosis is not sufficient information to inform treatment; clinicians need to know much more about a person to institute an effective therapy, including what, when, and how to use homework with each particular client.

Even if we put such foundational problems aside and rely on the results of comparative outcome studies, the research leading to the identification of empirically supported specific therapies for specific disorders has not produced unequivocal results for deciding on best practices. Comparative outcome studies, besides generating a new wave of turf wars connected to theories of psychopathology and change, show that the amount of variance that can be attributed to specific treatments appears to be meager at best, or even contradictory. This is surprising given that the intent of such studies is too accentuate differences in outcome between treatments, and that there is no doubt that many of the interventions considered essential in one form of treatment are eschewed by a contrasting treatment.

Many authors (e.g., Lambert, 2002; Lambert and Ogles, 2004; Orlinsky, et al., 2004) have commented on the absence of clinically meaningful differences between diverse treatments and suggested that a reasonable explanation for the small differences in effects found between different psychotherapies can be accounted for by the powerful effects of factors that are shared by almost all treatments. Most important among these variables is a strong therapeutic alliance, which is manifest by considerable agreement between therapist and patient about both the tasks and goals of therapy, as well as a positive affective bond characterized by trust and honesty; themes that repeat themselves throughout this book when discussions of homework compliance are offered. Wampold (2001) in an analysis of comparative effects, has suggested similar "common factors" explanations for the failure to find differences in school-based treatments and provided evidence that the outcomes of psychotherapy are more highly related to individual therapists than to school-based interventions (see also, Okiishi, Lambert, Nielsen, & Ogles, 2003).

In addition, three major task forces established by Divisions of the American Psychological Association have emphasized different aspects of psychotherapy that effect patient well being. These range from those that emphasize specific treatments in relation to specific disorders (e.g., Nathan & Gorman, 2002), to those that emphasize the importance of the therapist patient relationship based on research on the qualities of the therapeutic encounter and participant characteristics that induce effective change (e.g., Norcross, 2002), to recent efforts to distill empirically supported and cross-cutting "principles of effectiveness" that cut across specific treatments and attempt to do away with competition between diverse theoretical language systems by recognizing similarities across treatments (Castonguay & Beutler, 2005). Each task force makes many assumptions about the causal relationship between treatments and outcomes and attempts to distill the most important aspects of psychological interventions.

Collectively, the research literature is strongly supportive of the effectiveness of psychotherapeutic interventions across a variety of patient problems and disorders, but less supportive of the unique importance of particular treatments or therapeutic activities. Recognizing that there are many variables that influence how much patients change [with the most important being patient characteristics (Lambert & Barley, 2002)], one should not expect the contribution of homework to be large or even detectable unless it is absolutely essential to patient improvement. While treatment orientations vary in the amount of importance afforded homework, homework effects will be difficult to find unless they are indeed *essential* for a positive outcome, regardless of the importance it is theoretically afforded. The search for homework effects, viewed from the larger context of repeated failures to establish the importance of specific techniques that differentiate very diverse treatments, seems rather optimistic. Clinicians and theoreticians may consider homework as essential, but from the perspective of past research, the failure to detect an effect for specific activities like homework is expected. Investigations examining the necessity of specific therapeutic actions that directly or indirectly influence patient outcome have suggested that partitioning out effects for specific actions is difficult. Despite this difficulty, this volume can serve as an important guiding resource to organize future research on homework, such that the nature and limits of its influence can be illuminated.

IS HOMEWORK A COMMON FACTOR OR A UNIQUE INTERVENTION?

Within the context of searching for important variables that affect patient improvement, homework emerges as a therapeutic activity that can be viewed as both a common factor and one that is unique to specific treatments. On the one hand, between-session activity, whether directed by a therapist or initiated by a client and supported by a therapist, occurs constantly during psychotherapy and generates, at the very least, grist for the therapeutic encounter in virtually all treatments (Kazantzis & Lampropoulos, 2002). In a review of 500 outcome studies conducted between 1973 and 1980, 68% included self-help assignments" (Shelton and Levy, 1981). However, these findings are limited in that the Shelton and Levy analysis consisted of behavior therapy outcome treatments. Even less overt therapy interactions can be interpreted as homework and treated as an "assignment." Note, for example, Stricker's (Chapter 8) suggestion that dependent clients may interpret a question posed by the therapist as a homework prescription and initiate behaviors outside of therapy, perceiving that the therapist has recommended it. While not necessarily intended as homework, it can be argued (as does the author) that the newly initiated behaviors are a form of homework even though they are not easily separated or evaluated apart from the treatment as a whole. On the other hand, homework that takes the form of a complete and nearly independent activity with its own defining characteristics, such as a twelve-step self help group, can be more easily investigated as a specific treatment.

Although homework is universal enough to be considered a common factor across diverse psychotherapies, in the present context it will be viewed as a defining characteristic of the action oriented/directive treatments central to this book. Consider, for example, the place accorded homework in behavioral and cognitive behavioral psychotherapies. "Cognitive therapy is based on the premise that psychological disorders are associated with the meanings individuals give to events (rather than to the events themselves) and that these meanings are derived from a constellation of core beliefs and assumptions they developed as part of their learning histories" (Beck & Tompkins; Chapter 3). Beck and Tompkins emphasize six main purposes of homework within the cognitive therapy framework: Implementing solutions; increasing self-awareness; practicing cognitive, behavioral, and emotional skills; reinforcing what was learned in session; testing ideas; and preventing relapse. The overall purpose of all homework follows the ultimate purpose of cognitive therapy—to identify and modify maladaptive cognitions by learning new skills and practicing them between sessions.

Similarly, behavior therapy consists of a collaborative effort on the part of the patient and the therapist to understand the maintenance of problematic behaviors, and to develop strategies for change. Behavior therapy is unique from many other therapies in that it regularly incorporates homework into therapy as part of all treatment components. Advantages of homework from the behavior therapy perspective include the opportunity for patients to experiment with new behaviors in different contexts, and increasing feelings of self-efficacy when the homework is done outside the presence of the therapist, thereby teaching the client to be their own therapist. "Repeated practice strengthens this new stimuli-response, while weakening the old maladaptive responses" (Ledley and Huppert, p. 4, Chapter 2). Within-session structure usually consists of the first and last 10 minutes of the session consisting of homework review of the past week and homework planning for the next week (making up at least 40% of the typical session). A review of the previous week's homework is conducted in order to facilitate compliance, where difficulties and learning experiences are discussed.

Along similar lines, Neimeyer and Winter (Chapter 11) describe homework as complementary to the theoretical tenets of personal construct theory, explaining that "from its inception [Personal Construct Therapy] sought to extend therapy beyond the four walls of the consulting room through the judicious use of between-session assignments" (p. 2). According to the authors, homework is one method by which Kelly's "person as scientist" metaphor is enacted. In completing homework assignments, the client is thought of as the "principle investigator" in "field experiments" in which the client's behavior is the independent variable in the design (Kelly, 1991).

The same emphasis can be found in chapters that focus on the treatment of specific disorders rather than general chapters on therapeutic modality. For example, in their chapter on eating disorders, Schlam and Wilson (Chapter 16) explain, "Homework is absolutely essential to the effective use of CBT in the treatment of eating disorders and in the prevention of relapse. Adherence to homework assignments, including difficult assignments that provoke anxiety, is best achieved in the context of a strong relationship in which clients understand the rationale for the assignment and are able to articulate in their own words how the assignment may help them" (p. 31). Johnson's discussion (Chapter 15) on chronic pain emphasizes the importance of homework by asserting, "home practice, following initial in-session instruction and coaching *is* the treatment" (p. 3, original author emphasis).

Clearly paradigms differ in the extent they seek to use homework to directly enact the various tenets of the theory. For example, Twohig, Pierson, and Hayes (Chapter 7) describe specific, manualized homework techniques for each of six psychological techniques within Acceptance and Commitment Therapy. In order to help a client with the technique of Contact with the Present Moment in which the client is encouraged to experience the world directly as opposed to experiencing it as it is structured by the products of thought, clients may be given a homework assignment called the "Tin Can Monster Exercise" (Hayes, Strosahl, & Wilson, 1999). This contrasts sharply with homework assignments that are more specifically tailored to particular problems. For example, Clark (Chapter 18) describes CBT homework exercises that are "designed to challenge the faulty appraisals and beliefs of the obsession, to reinforce more adaptive evaluations of the obsession, and to encourage cessation of compulsions or neutralizing activities. Most of the homework assignments are based on exposure and response prevention but are modified into actual behavioral experiments that test out faulty appraisals and beliefs of OCD" (p. 18). These behavioral experiments take the form of directly investigating the unique faulty appraisals of each client.

It is obvious that homework is central to behavioral and cognitive-behavioral orientations as well as to some couple and family treatments, and that researchers and clinicians within these theoretical orientations have made the majority of contributions to understanding the requirements necessary for effective use of homework. It is also important to note that homework is not viewed as a defining characteristic of many mainstream therapies, as evidenced by authors of chapters in the current text who focus their efforts on only a particular variant of the larger, traditional approach. For example, Stricker (Chapter 6) acknowledges that homework is not integrated into mainstream psychodynamic therapy, and focuses on the assimilative psychodynamic approach, and Young and Mufson (Chapter 5), focus on treatment for depressed adolescents specifically, rather than the general interpersonal therapy approach. This lack of overall theory inclusion certainly gives rise to the possibility that many effective treatments do not regularly utilize homework, and still produce equivalent outcomes. It is, of course, unclear as to whether equivalent outcomes are alternately due to failure to assess therapist adherence and competence with manualized delivery employing homework, and/or poor methods of assessing patient compliance. Finally, Witty (Chapter 2) directly acknowledges the issue that homework is rarely employed within the client-centered approach, and focuses her effort on the small portion of time when homework is utilized in treatment.

HOMEWORK (BETWEEN-SESSION ACTIVITY) AND PSYCHOTHERAPY OUTCOME

Given the importance accorded homework in the directive therapies one would expect a substantial body of empirical evidence supporting its effective use. It is surprising to find that even in this Handbook, empirical evidence for the value of homework assignments is far from substantial. Several reasons for this situation exist. First, most attention in research studies has been devoted to the effects of overall treatments rather than to the single aspect of homework. To some degree this represents the level of maturity in the scientific exploration of cognitive-behavioral and related psychotherapies. We are still establishing overall treatment effects, and when the components of treatment have been considered, attention has been focused on theory-based mechanisms, rather than on mode of delivery or implementation.

Secondly, defining homework is problematic. Formulating a general definition that narrows homework activity to a discrete activity such that interventions that contain it are distinguished from those that do not, can only be accomplished with great difficulty when homework is embedded within treatment. Homework studies are more common and more easily accomplished when the homework activity represents an almost independent activity, such as self-exposure homework for phobia, rather than an inseparable aspect of overall treatment, such as supporting a patient's initiation of a new behavior that they have tried out in psychotherapy and want to practice the coming week.

As a reader of the present volume can see, the activities that fall under this rubric are very broad. The chapters in this volume define homework, variously, as a myriad of activities including: full-on adjuncts to therapy (e.g., 12-step program for substance abuse, undergoing assertiveness training), provision of self-help home reading materials with directed activities (e.g., treatments aimed at reducing sexual dysfunction), making a "simple" request of a patient that requires out of session activity (e.g., asking a patient to bring a spouse or family member to treatment), to completing forms and questionnaires that are filled out at home.

Despite the way in which homework is conceptualized and defined there is no difficulty in making homework the central topic of an entire book (such as the present one) that guides the reader towards applications with highly diverse patient populations. This diversity is recognized as an unavoidable outgrowth of theoretical divergence regarding what is helpful in treatment (e.g., restructuring family systems versus an activity that has direct effects on the individual) and a consequence of the diversity in patient problems (e.g., an activity related to testing beliefs about an event versus building a skill that is essential to daily functioning for a patient with TBI). Although expected, the level of diversity in definitions of what constitutes homework and suggestions for implementation does, however, create some difficulty with summarizing the effects of homework across studies. Indeed, when one witnesses the diversity of activities which pass under the rubric of "homework" it is easy to see the problem of summarizing the effects of homework on outcome. This problem was recognized early on in relation to the diversity of treatments that were lumped under the heading of "psychotherapy" and aptly termed the "uniformity myth" by Kiesler (1966). In his view it made little sense to sum across highly diverse treatments and to draw general conclusions that might not be true of any particular treatment.

Notwithstanding this diversity in the content of homework assignments, basic theoretical rationales for the use of homework and its impact exist. For example, the behavioral principle of generalization provides a basis for the process of including homework, and theories of behavioral conditioning assist in explaining patient motivation for engagement. Thus, although diversity of homework content is to be expected and was acknowledged by Kazantzis, Deane, and Ronan (2000) in a meta-analysis of homework effects, underlying foundational theories for the use of homework assignments have been identified [see Kazantzis & L'Abate (2005) for a summary].

As a beginning to understanding homework and treatment outcome we turn our attention to the research evidence as it exists. The most widely quoted and authoritative analysis of the effects of homework on treatment outcome is that of Kazantzis, Deane, and Ronan (2000). These authors reported a meta-analysis of all studies that met inclusion criteria, a surprisingly small number; 11 studies (the majority of which were published in the 1980s) examined the effect of homework on treatment outcome. Ten of eleven studies involved cognitive, behavioral, or cognitive-behavioral interventions. They also summed 16 studies that examined the relation between homework *compliance* and outcome, a topic we shall return to later. Unfortunately sample characteristics were not reported separately for the homework outcome studies and those examining compliance/outcome relations, but the nature of homework across studies was amazingly heterogeneous, with four of the 26 focusing on relaxation practice, three examining self-graduated exposure, and two on assertiveness training tasks. The remainder of studies used "a wide variety of homework assignments" (p. 193) or surprisingly, did not provide adequate information on the nature of homework.

Another limitation of this meta-analysis was the failure to discuss the nature of the comparison treatments with which the homework was compared, such that the effect size of $r = 0.36$ reported for the impact of homework on outcome cannot be easily interpreted.[1] Excluded details prevent the reader from easily ascertaining if a comparative treatment was examined, if random assignment to treatment conditions was accomplished, or even if the effect size comparison was between two bona fide treatments or between a treatment condition and a placebo control. This problem is compounded by the fact that effect sizes for each study comparison are not provided and so it is not clear which of the many comparisons are used for effect size calculation and which effect size came from which study. The nature of comparison groups and resulting effect sizes is an important concern. Generally, an effect size comparing outcomes from pre- to post treatment average around a $d = 1.2$, those comparing a placebo group and a treatment group average closer to 0.40, and those comparing a bona fide treatment with another bona fide treatment average somewhere between 0 and .2.

Thus the effect size $r = 0.36$ ($d = 0.77$) could be seen as indicating a relatively large effect with a high level of clinical meaningfulness, or of much less importance, depending upon the kind of control the homework group was compared to. Using Rosenthal and Rubin's (1982) criterion for interpreting an effect size, an effect size of $r = 0.36$ (see footnote 1) denotes that the success rate for groups who missed out on homework (no homework) is estimated to be 32% while the success rate for those in the homework condition is 68%. Another way of looking at this effect size is to simply square it and conclude that an effect size of $r = 0.36$ suggests homework accounts for 13% of the variance in outcome. These estimates are, of course, not so exact and one must keep in mind that the effect size statistic does not provide much information about the clinical significance of an individual patient's improvement. Thus, even if the overall effect size of the 11 studies reported in this meta-analysis is interpreted to warrant the conclusion that homework has a modest effect on patient outcome; the clinical meaningfulness of this finding with regard to the individual client is still unknown. The "true effect" for the individual client may be much less because clinical significance offers a higher standard for the amount of treatment gains needed to interpret the treatment as helpful.

Examination of each of the 11 studies does little to invoke confidence in the conclusion that homework rests on a firm empirical foundation with regard to its impact on outcome. The following examination of one of the 11 studies included in the meta-analysis illustrates this point. Gasman (1992) asked 88 of his patients whom he had asked to view videotapes of their psychodynamic treatment sessions, to retrospectively fill out a homemade 9-item questionnaire asking about the success of their treatment and their reaction to viewing the session videotapes. He also self-selected 49 of his past clients who had not seen videotaped therapy sessions to complete a modification of the same questionnaire. The questionnaire response rates were 94%

---

[1] The meta-analysis reports the effect size as an r rather the Cohen's d, but either statistic can be transformed to the other by applying a simple formula. The formula for converting r to d is $d = 2r/$ the square root of $1 - r^2$. Thus, an $r = 0.36 =$ a d of 0.77.

and 60%, respectively. Assessment of outcome was based on a single item: "Rate the success of your psychotherapy overall" which was rated on a 10- point scale (1 = "no effect", 10 = "complete success").

Results indicated that a select sub-sample of 50 patients from the videotape group provided an average rating of 6.8, and a sub sample of 26 from the treatment-as-usual "controls" provided an average rating of 5.04. The majority of those who responded to the questionnaire item found viewing sessions of their therapy to be helpful, with a single patient regarding it as harmful (with one-third of those who viewed their session videotape and half of the controls completing the questions by phone).

Because of the serious and numerous methodological problems with this study (poor outcome assessment, retrospective recall, a single therapist, biased sampling, incomplete data, etc.), we are almost sure that most practitioners and certainly researchers would regard this study as, at most, a pilot study (as the author did) and as undeserving of inclusion in a quantitative review of literature on the effects of homework. Despite the fact the analysis of the data produced a rather large effect size ($d = 1.37$; $r = 0.56$), the methodology of the study is so weak that it should be excluded from consideration.

Other studies included in the Kazantzis et al. (2000) review are better designed, but still have significant problems because they include treatments that did not compare homework with an appropriate control group. For example, Jannoun, Munby, Catlyn, and Gelder (1980) studied two home-based treatment programs for agoraphobia consisting of programmed practice in entering feared situations or a treatment based on resolving life problems. Both treatments took place in the patient's homes, both were offered as forms of self-help, and both involved spouses. In the exposure treatment, instructions for facing feared situations were offered and step-by-step instructions were given with the expectation that the patient would leave the house at least on a daily basis. Unfortunately, the most appropriate control, if an understanding of homework effects were the focus, would have been a similar exposure-based treatment without practice, rather than the placebo control that was employed. Thus the authors discuss the major findings and conclude that agoraphobia improves if anxiety is lowered regardless of the methods used to reduce anxiety (exposure or problem solving). The study might be more aptly interpreted as exposure versus control, rather than homework versus no homework.

Similarly, Jannoun, Oppenheimer, and Gelder (1982) used a methodology in studying a self-help treatment program for anxiety reduction that is inappropriate for estimating the effects of homework because the comparison group consisted of wait-list control patients instead of a treatment that excluded homework but was otherwise similar. They found that minimal therapist contact and directed practice in anxiety self-management produced greater improvements than the passage of time. There was no way of separating out the homework component of treatment from the effects of the overall, largely manual-directed anxiety management program. In sum, including the two aforementioned studies in an analysis of the size of homework effects is questionable.

Additionally, more carefully controlled and appropriate studies of homework are also reported in the Kazantzis et al. (2000) meta-analysis. Blanchard et al. (1991b), for example, examined the impact of home practice in thermal biofeedback on headache reduction. The experimental group received 12 sessions of in-session practice and additional home practice (with an assistant), and was compared with a randomly assigned in-session practice only group, and a self-monitoring group. Both treatment groups had better outcomes than the self-monitoring group, but no incremental improvements in headache reduction or hand-warming response could be found for the inclusion of homework, despite patient compliance with homework. The authors concluded that involving patients by encouraging them to be more responsible for their headache treatment could not be shown to be more effective than having them participate in a more passive role, where the therapists takes more control of the practice sessions. Kazantzis et al. also included a second study from this research group (Blanchard et al., 1991a) that focused on tension headache and deep muscle relaxation that reported similar findings—no effects for out of office practice.

Unfortunately, it is not possible to tell how the effect sizes from these two studies were calculated in the meta-analysis. The effect size of interest is the comparison between treatment-as-usual and treatment-as-usual-plus-home-practice, rather than the effect size between treatment-as-usual-plus-homework and the self-monitoring control group. In this latter case the effect size would be moderate, in the former it would approach zero, and if combined, the effect size would overstate the effects of homework.

Since the Kazantzis et al. (2000) review appeared, additional research has been conducted but it is beyond the scope of this chapter to attempt a full review of this literature. Certainly as more studies emerge a greater understanding of the role of homework will emerge. Instead we consider here a single well-designed study and its possible implications for practice. Park et al. (2001) reported a two-year follow-up of 68 (out of 80) phobic patients, about half of whom had a simple phobia with the rest agoraphobic or social phobic, who completed a 14-week randomized trial comparing therapist-accompanied exposure, self-exposure, or self-relaxation. The design included two types of treatment: (1) a condition intended to be the treatment of choice (exposure) and (2) a condition intended to be less potent (relaxation). Similarly, two types of treatment implementation were assessed: (1) therapist-assisted treatment and (2) homework (self-exposure)-enhanced treatment. The behavior therapy consisted of six 60-minute sessions with a therapist and assignment of homework (mean total amount of self-exposurehomework was 52 hours). Therapist assisted exposure consisted of six 90- minute sessions over 8 weeks, and average total homework time of 59 hours over 14 weeks. Measures of outcome were self-reportedratings of symptoms, satisfaction and use of other treatment.

Improvement (which was significant for the exposure conditions) was accomplished by week 14 and was maintained at two-year follow-up. Although clinician-accompanied exposure and self-exposure did not differon any measure, compliance with self-exposure homework (as rated by therapist) duringweeks 0–8 predicted more improvement two years later. Interestingly, those patients who recruited a relative or friend to help them with exposure had better outcomes at the end of treatment than those who did not, but at follow-up were more prone to lose gains than those who did not have this type of assistance. Patientswho failed to improve with relaxation by week 14 improved after asubsequent crossover to exposure. A need for more treatmentfor their phobias was still felt by 33 (49%) patients at the two-year follow-up.

This study suggests that the "right" treatment (i.e., exposure), could be offered either with therapist presence or as self-guided homework and have the same positive effect on patients suffering with phobic disorders, provided they go through the exposure practice. It provides some evidence for the use of collaterals to help with self-exposure, but indicated their use may be related to greater loss of gains two years post-treatment. If clinical practice were guided by only the results of this study, it would last eight weeks, exposure would be preferred over relaxation, self-guided homework would be preferred over therapist-accompanied exposure (for cost/benefit reasons), and use of collaterals to implement homework would be avoided, due to the probability of losing gains during the two years following treatment. Patients could be expected to wish they had more time with their therapist, a sizable portion would seek further treatment during the two years, and at least half would feel a need to undergo further treatment by the end of two years. Despite the demonstrated cost/benefit value of homework, the effect size for this type of intervention would approach zero.

Unfortunately, practice cannot be guided by a single study, and this particular study provides evidence to support (e.g,. homework) and argue against (e.g., use of collaterals) specific clinical practices. This study provides evidence of the complexity of outcomes that result from careful examination of the effects of interventions. In addition to the effect of homework on outcome, homework may alter treatment in other ways. For example, in their retrospective analysis of 25 years of face-to-face psychotherapy sessions with clients utilizing a number of treatment modalities, L'Abate, L'Abate, and Maino (2005) reported that homework assignments actually increased, rather than decreased, the number of treatment sessions. Not surprisingly, drawing conclusions regarding the impact of homework requires acknowledgement of a myriad of both therapy process and outcome variables.

SUMMARY

In general, the studies reviewed here suggest the difficulty of establishing the effects of homework on the variables that are claimed to make it an advantage—such as the maintenance of treatment effects, for which we could not find any support in the literature that we reviewed. It is important to note that within the context of the chapters in this text, few of the authors provided extensive, if any at all, independent empirical investigations and confirmation of the effects of homework on patient outcome, with most relying on the single meta-analysis of homework, or the theoretical/clinical assumption of effects. For example, Johnson (Chapter 15) acknowledges, "there is not much firm evidence for the efficacy of homework for psychological treatment of chronic pain. . . ." before detailing homework exercises employed for this condition (p. 2). Similarly, many of the studies described in this volume provide support for the type of treatment being offered without partitioning out the effects that are specifically due to homework. While understandably, dismantling out the specific effects of homework is difficult to do, this is an area of research that warrants attention. Others reported empirical studies that were primarily descriptive in nature and did not directly address the question of the relationship of homework to outcome. Lindenboim, Chapman, and Linehan (Chapter 13) addressed the role of homework in DBT with a description of one study detailing the average number of DBT homework skills practiced per day and another study in which clients rated their perceptions of the usefulness of the DBT homework skills on a 5-point scale. Similarly, Ellison and Greenberg (Chapter 4) refer to a study that discusses the procedure of homework and how to implement it in Emotion Focused Therapy, but does not appear to examine the effectiveness of the implementation of homework in the EFT approach.

In order for practitioners to feel confident that the homework they encourage their patients to engage in is based on an empirical foundation, a great deal more research must be undertaken with favorable results. Since homework has so many faces, this research is likely to take decades. Suggestions for future research will be provided shortly. Before turning to this task, some comments on homework compliance are in order.

HOMEWORK COMPLIANCE AND OUTCOME

Not only is there diversity in what is considered homework, there is diversity in the way a therapist makes an assignment, with implementation of assignments possibly being just as important as the content of the specific assignment itself. Effective use of homework assignments is a major factor that has an influence on outcome and its importance has been recognized within the writings of nearly all the authors of the chapters in this text. There will always be patients who fully engage in the treatment, by becoming involved in the change processes the treatment is attempting to promote, and those who do not. Compliance with homework, within the treatments that make it essential, is a central issue in creating treatments that fully engage all the patients in all the active ingredients of the treatment that are necessary for resolution of problems. As one author puts it: "In all cases, homework requires collaboration, judicious preparation, and careful timing in order to promote compliance and prevent relapse" (Gambescia & Weeks, p. 30, Chapter 20). These authors have found that homework that is intersystemic is most comprehensive since it addresses individual factors, relational problems, and internalized messages from the partners' families of origin. The emphasis on compliance in clinical practice and training reflects the belief that completion of assignments is highly related to positive outcomes and is reflected in relatively high research activity.

An indirect method of confirming the value of homework to patients is to show that there is a relationship between patient engagement in more or less homework and ultimate treatment outcome. A similar tactic has been used extensively within the experiential therapies to confirm the presumed theoretical importance of therapist offered facilitative conditions and patient improvement. As an example, consider recent research exploring the relationship between the therapeutic alliance and outcome, which has been summarized by Horvath and Symonds (1991). Such research has generally relied on correlational designs that have generated a substantial amount of research dating back over four decades. This research strategy is especially important when systematic experimental manipulation of a variable is considered unethical, e.g., having therapists intentionally disagree on goals and tasks, create a negative bond, intentionally misunderstand, be disrespectful, and phony, etc. Although such ethical concerns do not necessarily apply to the assignment of homework, where experimental manipulation of homework could be accomplished without ethical concerns, practical constraints can be just as problematic. For example, since the field has been most in need of establishing the overall effects of treatments, it has made little sense to use time, money, and energy with experimental manipulation of homework itself. Correlations between compliance and outcome can be derived from studies in which this interest is not central to the investigation.

Kazantzis et al. (2000, 2004) have provided the most authoritative analysis of findings in this area. In their 2000 meta-analysis, these authors concluded that the effect size for the relationship between compliance and outcome was an $r = 0.22$. The effect size r of 0.22 can be interpreted as indicating there was a 22% difference in outcome as a result of homework compliance across the 16 studies that met inclusion criteria (e.g., with the success rate for the compliant clients estimated to be about 61%, while that for the non compliant clients being 39%). This effect size reflects the average size of correlations found in investigations that did not require a control group or an experiment to compute. Alternately, it can be interpreted as the typical r squared, (0.22 squared = compliance accounts for approximately 5% of the variance in outcome).

In their more recent 2004 article Kazantzis et al., examined 32 studies on compliance and were more critical of the heterogeneity of methodology used to examine compliance and outcome. They suggest that the field would benefit from greater attention and uniformity in the timing and nature of compliance assessment. The reader who is interested in pursuing research on this topic should consult the Kazantzis et al. (2004) article for valuable guidelines. For example, the compliant or dependent client may be more likely to report doing homework but also inclined to report improvement as a way of pleasing the therapist or researchers. Therefore, the research should consider the feasibility of using multiple sources for studying both compliance and outcome. Of course, multiple sources have always been recognized to be of value for assessing outcome (Hill & Lambert, 2004) but are even more important in estimating compliance partly because the subjective experience of compliance is not the phenomenon of interest in compliance research whereas it is an essential aspect of outcome. Owing to the difficulty of separating the effects of compliance and outcome, it may be useful to identify homework compliance as the measured outcome variable.

As suggested above, not only are the methods of studying compliance complicated, but even when accomplished, the resulting correlations can be hard to interpret. Unfortunately, even if the best methodology is applied and an even stronger link between homework compliance and outcomes is established, there is no guarantee that a third variable isn't responsible for both engagement with homework and outcome. This has led to a number of studies that attempt to show that not only is compliance important but that it makes a contribution to outcome that is independent from other variables. Typical of research in this area is a study by Burns and Spangler (2000) that used structural equation modeling to examine the "causal" relationship between homework compliance and outcome in samples of 122 and 399 adult depressed patients who underwent cognitive behavioral psychotherapy. Although they found the typical correlation ($r = 0.19 - 0.21$) between ratings (clinician and patient) of compliance and outcome, the use of statistical controls allowed them to report that the correlation between homework compliance and outcome was not due to levels of patient depression and that those who are least depressed do not overestimate their engagement in homework. In addition, they found that pretreatment motivation did not relate to ratings of outcome or compliance, suggesting that positive effects of treatment were not due to this "extraneous" variable.

Once the relationship between compliance and outcome was calculated by eliminating measurement error, they were able to calculate the size of the relationship, if measured perfectly and some factors were factored out. In this case the relationship was found to be very large and was interpreted as suggesting that those patients who did homework changed substantially (about 16 points on the Beck Depression

Inventory), while those who did not, experienced almost no change (2–3 points on the Beck Depression Inventory). Unfortunately, certain information appears to be missing from the report of this research—such as the amount of improvement in depression that could be attributed to other aspects of the CBT treatment like variability due to in-session behaviors, activities, and interactions; specific therapists; and the like. The Burns and Spangler application of structural equation modeling tested for the possible mediating or moderating effects of demographic, therapist identities, medication, therapeutic empathy, and willingness in examining the homework compliance—outcome relationship. Nevertheless, other theoretically meaningful aspects of the mechanism by which homework produces its effects were *not* measured. Thus, as noted by Kazantzis, Ronan, and Deane (2001), the Burns and Spangler report is at fault for purporting to measure a *casual* relationship from correlational data.

Despite limitations and some confusion about the size of homework compliance effects, there is little doubt that compliance and outcome are related, and if we assume a causal relationship, then some justification can be made for the confidence that therapists place on the importance of ensuring compliance.

FUTURE RESEARCH DIRECTIONS

After reviewing the chapters in this Handbook and published research on the topic of homework, several directions for future research are apparent.

(1) Given the "essential" place given homework in the directive therapies, more experimental research in which homework is manipulated and compared with treatment without homework is essential. The most recent meta-analysis covering the 1980s and 1990s produced a mere 11 studies, and if design quality standards had been imposed a meta-analysis of results would not have been possible. The most logical research designs to implement would involve examining treatment effects through the isolation of various components, by separating components from, or adding components to, existing treatments. Dismantling and constructive research designs might be applied with some success to identify the essential aspects of homework assisted treatment (e.g., Borkovec, 1993).

However, the ambitious and hopeful researcher should be warned that the majority of studies that employ such designs fail to find that "essential" aspects are, in fact, essential (Lambert & Bergin, 1994). If fact such research shows that one can do away with almost all specific aspects of treatment without diminishing patient outcome. In an analysis of research using such designs, Ahn & Wampold (2001) examined component analyses conducted over an 18-year period and found that adding or removing components of treatment did not change the effects of the core treatment. These authors concluded that the lack of findings within these dismantling and constructive designs suggests "there is little evidence that specific ingredients are necessary to produce psychotherapeutic change" (p. 126). Nevertheless, there is always a chance that homework, of certain kinds, may be found to be essential.

(2) Research already underscores the importance of such factors as social support and the therapeutic alliance in positive outcomes (Lambert & Barley, 2001). It may be helpful to study these as moderating variables that aid in the degree of homework compliance, particularly with respect to more difficult or challenging assignments.

Given that research shows the alliance to be such a consistent contributor to outcome, the idea of its primacy in the completion of homework is an important area of further investigation. Certainly the importance of relationship factors in the use of homework is a repeated theme in nearly all chapters of this book and continued investigation of beliefs and practices in this area is needed.

(3) Directive therapies maintain that homework assignments are client specific and can be unique in nature. Future research may investigate differences between standardized homework for specific problems and unique homework for these same problems, while tracking the therapist's rationale for such decisions, and the client's outcome. Does the therapist's level of experience with directive therapy techniques affect the type of homework assigned, and is homework in directive therapy limited by a therapist with limited experience in directive therapies, which in turn may affect outcome.

(4) It would be of value to understand more about what happens when a homework assignment goes awry. How long does it take for the client to recover and try homework again? Does a bad experience with homework affect the therapeutic relationship? What does it do to the client and their sense of self-efficacy when an exercise that worked in the session, doesn't work at home? In general, it would be valuable to examine negative effects that arise from the use of homework as negative effects often provide more important learning than successes (Lambert, 2005).

(5) Most approaches that utilize homework interventions claim there is collaboration between the client and the therapist. This idea is based on therapist report and theory. Does the client, indeed, feel that this is collaboration, or does the client view it as a direct assignment from the therapist? In general, more process research on homework could be enlightening.

(6) For approaches that do not traditionally utilize homework in treatment, it may be of interest to explore the degree and nature of homework activity. Since these activities have been largely ignored in research within these treatments we do not really understand their contribution to client outcome. It would be interesting to know if differences in outcome between clients who participate in these types of treatments can be attributed to active engagement in self-initiated "homework."

REFERENCES

Ahn, H., & Wampold, B. E. (2001). Where oh where are the specific ingredients? A meta-analysis of component studies in counseling and psychotherapy. *Journal of Counseling Psychology, 48*, 251–257.

American Psychiatric Association (2004). *Diagnostic and statistical manual of mental disorders-IV* (5th ed.). Washington, DC: APA.

Anderson, E. M., & Lambert, M. J. (2001). A survival analysis of clinically significant change in outpatient psychotherapy. *Journal of Clinical Psychology, 57*, 875–888.

Blanchard, E. B., Nicholson, N. L., Radnitz, C. L., Steffek, B. D., Applebaum, K. A., & Dentinger, M. P. (1991a). The role of home practice in thermal biofeedback. *Journal of Consulting & Clinical Psychology, 59*, 507–512.

Blanchard, E. B., Nicholson, N. L., Taylor, A. E., Steffek, B. D., Radnitz, C. L.,& Applebaum, K. A. (1991b). The role of regular home practice in the relaxation treatment of tension headache. *Journal of Consulting & Clinical Psychology, 59*, 467–470.

Borkovec, T. D. (1993). Between-group therapy outcome research: Design and methodology. In L. S. Onken, J. D. Blaine, & J. J. Boren (Eds.), *Behavioral treatments for drug abuse and dependence* (pp. 249–290). Rockville, MD: National Institute on Drug Abuse.

Burns, D. D., & Spangler, D. L. (2000). Does psychotherapy homework lead to improvements in depression in cognitive-behavioral therapy? Or does improvement lead to increased homework compliance? *Journal of Consulting and Clinical Psychology, 68*, 46–56.

Castonguay, L. G., & Beutler, L. E. (Eds.). (2005). *Principles of therapeutic change that work.* New York: Oxford University Press.

Chiles, J. A., Lambert, M. J., & Hatch, A. L. (1999). The impact of psychological interventions on medial cost -offset: A meta-analytic review. *Clinical Psychology: Science and Practice, 2*, 204–220.

DeRubeis, R. J., Tang, T. Z., & Beck, A. T. (2001). Cognitive therapy. In K. S. Dobson (Ed.), *Handbook of cognitive-behavioral therapies* (2nd ed.). New York: Guilford.

Gasman, D. H. (1992). Double-exposure therapy: Videotape homework as a psychotherapy adjunct. *American Journal of Psychotherapy, 46*, 91–101.

Hannan, C., Lambert, M. J., Harmon, C., Nielsen, S. L., Smart, D. M., Shimokawa, K., & Hayes, S. C., Strosahl, K. & Wilson, K. G. (1999). *Acceptance and commitment therapy: An experiential approach to behavior change.* New York: Guilford.

Hill, C. E. & Lambert, M. J. (2004) Methodological issues in studying psychotherapy processes and outcomes. In M. J. Lambert (Ed.). *Bergin & Garfield's handbook of psychotherapy and behavior change* (5th Ed., pp. 84–135). New York: Wiley.

Horvath, A. O., & Symonds, B. D. (1991). Relationship between working alliance and outcome in psychotherapy: A meta-analysis. *Journal of Counseling Psychology, 38*, 139–149.

Jannoun, L., Munby, M., Catlin, J., & Gelder, M. (1980). A home-based treatment program for agoraphobia: Replication and controlled evaluation. *Behavior Therapy, 11*, 294–305.

Jannoun, L., Oppenheimer, C., Gelder, M. (1982). A self-help treatment program for anxiety state patients. *Behavior Therapy, 13*, 103–111.

Kazantzis, N., Deane, F. P., & Ronan, K. R. (2000). Homework assignments in cognitive and behavioral therapy: A meta-analysis. *Clinical Psychology: Science and Practice, 7*, 189–202.

Kazantzis, N., Deane, F. P., & Ronan, K. R. (2004). Assessing compliance with homework assignments: Review and recommendations for clinical practice. *Journal of Clinical Psychology, 60*, 627–641.

Kazantzis, N., & L'Abate, L. (2005). Theoretical foundations. In N. Kazantzis, F. P. Deane, K. R. Ronan, & L. L'Abate (Eds.), *Using homework assignments in cognitive behavior therapy* (pp. 9–33). New York: Routledge.

Kazantzis, N., & Lampropoulos, G. K. (2002). The use of homework in psychotherapy: An introduction. *Journal of Clinical Psychology: In Session, 58*, 487–488.

Kazantzis, N., Ronan, K. R., & Deane, F. P. (2001). Concluding causation from correlation: Comment on Burns and Spangler (2000). *Journal of Consulting and Clinical Psychology, 69*, 1079–1083.

Kelly, G. A. (1991). *The psychology of personal constructs.* New York: Routledge.

Kiesler, D. J. (1966). Some myths of psychotherapy research and the search for a paradigm. *Psychological Bulletin, 65*, 110–136.

L'Abate, L., L'Abate, B., & Maino, E. (2005). Reviewing 25 years of clinical practice: Homework assignments and length of therapy. *The American Journal of Family Therapy, 39*, 19–31.

Lambert, M. J. (2005). Emerging methods for providing clinicians with timely feedback on effective treatment: An introduction. *Journal of Clinical Psychology: In Session, 61*, 141–144.

Lambert, M. J. (Ed) (2004). *Bergin & Garfield's handbook of psychotherapy and behavior change* (5th ed.). New York: Wiley.

Lambert, M. J. (2002). Psychotherapy outcome research: Implications for integrative and eclectic therapists. In J. C. Norcross & M. R. Goldfried (Eds.), *Handbook of psychotherapy integration* (pp. 94–129). New York: Basic Books, Inc.

Lambert, M. J., & Barley, D. E. (2001). Research summary on the therapeutic relationship and psychotherapy outcome. *Psychotherapy, 38*, 357–361.

Lambert, M. J., & Bergin, A. E. (1994). The effectiveness of psychotherapy. In A. E. Bergin & S. L. Garfield (Eds.), *Handbook of psychotherapy and behavior change* (4th ed.) (pp. 143–189). New York: Wiley.

Lambert, M. J., & Ogles, B. M. (2004). The efficacy and effectiveness of psychotherapy. In M. J. Lambert (Ed.). *Bergin & Garfield's handbook of psychotherapy and behavior change* (5th ed.) pp. 139–193). New York: Wiley.

Nathan, P. E., & Gorman, J. M. (Eds.). (2002). *A guide to treatments that work* (2nd ed). New York: Oxford University Press.

Norcross, J. C. (Ed) (2002). *Psychotherapy relationships that work: Therapist contributions and responsiveness to patient needs.* New York: Oxford University Press.

Okiishi J., Lambert, M. J., Nielsen, S. L., & Ogles, B. M. (2003). In search of supershink: Using patient outcome to identify effective and ineffective therapists. *Clinical Psychology and Psychotherapy, 10*, 361–373.

Orlinsky, D. E., Ronnestad, M. H., & Ulrike, W. (2004). Fifty years of psychotherapy process-outcome research: Continuity and change. In M. J. Lambert (Ed.). *Bergin & Garfield's handbook of psychotherapy and behavior change* (5th ed.) pp. 307–390). New York: Wiley.

Park, J-M., Mataix-Cols, D., Marks, I. M., Ngamthipwatthana, T., Marks, M., Araya, R., and Al-Kubaisy, T. (2001). Two-year follow-up after a randomized controlled trial of self- and clinician-accompanied exposure for phobia/panic disorders. *British Journal of Psychiatry, 178*, 543–548.

Rosenthal, R., & Rubin, D. (1982). A simple, general purpose display of magnitude of experimental effect. *Journal of Educational Psychology, 74*, 166–169.

Roth, A., & Fonagy, P. (2005). What works with whom: A critical review of psychotherapy research (2nd ed.). New York: Guilford.

Shelton, J. L., & Levy, R. L. (1981). *Behavioral assignments and treatment strategies: A review of treatment strategies* Champaign, IL: Research Press.

Wampold, B. E., (2001). *The great psychotherapy debate: Models, methods, and findings.* New Jersey: Lawrence Erlbaum Associates, Inc.

CHAPTER 24

DIRECTIONS FOR THE INTEGRATION OF HOMEWORK IN PRACTICE

Dana L. Nelson, Louis G. Castonguay, and Fiona Barwick

Homework has been described as "the most generic of behavioral interventions—and one that greatly and immediately distinguishes behavior therapy from psychoanalysis" (Goisman 1985, p. 676). For decades, cognitive-behavioral approaches have indeed encouraged homework use as an effective behavioral intervention for specific problems, such as obsessions or compulsions and sexual dysfunction. Despite its association with and popularization by CBT, however, homework is no longer the narrow province of this theoretical tradition. As research has linked homework to better treatment outcomes and to long-term maintenance of treatment gains (Kazantzis, Deane, & Ronan, 2000), homework has earned the attention of therapists and researchers outside of CBT. A number of different therapies now actively encourage the use of homework, as many of the preceding chapters of this volume illustrate. Some researchers even argue that the acquisition and development of adaptive skills through between-session activities is a feature common to both cognitive-behavioral and dynamic therapies (Badgio, Halperin, & Barber, 1999). It may therefore be time to add homework to the list of so-called "common factors," which are viewed as active therapeutic ingredients cutting across theoretical orientations.

This chapter will address the conceptual convergence and, to a lesser extent, divergence across orientations on the subject of homework. First, we will define what is subsumed under the rubric of "homework." Next, we will discuss the debate over homework prescription. Then, we will articulate the various clinical or therapeutic advantages of homework that apply across orientations. Finally, we will identify the common principles underlying the use of homework in different approaches to psychotherapy. In distilling the information provided in each chapter, our aim is to offer therapists who subscribe to different orientations and clinicians who treat diverse populations a set of heuristics that will help them understand why homework is an important aspect of psychotherapy and a set of guidelines to help them use this important tool more effectively.

WHAT DO WE MEAN BY PSYCHOTHERAPY "HOMEWORK"?

Before we can discuss the use of homework in psychotherapy, we must understand what is meant by the term "homework." Does homework consist only of those activities recommended or assigned by the therapist for the client to do between sessions? Or does homework also include activities discussed in session but planned and developed by the client? Finally, does it or should it encompass therapy-relevant activities in which the client engages between session but which were not previously discussed with the therapist?

For some of us, the term "homework" evokes dim memories of childhood classrooms where teachers spelled out specific assignments, wrote them up on the blackboard, and expected them to be turned in the following day. Psychotherapy homework is sometimes much like this. Therapists from a number of different orientations may ask their clients to read psychoeducational materials, complete worksheets and diaries, or hand in written assignments. Therapists will also commonly suggest that clients pay attention to a particular thought, make note of a certain kind of experience, or try out a new behavior or activity during the week. Whereas this latter use of homework is more of a recommendation while the former is more of a command, describing both exercises as homework would probably provoke little disagreement.

Greater disagreement might arise over the inclusion of homework activities devised by or along with the client. Few of us were lucky enough to have teachers who allowed us to suggest or negotiate our own homework assignments. Yet, many of the preceding chapters emphasize the importance of collaboration between therapist and client in developing homework assignments. Collaboration gives clients greater choice in and control over their between-session activities, thereby increasing their investment in these activities and in therapy. Likewise, the term "homework" can even be extended to include client-initiated activities that bear upon treatment but that are not explicitly negotiated in session. As we will describe in the following section, some approaches consider the prescription of homework to be detrimental to clients and yet recognize the benefits of between-session activities that are initiated by clients. For the sake of respecting the different ways in which homework has been presented in the previous chapters, we thus have decided to define as "homework" any and all between-session activities that are relevant to treatment.

TO PRESCRIBE OR NOT TO PRESCRIBE?

Few therapists would disagree that it is beneficial for clients to engage in therapy-related activities between sessions. There is some debate, however, over whether prescribing or recommending such activities is in the client's best interest. Witty (this volume) points out that, although the use of prescribed homework may help in accomplishing the goal of symptom reduction, it may be detrimental to the realization of other goals such as client empowerment, increased personal authority, and the attainment of a more meaningful life. Coming from the perspective of client-centered therapy and thus committed to the principle of nondirectiveness (or self-directiveness), Witty stresses that unsolicited recommendations by the therapist could contribute to a power dynamic that undermines the client's personal autonomy and demonstrates a lack of trust in the client's self-realizing capacities.

Therapists who emphasize client potentiation and autonomy over symptom reduction maintain that therapists should not impose their own goals for treatment upon their clients by recommending homework, but rather should look to the client's experience as a guide for treatment. They do, however, support collaboration with or acceptance of activities initiated by the client, and they would elect to make recommendations should the client specifically request them. Furthermore, as in all types of therapy, it is assumed that clients will observe the world around them, engage in new activities or have new experiences, and then bring these observations and experiences to therapy for discussion. In other words, whether therapists prescribe homework activities or not, clients will engage in activities between sessions that will undoubtedly influence treatment.

At the opposite pole of the prescriptive spectrum lie cognitive-behavioral and other highly directive therapies. Therapists who identify with these orientations either disagree with the assertion that recommendations will have any detrimental effect or else contend that the benefits of prescribing homework outweigh any detrimental effects they might have. These therapists may believe that it would be ideal for clients to initiate and develop their own assignments; however, because they cannot count on clients to do so or to develop the most appropriate activities, and because the benefits of homework are so clear, these therapists endorse prescribing homework assignments as a guide for clients until they learn how to plan such activities for themselves. Not to prescribe homework, in their view, would be to let numerous and critical opportunities for helping clients pass them by.

Psychodynamic therapies fall between these two extremes. These forms of treatment tend to be relatively nondirective, and explicit homework assignments tend to be the exception rather than the rule. As Stricker (this volume) suggests, however, implicit or "quasi-homework assignments" are common even in the most traditional psychodynamic therapies. He points out that, even when therapists may not intend to make suggestions, clients may infer such suggestions from their questions or responses (e.g., "I wonder what would have happened if you had ..."). Occasionally, psychodynamic therapists will make explicit suggestions for out-of-session activities, but only with clients who are low in reactance and only for the achievement of specific goals, such as when insight has not led to subsequent behavior change. Freud himself wrote, "The pure gold of analysis [might be freely alloyed with] the copper of direct suggestion," (Freud, 1918, as cited in Strupp & Binder, 1984, p. 8) and is known to have suggested to some of his phobic patients that they engage in activities they previously had avoided (Alexander & French, 1946).

Likewise, humanistic therapies other than client-centered therapy fall along different points of the prescriptive spectrum. For example, emotion focused experiential therapy (EFT), as described by Ellison & Greenberg (this volume), frequently involves explicit suggestions for homework but usually frames these suggestions as activities or exercises for clients to try if they find them to be relevant and helpful, rather than as assignments they are necessarily expected to complete.

Although there are disagreements about the potential merits and dangers of prescribing homework, it is probably fair to say that most authors included in this book would agree that the benefits of homework are likely to depend more upon the completion of the homework than upon its discussion or prescription. In other words, whether they believe that homework should be prescribed or not, most therapists, regardless of orientation, consider clients' engagement in therapy-related activities outside of session to be beneficial. A most crucial question thus becomes: What are the benefits of homework beyond those gained from time spent with the therapist in session? We turn to this question next.

WHY USE HOMEWORK
IN PSYCHOTHERAPY?

Different theoretical orientations emphasize different rationales for the use of homework and for the benefits that accrue from it. Underlying these various rationales, however, are a number of common themes. What follows is a list of the themes we have extracted from the preceding chapters.

1. *The explicit use of homework communicates a message to clients about the nature of therapy.*
    In explicitly assigning homework, therapists communicate a message to clients about the nature of therapy and about the role of client. By asking clients to engage in activities outside of therapy—even by setting up the initial expectation of such activities—therapists let clients know that they must be active participants in treatment rather than passive recipients of it. Merely talking about their difficulties during sessions is not enough. This implicit psychoeducation is especially important for certain clinical populations. For example, in her chapter on older adults, DeVries (this volume) points out that this population may be more likely than others to regard therapy as a passive process and may need to be educated about the importance of an active, collaborative stance to the ultimate success of treatment.
    This implicit communication also increases clients' expectations about the process and outcome of psychotherapy—what Frank (1961) so eloquently describes as the provision of a "myth." According to Frank, increasing clients' expectations about therapy can lead to a reversal of demoralization and can promote the expectation of recovery. In turn, expectations of recovery, as we know from research on the placebo effect, can promote actual recovery. These cumulative effects play a crucial role in various forms of treatment. Epstein and Baucom (this volume), for example, describe how distressed couples usually seek therapy only after their relationships have deteriorated and previous attempts at self-help have failed. These couples are thus often skeptical that any treatment will work. Similar dynamics for couples entering treatment for sexual dysfunction have been described by Gambescia and Weeks (this volume). Epstein and Baucom therefore reason that therapists must convey to these distressed couples "some reason for hope that [they] can solve the problems they face" (p. 191). The recommendation of homework activities can serve as one means for implicitly communicating such a message.
2. *Homework assignments allow clients and therapists to gather information in order to better understand the nature of a problem and the use of therapy in addressing it.*
    The initial discussion between therapist and client of the factors that are contributing to current difficulties and of the reasons for seeking treatment is often inadequate in providing the therapist with a full understanding of all the issues that are relevant to treatment. Homework can help elaborate this initial picture. Therapists in more directive orientations will often ask clients to engage in information-gathering

between sessions. Clients might be asked to pay attention to the number of times they perform a certain behavior, such as purging in Bulimia Nervosa or ritualizing in Obsessive-Compulsive Disorder, or they might be asked to record their cognitions and concurrent emotions, as in Major Depressive Disorder or Generalized Anxiety Disorder. Obtaining this kind of data can help the therapist better understand the nature and severity of the client's problem.

Homework assignments continue to provide information throughout the course of treatment. This ongoing stream of data can be used as feedback to shape the approach to treatment. Clients' successful completion, or lack thereof, of the assigned activities lets the therapist know about the particular difficulties, specific strengths, and important contingencies that exist in clients' lives and that contribute to their problems. Several of the authors in this volume have stressed the importance of using feedback from homework exercises to tailor interventions to the particular needs and circumstances of each client. For example, in their discussion of using homework with families, Newcomb, Rekart, and Lebow (this volume) point out how homework assignments can be used to promote family involvement and to identify the constraints that maintain family difficulties as well as the strengths that the family can use to overcome them. Similarly, in their description of dialectical behavior therapy (DBT) with Borderline Personality Disordered patients, Lindenboim, Chapman, and Linehan (this volume) highlight the ways in which information from homework assignments is used to prioritize treatment goals and organize the focus of therapy sessions.

3. *Homework assignments give clients opportunities to raise awareness or achieve insight.*

The information-gathering that therapists often ask their clients to do early in treatment is also known as self-monitoring. Self-monitoring can raise clients' awareness of the problematic behaviors in which they engage and that might be contributing to their distress. These self-monitoring homework activities can sometimes be effective interventions by themselves. In their chapter on eating disorders, for example Schlam and Wilson (this volume) call attention to the fact that "self-monitoring food intake daily can decrease binge eating in the absence of any other intervention" (p. 281). Other authors who have contributed chapters to this volume comment on similar phenomena with different populations: Riso and Thase note that mood monitoring can correct the common misimpression among chronically depressed patients that they do not experience mood fluctuations, whereas Apodaca and Monti (this volume) observe that homework is useful in raising the awareness among substance users of the circumstances associated with abuse of alcohol or drugs and is an important component of several empirically supported treatment models for substance abuse.

Sometimes, however, self-monitoring alone is not enough to change destructive behaviors or cognitions. In such cases, therapists may ask clients to try out new behaviors, responses, or interactional strategies and observe the results of these changes. Based on their personal construct approach, for example, Neimeyer and Winter (this volume) use the metaphor of the "person as scientist" and liken homework to a "field experiment" (p. 152). These "field experiments" can furnish opportunities for clients to test out their hypotheses about the world and, using the data they gather from these experiments, revise their hypotheses as necessary.

Most cognitive-behavioral approaches would subscribe wholeheartedly to the conception of homework as an individual experiment in hypothesis testing. Although psychodynamic and humanistic approaches would be less likely to use this metaphor to describe homework activities, they implicitly ask clients to do the same thing. By asking questions that encourage exploration of the information that clients bring into session, the more nondirective (or self-directive) therapies subtly encourage clients to continue observing and investigating outside of session, thereby allowing them to acquire insight into their difficulties and to make sense of their experiences (see Gelso & Harbin, in press; Schottenbauer, Glass, & Arnkoff, in press). As such, whether therapists explicitly require or implicitly suggest that clients engage in between-session activities, they are advocating a general principle that is found in most therapeutic orientations: helping clients to develop a new perspective of self (Goldfried, 1980).

4. *Engaging in homework activities increases the amount of time clients spend doing therapeutic work.*

The average client spends approximately one hour per week in therapy. This means that for every hour spent in therapy, the client spends approximately 161 hours not in therapy. Subtract time for sleep, and a client still has over 100 hours of non-therapy time for every hour of therapy. Looking solely at time, therapists who want to impact a client's life are at a clear disadvantage in comparison to all the other influences acting on a client outside of therapy. Thus, it is not surprising that one of the rationales for using homework cited by almost every theoretical orientation is the fact that it extends the amount of time clients spend engaging in therapy-related activities.

Cognitive-behavioral therapists argue that more time means more practice—of skills, responses, associations, etc.—and that repeated practice strengthens learning (Goldfried, 2003). Psychodynamic therapists, on the other hand, reason that more time translates into more opportunities for gaining insight, which is not only is a goal in itself but can also be a catalyst for behavior change. While different orientations encourage different types of activities and emphasize different rationale for those activities, they seem to be in general agreement about the importance of homework's corollary benefit to effectively extend the amount of time clients spend doing therapeutic work. Almost all the authors in this volume who discussed the use of homework with specific clinical populations also emphasize this aspect of between-session activities. For older adults, brain-damaged patients, and individuals struggling with obsessive-compulsive disturbances or psychosis, all of whom may learn more slowly or may require more repetition, as well as for couples and families whose maladaptive interaction patterns have frequently been over-learned, practice is crucial to the successful outcome of treatment.

5. *Homework gives clients opportunities to engage in therapeutic work in different contexts outside of therapy.*

Homework not only extends the amount of time clients spend doing therapeutic work; it also increases the number of different contexts in which such work is done. This is important for several reasons. First, research in cognitive-behavioral psychology indicates that learning the same thing in different contexts promotes the retention of, and strengthens the associations for, what has been learned. Cognitive-behavioral therapists thus argue that clients not only should have many opportunities to practice new skills, but they also should have numerous contexts in which to practice them (Goldfried, 2003).

Moreover, homework extends therapeutic work into the client's natural environment. Most therapists, regardless of theoretical orientation, would agree that gains made in a therapeutic setting do clients little good if they do not translate into change outside of that setting. Circumstances and contingencies often exist outside of therapy that contribute to or help maintain clients' problems; thus without addressing prob-lems in their contexts, clients will be less likely to generalize changes made in therapy to their lives beyond the therapist's door. In that respect, homework serves as a tool to implement yet another general principle of change that cuts across different theo-retical orientations: facilitating ongoing reality-testing of clients' views and behaviors in their daily life experiences (Goldfried, 1980).

Several of the authors who contributed chapters to this volume offer examples of this crucial aspect of homework use. Clark (this volume), in his discussion of obses-sions and compulsions, comments upon the importance of homework for "ensuring the generalization of treatment gains to naturalistic settings that trigger obsessional symptoms" (p. 320). Lindenboim, Chapman, and Linehan (this volume) reiterate how the use of homework in DBT is essential for acquiring and strengthening effective be-havioral skills that will generalize to the client's natural environment. Leathem and Christianson (this volume) discuss how individuals with brain injuries often require the systematic implementation of behavioral cues in their everyday settings (e.g., pre-programmed cell phones or pagers and prominently posted lists of activities) in order to counter the deficits arising from their injuries. Johnson (this volume) points out that a major contributor to relapse in the treatment of individuals who suffer from chronic pain is the "failure to generalize behaviors learned during treatment to environments outside of treatment" (p. 88). Homework, in other words, is essential for generalizing therapeutic change.

Generalizing therapeutic change is also critically important in approaches that focus on interpersonal problems. As Young and Mufson (this volume) describe, in-terpersonal therapy is grounded in the belief that emotional or behavioral problems arise and are maintained in an interpersonal context. They attempt to address those aspects of clients' interpersonal relationships that may be contributing to the mainte-nance of their behavioral problems or detrimentally affecting their emotional health. The focus of these forms of treatment necessitates that clients try out new ways of relating in interpersonal contexts outside of therapy, making homework a crucial part of treatment.

Even in couple or family therapy, where significant others are present and ac-tive, not all interpersonal work can be done in session because not all interpersonal contingencies that are important to particular clients or specific problems will arise in session. Epstein and Baucom (this volume), who examine homework use with couples, as well as Newcomb Rekart and Lebow and Robbins, Szapocznik, and Pérez (both this volume), who consider homework use with families, spotlight homework's impor-tant role in helping clients. These authors argue that incorporating the skills gained in therapy into clients' everyday environments, where myriad factors can impinge upon and interfere with constructive interactions, is crucial for changing relationship patterns that have often become relatively automatic.

It is also important to note that some work cannot be done in therapy simply for pragmatic reasons. For example, therapists can use guided imagery to expose their clients to feared situations in session, but eventually clients will have to learn to face these feared situations in reality. Anxiety disorders, substance abuse disorders, and sexual disorders frequently necessitate extra-session work, both because the prob-lems occur primarily outside of the therapeutic context and also because it is often impractical, inappropriate, or unethical for therapists to accompany their clients in these activities.

Clark (this volume) underlines how crucial it is for clients struggling with obsessions and compulsions to incorporate the prevention techniques learned in homework exercises into their everyday life: what he terms "lifestyle exposure" (p. x). He also notes that self-directed exposure and response prevention (ERP), a technique that has been used successfully to treat Obsessive-Compulsive Disorder since its development in the 1960s, can be as effective as therapist-directed ERP. With substance-abusing clients, Riso and Thase (this volume) describe how "homework allows [them] to practice newly acquired skills in real-life problem situations [which] increases the likelihood that behaviors learned in treatment will more effectively generalize to clients' everyday lives" (p. 57). They note further that prescribing specific between-session tasks is an important component of several treatment modalities for substance abuse. In their contributory chapter on sexual dysfunction, Gambescia and Weeks (this volume) observe that improving effective communication and sexual technique requires that the couple verbalize sexual desires outside of the therapist's office and that they practice sexual techniques at home. The authors also point out that behavioral homework has been an integral part of the treatment protocol for sexual dysfunction since Masters & Johnson, and that it "... continues to provide the most direct and effective means of treating relational and sexual problems" and of preventing relapse (p. x).

Individual psychodynamic therapy does not focus on ecologically relevant homework activities to the same degree as cognitive-behavioral therapy. Traditional psychodynamic theory asserts that change occurs primarily in a unidirectional fashion, with insight leading to behavioral change. According to this view, problems that manifest outside of therapy can be addressed in session through insight-generating discussion. Stricker (this volume) notes, however, that assimilative psychodynamic therapists have moved away from this linear view of change. They theorize that behavior, cognitive-affective experience, and unconscious mental processes all affect one another in reciprocal fashion. They recognize that interventions made in any of these three domains will resonate throughout the system and affect the other domains. Thus, in instances where a client has achieved insight without subsequent behavioral, cognitive, or affective change, or where a client has difficulty achieving insight through discussion alone, the therapist might suggest out-of-session activities that would provide the client with experiences not possible in the therapeutic context. These novel experiences might help to bring about desired changes that failed to occur through insight alone, or they might provide the client with experiential learning that consequently leads to insight.

6. *Homework gives clients opportunities to engage in therapeutic work without the therapist present.*

Even after successfully practicing a new behavior or response in therapy, clients often believe that they would have been unable to do so without the reassuring presence of the therapist. Homework assignments help clients become less reliant upon their therapists by creating opportunities for them to practice what they have learned in the therapist's absence. Clients' realization that they can successfully manage problems on their own, or that they can effectively influence their own experiences, serves to increase their sense of self-efficacy. As Stricker (this volume) observes from the perspective of psychodynamic theory, "This sense of self-efficacy can be carried into future situations and will serve a preventative as well as a mutative function" (p. 109). An improved sense of self-efficacy may be particularly important for those clients whose belief in their own abilities to improve their situation has been compromised by previous unsuccessful attempts at change, a common occurrence, for example, in individuals suffering from chronic depression or pain.

Cognitive-behavioral therapists might argue that these are not only worthy goals in themselves, but that they act as positive reinforcement for more adaptive behaviors, further strengthening learning. Additionally, clients who come to believe that they have the power to improve their own lives are more likely to invest themselves in therapy, be motivated to make beneficial changes, and be optimistic about the future, all factors which contribute to positive outcome. Beyond these factors, practicing the work of therapy without the therapist present helps to ensure that clients will be able to act as their own therapists once treatment is over. Overseeing their own between-session treatment fosters clients' ability to manage their post-session treatment, both in maintaining treatment gains and in preventing relapse.

7. *Homework contributes to clients' consolidation or integration of in-session changes.*

Homework contributes to clients' consolidation of in-session changes because it provides clients with more opportunities to engage in therapy-relevant activities and to enter into therapeutic experiences in a variety of contexts, both inside and outside of session. Increased awareness of and insight into a problem, extended practice of more adaptive ways to manage the problem, and improved ability to generalize these gains to other contexts all make it more likely that clients will integrate their new ways of thinking, feeling, and behaving into their more intrinsic or habitual ways of reacting. Homework can help clients to reach a point where they no longer need to remind themselves to think, feel, or behave in a particular way. In other words, clients achieve real change by acquiring, reinforcing, and thus integrating new ways of being. This reflects what psychodynamic therapists have called the process of "working through."

GUIDELINES OR PRINCIPLES FOR THE EFFECTIVE USE OF HOMEWORK IN PSYCHOTHERAPY PRACTICE

In the previous section, we laid out and discussed various ways in which homework can enhance psychotherapy practice. Having addressed the question of *why* homework plays an important role in psychotherapy, we will turn our attention now to the question of *how* it best can be utilized.

Therapists from diverse orientations differ, sometimes drastically, in the kinds of homework assignments they encourage and in the types of prescriptive techniques they employ. Despite this fact, several common themes emerge from the preceding chapters as principles or guidelines for the most effective use of homework in psychotherapy. In the following section, we will delineate a number of these guidelines.

1. *Homework assignments should be communicated clearly and specifically.*

The authors of the preceding chapters uniformly recommend that therapists who choose to prescribe homework should strive to communicate such prescriptions clearly and specifically. Miscommunication has been cited as a leading cause of clients' noncompliance with therapists' recommendations. As a result, several chapter authors provide specific suggestions for avoiding such problems.

Beck and Tompkins and Ledley and Huppert (both this volume), for example, writing from the perspectives of cognitive and behavioral therapies, respectively, urge therapists to include specific details about when, where, for how long, and under what conditions homework tasks are to be completed. Likewise, in their description of brief strategic family therapy, Robbins, Szapocznik, and Pérez (this volume), suggest that therapists be specific about what they expect their clients to accomplish and confirm that clients understand the assignment by asking them to describe what they are going to do to carry it out. In their chapter on acceptance and commitment therapy (ACT), Twohig, Pierson, and Hayes (this volume) assert that it can be helpful to have clients practice an activity in session before asking them to complete an assignment on their own. Practicing together can help therapists more clearly communicate the assignment and can also allow clients an opportunity to clarify any parts of the assignment they may not have understood.

Communicating homework assignments clearly and specifically can be especially important when working with certain clinical populations. DeVries (this volume) points out that older adults often process information more slowly due to sensory and cognitive changes associated with normal aging. For such clients, she suggests presenting information more slowly and in several different modalities, such as verbal instructions and written handouts. She also suggests that therapists encourage clients to take notes during session to help them absorb new material. Johnson (this volume) describes impaired cognitive functioning in individuals suffering from chronic pain, and so advocates related strategies for ensuring that clients understand homework assignments well enough to successfully complete them. Leathem and Christianson (this volume) make similar suggestions for therapists treating patients with traumatic brain injury (TBI). As the authors point out, memory problems are a common in all types of brain injury, and therapists working with TBI clients should allow sufficient time during the session to ensure that homework assignments are understood, remembered, and repeated. They recommend keeping a folder for session notes, reading materials, and homework summaries. When working with individuals who experience psychosis, Dunn and Morrison (this volume) advocate providing these clients with written or audio-taped instructions of assignment details, as well as pre-printed assignment forms, in order to help them remember assigned activities.

2. *Homework assignments should be framed in a non-threatening manner.*

Whether they use the term "homework" or a less loaded term such as "exercise," "experiment," or "activity," therapists should try to frame homework in a way that is non-threatening to clients. Several chapter authors point out that clients may find the word "homework" intimidating or off-putting. Ledley and Huppert (this volume) point out that adolescent clients may associate the word "homework" with demands—even punishments—imposed upon them by adults in authority. They recommend that therapists working with adolescents try to frame assignments in the context of a game or a challenge. In their chapter on interpersonal therapy with adolescents, Young and Mufson (this volume) likewise acknowledge that adolescent clients may find the term "homework" aversive. They suggest framing assignments as "interpersonal experiments," in which the adolescent tries out different strategies for dealing with interpersonal problems in order to determine which is the most effective in producing the desired results.

Other authors point out that some adult populations may have similar negative reactions to the word "homework." Johnson (this volume), for example, calls attention to the fact that chronic pain patients often exhibit lower levels of educational achievement. Because the possible association of "homework" with unsuccessful school performance might reduce compliance, he advocates the use of alternative terms with this patient population. DeVries (this volume) also argues for the use of alternative terms when working with older clients, as do Apodaca and Monti (this volume) with substance users. These groups, like adolescents and chronic pain patients, may have a negative reaction and thus reduced compliance when recommendations are called "homework."

The framing issue is not just one of terminology. Whether therapists use the term "homework" or not, framing also includes the ways in which therapists introduce their recommendations and respond to noncompliance or partial compliance as previously mentioned, Ellison & Greenberg (this volume) describe giving homework as suggestions that clients can try if they find them to be relevant and helpful rather than assignments they are expected or obligated to complete. They advocate giving homework in a "spirit of exploration," where "client empowerment rather than compliance is the goal" (p. 68)

Although the issue of framing may be particularly salient when working with specific age groups or clinical populations, it is important to consider in almost all cases. Writing from a psychodynamic perspective, Stricker (this volume) notes that clients who are high in reactance (those who are reactant at being controlled by others) are likely to view direct, and even indirect, suggestions from the therapist as infringements on their personal autonomy and therefore as threatening. Clients who are low in reactance, on the other hand, may perceive such suggestions as supportive, indicating the therapist's interest and concern. Stricker advocates the use of direct suggestion sparingly and only when working with clients who are low in reactance. However, therapists who identify with orientations that advocate more frequent use of homework may still learn from this distinction and find it helpful to pay attention to questions of framing with highly reactive clients [see Castonguay (2000) for a consideration of this issue within the context of cognitive-behavioral therapy].

3. *The rationale for homework assignments, including the relevance of homework assignments to treatment goals, should be conveyed clearly and explicitly to clients.*

Although many of the preceding chapters on particular psychotherapy orientations discuss reasons for using homework and imply that such reasons should be communicated to clients, few discuss the importance of doing so explicitly. Ledley and Huppert, in their chapter on behavior therapy (this volume), are an exception. They point out that a clear understanding of the rationale for doing homework increases the likelihood that clients will comply with assignments, thus enhancing the effectiveness of homework interventions. Therapists who plan to prescribe homework regularly should explain to clients their rationale for doing so in the initial discussion of between-session activities. They might find it helpful to share with clients the general research demonstrating the benefits of homework. The rationale discussed earlier in this chapter may also be communicated to clients, as could the more specific rationales associated with particular theoretical orientations. Not only is such understanding likely to increase compliance, but it is also likely to contribute to clients' expectations for positive change, which, as we discussed earlier, has been associated with actual change.

Many of the chapters on particular clinical populations also emphasize the importance of providing clients with a clear and explicit rationale when assigning homework. Several of these authors echo the point made by Ledley and Huppert: for clients struggling with substance abuse, eating disorders, obsessions and compulsions, or psychotic symptoms, helping them to understand more clearly why homework assignments are important increases their compliance with and completion of, as well as the degree to which they benefit from, between-session activities. Johnson (this volume) points out that patients who suffer from chronic pain, for example, are often highly skeptical that psychological interventions can affect physiological pain. Thus, homework rationales must be presented in a way that agrees with clients' understanding of the nature of their problems and their expectations for treatment.

Also, regardless of whether they prescribe homework frequently or occasionally, therapists should ensure that clients understand how a particular assignment is relevant to long-term treatment goals. While this aspect of homework prescription is important when working with any population, it is especially important with certain populations. DeVries (this volume) observes that older adults especially may resist doing things that they don't perceive as meaningful. Obsessive-compulsive clients, as Clark points out (this volume), may be overwhelmed by the anxiety of giving up long-standing beliefs or rituals. Depressed clients are often doubtful that homework is going to help and fearful of experiencing distressing emotions. For all of these groups, the therapist's ability to articulate clearly and explicitly how homework assignments relate to specific goals in therapy can be crucial in promoting clients' cooperation. Furthermore, such communication not only increases compliance but also helps clients to connect their short-term learning with the longer-term changes they hope to achieve.

4. *Homework assignments should be tailored to clients' unique situations and needs.*

The chapter authors are united in emphasizing the importance of tailoring homework assignments to clients' unique situations and needs. Therefore, while they differ in the degree to which they are process-directive, the authors agree that the content and nature of homework should be sensitive to client differences rather than blindly prescriptive. As Gambescia and Weeks (this volume) point out in their chapter on couples dealing with sexual dysfunction, therapists should design "homework exercises . . . to fit the couple rather than trying to fit the couple to the exercises" (p. 353). Furthermore, as Beck and Tompkins (this volume) suggest, when designing homework for a particular client, therapists should be guided not only by their understanding of the client's difficulties (including level and type of symptomology as well as treatment goals), but also by their knowledge of the client's predilections, capacities, motivation, and practical factors in the client's life.

It may be especially important for therapists to keep this advice in mind when working with specific populations. For instance, Leathem and Christiansen (this volume) describe how clients with traumatic brain injuries can exhibit impairment in a wide variety of domains—physical, cognitive, emotional, and interpersonal—all of which can interact with and exacerbate each other. Interventions, including homework, must thus be specifically adapted to the widely divergent and highly complex deficits and needs of individual clients. Similarly, Johnson (this volume) encourages the thorough assessment of clients suffering from chronic pain. He points out that therapists' lack of awareness of clients' particular pain problems and history can prevent or hinder clients' successful engagement in treatment, including homework. DeVries (this volume) notes that older populations, too, show much greater variations in physical health, educational level, intellectual functioning, personal interests, and social circumstances than younger populations. Therapists need to be cognizant of these variations when planning specific homework activities.

Clearly, there are a number of different factors that therapists need to keep in mind when considering the unique situation of a particular client. The remaining guidelines are aimed at helping therapists tailor homework interventions to specific aspects of clients' unique situations.

5. *Homework assignments should be tailored to client capabilities and should make use of client strengths.*

In order to customize homework assignments for a particular client, therapists need to keep in mind a number of different aspects of the client's situation—including their capabilities, strengths, and resources. In interpersonal therapy, for example, Young and Mufson (this volume) recommend that therapists begin by assigning tasks at which clients are likely to succeed. This serves several purposes: it fosters self-confidence; it creates positive expectations for therapy; and it encourages compliance on current and future assignments. Such considerations are especially important for clients who have been demoralized by long-standing problems or previous failed attempts at change, such as those struggling with chronic pain or depression, long-term relational or sexual difficulties, obsessive-compulsive or substance abuse disorders. In a similar vein, Robbins, Szapocznik, and Pérez (this volume) advise therapists using brief strategic family therapy to assess clients' abilities before recommending an activity for homework. If therapists determine that clients do not yet have the necessary skills to complete a task successfully, they should help clients develop the requisite level of proficiency in session before asking them try a task on their own. In the meantime, they should assign clients a different task that has a greater likelihood of success.

Several authors focus on the importance of actively utilizing clients' strengths and resources in homework. For example, Ellison and Greenberg (this volume) emphasize the importance of developing clients' strengths, as opposed to focusing solely on their weaknesses, a perspective that reflects the philosophical assumptions of EFT. Stricker (this volume), representing the psychodynamic point of view, cites a recent article by Scheel, Hanson, and Razzhavaikina (2004), in which the authors assert that the playing to clients' strengths can enhance the acceptability of homework recommendations. This, in turn, can increase clients' motivation, sense of mastery, and compliance with assignments.

6. *Homework assignments should flow out of and build upon work that occurs in session and should be directly related to treatment goals.*

As Ledley and Huppert (this volume) point out, "the purpose of homework is not just for patients to *do* something, but to do something that will move along the therapy process" (p. 24). In order to fulfill this purpose, homework assignments should essentially be, as Neimeyer and Winter (this volume) so aptly put it, "between-session extensions of in-session work" (p. 398). Therefore, many of the activities developed by different therapeutic orientations are used to guide work outside of session as well as to focus work in session.

For example, in their chapter on EFT, Ellison and Greenberg (this volume) discuss different markers of emotional processing that can be used to determine the most appropriate activities in which to engage during the session as well as the most helpful activities to assign between sessions. These authors emphasize that therapists should not plan too far ahead in designing homework assignments. Rather, in order to engage in "hot teaching"—or the facilitation of situation-relevant learning while clients are emotionally aroused—they should take their cues from what arises in session to suggest homework that will further consolidate in-session learning.

In their chapter on brief strategic family therapy, on the other hand, Robbins, Szapocznik, and Pérez (this volume), recommend that therapists assign homework that is informed by their case conceptualizations based on diagnostic "enactments" (p. 137), or repetitions of a family's characteristic ways of behaving.

Both sets of authors underscore the importance of homework's relevance to in-session work and to treatment goals; their emphases, however, are different, with the former focusing on homework's relevance to moment-by-moment experience, while the latter focuses on its relevance to more general diagnostic patterns or conceptualizations.

7. *When possible, homework assignments should be developed collaboratively, and client initiated assignments should be encouraged.*

Nearly every author in this volume advocated working collaboratively with clients to develop homework assignments. Active collaboration ensures that assignments are tailored to clients' individual situations and needs and that they are experienced as personally relevant. Encouraging collaboration also helps therapists teach clients how to manage their own treatment, an important component of maintaining gains and preventing relapse once therapy has ended.

Ledley and Huppert (this volume) recommend that therapists ask clients what they think might be helpful to work on between sessions. If clients suggest assignments that are less optimal from the therapists' perspective, therapists should use Socratic questioning to lead clients toward more effective activities. A number of other authors, including Beck and Tompkins and Ellison and Greenberg (both this volume), argue that developing homework collaboratively increases the acceptability of an assignment and thus the likelihood of its compliance. Ellison and Greenberg further assert that collaboration increases the likelihood that assignments will resonate with clients, making them seem more personally relevant and also increasing the likelihood that clients will continue to practice homework assignments after treatment has ended.

In addition to fostering collaboration with clients in developing homework activities, therapists should encourage clients to initiate such activities themselves. Therapists can give such encouragement either explicitly, by suggesting that clients come up with their own ideas for activities, or implicitly, by reinforcing those ideas with which clients present them.

Stricker and Witty (both this volume) address the question of self-initiated homework within the contexts of relatively nondirective or self-directive treatments. As we discussed earlier in this chapter, client-centered therapists and others who are committed to the principle of nondirectiveness see the prescription of homework—through either explicit recommendation or implicit suggestion—as problematic, contributing to a power dynamic that undermines the client's personal authority and communicating a lack of trust in the client's capacities for self-realization. Client-initiated homework activities, however, allow clients to enjoy many of the previously mentioned benefits of homework while avoiding the potential negative effects of prescription. Of course, nondirective therapists cannot effect whether or not their clients initiate their own out-of-session activities (that is, while remaining truly nondirective); likewise, they may believe that active reinforcement of clients-initiated activities can communicate conditions of worth, just as explicit recommendations might. Nonetheless, even therapists who depend solely on clients' ability to self-direct treatment can use their knowledge of the beneficial effects of homework to better understand the process of therapeutic change.

Therapists who do not experience such reluctance about prescribing homework can likewise learn from their nondirective colleagues. Whether or not they believe that prescription or directiveness on the part of the therapist communicates a disempowering message to clients, they can probably agree that allowing or even encouraging clients to initiate their own activities communicates respect for clients' personal authority and trust in clients' self-realizing potential. Sending such a message to clients is likely to increase their self-confidence, promote positive expectations of therapy, and boost belief in their own abilities to affect change.

Stricker (this volume) also points out, as previously mentioned, that clients who are low in reactance are likely to do well in directive treatments, because they are more likely to perceive homework assignments that are explicitly recommended by the therapist as expressions of concern and support. Clients who are high in reactance, on the other hand, are more likely to see therapists' explicit homework recommendations as infringements of their personal autonomy. Thus, they may excel in less directive treatments where they can formulate their own ideas for homework, "taking tacit cues from the therapist, but also taking responsibility for the direction of the treatment" (p. x). When considering whether to prescribe specific homework assignments or whether to encourage self-initiated homework activities, therefore, therapists should keep in mind any personality characteristics, including reactance, which may affect clients' responses to therapists' recommendations.

When encouraging collaboration or self-initiated homework, therapists also need to be aware of clients' capabilities, including their levels of cognitive and emotional development. When working with adolescents and young children, for example, Ledley and Huppert (this volume) recommend giving these clients a choice between several tasks that the therapist deems appropriate. In this way, young clients who may be less well equipped to initiate or develop their own homework assignments are given opportunities to contribute to their treatment. On the opposite end of the age spectrum, older clients may have similar limitations stemming from cognitive deficits associated with aging. As DeVries points out (this volume), however, older clients need to feel that their age and life experience are respected by younger therapists. Encouraging such clients to actively collaborate in or initiate between-session activities that they find acceptable can promote their involvement with homework and their engagement with therapy more generally.

8. *Homework assignments should incorporate client feedback from previous assignments.*

In addition to utilizing in-session cues and working collaboratively with clients to develop homework assignments, therapists can customize homework by soliciting and incorporating clients' feedback from previous assignments. For example, Neimeyer & Winter (this volume) suggest that therapists who practice personal construct therapy conduct an "acceptance check" with clients after recommending a homework assignment (p. 164). If clients are uncomfortable with the therapist's recommendation or wish to change it in some way to make it more meaningful or relevant, they can negotiate a more acceptable assignment with the therapist. Furthermore, asking clients how they feel about an assignment and whether or not it is acceptable to them lets them know that they have a say in the process and that the therapist will not impose assignments on them that they are uncomfortable or unwilling to complete.

Likewise, when prior assignments are discussed in subsequent sessions, therapists can ask clients about any obstacles or difficulties they encountered when attempting the homework. They can also inquire about aspects of the assignment that clients found relevant and helpful versus those they found impractical and less useful. Several authors in this volume recommend that therapists spend at least 10 minutes of every session reviewing the previous week's homework assignment, soliciting feedback from clients, and discussing any difficulties they may have had in attempting it. As Gambescia and Weeks (this volume) suggest, clients' feedback from each exercise should serve as the foundation for the next exercise.

9. *Homework noncompliance should be recognized and used as an additional source of feedback.*

Many of the guidelines outlined above focus on promoting homework compliance as a way of increasing its effectiveness. Although several of the chapter authors argue that the best way to handle noncompliance is to use the aforementioned principles to forestall it, therapists are bound to encounter noncompliance at least occasionally. A common strategy for dealing with noncompliance, advocated by various approaches described in this volume, proposes using clients' noncompliance as a source of information about their difficulties and as a means of adapting assignments to their individual situations and needs. Newcomb, Rekart, and Lebow (this volume), for example, stress that therapists working with families should utilize feedback from "unsuccessful" as well as "successful" completion of homework in planning the next task. Likewise, within the context of brief strategic family therapy, Robbins, Szapocznik, and Pérez (this volume) urge therapists to recognize that clients' noncompliance or difficulties in completing an assignment can be a "great source of new and important information regarding the reasons why a family cannot do what is best for them" (p. 143). They advocate utilizing these opportunities to identify the interactional patterns that interfere with the family's ability to carry out the homework task and to construct homework assignments targeted at changing these problematic patterns.

Beck and Tompkins (this volume), describing a cognitive therapy approach to homework noncompliance, recommend that therapists first determine whether clients experienced practical difficulties and/or interfering cognitions in completing the assignment. If the difficulties were practical, such as illness, the therapist might suggest working on the assignment the following week. If lack of opportunity or unforeseen conditions made the activity difficult to start or finish—for example, a single mother is unable to find time alone to read or garden because her children are always around—the therapist and client might brainstorm different solutions to those obstacles in the environment that prevented the client from completing the assignment. These practical problems can even be made the focus of another homework assignment: the single mother is given the assignment of finding a regular babysitter so that she has an afternoon or evening to herself once a week. If, on the other hand, the therapist learns that interfering cognitions were responsible for clients' noncompliance (e.g., "If I try to do something, I'll fail," or "If I focus on my problems, I'll only feel worse"), Beck and Tompkins recommend that they use Socratic questioning to help clients evaluate and respond to these cognitions. Future homework assignments may then be designed to focus on responding to these cognitions. In all cases, by gathering information about clients' reasons for noncompliance, the therapist learns about additional difficulties that might be usefully addressed in therapy and incorporated into future homework assignments.

Partial compliance can likewise provide useful information to clients and therapists. The fact that a client has not fully complied with an assignment does not mean that learning has not taken place or that useful information has not been gained. Furthermore, as in the case of noncompliance, partial compliance can provide therapists with information about potential obstacles the client may have experienced in attempting to complete the assignment. As described above, this information can then be incorporated into future therapeutic work both in and out of session.

10. Therapists should help clients articulate what they have learned from both "successful" and "unsuccessful" homework assignments.

One of the important and distinctive benefits of assigning homework in therapy is the fact that it provides clients with additional opportunities for learning. It is thus helpful for therapists to assist clients in understanding and articulating exactly what they have learned from these activities. Ledley and Huppert (this volume) suggest asking clients to describe what they have learned from an assignment (e.g., "I don't *always* have panic attacks on subways," or "If I do have a panic attack, I won't actually die"). They also recommend recording these learning experiences so that clients have something to refer back to when they encounter similar difficulties in the future.

These same authors, like others in this volume, recommend that therapists review previous homework assignments in the following session, examining possible reasons for "success" or "failure." They encourage therapists to have clients make specific predictions before starting an assignment and evaluate these predictions after finishing it. Making predictions and evaluating them in the following session both can help clients become more cognizant of the "shifts in beliefs and feelings" that typically occur as a result of behavior change and also can "reinforce behavior change" itself (p. 24).

Young and Mufson (this volume) also recommend that prior homework assignments be reviewed in the following session. Consistent with the assumptions of interpersonal therapy, they urge therapists to conduct a "communication analysis" to better understand the interaction that took place. Where clients used less adaptive communication techniques, therapeutic work should focus on discussing and role-playing more helpful techniques; where clients completed their assignments "successfully," discussion should focus on the ways in which skills utilized by clients were effective in achieving the desired outcome. The authors stress the importance of reviewing not only "unsuccessful" attempts but also "successful" ones in order to help clients understand and articulate any changes—behavioral, cognitive, and affective—that occurred or might still need to occur.

CONCLUSIONS AND FUTURE DIRECTIONS

Although each of the chapters in this volume addresses the use of homework within a particular therapeutic approach or with a specific population, a number of similarities are apparent between them. These similarities, or common factors, may well represent robust consensus in the field about the benefits and implementation of homework in psychotherapy.

In this chapter, we have delineated a number of therapeutic advantages or reasons for using homework that we believe cut across therapies of different orientations and for different client populations. These are: (1) the explicit use of homework communicates a message to clients about the nature of therapy; (2) homework assignments allow clients and therapists to gather information in order to better understand the nature of a problem and the use of therapy in addressing it; (3) homework assignments give clients opportunities to raise awareness or achieve insight; (4) engaging in homework activities increases the amount of time clients spend doing therapeutic work; (5) homework gives clients opportunities to engage in therapeutic work in different contexts outside of therapy; (6) homework gives clients opportunities to engage in therapeutic work without the therapist present; and (7) homework contributes to clients' consolidation or integration of in-session changes. We have discussed each of these advantages from a trans-theoretical perspective, while also paying attention to the specific rationale of the particular approaches presented in the preceding chapters.

Likewise, we have delineated from the chapters a list of guidelines for clinicians who wish to incorporate homework more effectively into their treatment. These guidelines are: (1) homework assignments should be communicated clearly and specifically; (2) assignments should be framed in a non-threatening manner; (3) the rationale for homework assignments, including the relevance of homework assignments to treatment goals, should be conveyed clearly and explicitly to clients; (4) homework assignments should be tailored to clients' unique situations and needs; (5) homework assignments should be tailored to client capabilities and should make use of client strengths; (6) homework assignments should flow out of and build upon work that occurs in session and should be directly related to treatment goals; (7) when possible, homework assignments should be developed collaboratively, and client initiated assignments should be encouraged; (8) homework assignments should incorporate client feedback from previous assignments; (9) homework noncompliance should be recognized and used as an additional source of feedback; and finally, (10) therapists should help clients articulate what they have learned from both "successful" and "unsuccessful" homework assignments.

Although a substantial number of common therapeutic functions and guidelines related to homework have emerged from the preceding chapters, some noteworthy differences have also caught our attention. While the each of the aforementioned commonalities can be found in the majority of the chapters, there are several themes that are addressed by only a few of the authors or whose absence from some chapters is noticeable.

Unlike most other represented authors, for example, Stricker (this volume) discusses important individual differences that go beyond demographics or the diagnostic picture and that may interact with various aspects of homework use—from collaboration and self-initiation to compliance. Likewise, both Stricker and Ellison and Greenberg (both this volume) highlight the importance of utilizing clients' strengths in homework as well as addressing their weaknesses, a point that was neglected in many of the other chapters. Ledley and Huppert and Beck and Tompkins (this volume), on the other hand, addressed issues around specificity of assignments that were not as clearly expressed in other chapters. Witty (this volume) pointed out potential pitfalls of homework prescription that all of the other approaches neglected to address.

We encourage researchers and clinicians of all theoretical orientations and those working with all populations to thoughtfully consider the rationale and methods advocated by their colleagues from disparate approaches—not necessarily to change the foci of their own approaches, but to keep in mind valid points made by others and which they may not have considered. It would seem indicated, for example, that directive approaches such as CBT seriously consider the points made by Witty (this volume) concerning the potential power differential to which homework prescription could contribute. Likewise, we are convinced that client-centered therapists, like other humanistic therapists [such as Ellison and Greenberg (this volume)] can learn to pay more attention to the actual benefits of client-initiated homework, as a way to deepen and generalize the work done in session. Clearly, neither the directive nor nondirective therapists are likely to adopt the philosophies of the other; we believe, however, that each would benefit from an understanding of the other's arguments.

In closing, we would like to encourage both researchers studying the use of homework and therapists using it to think in terms of principles of change rather than specific techniques. As the chapters discussed here demonstrate, a variety of techniques can be used to serve the same function. In line with a position elegantly proposed by Goldfried (1980), therapists can therefore enlarge their repertoire by thinking in terms of principles underlying particular interventions rather than techniques prescribed by a specific manual or orientation. Examples of principles that have been emphasized herein include clients' development of new view of self, ongoing reality testing, and consolidation of learning. Other principles, such as increased expectation or remoralization, development of an alliance, and fostering positive experience can likewise be affected by the application of homework.

At the same time, and as Stricker (this volume) points out, it is important to recognize that the same technique can have different effects when used in different contexts. Therefore, we must keep in mind that the rationale and/or guidelines endorsed by various approaches may be more or less applicable within different orientations or with different populations. Again, this suggests that therapists should be guided by principles of change rather than a list of prescribed techniques when applying homework.

As demonstrated by the results of a recent Task Force (Castonguay & Beutler, 2005), clinicians can now rely on a substantial number of empirically based principles of change. Delineated for several types of clinical problems (dysphoric, anxiety, personality, and substance use disorders), these principles recognize the respective influence and constant interaction of variables related to participants (client and therapist), relationship, and techniques. Because many of these principles are consistent and/or complimentary with guidelines and therapeutic advantages described in this chapter, we believe that clinicians of different orientations might find them to be useful heuristic as they consider when, how, and why to encourage between-session activities

REFERENCES

Alexander, F., & French, T. M. (1946). *Psychoanalytic Theory: Principles and Applications*. New York: Ronald Press.

Badgio, P., Halperin, G., & Barber, J. (1999). Acquisition of Adaptive Skills: Psychotherapeutic Change in Cognitive and Dynamic Therapies. *Clinical Psychology Review, 19*, 721–737.

Castonguay, L. G. (2000). A common factors approach to psychotherapy training. *Journal of Psychotherapy Integration,10*, 263–282.

Castonguay, L. G., & Beutler, L. E. (Eds.) (2005). *Principles of therapeutic change that work*. New York: Oxford University Press.

Frank, J. D. (1961). *Persuasion and healing*. Baltimore: Johns Hopkins University Press.

Gelso, C. J., & Harbin, J. (in press). Insight, action, and the therapeutic relationship. In L. G. Castonguay & C. E. Hill (Eds.), *Insight in psychotherapy*. Washington, DC: American Psychological Press.

Goisman, R. M. (1985). The psychodynamics of prescribing in behavior therapy. *American Journal of Psychiatry, 142*, 675 – 679.

Goldfried, M. R. (2003). Cognitive-behavior therapy: Reflections on the evolution of a therapeutic orientation. *Cognitive Therapy and Research, 27*, 53–69.

Goldfried, M. R. (1980). Toward the delineation of therapeutic change principles. *American Psychologist, 35*, 991–999.

Kazantzis, N., Deane, F. P., & Ronan, K. R. (2000). Homework assignments in cognitive and behavioral therapy: A meta-analysis. *Clinical Psychology: Science and Practice, 7*, 189–202.

Scheel, M. J., Hanson, W. E., & Razzhavaikina, T. I. (2004). The process of recommending homework in psychotherapy: A review of therapist delivery methods, client acceptability, and factors that affect compliance. *Psychotherapy: Theory, Research, Practice, Training, 41*, 38–55.

Schottenbauer, M. A., Glass, C. R., & Arnkoff, D. B. How is insight developed, consolidated, or destroyed between sessions. In L. G. Castonguay & C. E. Hill (Eds.), *Insight in psychotherapy*. Washington, DC: American Psychological Press. (in press).

Strupp, H. H., & Binder, J. L. (1984). *Psychotherapy in a new key: A guide to time-limited dynamic psychotherapy*. New York: Basic Books.

CHAPTER 25

DIRECTIONS FOR HOMEWORK IN PSYCHOTHERAPY PREVENTION

T. Mark Harwood, Joselyne M. Sulzner, and Larry E. Beutler

All psychotherapy should be geared toward the prevention of future mental health episodes or to the reduction of decrements in functioning that necessitate a return to mental health treatment. In essence, a primary goal of psychotherapy should be relapse or recidivism prevention. Stated another way, although some therapists may foster a degree of patient dependence on the clinician at the outset of therapy, the ultimate goal is to increase patient independence. As the foregoing suggests, we will focus on individuals who have already engaged in psychotherapy and how the application of homework (or "personal therapy") can improve long-term outcomes for psychotherapy and prevent relapse.

All homework assignments seek to generalize interventions and skills practiced in the safe confines of the therapist's office to the real-world environment where functioning is contextually related. RCT research specifically geared toward the effects and acceptability of homework and the subsequent generalization of treatment-based change is limited (Detweiler-Bedell & Whisman, 2005; Kazantzis, Deane, & Ronan, 2000; Scheel, Hanson, & Razzhavaikina, 2004); however, some recent studies on the quality of homework compliance (i.e., the degree of learning) have provided some support for the generalizing effect that personal therapy exerts (e.g., Schmidt & Woolaway-Bickell, 2000; Woods, Chambless, & Stetekee, 2002). Additionally, few clinicians would disagree that the generalization of treatment elements are enhanced through homework. Generalization is extremely important because it increases the likelihood that new skills will be learned well and utilized if and when needed. For example, social skills training will be more effective when these skills are practiced and applied in the patient's social environment and not simply in the therapist's office.

Additionally, although the general principle of exposure is an important aspect of all treatments, exposure is also operating when one applies skills or tests beliefs in their real world environment. Given the reality that most patients see their therapists for only 50 minutes a week, "personal therapy" practiced outside the therapist's office extends the intensity of treatment and helps to consolidate and maximize gains. Homework and the generalization effect it produces are essential to recidivism/relapse prevention.

THE ISSUE OF COMPLIANCE

Homework completion is associated with patient motivation level. This finding begs the question—If homework improves outcomes, can practitioners be more effective if they increase patient motivation for homework completion? As the authors in the foregoing chapters have stated, the issue of compliance appears related to the presentation and fit of homework to the patient and their problem(s). In the effort to tailor homework, therapists should attend to a number of development and matching considerations. For example, homework needs to be relevant to the patient and their situation. Additionally, homework assignments need to be clearly developed/presented and their difficulty level should be appropriate to the patient's level of intellectual and emotional functioning. In a different vein, therapists must model the importance of homework's contribution to the therapy process by reviewing homework at each session. Of course, encouragement for any homework completed and successful problem solving for uncompleted homework also increases compliance levels.

When investigators examined how therapists integrate homework into therapy they identified a number of behaviors and strategies that predict acceptability of homework assignments. More specifically the following indicators of homework acceptability were identified in a number of studies: (1) patient beliefs that homework would be beneficial and relevant to their presenting problem (e.g., Kazantzis & Deane, 1999; Mahrer et al., 1994; Scheel, Conoley, & Ivey, 1998), (2) time, effort, and complexity (i.e., difficulty level) was considered reasonable (e.g., Reimers, Wacker, and Koeppl, 1987; Conoley, Conoley, Ivey, and Scheel, 1991), (3) homework built or expanded upon existing skills (i.e., shaping, generalizing, or maintaining behavior) (e.g., Conoley, Padula, Payton, and Daniels, 1994; Scheel, Hoggan, Willie, McDonald, and Tonin, 1998), and (4) the amount of encouragement and social influence from the therapist (e.g., Bryant, Simons, & Thase, 1999; Kazantzis & Deane, 1999). A recent study from Detweiler-Bedell and Whisman (2005) found that outcome was enhanced when therapists developed specific concrete goals that involved homework, discussed barriers to homework compliance among the less involved patients, and employed written reminders about homework. Shaw et al. (1999) found that the assignment of relevant homework was a key component of ratings of therapist competence and highly related to outcome.

Scheel, Hanson, and Razzhavaikina (2004) reviewed the outcome literature on homework process and developed an empirically derived six-phase model to improve acceptability and compliance. This six phase model consists of the following: (1) *client-therapist formulation* that included collaboration, skill level, fit and social influence, (2) *therapist delivery* that included specificity of the homework task, a convincing rationale for the homework that indicated the benefit that it provides, and a match between homework and the patient's ability level, (3) *client receipt* that includes the consideration of strategies for overcoming potential problems for homework completion, an evaluation of the patient's confidence level about their ability to complete the homework and renegotiation of an assignment when necessary, (4) *implementation* that may involve a contractual agreement or some other type of commitment to follow-through with assignments, (5) *therapist asks about homework experience* at each session and offers praise for any homework completed, and (6) *client report of homework experience* that involves an assessment and record of patient performance on homework.

When one considers the extant research, it simply makes clinical sense to believe that homework that is skillfully tailored to patients and their problem(s) would enhance motivation, compliance, and outcome.

Additional empirically derived dimensions that may be useful to consider relative to compliance/motivation and the goodness of fit for personal therapy involves patient predisposing characteristics not mentioned in the foregoing. These patient dimensions are extracted from the Systematic Treatment Selection model (STS; Beutler & Clarkin, 1990; Beutler, Clarkin, & Bongar, 2000; Beutler & Harwood, 2000), an empirically-derived and empirically-supported method of patient-treatment matching (Beutler et al., 2003). The STS patient dimensions were identified through an extensive search of the psychotherapy outcome literature that involved over 300 peer-reviewed journal articles. A number of patient characteristics were distilled to four primary dimensions that have been systematically evaluated over a period that spans more than a decade (Beutler et al., 1991; Beutler & Clarkin, 1990; Beutler et al., 2003; Karno, Beutler, & Harwood, 2002).

Recently, this STS treatment model was investigated employing a randomized clinical trial (RCT) design as a complete treatment package called Prescriptive Psychotherapy (PT; Beutler and Harwood, 2000; Beutler et al., 2003). More specifically, a patient population comprised of depressed and stimulant abusing patients was randomly assigned to one of three treatment conditions: a standard Cognitive Therapy for substance abuse (CT; Beck et al., 1993), a contrasting Cognitive-Narrative Therapy (NT; Gonçalves, 1995), and a Prescriptive Therapy (PT; Beutler & Harwood, 2000). The PT condition selectively applied interventions from both of the other two treatments via an Aptitude by Treatment Interaction (ATI) model. PT was developed with the practitioner in mind and it represents a combination of all of the patient-treatment matching dimensions (Beutler and Harwood, 2000).

Hierarchical Multiple Regression was utilized in the analyses from the forgoing RCT and residualized change scores were calculated and employed to eliminate regression to the mean effects. Entry of predictor variables was designed to provide the most stringent test of the hypotheses regarding patient-treatment fit (Beutler et al., 2003). That is, patient variables were entered first, followed by treatment variables and the strength of the therapeutic alliance. In the final step, the patient-treatment matching interaction variables were entered—this allowed us to examine if our patient-treatment matching interaction variables contributed variance to the prediction over and above the variance contributed by the patient, therapy, and alliance variables. The strength of the therapeutic alliance was measured with the Revised Helping Alliance Questionnaire, Patient version (HAq-P-II; Luborsky et al., 1996)

Findings from our investigation indicated that the fit between patient and therapy played a stronger predictive role in Hamilton Rating Scale for Depression scores (HRSD; Endicott, Cohen, Nee, Fleiss, & Sarantakos, 1981) than treatment interventions, alliance, or patient characteristics. Further, the predictive strength of the patient-treatment matching variable was greater than each of the other three sets of predictors at end of treatment and the predictive strength of the matching variables improved even further at six-month follow-up (Beutler et al., 2003).

More specifically, approximately 90% of the variance at end of treatment and at six-month follow-up for HRSD residual changes scores were accounted for by the four sets of predictors but the greatest predictor was the matching variable for all four patient dimensions. The finding for the HRSD translated to an effect size (r) of 0.94 ($p < 0.01$). Outcome estimates at end of treatment and follow-up were similar but somewhat lower compared to findings on the HRSD. For example, on the study's other major outcome measures: Beck Depression Inventory (BDI-II; Beck, Steer, & Brown, 1996), Addiction Severity Index (ASI; McLellan, Luborsky, Woody, & O'Brien, 1980), and Time-Line Follow Back (TLFB; Sobell & Sobell, 1992), the smallest effect size (r) was 0.67 ($p < 0.01$) on the TLFB. All of the estimated effect sizes from each of the regression analyses indicate clinically meaningful change.

The STS model rests on the premise that patients are individuals who bring unique proclivities to the treatment experience that are independent of diagnosis and important to treatment effectiveness. In other words, not all depressed patients are the same because each patient has unique predisposing characteristics that impact on the usefulness of various treatment interventions. For example, some patients have the predisposition to respond favorably to a symptom-focused treatment but they may be relatively unresponsive or they may react negatively to an insight-oriented treatment. The patient dimension of coping style informs the practitioner in the selection of insight versus symptom-focused treatment. If patients are predisposed to respond differentially to treatment focus, they may also respond differentially to homework focus.

STS or its condensed and practitioner-friendly variant, Prescriptive Psychotherapy (PT), provides a useful guide for clinicians in their selection of various treatment interventions. Patient-matching dimensions are translated to the level of strategies and principles that subsume families of interventions. That is, practitioners are guided to families of interventions and they have the flexibility to select from a wide variety of treatment elements. The STS and PT models afford the clinician maximum flexibility in the selection of interventions. For example, when the principle of exposure is indicated, the therapist can select among many exposure-based interventions and apply the types of interventions that fit the patients coping style or other predisposing dimension.

In addition to coping style, reactance or resistance level, level of subject distress, and functional impairment level are the primary patient characteristics that must be assessed and considered in fitting treatment to the patient. A brief discussion of each of these dimensions follows. The interested reader is directed to two illustrative texts, Prescriptive Psychotherapy (Beutler and Harwood, 2000) and its companion text Systematic Treatment Selection (Beutler, Clarkin, and Bongar, 2000), for a thorough explanation and guide to patient-treatment matching.

A BRIEF INTRODUCTION TO THE STS MODEL

As previously indicated, within the STS model coping style informs the selection of an insight focus or symptom-change focus for treatment. More specifically, those who have an internalizing style of coping respond well to insight-focused treatment. These individuals also respond to symptom-focused treatment and a symptom-focus may be necessary at the initiation of treatment when problematic behaviors and reactions need to be eliminated or reduced in order to stabilize the patient for further insight-based treatment or some combination of insight- and symptom-focused treatment.

Coping style, as with all of the patient dimensions, may be determined in one of two ways. First, coping style is easily obtained by computing an internalization ratio (IR; Beutler & Harwood, 2000) from the MMPI-2 (Butcher, 1990). A combination of eight clinical scales configured as a ratio provides the clearest indication of what type of coping style characterizes the patient's dominant pattern of perception and behavior. More specifically, four scales suggestive of an externalizing style of coping comprise the numerator and four scales suggestive of an internalizing style make up the denominator. An externalizing coping style is suggested if the IR is high (greater than 1.0). These patients tend to be more impulsive and under-controlled than the average patient. Conversely, if the IR is less than 1.0, an internalizing coping style suggestive of patients lower than average on impulsivity and higher than average in self-inspecting behaviors. The formula we have used to create the internalization ratio is:

$$IR = Hy + Pd + Pa + Ma/Hs + D + Pt + Si$$

For an assessment alternative, practitioners may wish to employ the STS Clinician Rating Form—Computer version (STS; Beutler & Williams, 1995) or the paper and pencil version that comes in both clinician and patient versions. The STS-Clinician Form is a computer-interactive clinician or patient based assessment procedure developed specifically to assess all of the patient dimensions that are important to Prescriptive Psychotherapy, including coping style. A second method for gauging coping style involves the clinician directing attention to indicators or cues based on patient history and in-therapy behavioral cues. For example, patients who have experienced problems with authority, are gregarious, and relatively immature in feelings and behavior characterize externalizers. Conversely, patients who rarely act out, tend to ruminate, and are thought of as shy characterize internalizers. Although not exhaustive, Table 25.1 provides some examples of behavioral cues indicative of an internalizing or externalizing coping style.

Resistance level (or reactance level) informs the level of therapist directiveness in treatment. Specifically, among those who perceive the therapist as a threat to their autonomy, non-directive interventions are indicated. Conversely, among those with low levels of reactance, patients respond well to either directive or non-directive interventions; however, these individuals appear to respond best to directive interventions.

Resistance informs therapist directiveness level. Resistance can be measured with the Therapeutic Reactance Scale (TRS; Dowd, Milne, & Wise, 1991) or trait resistance potential can be quantified from a composite of various MMPI-2 subscales reflecting dominance, problems with authority, and resistance to control. The STS-Clinician

TABLE 25.1. Indicators of coping style

Internalizers tend to:	Externalizers tend to:
1. feel hurt rather than feel angry	1. react to frustration with overt anger
2. lack self-confidence	2. be socially gregarious and outgoing
3. like to be alone	3. insist on having things his/her way
4. be quiet in social gatherings	4. not take responsibility for problems
5 worry or ruminate before taking action	5. be impulsive
6. be introverted	6. have an inflated sense of importance

TABLE 25.2. Resistance potential behavioral cues

Low resistance potential is indicated by patients who:	High resistance potential is indicated by patients who:	Specific signs of state-like resistance include:
1. usually follow advice of those in authority 2. avoid confrontation with others 3. have a history of accepting and following directions from those in authority	1. are distrustful and suspicious of others 2 resent those who make the rules 3. have tried to "get even" when provoked	1. having trouble understanding or following directions 2. becoming overtly angry at the therapist 3. lateness or avoiding appointments

Form can also be used to provide a measure of resistance that is more situation specific than the MMPI-2 composite and not as specific to psychotherapy as the TRS. Resistance can also be gauged through attention to in-session behaviors. In fact, resistance has a state component and the therapist should remain vigilant to state resistance levels throughout therapy. High levels of state-like resistance are evidenced by behaviors such as treatment session no-shows or late arrivals, frequent arguments with the therapist or failing to follow/understand the therapist. Table 25.2 provides some brief examples of behavioral cues to resistance level.

Subjective Distress or emotional arousal informs the level of emotionally arousing material or intervention style. Emotional arousal is associated with motivation and a curvilinear relationship between arousal levels and treatment effectiveness exists. That is, too little arousal results in low motivation for treatment while too much arousal results in an inability to engage effectively in treatment. Therapists need to select interventions and homework to maintain a moderate level of arousal that is appropriately motivating.

The dimension of subjective distress may be assessed through the State-Trait Anxiety Inventory (STAI; Spielberger, Gorsuch, Lushene, Vagg, & Jacobs, 1983). We have used the convention of one standard deviation above or below the normative mean to respectively indicate high or low subjective distress. Assessment alternatives for the dimension of subjective distress include the STS-Clinician Form and an evaluation of in-session behavioral cues and self-esteem. In general, unsteady or shaky voice, psychomotor agitation, and difficulty concentrating are reliable indicators of excessive emotional arousal. Lower emotional arousal may be indicated by an absence of the foregoing. See Table 25.3 for additional in-session cues indicating level of emotional arousal.

Functional impairment informs the level of treatment intensity. For those who are experiencing high levels of functional impairment, more intensive therapy (i.e., more

TABLE 25.3. Indicators of emotional arousal/subjective distress

Clinician ratings	Patient report	Self-esteem
1. Low energy level 2. Stoic and unexpressive 3. Worries a lot 4. Is anxious	1. Anxiety or unhappiness 2. Future feels uncertain 3. Feels like crying often 4. Difficulty with decisions	1. Overly self-critical 3. Feels like crying often 3. Low confidence level 4. Feels unhappy or sad

TABLE 25.4. Indicators of impairment level

Disturbed family/household	Social isolation	Poor social support
1. Has little or no contact with most family/household members	1. Seeks to be alone	1. Has no more than one friend who shares common interests
2. Has been kicked out of their home	2. Avoids social gatherings	2. Feels lonely most of the time, even when with others
3. Avoids being around one or more family members	3. Not comfortable with others	3. Doesn't seek other's help during crisis
	4. Has withdrawn recently from family or friends	

frequent sessions) is indicated. For those with low levels of functional impairment, patients will do well with one session per week.

Functional Impairment can be measured via an assessment of the patient's current circumstances and patient history. Beutler, Clarkin, and Bongar (2000) reduced level of impairment to three indices. The first of these indices is the presence of family problems in either the nuclear or the contemporary family. Social isolation and withdrawal comprise the second index of impairment. The final index of impairment stems from the presence of supportive relationships. In essence, relatively low levels of functional impairment are indicated when patients are experiencing regular family interaction, have friendships, and are involved in social activities. The Global Assessment of Functioning (GAF) from the DSM-IV-TR is also an indicator of functional impairment. We have used the convention that classifies a patient as moderately impaired if they have a GAF <59 and they report having less than three family members or friends who could provide social support. For these moderately impaired patients, sessions should be scheduled bi- or tri-weekly (2–3 sessions/week). Treatment should continue at this intensity until patients demonstrate clinically meaningful improvement in functioning for at least two weeks. Table 25.4 provides some concrete examples of indicators of disturbed family/household functioning, social isolation, and poor social support. The interested reader is directed to Beutler and Harwood (2000) for a more comprehensive list of behavioral/social indicators for each of the foregoing Prescriptive Psychotherapy patient dimensions.

FITTING HOMEWORK TO THE PATIENT

Based on the previously discussed dimensions, we can make the following tentative conclusions with respect to the development and assignment of homework to fit the unique proclivities and predispositions of patients. The matching of homework specifically based on patient predisposing dimensions has not been examined empirically; however, there is no reason to believe that the success of homework assigned in this manner would be any less successful than the empirically supported STS model of patient-treatment matching with in-session interventions. As alluded to previously, the complexity of the matching PT and STS models can not be completely represented here given the parameters of this chapter; therefore, the interested clinician is encouraged to consult Beutler, Clarkin, and Bongar (2000) or Beutler and Harwood (2000) for a complete discussion of the issues involved in skillfully matching treatment strategies and interventions to patient predisposing dimensions.

COPING STYLE AND HOMEWORK

When selecting or suggesting or collaborating with patients to develop specific homework assignments, the therapist may wish to consider the patient's dominant pattern of coping. A coping style characterized by externalization may not match well with homework that is insight focused. To increase compliance as well as the likelihood and magnitude of good outcome, clinicians can suggest or select from homework that can be conceptualized and applied in a symptom-focused approach. Examples of homework that may be readily employed in a symptom-focused manner include stimulus control procedures, mastery imaging, graded task assignment, activity scheduling, activity regulation, interpersonal skills training, a focus on the nature of automatic thoughts, reattribution of responsibility evidence analysis in conjunction with the Daily Thought Record (DTR), and exercise (Beutler and Harwood, 2000). The focus of the homework when presented, reviewed and used in therapy should remain at the symptom level throughout treatment.

For internalizers and following a reduction of any at risk behaviors for a period of at least one week, the clinician may wish to employ homework in an insight-focused manner. In other words, as problematic behaviors come under control, the nature of internalized coping styles necessitates a shift of focus from one of symptom change to one of insight and awareness. Therapists are usually able to successfully make this shift somewhere between the fourth and tenth session. Clinicians may slowly integrate an insight-focus on homework into the already established symptom-focused personal therapy. This thematic shift is associated with the use of procedures that support the strategic objective of increasing emotional awareness and understanding schematic processes. More specifically, sometime between sessions four and ten, treatment and homework should be shifted to focus on enduring thoughts and expectations that transcend the problems presented (Beutler and Harwood, 2000). Insight focused personal therapy may employ a wide array of techniques; however, these techniques should be developed to follow relevant *themes* that have been defined and identified as problematic. The Daily Thought Record (DTR) and downward arrow techniques are two examples of homework assignments that lend themselves well to an insight-focus; however, most types of homework assignments can be creatively adapted to provide or generate interpretations and questions that induce insight. Patients will begin to generate more perceptiveness from their personal therapy as treatment continues and as clinicians continue to focus on insight and awareness.

RESISTANCE

The resistance dimension has the most relevance to the issue of compliance. As previously stated, resistance has both trait and state dimensions. Therefore, the clinician must remain vigilant to the in-session cues that telegraph rising levels of resistance in the patient and adjust their stance accordingly (Beutler & Harwood, 2000). One suggestion that has been repeatedly made throughout the foregoing chapters involves the use of a name for these assignments other than homework. The word "homework" may have negative associations for some individuals and it may generate resistance. On the other hand, labels like "personal therapy" or "life skills" may increase patient motivation and compliance. Before moving on, it is worthwhile to note that in the early stages of treatment therapists should be relatively more process-directive with respect to homework rather than content-directive. That is, even among patients with low levels of trait resistance, it may be more productive for clinicians to attend to the process of homework assignment and those elements that increase the likelihood of acceptability (Scheel, Hanson, & Razzahavaikina, 2004) rather than taking a directive stance on homework assignment or content.

With the foregoing caveat in mind, the use of personal therapy is typically not a problem among those with low levels of resistance and research indicates that many of these individuals actually benefit from therapists who take a directive stance in treatment (Beutler et al, 2003). Therefore, clinicians may be somewhat more directive in life-skills assignment as long as they remain vigilant to state resistance levels that may be more easily activated in the early stages of treatment when trust is still developing. In general, therapists can feel comfortable selecting and assigning specific, structured, and active homework tasks among those with low levels of trait and state resistance. Any of the homework interventions previously named are candidates for assignment with low-resistance patients. Of course, the way that life-skills are employed in the therapy session ultimately depends on whether the patient manifests externalized or internalized coping strategies. For example, among those with low resistance and an internalizing coping style, interpersonal techniques (IPT; Klerman, Weissman, Rounsaville, & Chevron, 1984) or directed experiential techniques (Daldrup, et al., 1988) may be very useful treatments—homework consistent with the themes of these manualized treatments may increase their effectiveness. Because patient independence is a general treatment goal, clinicians will want to eventually become less directive in an effort to foster some "personal directiveness" on the part of the patient in both therapy and life-skills development and application.

Among those who are high on either state or trait resistance, therapists will want to be as non-directive as possible in the development and assignment of life-skills. Process-directive is the dominant mode at any stage of treatment for therapists working with patients high in trait resistance—clinicians will be more successful if they "suggest" rather than assign homework and the work itself should be self-directed (Beutler & Harwood, 2000). For example, the personal therapy should be derived from and accompanied by self-help workbooks. The patient should select from a predetermined list of homework/self-help books and they should be responsible for self-monitoring their success in treatment goals with little effort from the therapist with respect to collecting or checking homework. The therapist can show interest in the patient's personal therapy by asking about homework completion instead of checking or collecting the patient's work. Paradoxical interventions may be employed in cases of extreme and persistent resistance. For example, a patient may be encouraged to avoid engaging in life-skills for a while (Beutler & Harwood, 2000).

SUBJECTIVE DISTRESS

According to the STS model, the likelihood of therapeutic change is greatest when patient emotional stress is moderate and not excessively high or low (Beutler & Harwood, 2000). The therapist should keep in mind that there are three levels of emotional reactivity: chronic, moderately reactive, and immediately reactive (Beutler & Harwood, 2000). In general, procedures that confront are emotionally arousing while procedures that provide structure and support reduce emotional arousal. Among those experiencing excessive emotional arousal, behavioral and cognitive stress management procedures can reduce arousal levels and these activities lend themselves very well to personal therapy or life skills—patients need to generalize these skills to their everyday life. It may be somewhat more difficult to provide homework assignments that produce emotional arousal; however, assignments that involve confrontational, experiential, or unstructured procedures are recommended. Therapists who are creative will be able to develop homework that keeps the patient motivated to change.

Coping style should be considered when assigning homework that is relevant to Subjective Distress. For example, internalizers who require an increase in arousal level will respond best to techniques or strategies that present or raise distressing thoughts, images of past events, or unwanted feelings. Conversely, externalizers who need to have their emotional arousal level raised should be confronted with unwanted external consequences (e.g., external control, feared events) or avoidance behavior (e.g., phobic objects) in an effort to maintain a moderate level of discomfort until dissipation occurs (Beutler & Harwood, 2000). The therapist should make an effort to gauge the level of distress generated by each homework assignment because extremely high or low levels of distress will hinder compliance and effectiveness.

FUNCTIONAL IMPAIRMENT

In general, as a patient's functional impairment increases, treatment intensity should also be increased. In other words, the frequency of treatment sessions should be higher among those who are experiencing the greatest amount of social or occupation impairment. Highly impaired patients may also require a more intense level of personal therapy. Of course, personal therapy should be developed with the understanding that homework can be overwhelming and problematic for those who are already experiencing impairment. The clinician should attempt to develop homework that is relatively easy to complete, at least at the outset, and homework may be assigned frequently to increase the intensity of personal therapy. Intensity can be maintained by assigning a variety of personal therapy or life skills activities. Additionally, increasing the length of various homework assignments may be helpful at times. The integration of 12-Step programs or other support groups and bibliotherapy may be particularly helpful and can be considered to be personal therapy activities.

SUMMARY AND CONCLUSIONS

There is general agreement that along with the delivery of psychosocial treatment, the application of homework or personal therapy enhances outcome and reduces the likelihood of relapse. When relapse does occur, homework may attenuate the severity or chronicity of distressing episodes.

It makes sense that if homework is beneficial to psychotherapy outcome, clinicians can improve on outcome (both in magnitude and likelihood) if they increase or maintain both motivation for homework and motivation for therapy. Tailoring homework along a number of patient dimensions would appear useful in the foregoing endeavor.

Clinicians already agree that homework should be relevant to the patient's problem(s) and it should be clearly presented and measurable. Additionally, collaboration in homework development may be helpful; therapists should recognize when homework is completed or attempted, problem-solving should be employed if homework is not attempted or only partially completed, and it is important to always review the homework. What is not generally recognized is the utility of formal and systematic application of various personal therapy assignments as guided by information obtained on patient predisposing treatment-matching dimensions.

As previously stated, the Systematic Treatment Selection model and Prescriptive Psychotherapy have been empirically supported recently via RCT investigation (Beutler et al., 2003). More specifically, each of the patient-treatment matching dimensions (i.e., coping style, resistance, subjective distress, and functional impairment) have been supported over the years through a number of studies and PT was recently supported as a complete treatment package incorporating all of the dimensions simultaneously (Beutler, et al., 1991; Beutler, et al., 2003; Beutler, Machado, Engle, & Mohr, 1993; Karno, Beutler, & Harwood, 2002).

Numerous empirical investigations provide evidence of the utility of systematically matching patient characteristics with treatment dimensions. Based on the forgoing, it would make good clinical sense to try and improve on matching personal therapy to the patient—given the amount of support that our matching dimensions have garnered over the years, STS and PT would seem to be a logical and practical method in this endeavor. Indeed, when therapists correctly match treatment interventions to patient dimensions, both magnitude of change and likelihood of change are enhanced—the same effect is quite possible with respect to personal therapy developed for application outside of the clinician's office.

In a different vein, it may be possible, in some instances, to prevent the need for psychotherapy through public education. For example, educating the public about the importance of healthy social support networks may be a preventive measure for some individuals. Relatedly, increasing awareness about community-based support groups and the utility of bibliotherapy may be corrective for some—for others such resources may prevent the worsening of symptoms. Prevention programs are already popular in areas such as teen pregnancy prevention programs in High Schools (Durlak & Wells, 1997) and child abuse prevention programs associated with parenting classes (Bugental, Ellerson, Lin, Raiiney, Kokotovic, & O'Hara, 2002). Perhaps it is time to focus on prevention programs in an effort to reduce the incidence or severity of some episodes of mental illness.

REFERENCES

Beck, A. T., Steer, R. A., & Brown, G. K. (1996). *Manual for the Beck Depression Inventory—II*. San Antonio, TX: Psychological Corporation.

Beck, A. T., Wright, F. D., Newman, C. F., & Liese, B. S. (1993). *Cognitive therapy of substance abuse*. New York: Guilford.

Beutler, L. E., & Clarkin, J. (1990). *Systematic treatment selection: Toward targeted therapeutic interventions*. New York: Brunner/Mazel.

Beutler, L. E., Clarkin, J. F., and Bongar, B. (2000). *Guidelines for the systematic treatment of the depressed patient*. New York: Oxford University Press.

Beutler, L. E. & Harwood, T. M. (2000). *Prescriptive psychotherapy: A practical guide to systematic treatment selection.* New York: Oxford University Press.

Beutler, L. E., Engle, D., Mohr, D., Daldrup, R. J., Bergan, J., Meredith, K., & Merry, W. (1991). Predictors of differential and self-directed psychotherapeutic procedures. *Journal of Consulting and Clinical Psychology, 59*, 333–340.

Beutler, L. E., Machado, P. P. P., Engle, D., & Mohr, D. (1993). Differential patient X treatment maintenance of treatment effects among cognitive, experiential, and self-directed psychotherapies. *Journal of Psychotherapy Integration, 3*, 15–32.

Beutler, L. E., Moleiro, C., Malik, M., Harwood, T. M., Romanelli, R., Gallagher-Thompson, D. & Thompson, L. (2003). A comparison of the Dodo, EST, and ATI factors among co-morbid stimulant dependent, depressed patients. *Clinical Psychology & Psychotherapy, 10*, 69–85.

Beutler, L.E., & Williams, O. B. (1995, July/August). Computer applications for the Selection of optimal psychosocial therapeutic interventions. *Behavioral Healthcare Tomorrow*, pp. 66–68.

Bryant, M. J., Simons, A. D., & Thase, M. E. (1999). Therapist skill and patient variables in homework compliance: Controlling an uncontrolled variable in cognitive therapy outcome research. *Cognitive Therapy & Research, 23*, 381–399.

Bugental, J. F. T., Ellerson, P. D., Lin, E. K., Rainey, B., Kokotovic, A., & O'Hara, N. (2002). A cognitive approach to child abuse prevention. *Journal of Family Psychology, 16*, 243–258.

Butcher, J. N. (1990). *The MMPI-2 in psychological treatment*. New York: Oxford University Press.

Conoley, C. W., Conoley, J. C., Ivey, D. C., & Scheel, M. J. (1991). Enhancing consultation by matching the consultee's perspectives. *Journal of Counseling and Development, 69*, 546–549.

Conoley, C. W., Padula, M. A., Payton, D. S., & Daniels, J. A. (1994). Predictors of client Implementation of counselor recommendations: Match with problem, difficulty level, and building on client strengths. *Journal of Counseling Psychology, 41*, 3–7.

Daldrup, R. J., Beutler, L. E., Engle, D., & Greenberg, L. S. (1988). *Focused Expressive: Psychotherapy: Freeing the overcontrolled patient*. New York: Guilford.

Detweiler-Bedell, J. B. & Whisman, M. A. (2005). A lesson in assigning homework: Therapist, client, and task characteristics in cognitive therapy for depression, *Professional Psychology: Research and Practice, 36*, 219–223.

Dowd, E. T., Milne, C. R., & Wise, S. L. (1991). The therapeutic reactance scale: A measure of psychological reactance. *Journal of Counseling and Development, 69*, 541–545.

Durlak, J. A. & Wells, A. M. (1997). Primary prevention mental health programs for children and adolescents: A meta-analytic review. *American Journal of Community Psychology, 25*, 115–152.

Endicott, J., Cohen, J., Nee, J., Fleiss, J., & Sarantakos, S. (1981). Hamilton depression rating scale. *Archives of General Psychiatry, 38*, 98–103.

Gonçalves, O. F. (1995). Cognitive narrative psychotherapy: The hermeneutic construction of alternative meanings. In M. J. Mahoney (Ed.), *Cognitive and constructive psychotherapies* (pp. 186–245). New York: Pergamon.

Karno, M., Beutler, L. E., & Harwood, T. M. (2002). Interactions between psychotherapy process and patient attributes that predict alcohol treatment effectiveness: A preliminary report. *Addictive Behaviors, 27*, 779–797.

Kazantzis, N., & Deane, F. P. (1999). Psychologist's use of homework assignments in clinical practice. *Professional Psychology: Research and Practice, 20*, 581–585.

Kazantzis, N., Deane, F. P., & Ronan, K. R. (2000). Homework assignments in cognitive and behavioral therapy: A meta-analysis. *Clinical Psychology: Science and Practice, 7*, 189–202.

Klerman, G. L., Weissman, M. M., Rounsaville, B. J., & Chevron, E. S. (1984). *Interpersonal psychotherapy of depression*. New York: Basic Books.

Luborsky, L., Barber, J. P., Siqueland, L., Johnson, S., Najavits, L. M., Frank, A., & Daley, D. (1996). The revised helping alliance questionnaire (Haq-II). *Journal of Psychotherapy Practice and Research, 5*, 260–271.

Mahrer, A. R., Gagnon, R., Fairweather, D. R., Boulet, D. B., & Herring, C. B. (1994). Client commitment and resolve to carry out postsession behaviors. *Journal of Counseling Psychology, 41*, 407–414.

McLellan, A. T., Luborsky, L., Woody, G. E., & O'Brien, C. P. (1980). An improved diagnostic instrument for substance abuse patients: The addiction severity index. *Journal of Nervous and Mental Disease, 168*, 26–33.

Reimers, T. M., Wacker, D. P., & Koeppl, G. (1987). Acceptability of behavioral interventions: A review of the literature. *School Psychology Review, 16*, 212–227.

Scheel, M. J., Conoley, C. W., & Ivey, D. C. (1998). Using client positions as a technique for increasing the acceptability of marriage therapy interventions. *American Journal of Family Therapy, 26*, 203–214.

Scheel, M. J., Hanson, W. E., & Razzhavaikina, T. I (2004). The process of recommending homework in psychotherapy: A review of therapist delivery methods, client acceptability, and factors that affect compliance. *Psychotherapy: Theory, Research, Practice, Training. 41*, 38–55.

Scheel, M. J., Hoggan, K., Willie, D., McDonald, K., & Tonin S. (1998). Client understanding of homework determined through therapist delivery. *Poster presented as the 106th Annual Convention of the American Psychological Association*, San Francisco.

Schmidt, N. B., & Woolaway-Bickel, K. (2000). The effects of treatment compliance on outcome in cognitive-behavioral therapy for panic disorder: Quality versus quantity. *Journal of Consulting and Clinical Psychology, 68*, 13–18.

Shaw, B. F., Elkin, I., Yamaguchi, J., Olmsted, M., Vallis, T.M., Dobson, K. S., et al. (1999). Therapist competence ratings in relation to clinical outcome in cognitive therapy of depression. *Journal of Consulting and Clinical Psychology, 67*, 837–846.

Sobell, L. C., & Sobell, M. B. (1992). Timeline follow-back: A technique for assessing self-reported alcohol consumption. In R. Z. Litten, & J. P. Allen (Eds.), *Measuring alcohol consumption: Psychological and biochemical methods* (pp. 41–72). Treatment Handbook Series, Number 4. Bethesda, MD: National Institute of Alcohol Abuse and Alcoholism.

Spielberger, C. D., Gorsuch, R. L., Lushene, R., Vagg, P. R., & Jacobs, G. A. (1983). *State-trait anxiety inventory*. Palo Alto, CA: Consulting Psychological Press.

Woods, C. M., Chambless, D. L., & Steketee, G. (2002). Homework compliance and behavior therapy outcome for panic with agoraphobia and obsessive compulsive disorder. *Cognitive Behaviour Therapy, 31*, 88–95.

INDEX

Printed in the United States of America.